Cognitive Models of
Speech Processing

ACL–MIT Press Series in Natural Language Processing
Aravind K. Joshi, Mark Liberman, and Karen Sparck Jones, editors

Cognitive Models of
Speech Processing

Psycholinguistic and
Computational Perspectives

edited by
Gerry T. M. Altmann

A Bradford Book
The MIT Press
Cambridge, Massachusetts
London, England

First MIT Press paperback edition, 1995

© 1990 Massachusetts Institute of Technology

This book was set in Times Roman by Asco Trade Typesetting Ltd., Hong Kong, and printed and bound in the United States of America.

Library of Congress Cataloging-in-Publication Data

Cognitive models of speech processing: psycholinguistic and computational
    perspectives/edited by Gerry T. M. Altmann.
        p. cm.—(ACL–MIT Press series in natural language processing)
    "A Bradford book."
    Includes bibliographical references.
    ISBN 0-262-01117-4 (HB), 0-262-51084-7 (PB)
    1. Computational linguistics. 2. Psycholinguistics. 3. Speech processing
systems. I. Altmann, Gerry T. M. II. Series.
P98.C54   1990
410'.285—dc20   89-78303
                                                                        CIP

Contents

Contents

Preface

The chapters in this book represent the outcome of a research workshop held at the Park Hotel Fiorelle, Sperlonga, 16–20 May 1988. Twenty-five participants gathered in this small coastal village in Italy, where the Emperor Tiberius kept a Summer house, to discuss psycholinguistic and computational issues in speech and natural-language processing.

The workshop itself would not have been possible without the very generous financial support of British Telecom International, who agreed not only to the funding of the 1988 meeting but also to the funding of further meetings of the workshop in subsequent years. Special thanks are due to John Matthews at BTI and Fred Stentiford at British Telecom Research Laboratories. Additional funding was provided by the American Association for Artificial Intelligence.

The original idea to run a research workshop in Italy on cognitive models of speech processing arose during a conversation one wet and windy night in Edinburgh with Anne Cutler, who was attending a linguistics conference at the university and simultaneously bemoaning the weather. The organization of this workshop would not have been possible without Anne's encouragement and support, as well as that of Ellen Bard and Richard Shillcock.

Thanks are also due to the local council of Sperlonga, which provided transport, and to Mr. and Mrs. Cosmo di Mille, owners of the Park Hotel Fiorelle, in which the workshop was held. The success of the workshop is in part a reflection of the amenities they offered and in particular the excellent food.

My thanks also go to my colleagues at the Centre for Speech Technology Research, University of Edinburgh, for their support and encouragement during the run-up to the workshop and to my colleagues at the Laboratory of Experimental Psychology, University of Sussex, for their support during the production of this book. I am grateful both to the authors themselves and to the following for participating in the review process during the production of the book: Paul Bertelson, Colin Brown, Chuck Clifton, Chris Darwin, Gary Dell, François Grosjean, Geoff Hinton, Steve Isard, Bob Ladd, Joanne Miller, Jane Oakhill, Patrizia Tabossi, and Roger Wales.

Final thanks must go to the participants themselves, without whom there would have been no workshop and whose patience while suffering my editorial meddling I greatly appreciate.

Cognitive Models of
Speech Processing

Chapter 1

Cognitive Models of Speech Processing: An Introduction

Gerry T. M. Altmann

The process of speech comprehension can be divided into a number of subprocesses ranging from those responsible for matching acoustic input against some internal representation of the words in the language to those involved in extracting meaning from the string(s) of lexical items hypothesized by the lexical-access process and constructing a message-level interpretation of the sentence. The modeling of speech comprehension, in common with other domains of cognitive modeling (e.g., visual perception), can be guided by the following three considerations: First, to what extent can the subprocesses involved in the comprehension process be assigned to separate informationally encapsulated modules (Fodor 1983)? Second, to what extent do these modules interact? And third, what kinds of computational architectures are suited to modeling these processes? This last consideration is closely linked to the previous two, since certain computational architectures lend themselves more or less naturally to the notions of subprocessing, information encapsulation, and interaction. Any attempt to model speech comprehension that considers not just the nature of the representations constructed during the comprehension process but also the kinds of information that affect the construction of these representations and the time course of such effects can be considered with these three questions in mind.

The development of models of spoken word recognition has been concerned primarily with the following issues:[1]

- The manner in which the acoustic input makes contact with the lexion
- The nature of any internal representations that mediate this process
- The nature of any particular strategies that may be used to facilitate this process
- The locus of word-frequency effects
- The factors that determine whether or not another lexical item competes with the item intended by the speaker

• The degree to which the existence of such competitors influences the process of recognizing the intended item (that is, the form and locus of competitor effects)

• The degree to which context can influence this process, and the manner in which this influence is exerted

In addition, the development of models of the processes traditionally associated with sentence processing has recently focused on topics which include the following:[2]

• The nature of the information accessed from the lexicon and the use to which it is put during sentence processing

• The separation of the processes responsible for sentence processing into distinct modules

• The relationship between such higher-level processes as syntactic analysis (which has tended to be studied in the visual domain rather than the auditory domain) and properties of the sentence unique to the spoken form, such as the prosodic attributes of a sentence

The chapters in the present volume address the issues listed here. The purpose of the present introduction is to provide a brief overview of the main issues, with pointers to the relevant chapters in this collection, and with particular emphasis on addressing the three considerations described earlier.

Lexical Segmentation

There are a number of properties of the raw acoustic input that make the task of spoken-word recognition, and speech comprehension in general, particularly difficult. One such problem is that the input is not conveniently divided into acoustic segments that correspond neatly to the individual words uttered by the speaker. Since individual words can be identified from the acoustic input, it follows that the process of lexical access is able to overcome this lack of overt segmentation. At issue is exactly how the processor manages this, that is, how it decides where in the input a new word begins.

There are a number of solutions to this problem. Cutler (this volume) cites a computational study by Briscoe (1989) in which four different segmentation algorithms were assessed within the context of automatic continuous-speech recognition. The first strategy was simply to initiate lexical access (that is, to decide that a word potentially started) at each and every phoneme in the input. The problem here was that the system was soon overwhelmed by the sheer number of lexical hypotheses that this strategy induced. A second strategy was a more constrained version of this: lexical access was initiated at the onset of the sentence and then only subsequently at the offset of each word successfully found in this way (see Cole and Jakimik 1980). This worked well except when only partial phonetic information about the identity of each phoneme was made available. Moreover, evidence discussed by Shillcock (this volume) suggests that this strategy is not an adequate reflection of human processing. Shillcock reports activation of the lexical item *bone* in a word such as *trombone* even though the sequence *trom* is not a valid word. According to the strategy of word-offset segmentation, lexical access should not be initiated at the offset of *trom*, because it is not a real word, and consequently, the word *bone* should not be activated. A third strategy simulated in the Briscoe study initiated lexical lookup at each syllable boundary, and the fourth strategy initiated lookup at the onset of each strong syllable, that is, each syllable containing a full, unreduced vowel (Cutler and Norris 1988). This last strategy was favored in the computational trials.

The role that syllables play during lexical access has been the subject of considerable discussion within the literature (and elsewhere). On the one hand, researchers like Segui et al. (this volume) and Mehler et al. (this volume) argue that the syllable, irrespective of its strength, is the fundamental unit of perception on which basis lexical access is initiated. On the other hand, persuasive evidence reviewed in the chapter by Cutler suggests that strong syllables are the units of access, at least in the English language. This latter point is important, since a language like French does not distinguish between strong and weak syllables—they are all, in effect, strong. Thus for a language like French the operations of a strategy of segmenting at strong syllables and those of a strategy that simply segments at all syllable onsets would be indistinguishable, as Cutler points out.

Cutler suggests that the strategy that she and Dennis Norris have identified, the Metrical Segmentation Strategy (Cutler and Norris 1988), "is best thought of as the operation of an autonomous and automatic device, the purpose of which is to initiate lexical access attempts with maximum efficiency." However, there is some controversy over whether spoken-word recognition uses such an explicit device and whether the results reported by Cutler and Norris can be explained only by recourse to an explicit device. Bard (this volume) suggests an alternative explanation of the results that originally motivated the Metrical Segmentation Strategy. Bard's account assumes that each new syllable spawns a lexical-access process and thereby activates a cohort of competing lexical candidates (Marslen-Wilson and Welsh 1978, Marslen-Wilson 1987). She suggests that a crucial difference between weak and strong syllables is that weak syllables will lead to the weak activation of quite a number of lexical candidates while strong syllables lead to the strong activation of only a few lexical candidates. Consequently, the manipulation of the metrical properties of a stimulus (e.g., strong versus weak syllables) results not simply in differences in syllable structure but also in differences in activation pattern across competing lexical hypotheses. Bard suggests that what have been interpreted as differences in lexical segmentation can alternatively be interpreted as differences in activation and competition among lexical candidates without the postulation of an explicit segmentation device.

The available evidence suggests that the syllable, in one form or another, is a fundamental unit of perception.[3] Moreover, there is compelling evidence in support of some form of segmentation strategy (see the chapters by Cutler and by Segui et al.). Yet whether or not there exists an explicit, autonomous subprocessor whose sole responsibility is to segment the speech stream according to a particular strategy is still to some extent an open issue. Bard's proposals, based on an interactive-activation model of spoken-word recognition (Marslen-Wilson 1987, McClelland and Elman 1986), question the existence of such a device.

Interactive-Activation Architectures

Early versions of the cohort model of spoken-word recognition (Marslen-Wilson and Welsh 1978, Marslen-Wilson and Tyler 1980) suggested that the acoustic input available at a particular point in time activates the set of all lexical candidates compatible with that input, with disconfirming evidence causing members of the cohort to drop out. The shortcomings of this model are well documented in Norris 1986 and Marslen-Wilson 1987. One reason for its demise was the assumption in the original cohort model that the matching process between acoustic input and each member of the cohort was an all-or-none process—either the input matched, in which case the cohort member was on, or there was a mismatch, in which case it was off. This relied on too perfect a match (a similar problem existed with the manner in which the original cohort model matched each member of the cohort against the context). The revised cohort model (Marslen-Wilson 1987) overcame this problem by proposing that the cohort consists of elements whose activation levels are not all-or-none, as in the original, but are determined by goodness of fit to the acoustic input, with higher-level processes evaluating the most highly activated elements, in parallel, for integration into the utterance interpretation. A further reason for the demise of the original model was the increasing evidence that word frequency can affect the activation levels of lexical candidates in the initial stages of the access process (Marslen-Wilson, this volume; Zwitserlood 1989). Activation could not, therefore, be the all-or-none state that the initial cohort model assumed.

TRACE (McClelland and Elman 1986) is a computational simulation of word recognition based on a localist parallel-distributed-processing (PDP) system. It was similar in many respects to the revised cohort model, although it stopped short of any higher-level interpretive component. TRACE differs in one crucial respect from the revised cohort model in that it assumes inhibitory links between competing hypotheses. Thus a strongly active candidate will suppress the activation of a weakly active competitor, which thereby increases the difference in level of activation between the two. Bard's account of the data supporting strong-syllable segmentation relies on just such a relationship between competing items.

Frauenfelder and Peeters (this volume) describe a number of simulations using TRACE. These simulations illustrate the role of inhibition in the model and the manner in which the model deals with examples of words embedded within other words similar to those investigated in human studies by Shillcock (this volume). Norris (this volume) describes a rather different PDP model of word recognition. It differs from TRACE in the manner in which temporal information is encoded in the system and by virtue of being truly distributed. Briefly, TRACE encodes temporal (or sequential) information by using a bank of feature detectors, one for each time-slice, which are exposed to the acoustic input. Thus a particular phoneme unit will receive activation from one element of the bank at time t_n and from a "neighboring" element in the bank at t_{n+1}. Each phoneme unit receives input across six time slices in all, and there is a copy of each phoneme unit centered on every three time-slices (they overlap). Similarly at the word level, there is one copy of each word unit centered over every three time slices, and thus any one word unit receives activation, mediated by the phoneme units, from more than one time slice. In Norris's dynamic network, based on work with recurrent networks by Jordan (1986), temporal information is encoded by way of a feedback loop, from the hidden layer of a three-layer network (input, hidden, output) to the input layer.[4] This feedback loop incorporates a time delay of one cycle, and thus the activation of an input unit is determined both by activation from the input and by the previous activation state of the hidden units. In other words, the activation depends on both the current input and the previous input(s).

Further differences between the two simulations are that the dynamic network is essentially a learning network using standard back-propagation techniques and distributed representations while TRACE uses local representations and preset parameters, so no learning is involved. One consequence of this difference in architecture is that within TRACE there are identifiable levels of local representation corresponding to the feature, phoneme, and word levels. This is not to say that there are identifiable subprocesses corresponding to each of these levels. There exist mutually excitatory links between the phoneme units and the words containing those phonemes (and similarly for the feature-phoneme interface) that ensure that there is not a simple sequential flow of information up through the distinct levels of representation. However, the dynamic network does not even contain these distinct levels of representation.[5]

A crucial feature of interactive-activation models is that active elements compete with one another. Competition can manifest itself in these models in a number of ways. On the one hand, competition between lexical hypotheses may be indirect, insofar as there is no direct effect of the activation level of one candidate on the activation level of another (as in the revised cohort model). In such a case, competition is manifested in terms of some higher-level decision process favoring the most highly activated candidate. On the other hand, competition between hypotheses can be more direct, with an inhibitory relationship between the competing candidates. In this case, competition is manifested when the activation level of one candidate supresses, or is suppressed by, the activation level of another (as in TRACE). A number of studies have addressed this issue (see Bard, this volume, for a discussion), with particular interest focusing on how the recognition of one word is influenced by properties of the competing word hypotheses.

Competitor Effects during Spoken-Word Recognition

Marslen-Wilson (this volume) shows how in principle the frequency of a competitor can affect the time course of the recognition of a target word. Thus, the time to recognize a word like *speech* is dependent not simply on the existence of competitors like *specious* and *speed* but also on their frequencies. If the target word (that is, the actual word as defined by some later acoustic input) is much higher in frequency than a competitor, the rise in activation of the target will be much greater than the rise in the activation of the low-frequency competitor. Thus the two will be distinguished between sooner than in the converse case, where the target word is much lower in frequency than a competitor, whose activation level will consequently rise much faster than the target. Marslen-Wilson reports results consistent with these predictions.

One important feature of the cohort model is that the evaluation of highly active competitors prior to their integration into the utterance interpretation takes place *in parallel*. Marslen-Wilson (1987) claimed that as a consequence of this parallel evaluation, there should be no effect on recognition of the number of competitors with which the target has to compete. This is in marked contrast to a model of spoken-word recognition put forward by Luce (1986), in which the number of competitors, or rather the "neighborhood density," is supposed to influence the extent to which a decision can be made to choose one candidate hypothesis over its neighbors, or competitors (also see Luce et al., this volume), Luce's Neighborhood Activation Model (NAM) differs in at least one other important respect from the revised cohort model.

In the cohort framework a competitor is defined as such only at a particular point in time, and it is a competitor because it shares the same input sequence, which for the sake of the argument I shall take to be a sequence of phonemes (but see Marslen-Wilson 1987 for discussion). Thus in cohort terms, the words *speech* and *Sperlonga* are competitors if the only available input corresponds to the phoneme sequence /sp/. They are no longer competitors by the time the following vowel has been encountered. Thus competition is defined *over time*. NAM has little to say, however, about the time course of activation or about the time course of frequency and competitor effects. Thus, whereas the competitor pairs *speech/beach* and *speech/speed* are distinguished in the cohort model because their phonemic specifications diverge at different times, they are not distinguished in NAM.

Luce et al. describe a number of experiments that demonstrate the effects of neighborhood density and neighborhood frequency on word recognition. Within the model, word-decision units compute values based on the acoustic-phonetic pattern of a word, its frequency, and the overall pattern of activity in the decision system as a whole. Thus frequency and neighborhood effects exert their influence by biasing a decision, as opposed to directly modifying the activation level of a cohort member (see Luce et al., this volume, for further discussion of the relationship between NAM and other models of word recognition).

Marslen-Wilson's (1987) data suggest that the number of competitors (that is, the size of the cohort) does not influence the time course of the recognition process. Yet Luce's work suggests that the number of competitors does influence the process.[6] The issue is further complicated by Shillcock's findings on embedded words (this volume). Shillcock reports that the amount of priming from a word like *report* to a related probe such as *wine* (and by implication the degree to which *port* is activated) is unrelated to the size of the cohort at *re*. Instead, Shillcock finds a correlation with the degree of phonemic divergence at *re*, that is, the number of different phonemes that could possibly follow *re* (e.g., *reb*el, *rec*ant, etc.), irrespective of how many words are in the cohort defined by each such phoneme continuation (*rec*ord and *rec*ant belong to the same cohort and count as a single divergence).[7] Moreover, although Shillcock found no correlation between activation of the embedded word and the overall frequency of the carrier, he did find a correlation with the frequency of the highest-frequency member of the cohort generated by the first syllable of the carrier (i.e., *re* in *report* or *trom* in *trombone*).[8] Shillcock points out several implications of these results for interactive-activation models such as TRACE.

Just how competitor effects manifest themselves in the recognition system is still an open question. As suggested earlier, within the interactive-activation framework they can be manifested either as changes in activation levels brought about by mutual inhibition between competing elements or as biases applied to the decision on whether to incorporate one item or another into the utterance interpretion.[9] A similar issue applies to the effects on word recognition of higher-level context. Can context affect the activation levels of compatible words directly, or are context effects more indirect?

Context Effects in Word Recognition and the Architecture of the Recognition System

Exactly this last issue has been addressed in a number of studies by Samuel (see his chapter in this collection for a comprehensive review) and by Connine (Connine 1987; Connine, this volume; Connine and Clifton 1987). Both sets of studies were concerned with the manner in which different kinds of high-level information can or cannot affect the perception of relatively low-level phonemic contrasts. In particular, they were concerned with the effects of lexical and sentential context on phonemic identification.

Samuel (1981, 1987) used the phoneme-restoration effect, in conjunction with a signal-detection analysis, to discover whether these two kinds of contextual information, lexical and sentential, manifested themselves in the same way. Phoneme restoration occurs when a part of a word is either excised or masked by noise and yet the word appears to the perceiver still to contain the excised/masked segment. There are two basic conditions in Samuel's version of the signal detection task: in one, a particular segment is masked by noise, and in the other, that segment is actually replaced by noise. The subjects' task is to identify whether a given stimulus is intact but with noise *added* over the crucial segment or whether it contains a segment that has been *replaced* by noise. If phoneme restoration involves the actual perception of a segment that is in fact missing, there should be only poor discrimination between the added condition and the replaced condition. If the restoration effect is *postperceptual*, there should be good discrimination between the two conditions.

Samuel (this volume) reports a number of studies that made use of this task. These studies suggest that whereas lexical context (manipulated by comparing real words with nonwords) does lead to *perceptual* restoration, sentential context (manipulated by using predictable sentence frames around the target words) does not.[10] Interestingly, Samuel also reports results that suggest that the more lexical competition there is, the stronger the perceptual-restoration effect, but also the stronger the (postperceptual) bias to report such stimuli as intact.[11] Samuel concludes on the basis of these results that the architecture of the recognition system is partially modular: high-level sentential information (syntactic or semantic) is not used by the component responsible for lower-level speech perception, while lexical information is (this latter finding violating informational encapsulation of the perceptual process).[12]

Such a conclusion places considerable constraints on the form that computational models should take. In a PDP framework, the implication is that there should not be *mutually* excitatory links between any higher-level sentential level and the word level (however these levels are represented). In this respect, the findings are consistent with Marslen-Wilson's (1987) revised cohort model, with prelexical interactive activation and postperceptual decision-based selection among the alternative lexical hypotheses. Similar conclusions can be reached on the basis of a number of studies by Connine and her colleagues.

Connine (this volume) describes results very similar to those described by Samuel though she uses a very different methodology. Like Samuel, Connine was interested in the distinction between lexical and sentential effects on perception, but within the paradigm of categorical perception, specifically, the "identification-function-shift paradigm." This involves creating a continuum of sounds between, for example, *dice* at one extreme of the continuum and *tice* at the other. Ganong (1980) used similar materials and showed that subjects tended to label stimuli that fell midway along the continuum so that a real word was formed (favouring *dice* in this example).

Connine used a speeded judgement task and compared the pattern of reaction times to stimuli that were either midway in the continuum or at the continuum endpoints under conditions that were known to involve postperceptual biases (e.g., monetary payoffs, with certain responses leading to greater financial reward) and others that did not. She found that the identification curves and associated patterns of reaction times were the same in both the monetary-payoff condition and in the condition in which sentential context was used to bias subjects' identification of the stimuli. On the other hand, lexical contexts (Ganong 1980), which also biased subjects' identification of the stimuli, led to a very different pattern of reaction times. On the basis of the similarity between the effects of sentential context and the obviously postperceptual effects of monetary payoff, Connine concluded, like Samuel, that the effects of sentential context are also postperceptual.[13]

The studies by Connine and Samuel demonstrate, like Marslen-Wilson 1987, that sentential context *does* influence lexical processing, albeit in a way different from the way in which lexical processing can influence phoneme recognition. In the following section I consider two computational architectures for processing sentential information and the degree to which they naturally capture the kinds of interaction suggested by the empirical data.

Computational Models and Syntactic Effects on Lexical Access

There has recently been a growing debate between advocates of "classical" architectures for modeling human cognitive processes and advocates of models based on parallel distributed processing, which do not make explicit use of symbolic computation.[14] In this section I shall consider an example of each kind of model and the implications of these distinct architectures for modeling the interaction between higher-level sentential information and lexical access.

Thompson and Altmann (this volume) describe an architecture based on the Active Chart Parser (Thompson and Ritchie 1984) that permits various different kinds of interaction between syntactic processing and lexical access. The Chart is an explicit representation of each lexical or syntactic hypothesis and the state of these hypotheses across time. It is thus explicitly symbolic. For the purposes of discussion, lexical access is the mapping between *phoneme sequences* in some phoneme lattice and an internal tree-structured lexicon. Of particular concern is the manner in which syntactic information can be used to filter out spurious lexical hypotheses, that is, hypotheses that are inappropriate in a particular syntactic context. We distinguish between a number of alternative mechanisms for handling the interaction between syntactic information and lexical search. At one extreme, syntactic information serves merely to filter out hypotheses that, despite their inappropriateness in the syntactic context, are nonetheless entered onto the Chart as bona fide lexical candidates. At the other extreme, a mechanism is provided for allowing syntactic *expectations* to modify the lexical search itself, that is, to modify the manner in which the processor attempts to map sequences of phonemes in the input against branches of the tree-structured lexicon. In between are various intermediary mechanisms that, although more powerful than simple filtering insofar as they prevent the activation of certain syntactically inappropriate lexical candidates, do not interfere with the mechanics of the lexical-search process itself.[15]

The different mechanisms for achieving similar degrees of syntactic filtering are accompanied, within our framework, by differences in the degree to which the informational encapsulation of lexical search is violated by information derived from the higher module of syntactic analysis.[16] Whether or not one chooses to violate the informational encapsulation of the lexicon depends in part on issues relating to computational efficiency, since the mechanism for preventing the access of syntactically erroneous lexical candidates that *does not* violate the encapsulation of lexical search is in fact more complex than the equivalent mechanism that *does* violate encapsulation.

The notion that information can be encapsulated depends on the ability to identify distinct levels of representation and process within the computational system. Earlier the notion of such identification was introduced in connection with the differences between TRACE and the dynamic network model of lexical access proposed by Norris. In TRACE, distinct levels of representation exist (the feature level, the phoneme level, and the word level), whereas in the dynamic net there is no explicit intermediate level of representation that mediates processing between the input and output units. Elman (this volume) describes an architecture similar to that used by Norris and shows that, at least within the syntactic domain, the network can nonetheless acquire internal representations that map onto syntactic structures. However, there is neither an explicit grammar nor explicit hypothesization of syntactic structure. What structure there is, is merely inferred on the basis of similarities in activation patterns across the hidden units for different inputs and changes in these patterns through time. In the Chart framework, on the other hand, syntactic processing is brought about by explicit rules of grammar causing the creation of explicit syntactic hypotheses.

Both Connine's and Samuel's work suggest that the interaction between lexical knowledge and phonemic identification is qualitatively different from that between sentential context and lexical processing. Within a framework like the Chart, the different intermediate levels of representation and process and the various kinds of interaction that occur between them can be explicitly modeled.[17] In a PDP learning network, which must learn the input/output mapping for itself, these intermediate representations and accompanying interactions cannot be modeled in the same way. In view of the black-box nature of PDP learning systems, it is unclear just what control on the modeling of these interactions there really is. In a system like TRACE, which does maintain distinct levels of representation, such modeling is possible by explicitly modifying the nature of the links between the different levels (from being bidirectional to unidirectional, from allowing both excitation and inhibition to only allowing one or other, and so on). In a recurrent network these parameters are set by the system itself as it learns. To the extent that such networks are nonmodular with no autonomous levels of representation (see McClelland et al., 1990, for this claim as applied to a recurrent network operating in the domain of syntactic/thematic processing), it follows that the notion of interaction between explicitly identifiable levels of processing is inapplicable. If the task is to model the phenomena identified by Connine and Samuel, it is thus unclear whether a recurrent network could successfully capture the qualitative differences between the various interactions and phenomena they have observed.

Lexical Information and Sentence Processing

Thus far my main concern has been with lexical access: the process by which individual words are recognized from the speech stream and the manner in which this process might be influenced by higher-level sentential information. In this section I move more explicitly into the domain of sentence processing and consider the nature of the information accessed from the lexicon once a word has been recognized, the manner in which this information is then used during sentence processing, and the degree to which the processes responsible for extracting the meaning of a sentence can be divided into distinct informationally encapsulated modules.

Tanenhaus, Garnsey, and Boland (this volume) describe a number of studies that address the first question, the nature of the information that is made available when a word is recognized. Specifically, they are concerned with the time course with which lexical information is accessed and used during sentence comprehension. There are a number of different ways in which lexical information might be used during sentence processing. One possibility is that only very superficial information concerning, for instance, the syntactic class of a word might be made available to begin with. This information would then be used by the human parser to build an initial syntactic representation of the sentence. Only after this process has been initiated might the system access and use more detailed information concerning, for instance, a verb's subcategorization features (such as the argument structure it expects, and so on) in order to filter out inappropriate structures. A second possibility is that this more detailed information is made available straight away and is used to guide the building of the syntactic representation in the first place. An independent issue is whether the lexical information concerning the argument structure of a verb is in fact syntactic or whether it might instead be thematic and specify the semantic roles played by the arguments of the verb. Tanenhaus, Garnsey, and Boland report a number of studies aimed at distinguishing between these various viewpoints.[18]

Tanenhaus et al. suggest that if lexical information is used very early on to help guide the parser's decision, there will be circumstances in which certain syntactic structures or dependencies will be proposed before direct syntactic evidence for their existence is encountered. One way in which they investigated this possibility was to use materials containing "filler-gap dependencies," as in "Which monsters did Ulysses escape from _____ during his voyage?" At issue here is the role that lexical information about the main verb can play in influencing the assignment of a filler (*monsters* in this case) to a particular gap (marked with the dash). Tanenhaus et al. describe a methodology for determining whether or not a filler has been associated with a particular gap and then for assessing whether verb-control information is used to guide the assignment (as opposed to ruling the assignment out once it has been made). To do this, they investigated filler-gap assignments with sentences containing different verbs that have different argument structures and hence require different filler-gap assignments, as well as with sentences containing the same verb but different potential fillers, only some of which are compatible as fillers for a particular gap. The results they obtained are consistent with the view that verb-control information is accessed immediately and used to guide the parser's decisions[19] and that the accessed information is *thematic* rather than *syntactic* (Tanenhaus et al. 1990, but also see Fodor, this volume, for a discussion).

The issues that Tanenhaus, Garnsey, and Boland consider imply that there is some division of labor between different processes, for instance, between a syntactic processor and a thematic processor. Frazier (this volume) further considers the nature of this subdivision, with particular emphasis on how and whether these processes are modular. Frazier divides sentence processing into four modules. The first two modules are concerned primarily with structural properties of the lexical input. One of these computes the syntactic-constituent structure of the sentence using only syntactic information (such higher-level information as thematic information is not used to guide this construction process at all). The second syntactic module is concerned more with computing the binding relations between elements in the sentence (e.g., filler-gap dependencies). The third module computes thematic-role assignments. And the fourth and final module computes referential relations (i.e., it establishes referents within some model of the discourse). Frazier cites a number of studies that further investigate the workings of the thematic module and concludes that it considers alternative assignments in parallel and assigns thematic roles only when all the potential arguments (role fillers) have been encountered.[20]

Frazier acknowledges that the modules responsible for thematic and referential processing are not informationally encapsulated. The thematic module requires access to general world knowledge (to assess the plausibility of a thematic assignment), and the referential module requires access to information about the discourse context. Thus these two modules cannot be modules in the Fodorian sense. J. D. Fodor (this volume) considers this point and concludes that only a small change in Frazier's specification is needed to preserve J. A. Fodor's (1983) conception of modularity. Briefly, there are two major ways in which one can model the interaction between the thematic and syntactic processors during the resolution of syntactic ambiguity. According to one model, the thematic module actively directs the syntactic module to attempt a particular analysis, what Crain and Steedman (1985) termed a "strong" interaction, while according to the other model, the thematic module simply rejects an implausible syntactic analysis and thereby causes the syntactic processor to try again. The essential difference here is that in the latter case the thematic processor does not dictate the form of the analysis to be attempted (if it did, as in the first model, this would violate information encapsulation). However, as Fodor points out, Frazier would not advocate such a model, since on her view, shared by Tanenhaus et al. (1990), the thematic processor serves as an interface between linguistic and nonlinguistic knowledge.[21] For Frazier, this means that the thematic processor knows too much about grammar to be relegated to being a simple filter.

The nature of the interaction between the syntactic module and other modules making up the language-comprehension system is still the subject of considerable debate (e.g., Altmann and Steedman 1988; Crain and Steedman 1985; Ferreira and Clifton 1986; Fodor, this volume). Typically, however, the main concern has been over the relationship between syntax and higher-level information (whether it is thematic or pragmatic) and the interactions between these two types of information. In the following section I consider a further relationship, that between syntactic analysis and the prosodic attributes of a sentence, that is, sentence attributes which are generally manifested only in the spoken form of the sentence.

Syntactic Processing and Intonational Structure

An important aspect of sentence processing is the integration of the information conveyed by the sentence with information contained within some internal model of the discourse within which the sentence plays a part. This process of integration must necessarily be sensitive to whether the information conveyed by a part of the sentence provides "given" information, that is, already known to the hearer (or assumed by the speaker to be known to the hearer), or new information, that is, not already known to the hearer (Halliday 1967). Prosody and intonational structure are together one way of conveying these distinctions to the hearer, with the main sentential pitch accent falling on the new information and with prosodic phrase boundaries demarcating the given/new structure of the sentence.

Steedman (this volume) points out that several current theories of prosody and intonation assume a level of representation corresponding to intonational structure that is independent of the level that corresponds to surface structure. The motivation for postulating this independence is in part that although intonational phrases can correspond to units that are not traditional syntactic constituents, there are constraints on the freedom with which intonational phrases can be mapped onto such units. Not all conceivable substrings of a sentence can correspond to an intonational phrase. Traditional theories of metrical phonology thus introduce this independent level of representation to provide an additional level of constraint on the mapping between surface structure and intonational structure. In essence, this extra level of constraint is needed simply because the syntactic structures defined by the grammar do not match up with the phrasal structures defined by the rules of metrical phonology. Steedman suggests that by adopting an alternative grammatical formalism to those favored by metrical phonologists, namely combinatory categorial grammar (CCG) (Steedman 1985, 1987), an appropriate match between syntax and intonational structure can be found.

An important feature of CCG is that it assigns nonstandard constituent structures to input strings. They are nonstandard because English has traditionally been thought of as a right-branching language, whereas CCG generally assigns *left*-branching structures to the input. One consequence of this is that the grammar thus allows, under certain assumptions concerning the relationship between syntactic and semantic rules, *incremental left-to-right* interpretation. In other words, it allows a comprehension device to interpret a sentence, and integrate the information conveyed by that sentence into a representation of the discourse, more or less as each word is enountered. The benefits of this are that it in principle allows the early and efficient rejection of semantically and pragmatically inappropriate analyses (see Altmann and Steedman 1988 for further elaboration). In view of the incremental real-time nature of human sentence processing (Marslen-Wilson 1975, Marslen-Wilson and Tyler 1980, Tanenhaus et al. 1985),[22] there is some psycholinguistic motivation, in addition to the purely linguistic motivation (Steedman 1985, 1987), for adopting a grammar that permits such processing.

CCG treats as well-formed constituents substrings that under the more traditional grammatical formalisms would not be considered well formed. However, there are constraints on which substrings can be considered in this way. Not all substrings can be interpreted as well-formed constituents. Steedman (this volume) shows that those substrings that *cannot* be interpreted as well-formed constituents within CCG are exactly those substrings that, according to conventional metrical phonology, cannot form an intonational phrase. The converse, that all permissible constituents as defined by CCG can also be intonational phrases is also true.[23] There is thus a complete match between the syntactic structures defined by CCG and the intonational phrases defined by the rules of metrical phonology. From this complete match it follows that it is no longer necessary, within the framework provided by CCG, to postulate the intermediary level of intonational structure that is assumed by other theories of metrical phonology.

CCG exactly satisfies the requirements of a metrical phonology because it assigns a nonstandard constituent structure to each sentence. However, as Joshi (this volume) points out, there are a variety of grammatical formalisms that, like CCG, can provide nonstandard analyses. Joshi demonstrates that at least one of these, the Tree-Adjoining Grammar (TAG), also permits the flexibility required to support intonational phrasing without postulating an intermediate level of structure.

Steedman's and Joshi's approach to intonation is to use a grammatical formalism to define the possible locations of intonational phrase boundaries. What they do not attempt to do, however, is to show how a syntactic parsing device might *use* intonational boundaries to guide its operations. Such an account is given by Marcus and Hindle (this volume).

Marcus and Hindle suggest that intonation breaks (or phrase boundaries) serve to restrict the assignment of theta roles to potential fillers (that is, lexical items that can be assigned a theta role).[24] Specifically, they suggest that uninterpreted tree descriptions (corresponding more or less to the major syntactic constituents) are output by a phrase-structure analyzer. As they are output, a theta-role mechanism immediately attempts to assign theta roles to the lexical items it encounters. Marcus assumes that the theta structure, or theta grid, of any verb is immediately available (see Tanenhaus, this volume). However, intonation boundaries force the parsing mechanism to terminate the current (and any previously unterminated) constituent(s). This prevents the theta-role mechanism from immediately filling an empty role in the theta grid with *the first potential filler* (which can only be found in the description tree for the next constituent). Instead, the theta-role mechanism leaves the role unfilled, allowing a subsequent mechanism to choose a *different* assignment. Thus, the short-sighted theta-role mechanism cannot assign a filler on one side of an intonation break to a role on the other side. Only a subsequent, more long-sighted mechanism can do this. Marcus's examples of the workings of his parser illustrate this process and show how appropriate intonation breaks can cause the parsing device to avoid constructing inappropriate syntactic analyses (and hence "garden-pathing") by preventing the theta-role mechanism from filling an empty role with the first possible filler.

Unlike Steedman's grammatical formalism, Marcus's theory is a processing account. Within this account the role of intonation breaks is not as a *guiding* influence on theta-role assignment. The interaction here is indirect, in that intonation breaks signal the parser to terminate a constituent, and it is due to the short-sightedness of the theta-role mechanism that this has the effect of modifying theta-role assignments. Whereas Marcus attempts to relate intonational structure to processing, Steedman attempts to relate it to grammar. The aims of the two accounts are very different. It remains to be seen how the two accounts can be reconciled.

Summary and Concluding Remarks

The chapters in this volume cover a wide range of topics from models of lexical access, through models of the interaction between lexical access and higher-levels of sentential interpretation, to models of sentence processing and its relationship to intonation. Within the domain of lexical access there is a general consensus, at least among the contributors to this volume, that such notions as interactive activation, inhibition, and competitor effects are fundamental to modeling the mapping between acoustic input and the internal lexicon. There is also agreement over the form of the interaction between this mapping process and information in the sentential domain. Whereas lexical information appears to be capable of altering the percept of the individual sound segments making up the word, sentential information only has a much more indirect effect on the lower-level processes. There is less consensus, however, among researchers at this higher sentential level. Some argue that syntactic processing is relatively immune to higher-level semantic/pragmatic effects, with the latter exerting their influence only during a later stage of processing, while others argue that semantic/pragmatic information can be used during the earliest syntactic analysis. These issues are far from settled, and further research is required to resolve these different views.

Spoken-word recognition and sentence processing have traditionally been considered as two separate domains of study. However, speech comprehension, and speech processing in general, does not simply stop once the acoustic input has been matched against the internal lexicon. One outcome of recent research on computational models of the higher-level processes responsible for the construction of an utterance-level interpretation of the acoustic input has been the demonstration that these higher-level processes need not be too different in form, in terms of their computational implementation, from the lower-level processes traditionally associated with spoken-word recognition. Consider PDP models of sentence interpretation (e.g., McClelland et al. 1990). Whether or not researchers can construct a unified model of speech processing remains to be seen. As indicated earlier, it is unclear whether a model based solely on the principles of PDP learning systems can successfully model the different kinds of interactions among the different conceptual levels within the system. Of course, whether it does or not is to a certain extent irrelevant if the correct *behaviors* are nonetheless elicited.

The intention of this particular collection of papers has been to highlight contemporary issues in the cognitive modeling of speech processing. One of the more important developments in cognitive modeling in recent years has been the increased exchange of ideas and concepts between the computational and psycholinguistic domains. The chapters in this volume constitute just such an exchange and emphasize bringing together the psycholinguistic and computational perspectives on cognitive modeling.

Notes

1. This list is not exhaustive but is intended only to cover the main issues dealt with by the accompanying papers in this volume. For further review, see Tyler and Frauenfelder 1987.

2. Further discussion of current issues in sentence processing can be found in Altmann 1989.

3. See the chapters by Segui et al. and by Mehler et al. for further discussion of the syllable as the unit of perception. The former chapter is concerned primarily with adult perception, while the latter argues that the syllable is the perceptual unit on which basis the infant acquires a lexicon in the first place. My chapter on lexical statistics reviews the evidence from computational studies of large lexicons, which suggests that stressed syllables convey more information about the identity of the word in which they occur than do unstressed syllables.

4. In fact, feedback is via a set of state (or context) units (see the chapter by Norris for further details).

5. There is no reason why, during the learning phase, the network couldn't *acquire* distinct levels of representation. In other words, learning could lead to the emergence of a division of labor within the hidden units. See the chapter by Elman for an example of a network that does acquire internal representations.

6. Marslen-Wilson's (1987) conclusions were based on reaction-time studies with nonwords, while Luce's conclusions were based on a combination of word and nonword studies.

7. This corresponds, within the context of a tree-structured lexicon, to the notion of a branching factor.

8. For further discussion of Shillcock's work, see the chapter by Charles-Luce et al. This chapter describes data on the recognition of such words as *lighthouse* and bears additionally on the issues considered in the chapter by Cutler.

9. See the chapter by Bard for a detailed theoretical discussion of this distinction and of the role of inhibition in models of spoken-word recognition.

10. Samuel (this volume) reports a study by Dewitt and Samuel that suggests parallel effects from nonspeech stimuli in the music domain: melodic information did not have any perceptual effect on note discrimination, while scale information did.

11. Samuel argues that these two influences can be discriminated between with the signal-detection methodology. See the chapter by Tyler for a discussion.

12. Samuel points out, though, that modularity can be preserved if it is assumed that the lexicon is embedded within the perceptual module.

13. See the chapter by Tyler for further discussion of both Samuel's and Connine's results.

14. This is not the place to continue, or even to comment on, the debate. The reader is referred to Fodor and Pylyshyn 1987 for a summary of the main arguments. The Fodor and Pylyshyn paper is one of a number of papers making up a special issue of the journal *Cognition*. See that issue for further discussion of topics concerned with the connectionist paradigm. See also McClelland, St. John, and Taraban 1990 for a reply to Fodor and Pylyshyn's charges against connectionism.

15. Activation is not a concept that fits naturally within the Chart framework, but see the chapter by Thompson and Altmann for further discussion of the relationship between Marslen-Wilson's (1987) distinctions between access, selection, and integration on the one hand and processing on the Chart on the other.

16. Note that the term *module* is used here not in the original sense intended by Fodor (1983) but in its more informal sense.

17. As in the chapter by Thompson and myself, no claim is made about the psychological status of either the Active Chart Parser or the tree-structured lexicon.

18. See Fodor's chapter, which comments on the chapters by Tanenhaus et al. and by Frazier, for further discussion of these distinctions.

19. This runs counter to Mitchell's (1987, 1989) claims that verb-subcategorization information is *not* immediately used during sentence processing but *is* used to filter out inappropriate syntactic analyses.

20. Note that this view is different from that advocated by Tanenhaus et al., who would not necessarily agree with the claim that thematic assignments are made only once all the potential arguments have been encountered.

21. See Fodor's chapter for further discussion and for differences between a serial interpretation of thematic processing (advocated by Frazier) and a parallel interpretation, in which thematic information is used to select among alternatives, a view that conforms more with that held by Tanenhaus and colleagues (this volume, 1989; see also Clifton and Ferreira (1989) and Steedman and Altmann (1989) for further discussion of this issue).

22. Also see the papers in a special issue of the journal *Language and Cognitive Processes*, vol. 4 (1989), no. 3/4, on parsing and interpretation for further discussion of incremental processing and real-time interpretation.

23. See Steedman (this volume) for a discussion, and see Joshi (this volume) for a related discussion of some shortcomings of the CCG approach to defining intonational structure.

24. See the chapter by Fodor for the distinction between theta role and thematic role. The distinction does not need to be elaborated for the purposes of this summary.

References

Altmann, G. T. M. 1989. Parsing and interpretation: An introduction. *Language and Cognitive Processes* 4, no. 3/4: 1–20.

Altmann, G. T. M., Steedman, M. 1988. Interaction with context during human sentence processing. *Cognition* 30: 191–238.

Briscoe, E. J. 1989. Lexical access in connected speech recognition. Twenty-Seventh Annual Congress of the Association for Computational Linguistics, Vancouver.

Clifton, C., and Ferreira, F. 1989. Ambiguity in context. *Language and Cognitive Processes* 4, no 3/4: 77–104.

Cole, R. A., and Jakimik, J. 1980. A model of speech production. In R. A. Cole (ed.), *Perception and Production of Fluent Speech*. Hillsdale, N.J.: Erlbaum.

Connine, C. M. 1987. Constraints on interactive processes in auditory word recognition: The role of sentence context. *Journal of Memory and Language* 26: 527–538.

Connine, C. M., and Clifton, C. 1987. Interactive use of lexical information in speech perception. *Journal of Experimental Psychology: Human Perception and Performance* 13: 291–299.

Crain, S., and Steedman, M. J. 1985. On not being led up the garden path: The use of context by the psychological parser. In D. Dowty, L. Karttunen, and A. Zwicky (eds.), *Natural Language Parsing: Psychological, Computational, and Theoretical Perspectives*. Cambridge: Cambridge University Press.

Cutler, A., and Norris, D. 1988. The role of strong syllables in segmentation for lexical access. *Journal of Experimental Psychology: Human Perception and Performance* 14: 113–121.

Ferreira, F., and Clifton, C. 1986. The independence of syntactic processing. *Journal of Memory and Language* 25: 348–368.

Fodor, J. A. 1983. *The Modularity of Mind*. Cambridge: MIT Press.

Fodor, J. A., and Pylyshyn, Z. W. 1987. Connectionism and cognitive architecture: A critical analysis. *Cognition* 28: 3–71.

Ganong, W. F. 1980. Phonetic categorization in auditory word perception. *Journal of Experimental Psychology: Human Perception and Performance* 6, no.1: 110–125.

Halliday, M. A. K. 1967. Notes on transitivity and theme in English. Part 2. *Journal of Linguistics* 3: 199–244.

Jordon, M. I. 1986. Serial order: A parallel distributed processing approach. Institute of Cognitive Science, report 8604. University of California, San Diego.

Luce, P. A. 1986. Neighborhoods of words in the mental lexicon. Doctoral dissertation, Indiana University, Bloomington, Indiana.

McClelland, J. L., and Elman, J. L. 1986. The TRACE model of speech perception. *Cognitive Psychology* 18 : 1–86.

McClelland, J. L., St. John, M., and Taraban, R. 1989. Sentence comprehension: A parallel distributed processing approach. *Language and Cognitive Processes* 4, no. 3/4: 287–336.

Marslen-Wilson, W. D. 1975. Sentence perception as an interactive parallel process. *Science* 189 : 226–228.

Marslen-Wilson, W. D. 1987. Functional parallelism in spoken word recognition. *Cognition* 25 : 71–102.

Marslen-Wilson, W. D., and Tyler, L. K. 1980. The temporal structure of spoken language understanding. *Cognition* 8 : 1–71.

Marslen-Wilson, W. D., and Welsh, A. 1978. Processing interactions during word recognition in continuous speech. *Cognitive Psychology* 10 : 29–63.

Mitchell, D. C. 1987. Lexical guidance in human parsing: Locus and processing characteristics. In M. Coltheart (ed.), *Attention and Performance*, vol. 12. Hove, U.K.: Erlbaum.

Mitchell, D. C. 1989. Verb-guidance and other lexical effects in parsing. *Language and Cognitive Processes* 4, no. 3/4: 123–154.

Norris, D. 1986. Word recognition: Context effects without priming. *Cognition* 22 : 93–136.

Samuel, A. 1981. Phoneme restoration: Insights from a new methodolgy. *Journal of Experimental Psychology: General* 110 : 474–494.

Samuel, A. 1987. The effect of lexical uniqueness on phonemic restoration. *Journal of Memory and Language* 26 : 36–56.

Steedman, M. 1985. Dependency and coordination in the grammar of Dutch and English. *Language* 61 : 523–568.

Steedman, M. 1987. Combinatory grammars and human sentence processing. In J. Garfield (ed.), *Modularity in Knowledge Representation and Natural Language Processing*. Cambridge: MIT Press.

Steedman, M. J., and Altmann, G. T. M. 1989. Ambiguity in context: A reply. *Language and Cognitive Processes* 4, no. 3/4: 105–122.

Tanenhaus, M. K., Carlson, G., and Seidenberg, M. S. 1985. Do listeners compute linguistic representations? In D. Dowty, L. Karttunen, and A. Zwicky, (eds.), *Natural Language Parsing: Psychological, Computational, and Theoretical Perspectives*. Cambridge: Cambridge University Press.

Tanenhaus, M. K., Carlson, G., and Trueswell, J. C. 1989. The role of thematic structures in interpretation and parsing. *Language and Cognitive Processes* 4, no. 3/4: 211–234.

Thompson, H. S., and Ritchie, G. D. 1984. Implementing natural language parsers. In T. O'Shea and M. Eisenstadt (eds.), *Artificial Intelligence: Tools, Techniques, and Applications*. Harper & Row.

Tyler, L. K., and Frauenfelder, U. H. 1987. The process of spoken word recognition: An introduction. *Cognition* 25: 1–20.

Zwitserlood, P. 1989. The locus of the effects of sentential-semantic context in spoken-word processing. *Cognition* 32: 25–64.

Chapter 2
Lexical Hypotheses in Continuous Speech

Richard Shillcock

Spontaneous, continuous speech contains very few completely reliable cues to the location of word boundaries. Listeners, however, are rarely conscious of any difficulty in resolving such an inherently ambiguous signal into a stream of words perceived clearly and immediately, which are quickly incorporated into a message-level interpretation. Numerous incorrect and inconsistent word hypotheses are necessarily considered by the processor. This paper demonstrates the existence of one particular type of erroneous hypothesis and considers the implications for the general process of word recognition in continuous speech. Figure 1 is a spectrogram of the two-word utterance *recognize speech*. It demonstrates the problem that there is no single reliable physical cue, such as the spaces between words in text, to inform the processor that a new word starts at a particular point in the signal. Even if this speech is reliably converted into a sequence of phonemes, as in figure 2, it still presents an ambiguous picture. While there is only one intended parse of the sequence into words, there are a number of erroneous hypotheses that are homophonous with parts of the target word, like *wreck* and *nice* in *recognize*. In other cases the erroneous hypothesis might span a word boundary, as when the phrase *let us* is mistaken for *letters*, for instance.

Figure 2 is taken from the output of an automatic speech recognizer. Does the same problem exist on the same scale for the human speech processor? Although listeners are only rarely aware of the problem, occasionally noticing a segmentation error such as *Sue did her theories* for *suited her theories*, there is good reason to believe that erroneous hypotheses are continually generated by the processor without the listener being conscious of them. First, the processor cannot avoid entertaining a range of word-initial competitors: *mar* could be a word in itself or it could go on to become *mark, market, marquis,* and so on. Second, many non-word-initial hy-

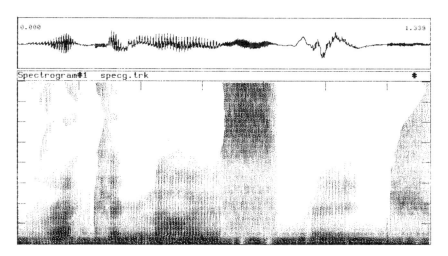

Figure 1
A spectrogram of the two words *recognize speech.*

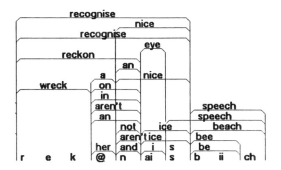

Figure 2
A machine's attempt to parse phonemes into words.

potheses (*nice* in *recognize*) should be entertained partly because it is generally safer for the processor to overgenerate hypotheses than to risk excluding the correct hypothesis and partly because segmentation cues other than substantial pauses are unreliable and generally only signal the probability of a boundary at a particular point (Lehiste 1972; Nakatani and Dukes 1977; Harrington, Watson, and Cooper 1988). In some cases there will be no means of distinguishing syllable boundaries from word boundaries using only low-level cues: the syllable boundary in *trombone* might be mistaken for a word boundary were it not for the lexical-level knowledge that *trom* is not a word; syntactic information may be required to prevent *terrain* being parsed as *to rain*. Third, the segmentation strategy suggested by Cutler and Norris (1988) and Cutler and Carter (1987), in which a metrically stressed syllable signals a word boundary, actually predicts a false alarm rate of the order of 16 percent in spontaneous continuous speech (Shillcock and Bard, forthcoming) in which incorrect word-medial boundaries are generated. For these reasons, then, we might expect the human listener to produce erroneous hypotheses something like those in figure 2 prior to word recognition.

The progress of correct segmentation decisions and correct word recognitions was central to earlier models of word recognition (Marslen-Wilson and Welsh 1978, Cole and Jakimik 1980), but it plays much less of a role in current models. The earlier models employed what Frauenfelder (1985) termed a postlexical strategy for ensuring correct segmentation decisions. Given speech of adequate quality, correct word recognition usually trails behind the input by no more than one or two syllables (Marslen-Wilson 1973), with recognition often occurring before the acoustic offset of the word. In principle, a word such as *evict* may be recognized before its final segment, as it is already unique in the lexicon at that stage: its uniqueness point is before the final segment. If a word has been correctly recognized before its offset and its phonological code accessed, the end of the word may be calculated in advance, and the beginning of the next word correctly predicted. If this postlexical strategy were able to operate consistently, it would leave only the temporary ambiguities of the *mar*, *mark*, *market* category. Indeed, research inspired by the original version of the cohort model has tended to concentrate on the process whereby the set of initially homophonous words is reduced until only the target word remains. In research on auditory word recognition, competition between word hypotheses has usually meant competition between words that share initial segments, like the cohort *mar*, *market*, *marlin*, *marquis*, etc.

It is now clear, however, that the postlexical strategy has only a limited role. Luce (1986a) demonstrated that some 60 percent of words in continuous speech do not possess uniqueness points: like *mar*, they can be extended to form longer, completely unrelated words. In these cases the beginning of the next word cannot be reliably predicted. Additionally, Bard, Shillcock, and Altmann (1988) have demonstrated that approximately one in five correctly recognized words in spontaneous, continuous speech requires subsequent context for recognition to occur. Finally, there is suffixing: since it is a relatively unattractive option for the lexicon to store each differently suffixed version of each word, the processor may have identified the stem of the previous word but still have the task of identifying its suffix, often in the face of considerable phonological reduction. In view of Luce's finding, the postlexical strategy seems best suited to longer, content words, which are precisely the words that often end with a poorly specified suffix. Even for longer words that do possess uniqueness points, the postlexical strategy may not be very effective at all.

In short, the processor is frequently confronted by stretches of input representing two or more words in which there are no reliable indications of where the word boundaries might be and in which the processor may be forced to recognize a word in the absence of word-boundary information.

Current models of word recognition, such as the revised cohort model (Marslen-Wilson 1987) and TRACE (McClelland and Elman 1986), have accommodated these facts. These models do not require prior segmentation. Instead, segmentation is the result of recognition. The early version of the cohort model stressed the role of the *word-initial cohort*, the candidate set generated by the first 150 msec or so of the word. The model achieved extreme economy by assuming prior segmentation and by making correct, sequential, categorical decisions about the identity of phonemes, but it ran an unacceptable risk in that it required some unspecified kind of backtracking in cases where recognition failed either because the segmentation information was unreliable or consecutive categorical decisions about phonemes could not be made. In the revised version of the cohort model, the representation of a word is activated to the extent that there is a correspondence between the stored representation and the input. This allows the processor to cope with signal variability. It is far less likely to fail to recognize a word as a result of the poor specification of a single phoneme, for instance: *shigarette* will activate *cigarette*. This means, however, that word-internal stretches of the signal that happen to match words in the lexicon will cause the momentary activation of those candidates. When the preceding and subsequent input fails to match, their activation levels return to their resting levels. Alternatively, these word-internal candidates might be assessed against the developing message-level interpretation and dismissed only somewhat later. There is no necessary contradiction between this state of affairs and the attribution of a special role to the initial segments of a word. As Marslen-Wilson (1987) points out, this revised cohort will be functionally little different from the original notion of the cohort.

In TRACE, when the input supports the presence of a particular phoneme, this adds to the activation level of all of the words in the lexicon that contain that phoneme at any point. As Frauenfelder and Peeters (this volume) demonstrate, TRACE generates severe constraints on the activation levels that embedded words may reach. Nevertheless, TRACE in principle permits the activation of embedded words that violate the intended segmentation; the precise activation level reached by such words depends on the network parameters chosen and on the set of competing words in the lexicon in any particular case. Note that small activation levels need to be the judged against the criteria set by whatever apparatus for multiple semantic assessment sits above the network in the larger model.

Both of these models of word recognition in principle permit the generation of a wide range of erroneous lexical hypotheses. The target word is unlikely to be excluded from this set of activated words. The cost lies in the potentially large size of the set of activated words. The means by which the processor contains this enlarged volume of activation thus becomes important, and attention has recently moved to the competition between lexical hypotheses.

The TRACE model is computationally explicit about this competition: the activation level of the representation of a particular word is determined partly by its correspondence to the input and partly by the state of activation of the representations of all of the other words in the lexicon, since TRACE contains inhibitory connections between all of the representations at the same level and excitatory interlevel connections. Marslen-Wilson notes that TRACE fails to predict Zwitserlood's (1985) demonstration of the parallel activation of word hypotheses that match a certain input: the input *cap-* activates both *captain* and *captive*, for instance. He argues that TRACE predicts that these active hypotheses should be inhibiting each other, with the result that there is very little early activation of either candidate until after their separation point, when the hypothesis that matches more of the input outstrips all of the others. It is difficult to assess such an argument: in principle, winner-take-all architectures like that of

TRACE tend not to allow the equal parallel activation of competing hypotheses, but in reality, it is possible to set the various parameters that govern activation and inhibition so as to permit something like this. (In fact, with the parameter settings used by McClelland and Elman the mutual inhibition of two word-initial competitors suppresses their activation only relatively slightly.)

Marslen-Wilson (1987) is less explicit about the nature of the competition that the revised cohort model permits between active candidates, although he cites work by Zwitserlood (1985) that suggests that the determining factor in the competition between two word hypotheses is the frequency *difference* between them. The cohort model does not, however, possess TRACE's lateral inhibition. (See Bard, this volume, for a discussion of different forms of competition between activated word hypotheses.) The cohort model still involves multiple semantic assessment: as in the original version, it is not necessary for the winning hypothesis to be the most highly activated hypothesis, as all of the activated hypotheses are assessed in parallel for their plausibility in the context of the higher-level message. However, in discussion of situations in which the process of selection apparently runs to completion without the intervention of the parallel semantic assessment of the candidate set, Marslen-Wilson suggests that a word is recognized once its level of activation becomes criterially different from that of its closest competitor. (See Marslen-Wilson, this volume, for a fuller discussion of competition between active word hypotheses.)

In summary, some models of word recognition do not rely on prior segmentation.[1] In principle, these models allow overlapping hypotheses to be simultaneously entertained; these will include competitors that do not have synchronized onsets, like *trombone* and *bone*. If such models require the emergence of a winning hypothesis, then efficient functioning calls for an architecture that allows the correct hypothesis to emerge as quickly as possible once information has arrived that uniquely favors that hypothesis. It is also in the interests of the processor that the activation levels of the unsuccessful competitors are quickly returned to their resting levels so as not to prejudice the recognition of the next word. The optimal performance of the processor would involve activating no more hypotheses than were actually necessary to guarantee the generation of the target hypothesis.

The issues are, first, does the human speech processor pursue erroneous hypotheses such as *bone* in *trombone* in continuous speech, as predicted by the models of word recognition discussed above? Second, do the constraints on the generation of these hypotheses indicate the means by which the processor contains the general volume of activation in the lexicon? Finally, are these constraints captured by the architectures of the models?

Is there any evidence that listeners actually generate such erroneous hypotheses when they process speech? Swinney (1981) refers to a study by Prather and Swinney (1977) that employed the technique of cross-modal priming to investigate precisely this question. The strength of this technique is that the subject listens carefully to a complete auditory stimulus— a single word or an utterance—and monitors it only for meaning. This is a relatively normal listening task in comparison with techniques that require the subject to monitor the speech for a particular phoneme, for instance. At some point in the speech, a word or nonword appears on a screen in front of the subject, who is then required to perform a timed lexical decision, pressing a *yes* button if a real word has been presented. If the speech has caused a lexical entry to be accessed and activated, this is reflected in a facilitation of the visual lexical decision about a semantically related word when compared to a matched unrelated control word in a different condition of the experiment: hearing *bank* facilitates the visual recognition of *money*. Moreover, the technique is able to reflect the access of lexical entries of which the listener is unaware: *bank* in a context that indicates its money meaning will also cause the momentary activation of the river meaning.

In Prather and Swinney's cross-modal priming experiment, subjects were auditorily presented the word *boycott*. The recognition of a visual probe word related to *boy* was facilitated when it was presented at a point halfway through *boycott*, whereas in a different condition of the experiment there was no facilitation of a visual probe word related to *cot* presented at the end of *boycott*. The implication of Swinney's result is that the *boy* hypothesis is activated halfway through *boycott*, which is not surprising, since the two words are homophonous up to that point, but that the *cot* hypothesis is not activated despite a similar close match with the input.

This led Swinney to formulate a "minimal accretion principle," which states that the first potential word encountered in the speech stream is momentarily activated (*boy*), and that immediately subsequent potential words (*cot*) are not activated in cases where this subsequent information can combine with the earlier material to form a larger word (*boycott*). This late-closure principle was implicit in the early version of the cohort model, with its narrowing down of the word-initial cohort: the input corresponding to the first two phonemes of *boycott* define a word-initial cohort of candidates including *boy*, *boycott*, *boisterous*, etc., and as additional information arrives, more and more candidates fail to meet the specification and are dismissed, a process that eventually leaves only the target word. Swinney's minimal accretion principle means that the cohort must be reduced until only the target word remains. For *boycott*, a new word-initial cohort may not be generated anywhere else in the word, as this would leave either a nonword (*boyk*) or a cohort with more than one entry (*boy*, *boycott*, etc.).

Swinney's minimal accretion principle is consistent with the early version of the cohort model and is subject to some of the same criticisms: it helps the processor to constrain the number of hypotheses entertained, but it embodies the postlexical strategy in that it relies on words being sequentially recognized at or before their offsets. Also, it fails to give both readings in examples like *no notion* versus *known ocean*. The principle involves an unacceptably high risk of failure, and it does not specify the details of recovery from that failure.

There are a number of reasons for doubting the generality of Swinney's finding. Unfortunately, the materials Swinney used are not listed in the review article in which he mentions the experiment, so the following points are addressed to the one example of *boycott*.

First, *boycott* is stress-initial: lexical stress falls on the first syllable, although there is typically little or no phonological reduction in the second syllable. There have been several suggestions that stressed syllables should receive some kind of privileged status in lexical access (Cutler 1976, Bradley 1980, Grosjean and Gee 1984, Huttenlocher 1984). If this is so, Swinney's results might have been different for a stress-final word like *guitar*, in which the second, stressed syllable is also a word, *tar*.

Second, *boycott* is monomorphemic. Erroneous lexical hypotheses that are not word-initial are perhaps more likely to be found in words that begin, or appear to begin, with a prefix. Various models of lexical access include a process corresponding to prefix stripping together with a stem-ordered lexicon, so that a prefixed word is accessed via its stem (Taft 1979, Jarvella and Meijers 1983). These models predict that a word like *delight* might cause the activation of *light* as the processor assesses the putative stem of that word. The processor would need to treat genuine prefixes and pseudoprefixes alike in this respect.

Third, the subjects in Swinney's experiment appear to have heard only an isolated word. Continuous speech is an inherently ambiguous signal; the human speech processor may be unable to avoid certain erroneous word hypotheses in continuous speech. The situation may be very different, however, when the subject is expecting only an isolated word.

Fourth, the first syllable of *boycott* is not only homophonous with *boy*, but the two are also orthographically identical, whereas the second syllable is only homophonous with *cot*. Jakimik, Cole, and Rudnicky (1985) suggest that this difference may be important in determining priming effects. For these four reasons, Swinney's minimal accretion principle may be an underestimation of the extent to which the processor generates erroneous word hypotheses.

The First Experiment

In the first experiment the cross-modal priming technique was used to determine whether or not listeners actually entertained these critical erroneous hypotheses that are not word-initial with respect to the target word. (Fuller experimental details are given in Shillcock 1990.)

The critical word in each sentence was a two-syllable word, with a weak-strong stress pattern, in which the second syllable was homophonous with a semantically unrelated word: *guitar*, which contains *tar*, for instance. The critical word was either prefixed (*descend*) or monomorphemic (*trombone*). In addition, the second syllable of the word was either orthographically identical to, and homophonous with, the unrelated word (*bone* in *trombone*) or simply homophonous with that word (*send* in *descend*). Relatively few words in the language satisfy all of these criteria; accordingly, the prefixed category contained a number of words, such as *defeat*, whose morphological complexity is debatable. However, all of the words in this category began with a syllable that commonly occurs as a prefix. If the processor is really involved in some form of prefix-stripping, it must treat all word-beginnings that are homophonous with a prefix as potential prefixes.

The two versions of each experimental sentence resembled (1) and (2) below. In (1) the critical word was the two-syllable word; in (2) the critical word was the relevant monosyllabic word embedded in the same minimal context.

(1) He carefully placed the trombone on the table.

(2) He carefully placed the bone on the table.

A close associate of the monosyllable, generally a hyponym (*rib* in the case of *bone*) or a matched unrelated control word (*bun*), acted as the visual probe word.

The construction of the materials and the design of the experiment allowed the two contrasts, orthography and prefixing, to be studied in-

Table 1
Mean reaction times (in msec) for monomorphemic and prefixed words. $N = 32$.

	Related probe (*rib*)	Unrelated probe (*bun*)
One-syllable word (*bone*)	743.7	779.4
Two-syllable word (*trombone*)	765.2	772.8

Table 2
Mean reaction times (in msec) for the monomorphemic words. $N = 32$.

	Related probe	Unrelated probe
One-syllable word	755.7	783.7
Two-syllable word	746.8	780.1

dividually, as the 48 critical words fell equally into the four different combinations of the two factors. Sentence (1), for instance, falls into the monomorphemic and orthographically identical category. An analysis employing data from all of the items produced the means shown in table 1, in which only normal, whole-word priming appears to be happening. Significant priming occurred only for the one-syllable auditory word: *rib* is only primed by *bone*, which is what was expected. Scheffé tests revealed that this *bone-rib* priming was significant at $p < .005$. This is good news for the traditional strictly left-to-right view of things.

Separate analyses for the prefixed and monomorphemic words proved to be rather more interesting, however. They revealed that the results for the whole data masked an important distinction. For the monomorphemic subset, the means, shown in table 2, demonstrate priming by both types of auditory word, *bone* and *trombone*. The priming effect was significant: $F_1(1, 28) = 9.04, p < .01; F_2(1, 23) = 5.30, p < .05$. Although there is very slightly more priming by the two-syllable word, the interaction was not significant. In short, the monomorphemic two-syllable words produced quite erroneous priming equal to the legitimate priming produced by the monosyllabic word.

When just the prefixed set of words was analyzed, the means were as in table 3. In table 3 the effect has swung around. After the two-syllable word there were longer lexical decision times for the related probe word in comparison with the control word: after *report* it took subjects longer to recognize *wine* than the unrelated control word *dirt*. The interaction was significant only in the F_1 analysis, however: $F_1(1, 28) = 9.54, p < .005$; $F_2(1, 23) = 2.96, p < .1$.

Table 3
Mean reaction times (in msec) for the prefixed words. $N = 32$.

	Related probe	Unrelated probe
One-syllable word	731.7	775.2
Two-syllable word	783.6	765.5

The differences in orthography proved to have no interesting implications. Post hoc analyses indicated an important role for word frequency in any explanation of the results. The two-syllable monomorphemic words were lower in frequency than the prefixed words: a mean of 17 compared with 40, measured in terms of numbers of samples in Francis and Kučera (1982). If there is competition between the carrier word and the embedded word, the embedded word should receive less activation when it is competing with a high-frequency carrier word. There was, however, no significant correlation between the priming obtained and the frequency of the two-syllable word which suggests that the frequency of the carrier word does not provide a complete explanation of the results. The level of activation attained by the embedded word was predicted by the frequency of the most frequent word in the word-initial cohort generated by the first syllable of the two-syllable word (*give* in the case of *guitar*). For both groups of stimulus materials combined, the correlation was $-.291$, d.f. $= 46$, $p < .025$, and for the monomorphemic group alone $r = -.379$, d.f. $= 22$, $p = .05$; the correlation was not significant for the prefixed group alone, $r = -.072$, d.f. $= 22$, n.s.

This first experiment demonstrated, then, that for the monomorphemic words, erroneous lexical hypotheses were generated that did not reflect a strictly sequential, deterministic parsing of the speech input into words, even in high-quality, read speech. These results are inconsistent with those models of word recognition that embody such processing. The results confirm the general principle, inherent in the revised cohort model and TRACE, that lexical hypotheses may be generated on the basis of goodness of fit between a lexical entry and some part of the input regardless of the segmentation of the target stimulus. The results are evidence against the more detailed prediction from TRACE that word-final embedded words will be effectively suppressed in most cases by the activation of the target word (Frauenfelder and Peeters, this volume). In the case of the monomorphemic words, a hypothesis still seems to be generated even if there is strong competing evidence in the form of an unresolved word hypothesis.

TRACE predicts that even in the optimum case of a word like *appeal*, which has only one phoneme in its first syllable, the embedded word corresponding to the second syllable will attain only a short-lived activation level that is substantially less than it would reach in isolation. This suppression of the embedded word is even more effective in words with larger initial syllables, like *guitar*, and is more or less complete with words like *confine* and *trombone*. (In this respect TRACE accurately reflects the strictly left to right behavior of the early cohort model on which it is based.) A number of points may be made about these predictions. First, it is difficult to assess the more quantitative predictions of TRACE: a small amount of activation may be sufficient to qualify a lexical entry for semantic assessment in parallel with many other hypotheses. Second, a more psychologically realistic version of TRACE would allow differences in the acoustic realization of segments to be reflected in the size of the activations they engender at the different levels; phonological reduction would result initially in smaller amounts of activation at all levels. The recognition of weak-strong words, like *guitar*, in which the vowel in the first syllable can be reduced to the point of elision should typically involve only a slow initial rise in activation level as the *guitar* hypothesis competes with many other weakly activated hypotheses. The more reliably articulated second syllable should then add disproportionately to the activation level of the word. Overall, such an amendment to TRACE should allow word-final embedded words in weak-strong words a larger amount of temporary activation. Third, Frauenfelder and Peeters's simulations ignored word frequency. If frequency is allowed to have its effect in the early stages of access and activation, which gives more-frequent words higher resting levels or shorter rise times, then embedded words in any position in carrier words should be more intrusive, since short words tend to be more frequent than long words. On the other hand, TRACE does accommodate the apparent importance of the most frequent competitor in the word-initial cohort (*give* for *guitar*): TRACE predicts an antagonistic relationship in which a high-frequency word-initial competitor (*give*) may inhibit both the carrier word (*guitar*) and the embedded word (*tar*) (Shillcock 1989). In summary, in view of the previous points about the interpretation of TRACE's predictions, the results for the monomorphemic words offer mixed support for the TRACE model, confirming the ability of the processor to generate lexical hypotheses solely on the basis of goodness of fit with the input and demonstrating frequency-based competition but providing no support for some of the more detailed predictions in which the realization of different segments is idealized.

The behavior of the prefixed items suggests that the activation of word-final embedded words is not the whole story, however. The processor does not generate such hypotheses in every possible instance. In just those words where an erroneous priming effect was most expected, the prefixed ones, there was no activation. In fact, there was inhibition, although the failure of the F_2 analysis to reach statistical significance indicates that word-to-word variation in this effect prevents generalization to all similar words. There appears to be some kind of principled constraint on the simultaneous activation of lexical hypotheses that do not share the same onset.

If the overall results are viewed as embedded-word activation in mono-morphemic carrier words and no embedded-word activation in prefixed words, this offers a certain support for TRACE, which itself predicts a prefixing effect (Shillcock 1989). TRACE's prefixing effect may be summarized as follows. If the principle source of inhibition of a word-final embedded word is the carrier word, the presence of activated hypotheses competing with that word will depress its activation curve and prevent it from inhibiting the embedded word so strongly. Competitors of the carrier word can therefore indirectly increase the activation level of the embedded word (Frauenfelder and Peeters, this volume). Other patterns of competition emerge, however, in larger lexicons that resemble the mental lexicon more closely in that they contain substantial groups of prefixed words.[2] The result is that a substantial word-initial cohort in which the words are homophonous for the first syllable but diverge thereafter causes the suppression, rather than the activation, of a word-final embedded word. This effect is reversed when the word-initial cohort intrudes into the second syllable so that the words share the whole of the first syllable plus the first phoneme (or the first few phonemes) of the second syllable (i.e., the embedded word itself). In this case the activation level of the embedded word is increased. The reason for these differing effects of word-initial competition lies in top-down activation from the word level to the phoneme level. The node representing the first phoneme of the embedded word achieves a high activation when a substantial proportion of the currently activated words predict that phoneme in that position, which thus lends the embedded word hypothesis greater initial support. Post hoc analyses investigated the role of the word-initial cohort, with cohorts being calculated using a 20,000-word computerized dictionary (Francis and Kučera 1982) and the MRC Psycholinguistic Database and taking account of possible reductions in cases of words with first syllables containing schwa. There was no significant correlation between the amount of erroneous priming and the size of the word-initial cohort generated by the first syllable of the word, despite the overall difference in mean cohort size between the two groups. There was, however, an effect of the degree of divergence in the cohort at the phoneme representing the beginning of the embedded word: for *report*, for instance, the number of different phonemic continuations of *re-* were counted (*reb-*, *rec-*, *reg-*, etc.) in the 22,350 phonemically transcribed words in the MRC Psycholinguistic Database (Coltheart 1981) that also appear in Francis and Kučera 1982. There was a significant negative correlation overall between amount of priming and the number of different continuations, $r = -.310$, d.f. $= 46$, $p < .025$.

In summary, TRACE predicts that there will be less activation of word-final embedded words when there is a substantial word-initial cohort that diverges mainly after the first syllable, as in prefixed words like *report* where there are many words beginning *re-* that continue in a variety of ways in the second syllable. This prediction is supported by the data if the materials are divided into monomorphemic and prefixed words: in the prefixed group the mean word-initial cohort was larger and had a greater number of different continuations into the second syllable in comparison with the monomorphemic group. The initially counterintuitive direction of the results (priming was predicted to be more likely in the prefixed group than in the monomorphemic group) is thus no longer puzzling. Since the inhibition was not statistically robust (it failed to generalize to all of the prefixed items), it will not be further discussed here.

The conclusions from the first experiment are, first, that the processor is able to activate hypotheses on the basis of a satisfactory match with the input, irrespective of possible segmentation violations. Second, this does not always happen. The suppression of embedded-word hypotheses may be explained by a combination of a frequency-based explanation and a prefixing-explanation. The small number of suitable prefixed and monomorphemic words in the language limit the possibility of using the cross-modal priming technique to distinguish the precise contribution of the two explanations.

If the level of activation an embedded word reaches is dependent upon the competition from the word-initial cohort, as interactive-activation models such as TRACE suggest, manipulating this cohort should affect priming in an experiment such as the one described above. The overall size of the word-initial cohort is the feature that determines word-initial competition in the most obvious way: the larger the word-initial cohort, the larger the number of activated hypotheses. Post hoc analyses of the data from the first experiment revealed no significant correlation between size of the word-initial cohort and the level of priming. The second experiment was designed to test in a more controlled and direct way the hypothesis that it is simple, overall size of the word-initial cohort that determines the activation level of the embedded-word hypothesis.

The Second Experiment

A second cross-modal priming experiment, identical in most of the technical detail to the first experiment, was carried out to contrast the effects of large and small cohorts of word-initial competitors on the activation of word-final embedded words. Sentences (3) and (4) illustrate the crucial contrast. (Sentences (3) and (4) are in fact not typical of the materials used in that most of the pairs of words possessed weak-strong stress patterns.)

(3) I heard that the *combat* had been very fierce.

(4) I heard that the *wombat* bad been very fierce.

The first syllable of *combat* defines a large cohort of words, whereas there are only one or two other words in the language with an initial syllable homophonous with *wom-*.

Table 4 shows that the resulting means provide no evidence for the hypothesized effect of cohort size. The interaction between priming and cohort size was not significant ($F_1(1, 36) = 0.31$, n.s.). The overall priming effect is slightly less robust in this study ($F_1(1, 36) = 4.22, p < .05$). Because very few words in the language obey the necessary constraints, the stimulus materials contained pairs of both prefixed and monomorphemic words, both types of pairs conforming to the cohort size distinction under study. The presence of the former adversely affected the overall priming effect. The materials also contained a small number of pairs of words in which the criterion of the weak-strong stress pattern was compromised, as in the word *combat*, for instance. This may also have reduced the level of activation achieved by the embedded word.

Table 4
Mean reaction times (in msec) for large and small word-initial cohort words. $N = 40$.

	Related probe	Unrelated probe
Large-cohort word	807.1	842.0
Small-cohort word	808.3	830.0

The conclusion from this experiment agrees with the post hoc analysis of the first experiment: the simple size of the word-initial cohort does not have any significant effect on the activation level of an immediately subsequent hypothesis. If the prefixing explanation that emerged from TRACE is correct, the word-to-phoneme level of excitation that crucially interferes with the activation of the embedded word is brought about by some more detailed aspect of the word-initial cohort that is not satisfactorily captured simply by its overall size. The simple measure of size ignores the frequencies of the words involved and the fine detail of the predictions they make about the rest of the word. The activation of the embedded word may be more dependent on some such more fine-grained measure, such as the degree of divergence of the word-initial cohort, as in the first experiment.

The Third Experiment

The third experiment, carried out by Sarah Lowe, uses a different technique —the identification of words in white noise—to explore the same issue of competition between words (see Shillcock and Lowe 1988 for fuller technical details). We saw that listeners often entertain erroneous monosyllabic word hypotheses that map onto the final syllables of polysyllabic words, which means that monosyllables and polysyllables are competing. What happens, though, when only the monosyllabic word is heard? Is the polysyllable also accessed? When *sheen* is heard, is *machine* also accessed? If it is, the ensuing competition comparable to that between word-initial competitors like *pry* and *private*?

The first problem is that we do not really know the ground rules governing the competition between short words and long words. In TRACE, for instance, there are conventions concerning the contribution of phoneme-level activation to word-level activation and concerning the mutual inhibition of partially overlapping hypotheses, which determine that when a shorter word is competing with an initially homophonous longer word, the former rises in activation more quickly at first. The activation levels eventually cross over when additional segments arrive in support of the longer hypothesis, which means that the longer-word hypothesis achieves a higher final level than could ever be reached by the shorter-word hypothesis. (See the chapter by Frauenfelder and Peeters, this volume, for detailed discussion on this point.) Does this reflect in any way what goes on in the human speech processor? Is the competition between low-frequency *pry* and high-frequency *private* the same (over the acoustic lifetime of *pry*) as the competition between low-frequency *robe* and high-frequency *road*? The scale of the problem, at least in its very pure form involving completely homophonous competitors, is small: there are very few instances in the language of rare monosyllabic words like *pry* that have a relatively high-frequency polysyllabic competitor like *private*. Shorter words tend to be more frequent than longer words in English. However, when partially matching competitors are taken into account (*brine* and *private* are partial, initial competitors, for instance) the problem becomes a general one of finding the best mechanism to mediate the competition between lexical hypotheses.

Luce (1986a) defined the neighborhood of a word as consisting of all the words that may be generated from that word by the addition, deletion, or substitution of a single segment. Luce found a significant effect of mean neighborbood frequency and mean neighborhood density when subjects were asked to identify monosyllabic words in white noise. Luce's study, in common with other experiments on competition between word hypotheses, investigated the competition between words of similar, or closely similar, length. The pilot study described below compares the recognition in noise of monosyllabic words that are homophonous either with the first or the last syllable of a relatively high-frequency polysyllabic word. It was predicted that words with high-frequency word-initial competitors (like *pry*) would be recognized less accurately than words without such competitors. It was not predicted that *pry* heard in white noise would necessarily generate the mistaken response *private*, particularly because of the length difference. Rather, the presence of the strong competitor should simply muddy the waters and provoke monosyllabic errors. The results from the words with high-frequency word-final competitors (like *sheen*) are of considerable interest because there is no clear prediction. If straightforward competition occurs, as in *pry*, then *sheen* type words should be recognized less well than words with no word-final competitors, but if this type of competition between lexical hypotheses does not occur, it is even arguable that facilitation of *sheen* type words may occur on the grounds that *sheen* occurs commonly as a syllable, if not as a word.

In terms of frequencies calculated from Francis and Kučera 1982, the stimulus materials contained 17 low-frequency monosyllabic words (mean frequency = 4) that have word-initial high-frequency competitors (mean frequency = 89) (e.g., *pry*, *private*) and 18 low-frequency monosyllabic words (mean frequency = 5) that have word-final high-frequency competitors (mean frequency = 69) (e.g., *vent*, *prevent*). We matched 36 monosyllabic control words with no corresponding high-frequency competitor

Table 5
Percentages of correct responses for the different word groups. $N = 15$.

	With competitor	Without competitor
Word-initial homophone (*numb, number*)	64.3	71.7
Word-final homophone (*sheen, machine*)	76.6	70.0

as closely as possible for length and frequency (mean frequencies for the groups were 3 and 4, respectively). All of the words that subjects heard were monosyllabic. The relatively small numbers of items available reflects the relationship between frequency and word length in English. The constraints on assembling the stimulus materials unfortunately did not allow the morphological complexity of the high-frequency polysyllabic competitor to be controlled. The polysyllabic competitors in the word-final group were predominantly pseudoprefixed (e.g., *prevent*).

Subjects were told that they would hear words spoken against a background of white noise and that their task was to identify the words as accurately as possible. Pretesting determined a suitable S/N ratio that would produce an error rate of approximately 30 percent.

The mean error rate was 31.1 percent. The percentages of correct responses for the different groups of words are shown in table 5. The right-hand column refers to the matched control words with no high-frequency competitor. Analysis of variance showed that the interaction evident in the table was significant: $F_1(1, 14) = 7.28$, $p < .02$. The difference between the with-competitor groups of words was significant in a Scheffé test, $p < .05$. Inspection of the error data revealed that when subjects failed to report the target word, they responded not with the polysyllabic competitor but with a monosyllable that differed from the target by one or two segments.

The results of this pilot study should be interpreted with considerable care for a number of reasons. First, the effect may not be generalizable over all of the items. The interaction in the analysis by materials was not significant. Second, the potential effect of type of competitors (word-initial or word-final) was confounded with the potential effect of prefixing: the majority of the word-final competitors (like *prevent*) had prefixlike first syllables, whereas all of the word-initial competitors (like *private*) were monomorphemic. Third, because of the scarcity of suitable materials it was not possible to match the words as closely as desired for their inherent intelligibility or to control the words for their lexical neighborhoods (the number of words different by only one segment). However, a post hoc analysis revealed a nonsignificant correlation between the number of lexical neighbors and the error score.

Recognition rates for the two groups of experimental items differed in that the words with high-frequency word-initial competitors were recognized significantly less reliably than the words with high-frequency word-final competitors. These results suggest that the competitor effects between monosyllabic words, reported by Luce (1986a, 1986b), are also found between monosyllabic and polysyllabic words that are initially homophonous. A high-frequency word inhibits the activation of a concurrently activated low-frequency word, and when the high-frequency word is a polysyllabic word, the inhibition begins with the early segments of the word. Polysyllabic words seem not to rely on their length advantage: even with infrequent monosyllabic words (which have a double disadvantage in recognition) the competition appears to begin in the early segments of the polysyllable, which thus adversely affects the recognition of the monosyllable. In the present study the effects of competition were predicted on the basis of the presence of a *single* higher-frequency competitor rather than, as with Luce, the entire neighborhood of the word. Finally, the results suggest that word-initial and word-final competition are not completely comparable. If the activation of erroneous word-final hypotheses were a completely general phenomenon, we might expect comparable competitor effects in both cases. This study, however, is a pilot study using a relatively crude technique. It does not allow us to conclude that actual facilitation occurred in the case of the monosyllables with word-final competitors, nor does it reveal the precise role of prefixed competitors.

Conclusions for Methodologies

Studying competition between word hypotheses calls for particularly subtle methodologies, particularly in the auditory modality, where the effects of competition may be expected to be quite transient: speech reaches the processor over time—a monosyllabic word might occupy 200 to 500 msec—and many of the effects of competition will have disappeared by the time the end of the word has been reached. Consecutive presentation of *coal* and *coat*, for instance, may not reveal any competition between the two. Marslen-Wilson's cross-modal repetition-priming methodology, in which the auditorily presented *co-* or *coat* is followed with the visually presented *coat* (discussed in this volume), is one means of studying the phenomenon, but it is necessarily limited to the case of competition between words with simultaneous onsets. In addition, it is difficult to compare the behavior of different words because of the necessity of controlling for their orthographic neighbors: responses in a visual lexical decision task reflect the presence of higher-frequency orthographic neighbors (Grainger et al. 1988). (This added complexity still allows comparisons to be made of the different amounts of priming at different points within the word, of course.)

The use of word-initial homophones like *pry* and *private*, as in the third experiment, is one possible way of circumventing the fact that the effects of competition in auditory word recognition are very transient. Toward the end of *pry* there will be cues involving duration and declination and signaling that the word is more likely to be a monosyllable, but these cues should cause less decisive changes in the activation levels of the two competing words than the presence of a phone that unambiguously favors one of the competitors. The effects of competition in auditory word recognition should be most easily demonstrable using such monosyllables and comparing them with monosyllables that have no high-frequency competitor.

Priming by word-final embedded words offers a means of studying competition when the word onsets are not simultaneous. Processing the auditory stimulus is as normal as possible, since the visual word does not appear on the screen until the auditory word has ended and subjects do not typically perceive even the temporal relationship between the critical auditory word and the visual word. As a technique, the limitations lie in the fact that very few words in the language conform to all of the necessary constraints. One might speculate that the general shape of the phenomenon would survive even if bisyllabic nonwords were used in which the second syllable constituted a monosyllabic word; this would allow a more comprehensive manipulation of some of the variables.

Conclusions for Models of Word Recognition

What conclusions may be drawn from the experiments described above, and what implications do they have for modeling word recognition?

First, erroneous lexical hypotheses are often activated when there is a sufficiently close match with the input; in some instances when there is a close match with the input, there is inhibition. As well as supporting models that effectively ignore segmentation information, these results are consistent with the proposals by Cutler and Norris (1988) that strong syllables, those containing a full vowel, are interpreted by the processor as evidence for word onsets and that such syllables trigger segmentation. Their metrical segmentation strategy does not stipulate anything about the nature of the competition that follows the generation of overlapping hypotheses, so that the production of inhibition or facilitation by the embedded word is equally valid evidence for segmentation; *no* effect either way is the only result that would constitute evidence against the strategy. (A fuller treatment of the metrical segmentation strategy is to be found in the chapter by Cutler, this volume.)

Second, there are competing answers to the question of what predicts whether there will be activation or inhibition of the erroneous hypothesis. These answers involve progressively more of the competing words. The first answer involves only the two-syllable word and states that the more frequent the two-syllable word, the smaller the level of activation of the embedded word and the smaller the priming. The associations of priming with the less frequent words, like *trombone* or *cadet*, and inhibition with the more frequent words, like *report* or *confine*, seem to bear this out. There was, however, no significant correlation between priming and frequency of the two-syllable word, which suggests that the complete explanation contains more than this. The second answer involves a single competitor. The apparent role of the frequency of the most frequent word in the word-initial cohort (at least in the monomorphemic words) suggests that partially overlapping competitors in the word-initial cohort (*give* and *guitar*, for instance) need to be considered. (Note that this frequent competitor will rarely be the target two-syllable word itself.) This account seems to agree with the results of cross-modal priming experiments by Zwitserlood (1985), reviewed in Marslen-Wilson 1987, to the effect that when two words have both been activated by a shared first syllable, the more frequent of the two is activated more, the determining factor being the frequency difference between them. A determining role for the most frequent word-initial competitor, with no effect of overall cohort size, is accommodated by a winner-take-all architecture like TRACE. The third answer, the prefixing effect predicted by TRACE, involves the wider word-initial cohort. This explanation is attractive because it accounts for very counterintuitive data. Differentiating between these three accounts may well require techniques other than cross-modal priming. The TRACE model accommodates all of these accounts (Shillcock 1989).

The second conclusion qualifies the prefixing explanation from TRACE: the simple, overall size of the currently activated set of hypotheses—the word-initial cohort generated by the first syllable in this case—is not important in determining the activation level of a newly activated hypothesis. This result agrees with one reported by Marslen-Wilson (1987) to the effect that the number of alternatives that the processor has to assess at the point of transition when a potential word becomes a nonword has no bearing on the speed of the nonword response. (Marslen-Wilson's conclusion is that such assessment is carried out in parallel.) It also agrees with the finding of Grainger et al. that in visual word recognition the number of higher-frequency orthographic neighbors (words the same length as, but one letter different from, the target word) has no cumulative competitive effect; there is no significant difference between the effects of just one higher-frequency competitor and many. Coltheart et al. (1977) had similarly found no effect of number of competitors. Back in the auditory modality, Luce (1986b) presents data from two tasks that are relevant to the issue of whether overall cohort size can exert an effect. A task involving the identification of a word in white noise revealed an effect of neighborhood density (the number of words that are one segment different from the target word): words in high-density neighborhoods were identified less accurately than those in less dense neighborhoods. In the second task used by Luce, an auditory lexical-decision task, there was a significant effect of neighborhood density for low-frequency words: words in high-density neighborhoods were judged to be words more accurately than words in low-density neighborhoods. When reaction times were analyzed, there was a significant effect of neighborhood density only for high-frequency words: words in low-density neighborhoods were responded to faster than words in high-density neighborhoods. There was no such effect for low-frequency words. The reported effect of neighborhood density for high-frequency words resembles an effect of cohort size, even though no account was taken of the temporal dimension and only monosyllabic words were considered. Although the lack of an effect for the low-frequency words is consistent with the studies reported above, the neighborhood-density effect for high-frequency words does resemble an effect of overall cohort size. This result is difficult to interpret, however, first because the decisions subjects made were simply ones of lexical status rather than actual identification of the words involved, and second because an analysis in terms of neighborhood density and mean neighborhood frequency does not preclude the explanation that the observed effects may be due to the presence of *just one* higher-frequency neighbor.

There is, therefore, wider support for the claim that overall cohort size is irrelevant. The alternative is some more detailed aspect of the competition occurring *within* the word-initial cohort. One measure that emerged in the first experiment was the number of different phonemic continuations allowed by the first syllable of the word. Measures at this level of specificity are more likely to predict the priming described.

The third conclusion, this one from experiment three, is that word-initial competition from at least one high-frequency polysyllabic competitor seems to be sufficient to prejudice recognition in white noise. There was not an equivalent competition when the polysyllabic competitor was a word-final competitor. Grosjean and Gee (1987) present the outlines of a model of word recognition that emphasizes some of the prosodic information available to the listener, and they suggest the efficacy of accessing word hypotheses by means of their stressed/salient syllables: *number* would be accessed by its first syllable, and *prevent* by its second syllable. This predicts equal competition from the two types of high-frequency polysyllabic words when the corresponding monosyllabic words are processed. The present results do not show equal competition and represent evidence against a general strategy of accessing words by their strong syllable.

Finally, the process of word recognition appears to involve slightly more momentary activations of words than was previously realized. While this makes preparation of stimulus materials an even more vexing task, it also presents us with further data with which to test models of word recognition. In testing such models it is crucially important to make computationally explicit predictions about the recognition of any particular word in the context of the rest of the lexicon and all of the diverse influences that competing words are capable of producing.

Acknowledgments

I would like to thank Jeff Elman for making TRACE available and Uli Frauenfelder and an anonymous reviewer for comments on an earlier version of the paper. This research was carried out under SERC grant GRE/19541.

Notes

1. This includes the model proposed by Grosjean and Gee (1987), who suggest that because the stressed syllable in a word is generally an acoustically reliable and salient part of the input, it is used to contact all of the words in the lexicon that contain that syllable.

2. TRACE instantiates the "full-listing hypothesis": every version of a prefixed stem is simply listed as a separate word. TRACE's word-initial cohorts may contain without distinction such prefixed, pseudoprefixed, and monomorphemic words as *derail, deploy, delight*, etc.

References

Bard, E. G., Shillcock, R. C., and Altmann, G. T. M. 1988. The recognition of words after their acoustic offsets in spontaneous speech: Effects of subsequent context. *Perception and Psychophysics* 44 (5): 395–408.

Bradley, D. 1978. Computational distinctions of vocabulary type. Doctoral dissertation, MIT.

Bradley, D. 1980. Lexical representation of derivational relation. In M. Aronoff and M-L. Kean (eds.), *Juncture*. Saratoga, Calif.

Cole, R. A., and Jakimik, J. 1980. A model of speech production. In R. A. Cole (ed.), *Perception and Production of Fluent Speech*. Hillsdale, N.J.: LEA.

Coltheart, M. 1981. The MRC Psycholinguistic Database. *Quarterly Journal of Experimental Psychology* 33A : 497–505.

Coltheart, M., Davelaar, E., Jonasson, J. T., and Besner, D. 1977. Access to the mental lexicon. In S. Dornic (ed.) *Attention and Performance*, vol. 6. London: Academic Press.

Cutler, A. 1976. Phoneme monitoring reaction time as a function of preceding intonation contour. *Perception and Psychophysics* 20 : 55–60.

Cutler, A., and Carter, D. M. 1987. The predominance of strong initial syllables in the English vocabulary. *Computer Speech and Language* 2 : 133–142.

Cutler, A., and Norris, D. 1988. The role of strong syllables in segmentation for lexical access. *Journal of Experimental Psychology: Human Perception and Performance* 14 : 113–121.

Francis, W. N., and Kučera, H. 1982. *Frequency Analysis of English Usage*. Boston: Houghton Mifflin.

Frauenfelder, U. H. 1985. Cross-linguistic approaches to lexical segmentation. *Linguistics* 23 : 669–687.

Grainger, J., O'Regan, J. K., Jacobs, A. M., and Segui, J. 1988. On the role of competing word hypotheses in visual word recognition: The orthographic neigbourhood effect. *Perception and Psychophysics* 45 (3): 189–195.

Grosjean, F., and Gee, J. 1984. Another view of spoken word recognition. Working paper, Northeastern University.

Grosjean, F., and Gee, J. 1987. Prosodic structure and spoken word recognition. *Cognition* 25 : 135–155.

Harrington, J., Watson, G., and Cooper, M. 1988. Word-boundary identification from phoneme sequence constraints in automatic speech recognition. Paper presented at the Twelfth International Conference on Computational Linguistics, Coling '88, Budapest.

Huttenlocher, D. P. 1984. Acoustic-phonetic and lexical constraints in word recognition: Lexical access using partial information. M.Sc. thesis, MIT.

Jakimik, J., Cole, R. A., and Rudnicky, A. I. 1985. Sound and spelling in spoken word recognition. *Journal of Memory and Language* 24 : 165–178.

Jarvella, R. J., and Meijers, G. 1983. Recognizing morphemes in spoken words: Some evidence for a stem-organized mental lexicon. In G. B. Flores d'Arcais and R. J. Jarvella (eds.), *The Process of Language Understanding*. New York: Wiley.

Lehiste, I. 1972. The timing of utterances and linguistic boundaries. *Journal of the Acoustical Society of America* 51:2018–2024.

Luce, P. 1984. A computational analysis of optimal discrimination points in auditory word recognition. *Research on Speech Perception Progress Report* (Indiana University) 10:1–8.

Luce, P. 1986a. A computational analysis of uniqueness points in auditory word recognition. *Perception and Psychophysics* 39:155–159.

Luce, P. 1986b. Neighbourhoods of words in the mental lexicon. Research on Speech Perception, technical report no. 6. Bloomington, Ind.: Department of Psychology, Speech Research Laboratory.

McClelland, J., and Elman, J. 1986. The TRACE model of speech perception. *Cognitive Psychology* 18:1–86.

Marslen-Wilson, W. D. 1973. Linguistic structure and speech shadowing at very short latencies. *Nature* 244:522–523.

Marslen-Wilson, W. D. 1987. Functional parallelism in spoken word-recognition. *Cognition* 25:71–102.

Marslen-Wilson, W. D., and Welsh, A. 1978. Processing interactions during word-recognition in continuous speech. *Cognitive Psychology* 10:29–63.

Nakatani, L. H., and Dukes, K. D. 1977. Locus of segmental cues for word juncture. *Journal of the Acoustical Society of America* 62:714–719.

Prather, P., and Swinney, D. 1977. Some effects of syntactic context upon lexical access. Presented at a meeting of the American Psychological Association, San Francisco, August 26, 1977.

Shillcock, R. C. 1989. Competitor effects in auditory word recognition: Implications for interactive-activation models of word recognition. *Proceedings of Eurospeech '89*, 2:388–391.

Shillcock, R. C. 1990. Competition between lexical hypotheses in auditory word recognition. Submitted.

Shillcock, R. C., and Bard, E. G. Forthcoming. The role of prosodic units in speech recognition.

Shillcock, R. C., and Lowe, S. 1988. The effects of competition on auditory word recognition. *Work in Progress*, no. 21, pp. 43–50. Department of Liguistics, University of Edinburgh.

Swinney, D. 1979. Lexical access during sentence comprehension: (Re)consideration of context effects. *Journal of Verbal Learning and Verbal Behaviour* 18:645–659.

Swinney, D. 1981. Lexical processing during sentence comprehension: Effects of higher order constraints and implications for representation. In T. Myers, J. Laver, and J. Anderson (eds.), *The Cognitive Representation of Speech*. North-Holland.

Taft, M. 1979. Recognition of affixed words and the word frequency effect. *Memory and Cognition* 7:263–272.

Zwitserlood, P. 1985. Activation of word candidates during spoken word-recognition. Paper presented to Psychonomic Society Meetings, Boston, Mass.

Chapter 3

Lexical Segmentation in TRACE: An Exercise in Simulation	Uli H. Frauenfelder and Guus Peeters

1 Introduction

This paper examines the innovative solution to the problem of lexical segmentation and recognition found in the interactive-activation model TRACE (McClelland and Elman 1986). The problem of segmenting a continuous and overlapping sensory input into discrete words is resolved in TRACE not at the level of a bottom-up analysis of phonetic or prosodic boundary cues but rather at the lexical level. Indeed, a multitude of different lexical hypotheses based on competing segmentation analyses are activated, and the inappropriate hypotheses are eliminated via inhibition. By means of a series of simulations we investigate the processes of excitation and inhibition that produce this segmentation behavior in TRACE.

Unlike most other models of spoken-word recognition, TRACE does not segment the sensory input to identify selected points (e.g., word boundaries) that provide the basis for the alignment between the input and the discrete entries in the lexicon. In other words, TRACE does not restrict the lexical search space activated for a particular stretch of speech to those lexical candidates aligned with the point of segmentation. Rather, lexical hypotheses for all the words in the lexicon are in constant contention for recognition at every processing moment. Thus the activation level of every lexical unit continuously changes as a function of the incoming signal. The dynamics of interactive activation allow TRACE to converge on a single lexical candidate despite the mass of lexical candidates contending for recognition.

Before examining the intricate interplay between the activation and inhibition responsible for segmentation in TRACE, we will briefly consider some alternative proposals for handling the segmentation and alignment problems. There are several alternative proposals that generate a relatively small and restricted set of lexical hypotheses by making more perceptual commitments at the lower levels on the basis of additional information. The nature and number of activated lexical hypotheses depends critically upon two different factors: the parts of the speech input allowed to activate these hypotheses and the required goodness of fit between this input and the lexical hypotheses.[1] In the following discussion we will be concerned with the way in which different models specify the former factor. Clearly, the number of lexical hypotheses can be greatly reduced when only restricted parts of the speech input are allowed to generate lexical hypotheses.

In the case of *positional alignment* only those lexical items that are aligned with a specific position are considered for recognition. Cole and Jakimik (1980) and Marslen-Wilson and Welsh (1978) developed models based upon *initial alignment*. Here, only word onsets are allowed to generate the lexical hypotheses entering into competition for recognition. Restricting the lexical search space in this fashion leads, of course, to major reductions in the number of activated lexical hypotheses. We should point out, however, that this approach to segmentation presupposes that listeners know which part of the speech input corresponds to word onsets. Unfortunately, the segmentation problem has received little attention within the framework of these models.

Lexical hypotheses can also be restricted by requiring that they match certain salient parts of the input irrespective of the position of these parts. An example of what we will call *landmark alignment* can be found in a model proposed by Grosjean and Gee (1987). In this model the stressed syllable is chosen to serve as the unit of alignment because of its perceptual saliency. It defines which lexical hypotheses are entertained. All words containing the recognized stressed syllable in any position are activated.

Finally, positional and landmark alignment approaches are combined in the metrical segmentation strategy (MSS) advanced by Cutler and Norris (Cutler, this volume; Cutler and Norris 1988). Here listeners are assumed to segment the speech input whenever they encounter a metrically strong syllable. When such a syllable is detected, a word boundary is postulated immediately before the onset of this syllable, and lexical candidates beginning with this syllable are activated.

Clearly, there are large differences in the number and nature of the lexical hypotheses assumed to be activated by these diverse approaches to alignment and segmentation. In evaluating these solutions, we must bear in mind two opposed constraints. By restricting the lexical search space too much on the basis of unreliable segmentation decisions, a model runs the risk of never including the intended word in this search space. Alternatively, a model not sufficiently discriminating in its segmentation decisions may be left with too many hypotheses to converge upon the correct lexical candidate.

To get a better understanding of where the best compromise between these two approaches lies, it is useful to explore the costs and benefits of the extremes. It is in this spirit that we present a simulation exercise with TRACE that aims at understanding and assessing TRACE's approach to lexical segmentation. Our study constitutes a continuation of the original investigation of segmentation in TRACE by McClelland and Elman (1986). By means of a series of simulations of increasing complexity, we scrutinize the mechanisms of excitation and inhibition underlying its segmentation behavior.

In section 2 we will first motivate our decision to restrict the discussion to the particularly thorny problem of segmenting and recognizing words within words. Then in section 3 we will present a short overview of the structure of TRACE. Section 4 reports a series of simulations that illustrates and analyzes the processes of interactive activation. Finally, section 5 presents some conclusions about the segmentation behavior of TRACE.

2   The Problem of Lexical Embedding

We will limit ourselves in this paper to the segmentation problems that arise from the lexical ambiguity inherent in strings of segments. Imagine, for instance, that a listener hears the sequence *abc* in which the strings *a*, *b*, *abc* are all words in the language (e.g., carpenter). We can ask how the listener deals with this ambiguity. Which lexical hypotheses are activated during the processing of such sequences, and how does the listener converge upon the correct one(s)?

This kind of lexical ambiguity is extremely common in many languages. This should not come as a great surprise, since the basic building blocks of words—phonemes and syllables—are themselves often words. With the advent of computerized dictionaries it has become possible to give a precise characterization of the amount of overlap and embedding found in the lexicon.

Lexical database analysis
Initial efforts in this direction, under the influence of models assuming positional alignment have focused on the overlap that exists at the begin-

ning of words. For example, Luce (1986) performed a statistical analysis of a 20,000-word computerized American English dictionary to determine how often words overlap in their onsets. His results showed that when word frequency is taken into account, 38 percent of all words in his lexical database are *not* unique at their offsets. By *unique* we mean that there is no other word in the lexicon sharing the initial part of the target word. This means that over a third of the words included in his analysis constitute the initial portion of longer carrier words. Obviously, this is especially the case for shorter words. Over 94 percent of words of two phonemes, 74 percent of words of three phonemes, and 35.6 percent of words of four phonemes became unique only after their offset. The work of Luce makes it quite evident that such overlap is not rare but in fact so common that every model must address the problem.[2]

We wanted to extend Luce's analysis to lexical embedding in positions other than the word-initial position. We took the CELEX lexical database for Dutch, excluded compounds, and reduced the number of derivationally related words. This provided us with a corpus of 9,985 words that we analyzed for lexical overlap in three different positions: word-onset, word-internal, and word-offset. The computations involved taking all the words in the database (ranging in length from 1 to 16 phonemes) and determining whether each of these words occurred in a longer word in one of the three positions examined.

Table 1 gives the total number of words of each length as well as the number and the percentage of these words that were found as substrings in longer words in one of the three different positions distinguished. The results for the initial position closely match those obtained by Luce. More important, we see that the amount of overlap in word-initial position does not differ much from that in either word-final or word-internal position. Indeed, for all three positions we find an extremely high percentage of short words embedded in longer words. This result is all the more striking because we used a database that gives a very conservative measure of lexical overlap; compounds were excluded from the analysis, and the results were not weighted by frequencies.

The results of our analysis of the Dutch lexicon show the existence of considerable embedding in the three positions examined. They suggest that listeners have many potential lexical candidates to contend with if all embedded words are activated during lexical processing. These lexical statistics raise some important questions about the processing of words within words. First, which words embedded within carrier words are

Table 1
Percentages of words found as substrings in longer words

Length	Number	Onset	% onset	Middle	% middle	Offset	% offset	Total	% total
1	6	6	100.0	6	100.0	6	100.0	6	100.0
2	124	110	88.7	122	98.4	108	87.1	124	100.0
3	954	583	61.1	613	64.3	552	57.9	816	85.5
4	1,542	479	31.1	424	27.5	432	28.0	825	53.5
5	1,699	259	15.2	170	10.0	195	11.5	472	27.8
6	1,626	147	9.0	67	4.1	86	5.3	263	16.2
7	1,378	76	5.5	30	2.2	51	3.7	151	11.0
8	1,056	49	4.6	23	2.2	19	1.8	86	8.1
9	715	11	1.5	6	.8	5	.7	21	2.9
10	423	13	3.1	6	1.4	3	.7	22	5.2
11	231	6	2.6		.0		.0	6	2.6
12	126	1	.8		.0		.0	1	.8
13	72		.0		.0		.0		.0
14	18		.0		.0		.0		.0
15	10		.0		.0		.0		.0
16	5		.0		.0		.0		.0
Total	9,985	1,740	17.4	1,467	14.7	1,457	14.6	2,793	28.0

actually activated during processing, and second how much acoustic information is actually required by the listener to resolve the lexical ambiguity?

Human performance data

Although there is still relatively little psycholinguistic research investigating lexical segmentation, there are some findings that relate to both of these questions. The first concerns the time course of word recognition with as dependent variable the amount of acoustic information required to access words in fluent speech. Specifically, these studies investigate how much of the following context of a given word must be analyzed before this word can be identified. The second type of data informs us about lexical activation, that is, which lexical candidates are activated, even if only momentarily. We will consider these two data sources in turn, since they each impose constraints upon models of lexical processing.

Amount of stimulus information and the gating data   Several *gating* studies suggest that listeners do not systematically recognize words as they are heard. Grosjean (1985) determined how much acoustic signal listeners needed to identify words in sentence contexts. He presented subjects with short sentences in which relatively infrequent monosyllabic nouns were preceded and followed by uninformative contexts. These target nouns as well as their following context were presented in increasing chunks of 50 msec to subjects who had to write down what they thought they heard. The results showed that subjects often did not identify words before their acoustic offsets. In fact, more than half of the monosyllabic words were recognized after their offsets. Among the reasons given by Grosjean for this delayed recognition was the fact that some of the stimuli used were potential parts of longer words.

Bard, Shillcock, and Altmann (1989) also investigated the recognition of words by means of the gating procedure, but in conversational speech. They found that about 20 percent of the words were recognized after their ends and concluded that such late recognition was a rather common phenomenon. Again, the words whose recognition was the most delayed with respect to their offsets were generally short, probably because they were phonologically less redundant and in some cases parts of longer words. These two gating studies convincingly demonstrate that in many instances, including the word-within-word cases, listeners recognize words only when their following context has been analyzed.

Lexical activation and cross-modal priming   Valuable information about which lexical candidates are activated during the processing of fluent speech comes from studies using *cross-modal priming* (Swinney 1979). This task provides a measure of the degree to which specific spoken words are activated during sentence processing. Subjects listen to spoken words presented in sentence contexts and see a visual proble word immediately after hearing the critical word. This spoken word facilitates lexical decisions about the semantically related visual proble in comparison to the decision latencies to some unrelated visual word. The precise amount of facilitation is interpreted as a measure of the activation of the spoken word.

Zwitserlood (1989) has shown that the initial fragment of a spoken word activates competing lexical candidates that share this fragment. These results reveal the activation of the semantic codes of several lexical candidates that match the sensory input. Upon hearing the sequence *par*, the listener activates diverse lexical hypotheses beginning with this sequence, such as *party* and *park*.

Results reported by Shillcock (this volume) suggest that embedded lexical candidates other than those aligned with the onsets of words are also activated during processing. Using the same technique, Shillcock presented subjects with sentences in which the second syllable of the target bisyllabic word was also a word (e.g., *bone* in *trombone*). He found evidence for the activation of the embedded word *bone*. These results are important because they call into question models that assume that only lexical candidates with aligned word onsets are activated. It is therefore of particular interest see how TRACE handles such embedded sequences.

3   The Structure of TRACE

In this section we will present a brief overview of the structure of TRACE. (For a more complete description, see McClelland and Elman 1986.)

A static description of TRACE

The units   The TRACE model is made up of distinctive feature, phoneme, and word units that each represent hypotheses about the sensory input. At the feature level there are 7 dimensions or features. Each of these features have 9 possible values represented as separate units. The majority of these features come from phonological theory (e.g., consonantal, vocalic, etc.). In addition, there are 15 different phoneme units (including the hyphen, which represents a word boundary) and a variable number of word units (specified by the user). The feature, phoneme, and lexical units can range in activation from $-.3$ to 1.0. The resting level for feature and phoneme units is $-.1$ and that for word units is $-.01$.

These three types of units are organized hierarchically and are aligned with one another and with time in a precise fashion. At the lowest level, detector units for distinctive features are aligned with the *elementary time slices* so that all feature units are duplicated for each time slice. Each phoneme unit spans 6 of these elementary time slices. Furthermore, a new unit for each phoneme begins every 3 elementary time slices or every *phoneme* time slice. As a consequence, adjacent phonemes overlap in 3 elementary time slices. Each word spans its constituent phonemes and hence the time slices that these phonemes cover. As with phonemes, a new copy of each *word token* begins at every phoneme time slice. Thus the hypothesis that a particular word is present in the input is repeated at every phoneme time slice. A word token is identified by the time slice at which it begins.

Connectivity pattern   In TRACE there are facilitatory connections between units on adjacent levels (feature-phoneme, phoneme-word, and word-phoneme) and inhibitory connections between units within levels (feature-feature, phoneme-phoneme, and word-word). These connections exist not only between (phoneme and word) units from the same time slice but also to a lesser degree between units in different time slices.

The excitatory or inhibitory influence of one unit upon another is proportional to the level of activation of the first unit and depends upon the strength of the connection between the two units. The connection strengths are weighted for each distinct type of connection. These weights are set as values of parameters given to TRACE (default values can be found in McClelland and Elman 1986, table 3). The resting level, the minimum and maximum activation values, and the decay rate of the units are also defined in this parameter set.

A dynamic description of the model

Bottom-up excitation   The bottom-up flow of activation begins when TRACE receives some input. This so-called mock input (not real speech but a phonetic transcription) is presented to the feature level. We will refer to the input in terms of segments to distinguish it from TRACE's internally represented phonemes. The feature units excite the appropriate phoneme units (e.g., the voiced feature activates all voiced phonemes). A phoneme unit whose activation level is raised from its resting level of $-.1$ to 0 begins to activate every word unit to which it is connected. The amount that this phoneme unit excites connected word units depends on the activation level of the phoneme unit and the connection strength between the two units. It is independent of the length of the word itself or the position of the phoneme in the word (i.e., the phoneme /t/ equally excites word units containing it in initial, medial, or final position).

Top-down excitation   TRACE also allows word units to excite their constituent phoneme units. Again, the amount that a particular word activates its phonemes is proportional to the level of activation of the word unit and the connection strength between the units. Phonemes located in different positions in the activated word receive the same amount of top-down excitation.

Lateral inhibition   There is also a flow of negative activation or inhibition between units at the same level. The degree to which one (phoneme or word) unit can inhibit another depends on the connection strength, the inhibiting unit's activation level, and the amount of overlap between the two units. Overlap is defined in terms of the amount of shared length (measured in phonemes) between the two respective words. Since longer words overlap more, they also inhibit each other more. Inhibition reduces the number of serious rival hypotheses at each level by allowing the units having the most activation to suppress the other less activated units.

Global activation flow   As input is received by TRACE, units at different levels progressively become activated above or below their resting level. During each processing cycle, all the different types of units are simultaneously updated to new values that depend on the activation of the units they are connected to, and the input for the feature units. The change in activation of a particular unit from one cycle to the next depends roughly upon the amount of bottom-up and top-down excititation it receives minus the amount of inhibition it receives from every other activated unit at the same level and minus the amount it decays from cycle to cycle.

Recognition
A particular word or phoneme is assumed to be recognized when the activation of one of its token units at a particular time slice is sufficiently higher than the activation of all other units at the same level for that

particular time slice. To determine when a given phoneme unit is recognized, it is common (McClelland and Rumelhart 1981, McClelland and Elman 1986) first to increase the differences between activated units by exponentially transforming the activation values (a_i) of all units at a particular time slice into response strengths (S_i) according to the formula $S_i = e^{ka_i}$. The constant k in the expression determines the extent to which high and low activation values separate. The response probability, $p(R_i)$, of a particular unit is then calculated as the response strength of this unit divided by the sum of the response strengths of all units for that time slice. Hence, we get the probability of choosing unit i out of the total set of units in terms of the Luce choice rule (1959):

$$p(R_i) = \frac{S_i}{\sum_j S_j}$$

Here j indexes the members of the alternative set of activated units. A phoneme is said to be recognized when its response probability exceeds a certain threshold value (e.g., 0.9 in McClelland and Elman 1986).

Segmentation

In TRACE, segmentation and recognition are the by-products of excitation and inhibition. As McClelland and Elman (1986, p. 61) put it, "Word indentification and segmentation emerge together from the interactive activation process, as part and parcel of the process of word activation." Once a word is recognized, its endpoints can be identified. TRACE can, however, appeal to a phoneme, the word-boundary symbol (-), to assist in the segmentation process.[3] These authors acknowledge that future models will need to exploit other cues, like syllabification and stress, but point out that even without these additional sources of information, TRACE manages to segment surprisingly well. The key to understanding this segmentation behavior is in characterizing the interactive activation process. The goal of the following simulations is precisely this.

4   Segmentation Simulations

In this section we present a series of simulations that explore the way in which TRACE segments and recognizes a longer word or shorter words embedded in this longer word. By comparing the activation curves for these words in simulations with varying lexica and parameter settings, we hope to elucidate the interactive activation mechanisms at the origin or TRACE's segmentation behavior.

Table 2
Relations between carrier sequences and embedded
sequences

	Carrier sequence	
Embedded sequence	A word	B nonword
1	word, word	word, word
2	nonword, word	nonword, word
3	word, nonword	word, nonword
4	nonword, nonword	nonword, nonword

To characterize the segmentation problem, it is useful to introduce some terminological distinctions between different types of strings and embedded substrings. First, a *carrier sequence*, either a carrier word (CW) or carrier nonword (CNW), is any stretch of speech made up of smaller units of words and nonwords. Second, *embedded sequences* are substrings making up the carrier sequence. The embedded strings, either *embedded words* (EW) or *embedded nonwords* (ENW), can be found initially and finally in the carrier string. Table 2 depicts some possible relations between carrier and embedded sequences according to the lexical status of each. Overlapping embedded words are not considered here. It should be noted that these definition are recursive in that an embedded word can itself be a carrier word.

In the seven simulations to be presented, we will consider several of these cases. We will use the term *targets* to refer to the (embedded or carrier) words that correspond exactly to the entire input. *Competitors*, in contrast, are the (embedded or carrier) words that only partially match the input. It is possible to have more than one target by including the boundary symbol (-) within the input sequence. The final two simulations differ from the first five simulations in their use of this symbol to assist in segmentation. We begin by examining case 3A, in which a carrier word contains an initially embedded word.

Segmentation without boundary markers

Simulation 1   This simulation examines the activation and recognition of EWs and CWs with small lexica to study the mechanisms of interactive activation and the role of word length therein.

The input consisted of eight pairs, each pair consisting of a carrier word (e.g., *carpet*) and an embedded word (e.g., *car*) that makes up the beginning

Table 3
Input words

CW	EW	CW	EW
partial	par	secret	seek
crucial	crew	target	tar
barber	bar	stupid	stew
carpet	car	butler	but

of the carrier word. All 16 words were given to TRACE accompanied boundary symbols (e.g., "-car-"). The words tested are listed in table 3.

These input words were presented to TRACE with two different types of lexica. These lexica defined the two conditions of this simulation. The baseline condition establishes the activation curve for each word when it is the only item in the lexicon and hence unaffected by any other word. In the competitor condition each CW and its matched EW comprise the two-word lexicon. The activation curve obtained here for each target word reflects the inhibiting influence of its competitor.

Default values for parameters were used. Word frequency was not active.

The simulation was run through 90 successive cycles, as were all the other simulations in this study.

The mean activation values for every cycle were obtained for the eight pairs of words tested. We see plotted in figure 1 the mean activation curves for these words in the baseline and the competitor conditions.

Figure 1 shows that the CW (*carpet*) reaches a higher overall activation level than the EW (*car*) both in the baseline and competitor conditions. This reflects the relationship between the number of phonemes in a word (its word length) and the activation level it ultimately reaches. Figure 1 also shows that the activation curves for the two target words differ according to whether they are alone in the lexicon or whether their respective competitor is also present: the entire curve of the EW target word is attenuated when the competitor is present. This reduction in activation is attributable, of course, to the inhibition of the target word by its competitor.

To get a complete picture of the inhibition at work here, we must also examine the activation curves of the competitors. Indeed, since inhibition is bidirectional, we need to consider both the inhibitory influence of the target upon the competitor and the influence of the competitor upon the target. We will first discuss the former case of inhibition.

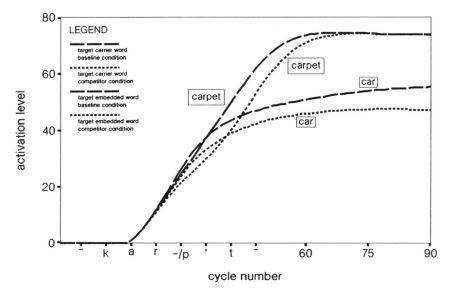

Figure 1
The activation curves for target embedded and carrier words in the baseline and the competitor conditions. In the example here the embedded word is *car*, and the carrier word is *carpet*.

We see in figure 2 that both competitors are as strongly activated as their respective target words through the first three or four segments of the input. At this point, however, they diverge not only from their corresponding target words but also from each other. Although the EW competitor reaches a higher activation level than the CW competitor, it subsequently drops rapidly below its resting activation level. In contrast, the CW competitor continues to rise parallel to its EW target, albeit at a lower activation level.

The difference in the activaticn curves of the two competitors is due to the differential amounts of inhibition they receive from their respective target words. Recall that the amount that one lexical unit inhibits another is directly proportional to its own level of activation. Further, the level of activation of the inhibiting unit depends upon the amount it matches the input. The additional matching input (e.g., "pet-") gives the target CW much more activation relative to its EW competitor, thereby allowing it to suppress its competitor completely. In contrast, the input corresponding to the target EW differs in its match with the competitor CW in only the boundary symbol. Consequently, the EW is activated not much more than

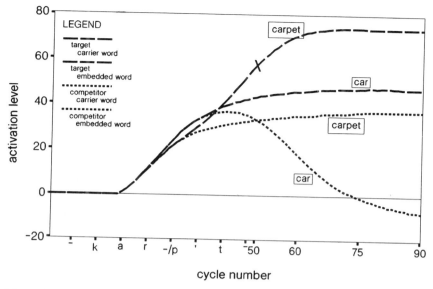

Figure 2
The activation curves for target embedded and carrier words and their respective carrier and embedded competitors, all in the competitor condition. The recognition point of the target word is marked with an X.

its CW competitor and can only prevent the competitor from reaching the same level of activation but cannot not suppress it.

Now let us turn to the inhibitory influence of the competitor upon the target word. Figure 3 presents a measure of this inhibition by taking the difference between the activation curves for the target words in the baseline and competitor conditions (shown in figure 1).

Although both target words are inhibited about equally by their respective competitors early on, the CW target is soon inhibited by its EW competitor. After this inhibition reaches its maximum at the end of the target word, it quickly drops off, so that by cycle 75 there is no more inhibition. In contrast, the EW target is increasingly inhibited across time.

How are we to understand this difference in the amount of inhibition that the target words suffer from their respective competitors? The EW target is increasingly inhibited because it is unable to inhibit its CW competitor effectively, which allows the latter in turn to continue to inhibit this target. The situation is quite different for the CW target word, which inhibits its EW competitor so effectively that this competitor cannot exert a reciprocal inhibitory influence except for the initial inhibitory peak.[4]

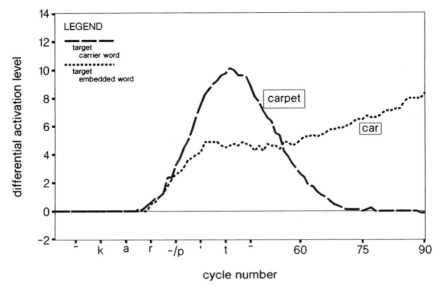

Figure 3
The amount of inhibition of the target word by the competitor as reflected by the differences between the activation curves of the target embedded and carrier words across the baseline and competitor conditions.

We have now examined the bidirectional inhibition between the target and the competitor words and have seen that the CW target inhibits its shorter competitor more than the EW target can inhibit its competitor. This asymmetry in inhibition has important consequences on the recognition and segmentation of target words. We computed the moment at which TRACE recognized the different target words.[5] Figure 2 shows that the CW target word is recognized at approximately cycle 50. The situation is different for the EW target word, which is never recognized according to the criterion we have adopted here. Since it receives less bottom-up activation, it cannot sufficiently inhibit its CW competitor. The difference in activation between the two is not great enough for the target to be recognized.

Simulation 2 The preceding simulation used extremely small lexica to uncover the underlying mechanisms of activation and inhibition in TRACE. However, they do not provide a fair test of its performance on the recognition of words within words. In the following simulations we will progressively increase the complexity of the simulations to approximate more

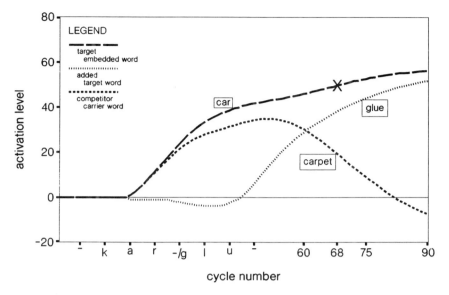

Figure 4
The activation curves for a target embedded word, added word, and competitor carrier word. In the example here the target embedded word is *car*, the added word *glue*, and the carrier word *carpet*. The recognition point of the target embedded word is marked with an **X**.

realistic conditions. In simulation 2 we examine how the recognition of EWs is influenced when they are followed by another monosyllabic word (case 1B of table 2, where the EW *car* is followed by another word, *glue*). The gating results presented above suggest that listeners must often continue their analysis of the signal into the next word to be able to identify the previous one.

This simulation investigates whether the EW can be recognized when it is followed by another short word that can compete with the carrier word.

In the input, each of the eight EWs used in the preceding simulation were followed by different monosyllabic words having three input segments (e.g., "-carglue-") that differ from the last three phonemes of the CW.

A three-word lexicon including the EW, the CW, and the added word was used for each input.

Figure 4 shows the activation curves of the EW target, the CW competitor, and the monosyllabic word added after the EW target. The most striking result is the change in the activation curve of the CW competitor. If we compare its activation curve here with the one in the preceding simulation (figure 2), we notice that although the curves begin identically, the activation of the CW drops dramatically when the added word begins to be activated. This latter word overlaps with the CW competitor and therefore strongly inhibits it. With this competitor inhibited to low activation levels, the EW target is less inhibited and reaches an activation level high enough with respect to its competitor to be recognized at approximately cycle 68.[6] This simulation illustrates the role that competition between lexical units plays in the segmentation process. Since competition is restricted to lexical units that overlap in time, the added word inhibited the CW but did not alter the activation curve of the EW.

Simulation 3 The preceding two simulations have been conducted on extremely small lexica to simplify and make more understandable the complex interactions taking place between the different lexical units. In simulation 3 we will repeat the previous simulations with a larger lexicon, Phonolex. By using this lexicon, we can study the inhibiting role of a greater number of competitors on the recognition and segmentation processes.

The input is the same as in simulation 1.

We used a lexicon made up of 211 words of different lengths. Following McClelland and Elman (1986), who used essentially the same lexicon, we will refer to this lexicon as Phonolex. The second syllable of the carrier word is never a word in this lexicon.

Figure 5 gives the activation curves for both CW and EW targets as well as those for their competitors and shows that both the EW and the CW are recognized.

Unlike in simulation 1, the EW target now gets enough differential activation to be recognized even when it is not followed by another word, as in simulation 2. It is recognized because its CW competitor is never highly activated, due to the inhibition that this competitor receives from other words in the lexicon. The CW target is recognized as in the competitor condition of simulation 1, but approximately five cycles later owing to the additional inhibition it receives.

We can quantify the inhibition coming from the other words in the lexicon (excluding that from the CW and EW competitors) by taking the difference between the activation curves of the EW and CW targets and their competitors in the competitor condition of simulation 1 and in this simulation. We see these differential activation curves plotted in figure 6.

Figure 6 shows that the longer words (the CW target and CW competitor) suffered the most inhibition from the other words in the Phonolex lexicon. First, we see that the CW competitor is increasingly inhibited by

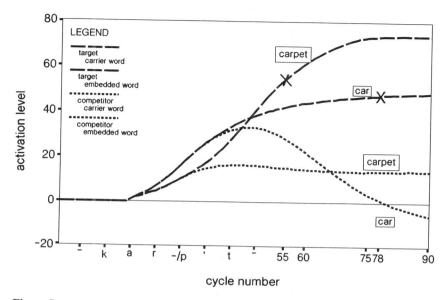

Figure 5

The activation curves for target embedded and carrier words as well as their respective carrier and embedded competitors in the Phonolex condition. The recognition point of the target word is marked with an **X**.

the other words. This is, of course, vital for the recognition of the EW, which is less inhibited and more easily attains sufficient activation to be recognized. The inhibition curve for the CW target also reveals a marked inhibitory influence from the other words in Phonolex. In contrast, both EW competitors and targets submit to considerably less inhibition than these longer words. So what emerges clearly from this simulation is that the amount of inhibition a word receives is a function of its length. Longer words suffer more inhibition from other words in the lexicon than shorter words, since they overlap in more phonemes.

Simulation 4   The preceding simulations have concentrated upon the recognition of carrier words and of embedded words that overlap with the beginning of these carrier words. We now look at input sequences made up of words that are embedded in the final rather than in the initial position of the carrier words (case 2A in table 2). This is of interest for two reasons. First, our analysis of the Dutch database has shown that words embedded at the ends of carrier words occur as frequently as initially embedded words. Second, psycholinguistic evidence suggests that words embedded

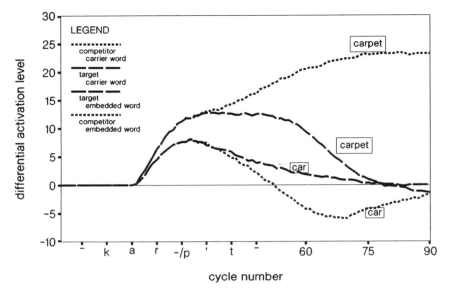

Figure 6
The amount of inhibition of the target words by all their competitors as reflected by the difference between the activation curves of target embedded and carrier words in the competitor and Phonolex conditions.

word-finally can also be activated during lexical processing (Shillcock, this volume).

Simulation 4 compares the activation of CWs and their finally embedded EWs when the CWs were given as input.

Ten CWs were presented as input to TRACE. The first syllable of the CW was a nonword, but the second syllable was a word (e.g., *precede* = *pre + seed*).

Phonolex with a few words added was used. Here, as in the following simulations, the word boundary symbol was also included in the lexicon.

Figure 7 shows the average activation curves for both the CW and the EW. As in the preceding simulations, the longer CW (*precede*) dominates the EW (*seed*) and is recognized. The EW hardly rises above its resting level, since it is strongly inhibited by the CW, which is highly activated by the time the input corresponding to this embedded words is received. The low activation level attained by the finally embedded words here contrasts strikingly with the activation of the initially embedded words in simulation 3. This difference in activation between initially and finally embedded words was also reported by McClelland and Elman (1986).

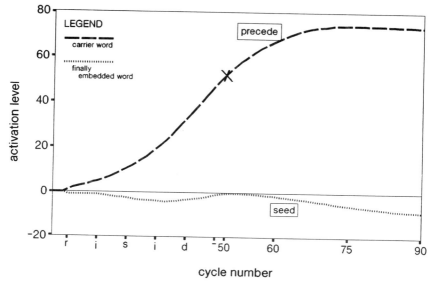

Figure 7
The activation curves for a target carrier word and the final embedded word in the Phonolex condition. In the example here the embedded word is *seed*, and target carrier word is *precede*. The recognition point of the target CW is marked with an X.

Simulation 5   To make a more direct comparison between the activation of the initially and finally embedded words, we ran another simulation using inputs consisting of carrier words made up of both initially and finally embedded words. Such inputs (case 1A in table 2) are also of interest for another reason. These sequences are completely ambiguous, since they can be interpreted either as a single carrier word or as two embedded words. By comparing the activation level of the carrier word with that of the two embedded words, we can discover TRACE's preferred interpretation of these ambiguous sequences.[7] If, as in the preceding simulations, word length plays a determining role, the target carrier word should again dominate the shorter words. On the other hand, if the carrier word is sufficiently inhibited by the two embedded words, the EWs and not the CW can be recognized.

Simulation 5 tests for the segmentation preferences of TRACE when it is presented with ambiguous input strings (one CW or two EWs). It also compares the activation of the initially and finally embedded EWs.

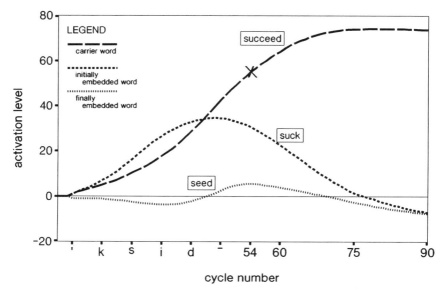

Figure 8
The activation curves for a target carrier word and its two embedded words in the Phonolex condition. In the example here the initial embedded word is *suck*, the final embedded word *seed*, and the input carrier word *succeed*. The recognition point of the target CW is marked with an **X**.

TRACE received as input 10 CWs whose first and second syllable was a word (e.g., *succeed = suck + seed*). In order to compare the results of this simulation with the preceding one, the same second syllable (e.g., *seed*) was used.

Phonolex with a few words added was used.

We turn first to a comparison of the activation curves of the carrier and embedded words. Figure 8 shows that TRACE has a clear preference for analyzing the ambiguous input as a single longer word. Indeed, only the carrier word is recognized; neither embedded word is sufficiently activated. Thus, owing to its longer length and to the correspondingly greater bottom-up activation it receives, the carrier word can withstand the inhibiting influence of the embedded words and can be recognized.

Figure 8 also reveals a striking difference in the activation levels reached by initially and finally embedded EWs. While the initial EW (*suck*) is strongly activated, the final EW (*seed*) is activated only slightly above its resting level. The latter is strongly inhibited by the CW, which is highly activated by the time that the input corresponding to this embedded word

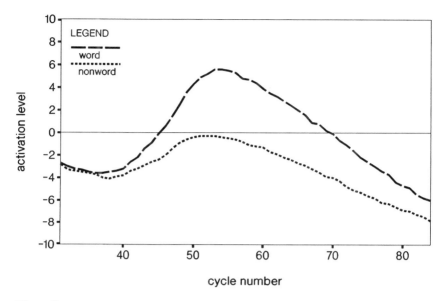

cycle number

Figure 9
The activation curves for a finally embedded word (*seed*) when the initially embedded item was either a word (*suck seed*) or a nonword (*pre seed*).

is received. Nonetheless, if we compare the activation curves for the finally embedded words in this simulation and in the previous one (where the initial embedded sequence is a word and a nonword, respectively), we obtain the differences shown in figure 9.

The final EWs that are preceded by an initial EW are activated more than those preceded by an embedded nonword. The greater activation level attained by the former EWs is the result of the inhibiting influence that the initial EW exerts upon the CW. Since the activation level of the CW is reduced, it is less effective in inhibiting the final EW.

The influence of CW competitors   If the inhibition of the carrier word by the initially embedded word explains the increased activation level of the finally embedded word, we also expect this activation to increase as a function of the number of competitors of the carrier word or its cohort size. To confirm this prediction, we conducted a further TRACE simulation in which we successively increased *the number of competitors of the carrier word* (*succeed*) and evaluated the effect of this manipulation upon the activation level of the finally embedded word (*seed*).

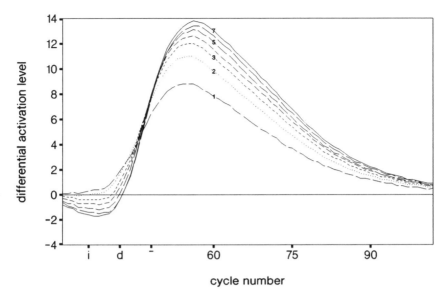

Figure 10
The differential activation curves for the finally embedded word *seed* as a
function of the number of competitors (1 to 7) of its carrier word *succeed*.

In the first run of this simulation we included in Phonolex the initially
embedded word *suck* as the primary competitor of the carrier word (as in
simulation 5). In subsequent runs we progressively increased the number
of competitors that matched the carrier word through the third segment
but deviated in the fourth and subsequent segments (e.g., *sucker* and
sucked). The length of these competitors varied from four to six phonemes.
Figure 10 presents the differential activation curves for the EW (*seed*) as
a function of the number of competitors of its CW (one to seven).

These plots were derived by taking the activation differences between
the curve for the EW in a simulation run (comparable to simulation 4)
without any CW competitors and the curves resulting from the systematic
addition of competitors into the lexicon. We see the expected elevation of
the activation level attained by the EW with the increasing number of CW
competitors. This activation gain is not constant, however. The largest
increase in the activation level of the finally embedded word is attributable
to the presence in the lexicon of the initially embedded word; the other
competitors produce less activation. The importance of this second factor,
the lexical status of the initially embedded sequence (word versus nonword),
was confirmed in further simulations. In addition, *the length of the initially*

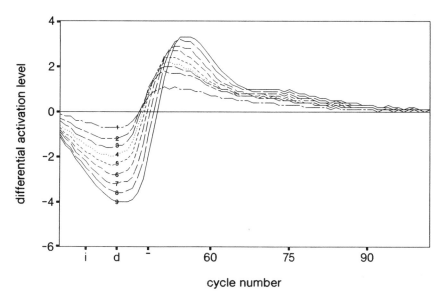

Figure 11
The differential activation curves for the finally embedded word *seed* as a
function of the number of competitors (1 to 9) of its carrier word *succeed*. The
competitors all were the same length.

embedded word was shown to correlate negatively with the activation level
reached by the finally embedded word. As the length of the initially
embedded word increases, so does the delay in the arrival of the finally
embedded word. The later this embedded word arrives, the more activated
the carrier word has become and the more this carrier word can inhibit the
finally embedded word.

Additional simulations also revealed the influence a fourth important
factor, *the length of the competitors*. In a series of runs, nine competitors
that overlapped the carrier word in its first five phonemes but matched
only in the first three (e.g., *sucker*) were successively added to the lexicon.
The differential activation curves for the EW with an increasing number
of CW competitors are shown in figure 11.

The results of this simulation show major fluctuations in the differential
activation curves for the embedded word with respect to its baseline.
During (and even before) the time cycles when the input corresponding to
the embedded word is received, this finally embedded word is inhibited not
only by the carrier word but also by its competitors, which also become
competitors of the embedded words to the extent that they overlap.

Relating simulation and human data   These simulations illustrate some precise predictions that TRACE makes about the activation of embedded words. The fact that TRACE can predict patterns of activation and word recognition in such quantitative detail makes it an extremely attractive model. One is tempted to test all of the predictions experimentally.[8] Unfortunately, moving from simulations to the experimental domain has its problems. It is not at all obvious, for example, how to relate the level of activation of a word in TRACE to the values measured (e.g., reaction times) during its processing by humans in experiments. Moreover, establishing correspondences between the time course of this activation, the moment of the experimental measurement, and the time course of human processing presents another serious challenge. Despite these difficulties, it is important to confront simulation with experimental data and eventually even to take the step from qualitative to quantitative comparisons.

As we noted above, Shillcock has obtained findings concerning the activation of embedded words that are directly relevant in this connection. In his first experiment he examined the activation of finally embedded words while manipulating the morphological complexity (monomorphemic versus bimorphemic) of the carrier word. He found evidence for lexical activation only for monomorphemic carriers. In his second experiment he varied the cohort size of the carrier word to examine the influence of the number of competitors of the carrier word on the activation of the embedded word. No evidence for activation of the embedded word was found, irrespective of the cohort size of the carrier word.

Relating these findings to the results of the preceding TRACE simulations is not a simple chore, for the reasons given above. First, it is difficult to decide whether the relatively low activation levels attained by the EW (less than 15 activation units) actually constitute a prediction of activation. Second, we don't know how the reaction-time measurements to visual probes taken at the end of a spoken word relate to the time cycles in the simulations at which the embedded words are most activated (approximately 300 msec after word offset in figure 10). The comparison between our simulation and the experimental data is further complicated by the fact that the activation patterns obtained in TRACE are determined by the properties of the words and their competitors that were not controlled in Shillcock's experiments. Our simulations have shown that the length and lexical status of the initial part of the carrier word and the number and length of the competitors of the carrier word all determine when and how much the embedded word is activated above its resting level. On the other hand, the experiments showed the effect of a variable, the frequency of the competitor, that was not included in the simulations. Because of these difficulties associated with relating experiments to simulations, it is premature to evaluate TRACE's performance on the basis of Shillcock's data. It is crucial nonetheless to run further experiments that systematically study lexical activation with stimuli controlled for the relevant factors.

Word length and word overlap   The preceding simulations allow us to draw some conclusions about the role the *word length* and *word overlap* play in the segmentation behavior of TRACE. Word length influences not only the amount of bottom-up activation a given word token receives but also the amount of lateral inhibition between word tokens.

Although short words initially increase more quickly in activation than longer words, they ultimately never reach the same activation level. This is because there is simply more bottom-up evidence (segments) supporting longer words than shorter words. This can be seen in figure 12, which presents the activation curves for word strings of varying lengths (*p*, *pl*, *plu*, *plut*, etc.). When each of these word strings was presented to TRACE, it was the only entry in the lexicon. Our purpose was to get a pure measure

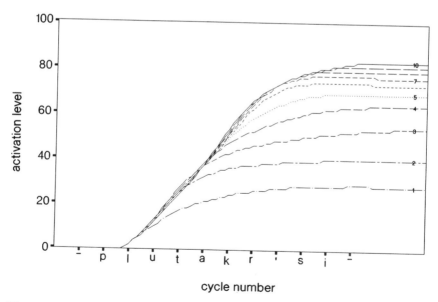

Figure 12
The activation curves for word strings of different lengths (1 to 10 phonemes) as input and as the only entry in the lexicon. In the example here the word strings are *p*, *pl*, *plu*, . . . , *plutocracy*.

of bottom-up activation without inhibition from competitors. Figure 12 shows that the activation level attained is a clear function of word length.

Since the length of a word partially determines its level of activation and since the inhibiting influence of this word upon other words depends upon its own activation level, word length also determines the inhibitory influence of one word upon another. As simulation 1 showed, longer words receive more bottom-up activation, and consequently, they effectively inhibit short ones. Indeed, TRACE revealed a definite preference for recognizing longer words when presented a completely ambiguous sequence (one that was a CW or two EWs), as shown in simulation 5.

Because of the advantage that long words appear to enjoy, we might wonder how shorter words ever have a chance of being recognized. To compensate, TRACE includes a counterbalancing mechanism in the computation of inhibition. Indeed, the strength of the inhibition between two different word tokens is made to depend upon the amount of overlap (i.e., the number of shared phonemes) between these two tokens. As a result, long words are inhibited more by other (long) words than short words are. This can best be illustrated by considering a simplified lexicon containing three words (two long and one short, all with the same level of activation). The short word inhibits the long words as much as the long words inhibit the short word, since they overlap the same number of phonemes (the length of the short word). This amount of inhibition is less, however, than that found between the two long words, which overlap in more phonemes and inhibit each other more strongly. By computing inhibition between units in this fashion, TRACE prevents longer words from completely dominating shorter words. This effect explains why, unlike in simulation 1, the embedded word was recognized in simulation 3. In this latter simulation all the longer competitors in Phonolex inhibited the CW competitor.

This series of five simulations suggests some tentative conclusions about the underlying mechanisms of interactive activation. In particular, they have shown that both absolute word length of the target and relative length with respect to the competitor words is important in determining the recognition and segmentation performance of TRACE. However, it is obvious that the results of these simulations cannot be explained only in terms of word length.

In the following simulations we will examine two other factors, *match* and *alignment*, that also play a central role in determining word activation. The first concerns the identity relationship, and the second the temporal relationship between a given input sequence and the internal representations of words. The preceding simulations already provide us with some examples of the effect that these two factors have. In simulation 2 the longer carrier word quickly loses its activation with the arrival of the mismatching input corresponding to the added word. Furthermore, the differential activation of initially and finally embedded words in simulation 5 is attributable to the other factor, alignment. The former word is initially aligned with the input, and the latter is not.

Segmentation with boundary markers

Since we have been concerned primarily with input sequences that match and are aligned with target word tokens, the effect of mismatch and misalignment has not sufficiently some to light. In the following simulations we examine more closely the role played by these two important factors in lexical activation. More precisely, we follow the suggestion of McClelland and Elman (1986) who claim that a boundary symbol separating two embedded words suffices for them to be recognized. The insertion of this symbol in the input leads to mismatch or misalignment (or even both) with the word tokens. The following simulations examine the segmentation behavior of TRACE under these conditions.

Simulation 6   The input is the same as in simulation 5 with the exception that the boundary symbol separated the two EWs (e.g., "-suck-seed-").

The lexicon is the same as in simulation 5.

Figure 13 shows the activation curves for the two embedded words and for two tokens of the carrier word. CW1 starts at the same phoneme time slice as the initially embedded EW, and CW2 starts on the next phoneme time slice.

Unlike in the previous simulation, both EWs are strongly activated and recognized. In contrast, CW1 ceases to gain in activation after the boundary symbol is received. Although CW1 matches the three input segments following the boundary symbol, it is two phoneme time slices out of alignment with this input and therefore receives little, if any, additional bottom-up excitation from it. The situation is different for CW2, which is only one phoneme time slice out of alignment with both the initial three segments (shifted to the right) and the final three segments (shifted to the left) of the input. As figure 13 shows, this token becomes considerably more activated than CW1. We can conclude that misalignment of two phoneme time slices (the length of a phoneme) actually constitutes a total mismatch between the input and the word token (CW1), whereas misalignment of a single phoneme time slice in CW2 still produces a partial match that leads to some bottom-up activation.

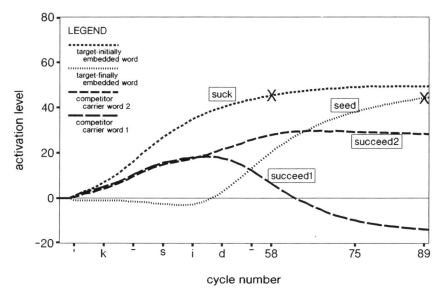

cycle number

Figure 13
The activation curves for two tokens of the carrier word (CW1 and CW2) and its two embedded words, all in the Phonolex condition. In the input the two embedded words were separated by the boundary symbol. In the example here the embedded words were *suck* and *seed*, and the carrier word *succeed*.

Simulation 7   In the previous simulation we investigated how the insertion of the word-boundary symbol modified the segmentation of the ambiguous sequence in favor of the two-embedded-word reading. This symbol led to a reduction in the activation of the carrier word by introducing a mismatch between the boundary symbol and the carrier word and by shifting the remaining (previously matching) input out of alignment so that the carrier word could not benefit from this input. In this final simulation we will explore the way in which this symbol can create not only mismatches but also new alignments. In particular, we investigate what happens when TRACE receives an input sequence (made up of two embedded words separated by an intervening segment) that closely matches another longer word in the lexicon (e.g., *cat-log* versus *catalog*).

Ten sequences of two short words separated by the word-boundary symbol were given as input (e.g., "-cat-log-").

The lexicon was Phonolex with a few additional words.

Figure 14 shows the activation curves for the two short words and for the competitor carrier word. The pattern of results obtained here is surpris-

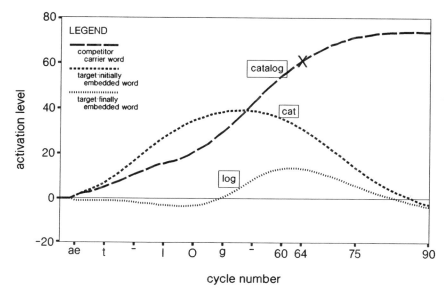

Figure 14
The activation curves for the carrier word *catalog* and its two embedded words *cat* and *log*. In the input the two embedded words were separated by the boundary symbol. The lexicon was Phonolex.

ing. It is the competitor carrier word rather than either of the embedded target words that is recognized despite the fact that this competitor mismatches the input in its fourth phoneme. This incorrect segmentation and recognition is a result of including the word-boundary symbol among the phonemes. The boundary symbol causes the recognition of the CW by shifting the input corresponding to the final embedded word into alignment with it. As a consequence, the CW is further activated by this input and is recognized. This simulation shows that the presence of the word boundary symbol does not guarantee correct segmentation and recognition.

Match and alignment   The preceding simulations have served to illustrate the role played in TRACE by match and alignment. In this section we consider more closely how these factors determine lexical excitation and inhibition. The level of activation that a word token reaches is obviously a function of the extent to which it matches or mismatches the input sequence. In general, when there is a complete match, the word token is strongly activated. However, a complete match with part of the input does not guarantee that the lexical token will become highly activated.

Simulation 5 showed that a word token like *seed* never increased much in activation despite its perfect match with part of the input (*preseed*). This is because the lexicon contained a longer overlapping token, *precede*, that was aligned with the onset of the input. Indeed, such word tokens have a clear activation advantage over overlapping word tokens that match later parts of the input. This advantage is due to the fact that initially aligned words become activated before the overlapping noninitially aligned words, and consequently, they are in a position to inhibit the latter and prevent them from being activated.

Word tokens that mismatch the input also generally do not become activated. The most common type of mismatch is found when the input simply differs or diverges from the word token. This type of mismatch is not analyzed in much detail here, since we used input consisting of words within words, where there is no such mismatch. Simulation 2, however, showed the deactivating effect of an input (e.g., *carglue*) on mismatching lexical tokens (*carpet*). A second type of mismatch results from misalignment, which can be caused by the insertion of the word boundary symbol, as in the simulations presented above. This symbol pushes the carrier word out of alignment and causes it to mismatch the input. Such mismatch by misalignment leads to the segmentation of the two embedded words making up a longer carrier word.

Both of these types of mismatch can affect the activation of the target in two different ways. First, since a mismatching word token receives little or no bottom-up support from the input, its level of activation stays constant or even decreases through decay. Second, competitors that do match the input are activated and inhibit the mismatching token. It is by means of inhibition of this kind that inappropriate lexical tokens are eliminated from contention in the recognition process. Segments in the input do not directly inhibit word tokens that mismatch them, but they activate other lexical units that do the inhibitory work. We expect inhibition to work in this way in a model allowing only facilitatory connections between units at different levels and inhibitory connections within levels.

5 Conclusion

This paper has been concerned with the way TRACE deals with the problem of lexical segmentation and recognition in the cases of lexical overlap. Lexical statistics derived from the CELEX database for Dutch have revealed that such overlap is extremely common in the lexicon. This overlap is not restricted to the initial position but is also abundant word-internally and word-finally. Indeed, the majority of short words are to be found embedded somewhere within longer morphologically unrelated words. The frequency of such embedding raises important processing questions about which lexical hypotheses are activated during the processing of lexically ambiguous stretches of speech and how inappropriate ones, if activated, are dispensed with.

As we have seen, TRACE provides some clear answers to these questions. In particular, bottom-up excitation and lateral inhibition lead to definite preferences in segmentation. For example, TRACE recognizes ambiguous stretches of speech as a single longer carrier word rather than as shorter embedded words. Levelt and Flores d'Arcais (1987) and Swinney (1982) have also suggested a similar processing preference for longer words. We have not yet conducted the lexical database queries and text analyses necessary to assess the probability with which this segmentation strategy will succeed (and not *suck seed*). However, our intuitions suggest that this segmentation analysis is indeed appropriate more often than not.

More generally, TRACE allows every word to contend for recognition at every moment in time, in contrast to the models presented in the introduction, which severely restrict the set of lexical hypotheses considered for a given stretch of speech. This is possible because TRACE duplicates lexical hypotheses for every word at every phoneme time slice, which produces a very high number of word tokens that can potentially be activated (the product of the number of phoneme time slices and the number of words in the lexicon). Although many word tokens quickly become excited above their resting level when an input is first received, large differences between the activation levels of these tokens also arise at these early stages of processing. Those word tokens that match and are aligned with the onset of the input steadily gain in activation and inhibit the other word tokens below their resting level. Not only the mismatching word tokens are inhibited, but also those tokens starting at later time slices, that is, those corresponding to other segmentations. If there is a sufficient match with the input, these inhibited tokens can still become activated (as was the case for finally embedded words) despite their initial mismatch or misalignment with the input. Thus there is no closed set of lexical hypotheses that depend upon a specific segmentation; words starting at any point in time have a chance of being recognized. Furthermore, since inhibition is restricted to word tokens that overlap, those tokens that begin after the offset of the activated word tokens are not inhibited by these tokens and are free to increase in their activation level. By defining which word tokens can inhibit each other in this way, TRACE tends to find the best-fitting match(es) for any input except in certain cases. In particular, since TRACE has a preference for words that provide the longest fit with the input, it sometimes commits itself to erroneous lexical hypotheses to such an extent that it can no longer recover the correct analysis.

Although the results of our simulations and those of McClelland and Elman (1986) present a relatively positive picture of TRACE's segmentation performance, further tests and modifications are still required. TRACE's performance needs to be tested in more realistic simulations than the ones presented here, which used a highly restricted lexicon and simplified input. First, the small lexica differed from the normal adult English lexicon in its higher proportion of short words (resulting in less lexical embedding) and lower proportion of similar and potentially confusable words (resulting in a smaller number of competitors). Second, future simulations should use longer continuous input strings. Clearly, the input of individual words or word pairs is much easier to segment and recognize than normal continuous speech. Furthermore, this input provided TRACE with some very useful segmentation information in the simulations. The fact that the onset of the input systematically corresponded to the onset of the words to be recognized meant that a part of the segmentation problem was solved for TRACE. This is especially true in view of the importance of onset alignment; the first activated words easily dominate all others. Third and finally, it is important to test predictions of TRACE experimentally and to use conflicting results to constrain or modify the model.

The multiple representation of the same lexical hypothesis for different moments in time allows TRACE to test every segmentation. Although this brute-force approach to time produces nice results, it is both uneconomical and psychologically unrealistic. In addition, this representation prevents the model from being able to learn, since the connection strengths between units can only be learned locally (i.e., for one time slice) and cannot be generalized over the entire network. Recently, alternative solutions to the representation of time using dynamic nets have been proposed by Elman (this volume), Jordan (1986), and Norris (this volume).

In sum, we have presented seven related simulations that shed some light on the remarkable ability of TRACE to segment and recognize words despite the large number of activated lexical candidates. One is tempted to ask whether this ability emerges from TRACE's structure or whether it is attributable to the specific parameter settings used. To address this question properly, it is necessary to modify the parameters and to evaluate the consequences of these modifications on the simulation results.

Since we believe that the credit should go to the interactive activation mechanism and the specific architectural assumptions of TRACE, our approach has been to ignore the effect of parameter variation. Indeed, we found it necessary to hold the parameters constant to understand the architecture of TRACE and to provide a fair test of the model. In all of our simulations we used the same values for the parameter set and the decision rule. McClelland and Elman originally proposed these default parameters and also used them in most of their successful simulations of diverse perceptual phenomena. These authors claim, "The qualitative behavior of the model was remarkably robust under parameter variations" (p. 22).

Our strategy of focusing on TRACE's internal structure has brought new insights into the interactive activation mechanism and its complex interaction with the architecture of TRACE. In addition, the simulation exercises here have identified four factors that play a decisive role in determining TRACE's segmentation and recognition behavior: the length of the word tokens, the amount of overlap between word tokens, and the match and the alignment between the input and the word tokens. We assume that further simulations will confirm the importance of these *emergent* properties of the model (even with different parameters). To avoid TRACE's submergent properties, however, these simulations will be left for future research.

Acknowledgments

The authors would like to thank Jeff Elman for making TRACE available to us and Ellen Bard, Gary Dell, and Arthur Samuel for comments on an earlier version of this paper. Thanks also go to CELEX for providing access to the Dutch database.

Notes

1. There are at least two further factors that determine which lexical hypotheses are activated: the nature of the lexical representation and context. Models defining lexical representation in terms of syllabic as opposed to phonemic units would presumably not activate the same subset of lexical hypotheses. Lexical hypotheses would also vary according to whether context can propose new lexical hypotheses or simply dispose of those already active. These factors are not considered here.

2. These statistics provide only a conservative estimate of the amount of lexical overlap, since they are based on citation forms, assume phonemic representations, and require a perfect match. If fluent speech is analyzed with a relaxed goodness-of-fit criterion, there is even more lexical overlap.

3. To increase the efficiency (or activation) of the word boundary phoneme, these authors included it in the lexicon. As a lexical unit, it provides top-down feedback to the phoneme boundary unit and consequently strengthens the latter's segmenting ability.

4. We have determined the cause of this rather curious inhibitory peak upon the CW target. It results from the fact that the EW competitor is initially activated faster than its CW target and can inhibit this target proportionately more. In principle, one would not expect a difference in the initial rate of activation of words matching the same input string but differing length. In fact, there is! We can see the reason for this in the baseline condition presented in figure 1. There the EW is activated more quickly than the CW despite the fact that both targets are alone in their respective lexica. Consequently, this effect cannot be due to inhibition from other words but is attributable to inhibition from other tokens of the same word starting at different time slices. TRACE allows tokens of the same words starting at different time slices to inhibit each other. This inhibitory influence is greater for longer words than for shorter ones, since there is more overlap between longer tokens. The slower activation of the longer target word with respect to its shorter competitor is the indirect cause of the inhibitory peak for this CW target found in figure 3.

5. We computed the moment a word is recognized following the same procedure as for the recognition of phonemes described in section "Recognition." We used a response probability of .90 to define recognition and included only those words with positive activation values in the computation. McClelland and Elman (1986) did not compute recognition times for words, although they imply that a word is recognized when it dominates all other word candidates. Their use of a qualitative definition of word recognition is understandable in view of the problems inherent in specifying the moment of word recognition. For example, to define when a given phoneme or word is recognized, it is necessary to decide which target tokens and which competitor tokens enter the function determining recognition. We restricted the set of tokens to only those initially aligned with the target (i.e., tokens sharing the same initial time slice).

6. We conducted an additional simulation in which *glue* was replaced in the lexicon by the boundary symbol and the input "-car-" was given. In this simulation too the target embedded word was recognized, but at a later moment than in simulation 2.

7. McClelland and Elman point out that TRACE prefers to interpret an ambiguous sequence (/parti/) as a longer carrier word (*party*) over the embedded reading *par + tea*). They appear to have based their conclusions on one example. In this simulation we intend to extend this result to a larger sample of inputs.

8. Other attempts at testing some predictions of TRACE concerning its activation flow can be found in Frauenfelder, Segui, and Dijkstra 1990 and Peeters, Frauenfelder, and Wittenburg 1989.

References

Bard, E. G., Shillcock, R. C., and Altmann, G. T. M. 1989. The recognition of words after their acoustic offset: Effect of subsequent context. *Perception and Psychophysics* 44:395–408.

Cole, R. A., and Jakimik, J. 1980. A model of speech perception. In R. A. Cole (ed.), *Perception and Production of Fluent Speech*. Hillsdale, N.J.: Lawrence Erlbaum Associates.

Cutler, A., and Norris, D. 1988. The role of strong syllables in segmentation for lexical access. *Journal of Experimental Psychology: Human Perception and Performance* 14, no. 1: 113–121.

Frauenfelder, U., Segui, J., and Dijkstra, T. 1990. Lexical effects in phonemic processing: Facilitatory or inhibitory? *Journal of Experimental Psychology: Human Perception and Performance* 16, no. 1: 77–91.

Grosjean, F. 1985. The recognition of words after their acoustic offset: Evidence and implications. *Perception and Psychophysics* 38:299–310.

Grosjean, F., and Gee, J. P. 1987. Prosodic structure in spoken word recognition. *Cognition* 25, nos. 1–2: 157–187.

Jordan, M. I. 1986. Serial order: A parallel distributed processing approach. Institute for Cognitive Science, report 8604, University of California, San Diego.

Levelt, W. J. M., and Flores d'Arcais, G. B. 1987. Snelheid en uniciteit bij lexicale toegang. In H. F. M. Cromback, L. J. Th. van der Kamp, and C. A. J. Vlek (eds.), *De psychologie voorbij: Ontwikkelingen rond model, metriek en methode in de gedragswetenschappen*. Lisse: Swets and Zeitlinger.

Luce, P. A. 1986. A computational analysis of uniqueness points in auditory word recognition. *Perception and Psychophysics* 34:155–158.

Luce, R. D. 1959. *Individual Choice Behavior*. New York: Wiley.

McClelland, J. L., and Elman, J. L. 1986. The TRACE model of speech perception. *Cognitive Psychology* 18:1–86.

McClelland, J. L., and Rumelhart, D. E. 1981. An interactive activation model of context effects in letter perception: Part 1, An account of basic findings. *Psychological Review* 88:375–407.

Marslen-Wilson, W. D., and Welsh, A. 1978. Processing interactions and lexical access during word recognition in continuous speech. *Cognitive Psychology* 10:29–63.

Peeters, G., Frauenfelder, U. H., and Wittenburg, P. 1989. Psychological constraints upon connectionist models of word recognition: Exploring TRACE and alternatives. In R. Pfeifer, Z. Schreter, F. Fogelman, and L. Steels (eds.), *Connectionism in Perspective*. Amsterdam: Elsevier.

Swinney, D. A. 1979. Lexical access during sentence comprehension: (Re)consideration of context effects. *Journal of Verbal Learning and Verbal Behavior* 18:645–659.

Swinney, D. A. 1982. The structure and time-course of information interaction during speech comprehension. In J. Mehler, E. C. T. Walker, and M. F. Garrett (eds.), *Perspective on mental representations*. Hillsdale, N.J.: Lawrence Erlbaum Associates.

Zwitserlood, P. 1989. The locus of the effects of sentential-semantic context in spoken-word processing. *Cognition* 32, no. 1: 25–64.

Chapter 4

A Dynamic-Net Model of Human Speech Recognition

Dennis Norris

Speech is a signal that varies over time, but standard feed-forward networks have no way of handling the temporal component of speech directly. In fact, this is one case where parallel distributed processing suffers from being too parallel. Feed-forward nets can only work with patterns that can be presented simultaneously to all input nodes. There is no simple way to make such nets deal with an input pattern that unfolds over time. The usual solution adopted to this problem is to recode the time dimension as a spatial dimension. That is, the dynamic speech signal is treated as if it were a static plot of the waveform or a spectrograph. The recognition problem can then be solved in the spatial domain rather than the time domain. So rather than having to deal with a dynamically varying signal, we can deal with a static representation in which all parts of the signal are present simultaneously. However, although moving the problem from the time domain to the spatial domain does at least enable feed-forward nets to get a grip on the task, dispensing with time tends to generate difficulties of its own. Simple networks with a single layer of hidden units (e.g., Elman and Zipser 1987; Landauer, Kamm, and Singhal 1987) suffer from a number of serious limitations. While it is relatively simple to train a net to recognize a single token of a word located at a fixed position in the net, there is no simple way to ensure that the net will generalize from this learning experience to recognize a different token of the same word spoken at a different rate or even the same token beginning at a different location in the net. To solve the latter problem, TRACE (McClelland and Elman 1986), for example, has had to use multiple location-specific word units. In effect, there has to be a complete lexical net beginning at each location where a word might start.

Table 1
Patterns of input

Time	t_1	t_2	t_3	t_4	t_5	t_6	t_7	t_8	t_9	t_{10}
Training pattern	1	0	1	0	1	0	1	0	1	0
Phase shifted	0	1	0	1	0	1	0	1	0	1
Slow	1	1	0	0	1	1	0	0	1	1
One element lengthened	1	0	1	0	0	1	0	1	0	1

The Invariance Problem

The problems that simple feed-forward nets face can be seen more clearly by considering the patterns shown in table 1. Assume that a network of the form shown in figure 1 is trained to recognize a pattern consisting of alternating 1s and 0s. To the human observer a phase-shifted version of the pattern that begins with a 0 rather than a 1 appears very similar to the original pattern. In speech terms, this second pattern might well be an instance of the first pattern starting at a slightly different point in time. However, as far as the network is concerned, these two patterns produce maximally different inputs. Every node of the network that received a 1 as its input with the training pattern now receives a 0 with the phase-shifted pattern. If we want the network to respond in the same manner to both of these patterns, we have to explicitly train it how to respond to each pattern separately. We can't simply train it with one pattern and hope that it will generalize to what we as humans think are "similar" patterns. The net will also have a problem making appropriate generalizations to patterns that are stretched or compressed. If the input cycles through levels of 1s and 0s at half the rate of the training pattern, only half the input nodes will receive the same input as they did with the training pattern. Even if only a single element in the pattern is lengthened, all subsequent inputs will be out of phase.

   It might seem that shifting a pattern out of phase by a single time slice shouldn't really make all that much difference. After all, each input is going to the node next to the node it was presented to during training. Surely that must be better than a large phase shift where the inputs now go to nodes a long way from their original input nodes. However, the input nodes have no intrinsic ordering in the network. In terms of connections, all nodes are equally close together (or equally far apart). In a network such as figure 1, nodes that are drawn close together are no more strongly connected than nodes that are drawn far apart. We get the impression that input

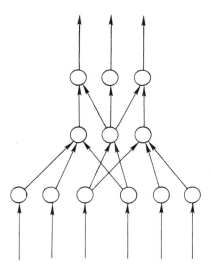

Figure 1
A simple feed-forward network. (Not all connections are shown.)

nodes are ordered from the way in which we represent networks in two-dimensional diagrams.

All of these difficulties with simple feed-forward nets are examples of the invariance problem. We want a net that produces invariant output despite the fact that the input may be transformed or distorted in ways that don't alter the way in which we wish to classify the input. We want to be able to recognize words despite changes in rate of speech, fundamental frequency, voice quality, etc.

Speech as a Sequence of Events

The problems of recognizing patterns that vary in onset time or rate stem from the failure of simple feed-forward nets to make appropriate generalizations in the time domain. They fail to accommodate temporal variability either with respect to changes in the duration of the signal or changes in the onset time of the signal. To overcome these problems, we need to develop an architecture that acknowledges that speech can be characterized as a sequence of events (phonemes, syllables, words) in which the temporal location and absolute duration of the events is of secondary importance to their ordering. The word *cat* can be characterized as the ordered sequence of phonemes /k/, /a/, /t/. The point in time at which the sequence appears obviously makes no difference to the identity of the word, and within limits, neither does the duration of the individual phonemes.

Network Architectures for Sequence Perception and Production

One possible approach to sequence perception is to use recurrent nets and employ an extension of the back-propagation technique (Rumelhart, Hinton, and Williams 1986) to permit the error term to be propagated back through time (see, e.g., Watrous, Shastri, and Waibel 1987). However, a severe drawback with this method is that it is computationally very expensive, particularly in terms of its demands on storage. In effect, the net has to be duplicated for each time slice. Lengthy sequences thus place enormous demands on memory. A rather more economical approach to the problem is suggested by the work of Jordan (1986) on sequence production. This work also uses a recurrent net, but the architecture is sufficiently simple to permit the use of the standard back-propagation algorithm.

Jordan has shown how a simple net with a single layer of hidden units can learn to produce sequences when supplemented by recurrent links (see figure 2). In Jordan's scheme the output of the network is fed back to a set of units termed state units. The state units serve to encode the current

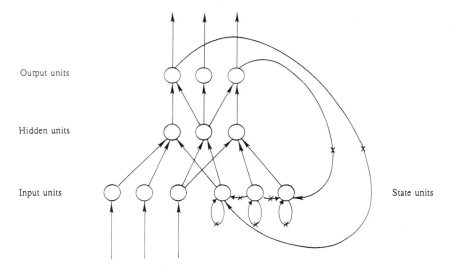

Figure 2
A Jordan net. Links marked x have delays of one time unit. (Not all connections are shown.)

state of the network. The output of the net is thus a function of both the activation of the input, or "plan units," and the activation of the state units. The state units are connected to each other and also have recurrent links to themselves. This ensures that the network's behavior is determined not only by its immediately preceding state but also by earlier states. The network can be trained to produce different output sequences in response to different inputs to the plan units. Because the recurrent links in the net have constant weights, learning in this net is very simple. Learning can be based on the standard back-propagation algorithm, and there is no need to propagate the error term back through time.

However, for speech recognition we really need a network that works the other way round. That is, we want different sequences of input patterns to produce different patterns on the output units. We want the network to recognize rather than produce sequences. In fact, this net will do precisely that if we hold the output pattern constant while we present the input sequence to the plan units. The net can be taught to classify sequences and to produce a different output pattern for each input sequence. Moreover, the recognition task can be performed with a simpler network architecture than that required for production. First, we can dispense with the self-recurrent links on the state units and with the links between the state units. In Jordan's production net these links were present to ensure that the state units represented a decaying average of past outputs. This enables the net to reproduce lengthy sequences, even when the sequences contain identical subsequences. If activity in the state units were determined simply by the last n outputs, the net would be unable to produce different sequences with common subsequences of length greater than n or single sequences with repeated subsequences greater than n.

In the sequence recognition net shown in figure 3, the output of the state nodes is determined by the previous output, which in turn is determined by the previous output of the state nodes. So because of the feedback loop, even inputs many cycles earlier in time will continue to exert at least some influence on the current state.

If the net in figure 3 were used as a production net, the next state would always be determined solely by the current values of the plan and output units. Given that the input to the plan units is constant throughout a sequence, this would mean that no element in the sequence could be repeated.

However, in the recognition net, the output should never stabilize until the input has been recognized. Unlike the production net, the output is not being driven through a set of predetermined output patterns that may

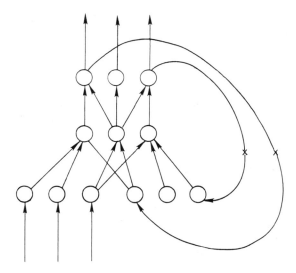

Figure 3
A dynamic net for recognition. Links marked x have delays of one time unit.
(Not all connections are shown.)

be repeated. The output is moving towards a single stable pattern that represents the classification of the input. If any two patterns that should be classified differently produce the same output pattern at any point, this can only be because the sequences are identical up to that point or because they differ at some point so far in the past that the relevant differences are no longer having a significant influence on the state. The links between the state nodes can therefore be dispensed with because the output never cycles through identical states that must be distinguished.

If we envisage a word-recognition system with a large number of output nodes, each representing a different word, and a relatively small number of hidden units, it would clearly be more economical to adopt a network structure like that shown in figure 4, where the feedback is taken from the hidden units. Given that the output units are driven by the hidden units, the hidden units themselves provide an equally good source of state information. If the output units changes, so must the hidden units. We can therefore derive the state information from either the output units or the hidden units, whichever are fewer.

As in Jordan's net, the feedback links have a constant weight. In the present case all feedback links have a weight of 1. Networks with this architecture can be trained with the standard back-propagation algorithm

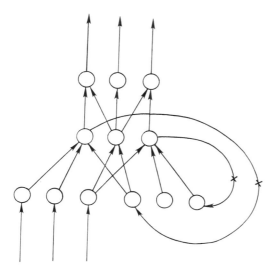

Figure 4
A dynamic net for recognition with feedback from hidden units. Links marked **x** have delays of one time unit. (Not all connections are shown.)

if the target pattern is present throughout the presentation of the input sequence during training. Training such a net is thus computationally far simpler than a recurrent net in which the error must be propagated back through time.

Tests of the Network

One of the central motivations for proposing a network of this form was the hope that by treating the input as a temporal sequence of events rather than as a static pattern, the network would exhibit more appropriate generalization in the time domain. To test the recurrent net's ability to generalize in the time domain, a net was trained to recognize a set of 27 sequences. There were two versions of each sequence designed to represent different rates of input. The two versions could, for example, be considered to represent tokens of the same word spoken at different rates. In the "slow" version of each sequence, each element of the sequence remained constant for 3 units of time. In the "fast" version each element was presented for only 1 unit of time.

After training on the complete set of such pairs, the test of the network was to see how well it would classify the same sequences presented at an

Table 2
Forms of stimuli for testing the network

Number represented	3	3	3	1	1	1	2	2	2
Training pattern	| 001 | 001 | 001 | 100 | 100 | 100 | 010 | 010 | 010 |								
Number represented	0	0	0	0	0	0	3	1	2
Training pattern	| 000 | 000 | 000 | 000 | 000 | 000 | 001 | 100 | 010 |								
Nunber represented	0	0	0	3	3	1	1	2	2
Test pattern	| 000 | 000 | 000 | 001 | 001 | 100 | 100 | 010 | 010 |								

Training set: $3n\,3n\,3n + 1n\,1n\,1n = 54$ stimuli, 27 response categories. Test set: $2n\,2n\,2n$

intermediate rate. In these test stimuli each element of the sequence appeared for 2 units of time. Would the net be able to classify these stimuli correctly even though it had never been presented with sequences at the intermediate rate?

The stimuli took the form shown in table 2. There were two training stimuli in each of the 27 response categories. The basic element or time slice in each stimulus was a three-bit binary pattern. The individual elements of the patterns differed according to which one of the three bits were set. The stimuli were formed from all possible combinations of the three basic three-bit patterns. All stimuli were preceded by a pattern element in which all three bits were set to 0. In the long version of the stimuli, each pattern element was repeated three times and followed by a final 0 element. In the short version each element appeared only once. The following seven pattern elements were set to 0. In the test stimulus each pattern element appeared twice and the following four elements were set to 0.

The recurrent network had 3 input units, 30 state units, 30 hidden units, and 27 output units. On each cycle of the net, successive three-bit elements of the stimulus were presented as input to the net. Activation in the net was reset to 0 in between each stimulus. For comparison, a feed-forward net was trained to classify the same stimuli. The feed-forward net had 33 input units, 30 hidden units, and 27 output units. An entire 33-bit stimulus pattern was presented as input to the net on each learning trial. After both nets had learned to classify all 54 training stimuli correctly, learning was turned off and the net was tested on the 27 test stimuli. The criterion for learning was the same for both nets.

The feed-forward net correctly classified 9 out of the 27 test patterns, whereas the recurrent net classified 23 of the test patterns correctly. The performance of the recurrent net is therefore much better than that of the feed-forward net. However, the feed-forward net is actually much worse than these figures indicate. Although it does make the correct generalization on one-third of the stimuli, it is not generalizing across spatial positions at all. As might be expected, it is simply averaging across the values of the patterns at each location.

By using all 27 combinations of the 3 basic pattern elements, I have included 3 patterns consisting simply of a single element repeated either 3 or 9 times. The feed-forward net will correctly classify the test pattern because it is more like the average of the two training stimuli for that sequence than it is like any other stimuli. Because the patterns are all right-justified, the same is true for any pattern of the form AAB, of which there are 6. Therefore, the only sequences that the feed-forward net gets right are those where it can achieve the correct result by simply averaging across each of the 27 positions in the pattern. So, if we consider only those stimuli that require temporal (spatial) generalization to classify correctly, the recurrent net scores 14/18, compared with 0 for the feed-forward net.[1]

Detecting Patterns in Continuous Input

As already mentioned, feed-forward nets with a single layer of hidden units have a major problem with position invariance. One solution is simply to train the net to recognize the stimulus in all possible positions. A hard-wired net like TRACE uses a large number of position-sensitive word units. In effect, there is a complete lexical network starting at each location where a word might begin. An alternative is to train a multilayered net to develop position-invariant detectors (Fukushima and Miyake 1982, Hinton 1987, Mozer 1987). However, the recurrent net completely avoids the need for any of these more complex solutions to achieve translation invariance in the time domain. Because the net operates by scanning through the input a slice at a time, the problem of aligning the input with the net simply never arises. The net learns to recognize sequences of inputs and is quite indifferent as to where the sequence begins.

The Plausibility of the Recurrent Net as a Psychological Model

The bulk of our knowledge of the temporal characteristics of human word recognition comes from work by Marslen-Wilson and his colleagues (Marslen-Wilson 1984, Marslen-Wilson and Tyler 1980, Marslen-Wilson and Welsh 1978). In a number of studies Marslen-Wilson has demonstrated that the point at which human listeners can identify a word is strongly correlated with the point at which that word diverges from other words in the language. So, for example, the word *kangaroo* can be identified as soon as the listener hears the phoneme /g/, since at that point *kangaroo(s)* is the only word in the language consistent with the acoustic input. In other words, under ideal conditions, listeners can identify the word at the earliest possible point in time. Similarly, listeners can determine that *tregible* is not a word as soon as they hear the phoneme /g/, since at that point the input ceases to be compatible with any word in the language. Marslen-Wilson explains these findings in terms of the cohort model. In the cohort model each word in the language is associated with an active computational unit. Each unit monitors the input and drops out of the cohort of active units whenever it detects a mismatch between the input and the word it represents. The word is recognized as soon as the cohort is reduced to a single element.

The major problem for the first version of the cohort model was that it proceeded by a series of all-or-none decisions. That is, the units in the cohort permanently dropped out as soon as any mismatch with the input was detected. This meant that any distortion in the input, such as might be caused by slight mispronunciation, would be detected as a mismatch by the relevent element and that unit would drop out of the cohort. The model would thus be unable to indentify the word. The present model manages to combine the desirable properties of the cohort model, in particular, its emphasis on the left-to-right nature of processing, while at the same time avoiding the problems associated with an all-or-none decision mechanism. But to what extent does the present model display the characteristics of human word recognition described by Marslen-Wilson?

To examine the models ability to model the left-to-right nature of human word recognition, a net with 11 input units, 20 hidden units, 20 state units, and 50 output units was trained to identify a set of 50 "words."

As the primary concern here was with the left-to-right processing char-acteristics of the model, it seemed premature to use real speech as input. I therefore decided to begin by coding segments in terms of binary speech features. In fact, since the left-to-right behavior of the model should be independent of the segments and the featural representation chosen, I decided to simplify matters by deriving the input to the model from the orthographic form of the words. Each orthographic consonant was coded in terms of the features of its nearest phoneme. Each was represented by a set of 11 features based on Lehmann 1972.

The 50 words in the training set were constructed from a set of 25 words varying in length between four and seven letters. The remaining 25 words in the training set were constructed by reversing the order of the letters in each of the 25 original words. This manipulation was designed to facilitate comparisons between pairs of words that differed in either their initial or their final letters. For a pair of words differing at their initial letters, the reversed versions served as a control pair differing in their final letters, and vice versa.

During training, the words were input to the net one phoneme/letter at a time with no breaks or silences between words. The order of presentation of the words was randomized between training epochs. One output unit was assigned to represent each word and the target output pattern was present throughout the presentation of each word.

After training, the net does a very good job at identifying words from the continuous input stream, especially with longer words. Most of the net's errors occur at points where, in the absense of any cues to lexical segmentation, there is some local ambiguity in the analysis of the input. This aspect of the net's performance will be discussed in more detail later. Because the net is rather small, there was some concern that long words differing only in their initial phoneme might prove difficult to discriminate owing to limitations in the net's memory capacity. However, this proved not to be a problem with the test set of words.

To test the net's ability to model the psychological data, activity in the net was zeroed before presenting each word. This effectively simulates presenting each word in isolation and ensures that the initial state of the net does not exert a bias in favor of some words rather than others. In accordance with the findings of Marslen-Wilson and his colleagues, the net was able to identify most words reliably at the point where they became unique in the net's 50-word lexicon. Table 3 shows the results of presenting the net with the words *delimit* and *deliver*. While *delimit* and *deliver* were both activated during the first 4 letters/phonemes (0.319 and 0.458 respectively), presentation of the *m* causes *delimit* to become highly activated (0.826), while *deliver* drops to near zero (0.06). This result reflects both of the central properties of the cohort model. Words can be identified as soon as they become unique, and also, words cease to become activated as soon as the input becomes inconsistent.

As noted earlier, one of the major problems with the cohort model is its reliance on all-or-none decisions; the system must be able to identify slightly mispronounced or distorted words. Unlike the cohort model, the present model is not completely disrupted by small distortions, particularly in longer words. Table 4 shows the results of presenting the net with *goronet* and *horonet*, distortions of *coronet* in the training set. Only *goronet*, in

Table 3
Activation levels of the three most highly activated items in the net's lexicon after the presentation of successive phonemes/letters

Input	Word	Activation	Word	Activation	Word	Activation
Input: deliver						
d	dloc	0.105	damp	0.096	toob	0.014
e	deliver	0.421	delimit	0.375	dish	0.039
l	deliver	0.336	delimit	0.321	dloc	0.008
i	deliver	0.458	delimit	0.319	disk	0.061
v	deliver	0.854	ksid	0.175	delimit	0.059
e	deliver	0.781	ksid	0.233	fear	0.048
r	deliver	0.854	ksid	0.302	fear	0.174
Input: delimit						
d	dloc	0.105	damp	0.096	toob	0.014
e	deliver	0.421	delimit	0.375	dish	0.039
l	deliver	0.336	delimit	0.321	dloc	0.008
i	deliver	0.458	delimit	0.319	disk	0.061
m	delimit	0.826	deliver	0.060	mlac	0.019
i	delimit	0.770	deliver	0.043	disk	0.042
t	delimit	0.776	disk	0.079	deliver	0.016

which the /g/ is featurally very similar to the /c/ in *coronet*, actually activates *coronet*. The mismatch of the initial /h/ in *horonet* is too great to cause any activation of *coronet*.

The results of unpublished studies by Marslen-Wilson and Zwitserlood (1987) and by Marslen-Wilson, Brown, and Zwitserlood (in preparation), which demonstrate the importance of the beginnings of words over the ends of words, are also handled correctly by the network. These studies used the cross-modal priming technique to examine the extent to which minimally different pairs of words activate each other, depending on whether they differ in their initial phoneme or in their final phoneme. The question was whether words such as *take* and *tape*, which differ in their final phonemes, would activate each other more strongly than would *taker* and *baker*, which differ only in their initial phonemes (note that the experiments were actually performed in Dutch). If auditory lexical access is largely a matter of computing an overall similarity metric between the input and the stored representation of the word, words in both pairs should activate each other equally. Whether the words differ at the beginning or at the end should make no difference. All that should matter is the size of

Table 4
Activation levels of the three most highly activated items in the net's lexicon after the presentation of successive phonemes/letters

Input	Word	Activation	Word	Activation	Word	Activation
Input: coronet						
c	ksid	0.182	calm	0.171	coroner	0.156
o	coroner	0.310	cold	0.235	coronet	0.073
r	coroner	0.769	coronet	0.244	cold	0.039
o	coroner	0.788	coronet	0.259	bounded	0.010
n	coroner	0.776	coronet	0.267	tenoroc	0.025
e	coroner	0.763	coronet	0.233	calm	0.046
t	coronet	0.615	coroner	0.430	tenoroc	0.072
Input: goronet						
g	calm	0.250	ksid	0.195	coroner	0.110
o	cold	0.283	coroner	0.196	coronet	0.049
r	coroner	0.737	coronet	0.219	cold	0.035
o	coroner	0.796	coronet	0.291	bounded	0.006
n	coroner	0.782	coronet	0.285	tenoroc	0.010
e	coroner	0.786	coronet	0.289	calm	0.011
t	coronet	0.673	coroner	0.470	tenoroc	0.033
Input: horonet						
h	finish	0.011	raef	0.007	flash	0.007
o	raef	0.332	hurt	0.082	tripe	0.016
r	raef	0.136	hurt	0.011	hsart	0.005
o	raef	0.038	rood	0.031	hurt	0.012
n	rood	0.051	damp	0.032	toob	0.013
e	damp	0.037	tripe	0.032	trash	0.007
t	damp	0.463	toob	0.022	taeb	0.010

the difference. However, if lexical access is based on a left-to-right decision mechanism, such as that employed in the cohort model, a word should not activate other words with different initial phonemes. This is precisely the pattern of results that Marslen-Wilson and his colleagues found. It is also the pattern of behavior produced by the model. As table 5 shows, neither *baker* nor *taker* activates the other. However, *rekab* and *rekat* (which are reversed versions of *baker* and *taker* and which are both in the model's lexicon) activate each other right up until presentation of the final phoneme/letter. When two words differ only in their initial phoneme, neither word will activate the other unless the initial phonemes are very similar and the words are fairly long. Table 6 shows a similar example using the words *coronet* and *coroner*.

So far I've emphasized how the strongly left-to-right properties of the network give it the ability to provide a very natural account of the cohort-like attributes of human spoken-word recognition. In common with the cohort model, however, it suffers from being *too* left-to-right. All its decisions are made without the benefit of look-ahead. Subsequent input can never force the model to revoke an earlier decision. Consider what happens when the model hears *catalog*. After hearing *cat* the most active word may be *cat*. However, as further information comes in, the activation of *cat* will rapidly decrease, while the activation of *catalog* will increase. The network somehow wants to know that the initial activation of *cat* should be ignored because it was actually caused by the word *catalog*. As the chapter by Shillcock shows, the network is right to activate *cat* as soon as possible without waiting for further information to become available. However, some mechanism must be provided whereby this initial decision can be reassessed in the light of new information. In TRACE this is achieved by having multiple lexical networks whose interpretations of the input compete with each other to find the optimum analysis of the input. These networks can take account of new information as it arrives to revise the initial analysis of the input. A similar approach could be adopted here by duplicating the network over a number of time slices. By interconnecting the hidden units of adjacents nets, each net could be made to take account of right context as well as left context. One advantage of such an architecture would be that it would only need to be expanded to deal with enough right context to resolve potential ambiguities with inputs like *catalog*. A single net is already capable of memorizing left context in its state units. Unlike TRACE, it would still maintain its ability to cope with temporal variability in the signal.

Table 5
Activation levels of the three most highly activated items in the net's lexicon after the presentation of successive phonemes/letters

Input	Word	Activation	Word	Activation	Word	Activation
Input: baker						
b	beat	0.131	pound	0.022	damp	0.020
a	beat	0.043	paeh	0.039	pmad	0.003
k	baker	0.924	beat	0.008	hurt	0.005
e	baker	0.950	beat	0.006	hurt	0.006
r	baker	0.863	border	0.052	deliver	0.009
Input: taker						
t	tenoroc	0.087	toob	0.072	trash	0.069
a	taker	0.316	taeh	0.283	taeb	0.178
k	taker	0.945	tenoroc	0.042	taeb	0.025
e	taker	0.970	taeb	0.018	hurt	0.016
r	taker	0.958	taeb	0.024	hurt	0.009
Input: rekab						
r	raef	0.125	rood	0.120	renoroc	0.111
e	renoroc	0.199	rekat	0.161	reviled	0.137
k	rekat	0.594	rekab	0.295	renoroc	0.030
a	rekat	0.603	rekab	0.201	renoroc	0.027
b	rekab	0.719	rekat	0.099	reviled	0.031
Input: rekat						
r	raef	0.125	rood	0.120	renoroc	0.111
e	renoroc	0.199	rekat	0.161	reviled	0.137
k	rekat	0.594	rekab	0.295	renoroc	0.030
a	rekat	0.603	rekab	0.201	renoroc	0.027
t	rekat	0.899	redrob	0.056	rekab	0.027

Table 6
Activation levels of the three most highly activated items in the net's lexicon
after the presentation of successive phonemes/letters

Input	Word	Activation	Word	Activation	Word	Activation
Input: coroner						
c	ksid	0.182	calm	0.171	coroner	0.156
o	coroner	0.310	cold	0.235	coronet	0.073
r	coroner	0.769	coronet	0.244	cold	0.039
o	coroner	0.788	coronet	0.259	bounded	0.010
n	coroner	0.776	coronet	0.267	tenoroc	0.025
e	coroner	0.763	coronet	0.233	calm	0.046
r	coroner	0.875	coronet	0.070	calm	0.024
Input: coronet						
c	ksid	0.182	calm	0.171	coroner	0.156
o	coroner	0.310	cold	0.235	coronet	0.073
r	coroner	0.769	coronet	0.244	cold	0.039
o	coroner	0.788	coronet	0.259	bounded	0.010
n	coroner	0.776	coronet	0.267	tenoroc	0.025
e	coroner	0.763	coronet	0.233	calm	0.046
t	coronet	0.615	coroner	0.430	tenoroc	0.072
Input: renoroc						
r	raef	0.125	rood	0.120	renoroc	0.111
e	renoroc	0.199	rekat	0.161	reviled	0.137
n	renoroc	0.955	rekat	0.034	reviled	0.025
o	renoroc	0.988	coroner	0.023	dloc	0.019
r	renoroc	0.992	damp	0.080	coroner	0.030
o	renoroc	0.985	coroner	0.102	damp	0.025
c	renoroc	0.952	dloc	0.049	door	0.044
Input: tenoroc						
t	tenoroc	0.087	toob	0.072	trash	0.069
e	tenoroc	0.932	damp	0.052	taker	0.050
n	tenoroc	0.961	damp	0.061	truh	0.014
o	tenoroc	0.986	taker	0.014	coroner	0.013
r	tenoroc	0.966	taker	0.021	coroner	0.020
o	tenoroc	0.996	coroner	0.030	pound	0.029
c	tenoroc	0.959	coroner	0.033	pound	0.023

Note

1. Interestingly, the time-delay neural net (Waibel et al. 1988), which in its simplest form is equivalent to training the feed-forward net described here to recognize the input patterns in all possible input positions, performs as well as the dynamic net.

References

Elman, J. L., and Zipser, D. 1987. Learning the hidden structure of speech. Institute for Cognitive Science report 8,701, University of California, San Diego.

Hinton, G. E. 1987. Learning translation invariant recognition in a massively parallel network. In *Proceedings of the Conference on Parallel Architectures and Languages, Europe*. Eindhoven, the Netherlands.

Fukushima, K., and Miyake, S. 1982. Neocognition: A new algorithm for pattern recognition tolerant of deformations and shifts in position. *Pattern Recognition* 15:455–469.

Jordan, M. 1986. Serial order: A parallel distributed processing approach. Institute for Cognitive Science report 8,604, University of California, San Diego.

Landauer, T. K., Kamm, C. A., and Singhal, S. 1987. Teaching a minimally structured back-propagation network to recognize speech sounds. Unpublished manuscript, Bell Communications Research, Morristown, New Jersey.

McClelland, J. L., and Elman, J. L. 1986. The TRACE model of speech perception. *Cognitive Psychology* 18:1–86.

Marslen-Wislon, W. D. 1984. Function and process in spoken word recognition. In H. Bouma and D. G. Bouwhuis (eds.), *Attention and Performance*, vol. 10, *Control of Language Processes*. Hillsdale, N.J.: Erlbaum.

Marslen-Wilson, W. D., Brown, C. M. B., and Zwitserlood, P. In preparation. Spoken word-recognition: Early activation of multiple semantic codes. Max Plank Institute, Neijmegen.

Marlsen-Wilson, W. D., and Tyler, L. K. 1980. The temporal structure of spoken language understanding. *Cognition* 8:1–71.

Marslen-Wilson, W. D., and Welsh, A. 1978. Processing interactions and lexical access during word-recognition in continuous speech. *Cognitive Psychology* 10:29–63.

Marslen-Wilson, W. D., and Zwitserlood, P. 1987. Accessing spoken words: The importance of word onsets. Unpublished manuscript, Max-Planck Institute for Psycholinguistics, Nijmegen.

Mozer, M. C. 1987. Early parallel processing in reading: A connectionist approach. In M. Coltheart (eds.), *Attention and Performance*, vol. 12. Hove, England: Erlbaum.

Robinson, A. J., and Fallside, F. 1987. The utility driven dynamic error propagation network. Unpulished manuscript CUED/F-INFENG/Tr. 1. Cambridge University Engineering Department.

Rumelhart, D. E., Hinton, G. E., and Williams, R. J. 1986. Learning internal representations by error propagation. In D. Rumelhart, J. McClelland, and the PDP Research Group, *Parallel Distributed Processing: Explorations in the Microstructure of Cognition*, vol. 1. Cambridge: MIT Press.

Waibel, A., Hanazawa, T., Hinton, G., Shikano, K., and Lang, K. 1988. Phoneme recognition using time-delay neural networks. *IEEE Transactions on Acoustics, Speech, and Signal Processing*.

Watrous, R. L., Shastri, L., and Waibel, A. H. 1987. Learned phonetic discrimination using connectionist networks. In J. Laver and M. A. Jack (eds.), *Proceedings of the European Conference on Speech Technology*, Edinburgh: CEP Consultants.

Chapter 5

Exploiting Prosodic Probabilities in Speech Segmentation

Anne Cutler

Recognizing Continuous Speech

Shillcock (this volume) has shown that listeners hearing the word *trombone* in a sentence momentarily entertain the hypothesis that they might be hearing the word *bone*. Why does this happen? Surely speech recognition would be more efficient if listeners accessed only the lexical representations of words that really occurred and not also words that might be embedded within occurring words?

It is the argument of this chapter that Shillcock's finding arises naturally from a strategy used by listeners to deal with the problems of speech segmentation. The essence of the segmentation problem is that word boundaries in continuous speech are not reliably marked. Recent studies of human speech processing have suggested that listeners may use heuristic strategies for overcoming the absence of word-boundary information. Such strategies may allow listeners to guide their attempts at lexical access by postulating word onsets at what linguistic experience suggests are the most likely locations for word onsets to occur.

Cutler and Norris (1988) have proposed such a strategy based on metrical structure. In a stress language like English, syllables can be either strong or weak. Strong syllables contain full vowels, while weak syllables contain reduced vowels (usually a schwa). Cutler and Norris found that listeners were slower to detect the embedded real word in *mintayf* (in which the second vowel is strong) than in *mintef* (in which the second vowel is schwa). They suggested that listeners were segmenting *mintayf* prior to the second syllable, so that detection of *mint* therefore required combining speech material from parts of the signal that had been segmented from one another. No such difficulty arose for the detection of *mint* in *mintef*, since the weak second syllable was not segmented from the preceding material.

Cutler and Norris proposed that in continuous speech recognition in English, listeners generally approach the problem of segmentation for lexical access by applying a metrical segmentation strategy (MSS): strong syllables are taken as likely lexical (or content) word onsets, and the continuous speech stream is segmented at strong syllables so that lexical-access attempts can be initiated. This explains why *bone*, even when it is embedded in *trombone*, should be momentarily considered to be a possible new word: *bone* is a strong syllable.

The success rate of such a strategy depends, of course, on how realistically it reflects the structure of the language. Hypothesizing that strong syllables are likely to be lexical word onsets and that weak syllables are not will only prove to be an efficient strategy for detecting actual word onsets if most lexical words actually begin with strong syllables and not with weak syllables. As the next section shows, the MSS is indeed well adapted to the characteristics of the English vocabulary.

Assessing Prosodic Probabilities for English

To estimate the success rate of the MSS, Cutler and Carter (1987) examined the metrical structure of word-initial syllables in English. First they looked at the metrical structure of words in the English vocabulary. The MRC Psycholinguistic Database (Coltheart 1981, Wilson 1988) is a lexicon of over 98,000 words and is based on the *Shorter Oxford English Dictionary*. Over 33,000 entries have phonetic transcriptions. Figure 1 shows the metrical characteristics of the initial syllables of the transcribed words in this lexicon divided into four categories: monosyllables (such as *bone* and *splint*), polysyllables with primary stress on the first syllable (such as *lettuce* and *splendour*), polysyllables with secondary stress on the first syllable (such as *trombone* and *psychological*), and polysyllables with weak initial syllables (in which the vowel in the first syllable is usually schwa, as in *averse* and *trapeze*, but may also be a reduced form of another vowel, as in *invest* and *external*). Words in any of the first three categories satisfy the MSS. It can be seen that these categories together account for 73 percent of the words analyzed.

In English the most common word *type* (as opposed to token) is clearly a polysyllable with initial stress. However, individual word types differ in the frequency with which they occur. Frequency-of-occurrence statistics (Kučera and Francis 1967) are listed in the MRC Database, and Cutler and Carter found that the mean frequency for the four metrical word categories did indeed differ. First, monosyllables occur on average far more

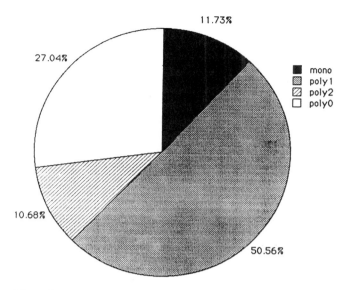

Figure 1
Metrical structure of the initial syllable of words in the MRC Psycholinguistic
Database (mono = monosyllabic words; poly 1 = polysyllabic words with initial
primary stress; poly 2 = polysyllabic words with initial secondary stress; poly
0 = polysyllabic words with weak initial syllable).

frequently than any type of polysyllable. (Note that to analyze frequency
of occurrence, Cutler and Carter considered only the lexical, or content,
words in the database and excluded the grammatical, or function, words
which accounted for less than 1 percent of the phonetically transcribed
words. These were overwhelmingly monosyllabic and of high frequency;
their inclusion would have inflated the mean frequency of monosyllables
still further.) Second, within the set of polysyllables, words with strong
initial syllables occur somewhat more frequently than words with weak
initial syllables. If the type counts in figure 1 are multiplied by their mean
frequencies, one can estimate that although there are more than seven times
as many polysyllables in the language as there are monosyllables, average
speech contexts are likely to contain almost as many monosyllables as
polysyllables. Moreover, only about 17 percent of lexical tokens in most
speech contexts will begin with weak syllables.

Cutler and Carter tested this estimate against a natural speech sample,
the *Corpus of English Conversation* (Svartvik and Quirk 1980), using the
frequency count of this corpus prepared by Brown (1984). The London-
Lund corpus consists of approximately 190,000 words of spontaneous

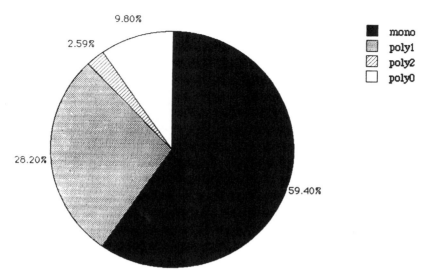

Figure 2
Metrical structure of the initial syllable of lexical words in the *Corpus of English Conversation* (mono = monosyllabic words; poly 1 = polysyllabic words with initial primary stress; poly 2 = polysyllabic words with initial secondary stress; poly 0 = polysyllabic words with weak initial syllable).

British English conversation. Figure 2 shows the distribution of metrical categories for lexical words in this corpus. The three categories with strong initial syllables account for 90 percent of the tokens; only 10 percent of the lexical words have weak initial syllables.

Although figure 2 covers all the lexical words in the London-Lund corpus, it actually accounts for only 41 percent of all words in the sample; the majority of words in the corpus are grammatical words. But because hardly any grammatical words have more than one syllable, figure 2 nevertheless accounts for 51 percent of all *syllables*. In fact, with some reasonable assumptions it was possible to compute the probable distribution of syllables in this speech sample. Cutler and Carter assumed that grammatical words such as *the* and *of* were in general realized as weak syllables. If so, the most likely distribution of syllables is that given in table 1. It can be seen that about three-quarters of all strong syllables in the sample were the sole or initial syllables of lexical words. Of weak syllables, however, more than two-thirds were the sole or initial syllables of grammatical words.

Thus a listener encountering a strong syllable in spontaneous English conversation seems to have about a three to one chance of finding that

Table 1
Strong (full) syllables versus weak (reduced) syllables in the *Corpus of English Conversation*

	Strong	Weak
Sole or initial syllable of lexical word	74%	5%
Noninitial syllable of lexical word	12%	23%
Sole or initial syllable of grammatical word	11%	69%
Noninitial syllable of grammatical word	3%	3%
Total number of syllables	93,989	145,888
Percentage of syllables in corpus	39%	61%

strong syllable to be the onset of a new lexical word. A weak syllable, on the other hand, is most likely to be a grammatical word. It seems, therefore, that English speech indeed provides an adequate basis for the implementation of a segmentation strategy such as Cutler and Norris's MSS, whereby strong syllables are assumed to be the onsets of lexical words.

Testing the Performance of the Metrical Segmentation Strategy

Cutler and Carter tentatively proposed some characteristics of an algorithm for implementing the MSS. In their proposal they suggested that listeners might not only assume strong syllables to be the onsets of lexical words but also take into account the likely distribution of weak syllables. The algorithm in outline has six steps:

1. Assume separate lexical (L) and grammatical (G) lists.
2. If the initial syllable of the input is weak, go to the G list. If it is strong, go to the L list.
3. The lookup process in each list returns the longest candidate consistent with the input up to a strong syllable.
4. Occurrence of a strong syllable terminates the current lookup process and initiates a new L lookup.
5. If either lookup fails, the input is submitted to the other list.
6. If both lookups fail, backtracking is necessary; that is, a previous decision must be canceled (e.g., by accepting a shorter candidate word, by undoing the word assignment of the previous syllable and attaching it to the current input, by continuing the current lookup process into a following strong syllable, etc.).

The performance of this algorithm on the London-Lund corpus can only be assessed by considering all words in context, which, in view of the size of the corpus, was impracticable. Cutler and Carter therefore created a minicorpus specifically to test the algorithm. A native speaker read onto tape a 97-word passage, and phonetically trained listeners noted which syllables were strong and which were weak. The algorithm given above performed extremely well, assigning 82 percent of all words (including 92 percent of lexical words) to the correct list on the first pass.

Cutler and Carter did not compare the performance of the MSS with that of other strategies. However, a 1989 study by Briscoe did undertake such a comparison. In this study the performance of three other routines for generating lexical hypotheses in continuous-speech recognition was compared with the performance of the MSS. The basis of Briscoe's comparison was the number of partial lexical hypotheses that the four strategies generated.

The three comparison strategies were loosely based on other existing proposals in the psycholinguistic literature.

1. Lexical-access attempts were initiated at each new phoneme.
2. Lexical access was tried at each syllable boundary.
3. Lexical access was initiated at sentence onset and subsequently at the conclusion of each successful lexical access. This amounts to a word-by-word segmentation, which is assumed in many automatic systems for continuous-speech recognition.
4. Lexical-access attempts were initiated at the onset of each strong syllable. This strategy was based on the specific proposals for the implementation of the MSS in Cutler and Carter 1987 and listed above.

Each strategy was implemented, and their respective performances were compared on a string of phonetic segments transcribing one sentence from the 97-word passage produced for Cutler and Carter's test of the MSS. Three transcription levels were used:

a. A fine-class transcription, in which each phoneme was explicity identified
b. A fine-class transcription of strong syllables with a broad-class transcription of weak syllables into such broad categories as vowel, stop consonant, nasal, etc.
c. A midclass transcription of strong syllables into more constrained categories such as voiced stop, back vowel, etc., again with a broad-class transcription of weak syllables

At transcription level (a), strategies 3 and 4 produced noticeably fewer lexical hypotheses than strategies 1 and 2, but this is only to be expected, since if all segmental information is available, the number of lexical hypotheses is simply a function of the number of segmentation points. The more frequent the segmentation points (phonemes or syllables versus strong syllables or words), the more hypotheses will be generated. In particular, the performance of strategies 3 and 4 at level (a) was very similar, even in their errors (both, for instance, treated *rainbow* initially as two words). Performance of the four strategies at transcription levels (b) and (c), however, is a more interesting comparison, since these levels of accuracy arguably offer a more realistic approximation of the likely information available to any recognizer. And it is at these levels that the greatest difference between the strategies appeared: at levels (b) and (c), strategy 4 performed much better than all three of the other strategies, producing significantly fewer partial lexical hypotheses. Interestingly, strategy 3, the word-by-word segmentation routine, which seems superficially to be the most common sense approach, produced an enormously increased number of hypotheses at level (c). Note that Harrington and Johnstone (1987) have computed that most English sentences of reasonable length allow millions of possible parses with broad- or middle-class phonetic transcription. At level (c) strategy 3 in fact produced very many more potential parses than did strategy 2, which includes the constraint that new words can only begin at syllable boundaries. This suggests that some constraint on which segment boundaries potentially begin words is virtually indispensible. A further aspect of Briscoe's study is that at level (c) the MSS-based strategy 4 was tested in two versions: one in which there was a single lexicon and segmentation was attempted only at the onsets of strong syllables, and one in which the lexicon was split into separate lexical and grammatical word lists and a weak syllable was initially looked up in the latter list. This second version performed best of all.

Thus on Briscoe's metric of counting lexical hypotheses (which amounts to an assessment of wasted effort in speech segmentation), the MSS is particularly well adapted to dealing with continuous spoken English and is more robust than alternative strategies in coping with the effects of reduction of fine-grain information. Since such reduced information might be argued to be all that the recognizer has to work with in many speech situations, it appears, at least from this limited study, that the MSS is the most realistic of the strategies Briscoe contrasted.

These tests strongly indicate that the MSS is a realistic strategy and should perform well on continuous spoken English. Some relevant evidence from human speech recognition is described in the next section.

Predicting Listeners' Segmentation Performances

Cutler and Norris's 1988 experiment, which motivated their proposal of the strategy, presented listeners only with nonsense bisyllables. Some evidence that listeners may indeed use the strategy in the segmentation of continuous speech was subsequently produced. This evidence comes from segmentation errors, the way in which word boundaries tend to be misperceived.

The absence of reliable correlates of a word boundary makes misperception of the location of a word boundary in speech easy in principle. Butterfield and Cutler (1988) examined listeners' misperceptions of continuous speech in the light of Cutler and Norris's proposed MSS. If listeners are indeed assuming strong syllables to be word-initial and weak syllables to be non-word-initial, word boundary misperceptions should be very unequally distributed across the four possible types of errors. Specifically, erroneous insertion of a boundary before a strong syllable and erroneous deletion of a boundary before a weak syllable should prove to be relatively common, whereas erroneous insertion of a boundary before a weak syllable and erroneous deletion of a boundary before a strong syllable should be relatively rare. Butterfield and Cutler examined both spontaneous and experimentally elicited misperceptions.

Psycholinguists have for many years collected and analysed the slips of the ear that occur in conversation, and in fact, many of these contain word-boundary misplacements. Butterfield and Cutler examined all the errors listed in published studies of slips of the ear (Bond and Garnes 1980; Browman 1978, 1980; Celce-Murcia, 1980; Garnes and Bond 1975, 1980) plus all the slips of the ear included in a speech error collection that I had assembled over several years. Among these slips, over one hundred involved misplacement of a word boundary across at least one syllabic nucleus. (We excluded errors in which a boundary was misplaced across only one or two consonants such as *up with Anne → up a fan* because they are irrelevant to the hypothesis about metrical syllable structure.) Some slips in fact involved more than one misplaced boundary (such as *for an occasion → fornication*).

Some examples of errors are shown in table 2. Butterfield and Cutler found in this set of naturally occurring errors precisely the pattern predicted by the MSS: insertions of a word boundary before a strong syllable (*disguise → the skies*) and deletions of a word boundary before a weak syllable (*ten to two → twenty to*) outnumbered by more than two to one

Table 2
Slips of the ear

Coke and a Danish	→	Coconut Danish
it was illegal	→	it was an eagle
ten to two	→	twenty to
disguise	→	the skies
reverse	→	your purse
my gorge is rising	→	my gorgeous ...
by tonight	→	butter knife
she'll officially	→	Sheila Fishley
she's a must to avoid	→	she's a muscular boy
variability	→	very ability
in closing	→	enclosing
effective	→	effect of
paint your ruler	→	paint remover

insertions of a boundary before a weak syllable (*variability* → *very ability*) or deletions of a boundary before a strong syllable (*in closing* → *enclosing*).

However, Butterfield and Cutler found that the contextual information available for these errors was insufficient to determine what opportunities the listeners had had for word-boundary misplacement. Thus the statistical significance of the asymmetric distribution of the natural slips was impossible to ascertain. It was possible, though, to carry out a statistical comparison of the relative frequency of the words that were actually spoken versus the words that were erroneously perceived. After all, it may simply be the case that when listeners are presented with an utterance that for some reason is difficult to perceive, they reconstruct a plausible version. In this case the distribution of word-boundary misperceptions across strong and weak syllables may simply fall out of the fact that, as Cutler and Carter (1987) showed, words with strong initial syllables tend to have a higher frequency of occurrence than words with weak initial syllables. Of course, this frequency analysis was not simple to perform. First, many of the slips of the ear involved proper names, the frequency of which is impossible to assess. Second, grammatical words such as *the* and *of* have such a high frequency of occurrence that any error that includes a grammatical word not in the target utterance will necessarily have a higher mean frequency of occurrence than the target, whereas any error omitting a grammatical word present in the target will necessarily have a lower mean frequency of occurrence than the target. However, it seems reasonable to suppose that if frequency effects are operative, they should show up in the lexical words analyzed separately from the grammatical words. For instance, it would not seem particularly surprising were *She wants a cot and blanket* to be heard as *She wants a cotton blanket*, and although the mean frequency of *cot* and *and* is higher than the frequency of *cotton*, it is surely more relevant that the frequency of *cot* alone is lower than the frequency of *cotton*. Thus Butterfield and Cutler simply compared the frequency of lexical words in targets and errors.

The results of the frequency analysis showed, unsurprisingly, that there was a general tendency for word-boundary insertions to result in errors containing higher-frequency words than the target and for word-boundary deletions to result in errors containing lower-frequency words than the target. This is unsurprising because boundary insertions are likely to produce a percept containing shorter words, while boundary deletions are likely to produce a percept containing longer words, and as is well known, shorter words tend to be more frequent than longer words. This predictable effect is less important than the fact that less than half of the errors overall contained higher-frequency words than their targets. Overall there was *no* significant tendency for errors to contain higher-frequency words than targets. Moreover, there was no significant difference in the nature of the frequency effect between the two types of errors predicted by the MSS and the two types of errors not predicted.

Thus the evidence from spontaneous slips of the ear suggests that listeners do indeed rely on a strategy of assuming that strong syllables begin words. However, slips of the ear occur infrequently and are difficult to collect. As noted above, they are also difficult to analyze in many ways. Therefore, Butterfield and Cutler followed up their analysis of spontaneous misperceptions with an experiment involving deliberately induced misperceptions. In this study, unpredictable utterances (e.g., "achieve her ways instead") were presented to listeners at a level minimally above their threshold for speech reception (which was determined separately for each listener in an extensive pretest). The subjects' task was to write down what they thought was said.

Some sample responses are listed in table 3. Excluding responses that were entirely correct, consisted of no responses, or consisted of only a few syllables, those responses that preserved the number of syllables (six) in the target utterance comprised nearly half of the responses. Of these 40 percent contained word-boundary misplacements. Some responses contained more than one boundary misplacement, so the total number of errors

Table 3
Example responses to faint speech

Stimulus	Responses
achieve her ways instead	a cheaper way to stay
	the chief awaits his men
soon police were waiting	soon the beast will waken
	soon to be awakened
conduct ascents uphill	the doctor sends her bill
	conduct a sense of ill
sons expect enlistment	some expect a blizzard
	sons expected missing
dusty senseless drilling	dust is senseless ruin
	thus he sent his drill in

available for analysis was 257. The distribution of these errors across the four possible error classes is shown in table 4. It can be seen that exactly the pattern predicted by the proposed strategy emerges: erroneous insertions of word boundaries before strong syllables and deletions of word boundaries before weak syllables greatly outnumber insertions of boundaries before weak syllables or deletions of boundaries before strong syllables.

Because the opportunities for each type of error could be determined exactly in this case, the difference could be evaluated statistically. Butterfield and Cutler found that it was indeed significant. Moreover, analysis of only the first missegmentation in each response (on the grounds that later word choices to a certain extent follow from earlier choices) revealed the same pattern—far more insertions before strong syllables than before weak and far more deletions before weak syllables than before strong—with the same level of statististical significance. And once again a comparison of the frequency of lexical words in the targets and in the errors showed no overall preference for higher-frequency responses and no significant difference in frequency effects across the responses that were predicted by the strategy and those that were not.

Note that this lack of a frequency effect is here, as with the spontaneous slips of the ear, strong evidence against any interpretation of the pattern of results in terms of simple plausibility of responses. If subjects had simply been choosing likely responses, their responses would have tended to be of higher frequency than the (improbable) stimuli; they were not. Moreover, it is also evidence against simple random choices of words as responses, since the skew in the frequency distribution of the English vocabulary is

Table 4
Frequencies of boundary misplacements in response to faint speech

Boundary misplacement	No. of occurrences
Insertion before a strong syllable (*sons expect enlistment → some expect a blizzard*)	144
Deletion before a weak syllable (*achieve her ways instead → a cheaper way to stay*)	52
Total no. of misplacements predicted by the MSS	196
Deletion before a strong syllable (*soon police were waiting → soon to be awakened*)	13
Insertion before a weak syllable (*dusty senseless drilling → thus he sent his drill in*)	48
Total no. of misplacements not predicted by the MSS	61
Total no. of misplacements	257

such that random choices predict that responses should have tended to be of *lower* frequency than the stimuli; again, they were not.

One further characteristic of the error pattern in this experiment is worthy of note. Although word-boundary insertions before weak syllables, which are predicted to be relatively uncommon, are indeed the second rarest type of error, they nevertheless occur four times as often as the rarest type of error, boundary deletions before strong syllables. From Cutler and Carter's examination of natural speech, one can predict the prosodic probabilities of weak syllables and hence the way they are most likely to be misperceived. In the spontaneous speech corpus that Cutler and Carter examined, more than two-thirds of all weak syllables were monosyllabic grammatical words. Thus one might predict that a weak syllable in faintly perceived speech is most likely to be perceived as a monosyllabic function word. A subsidiary prediction about the misperception data might then be that erroneous insertions of word boundaries before weak syllables should tend to involve erroneous reports of monosyllabic function words.

This is indeed the case. Exactly two-thirds of the boundary insertions before weak syllables (32 out of 48 cases) involved monosyllabic function words (such as *dusty senseless drilling → thus he sent his drill in*). Examination of the natural slips of the ear showed that a large number of the erroneous insertions of word boundaries before weak syllables in that corpus also involved monosyllabic function words (e.g., *descriptive → the script of*). Word-boundary misplacements by human listeners therefore seem to reflect the prosodic probabilities of English remarkably accurately. The initial statement of the MSS, which referred only to lexical word boundaries, may underestimate the degree to which the segmentation of continuous speech is driven by prosodic probability.

A complete implementation of the MSS would certainly have to take into account the distribution of strong and weak syllables with respect to different types of word boundaries. Cutler and Carter's tentative algorithm was deliberately oversimplified in an attempt to see how well the crudest implementation would perform. In that their algorithm distinguishes lexical from grammatical word hypotheses, it does in fact predict the predominance of grammatical words among weak-initial-syllable responses. However, its assumption that the longest word consistent with the input is accepted obviously has to be modified to take into account contextual acceptability. Cutler and Carter suggest several other ways in which their outline proposal can be substantially refined. Some further considerations involved in applying the MSS are discussed in the next and final section.

Conclusion: Applying a Metrical Segmentation Strategy

This chapter has argued that the absence of reliable word-boundary information in continuous speech can in part be overcome by exploiting the prosodic probabilities of the language. In English, where there is a strong likelihood that lexical words will begin with strong syllables, a strategy of assuming that a strong syllable is likely to be the onset of a new lexical word and that a weak syllable is not will successfully locate most lexical word boundaries. Evidence from human perceptual performance suggests that listeners do make use of such a segmentation strategy.

What exactly is a segmentation strategy? Let us first consider the term *segmentation*. It is important to be clear that this notion is logically distinct from a process of *classifying* the speech signal. A traditional preoccupation of psycholinguistics has been the search for units of perception, that is, the postulated prelexical units of representation into which incoming speech signals are translated in order that lexical entries (presumably coded in terms of the same units) may be accessed. Among such postulated units are phonemes (Foss and Gernsbacher 1983) and syllables (Mehler 1981, Segui 1984). Clearly, the process of turning a continuous speech signal into a sequence of labeled discrete units involves dividing up the signal or segmenting it; that is, classification logically entails segmentation. But, as Norris and Cutler (1985) have argued in more detail, the reverse is not true. Simply making a division at a particular point in the signal does not necessarily imply that what is on either side of the division point is assigned a label, that is, classified.

Thus Cutler and Norris (1988) were able to point out that the MSS is compatible with a model of speech perception involving classification and also with a model involving no classification. They suggested, for instance, that in a model involving a phonemic level of representation, the occurrence in the input of one of a specified set of phonemes (the set of full vowels) could instigate a lexical-access attempt that starts either from that vowel or from its preceding syllabic onset. On the other hand, in a model involving no prelexical classification, a segmentation device could monitor the incoming signal for a high-energy quasi-steady-state portion of a specified minimum relative duration (full vowels are, after all, among the most readily identifiable portions of speech signals). Whenever this specification was met, the segmentation device could divide the speech at a point suitably prior to the onset of the steady state and again instigate a lexical-access attempt from that point, with the input to the lexicon being a relatively untransformed portion of the speech signal, of which only the onset need be defined.

Thus, although the metrical segmentation strategy is based on the distinction between strong and weak syllables, syllables per se are not part of its operation. It is really the strong and weak *vowels* that matter. On any implementation of the strategy, the occurrence of a full vowel must trigger segmentation. But segmentation probably does not then occur precisely at the vowel itself, if only because it is more efficient to locate the actual onset of the word. In principle, lexical access *can* be based on strong vowels; one could, for instance, imagine a lexicon in which *hat*, *bedazzle*, *straggler*, etc., were all in some sense stored together. But there is no doubt that accurate location of the word onset is more useful, and for the MSS this means locating the left boundary of the syllable in which the detected vowel occurs. The right boundary is quite unimportant, especially in an implementation of the MSS such as that proposed by Cutler and Carter (1987), in which the lookup process starts at each strong syllable and *continues*, if necessary, over subsequent weak syllables, returning in each case the longest candidate consistent with the input.

Location of a syllable's left boundary means correctly attaching the syllabic onset to the vowel. In English, onsets can be null, or they can contain up to three phonemes (e.g., *oak*, *soak*, *stoke*, and *stroke* are all English words). There is evidence that consonant cluster onsets in English are perceived as integral units (Cutler, Butterfield, and Williams 1987); this could facilitate the process of locating the left boundary of a syllable if a strong vowel is detected.

The importance in the MSS proposal of the vowel plus its preceding onset means that the proposal resembles other models in the literature that share this feature, for example, the notion of demisyllables as representational units (Fujimura and Lovins 1978) and the consonant-vowel units that figure in Dogil's (1986) "pivot parser." But it is nevertheless not a proposal about representational units, i.e., about classification. It is only a proposal about segmentation for lexical access, about locating those points in a continuous speech signal that are the most efficient points from which to initiate attempts at lexical access.

The second component in the proposal for a segmentation strategy is the notion of *strategy*. It is not intended that this should be considered as a conscious operation on the listener's part. The prelexical level is presumably not a processing level open to conscious inspection and control. Metrical segmentation is best thought of as the operation of an autonomous and automatic device, the purpose of which is to initiate lexical-access attempts with maximum efficiency, i.e., with as little waste as possible. Its operation should be guided by experience, probably by very early experience with one's native language.

Thus native speakers of different languages might use a number of different variants of the same basic type of segmenting device. The MSS is a specific proposal about how such a device operates for a free-stress language like English. But even in languages with other prosodic structures there might still be quite similar possibilities for segmentation routines. In a fixed-stress language like Polish, for instance, the relationship between stress placement and lexical-word boundaries might well be exploited by a segmentation device. Segmentation of nonstress languages like French does not have such an obvious prosodic basis, since in such languages there is no opposition between strong and weak syllables; all syllables are effectively equal in their contribution to linguistic rhythm. But much the same sort of device may still operate. For instance, with no prosodic basis for distinguishing likely word-initial syllables from likely noninitial syllables, a segmentation device of the general type embodied by the MSS might treat all syllables as equally likely to begin a word and simply segment speech signals at the onset of every syllable. There is evidence that simple syllable-based segmentation does indeed occur in the perception of French (Cutler, Mehler, Norris, and Segui 1986).

The metrical segmentation strategy may be only one of a number of operations that participate in the recognition of continuous speech. Its particular contribution is to increase the efficiency of the initial process of lexical access. Evidence from comparative implementations suggests that its contribution to efficiency is high, even though the exigencies of experimental design mean that its operation in human recognition can best be appreciated from its occasional failures, such as finding *bone* in *trombone*.

References

Bond, Z. S., and Garnes, S. 1980. Misperception of fluent speech. In R. Cole (ed.), *Perception and Production of Fluent Speech*. Hillsdale, N.J.: Erlbaum.

Briscoe, E. J. 1989. Lexical access in connected speech recognition. *Proceedings of the Twenty-Seventh Congress, Association for Computational Linguistics*, Vancouver.

Browman, C. P. 1978. Tip of the tongue and slip of the ear: Implications for language processing. *UCLA Working Papers in Phonetics* 42.

Browman, C. P. 1980. Perceptual processing: Evidence from slips of the ear. In V. A. Fromkin (ed.), *Errors in Linguistic Performance: Slips of the Tongue, Ear, Pen, and Hand*. New York: Academic Press.

Brown, G. D. A. 1984. A frequency count of 190,000 words in the London-Lund Corpus of English Conversation. *Behavior Research Methods, Instrumentation, and Computers* 16:502–532.

Butterfield, S., and Cutler, A. 1988. Segmentation errors by human listeners: Evidence for a prosodic segmentation strategy. *Proceedings of SPEECH 88* (Seventh symposium of the Federation of Acoustic Societies of Europe), pp. 827–833. Edinburgh.

Celce-Murcia, M. 1980. On Meringer's corpus of "slips of the ear." In V. A. Fromkin (ed.), *Errors in Linguistic Performance: Slips of the Tongue, Ear, Pen, and Hand*. New York: Academic Press.

Coltheart, M. 1981. The MRC Psycholinguistic Database. *Quarterly Journal of Experimental Psychology* 33A:497–505.

Cutler, A., Butterfield, S., and Williams, J. N. 1987. The perceptual integrity of syllabic onsets. *Journal of Memory and Language* 26:406–418.

Cutler, A., and Carter, D. M. 1987. The predominance of strong initial syllables in the English vocabulary. *Computer Speech and Language* 2:133–142.

Cutler, A., Mehler, J., Norris, D., and Segui, J. 1986. The syllable's differing role in the segmentation of French and English. *Journal of Memory and Language* 25:385–400.

Cutler, A., and Norris, D. 1988. The role of strong syllables in segmentation for lexical access. *Journal of Experimental Psychology: Human Perception and Performance* 14:113–121.

Dogil, G. 1986. Phonological pivot parsing. *Proceedings of COLING 86—Twelfth International Conference on Computational Linguistics*, Bonn.

Foss, D. J., and Gernsbacher, M. A. 1983. Cracking the dual code: Toward a unitary model of phoneme identification. *Journal of Verbal Learning and Verbal Behavior* 22:609–632.

Fujimura, O., and Lovins, J. B. 1978. Syllables as concatenative phonetic units. In A. Bell and J. B. Hooper (eds.), *Syllables and Segments*. Amsterdam: North-Holland.

Garnes, S., and Bond, Z. S. 1975. Slips of the ear: Errors in perception of casual speech. *Proceedings of the Eleventh Regional Meeting, Chicago Linguistic Society*, pp. 214–225.

Garnes, S., and Bond, Z. S. 1980. A slip of the ear? A snip of the ear? A slip of the year? In V. A. Fromkin (ed.), *Errors in Linguistic Performance: Slips of the Tongue, Ear, Pen, and Hand*. New York: Academic Press.

Harrington, J., and Johnstone, A. 1987. The effects of word boundary ambiguity in continuous speech recognition. *Proceedings of the Eleventh International Congress of Phonetic Sciences*, vol. 3, pp. 89–92. Tallinn, Estonia.

Kučera, H., and Francis, W. N. 1967. *Computational Analysis of Present-Day American English*. Providence: Brown University Press.

Mehler, J. 1981. The role of syllables in speech processing. *Philosophical Transactions of the Royal Society* B295:333–352.

Norris, D., and Cutler, A. 1985. Juncture detection. *Linguistics* 23:689–705.

Segui, J. 1984. The syllable: A basic perceptual unit in speech processing. In H. Bouma and D. G. Bouwhuis (eds.), *Attention and Performance*, vol. 10. Hillsdale, N.J.: Erlbaum.

Svartvik, J., and Quirk, R. 1980. *A Corpus of English Conversation*. Lund: Gleerup.

Wilson, M. D. 1988. MRC Psycholinguistic Database: Machine-usable dictionary, version 2.0. *Behavior Research Methods, Instrumentation, and Computers*, 20:6–10.

Chapter 6

Similarity Neighborhoods of Spoken Words	Paul A. Luce, David B. Pisoni, and Steven D. Goldinger

A fundamental problem in research on spoken-word recognition concerns the processes by which stimulus information in the acoustic-phonetic waveform is mapped onto lexical items in memory. Clearly, in view of the enormous size of the adult mental lexicon, isolating the sound pattern of one word from tens of thousands of others in memory is no trivial problem for the listener, and yet this process of discrimination normally appears to proceed effortlessly and with little error. How can we characterize the human's amazing ability to efficiently isolate the sound pattern of a given word from among the myriad possible alternatives?

The set of studies reviewed below was aimed at addressing this important question. In particular, these studies investigated the organization of the sound patterns of words in memory and the implications of this organization for spoken-word recognition. Since one of the primary tasks of the word-recognition system involves discriminating among lexical items, the study of the organization of words in memory takes on considerable importance, especially if it can be demonstrated that these relations influence the ease or difficulty of lexical discrimination and subsequently word recognition and lexical access. Landauer and Streeter (1973) and Luce (1989a) have demonstrated that words vary substantially not only in the number of words to which they are similar but also in the frequencies of these similar words. These findings suggest that both similarity and frequency relations among words may mediate lexical discrimination.

The classic issue of word frequency takes on an important role in the investigation of the organization of the sound patterns of words. Numerous previous studies have demonstrated that the ease with which spoken words are recognized is monotonically related to experienced frequency as measured by some objective count of words in the language (Howes 1957, Newbigging 1961, Savin 1963, Soloman and Postman 1952). However, little work has been devoted to detailing the interaction of word frequency and similarity relations among words (see, however, Triesman 1978a, 1978b). If word frequency influences the perceptibility of the stimulus word, it may likewise affect the degree to which similar words are treated as likely candidates for recognition. Frequency is important, then, in further specifying the relative competition among items that are to be discriminated among.

The particular mechanisms by which frequency affects word perception are at present controversial. In particular, it is unclear whether frequency affects activation levels, the rates of activation, thresholds, or perceptual-decision mechanisms. The goal of the present research is aimed in part at demonstrating that at least some portion of the word-frequency effect is due to perceptual biases that affect selection of one word from a set of similar words.

The experiments summarized below were aimed specifically at examining the effects of similarity neighborhoods on auditory word recognition. A *similarity neighborhood* is defined as collection of words that are phonetically similar to a given stimulus word. We computationally estimated similarity neighborhoods using a 20,000 word on-line lexicon based on *Webster's Pocket Dictionary* (which in turn is based on *Webster's Seventh Collegiate Dictionary*, 1967). Each entry in this lexicon contains an orthographic representation, a phonetic transcription, a frequency count based on the Kučera and Francis (1967) norms, and a subjective familiarity rating on a seven point scale ranging from "Don't know the word" (1) to "Know the word, and know its meaning" (7) (Nusbaum, Pisoni, and Davis 1984). Examples of entries in the lexicon are shown in table 1.

The general procedure for determining the composition of a similarity neighborhood for a particular stimulus word using the computerized

Table 1
Examples of entries in Webster's lexicon

Orthography	Transcription	Frequency	Rating
baby	b'e < bi	62	7.00000
bachelor	b'@C-1X	6	7.00000
bacillus	bx-s'I*lxs	2	3.08333
back	b'@k	967	7.00000
bacon	b'e < k|n	10	7.00000
bad	b'@d	142	7.00000
bade	b'@d	1	3.25000

lexicon was as follows: A given phonetic transcription (the stimulus word) was compared to all other transcriptions in the lexicon (the potential neighbors).[1] By comparing the phonetic transcription of the stimulus word with all other phonetic transcriptions in the lexicon, it was possible to determine the extent to which a given stimulus word was similar to other words (i.e., the neighborhood density or confusability). In addition, it was also possible to determine the frequency of the neighbors (i.e., the neighborhood frequency) as well as the frequency of the stimulus word itself. Thus, three variables relating to the similarity neighborhood were of interest: stimulus word frequency, neighborhood density of confusability, and neighborhood frequency.

The precise hypotheses concerning the effects of similarity-neighborhood structure that were tested were as follows: First, it was proposed that stimulus words occurring in highly dense or confusable neighborhoods would be recognized less accurately and less quickly than words occurring in sparse or less confusable neighborhoods. This hypothesis was motivated by the assumption that high-density neighborhoods result in a high degree of competition among phonetically similar items activated in memory. Second, it was hypothesized that stimulus words having high-frequency neighbors would be identified less accurately and less quickly than those with low-frequency neighbors. The effects of neighborhood frequency were predicted under the assumption that frequency affects the degree of competition among items, high-frequency neighbors being stronger competitiors than low-frequency neighbors. Third, it was predicted that high-frequency words would in general be identified more easily than low-frequency words. It was further predicted, however, that effects of stimulus-word frequency would be mediated by the nature of the similarity neighborhoods in which the stimulus word resides in the mental lexicon.

Four experiments examining the effects of similarity neighborhoods on auditory word recognition are reviewed:

• Perceptual identification of words in noise
• Auditory lexical decision
• Auditory word naming
• Primed perceptual identification

Each of these experiments demonstrates that similarity-neighborhood structure has robust effects on the speed and accuracy of auditory word recognition. Furthermore, these experiments provide support for a model of spoken-word recognition, the neighborhood-activation model, that characterizes the processes of spoken-word recognition in terms of neighborhood activation and frequency-biased decision.

Evidence from Perceptual Identification

Luce (1986b) has developed a means of quantifying the effects of similarity-neighborhood structure on the perceptual identification of spoken words called the neighborhood-probability rule. This rule gives a single expression that simultaneously takes into account stimulus-word intelligibility, stimulus-word frequency, neighborhood confusability, and neighborhood frequency. Based on Luce's (1959) general biased choice rule, this rule has the form

$$p(\text{ID}) = \frac{p(\text{stimulus word}) \times \text{freq}_s}{p(\text{stimulus word}) \times \text{freq}_s + \sum_{j=1}^{n} \{p(\text{neighbor}_j) \times \text{freq}_j\}}.$$

The *neighborhood-probability rule* states that the probability of correct identification of the stimulus word is equal to the frequency-weighted probability of the stimulus word ($p(\text{stimulus word}) \times \text{freq}_s$) divided by the frequency-weighted probability of the stimulus word plus the sum of the frequency-weighted probabilities of the neighbors ($\sum_{j=1}^{n} \{p(\text{neighbor}_j) \times \text{freq}_j\}$). In general, this rule states the probability of choosing the stimulus word from among its neighbors. In additions, the probabilities of the stimulus word and its neighbors are weighted by their frequencies of occurrence as given in Kučera and Francis 1967. These frequency weights serve to increase, to greater or lesser degrees, the probabilities of the stimulus word and its neighbors according to their objective rates of occurrence.

To obtain independent estimates of the probabilities of the stimulus word and its neighbors, the probabilities were estimated from confusion matrices for all possible initial consonants, vowels, and final consonants (a complete description of the rule and how it was computed can be found in Luce 1986b). For example, to determine the probability of the stimulus word /kaet/, the separate probabilities for /k/ given /k/ (which we express as $p(\text{k}|\text{k})$), /ae/ given /ae/ ($p(\text{ae}|\text{ae})$), and /t/ given /t/ ($p(\text{t}|\text{t})$) were obtained from confusion matrices for initial consonants, vowels, and final consonants, respectively. These independent probabilities were than multiplied to give an estimate of the stimulus-word probability.

Computation of the probabilities of the neighbors was carried out in an analogous manner. For example, to determine the probability that /kɪd/ is a neighbor of the stimulus word /kaet/, the confusion matrices were once again consulted. In the case of computing neighbor probabilities, however, the conditional probability of /kɪd/ given /kaet/ was computed by finding the component probabilities /k/ given /k/ ($p(\text{k}|\text{k})$), /ɪ/ given /ae/ ($p(\text{ɪ}|\text{ae})$), and /d/ given /t/ (p(d|t)). These component probabilities were then multiplied to give an estimate of the neighbor probability.

By means of this method of computing stimulus word and neighbor probabilities, the neighborhood-probability rule can be computed with the computerized lexicon. Basically, this method involves comparing a given stimulus word to potential neighbors in the lexicon and computing the respective probabilities. These probabilities can then be weighted by the frequencies of occurrences of the words to which they correspond and entered into the rule to generate an estimate of the probability of identifying a stimulus word, given its frequency, the confusability of its neighborhood, and the frequencies of its neighbors.

A number of properties of the neighborhood probability rule are worthy of mention. First, the intelligibility of the phonemes of the stimulus word itself will in part determine the role of the neighbors in determining the predicted probability of identification. Stimulus words with high phoneme probabilites (i.e., words with highly intelligible phonemes) will tend to have neighbors with low phoneme probabilities because all probabilities in the confusion matrices are conditional. Likewise, stimulus words with low phoneme probabilities (i.e., those with less intelligible phonemes) will tend to have neighbors with relatively higher phoneme probabilities. However, the output of the neighborhood-probability rule is not a direct function of the stimulus-word probability. Instead, the output of the rule is dependent on the existence of lexical items with phonemes that are confusable with the phonemes of the stimulus word. For example, a stimulus word may contain highly confusable phonemes, but if there are few actual lexical items (neighbors) that contain phonemes confusable with those of the stimulus word, the sum of the neighbor-word probabilities will be low. The resulting output of the neighborhood-probability rule will therefore be relatively high. Likewise, if the phonemes of the stimulus word are highly intelligible, but there are a large number of neighbors with phonemes that are confusable with the stimulus word, the probability of identification will be reduced. In short, the output of the neighborhood-probability rule depends on both the intelligibility of the stimulus word and the number of neighbors with phonemes that are confusable with those contained in the stimulus word. Thus, intelligibility of the stimulus word, confusability of the neighbors, and the nature of lexical items all act in concert to determine the predicted probability of identification.

Note also that the frequencies of the stimulus word and the neighbors will serve to amplify to a greater or lesser degree the probabilities of the stimulus word and its neighbors. In the long run, high-frequency stimulus words are predicted to produce higher levels of performance. Likewise, high-frequency neighbors are predicted to reduce identification performance. However, because frequency in this rule is expressed in terms of the relation of the frequency of the stimulus word to the frequencies of its neighbors, the absolute frequency of the stimulus word determines predicted identification performance only in concert with the frequencies of the neighbors of the stimulus word. Thus, of two stimulus words of equal frequency, the stimulus word with neighbors of lower frequency will produce a higher predicted probability of identification than the stimulus word with neighbors of higher frequency. Simply put, this rule predicts that neighborhood composition will play a role in determining predicted identification prerformance in terms of the combined effects of the number and nature of the neighbors, the frequencies of the neighbors, the intelligibility of the stimulus word, and the frequency of the stimulus word.

Luce (1989b) tested the predictions of the neighborhood-probability rule by selecting four sets of high-frequency words and four sets of low-frequency words that varied in terms of stimulus-word probability and frequency-weighted neighborhood probability (see also Luce 1986b). Two levels of stimulus-word probability (high and low) were orthogonally combined with two levels of frequency-weighted neighborhood probability (high and low) for a total of 8 cells. Using the methods of determining stimulus-word probability neighborhood confusability described above, we assigned 50 consonant, vowel, consonant (CVC) words to each of the 8 cells (2 levels of stimulus word frequency $\times 2$ levels of stimulus word probability $\times 2$ levels of frequency-weighted neighborhood probability).[2] These 400 words were randomized, mixed with white noise at a signal-to-noise ratio of $+5$ dB, and presented to subjects for identification.

The results of this experiment are presented in figure 1. Results for the high-frequency words are shown in the top panel; results for the low-frequency words in the bottom panel. Solid lines indicate words with high stimulus-word probabilities; dotted lines indicate words with low stimulus-word probabilities. Frequency-weighted neighborhood probability is represented along the x axes; percent correct identification is represented along the y axes.

The result of this experiment clearly support the predictions of the neighborhood probability rule. First, words with high stimulus-word probabilities were consistently identified more accurately than words with low stimulus-word probabilities $(F(1, 37) = 111.60, p < 0.05)$. More interesting, however, was the finding that words with high frequency-weighted neighborhood probabilities were identified less accurately than words with

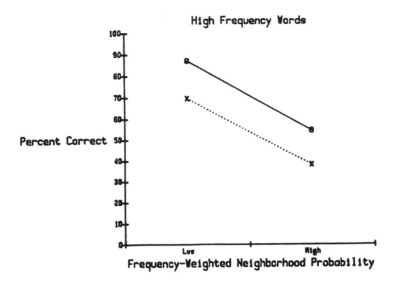

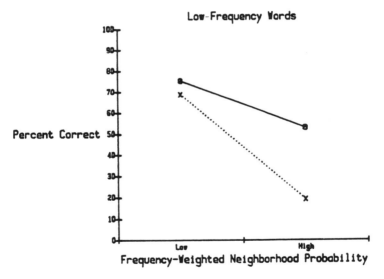

Figure 1
Percent correct identification of spoken words. The upper graph shows the
results for high-frequency words; the lower graph shows the results for
low-frequency words. Frequency-weighted neighborhood probability is shown
on the *x* axes. Low stimulus word probability is indicated by solid lines, and high
stimulus word probability is indicated by dotted lines.

low frequency-weighted neighborhood probabilities ($F(1, 37) = 353.60, p < 0.05$). That is, words occurring in neighborhoods densely populated by high-frequency words were identified less accurately than words occurring in neighborhoods sparsely populated by low-frequency words.

Not surprisingly, high-frequency words were on the average identified more accurately than low-frequency words ($F(1, 37) = 9.38, p < 0.05$). However, of interest is the finding that high-frequency words were not always identified at higher levels of accuracy. In particular, high-frequency words residing in dense, high-frequency neighborhoods were identified less accurately (46.33 percent overall) than low-frequency words residing in sparse, low-frequency neighborhoods (72.00 percent overall), as predicted by the neighborhood-probability rule.

These results support the hypothesis that accuracy in identifying spoken words in noise is dependent on characteristics of the similarity neighborhood. The results demonstrate that increased neighborhood competition reduces accuracy of identification and that this competition is influenced by both the number of possible neighbors and their frequencies of occurrence. Furthermore, these results demonstrate that effects of stimulus-word frequency are mediated by the composition of the similarity neighborhood.

Evidence from Auditory Lexical Decision: Nonwords

Although the previous results strongly implicate the role of similarity neighborhoods in spoken-word recognition, the findings are restricted to identification of words degraded by white noise. To test the generality of these effects to stimuli that are not degraded, Luce (1986b) tested subjects on an auditory lexical-decision task using specially constructed nonword stimuli varying neighborhood density and frequency. Examining decisions to nonwords was motivated by a 1987 study by Marslen-Wilson that failed to find effects of set-size (neighborhood density) on reaction times to nonwords in a lexical-decision task. Since we have obtained such effects for perceptual identification, it is of crucial importance to determine if such effects can also be obtained in a task in which the stimuli are not purposeful made difficult to perceive through stimulus degradation.

Luce (1986b) generated a set of consonant, vowel, consonant (CVC) nonwords modeled on the statistical properties of actual words occurring in *Webster's Pocket Dictionary*. Each of these nonwords had admissible initial consonant, vowel (CV) sequences; vowel, final consonant (VC) sequences; and initial consonant, final consonant (C__C) sequences. In addition, because of this manner of stimulus construction, each of the nonwords diverged from real words at the final phoneme. From this set of nonwords, 400 stimuli were selected that fell into one of four cells: high neighborhood density and high neighborhood frequency, high neighborhood density and low neighborhood frequency, low neighborhood density and high neighborhood frequency, and low neighborhood density and low neighborhood frequency.

Neighborhood density and neighborhood frequency were computed as follows: Each nonword was compared to each word in the Webster lexicon. A neighbor was defined as any word that could be converted to the nonword under analysis by the addition, substitution, or deletion of one phoneme in any position. For each nonword, the number of neighbors and the frequencies of these neighbors were tallied and used to assign the nonwords to one of the four cells in the design. These 400 nonwords are mixed with 400 words and presented for word/nonword decisions. Reaction times were measured from the onset of the nonword stimulus to the button-press response. Reaction times for correct nonword judgments are shown in figure 2.

Both neighborhood density and neighborhood frequency had demonstrable effects on nonword judgment times. Nonwords with many word

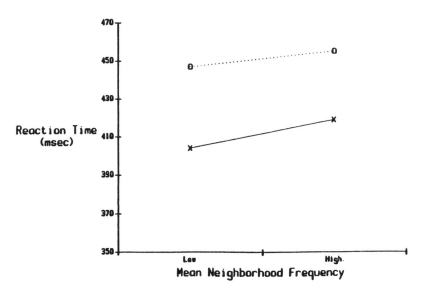

Figure 2
Reaction times to nonword stimuli in a task involving auditory lexical decisions. Mean neighborhood frequency is shown on the x axis. Low density items are represented by the solid line; high density items by the dotted line.

neighbors were responded to significantly more slowly than nonwords with few word neighbors ($F(1, 29) = 60.81$, $p < 0.05$). In addition, nonwords with high-frequency neighbors were responded to more slowly than nonwords with low-frequency neighbors ($F(1, 29) = 5.39$, $p < 0.05$). Thus we observed effects for both neighborhood density and neighborhood frequency on reaction times to make nonword judgments. These results demonstrate that similarity neighborhood effects are not contingent on presentation of degraded stimuli and have significant effects on processing times as well as on accuracy of identification.

Evidence from Auditory Word Naming

To further examine the effects of similarity neighborhoods on spoken-word recognition, Luce (1986b) performed an auditory word-naming experiment using word stimuli varying in frequency, neighborhood density, and neighborhood frequency. In this task, subjects were presented with a spoken word, which they were required to repeat as quickly as possible.

The motivation for using the naming paradigm came from recent findings in the literature on visual-word recognition on the role of word frequency in naming. Balota and Chumbley (1984) presented evidence that word-frequency effects are severely reduced in the visual-word naming task. Paap et al. (1987) have further argued that the visual-word naming task circumvents lexical access and thus circumvents access to frequency information.

These findings suggest an interesting means of dissociating effects of pattern similarity (e.g., density) and frequency and thus suggest the possibility of relegating the effects of frequency and multiple activation of neighbors to different levels of processing. In particular, the naming task was employed to determine if effects of frequency (both stimulus-word frequency and neighborhood frequency) lie at a later, decision stage of processing, whereas multiple activation of neighbors lies at some earlier stage. If the visual and auditory naming tasks are sufficiently similar, it may be hypothesized that frequency effects will be circumvented in the auditory naming task. However, activation of neighbors should not be affected by the task, because multiple patterns must still be activated and decided upon to identify the stimulus word.

To test this hypothesis, 400 CVC words were assigned to eight cells. These cells were constructed by orthogonally varying two levels of word frequency (high and low), two levels of neighborhood density (high and low), and two levels of neighborhood frequency (high and low). The method for determining similarity-neighborhood structure was identical to that used in the previous lexical-decision experiment.

Reaction times for naming the 400 stimuli were measured from the onset of the stimulus to the naming response. Results for the naming task are shown in figure 3. Because no significant interactions involving the three dependent variables of word frequency, neighborhood density, and neighborhood frequency were observed, only the mean reaction times for each level of the three variables are shown.

Only the effect of neighborhood density was significant ($F(1, 11) = 5.10$, $p < 0.05$). Words in high-density neighborhoods were named more slowly than words in low-density neighborhoods. We observed no effects of stimulus-word frequency ($F(1, 11) = 1.71$, $p > 0.05$) or neighborhood frequency ($F < 1.0$).

As hypothesized, significant density effects were observed in the absence of frequency effects. These results demonstrate that the naming task requires multiple activation of lexical items in memory but that word frequency information that may bias decision processes operating on these units is bypassed. Because the naming response requires a precise analysis of the phonetic properties of the stimulus word to build an articulatory plan for executing a response, biases not based on phonetic information (e.g., frequency biases) may hinder response generation. Because of the nature of the responses required by the naming task, therefore, subjects may optimize performance by focusing on discriminating among the phonetic patterns and ignoring higher-level lexical information. Thus frequency effects were not expected to affect naming times. However, because phonetic pattern must be isolated to make the naming response, neighborhood density was expected to influence the time need to generate the response. Indeed, precisely this pattern of results was obtained in the naming study (see Marslen-Wilson, this volume, for a similar finding).

The results of this study therefore demonstrate that neighborhood-density effects are clearly separate from frequency effects. Thus, the present study demonstrates that stimulus similarity and decision biases based on frequency are separable factors that have differential effects on the levels of processing in the word-recognition system.

Evidence from Primed Auditory-Word Identification

The three previous studies suggest two processes in spoken-word recognition: activation of multiple candidates in memory and frequency-biased decision processes. Furthermore, these studies demonstrate that activation

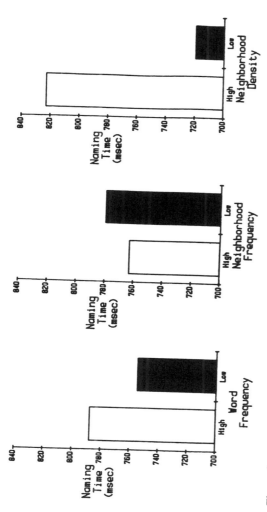

Figure 3
Reaction times for auditory-word naming. The left-hand graph shows the results for word frequency. The middle graph shows the results for neighborhood frequency. The right-hand graph shows the results for neighborhood density.

of multiple lexical items engenders costs to the word-recognition system in terms of speed and accuracy of processing.

Neither of these proposals is consistent with at least one popular theory of spoken-word recognition, namely cohort theory. The most recent version of cohort theory (Marslen-Wilson 1987) predicts neither processing costs associated with activation of multiple items nor frequency-biased decision processes. On this latter issue, cohort theory assumes that frequency adjusts the activation levels of items in memory and is not the product of postactivation decision processes.

To further investigate the issues of multiple activation and frequency in spoken-word recognition, Goldinger, Luce, and Pisoni (1989) recently conducted a priming experiment aimed at evaluating two crucial aspects of the effects of similarity-neighborhood structure on auditory-word recognition. The first concerned predictions based on the neighborhood-probability rule of inhibition from priming in spoken-word recognition. The second concerned the issue of the separation of activation and frequency bias.

The neighborhood-probability rule discussed earlier makes an interesting and somewhat counterintuitive prediction regarding priming by phonetically related items. Typically, in both visual- and auditory-word-recognition experiments, priming facilitates recognition of the target item. However, the neighborhood-probability rule predicts that in certain instances, inhibition should arise when a phonetically related prime is presented prior to a target item.

Recall that the rule states that identification performance may be characterized by the probability of choosing the stimulus word from among its neighbors. As the number and frequency of the neighbors increase, identification performance should decrease. Consider now the case in which a neighbor of the stimulus word is presented prior to the stimulus word itself (e.g., *bull* is presented immediately prior to *veer*), and subjects are required to identify the stimulus word. If we assume that some residual activation from the phonetically related prime (the neighbor) is present upon presentation of the stimulus word, this residual activation from the prime should increase the overall activity of words in the neighborhood and thus reduce the accuracy of identification of the stimulus word itself relative to an appropriate baseline condition (a phonetically unrelated prime-stimulus word pair, such as *gum* prior to *veer*). That is, priming with a neighbor should actually result in reduced identification of the stimulus word, because the residual activation from the neighbor prime will result in increased competition with the stimulus word for identification.

The neighborhood-probability rule also states that frequency serves to bias decisions and is not directly coded in the activation levels or thresholds of word units. This assumption follows directly from the results of the auditory-word-naming study, which demonstrated effects of neighborhood density in the absence of effects of word or neighbor frequency. If word-frequency information were encoded in the activation levels, such effects should not be possible.

In the present study, the frequencies of the primes and targets were manipulated in an attempt to further test the assumption that frequency is not coded in the activation levels of word units. Asssuming for the moment the frequency does in fact directly modify activation levels, one could argue that high-frequency primes should produre relatively more inhibition than low-frequency primes, simply because high-frequency primes should produce stronger competing activation levels in the neighborhood.

On the other hand, if frequency is not directly coded in the activation levels, high-frequency primes should not produce any more activation than low-frequency primes. In fact, low-frequency primes may be predicted to produce more inhibition than high-frequency primes.

The rationale for this prediction is as follows: All things being equal, low-frequency words should be identified less quickly and less accurately than high-frequency words. This prediction is not based on the assumption that high-frequency words have higher resting activation levels, lower recognition thresholds, or steeper activation functions than low-frequency words. Instead, the advantage of word frequency is assumed to arise because biased decisions regarding the stimulus input can be made more quickly and accurately for high-frequency words. Therefore, activation levels for acoustic-phonetic patterns corresponding to high- and low-frequency words are assumed to rise and fall at the same rates. However, we assumed that decisions can be made earlier for high-frequency words than for low-frequency words. This means that the activation of a high-frequency prime will begin to return to a resting level sooner than the activation of a low-frequency prime. Thus, target items following high-frequency should receive less competition from the residual activations of the primes than targets following low-frequency primes.

To test these hypotheses, Goldinger, Luce, and Pisoni (1989) generated CVC target items varying in stimulus-word frequency and neighborhood density and frequency. These target items were then paired with phonetically related primes that were either high or low in frequency. The phonetically related primes constituted the nearest neighbors of the target words that had no identical overlapping phonemes. Computation of primes from these neighborhoods was identical to that used in the perceptual-identification study discussed above. We imposed the restriction that none of the primes have any overlapping phonemes to guard against guessing strategies based on subjects' expectancies of overlap. In addition to phonetically related primes, unrelated primes for each of the target stimuli were also generated. The unrelated primes had a probability of 0 of being a neighbor of the target item.

On a given trial, a phonetically related or unrelated prime was clearly presented immediately prior to presentation of a target item mixed with white noise at a +5 dB signal-to-noise ratio. The subjects were required to identify the target word in each trial.

The results of this study of primed auditory-word identification are shown in figure 4. Light bars indicated conditions for neutral primes; dark bars show performance results for related primes. Mean percentages of correct target identification for high-frequency targets are shown on the left; mean percentage for low-frequency targets are shown on the right.

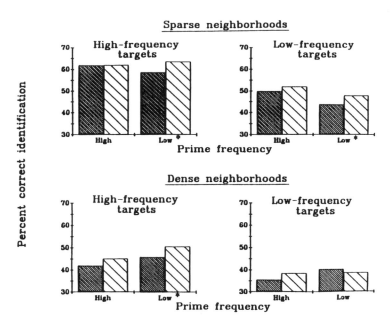

Figure 4
Percent correct identification for high- and low-frequency target words as a function of neighborhood density and prime frequency for related and unrelated primes. Light bars show performance results for neutral primes; dark bars show performance results for related primes.

Mean percentages of corrrect responses for prime-target pairs occurring in sparse neighborhoods are shown in the upper panel; mean percentages for dense neighborhoods are shown in the lower panel.

We obtained significant results for target-word frequency ($F(1, 59) = 164.00, p < 0.05$) and neighborhood density ($F(1, 59) = 248.28, p < 0.05$), replicating the effects of the perceptual-identification study. We also observed a significant main effect of priming ($F(1, 59) = 8.11, p < 0.05$). Post hoc Tukey Honestly Significant Difference analyses indicated that targets following related primes were identified significantly less accurately than targets following unrelated primes in three conditions, denoted by asterisks in figure 4. Note that significant effects of inhibition were obtained only for low-frequency primes, as predicated, with one exception. No inhibition was observed for low-frequency words occurring in high-density neighborhoods. Our failure to observe a significant effect may be due to the fact that in this condition the target item is already receiving a great deal of competition from other words in its neighborhood. Thus neighborhood competition may be so strong in this condition that any additional competition provided by the related prime preceding the target is undetectable. Nevertheless, as predicted by the neighborhood-probability rule, related low-frequency primes in all other conditions resulted in significant inhibition. These results demonstrate that phonetically related primes selected from the same similarity neighborhoods increase neighborhood competition via their residual activation and thus lower the probability of correct selection of target items from among their neighbors. In addition, only low-frequency primes produced significant levels of inhibition. This result is problematic for models that assume that frequency is coded in activation levels or thresholds. However, these results are easily accounted for by a model that separates activation and frequency-biased decision processes.

The Neighborhood-Activation Model

On the basis of these and other results (see Luce 1986b), we have proposed a model of spoken-word recognition that attempts to characterize the processes of neighborhood activation and selection. This model, called the neighborhood-activation model, is primarily a processing instantiation of the frequency-weighted-neighborhood-probability rule described above. Basically, the model assumes that a set of similar acoustic-phonetic patterns is activated in memory on the basis of stimulus input. We assume that the activation levels of these patterns are a direct function of their phonetic similarity to the stimulus input. Over the course of processing, stimulus input serves to resolve or refine a pattern. That is, as processing proceeds, the pattern corresponding to the stimulus input receives successively higher levels of activation, while the activation levels of similar patterns are attenuated.

Words emerge in the neighborhood-activation model when a system of word-decision units tuned to the acoustic and phonetic patterns are activated. The activation of the decision units is assumed to be direct, in the sense of logogen theory (Morton 1979) and cohort theory (Marslen-Wilson and Welsh 1978). In addition, as in cohort theory, the system of word units is assumed to be based only on the activation of acoustic and phonetic patterns. That is, word recognition is assumed to be, at least initially, completely driven by information contained in the speech waveform. Once the word-decision units are activated, they monitor a number of sources of information. The first source of information is the activation of the acoustic-phonetic patterns, which previously served to activate the decision units themselves. The word-decision units also monitor the overall level of activity in the decision system itself, much like processing units monitor the net activity level of the system in the TRACE model of speech perception (Elman and McClelland 1986, McClelland and Elman 1986). Finally, decision units are tuned to higher-level lexical information, which includes word frequency. This information serves to bias the decisions of the units by weighting the activity levels of the words to which they respond. The values that serve as the output of the decision units are assumed to be computed via a rule similar to the neighborhood-probability rule discussed above.

Word recognition in the neighborhood-activation model may be accomplished in a number of ways, according to the requirements of the task. In situations in which the stimulus input is degraded, word recognition is accomplished by evaluating the values computed by the decision units and selecting a response based on these values. When speeded responses are required, the subject presumably sets a criterion for responding that, once exceeded by the output of a decision unit, results in the recognition of a word. Word recognition is explicitly defined as the choice of a particular pattern by the system of decision units. Lexical access is assumed to occur once a decision unit makes all of the information it was monitoring available to working memory. Thus the decision units act as gates on the acoustic-phonetic and lexical information available to the processing system. If insufficient evidence for a word is provided by the decision system, the activation levels of the acoustic-phonetic patterns themselves may be consulted, and this would result in recognition of a nonword pattern.

The neighborhood-activation model places much of the burden of spoken-word recognition on the discrimination among similar acoustic-phonetic patterns corresponding to words and the decisions necessary for choosing among these patterns. In addition, the model accounts for word-frequency effects by allowing frequency information to bias the decisions of the word-decision units. However, because each word-decision unit computes values from its acoustic-phonetic pattern as well as the overall level of activity in the decision system, decisions should be context sensitive. Thus frequency is assumed to be a relative factor, not an inherent property or attribute of a word. That is, if many decision units are receiving strong frequency biases, a decision unit for a given high-frequency word may compute relatively low values. Likewise, a decision unit for a low-frequency word may quickly begin to output high values if there is little other activity in the system. Thus, effects to frequency are presumably not absolute but instead are highly dependent on the activity level of the decision system as a whole.

Other Models of Word Recognition

The neighborhood-activation model bears a strong resemblance to other models of spoken-word recognition, and many of the concepts incorporated in the model have precedents in previous accounts of auditory word recognition. However, as will be argued below, the model makes certain predictions that are inconsistent with current models of word recognition, in particular, with regard to the roles of frequency and similarity. We now turn to a discussion of two of the more influential models of word recognition to highlight the fundamental differences and similarities between the neighborhood-activation model and these models.

Logogen Theory

Morton (1969, 1979) has proposed a model of word recognition based on a system of "logogens" that monitor bottom-up sensory information and top-down contextual and lexical information. Information from either of these sources serves to drive a logogen toward its threshold. Once a threshold is reached, the information to which the logogen corresponds is made available to the processing system and a word is said to be recognized and accessed. Morton accounts for word-frequency effects in the logogen model by assuming that high-frequency words require less evidence to cross the threshold than low-frequency words. Morton thus refers to logogen theory as an evidence-bias model.

The resemblance between Morton's system of logogens and the system of word-decision units in the neighborhood-activation model is quite strong. Both logogens and word-decision units monitor top-down and bottom-up information. In addition, both logogens and word-decision units are assumed to prohibit information from becoming available to the general processing system until a decision on the identity of the word has been made. However, word-decision units differ from logogens in a number of important ways.

Perhaps the most crucial differences between logogens and the word-decision units hinges on the problem of accounting for the effects of similarity neighborhoods. Logogens are assumed to be independent processing units with no interconnections among lexical items in memory. The lack of cross talk among logogens makes it difficult to account for the findings that words in highly dense or confusable neighborhoods require more time for a response than words in less dense or less confusable neighborhoods. Because logogens are independent processing units, stimulus input should push a given logogen over its threshold after the same lapse of time regardless of whether the stimulus input activates many or few logogens. Granted, accuracy differences between dense and sparse neighborhoods may arise because there is a higher probability that logogens corresponding to similar words may surpass their thresholds prior to the logogen corresponding to the stimulus input. It is not so clear, however, how logogen theory would account for the effects of neighborhood density on reaction times. If word frequency is held constant, when presented with clearly specified phonetic information, as in auditory-word naming, the logogen corresponding to the stimulus input should always cross its threshold after the same amount of time regardless of the activity levels of other logogens.

The most difficult problem that the present set of results poses for logogen theory concerns the robust findings that frequency effects are dependent on the similarity neighborhood of the stimulus word. In the perceptual-identification study it was shown that certain classes of high- and low-frequency words are responded to at equal levels of accuracy if the neighborhoods of the words were equated. Because logogens corresponding to high and low frequency have different thresholds, low-frequency words should always require more evidence than high-frequency words in order to cross the thresholds. Because a single logogen has no knowledge of the activation levels of other logogens, it is difficult to explain within logogen theory how the frequencies of items in a neighborhood could influence recognition of the stimulus word.

In addition, logogen theory has no mechanism for explaining the results of the word-naming study. Recall that in the naming study we argued that word units must have been accessed by subjects in order to produce the effect of neighborhood density. However, no effects of word frequency and neighborhood frequency were observed. It is possible that the thresholds for logogens corresponding to high- and low-frequency words were temporarily equated because of some unspecified property of the naming task. However, not only is this solution extremely inelegant and unparsimonious, it seriously calls into question the fundamental claim of logogen theory that thresholds are intrinsic to the logogens themselves and arise over time as a function of degrees of exposure to words.

A final problem for logogen theory concerns the nonword data from the experiment involving auditory lexical decisions. Coltheart et al. (1976) have proposed that a nonword decision in the logogen model is executed when no logogen fires. However, because the activation levels within the logogens are not available for inspection (because of logogens are either above or below threshold), it is difficult to account for the finding that the number and nature of words activated by the nonword stimulus influences reaction time. As logogen theory stands, there is no means for evaluating the overall level of activity in the logogen system, and consequently there is no mechanism for making faster decisions to nonwords with fewer neighbors or lower-frequency neighbors. The nonword data from the experiment involving auditory lexical decisions are therefore problematic for a system of independent processing units that respond only upon surpassing an intrinsic threshold.

The neighborhood-activation model, on the other hand, provides a coherent description of these results by assuming that the decision units are interconnected and that frequency effects arise from biases stemming from higher-level sources of information. Modifications of logogen theory may possibly account for the present results, but it is very likely that the resulting model would bear a strong resemblance to the neighborhood-activation model. Nonetheless, there are important similarities between the neighborhood-activation model and logogen theory because the present model incorporates many ideas from logogen theory. In particular, the neighborhood-activation model assumes a system of word-decision units that serve as the interface between the acoustic-phonetic input and higher-level information, as proposed by logogen theory. However, owing to the interconnectedness of the system of word-decision units, the neighborhood-activation model is able to account for the effects of similarity neighborhoods, whereas logogen theory apparently is not.

Cohort Theory

Perhaps the most influential of current models of spoken-word recognition is cohort theory, proposed by Marslen-Wilson (Marslen-Wilson and Welsh 1978; Marslen-Wilson and Tyler 1980; Marslen-Wilson 1984, 1987). According to this theory, a cohort of words is activated in memory on the basis of the initial acoustic-phonetic input of the stimulus word. Words in the cohort are then eliminated by two sources of information: continued acoustic-phonetic input and top-down contextual information. That is, words in the cohort are ruled out or deactivated by continued processing of the stimulus information and by inconsistent contextual information. A given word is recognized when it is the only word remaining in the cohort.

Cohort theory has provided a number of valuable insights into the temporal processing of spoken words. In previous versions of the theory, no attempt was made to account for word-frequency effects. In the 1987 version of the theory, though, Marslen-Wilson has incorporated a mechanism for accounting for word-frequency effects by assuming that words in a cohort have differing levels of activation according to their frequencies of occurrence. Words with higher levels of activation take longer to eliminate from the cohort than words with lower levels of activation, which thus affords at least an initial advantage to high-frequency words. Because the latter version of cohort theory represents a significant improvement over the initial formulation of the theory, only this version will be considered in the present discussion.

Cohort theory and the neighborhood-activation model are similar in that both models assume bottom-up priority in the activation of items in memory. Furthermore, both models assume that items are activated and processed in parallel. In addition, both models state that items receive reduced levels of activity when disconfirming acoustic and phonetic information is presented. Unlike cohort theory, however, the neighborhood-activation model at this stage of formulation has little to say about the time course of effects in the word-recogniton system. This is primarily because the model was developed on the basis of data from subjects responding to very short words (which tend to be the most commonly used words in the language). Indeed, some aspects of cohort theory may have to be incorporated into the neighborhood-activation model to account for the recognition of longer words. Nonetheless, cohort theory and the present model do make fundamentally different predictions, at least for short stimuli.

Marslen-Wilson (1987) argues that because cohort theory is realized as a parallel system, there should be no effects of set size on word recognition. Words in a cohort are assumed to be activated at no cost. The neighborhood-activation model is also realized as a system of parallel processing units, but the fundamental claim of the neighborhood-activation model is that the nature and number of items activated in memory does influence the accuracy and speed of recogniton. This prediction stems from the claim that the word-decision units are sensitive to the overall level of activity in the decision system and are therefore influenced by the number and nature of competing items. Evidence to support this claim was provided by each of the experiments previously reported.

Marslen-Wilson (1987) argues that set size has no effect on recognition performance on the basis of a set of experiments examining lexical decisions for nonwords. He claims that if nonwords are matched at the point at which they diverge from words, there should be no effect of set size on reaction times. This contradicts the findings in the lexical-decision experiment reported earlier in which large effects of neighborhood density (i.e., set size) and neighborhood frequency were observed for nonwords. Recall that because of the manner in which these nonwords were constructed, each of the nonwords diverged from words at the third phoneme. Thus set size effects were demonstrated even when divergence points were equated. Since Marslen-Wilson's claim of no effects of set size are based on null results, the positive findings reported for the nonwords seriously calls this claim into question.

Indeed, each of the experiments reported previously fails to support the notion that the number of items activated in memory has no influence on recognition performance. Although Marslen-Wilson may object to the results from the perceptual-identification study, claiming that the use of noisy stimuli may induce postperceptual processes, the results from the lexical-decision study together with the auditory naming study clearly contradict a fundamental claim of cohort theory. Indeed, it is not even clear that the postulation of some vague postperceptual processes accounts for the results from the perceptual-identification study, which showed significant effects of neighborhood structure on identification performance. In short, the results of the present set of studies considered together refute a fundamental claim of cohort theory that activation of multiple lexical items in memory results in no processing costs to the system. The results of the naming study also provide counterevidence to the treatment of word frequency in the cohort theory. All words used in the naming study had approximately equal isolation points by virtue of their short length (see Luce 1986a). However, despite equivalent isolation points, high-frequency words were named no faster than low-frequency words, in contradiction to the predictions made by the most recent version of cohort theory (Marslen-Wilson 1987). In addition, because there was a strong effect of density, it cannot be assumed that lexical items were bypassed in the generation of the naming response. Thus the current version of cohort theory also fails to account for our results that frequency effects may be circumvented by task requirements.

Finally, the results of the priming study provide further evidence that high- and low-frequency words may not differ in absolute activation levels and that frequency effects come at a stage following activation. This conclusion is supported by the finding that only low-frequency primes resulted in significant levels of inhibition, a result that cannot easily be accounted for by models assuming that frequency is coded in activation levels or thresholds. As previously argued, an adequate model of spoken-word recognition cannot assume different inherent activation levels or thresholds for the units monitoring high- and low-frequency words. Instead, the effects of frequency are best described as biases on the decision units responsible for choosing among activated lexical items. By treating the effects of frequency as biases on the decision process, one can account for results demonstrating that the frequency effect varies according to task requirements (Pollack, Rubenstein, and Decker 1959) and in the face of higher-level sources of information (Grosjean and Itzler 1984). Thus the instantiation of frequency in the latest version of cohort theory is difficult to countenance. The neighborhood-activation model, however, provides a more principle explanation of the effects of word frequency on both the stimulus word and its neighbors.

Conclusion

The results reported in the studies discussed above suggest a perceptual and cognitive system optimized for the recognition of words under a variety of circumstances. This optimization is achieved by a simultaneous activation of alternatives based on stimulus input and by a sophisticated system that attempts to decide among these alternatives. The fact that the word recognition system is capable of considering numerous alternatives in parallel helps to assure the best performance of the system in the face of stimulus input that is often impoverished, degraded, or poorly specified. However, as the present set of experiments has shown, this optimization is not without its processing costs. Both the number and nature of the words activated by the stimulus input affect not only the accuracy of word recognition but also the time required to decide among the activated candidates. Nevertheless, such processing costs subserve the ultimate goal of speech perception, namely to maximize the speed and accuracy with which words are recognized in real-time.

Acknowledgments

This research was supported by NIH grant NS-12179 to Indiana University. We thank Gerry Altmann for many helpful comments and suggestions.

Notes

1. The precise methods by which a neighbor was defined varied as a function of the particular experimental paradigm employed and will be discussed in more detail below.

2. Each of the words in this study as well as the following studies were rated as highly familiar (5.5 or above) by subjects on a 7-point scale (see Nusbaum, Pisoni, and Davis 1984). This constraint on stimulus selection was imposed to ensure that the subjects knew the words to be presented.

References

Balota, D. A., and Chumbley, J. I. 1984. Are lexical decisions a good measure of lexical access? The role of word frequency in the neglected decision stage. *Journal of Experimental Psychology: Human Perception and Performance* 10:340–357.

Balota, D. A., and Chumbley, J. I. 1985. The locus of word-frequency effects in the pronunciation task: Lexical access and/or production frequency? *Journal of Verbal Learning and Verbal Behavior* 24:89–106.

Coltheart, M., Davelaar, E., Jonasson, J. T., and Besner, D. 1976. Access to the internal lexicon. In S. Dornic (ed.), *Attention and Performance*, vol. 6. Hillsdale, N.J.: Erlbaum.

Elman, J. L., and McClelland, J. L. 1986. Exploiting lawful variability in the speech waveform. In J. S. Perkell and D. H. Klatt (eds.), *Invariance and Variability in Speech Processing*, pp. 360–385. Hillsdale, N.J.: Erlbaum.

Goldinger, S. D., Luce, P. A., and Pisoni, D. B. 1989. Priming lexical neighbors of spoken words: Effects of competition and inhibition. *Journal of Memory and Language* 28:501–518.

Grosjean, F., and Itzler, J. 1984. Can semantic constraint reduce the role of word frequency during spoken-word recognition. *Perception and Psychophysics* 22:180–182.

Howes, D. H. 1957. On the relation between the intelligibility and frequency of occurrence of English words. *Journal of the Acoustical Society of America* 29:296–305.

Kučera, F., and Francis, W. 1967. *Computational Analysis of Present Day American English*. Providence R.I.: Brown University Press.

Landauer, T. K., and Streeter, L. A. 1973. Structural differences between common and rare words: Failure of equivalence assumptions for theories of word recognition. *Journal of Verbal Learning and Verbal Behavior* 12:119–131.

Luce, P. A. 1986a. A computational analysis of uniqueness points in auditory word recognition. *Perception and Psychophysics* 39:155–158.

Luce, P. A. 1986b. Neighborhoods of words in the mental lexicon. Doctoral dissertation, Indiana University, Bloomington, Indiana.

Luce, P. A. 1989a. Similarity neighborhoods of words in the mental lexicon: A computational analysis. Manuscript in preparation. Speech Research Laboratory, Psychology Department, Indiana University, Bloomington, Indiana.

Luce, P. A. 1989b. Stimulus context and similarity neighborhood structure. Manuscript in preparation.

Luce, R. D. 1959. *Individual Choice Behavior*. New York: Wiley.

McClelland, J. L., and Elman, J. L. 1986. The TRACE model of speech perception. *Cogitive Psychology* 18:1–86.

Marslen-Wilson, W. D. 1984. Function and process in spoken word recognition: A tutorial review. In H. Bouma and D. G. Bouwhuis (eds.), *Attention and Performance*, vol. 10, *Control of Language Processes*. Hillsdale, N.J.: Erlbaum.

Marslen-Wilson, W. D. 1987. Functional parallelism in spoken and recognition. In U. H. Frauenfelder and L. K. Tyler (eds.), *Spoken Word Recognition*. Cambridge: MIT Press.

Marslen-Wilson, W. D., and Tyler, L. K. 1980. The temporal structure of spoken language understanding. *Cognition* 8:1–71.

Marslen-Wilson, W. D., and Welsh, A. 1978. Processing interactions and lexical access during word recognition in continuous speech. *Cognitive Psychology* 10:29–63.

Morton, J. 1969. Interaction of information in word recognition. *Psychological Review* 76:165–178.

Morton, J. 1979. Word recognition. In J. Morton and J. D. Marshall (eds.), *Psycholinguistics 2: Structures and Processes*, pp. 107–156. Cambridge: MIT Press.

Newbigging, P. L. 1961. The perceptual reintegration of frequent and infrequent words. *Canadian Journal of Psychology* 15:123–132.

Nusbaum, H. C., Pisoni, D. B., and Davis, C. K. 1984. Sizing up the Hoosier mental lexicon: Measuring the familiarity of 20,000 words. Research on Speech Perception, progress report no. 10. Speech Research Laboratory. Psychology Department, Indiana University, Bloomington, Indiana.

Paap, K. R., McDonald, J. E., Schvaneveldt, R. W., and Noel, R. W. 1987. Frequency and pronounceability in visually presented naming and lexical-decision tasks. In M. Coltheart (ed.), *The Psychology of Reading*, vol. 12 of *Attention and Performance*. Hillsdale, N.J.: Erlbaum.

Pollack, I., Rubenstein, H., and Decker, L. 1959. Intelligibility of known and unknown message sets. *Journal of the Acoustical Society of America* 31:273–259.

Savin, H. B. 1963. Word-frequency effect and errors in the perception of speech. *Journal of the Acoustical Society of America* 35:200–206.

Soloman, R. L., and Postman, L. 1952. Frequency of usage as a determinant of recognition thresholds for words. *Journal of Experimental Psychology* 43:195–201.

Triesman, M. 1978a. A theory of the identification of complex stimuli with an application to word recognition. *Psychological Review* 85:525–570.

Triesman, M. 1978b. Space or lexicon? The word frequency effect and the error response frequency effect. *Journal of Verbal Learning and Verbal Behavior* 17:37–59.

Chapter 7

Activation, Competition, and Frequency in Lexical Access

William Marslen-Wilson

In current research into lexical access—into the means whereby the sensory signal is projected onto mental representations of lexical form—a certain consensus has begun to emerge about the basic properties of the form-based access and selection process. This consensus shares at least the following three basic assumptions:

- The activation metaphor is the appropriate one for representing the goodness of fit between sensory inputs and representations of lexical forms.
- Perceptual processing is based on a process of competition between simultaneously active candidates.
- The selection (or identification) decision is based on relations between levels of activation. Perceptual choice is made as the candidate emerges from among the welter of competing activation levels.

This leads to the kind of view schematically illustrated in figure 1. Here we see, for an event in the auditory modality, the joint activation of mulitple candidates, the emergence over time of the best candidate, and discrimination becoming possible as the level of activation (reflecting the computed goodness of fit) for the correct candidate reaches a criterial level of difference from the levels of activation of its competitors. Whether we represent these operations in terms of the levels of single points over time or as the differentiation of more distributed patterns of activation, the basic metaphor remains the same.

The research I am going to describe in this paper is intended to evaluate the correctness of this kind of view of lexical access and selection. In particular, I focus on the central claim that discrimination involves a process of competition, so that the outcome of the perceptual process is fundamentally *contingent* in nature. The timing and the outcome of the recognition process reflects not just the evidence that a particular word is present but also the evidence that other words, close competitors, are not

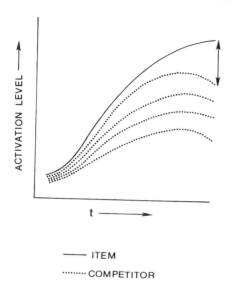

ITEM

········ COMPETITOR

Figure 1
Activation levels of the correct word candidate and its competitors over time

present. My colleagues and I investigate this question here by attempting to manipulate the activation level of a word's competitors. If other factors are held constant, the extent to which a given competitor is more or less active should affect the discrimination process. The variable we use to achieve these effects is the relative frequency of occurrence of words and their candidates.

This requires the further and more controversial assumption that frequency effects in lexical access reflect, at least in part, effects on activation levels—i.e., effects on the manner in which the access system responds to the sensory input—so that frequency cannot be written off just as an effect at the post-access decision stage. There is some evidence to support this, and certainly the evidence against it is by no means unequivocal (for a discussion, see Monsell, Doyle, and Haggard 1989). Furthermore, in this era of learning models it becomes increasingly implausible to suppose that frequency of experience is not somehow reflected in the basic organization of the way the system responds to sensory inputs (Seidenberg 1989, Monsell 1990).

If frequency can affect activation levels, variations in frequency should affect the primary relationship of items and competitors. Frequency differences change the relation between the activation levels of items and compe-

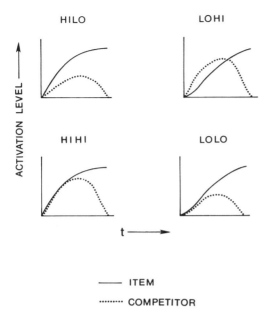

Figure 2
Effects of item and competitor frequency on item discriminability over time
(HILO = High-frequency item, low-frequency competitor; LOHI = Low-
frequency item, high-frequency competitor; HIHI = High-frequency item,
high-frequency competitor; LOLO = Low-frequency item, low-frequency
competitor)

titors and therefore affect the timing with which different candidates are
identified during perceptual processing. This is illustrated, again schematically, in figure 2.

If we stick with the auditory domain, where the signal is conveniently
distributed in time, we can see from this set of four graphs how the frequency
of an item and the frequency of its close competitors should interact to
determine the timing of lexical choice. The way in which they do this is by
changing the point at which the activation level of the item reaches the
point of criterial difference from the activation levels of its competitors.

Note that since we are working here in the auditory domain, we define
competitors sequentially, in terms of cohort membership, as we have
conventionally specified it (Marslen-Wilson 1987, Marslen-Wilson and
Tyler 1980). Thus, for example, *bribe* is considered to be a competitor for
bright, whereas *fright*, *light*, and *brute* are not. There is evidence to support this assumption both from behavioral data (Marslen-Wilson 1987,

Marslen-Wilson and Zwitserlood 1989, Zwitserlood 1989) and from the behavior of computer models such as TRACE (McClelland and Elman 1986, Frauenfelder and Peeters, this volume).

In particular, Marslen-Wilson and Zwitserlood (1989) showed that rhyme primes do not significantly activate the lexical representations of words with which they rhyme. Thus, for example, in a cross-modal semantic priming task, the auditory prime *fable* does not facilitate a lexical-decision response to the visual target CHAIR, despite the considerable phonetic overlap between *fable* and the word *table* (to which CHAIR is a close associate). Even a nonword rhyme prime (for example, *dable*) is ineffective in activating the lexical entry for the word it rhymes with (*table*). Subsequent research by Marslen-Wilson, van Halen, and Moss (1988) and by Moss and Marslen-Wilson (1989) shows that this failure of rhyme priming holds irrespective of the degree of similarity between the initial segment of a word and its rhyme. Even words that differ in only one phonetic feature (for example, *pill* and *bill*) do not prime each other. Words must apparently match at word onset—or else have perceptually ambiguous initial segments (Marslen-Wilson, van Halen, and Moss 1988)—if they are to enter the same word-initial cohort and thus be potential competitors.[1]

This view of the competitor environment differs from the proposals of Luce and his colleagues (Luce 1986; Luce, Pisoni, and Goldinger, this volume). In this research, the characteristics of a word's lexical neighborhood— the set of words that will be activated when that word is heard—are computed without reference to sequentiality. Luce treats both *bat* and *pad* as potentially equivalent competitors to the word *pat*. Despite Luce's successes in finding effects of neighborhood density computed on a nonsequential basis, it is clearly a problem for this approach that rhymes are such ineffective primes (Marslen-Wilson and Zwitserlood 1989). However, this may also reflect differences in experimental paradigm (see note 1).

If we assume for current purposes that competitors are indeed defined sequentially in auditory lexical access, figure 2 shows that the correct candidate should emerge most rapidly in the High-Low case, where a high-frequency word has only low-frequency competitors, and most slowly in the Low-High case, where a low-frequency word has a high-frequency cohort competitor. The High-High and Low-Low cases should be intermediate and not necessarily different from each other.

In other words, on this kind of story, frequency effects are at least in part relational effects. Low-frequency words are identified more slowly not just because they are infrequent in the language but also because they tend to have higher-frequency competitors. Conversely, high-frequency words tend to have lower-frequency competitors. In short, we are looking to see if item-frequency effects are shifted up or down by competitor frequency. In particular, a high-frequency competitor should slow you down, while a low-frequency competitor should speed you up, irrespective of item frequency. And remember, of course, that all these predictions depend just as much on the initial assumption that lexical access is a competitive and contingent process as they do on the assumptions about the nature of frequency effects.

Studies of Recognition Time

To test these questions, we constructed a set of stimuli that covaried the factors of Frequency and of Competitor in the manner illustrated in table 1. Specifically, we constructed four sets of 24 stimuli. Items in these four sets were matched for uniqueness points and for alignment points. These are two aspects of spoken words that it is essential to control for. The uniqueness point (UP) is the point in the word at which it becomes uniquely identifiable, in the sense of separating from the other members of its word-initial cohort (Marslen-Wilson and Welsh 1978, Grosjean 1980). Unless this point is held constant across sets, variations in UPs may be confounded with the experimental variables. The second point, referred to here as the alignment point (AP), is critical for tasks involving timed responses. If response times (RTs) to spoken words are to be measured, they need to be measured relative to equivalent points in the different words. If RTs are measured from word onset, the timing of the responses will be affected by possibly irrelevant differences in word-length. Instead, RTs need to be measured from a point that is informationally equivalent across different words. The difficulty, of course, is to determine the equivalent points in different words. Where, for example, are the equivalent measurement points in words like *steep* and *stone*, which differ quite

Table 1
Organization of the stimulus set

Group	Frequency	
	Item	Competitor
High-Low	High	Low
High-High	High	High
Low-High	Low	High
Low-Low	Low	Low

markedly in the temporal distribution of information about their final consonants (Warren and Marslen-Wilson 1987, 1988)?

We solved the problem of uniqueness points for these sets by using only monosyllabic words, all of which terminated in a consonant, and that became discriminable only when this final consonant was heard. We dealt with the problem of an alignment point by matching the phonetic properties of the last segment across stimulus sets. Each set contained 6 words terminating in voiced plosives (/b/, /d/, /g/), 14 terminating in unvoiced plosives (/p/, /t/, /k/), 2 in voiced fricatives (/z/, /v/), and 2 in unvoiced fricatives (/s/, /sh/). This meant that the alignment point (relative to which response time was measured) could be held constant across sets. For example, for any High-Low stimulus terminating in an unvoiced stop, there was a matched stimulus also terminating in an unvoiced stop for each of the three other sets. For each unvoiced stop the alignment point was set at the vowel offset (as for all these stimuli), which assured informational equivalence across sets.[2]

The four sets were as follows (see table 1 again). First, there were two sets of high-frequency stimuli, with mean frequencies for the two lists of 114 and 122. The two lists differed in their *competitor environments*, defined here in terms of sequential cohorts. Since the test words were all monosyllables, the pool of potential competitors was restricted to other monosyllabic words beginning with the same initial consonant and vowel as the test word but terminating in a different consonant or consonant cluster. We assume that words diverging earlier than this—that is, after the initial consonant—would not be significant competitors (especially for these test words, which become unique only with the final consonant).

The first list, labeled High-Low, contained words that had only low-frequency competitors. The mean frequency of the nearest competitor of these words was 5.2. An example is the word *book*, which only has competitors like *bush* and *bull*. This contrasted with the High-High words, each of which had at least one high-frequency competitor, with a mean frequency for the nearest competitor of 406. The word *light*, for example, has the high-frequency competitor *like* (as well as several low-frequency competitors).

If the faster response to high-frequency words is due to an intrinsic property of these words (such as more rapid activation), High-High and High-Low stimuli should be responded to equally quickly. If, however, the competitor environment also plays a role, High-Low stimuli should be responded to faster than High-High stimuli, since discrimination of High-High stimuli will be slowed down by the later separation of the high-frequency competitor.

The second set of contrasts involved two lists of low-frequency items, with mean frequencies of 3.9 and 4.1. One of these lists, labeled Low-Low, contained items that had only low-frequency competitors. The mean frequency of the nearest of these competitors was 4.6. The word *flock*, for example, has as its competitors words like *flog* and *flop*. The Low-Low list contrasted with the Low-High list, where each item had at least one high-frequency competitor, with a mean frequency of 125. The low-frequency word *streak*, for example, has the high-frequency competitor *street*.

Again, if responses to low-frequency words reflect solely the intrinsic properties of these words, there should be no difference between these two lists. If competitors matter, the Low-Low set should be faster than the Low-High set. The most radical outcome of the competitor theory of frequency effects is that the Low-Low list should not differ from the High-High list.

Experiment 1, lexical decision

The first experiment involved a lexical-decision task. Subjects heard a mixture of real words and nonwords, and their task was to indicate as rapidly as possible, by pressing either a yes or a no button, the lexical status of each item they heard ("Is this a word in English or not?"). Response-time was measured from the alignment point (vowel offset) for each stimulus, which was also carefully matched across lists. In previous research we had obtained strong frequency effects of matched sets of High-Low and Low-High stimuli.

The results are summarized in table 2. They show no effect whatsoever of competitor frequency for either of the two item-frequency pairs of lists, in contrast to the strong effect of item frequency itself. This is reflected in the analysis of variance, which reveals a significant main effect of frequency ($F(1, 95) = 18.10$, $p < .005$) but no effect of competitor ($F < 1$) nor any trace of an interaction between them ($F < 1$).

Table 2
Lexical decision times (msec from alignment points)

| | Item frequency | | |
	High	Low	Average
High competitor	405	480	442
Low competitor	411	476	443
Average	408	478	

The interpretation of this result is not, however, completely clearcut. The lexical-decision task encourages listeners to wait until the end of a word before responding, since it is only when they have heard all the word that they can be sure that it really is a word and hasn't turned into a nonword. The competitor effects that we are looking for, however, may well be rather transient phenomena, momentary delays as relative levels of activation readjust, which will have already been and gone by the time that the listener gets around to making the lexical-decision response.

Experiment 2, auditory repetition

We therefore ran the same stimuli in a second experiment, using the auditory repetition task.[3] The subjects heard only real words (the test words plus fillers), and their task was simply to repeat each word aloud as quickly as possible. There is no need here to wait until the very end of the word before responding, and earlier research using the shadowing task suggests that subjects do indeed not wait (Marslen-Wilson 1985). The results are summarized in table 3.

The outcome is again very clear. There is no effect at all of competitor frequency ($F < 1$), and there is a greatly reduced effect of item frequency ($F(1, 92) = 3.184, p = .08$). Responses average about 160 msec faster than in the lexical decision experiment, but this brings with it no sign of a competitor effect.

Experiment 3, gating

We then decided to check further on the properties of the stimuli by running the gating task on them. Perhaps the reason we were getting no competitor effect was that the stimuli didn't have the properties we had assigned to them. To find out about this, we gave subjects the different stimuli in gating sequences. This means that they hear the words as successive fragments, increasing in length with each gate. At the first gate they might hear the first 50 msec, at the second gate the first 100 msec, and so

Table 3
Auditory repetition latencies (msec from alignment points)

	Item frequency		
	High	Low	Average
High competitor	264	293	278
Low competitor	277	291	284
Average	270	292	

on by regular increments until the entire word had been heard. The subject's task after each fragment was to write down what they thought the word was or was going to become. They were also required to note down each time, on a scale of 0 to 10, how confident they were in the response.

Earlier research using the gating task (Grosjean 1980, Tyler 1984) suggests that responses in the gating task are sensitive to frequency effects and that low-frequency words tend to be identified later because higher-frequency candidates are initially preferred. Tyler's analyses show in detail how high-frequency candidates dominate over the first few gates, when the stimulus information is still ambiguous. These earlier experiments, however, were not run with stimuli explicitly contrasting item and competitor frequency in the way we have done here.

From the subject's gating responses we can compute two different measures. One of them, the *Recognition Point*, is the average point at which the subjects start to get the word right and at which they have 80 percent or more confidence in their choice.[4] This Recognition Point corresponds to the point where the sensory information about the word becomes completely unambiguous. The mean recognition points, given as msec from the alignment points, are shown in table 4.

There is no effect at all of competitor frequency ($F < 1$), and a very weak effect of item frequency ($F(1, 92) = 3.231, p = .08$). The Recognition Point is determined by the availability of unambiguous sensory information as to the identity of the word being heard, and the relationship of this to the alignment point has nothing to do with the frequency of competitors and not much to do with the frequency of the item. Note that since the alignment points for all these stimuli were set at vowel offsets, these mean Recognition Points fall on average well into the final consonant of the word. This is to be expected, since the words were selected to become discriminable only when this final segment had been identified.

Next is the gating *Isolation Point*, which is simply the average point where subjects start to get the word right. Confidence is not taken into account. These results are given in table 5.

Table 4
Mean gating recognition points (msec from alignment points)

	Item frequency		
	High	Low	Average
High competitor	+55	+68	+62
Low competitor	+55	+73	+64
Average	+55	+70	

Here finally we did find significant effects of competitor frequency $(F(1,92) = 11.023$, $p = .001$) and of item frequency $(F(1,92) = 5.963$, $p = .02)$. In other words, using a measure that requires the subject to make a response at a point where the sensory information is still ambiguous, we do find these elusive competitor effects. Note that these Isolation Points fall on average much earlier than the Recognition Points. In fact, for all except the Low-High stimuli the Isolation Point is reached before the alignment point, on the average between 13 and 46 msec before the end of the vowel. And while there is still a large difference between the Low-High and the High-Low groups (63 msec), the difference between High-High and Low-Low drops to only 9 msec.

We can also better understand what was happening in the lexical-decision and repetition experiments. Reaction times in these tasks correlate much more strongly with Recognition Points than with Isolation Points (see table 6). In fact, repetition and lexical-decision response times only correlate with Isolation Points to the extent that Isolation Points themselves correlate with Recognition Points. And if the responses in the two reaction-time tasks are tied to Recognition Points, then in both repetition and lexical decision, listeners seem to be waiting until they are sure they know what the word is before making the response. So perhaps that's why the effect of competitor frequency doesn't show up in these tasks.

To summarize the results so far, for three of these four measures we found no effect of competitor frequency. We got item-frequency effects varying from the strong to the marginal, but no trace of a competitor effect. This was for the three tasks that elicit "late" responses from listeners, tasks

Table 5
Mean gating isolation points (msec from alignment points)

	Item frequency		
	High	Low	Average
High competitor	−22	+17	−3
Low competitor	−46	−13	−30
Average	−34	+2	

Table 6
Correlations between gating measures and response-time measures (Pearson's r)

	Lexical decision	Repetition
Isolation Point	−.37	−.36
Recognition Point	−.69	−.65

where the listeners base their responses on secure knowledge of what the words are. For these monosyllabic stimuli this point was typically at the end of the word.

Lexical decision and repetition correlate very well with gating Recognition Points and not at all well with Isolation Points. What they all have in common, then, is the property that listeners are not making their responses until they are essentially certain, on bottom-up grounds, what the words are.

We do get effects of both item frequency *and* competitor frequency on gating Isolation Point, that is, when listeners are responding early before it has become certain what the word is. This effect is illustrated for the pair of words in figure 3, which shows how listeners' responses are affected early in the gating sequence by the presence of a high-frequency competitor and how this effect dies away when unambiguous sensory information becomes available.

The two words in the figure (*shark* and *sharp*) differ in the place of articulation of their final consonant. Information about this difference starts to become available in the signal toward the end of the vowel, but definitive information becomes available only after the stop closure at the release burst. This is reflected in the gating Recognition Points for these stimuli, which for each of them falls at or after the release burst. There is a big difference, however, in the gating Isolation Point for these words. For the word in the lower panel, *sharp*, which only has low-frequency competitors, the Isolation Point is reached early, in fact, even before the end of the vowel. The word in the upper panel, *shark*, in contrast, does have a higher-frequency competitor (the word *sharp*), and this has a strong effect. In fact, *sharp* is given as a response much more often than *shark* until very late in the word, so that the Isolation Point for *shark* falls very close to its Recognition Point.

The effects of gating Isolation Points show overall, then, that the frequency of the cohort competitors of a word can affect performance. They also show that the stimuli used in these experiments provided the appropriate contrasts. The Low-High stimuli in particular are treated as having higher-frequency competitors, and these are the responses given at the earlier gates.

But what the Isolation-Point results also mean, in conjunction with the Recognition-Point results and the results for the repetition and auditory lexical decision experiments, is that if there is any effect of competitor frequency in auditory word recognition, it is a *transient* effect that has dissipated by the time the end of the word is reached. We therefore cannot

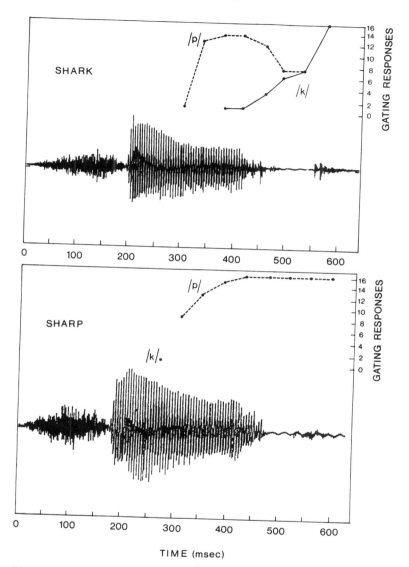

Figure 3

Gating responses for high- and low-frequency words with high- and low-frequency competitors plotted as a function of gate position relative to the acoustic waveform. The (low-frequency) response "shark" is coded as /k/ and the (high-frequency) response "sharp" as /p/.

hope to detect such effects using tasks that measure the state of the listeners' recognition system at the end of the word. Nor can we take the Isolation-Point results by themselves as demonstrating that there are transient competitor effects early in processing, since the technique does not rule out possible explanations in terms of bias or guessing effects.

The Cross-Modal Study

In this section I describe a further experiment that attempts to detect these transient effects using a quite different task, cross-modal repetition priming. This task not only allows one to pick up potential transient effects, but it also has the advantage of not being open to the same kinds of bias or guessing criticisms, since the subjects are never actually asked to respond to the spoken word at all.

To establish whether or not transient effects of competitor frequency exist, we need to test before all of the word has been heard and in particular before the sensory input has made it clear which word is actually being heard. To do this, we used a cross-modal repetition priming task, where subjects hear an auditory prime followed immediately by a visual probe. Their task is to make a lexical-decision response to the visual probe. What we were interested in is the way in which primes from different item or competitor frequency sets affect the response to the visual probe.

In choosing to use this task to investigate these issues, we were making two additional assumptions. The first of these concerns the organization of the lexical-access system. We assumed that there are two independent access routes, one for each modality, and that both of these feed into a central modality-independent evidence-collecting entity. This entity we call the *lexical entry* for the word in question. Thus, if there are cross-modal repetition effects, this is because the auditory prime has affected the state of the relevant modality-independent lexical entry, which in turn affects how this entry responds to subsequent input from another modality. Our second assumption, then, is that short-term repetition priming is due to the residual effects of the activation, by the spoken prime, of the relevant target representations.

The experiment used essentially the same stimulus set as before but with some modifications, because not all of the words used in the first round of experiments had suitable competitors.[5] A sample stimulus set from the four combinations of high and low item and competitor frequencies is given in table 7.

Table 7
Stimulus set for the cross-modal study

	High-High group	Frequency
Item	feel	211
Competitor	feed	212
Baseline	name	201

	High-Low group	Frequency
Item	dog	129
Competitor	dock	4
Baseline	jam	26

	Low-High group	Frequency
Item	robe	4
Competitor	road	317
Baseline	fish	30

	Low-Low group	Frequency
Item	swan	3
Competitor	swap	3
Baseline	trek	3

Across conditions, subjects always saw the same item as the visual probe. For example, FEEL is one of the 18 items in the High-High group (high-frequency items with high-frequency competitors). This item was preceded by one of three primes. So for the *feel, feed, name* set the visual probe FEEL was preceded either by the spoken word *feel*, by the competitor *feed*, or by the irrelevant prime *name*. When the probe is preceded by itself (visual FEEL is preceded by spoken *feel*), I refer to this as the *Same* priming condition. When the probe is preceded by a competitor word (FEEL is preceded by *feed*), I refer to this as the *Competitor* condition. And when the spoken word is both semantically and phonologically unrelated to the visual probe (FEEL preceded by *name*), I refer to this as the *Baseline* condition.[6]

Finally and most importantly, the auditory prime was either presented as a complete word (the late probe position) or as an incomplete fragment (the early probe position). In the early condition, subjects heard only the initial consonant and vowel of the word cut off 50 msec before the end of the vowel. We know from earlier research (Marslen-Wilson and Warren 1989, Warren and Marslen-Wilson 1987, 1988) that the nature of the final consonant is normally still indeterminate 50 msec before the end of the vowel preceding the consonant. Although the vowel out-transitions (the transitions out of the vowel into the next segment) contain partial cues to the manner, place, and voice of the final consonant, these cues only start to become available in the last 50 msec before vowel offset. This is corroborated by Isolation-Point results showing that words of this type first start to be reliably identified on average about 16 msec before the vowel offset (table 5).

The crucial condition in this experiment is therefore the early probe position. The visual probe appears immediately at the offset of the early prime, 50 msec before the end of the vowel, where the acoustic stimulus is still ambiguous between the item being probed and its competitor. Here, if anywhere, the transient effects of the competitor environment should be detectable. In the absence of clear sensory evidence to the contrary, the most highly activated candidate should be the most frequent one. This means that the effectiveness of an early prime in facilitating responses to the visual probe should depend on the frequency not only of the item but also of its competitor.

Specifically, the competitive activation hypothesis predicts that priming effects—the patterns of facilitation and interference—at the early position should reflect relative frequency of the items and the competitors. Thus, for High-Low stimuli, the system should facilitate the high item in both the early Same and early Competitor conditions. When the early prime [dɒ] is heard, for example, the candidate *dog*, being most frequent, should be more strongly activated than the competitor *dock* (see table 7), independently of whether the word that the fragment comes from is itself either *dog* or *dock*. This means that responses to the visual probe DOG will be facilitated relative to the baseline condition (responses following *jam*) in both the early Same and early Competitor conditions.

Conversely, for Low-High stimuli the system should favor the high competitor in both the Same and Competitor conditions, producing less (or even no) facilitation cross-modally. For the Low-High stimulus set in table 7, this means that the early prime [rəʊ] will initially trigger the strongest activation for the candidate *road* rather than the item *robe*. This in turn means that responses to the visual probe ROBE will tend not to be facilitated in either the early Same or the early Competitor condition.

Another way of looking at the predicted effects is in terms of the differences in the effectiveness of early and late Same primes across the four conditions. To the extent that the item approaches full activation at the early probe positions, there will be a relatively smaller increment at the late probe position, where we assume that the word in question is fully activated. Thus, if we look just at responses following same primes, the differential between early and late probe positions should be greatest for the Low-High case and smallest for the High-Low stimuli, with the High-High and Low-Low sets intermediate. Given the total amount of activation achievable by a given item (as reflected in the word-final probes), the extent to which an item achieves this at the early positions should reflect not only the frequency of the item itself, but also the frequency of its competitors.

The overall results of the experiment are summarized in table 8. This gives the mean response times for the three prime conditions (Same, Competitor, and Baseline) as a function of probe position—whether the visual probe occurred after an early or a late prime. The importance of these figures is that they show that one does obtain cross-modal priming effects using this paradigm and that these effects are tied to the relationship

Table 8
Overall effects of prime type and probe position (msec)

Probe position	Prime type		
	Same	Competitor	Baseline
Early	564	574	593
Late	467	624	592
Difference	−94	+50	−1

between the prime and the probe (as reflected in the strong interaction between prime type and probe position: $F(2, 136) = 113.46, p < .005$). In the Same prime condition there is a small amount of overall facilitation following the early probe (29 msec less than the baseline mean), with a big increase in facilitation following the late probe (125 msec faster than the baseline). The Competitor prime, in contrast, which also shows a small amount of facilitation at the early probe, shows evidence of marked interference following the late probe (32 msec slower than the baseline and 157 msec slower than the Same late prime). The baseline condition, in contrast, shows no effect at all of the early/late variable. Responses in this condition are clearly unaffected by the lexical identity of the prime.

Before moving on to look at the effects of probe position as a function of list type, we need to consider an unexpected aspect of the results. This is the finding of an effect of competitor frequency in the visual domain (table 9). These results are for the Baseline prime condition, where we know the auditory prime to be irrelevant to the subject's responses to the visual probes, since the early/late variaton has no effect in this condition. These results, collapsed across probe position, show that there *are* effects of competitor frequency both on response time and on error rate. Overall there is still an effect of item frequency ($F(1, 71) = 42.01, p < .005$), with high-frequency visual probes being responded to faster than low-frequency probes and with the same low error rate in both high-frequency conditions. For the low-frequency probes, however, we observed not only an effect of item frequency but also an effect of competitor frequency. Items in the Low-High group, with high-frequency close competitors, are responded to significantly more slowly than items in the Low-Low group and with a much higher error rate (subjects are much more likely to give a no response to a Low-High probe than to probes falling into any of the other conditions). Overall, there is not only an effect of competitor frequency for the Baseline condition ($F(1, 71) = 4.36, p < .05$) but also an interaction between Competitor and Item Frequency ($F(1, 71) = 6.16, p < .025$).

Table 9
Visual domain effects: responses following irrelevant primes

	Stimulus set			
	High-High	High-Low	Low-High	Low-Low
Mean response time (msec)	553	558	655	602
Percent error	2.9	1.6	13.3	6.0

Response times and errors are collapsed over probe positions (early/late).

Thus, although we could find no competitor frequency effect in auditory lexical decision, this effect is clearly present for visual lexical decision. For a number of reasons this is likely to be a real effect of competitor environment. First, we were able to demonstrate in a series of *post hoc* analyses that the visual probes for the four conditions are well matched for several variables that might otherwise have been sources of potential confounds. These variables include length in letters, bigram frequency, and neighborhood density (Coltheart et al. 1977). Second, in research published after we carried out the experiment described here, Grainger et al. (1989) report a similar effect for visually presented words in French. They do not find any effect of neighborhood size per se (as estimated by the method of Coltheart et al. 1977), but they do find an effect of having at least one orthographic neighbor of higher frequency than the stimulus word itself. This parallels the results here for the Low-Low and the Low-High groups, where the Low-High groups are defined as low-frequency words with at least one high-frequency neighbor.

I will return later in the paper to the implications of this visual-domain effect and of the resulting contrast between the modalities. In the meantime, the immediate practical implication of these findings is that we have to interpret the effects of the auditory prime in the Same and Competitor conditions as modulating competitor and item frequency effects that are already present in the visual domain. Remember that we assumed that these effects are mediated by the central, modality-independent entry for each lexical item, into which the inputs from each modality are fed. With this in mind I turn to the detailed results for these conditions.

The first set of predictions concerned the pattern of facilitation and interference at the early probe position, where the sensory input is still relatively ambiguous. The hypothesis here was that the responses should reflect the properties of the most frequent candidate, irrespective of whether it was the item or its competitor.

Figure 4 displays the relative amounts of facilitation (computed as differences between test and baseline scores) for the four frequency conditions at the early probe positions. The effects here follow the prediction: effects in both the Same and Competitor conditions are dictated by the most frequent candidate, irrespective of whether it is actually being heard or not.

The two critical conditions are High-Low and Low-High, where there is a large frequency asymmetry between the item and its closest cohort competitor. We observed for the High-Low group that there are large and equivalent amounts of facilitation following both the Same and the Competitor early prime (43 and 32 msec, respectively). That is, in each case the

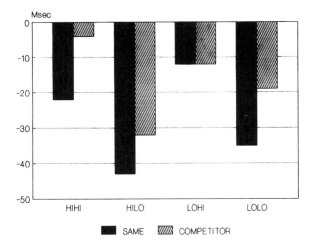

Figure 4
Facilitation effects (test versus baseline) at the early probe position plotted as a
function of experimental condition and prime type (Same or Competitor)

system is behaving as if the high-frequency Same prime is being heard. On
the other hand, for the Low-High group, where we can assume the competitor to be dominant, the amount of facilitation is very small for both prime
conditions (12 msec in each).

The two balanced frequency conditions (Low-Low and High-High)
produce intermediate effects. The slight asymmetry that these two conditions show in the effects of Same versus Competitor primes (also evident in
the High-Low condition) may reflect phonetic cues in the signal that are
starting to point to one candidate rather than another, even 50 msec before
vowel offset. Note that the Low-Low same prime, at 36 msec, is almost as
facilitating as the High-Low Same prime, at 43 msec. This matches the
pattern observed for the Isolation-Point data (table 5).

Figure 5 looks at the effects of the early Same primes from a different
perspective. It analyzes them in terms of the relative increase in facilitation
from the early to the late conditions. To the extent that the word is already
facilitated at the early position, lexical-decision responses to the visual
probe will benefit relatively less by hearing more of the word. The bar graph
gives the differences between test and baseline scores for the Same prime
condition at the early and late probe positions. The line graph gives the
increase from early to late as a percentage of the total amount of facilitation
at the late position (when all of the word has been heard).

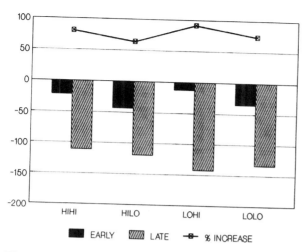

Figure 5
Lower panel (bar graph): facilitation effects in msec (test versus baseline) for the Same primes at early and late probe positions. Upper panel (line graph): the percent increase in facilitation from early to late expressed as a percentage of total facilitation at the late position

For the High-Low condition the item is expected to be relatively highly activated at the early position, since it is not only highly frequent itself but also has only low-frequency competitors. Here the increase from early to late is 64 percent. For the Low-High case, however, where one would predict very little facilitation of the low-frequency item at the early position, the increase is 92 percent. The Low-Low and High-High cases fall in between, with percent increases from early to late of 74 and 80 percent respectively.

This pattern of results, like the early effects displayed in figure 4, supports the hypothesis that evolved out of the first round of experiments. As the Isolation-Point gating results suggest, if one tests at a point in the word where its identity is still uncertain, level of activation reflects the relative frequency of different candidates.

To complete the presentation of the response times, figure 6 gives the results at the late probe position for the Competitor as well as for the Same primes. These results are for conditions in which the subject has heard all of the auditory prime word before seeing the visual target. Noteworthy here—an effect that bears more, perhaps, on the nature of the cross-modal effects involved—is the way in which frequency modulates the effects of the Competitor prime. Hearing the entire Competitor prime produces no

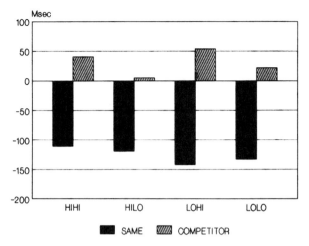

Figure 6
Facilitation and interference effects (test versus baseline) at the late probe
position plotted as a function of experimental condition and prime type (Same
or Competitor)

interference effects in the High-Low case. If the high-frequency visual
probe DOG is preceded by the complete low-frequency spoken word *dock*,
this produces no interference relative to the baseline condition. But in the
Low-High case, where a low-frequency visual probe like ROBE is preceded
by its complete high-frequency competitor (*road*), there is a marked increase in latency of 54 msec, which contrasts with the 6 msec increase for
the High-Low case. The Low-Low and High-High conditions, with interference effects for the late Competitor primes of 22 msec and 41 msec,
respectively, again show an intermediate pattern, but with the high-
frequency competitor clearly producing more interference than the low-
frequency one.

Finally, table 10 gives the details of the error rate for each combination
of experimental conditions. These error effects mirror, and in some cases
accentuate, the pattern obtained for response times. Apart from the overall
difference between high- and low-frequency probes—there are very few
errors in any of the conditions with high-frequency items—the most
striking effect is the error rate following late Competitor primes in the
Low-High condition. False negative responses (saying that a real word is
a nonword) are already high (13 percent) in the Low-High baseline conditions (in comparison with 6 percent for the Low-Low and an average of 2
percent for the High-Low and High-High conditions). But when the Low-

Tabel 10
Percentage of Errors (False Negatives)

| | Prime type | | | | | |
| | Same | | Competitor | | Baseline | |
Probe position	Early	Late	Early	Late	Early	Late
High-High	0.5	0.0	1.1	5.0	3.7	2.1
High-Low	2.5	1.0	1.5	2.1	0.6	2.5
Low-High	10.0	3.1	10.5	22.9	13.0	13.7
Low-Low	5.4	2.1	4.3	12.4	4.7	7.2

High visual probe is preceded by the complete Competitor prime, the error rate jumps to a remarkable 23 percent, which mirrors the large interference effect in figure 6. This is in contrast to an error rate of 12 percent in the Low-Low late Competitor condition and of only 2 percent in the comparable High-Low condition.

Conclusions

The key to understanding the pattern of results over the four experiments reported here turns out to be the unlooked-for contrast between the visual and auditory domains. In tasks like auditory lexical decision and repetition we saw no effects of competitor frequency. These emerged only when we probed early in the spoken word, before sufficient sensory information had become available to discriminate the between the item and its competitor. In contrast, in visual lexical decision—looking now at the responses in the baseline condition, where the auditory prime was irrelevant to the visual decision—we did see an effect of competitor frequency, without presenting incomplete or ambiguous stimuli.

How are we to explain these contrasts? We can do so as follows. In both the auditory and the visual domains there are immediate *transient* effects of frequency, triggered as soon as the relevant form representations are activated. It is possible, for example, that lexical representations corresponding to more-frequent words can be activated earlier, or on the basis of less input, than representations of less-frequent words. In any event, these effects have a time course, so that the early advantage of more-frequent candidates will rapidly become subsidiary to the dominant effects of the sensory input.

In *audition* the discriminating sensory input arrives relatively slowly over time, often as much as 400 to 500 msec downstream of the point at which cohort members start to get activated. By the time this discriminating input does arrive, given that subjects are waiting to make their responses until this point (as our auditory tasks clearly required), the *competitor*-frequency effect will have dissipated. All that is left is item-frequency effects, and these may even be postperceptual effects and not directly dependent on levels of activation.

In *vision*, by contrast, there is not this same gross temporal asynchrony between the arrival of the frequency effect, the arrival of the sensory information necessary for making the decision, and the initiation of the decision by the perceiver. This means that the competitor-frequency effects are still active (especially for low-frequency words) at the decision point. And since the lexical-decision task is a kind of signal-detection task, any factor that reduces the difference between signal and noise will both slow down responses and increase the number of false negatives.

In summary, the fact that we observed a competitor-frequency effect for visual lexical decision but not for auditory lexical decision reflects fundamental differences in the way information is delivered over time. This in turn reflects the contrasts between the two modalities in sequentiality and simultaneity. The state of affairs depicted in figure 2, which shows how competitor frequency should modulate item recognition time, does not, therefore, hold true for the auditory domain. The underlying processing mechanisms seem to be fundamentally the same in both modalities, being based on the same processes of competition between multiply activated candidates, but the way in which this competition affects access and recognition may, after all, be very different.

Acknowledgments

The research reported here developed out of a series of preparatory experiments carried out in collaboration with Colin Brown of the Max-Planck Institute for Psycholinguistics in Nijmegen. I am most grateful for his contribution. I would also like to thank Marie Jefsioutine, Vera Kamphuis, and Paul Warren for their help in running experiments 1 to 3. The cross-modal study was carried out under my supervision, and with the help of Paul Warren, by Martin Torevell and Chris Phillips as a third-year undergraduate project in the Department of Experimental Psychology at the University of Cambridge. I would also like to thank Lorraine Tyler for help and advice throughout. This research was supported by an MRC program grant awarded to myself and Lorraine Tyler.

Notes

1. These claims are being made about a task (cross-modal semantic priming) that involves high-level lexical representations operating at a modality-independent

level and in a semantic domain. In other tasks—for example, auditory-auditory form priming—it is possible that other kinds of prime-target relations will be effective, especially if the tasks are sensitive to low-level priming within a single modality.

2. We also attempted to hold constant across the four sets the phonetic relatedness of the competitors. We roughly balanced the nature of the differences in manner and place features between close competitors and items.

3. I use the term *repetition* here rather than *naming* because the use of the latter term makes it all too easy to treat as equivalent the task of reading a written word aloud with the task of repeating a word one has just heard. Both tasks involve producing a word, but the input routes are so different that I think different terms should be used.

4. The 80 percent criterion is relatively arbitrary. It could be 70 or 90 percent without greatly changing the location of the recognition point. But it is a sufficiently stringent criterion to ensure that the word really is definitely identifiable at this point in the gating sequence.

5. Not all of the test words in the first stimulus set had competitors with the appropriate properties to be presented as stimuli.

6. For the conditions where the item and competitor differed in frequency, the frequency of the baseline prime was set at a subjective midpoint between the frequency of the two test words.

References

Coltheart, M., Davelaar, E., Jonasson, J. T., and Besner, D. 1977. Access to the internal lexicon. In S. Dornic (ed.), *Attention and Performance*, vol. 6. New York: Academic Press.

Grainger, J., O'Regan, J. K., Jacobs, A. M., and Segui, J. 1989. On the role of competing word units in visual word recognition: The neighborhood frequency effect. *Perception and Psychophysics* 45: 189–195.

Grosjean, F. 1980. Spoken word-recognition processes and the gating paradigm. *Perception and Psychophysics* 28: 267–283.

Luce, P. A. 1986. Neighborhoods of words in the mental lexicon. Doctoral dissertation. Indiana University, Bloomington, Indiana.

McClelland, J. L., and Elman, J. L. 1986. The TRACE model of speech perception. *Cognitive Psychology* 18: 1–86.

Marslen-Wilson, W. D. 1985. Speed shadowing and speech comprehension. *Speech Communication* 4: 55–73.

Marslen-Wilson, W. D. 1987. Functional parallelism in spoken word-recognition. *Cognition* 25: 71–102.

Marslen-Wilson, W. D., and Tyler, L. K. 1980. The temporal structure of spoken language understanding. *Cognition* 8: 1–71.

Marslen-Wilson, W. D., van Halen, S., and Moss, H. 1988. Distance and competition in lexical access. Paper presented at the Psychonomics Society Meeting, Chicago.

Marslen-Wilson, W. D., and Warren, P. W. 1989. The lexical interpretation of phonetic cues. Manuscript submitted for publication.

Marslen-Wilson, W. D., and Welsh, A. 1978. Processing interactions and lexical access during word recognition in continuous speech. *Cognitive Psychology* 10: 29–63.

Marslen-Wilson, W. D., and Zwitserlood, P. 1989. Accessing spoken words: The importance of word onsets. *Journal of Experimental Psychology: Human Perception and Performance* 15: 576–585.

Monsell, S. 1990. The nature and locus of word frequency effects in reading. In D. Besner and G. W. Humphreys (eds.), *Basic processes in reading: Visual word recognition*. Hillsdale, N.J.: Erlbaum, in press.

Monsell, S., Doyle, M. C., and Haggard, P. N. 1989. Effects of frequency on visual word recognition tasks: Where are they? *Journal of Experimental Psychology: General* 118: 43–71.

Moss, H., Marslen-Wilson, W. D. 1989. Perceptual distance and competition in lexical access. Paper presented at the Experimental Psychology Society meeting, London, January.

Seidenberg, M. 1989. Visual word recognition and pronunciation: A computational model and its consequences. In W. D. Marslen-Wilson (ed.), *Lexical Representation and Process*. Cambridge: MIT Press.

Tyler, L. K. 1984. The structure of the initial cohort: Evidence from gating. *Perception and Psychophysics* 36: 417–427.

Warren, P., and Marslen-Wilson, W. D. 1987. Continuous uptake of acoustic cues in spoken word-recognition. *Perception and Psychophysics* 41: 262–275.

Warren, P., and Marslen-Wilson, W. D. 1988. Cues to lexical choice: Discriminating place and voice. *Perception and Psychophysics* 43: 21–30.

Zwitserlood, P. 1989. The locus of the effects of sentential-semantic context in spoken-word processing. *Cognition* 32: 25–64.

Chapter 8

Retroactive Influence of Syllable Neighborhoods	Jan Charles-Luce, Paul A. Luce, and Michael S. Cluff

The issue addressed by Richard Shillcock (this volume) and Anne Cutler (this volume) is how words in the absence of reliable phonetic cues to word boundaries are accessed in continuous speech. In part both Shillcock and Cutler showed effects of non-word-initial syllables on lexical access. Shillcock demonstrated that lexical hypotheses are initiated for noninitial syllables in monomorphemic bisyllabic words. In a cross-modal priming task he found that subjects' lexical decision times were faster when the visual probe was semantically related, rather than semantically unrelated, to the second syllable. For example, when auditorily presented *trombone*, subjects were faster to respond when the visual probe was *rib* than when it was *bun*. Shillcock suggests that the second syllable of *trombone* produced an independent lexical hypothesis that primed *rib*. Shillcock argues that these results are inconsistent with theories advocating sequential, deterministic parsing of the speech signal into words. Noninitial stressed syllables may initiate independent lexical hypotheses even though initial syllables may be unresolved (e.g., *trom-*).

Furthermore, lexical access may not always operate in a strictly left-to-right manner, and information carried in noninitial syllables may be important in helping to resolve preceding syllables. Cutler demonstrates that detecting the word *mint* embedded as the first syllable of a bisyllabic nonword takes longer in a strong-strong sequence (e.g., *mintayf* [mɪntef]) than in a strong-weak sequence (e.g., *mintef* [mɪntəf]). Cutler argues that in the strong-strong sequence (*mintayf*), lexical access is initiated twice, once for each strong syllable (see also Cutler and Norris 1988). Information from the end of the first syllable may be initially segmented as belonging to the second syllable. As a result, *mintayf* is initially segmented as *min-tayf*. When no word is found corresponding to the input of the second syllable, the listener must reassemble the missegmented speech signal to access the word *mint*. Consequently, detection times for *mint* are slowed in the strong-strong sequence as compared to the strong-weak sequence, where the initial segmentation is *mint-ef*. According to Cutler's model, weak syllables do not initiate segmentation. Hence, missegmentation does not occur, and no competition for [-t-] between syllables occurs in *mintef*. Thus when the bisyllabic word is strong-weak, only one lexical hypothesis is initiated because there is only one strong syllable. The *mintayf*-versus-*mintef* results show that noninitial syllabic contexts may affect resolution of preceding ambiguous syllables in lexical access. Strict left-to-right models of word recognition are not sufficient when missegmentation occurs and can only be successful if they allow some sort of principled backtracking during hypothesis matching.

Thus Shillcock's and Cutler's individual findings in part suggest that lexical access may not be a strictly sequential and deterministic process. Moreover, there is some evidence that a noninitial syllabic context may be significant in the resolution of a first syllable. However, retroactive resolution may depend not only on such factors as strong versus weak syllables, but also on the neighborhood structure of the individual syllables. To demonstrate this point, consider the results of a perceptual-identification task investigating spliced and natural spondees (Cluff and Luce 1989). A spondee is a bisyllabic, bimorphemic word composed of two monosyllabic, monomorphemic words. In English, spondees are compound words composed of varying parts of speech, for example, adjective + noun (*lighthouse*), noun + noun (*fencepost*), or verb + verb (*hearsay*). Note that spondees, while generally receiving primary stress on the first syllable, are metrically composed of two strong syllables. The second syllable is never phonetically reduced and therefore is never a weak syllable. Cluff and Luce found that the identification of an initial syllable occurring in a high-density, high-frequency neighborhood can be facilitated by a second syllable occurring in a low-density, low-frequency neighborhood.

Research by Luce (1986) has shown that identification of monosyllabic words is affected by stimulus-word frequency, neighborhood density, and neighborhood frequency (see also Luce, Pisoni, and Goldinger, this volume). Neighborhood density is defined as the number of words that are phonetically similar to the target word. Thus words may be in dense neighborhoods with many phonetically similar words or in sparse neighborhoods with few phonetically similar words. Neighborhood frequency refers to the frequency of the words within the neighborhood. Words may be in a neighborhood with high-frequency neighbors or in a neighborhood with low-frequency neighbors. In a perceptual identification task Luce found that performance increased as stimulus-word frequency increased and decreased as neighborhood density and neighborhood frequency increased. However, these results were based only on consonant-vowel-consonant (CVC) monosyllabic words. The purpose of the spondee investigation by Cluff and Luce was to extend the findings from monosyllabic words to bisyllabic words. In particular, the purpose was to determine how the neighborhood characteristics of each syllable of a spondee affect lexical access.

As already mentioned, spondees in general receive primary stress on the first syllable. Grosjean and Gee (1987) have proposed that stressed syllables are recognized first and that they provide the acoustic information necessary to initiate lexical access (see Cutler, this volume, and Cutler and Norris, 1988). However, because Cluff and Luce were interested in determining how neighborhood characteristics affect lexical access of bisyllabic words, stress was initially controlled. In the first set of results discussed below, stress was controlled for by digitally splicing together monosyllabic words that correspond with the two syllables of naturally occurring spondees. For example, for the spondee *lighthouse*, *light* and *house* were first recorded as individual words and then digitally spliced together using a waveform editor. These stimuli will be referred to as spliced spondees. The initial intent, then, was to determine the effects of similarity neighborhoods on syllables while controlling for possible stress differences across syllables.

Each syllable of the spondees had the pattern consonant-vowel-consonant, vowel-consonant, or consonant-vowel. To ensure that subjects had encountered the spondees previously, only spondees with a subjective familiarity rating of 4 or above on a 7-point scale were chosen, where 4 means familiar with the word but uncertain of its meaning and 7 means know the word and its meaning (Nusbaum, Pisoni, and Davis 1984). For the monosyllables composing the spliced spondees, only those with familiarity ratings of 6 or above were used. For both spondees and the monosyllables composing the spondees, familiarity and frequency were approximately equal across conditions. Frequency of spondees and monosyllables was determined by the Kučera and Francis (1967) word count.

In addition to these criteria for stimuli selection, frequency-weighted transitional probabilities were determined to ensure that the transitional probabilities from the first to the second syllable within a spondee and from the second to the first syllable within a spondee were approximately equal across conditions. The probabilities were computed using Webster's lexicon by determining the number of possible final syllables for a given

Table 1
Examples of spondee patterns

Pattern	Example
Easy-easy	jigsaw
Easy-hard	causeway
Hard-easy	bucksaw
Hard-hard	hearsay

initial syllable and the number of possible initial syllables for a given final syllable.

To gauge the effects of neighborhood density and neighborhood frequency, four sets of spliced spondees were created by independently manipulating the neighborhoods of each monosyllable of the spondees. (See Cluff and Luce 1989 for a detailed description of how neighborhoods were computed.) A monosyllable was either hard or easy. *Easy* signifies that the monosyllable is a high-frequency word in a low-density, low-frequency neighborhood. *Hard* signifies that the monosyllable is a low-frequency word in a high-density, high-frequency neighborhood. Thus, a spondee may have one of four bisyllabic patterns: easy-easy, easy-hard, hard-easy, and hard-hard. Examples of each of the four pattern types are presented in table 1.

Thirty-six spondees for each pattern type, a total of 144 spondees, were auditorily presented with a background of white noise at a signal-to-noise ratio of $+5$ dB. The subjects' task was to type the spondee they thought they heard.

Figure 1 shows the percentages of spliced spondees correctly identified. Each bar represents the mean percent correct averaged across first and second syllables for each pattern type.

The results of a one-way analysis of variance performed on the overall percent correct identification showed that subjects were best at identifying easy-easy spondees and worst at identifying hard-hard spondees ($F(3, 111) = 51.83, p < 0.05$). Thus performance is best when both syllables are in low-density, low-frequency neighborhoods. Performance is worst when both syllables are in high-density, high-frequency neighborhoods. Furthermore, Tukey Honestly Significantly Different tests revealed that percent correct identification differed significantly between all syllable structures. Easy-easy spondees were recognized most accurately, followed by hard-easy, easy-hard, and hard-hard spondees ($p < 0.05$). Thus identification is better for the hard-easy spondees than for the easy-hard

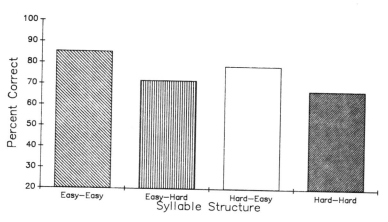

Figure 1
Percent correct identification of spliced spondees

spondees, which suggests differential effects of neighborhood structure on first and second syllables. To determine the locus of this asymmetry between hard-easy and easy-hard spondees, identification performance for the individual syllables making up the spondees was tested with an analysis of variance that was 2 × 2 × 2 (neighborhood structure × syllable position × neighborhood structure of the paired syllable). Percentages of correct identification by syllable type are shown in figure 2.

Easy syllables were recognized more accurately than hard syllables $(F(1, 37) = 165.93, p < 0.05)$. Second syllables were identified more accurately than first syllables $(F(1, 37) = 17.29, p < 0.05)$. Finally, syllables that were paired with easy syllables were recognized more accurately than those that were paired with hard syllables, regardless of neighborhood structure $(F(1, 33) = 18.34, p < 0.05)$.

The results for the second syllables show a systematic effect of neighborhood structure. Easy second syllables are identified more accurately than hard second syllables, regardless of the neighborhood structure of the first syllable. This was not the case, however, for the first syllables. Identification of easy first syllables is lower in easy-hard spondees compared with easy-easy spondees. Stated otherwise, a following hard syllable reduces perceptual identification of a hard first syllable. On the other hand, identification of a hard first syllable improves when a second syllable is easy in comparison with when they are hard. In fact, hard first syllables in hard-easy spondees were identified with an accuracy closer to that of easy first syllables and were not significantly different from easy syllables in easy-

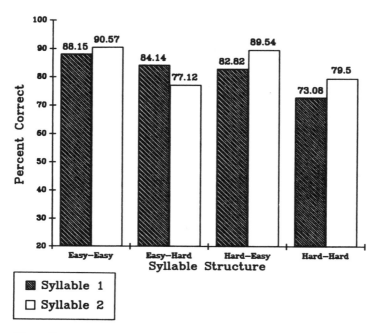

Figure 2
Percentages of correctly identified spliced spondees by syllable type

hard spondees ($p > 0.05$). This suggests that the identification of a hard first syllable was improved by a more easily recognized second syllable.

The results from the spliced spondees suggest, then, that there is some retroactive influence from the second to the first syllable in identification performance. Most interesting, an easy second syllable appears to help identification of a hard first syllable. Thus, a syllable in a low-density, low-frequency neighborhood may help resolve preceding ambiguity of a syllable in a high-density, high-frequency neighborhood. Where an earlier syllable cannot be resolved because of competition among its neighbors, a following easy syllable appears to aid in the resolution of hard syllables and consequently benefits lexical access to the whole word.[1]

Recall that stress was controlled in the spliced spondees. For those spondees each syllable was produced as a single word and then digitally spliced together to construct the spondee. In the next set of results the same 144 spondees were recorded in their entirety, rather than as component monosyllables. They were recorded in the same manner and by the same talker as the spliced spondees. The same four patterns and the same 36 spondees in each pattern type were used. Thus naturally produced easy-

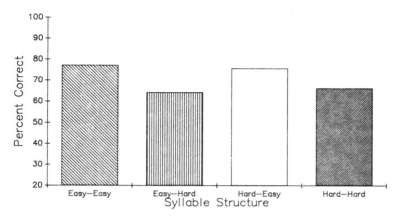

Figure 3
Percent correct identification of natural spondees

easy, easy-hard, hard-easy, and hard-hard spondees were presented for identification at a signal-to-noise ratio of +5 dB. The task was identical to the spliced spondee condition.

The results for the naturally produced spondees are presented in figure 3. Percent correct identification averaged across first and second syllables is given for each pattern type.

The results from the naturally produced spondees replicate the pattern of results from the spliced spondees. A one-way analysis of variance performed on overall spondee identification showed a main effect of neighborhood structure ($F(3, 99) = 33.36$, $p < 0.05$). Furthermore, when both syllables were in low-density, low-frequency (easy) neighborhoods, identification was better than when both syllables were in high-density, high-frequency (hard) neighborhoods (Tukey Honestly Significant Difference [HSD], $p < 0.05$). Also, identification is better when the second syllable is easy in comparison with when it is hard (Tukey HSD, $p < 0.05$).

Although the pattern of results is consistent with the spliced condition, overall identification for the natural spondees is somewhat attenuated from the spliced spondees. The overall decrement in performance appears to be due entirely to the second syllable. Percent correct is virtually identical for the first syllables for both the spliced and natural spondee conditions. This attenuation may be due to the fact that the second syllable does not carry primary stress. One consequence of this might be that the second syllable is less stressed and therefore somewhat shorter in duration in the natural condition than the spliced condition, where the second syllable was produced as an isolated word. However, measurements of each syllable showed that the mean duration of the second syllable is not shorter than the first syllable, irrespective of the syllable neighborhoods. Therefore, some other acoustic parameter associated with the production of the second syllables must explain the attentuation in performance (e.g., less clearly articulated overall, lower amplitude or pitch).

Nonetheless, the results from the natural spondees again show that the neighborhoods of the first syllables have little effect on the identification of the second syllables. We again performed an analysis of variance that was $2 \times 2 \times 2$ (neighborhood structure $\times$ syllable position $\times$ neighborhood structure of paired syllable) on accuracy scores for the individual syllables. Figure 4 shows percent correct identification for each pattern type for the natural spondee condition.

As with the spliced spondees, easy syllables were recognized more accurately than hard syllables ($F(1, 33) = 78.58, p < 0.05$), and syllables paired with easy syllables were recognized more accurately than those paired with hard syllables ($F(1, 33) = 5.76, p < 0.05$). The suggestion that overall at-

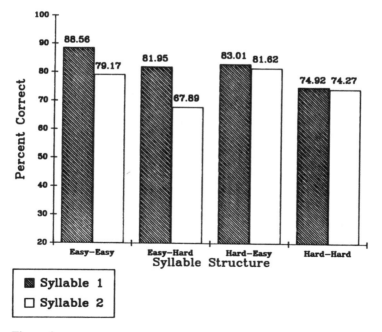

Figure 4
Percentages of correctly identified natural spondees by syllable type

tenuation of the results in the natural condition relative to the spliced condition is due to the second syllable was also confirmed. Second syllables were recognized less accurately overall than first syllables ($F(1, 33) = 146.00$, $p < 0.05$).

The results from natural spondees suggest the retroactive influence of second syllables. Easy-easy spondees are recognized more accurately than hard-hard spondees (Tukey HSD, $p < 0.05$). Furthermore, identification is better for the hard-easy spondees than for the easy-hard spondees, which reflects the asymmetrical effects of neighborhood structure on first and second syllables (Tukey HSD, $p < 0.05$). In particular, note that identification increases for hard first syllables when the second syllables are easy. As before, performance on hard first syllables for hard-easy spondees was not significantly different from performance on easy first syllables in easy-hard spondees (Tukey HSD, $p > 0.05$).

To summarize the two sets of spondee data, there appears to be differential effects of neighborhood structure on first and second syllables. An asymmetry in identification performance was found between hard-easy spondees and easy-hard spondees, regardless of whether the spondees were spliced or natural. Mean percent correct across syllables showed that identification was better for hard-easy than for easy-hard spondees. We suggest that this is the consequence of noninitial easy syllables' retroactively aiding in resolving the ambiguity of initial hard syllables. In general, spondees have a strong-strong metrical syllable structure because they have a primary-secondary stress pattern rather than a primary-reduced stress pattern. The second syllable never completely reduces to a schwa (ə). Assuming Cutler's model of lexical access (that is, strong syllables initiate lexical hypotheses), we believe lexical hypotheses are initiated independently for each syllable of the spondee (see Cutler and Carter 1987 and also Grosjean and Gee 1987). In addition, not only is there competition among neighbors of individual syllables of spondees; the easy second syllable also appears to retroactively facilitate access to the hard first syllable from among its neighbors.

Therefore, overall success in accessing a polysyllabic word may depend upon the composition of the word in terms of neighborhood characteristics of each syllable. We suggest that syllables may be activated independently and then assembled into words at a higher lexical node. Obviously, however, not all syllables will be complete words in and of themselves, as are the syllables composing a spondee. Nonetheless, it is reasonable to hypothesize that for such bisyllabic, monomorphemic words like *trombone*, two lexical hypotheses (one for each of the strong syllables) are initiated, as Shillcock's data (this volume) indicate. Morever, this also follows from the evidence suggesting that strong syllables boot lexical access.

Furthermore, as according to a syllable-based model of lexical access and recognition, the neighborhoods activated by each strong syllable may interact to facilitate the correction of erroneous lexical hypotheses. To again borrow one of Shillcock's stimuli as an example, for the word *trombone*, two independent lexical hypotheses are initiated by each of the strong syllables, *trom-* and -*bone*. We propose that the independent syllable hypotheses are resolved at some point and then assembled to access the single word *trombone*. Depending upon the neighborhoods activated by each syllable, lexical access of a bisyllabic word may be facilitated retroactively if the second syllable is in a low-density, low-frequency neighborhood. Access may not be facilitated if the second syllable is in a high-density, high-frequency neighborhood.

In words like Shillcock's pseudoprefixed bisyllabic words, the initial syllable is phonetically reduced and is therefore a weak syllable. Again on the assumption of Cutler's model, the weak initial syllables (prefixes) should not initiate lexical hypotheses or even segmentation (see Grosjean and Gee 1987). Although this is less clear at this time, we can conjecture that the second syllable acts retroactively to help resolve whether the preceding phonetic information is included with the second syllable or whether it stands alone as a function word (e.g., *a* in *avoid* versus *a void*). Thus, although prefixes cannot initiate lexical hypotheses in Cutler's model, it is possible that noninitial stressed syllables help to integrate the preceding syllable information retroactively.

We should note, however, that Shillcock (personal communication) may not agree with the argument of a syllable-based model of lexical access. In his cross-modal priming data he sees no evidence that *re-* in *report* would not activate lexical hypotheses for such words as *read* or *rim*. He attributes the failure in his study to activate the second syllables of pseudoprefixed words (e.g., -*port*) to competition from the longer words (*report*). However, where second syllables are activated in monomorphemic bisyllabic words (e.g., *trombone*), Shillcock feels that more likely to occur are coexisting, overlapping lexical hypotheses (*trombone* and *bone*) rather than independent syllable hypotheses that are later assembled at a lexical node.

Nonetheless, the combined findings from Shillcock, Cutler, and the spondee data suggest that non-word-initial strong syllables activate lexical hypotheses. Moreover, the spondee data suggest that noninitial syllables may retroactively influence the integration of preceding syllabic information. Specifically, when noninitial syllables are in low-frequency, low-density neighborhoods, they facilitate identification of initial syllables in high-frequency, high-density neighborhoods. As Shillcock and Cutler note for their own results, strict sequential models of lexical access cannot account for all aspects of lexical access in continuous speech. In particular, with regard to the spondee data, such models cannot account for the evidence showing that non-word-initial syllables in low-density, low-frequency neighborhoods help retroactively resolve initial syllables in high-density, high-frequency neighborhoods.

Acknowledgments

This work was supported by NIH Research Grant NS-12179 and NIH Training Grant NS-7134 to Indiana University. We would like to thank Gerry Altmann, Cynthia Connine, and Richard Shillcock for many helpful comments.

Note

1. It could be argued that the asymmetries in the data arise from differences in predictability from one monosyllable to another in the four cells. For example, *light* in *lighthouse* may predict *house* more than *hear* in *hearsay* predicts *say*. Two arguments can be leveled at such an objection. First, as previously mentioned, the frequency-weighted transitional probabilites were computed to assure no asymmetries in prediction from one monosyllable to the other. Second, as an empirical check on possible differences in prediction, Cluff and Luce (1989) recently completed a series of experiments using nonword spondees composed of the same monosyllables used in the present studies. If the various cells differed in predictability, one would expect the nonword spondees to show differential effects of predictability. This was not the case. In fact, for the nonword spondees, none of the asymmetries observed for the words were obtained.

References

Cluff, M. S., and Luce, P. A. 1989. Neighborhoods of spondees in spoken word recognition. Under review.

Cutler, A., and Carter, D. M. 1987. The predominance of strong initial syllables in the English vocabulary. *Computer Speech and Language* 2:133–142.

Cutler, A., and Norris, D. G. 1988. The role of strong syllables in segmentation for lexical access. *Journal of Experimental Psychology: Human Perception and Performance* 14:113–121.

Grosjean, F., and Gee, J. 1987. Prosodic structure and spoken word recognition. *Cognition* 25:135–155.

Kučera, F., and Francis, W. 1967. *Computational Analysis of Present Day American English.* Providence: Brown University Press.

Luce, P. A. 1986. Neighborhoods of words in the mental lexicon. Research on Speech Perception, technical report no. 6. Speech Research Laboratory, Psychology Department, Indiana University, Bloomington.

Nusbaum, H. C., Pisoni, D. B., and Davis, C. K. 1984. Sizing up the Hoosier mental lexicon: Measuring the familiarity of 20,000 words. In Research on speech perception, progress report no. 10, Speech Research Laboratory, Psychology Department, Indiana University, Bloomington.

Chapter 9

Competition, Lateral Inhibition, and Frequency: Comments on the Chapters of Frauenfelder and Peeters, Marslen-Wilson, and Others

Ellen Gurman Bard

It is now generally accepted that as listeners attend to a spoken word, they are simultaneously entertaining many candidate identities for it. The papers in this volume by Marslen-Wilson and by Frauenfelder and Peeters address models which explain how the competition among such candidates is realized. Competition models are attractive because they can account both for the recognition of isolated objects and for the segmentation of an individual object from a background in the same sensory modality. The price of this power is complexity, and the task which the authors of these two papers have set themselves is the exploration of some of that complexity.

Frauenfelder and Peeters agree with Marslen-Wilson that a spoken word is likely to be perceived as one of its candidate identities to the extent that the phonetic representation of the spoken word resembles the phonological representation of the candidate. The authors also agree, along the lines common to the cohort (Marslen-Wilson 1987) and TRACE models (McClelland and Elman 1986), that this sort of similarity provides a graded *bottom-up* contribution to the activation levels of the various lexical candidates.[1] Several areas are still under dispute: whether the *frequency of occurrence* of a word candidate also affects its activation level, whether competition among candidates involves *lateral inhibition*, and whether the *perceptual-choice criterion* determining when a candidate is recognized depends on the ratio of its activation level to total activation (as in the Luce (1959) choice rule used in TRACE) or only on the comparison with its closest competitor (as Marslen-Wilson effectively proposes).

The difficulty of reconciling their claims has several sources. First, there are differences in kind among the features of interest with respect both to their empirical verifiability and to their interrelationships. Second, competition models of word recognition are necessarily so complex that many of their characteristics remain unsupported by behavioral data. For this reason, arguments which appear to support a particular model may have to be taken more modestly to support some feature of that model and hence to count in favor of any model which allows the crucial feature the right sort of predictive value.

With this in mind I will begin by concentrating on the role of competition in recognition. Here I will discuss the difference between the features of competition models on which both Marslen-Wilson's and Frauenfelder and Peeters' papers focus: word frequency and lateral inhibition. Then I will assess the evidence presented for the involvement of these features in lexical access, and I will offer resolutions to some apparent contradictions. Finally, I will turn to the role of competition in the segmentation of words in running speech. Within a TRACE-like mechanism I will exemplify the framework I have established and show how this sort of competition model might account for word-segmentation results like those of Cutler (this volume), Cutler and Norris (1988), Butterfield and Cutler (1988), Shillcock (this volume), and Frauenfelder and Peeters (this volume) while retaining those features which account for effects in isolated-word recognition. If the full advantage of a competition model is to be realized, the model should have a form which makes this generalization possible.

Frequency and Lateral Inhibition in Lexical Access

The most obvious distinction to be made between frequency and lateral inhibition is that frequency is a property of a word and lateral inhibition is a property of a system of competition. The effects of frequency can be explored in a number of different tasks (Gernsbacher 1984, Brown and Watson 1987, Balota and Chumbley 1985), and predictions from these can be made about the expected results in word recognition. Making predictions about lateral inhibition is more complicated.

Because lateral inhibition is a characteristic of the way a system behaves, where a system is designed to model a particular behavior, its role cannot be determined by examining any tasks which the system does not model. It is not possible to take an independent measure of the degree of lateral inhibition which operates between two words like *dog* and *dock* and determine from that how long the recognition of *dock* should be delayed because *dog* is inhibiting it. In fact, it is difficult to make any predictions about the effects of lateral inhibition even in a straightforward instance of the task in question: the effects will depend on the parameters of the model and their settings. In models like TRACE there are many parameters to set. How much a very active competitor delays the recognition of another word depends on the function relating the activation of each competitor to the inhibition it contributes, the number of competitors permitted to contribute inhibition, limits placed on inhibition, etc., as well as on the prior activation level of the recipient of the inhibition and the decision rule which determines when any candidate can be recognized. Without accepting an entourage of parameter settings, we cannot make quantitative predictions.

Unfortunately, a model with lateral inhibition does not generally offer qualitative predictions which can be distinguished from those of mechanisms lacking inhibition. This is because lateral inhibition does not affect the ordinal characteristics of response strengths. The item most active on the grounds of bottom-up similarity to the stimulus and/or of frequency of occurrence will be the most active item after lateral inhibition is applied. What will have changed is the degree to which it is the most active. Because lateral inhibition makes the rich get richer and the poor get poorer, it will exaggerate differences, but it will never reverse their direction. For example, a model with lateral inhibition and one with simple, activation-based competition will both predict that the presence of competitors, particularly strong competitors, will delay the recognition of a stimulus. If lateral inhibition operates, the delay will be due to the flattening of the activation curve of the leading candidate through inhibition *and* to the addition of a competitor which the target item must come to dominate. Without lateral inhibition the delay is due to the latter alone.

This fact makes empirical assessments of lateral inhibition questionable. Because lateral inhibition has no effects on the ordinal accounts of results which usually characterize psychological models, it may be an inappropriate model feature at their level of refinement. I assume that a reservation of this kind and considerations of parsimony have kept Marslen-Wilson from including lateral inhibition in his discussions of competition among lexical hypotheses.

Insofar as psychological models now venture into interval or ratio measurement, however, it becomes appropriate to consider the utility of lateral inhibition. When Marslen-Wilson states that a word is recognized "when its activation level becomes criterially different from that of its close competitors" (1988), we should understand that the decision criterion is either an absolute difference in activation levels or a ratio between activation levels. These criteria presuppose some scale of measurement beyond

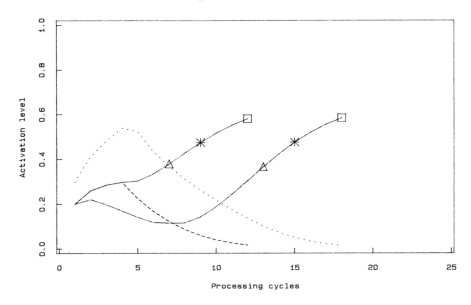

1a   Weak Targets with Lateral Inhibition

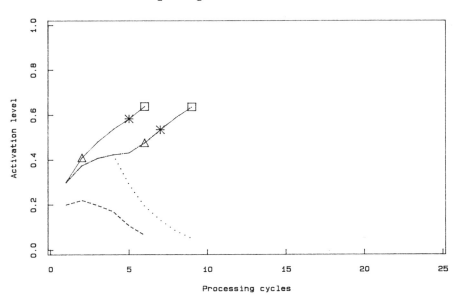

1b   Strong Targets with Lateral Inhibition

Figure 1
Activation levels and recognition points in systems with and without lateral
inhibition: ——— = target with weak competitor; – – – = weak competitor;

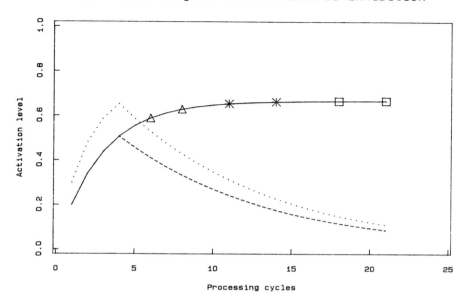

1c   Weak Targets without Lateral Inhibition

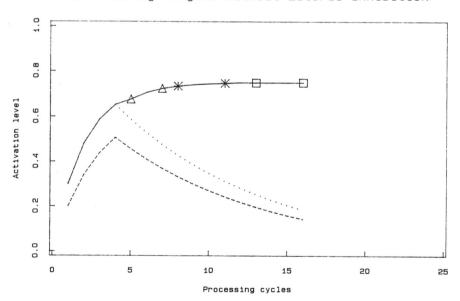

1d   Strong Targets without Lateral Inhibition

$-\cdot-\cdot$ = target with strong competitor; $\cdots$ = strong competitor; $\square$ = point of recognition with Luce rule (.9); $\triangle$ = point of recognition with Luce rule (.67); $*$ = point of recognition for $a_t = a_c + .4$.

the ordinal and give rise to a model in which lateral inhibition might have distinguishable effects.

In fact, the recognition criteria posited in the papers I am discussing make it possible to predict one difference between systems with and those without lateral inhibition: lateral inhibition will create an interaction between the effects of stimulus and competitor strengths, whereas simple competition will create only main effects. This follows from the fact that without lateral inhibition the strength of a word candidate as a competitor remains constant, whatever the strength of its own competitors. Strongly active competitors are more difficult to dominate than weaker, and they are equally more difficult to dominate, whatever the strength of the ultimately correct candidate. In a system with lateral inhibition, a candidate with weak competitors receives less inhibition and therefore functions in turn as a stronger competitor and a source of more lateral inhibition. The same candidate with strong competitors will become comparatively weaker and a source of attenuated inhibition. If there is a lower limit below which the inhibition contributed by a word cannot fall, the effect of a strong competitor is to compress the range of competition available from other active word hypotheses. Consequently, the same competitor-strength differences will produce smaller differences in the recognition of a strongly active target than in the recognition of a weakly active target.

This interaction is found in a simplified example based on TRACE. Figures 1a–b and 1c–d show activation curves for pairs of word elements in a single-layer system with and without lateral inhibition respectively. In each case the equations are those given in McClelland and Rumelhart 1988 with matched parameter settings except for gamma, the value of which determines the ratio of competitor activation to lateral inhibition.[2] In figures 1a and 1b, gamma is $-.5$, while in figures 1c and 1d, it is 0: there is no lateral inhibition. Both target and competitor receive input until the fourth cycle. Thereafter only the target is supported by input. The situation is thus analogous to the one which Marslen-Wilson examines, for in his cross-modal experiment the target word always diverges from its competitors at a known point.

Figures 1a and 1c contain curves for weakly active targets. Depending on the psychological model, targets might be weakly active because they are physically attenuated or because they correspond to lexical items with low frequencies of occurrence. Figures 1b and 1d contain curves for strongly active targets, corresponding to clear word tokens or frequent lexemes. In each figure the solid line follows the activation curve of the target in the case that it has a single weak competitor, the dashed line follows the activation of the weak competitor, the line of alternating dots and dashes follows the activation of the target when it has a single strong competitor, and the dotted line follows the activation of that strong competitor. In figures 1a and 1b, where lateral inhibition functions, the target activations are different with different competitor strengths. In figures 1c and 1d lateral inhibition is not used, and the target follows the same activation curve, however strong its competitor.

All four figures also show recognition points under several response criteria. The squares on the target lines mark the points where the targets are perceived under the Luce (1959) decision rule with the perceived stimulus controlling 90 percent of the available (exponentially transformed) activation. This is the sort of rule which Frauenfelder and Peeters used. The triangles mark perception points if targets must have two-thirds of the available (transformed) activation. Finally, the stars indicate recognition for targets under the simple criterion that the raw activation level of the target must be some arbitrary amount (here .4) greater than that of its nearest competitor. This is the sort of criterion which appears to underlie Marslen-Wilson's model. Table 1 records the differences in notional processing cycles between target recognition points for words with weak and strong competitors. Each such difference is a measure of the effect of competitor strength under one of the three criteria just described.

Figure 1 and table 1 show that lateral inhibition has two effects on recognition latencies under all these response criteria. First, it generally makes the recognition decision possible earlier. Second, it introduces the predicted interaction. With lateral inhibition operating (figures 1a and 1b), the effect of competitor strength on delay to recognition depends on target strength: the effect is larger for weak than for strong targets. Without

Table 1
Differences between recognition decision points for words with weak and strong competitors, measured in numbers of processing cycles

Decision rule	With lateral inhibition		Without lateral inhibition	
	Weak target	Strong target	Weak target	Strong target
Luce (.9)	6	3	3	3
Luce (.67)	6	4	2	2
$a_t = a_c + .4$	6	2	3	3

lateral inhibition (figures 1c and 1d) this interaction does not occur: the effect of competitor strength is the same for strongly and weakly active targets.

I will examine some real interactions in relation to the data presented by Marslen-Wilson in this volume. Meanwhile, it is sufficient to note that interactions and simple effects appear to imply different sorts of competition mechanisms, which otherwise remain indistinguishable.

Lateral Inhibition in Competition among Lexical Candidates

Frauenfelder and Peeters (this volume) present a number of simulations which use a frequency-free version of TRACE with lateral inhibition and test the effects of the nature and number of competing word candidates on the activation of words contained within other words. While the simulations are very useful, they clarify the role of competition rather than the role of lateral inhibition.

The simulations give a clear and easily digestible account of one useful function of competition: a word which would otherwise be dominated by a strong competitor may reach a level necessary for recognition if the lexion provides additional competition. In their figure 2 Frauenfelder and Peeters show how, if the lexicon contains only the two words, a shorter word embedded in a longer word is always barred by lateral inhibition from being recognized, as it is unable to suppress its longer competitor. With a larger lexicon (their figure 5) the longer word accrues more competitors because it contains phonetic material not corresponding to the shorter, embedded word but corresponding in part to other words in the lexicon. If these other competitors inhibit the activation of the carrier word, the embedded word has a chance of winning out in the end.

This view makes sense of a situation which is the bane of goodness-of-fit speech-recognition models: phonetic space is very full. Languages contain many words quite similar to other words, which induce finer and more difficult discriminations the more similar they are. Frauenfelder and Peeters show that words may be easier to recognize in running speech when competitors multiply. If lateral inhibition of carrier words by competitors destroys the dominant status of the carriers, the activation of small words will rise to respectable levels. In examples (1a) and (2a), *wreck* might otherwise be dominated by *recognize* and *pram* by *parameter*.

(1) a. That's a good way to wreck a nice beach.
     b. That's a good way to recognize speech.

(2) a. The afternoon was so hectic that she forgot she'd left the pram at her mother's.

b. The afternoon was so hectic that she forgot she'd left the parameter out.

Since there are many short words, ensuring that they can be recognized should be a goal of lexical access models.

While lateral inhibition contributes to TRACE's ability to achieve this goal, lateral inhibition per se does not create the effect. In Frauenfelder and Peeters' examples, the embedded word need not be recognized before its offset. It must merely be maintained long enough and with high enough activation to permit recognition if the proper kind of disambiguating information ever arrives or if the strong competitor dies away. Without lateral inhibition, of course, the competitor will not actually suppress the embedded word. Simple competition from an unsuppressed embedded word can prevent the carrier word from becoming sufficiently dominant to be recognized early and thereby end the access cycle. As long as the perceptual criterion depends on the proportion of all activation belonging to the most active item, the presence of any other items will reduce the leader's share and increase the time needed for the criterial share to be reached. Any benefit TRACE derives from the size of the competitor set owes as much to the ratio-based Luce decision rule as it does to lateral inhibition. Consequently, any case which Frauenfelder and Peeters make for the advantages of competition as instantiated in TRACE may not argue for lateral inhibition at all.

The case is at any rate intriguing. The simulations make at least two predictions which have been addressed in perceptual experiments. One set of simulations (their figure 4) shows that words embedded at the onset of nonwords will remain substantially activated even when the TRACE lexicon contains a competitor for the real words. Listeners monitoring for word-final consonants showed a word/nonword effect whether the target carrier was isolated or embedded at the onset of a longer nonword (Frauenfelder and Henstra 1988). This capacity is more useful than it might at first appear, because running speech does contain nonwords: words with postoffset uniqueness points are effectively words within sequences which become nonwords. The statistics collected by Luce (1986a) and by Frauenfelder and Peeters show that many words fall into this category.

In (3a), for example, *can* becomes unique only at the vowel of *trawl*, when, in my pronunciation, the [ɒ] contrasts with the [oᵘ] of *control*, as in (3b).

(3) a. They can trawl for hours and catch nothing but rubbish.

   b. They control the quotas.

The sequence [kəntɹɒ] is a nonword. The listener's task is to make it yield a recognition of the embedded word *can*. Frauenfelder and Peeters show that a system with lateral inhibition can account for such instances by preserving an active hypothesis for *can* into what might be the second syllable of *control*. The same result would presumably be achieved, however, if *can* were never inhibited and if the recognition of *control* were merely delayed by competition until at least its second vowel.

A second set of simulations (their figures 7 and 8) appear to make a predicition not fulfilled by experiment. In these figures a word embedded at the end of a word tends to be suppressed by the considerable activation achieved by its carrier before it began. *Seed* in *precede* and *seed* in *succeed* scarcely rise above resting level in these simulations.

Contrary to this prediction, Shillcock (this volume) reports that some word-final words (*bone* in *trombone*) are sufficiently activated to support cross-modal priming. Moreover, he finds no significant difference in priming strength for words embedded in carriers with small and large cohorts (*wombat* versus *combat*). Instead, *post hoc* investigations of his data show a negative correlation between the amount of priming and the frequency of the highest-frequency competitor to the carrier word. These results might be taken to follow Grainger et al. (1988) and Brown (1987) in casting the most frequent item as sole donor and all other competitors as recipients of lateral inhibition. Later we will see that a system with universal contribution of lateral inhibition could also produce Shillcock's results. Meanwhile, I must conclude that competition may account for some of the fine structure of spoken-word recognition, whether or not lateral inhibition is involved.

Word Frequency and Competition among Lexical Candidates

Shillcock's results, however, force us to consider the effects of word frequency on the activation of lexical hypotheses. Two questions are relevant here. The first is whether the frequency of any lexical competitor other than the correct one plays a role in determining the course of word recognition. And second, if there are any effects of competitor frequency, which competitors are involved? The first question deals with the contribution of frequency to the state of a system when a perceptual choice is made. The second deals with what the effective competitors of a word are.

Marslen-Wilson (this volume) proposes that competitor frequency is important because competition is realized as differences in activation levels, and activation levels are determined by the bottom-up fit of input to lexical hypothesis and by the frequency of occurrence of the hypothesized word. Items which are more frequent and more similar to the input rise in activation faster than other competitors. Although all competitors have this characteristic, the mechanism of perceptual choice depends only on the difference between the two most active elements, usually the target and the word which most closely resembles it. In Marslen-Wilson's cross-modal experiment the target and its competitor are virtually identical at the point in question. What distinguishes their activation levels, in this view, is their frequency of occurrence. As effects of stimulus frequency are well known, the work is intended to establish effects of competitor frequency.

Marslen-Wilson finds effects of target and competitor frequency on the points at which listeners achieve a consistently correct identification of gated words, but he seeks to confirm his results in a task less subject to postperceptual effects, a cross-modal lexical decision task. In this task, subjects hear a prime which may be either the onset or all of a target word, the onset or all of its most frequent competitor, or the onset or all of an unrelated control word. They then make a lexical decision about the visual version of the target. Though Marslen-Wilson's discussion focuses on the effects of competitor frequency, the results for the critical primes seem to show main effects of target frequency and competitor frequency but no interaction between them. This outcome is problematic, however.

The results just quoted are expressed in two derived measures. The simpler one is the difference between lexical decision reaction times in the test and control conditions (Marslen-Wilson, this volume, figure 4), a difference usually taken to represent a priming effect. The second derived measure reports test-control differences at the early position, when only the roughly homophonous onsets of the target and competitor word are heard, as a percentage of test-control differences at the late position, when the whole word is heard (Marslen-Wilson's figure 5). Both of these measures show only main effects. By the reasoning presented earlier, main effects without an interaction reflect a competition mechanism without lateral inhibition.

The raw reaction times give a different impression. While they also show the main effects, the raw scores produce exactly the interaction which should indicate the operation of lateral inhibition: there is a larger effect of competitor frequency on low-frequency target items than on high-frequency target times. Marslen-Wilson argues that the derived measures give a more legitimate account of frequency effects than the raw measures because the control condition yielded an uneven baseline (Marslen-Wilson, personal communication).

The control reaction times themselves appear to provide an uneven baseline because they display the same interaction between competitor and target frequency as the test reaction times (see Marslen-Wilson's table 9). Since the control reaction times follow primes which are unrelated to the target items in sound or meaning, the effects are not due to auditory priming of visual recognition. They reside, as Marslen-Wilson points out, in the visual modality. Even without priming, then, this modality shows effects of target frequency, competitor frequency, *and* their interaction.

The problem is not finding effects of competitor frequency in this paradigm; it is understanding the implications of the results. While the effects of competitor frequency in priming are attributed to the visual modality, the experiment is actually considering only some of the competitors of the visual target stimuli, their phonological competitors. But visual stimuli have visual competitors for which this experiment does not control. Thus far we know we have a visual effect, but we cannot be sure, in terms of all the competitors available, why we should have it.

It is also difficult to understand what model of cross-modal priming can support the analyses used. Marslen-Wilson claims that the activation of elements in auditory lexical access can be studied via reaction times for visual lexical decision not just because the cross-modal priming paradigm yields specific auditory effects but also because the mechanisms are "fundamentally the same in both modalities." But if the raw and derived measures have been interpreted legitimately, visual and auditory mechanisms are not analogous. As we have just seen, the auditory process appears to operate by simple competition, while the visual process appears to include lateral inhibition.

Moreover, if the mechanisms have these characteristics, it probably is not legitimate to take difference scores as indicating auditory effects. Lying behind this subtraction of control from test scores lurks an additive model of cross-modal priming: the visual activation of a target word with a particular set of competitors *plus* the contribution to the visual activation (whether of target or competitor) made by the activation of the auditory prime yields the state of the system which allows quicker or slower lexical decision on the target. But a visual lexical access system which incorporates lateral inhibition should not allow simple additive effects. Instead, it should create the now familiar interaction between (auditory prime) competitor frequency and (visual) target frequency: once the auditory contributions are added to the activation of the corresponding visual recognition elements, the whole system is affected by lateral inhibition. The effects of the competitor contributions should once more be magnified for rare visual targets, and the raw test reaction times should show an even more marked interaction than the raw controls. Since this does not happen, either the interpretation of the response measures or the model of cross-modal priming is incorrect.

Subtracting the control reaction times from the test reaction times removes the traces of this difficulty but not the real problem. What is needed is an elaborated account of the present visual effects to explain why the auditory priming patterns are found in the control conditions, as well as a model of cross-modal priming in the test conditions which will motivate the use of particular dependent variables.

Whatever the difficulties in interpreting results from this particular method, other techniques attest to a role for word frequency in determining competitor strengths. The isolation-point results in gating are among these (Marslen-Wilson, this volume). Marslen-Wilson (1987) cites results by Brown and Zwitserlood dealing, like the present ones, with auditory primes which represent the first, common part of two different words (*kapitein, kapitaal*). Priming was found to occur for both words in proportion to their frequencies. Shillcock (this volume) and Luce (1986b) also cite effects of competitor frequency.

This brings us to the second question: which competitors and hence which competitors' frequencies are important? Some results imply that all competitors are effective, because the number of competitors has effects on recognition (Frauenfelder and Peeters, this volume, and Luce 1986b). Marslen-Wilson's model gives all competitors a role and a contribution proportional to word frequency, but its decision rule depends only on the strongest competitor. Shillcock (this volume) and Brown (1987) contemplate a system in which only the most active competitor contributes lateral inhibition, so that the number of competitors is relatively unimportant.

In fact, a crucial role for a word's most frequent competitor and a negligible effect of the number of competitors both follow from what appears to be the usual shape of the frequency distribution of word-initial cohorts. Figure 2 displays the distribution of Francis and Kučera's (1982) frequencies of several word-initial cohorts. While the frequency ranges differ, the figure shows that Zipf's (1935) results on the lexicon as a whole appear to be replicated for individual cohorts. Many more words in each sample are of very low frequency than are of medial or high frequency, both absolutely and relative to the cohort's frequency range. The high end

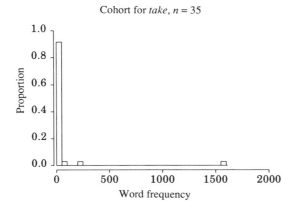

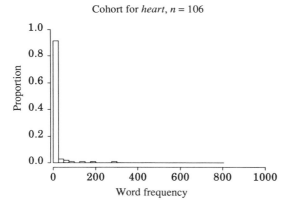

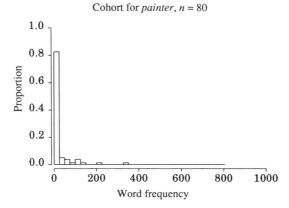

Figure 2
Frequency distributions of cohorts

Cohort for *to*, *n* = 29

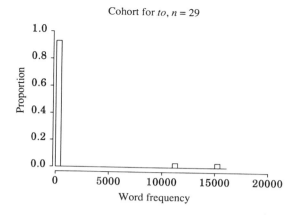

Cohort for *wombat*, *n* = 114

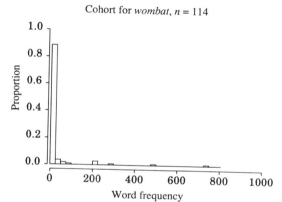

Cohort for *cohort*, *n* = 143

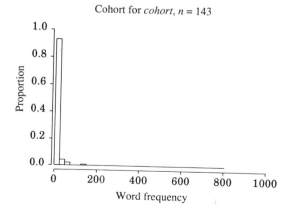

of the range is very much higher than the mode. In individual cohorts, where numbers of items are small, the member with the greatest frequency of occurrence is often an extreme outlier. If frequency is related to activation, this sort of distribution will contain competitors of vastly different importance.

This is the fact that allows the effect of a cohort or a neighborhood to be less than the sum of its unweighted parts. Activation proportional to frequency or log frequency, for example, will make an extremely frequent outlier the dominant competitor for any other member of the cohort. Since many of the competitors are so rare, their activation levels under this weighting will be low, and their number will have comparatively little effect either on the proportion of activation left to the target or on the total amount of lateral inhibition offered to it. To be recognized, then, a target item must compete with the outlier, if there is one. Whether or not there is a frequent outlier, the number and total activation of rare competitors is relatively unimportant. Consequently, there should be little difference between the predictions of a model whose perceptual-choice rule compares target and nearest competitor and one whose rule depends on target and total activation. No additional device is needed to identify the most frequent competitor to allow it sole access to lateral inhibition (Brown 1987). It identifies itself. Nor is it necessary to eliminate lateral inhibition in general to reduce the effects of cohort size.

Any such effects in the literature now bear reexamination. Frauenfelder and Peeters's findings on cohort size are based on simulations run without word frequency and assume that all competitors are a priori equal. In simulations with competitors weighted for frequency, results should be different. Luce's neighborhood activation model does weight competitor neighborhoods for mean frequency, but it also makes use of neighborhood density, which should be roughly proportional to cohort size. Luce 1986b did report effects for neighborhood density, but these may actually be frequency results in disguise. As high-frequency lexemes are relatively rare in the mental lexicon, a great many lexemes might be sampled before a high-frequency lexeme was found. Whatever their mean frequency, high-density neighborhoods, which contain many lexemes, have more opportunities than low density neighborhoods to contain an unusually high-frequency item which will compete strongly with the target.

In summary, we have now seen that models of competition in lexical access may account for the same phenomena whether or not they depend on lateral inhibition to facilitate competition. Actually distinguishing the empirical results of models with and without lateral inhibition is difficult. The results of Marslen-Wilson's cross-modal priming experiment displayed the required characteristics, but attributing them to particular perceptual mechanisms is problematic. We have also seen that a system in which word frequency contributes to the effectiveness of competitors conforms to much of the experimental evidence if it is generally the case that the frequency distribution of a cohort or neighborhood contains few but extreme outliers. To the extent that the outlier is extreme, there will be little difference between the predictions of perceptual-choice rules which compare the two most active candidates and those which compare the most active with the total activation. The net result is to offer support to competition models of any sort which include frequency in their determination of competitor strength.

Competition and the Segmentation Problem in Spoken-Word Recognition

It will be instructive to see whether such a model can fulfill the second role of competition models in perception: to segment the objects of perception out of their natural background. This section presents an account of lexical competition within a variant of TRACE which has the characteristics described above. The question to be explored is whether such a model can account for word segmentation results produced by Cutler and her colleagues while retaining the characteristics which reflect the results discussed earlier.[3]

The principal segmentation phenomenon to be explained is described as a metrical segmentation strategy in which strong syllables, defined as those with nonschwa, nonreduced vowels, are used as indicators of word onsets (Cutler, this volume; Cutler and Carter 1987; Cutler and Norris 1988). Because these syllables often mark the onsets of content words in English, Cutler notes that a segmentation mechanism based on strong syllables will be most successful if each strong syllable is then used to generate lexical hypotheses corresponding to content words. Weak syllables themselves are not supposed to induce word segmentation. If the longest available word is followed by a weak syllable, however, that syllable is used to access a list of function words. Because functors are usually without metrical stress (consider *of* in *list of function words*), it makes sense to entertain the hypothesis that a word starting with a weak syllable is a function word. In either case, lexical access is initiated less often than it might be if no segmentation device were present and access processes were constantly initiated.

This model is proposed not only to reflect the distributional facts of the language (Cutler and Carter 1987) and to impose some economies on processing (Briscoe 1989) but also to account for two principal groups of experimental results. In the first of these (Cutler and Norris 1988) listeners monitored faster for monosyllabic words at the onsets of bisyllabic non-words when the second syllable was weak (as in *mintesh*). The increased reaction times for cases in which the second syllable was strong (as in *mintayve*) were attributed to the segmentation mechanism, which imposed a boundary before the last segment of the embedded word ([t]) to use that segment as the onset of a strong syllable (-*tayve*). Increased reaction times were found only in conditions where the last segment of the embedded word was adjacent to the strong vowel (as in *mintayve*) and not where another segment intervened (as in *thintayve*). Listeners presumably had to recover from their error in the *mintayve* case before they could recognize *mint*.

The second group of results is less straightforward. To replicate results on spontaneous slips of the ear, Butterfield and Cutler (1988) presented strings of words in which strong and weak syllables alternated under signal-to-noise ratios which made them barely audible. When listeners made word-boundary errors in their attempts to identify stimuli, they showed a strong tendency to place word boundaries before strong syllables. When they did place spurious boundaries before weak syllables, they usually supplied monosyllabic function words. As the responses were on average no more frequent than the stimuli, the authors concluded that the listeners were not just guessing words at random but were actually using the proposed strategy as an aid to lexical access.

The difficulty is that the materials in this experiment did not reflect the distribution of English word-initial syllables. Some 60 percent of the content words here were strong initial, while in the London-Lund corpus the proportion is 90 percent (Cutler and Carter 1987). In general, English phrases with the rhythmic structure of the stimuli in this experiment should contain more strong-onset content words than the stimuli did just because of the properties of the available words. Listeners need not have been guessing at random to exploit the English lexicon in this way. Conforming to what they could hear and to the constraints of English syntax, they still had largely strong-onset content words and weak-onset functors to choose from. Deviations toward the norm should not be surprising.

Cutler (this volume) is certainly correct in concluding, "Word boundary misplacements by human listeners ... seem to reflect the prosodic prob-abilities of English remarkably accurately." The question is whether they do so by making word-boundary, as opposed to word-identity, decisions. In effect, this is a question of which kind of parsimony is preferable: parsimony in terms of lexical-access *operations*, which could be achieved by restricting attempts at lexical access to material starting at a hypothesized boundary, or parsimony in terms of lexical-access *apparatus*, which could be achieved by having no additional mechanism for locating boundaries prelexically.

The additional mechanism demanded by the metrical segmentation strategy depends on two problematic binary switches. The first of these determines whether a syllable is strong or weak. The second determines whether to seek the current word in the content or functor lexicon. Both reflect perfectly legitimate binary distinctions in linguistic theory which may be impossible to make prelexically for running speech.

Consider the strong-weak distinction. Cutler describes it in terms of vowel length and quality: A strong syllable will be reported where certain segments are recognized or where an acceptably long "high-energy quasi-steady-state portion" of input is identified. A weak syllable will contain a vowel which is shorter, more central, or lower in energy than some canonical version. While these are good general descriptions, a listener making decisions on individual syllables may need to appeal to calculations over much longer portions of speech to determine, for example, the length of clear local instances of strong syllables, the speaker's use of the vowel space, the local speech rate, its effects on vowel duration and location, and the intended identity of the vowel. And if, for example, a listener needs to know what the intended vowel is in order to categorize its syllable as weak or strong, it will be awkward if the vowel cannot be uniquely identified before the carrier word is recognized. In fact, segments are not always uniquely identifiable prelexically. This is why both TRACE and the more recent accounts of the cohort model (Marslen-Wilson 1987) allow the same input to activate a number of phonetic (and lexical) candidates to varying degrees.

Moreover, the metrical segmentation strategy has an ecological advantage only where perceptual and distributional strong/weak distinctions coincide. Disagreement between online judgements during speech perception and the considered judgments of linguists analyzing corpora or writing dictionaries are not unlikely. Where disagreement produces higher false-alarm rates than those estimated from corpus analyses, parsimony of operations diminishes. Failures to recognize strong syllables will abort necessary segmentation and access processes. To the extent that the perceptual boundary between weak and strong syllables is fuzzy, these perceptual-error rates must be added to the theoretical-error rate calculated from expert judgments.[4]

The dichotomy between function words and content words is also troublesome for reasons having to do with the processing of speech. While they may be orthographically distinct, weak-onset function words and weak affixes on content words are often homophonous in fluent speech, as the examples in (4) and (5) illustrate.

(4) a. strength in his hand
    b. strengthen his hand

(5) a. good terrain
    b. good to rain

The correct segmentation of strings like (4) and (5) actually depends on the interpretation of each full utterance. Yet Cutler and Carter's late closure principle forces (4b), while the strong-onset rule forces (5b). While function and content words have metrical characteristics, the distribution of such words in sentences is controlled by syntax. Any prelexical strategy for characterizing words which has as its strength the fact that it is autonomous will have as its weakness the fact that it fails to use the appropriate higher-level information. Cutler (this volume) notes that some sensitivity to context is a necessary addition to the metrical segmentation strategy. Yet if higher-level information blocks an incorrect choice in examples like these, the work of categorizing words as contentive or functor is being done by the higher levels and not by the segmentation algorithm.

Moreover, the treatment of the functor-contentive distinction would seem to make a predicition which is not met. When a weak syllable follows the end of a word, the functor lexicon should be accessed. Compared to the content-word lexicon, the functor lexicon should be small, and the number of competitors for any item minimal. With a smaller set to choose from, it should be easy to recognize function words. But it is not. Bard, Shillcock, and Altmann (1988) found that function words in spontaneous speech were harder to recognize by their offsets than content words. They argued that the delay derives from the fact that functors are usually such unintelligible word tokens that they depend heavily on higher-level information for their recognition. Because this information is found in both the subsequent and the preceding context, it is unlikely to be fully available during the course of the word. Because of the problems of distinguishing function words from their acoustic competitors and because of the location of the information capable of aiding this discrimination, it will take more than a weak-strong switch to identify function words.

However unsatisfactory the two switching mechanisms are, the metrical segmentation strategy exploits a general correspondance between stress and word types which could streamline lexical access. A TRACE-like competition model of the sort discussed earlier is capable of exploiting these regularities without resorting to prelexical word segmentation. The model would initiate lexical access operations by attempting to match onsets of words in the mental lexicon to any part of the input. Since, with few exceptions, words begin only at the beginnings of syllables, the model would actually be forced to generate lexical hypotheses which started at syllable onsets. Shillcock's results suggest, of course, that medial syllables do induce lexical access. If the activation level of competing word hypotheses depended jointly on similarity to the input and frequency of the word, as Marslen-Wilson's results suggest, and if the lexicon reflected the regularities discovered by Cutler and Carter (1987), the resulting model should offer at least some of the benefits of the metrical segmentation strategy.

A competition model of this sort does not need a weak-strong switch, because weak and strong syllables will tend to distinguish themselves on grounds of intelligibility, that is, on grounds of the size and activation level of the cohorts they engender. The model does not need a functor-contentive switch because of the distribution of strong and weak initial syllables in the lexicon. A closer look at the consequences of these facts should help us see how this model could account for the experimental results in the area.

First, consider the intelligibility differences between weak and strong syllables. Weak syllables should engender cohorts which make recognition difficult for several reasons connected with their unintelligibility, variously defined. First, a weak syllable may represent several different phonological syllables, in the sense that a single weak vowel may be the realization of various abstract vowels in the linguistic representation of word stems. While all the italicized syllables in (6) may be represented by the same weak syllable [fə], they might be expected to correspond to different abstract representations.

(6) a. *fa*miliar
   b. *for*gotten
   c. *for*
   d. *fe*rocious

The [fə] in (6a) alternates phonologically with [fæ] (as in *family*). The one in (6d) is arguably a version of [fi] (as in *feral*), and so on. Second, a weakened syllable pronounced in context may represent different citation-form syllables. The [fə] in (6d) is probably still [fə] in careful pronunciation of the isolated word. In (6b) and (6c) the isolated form probably begins with [fɔ]. Third, weak syllables can be weak enough to lose their vowels altogether. Example (6d) could readily be pronounced [fɹoᵘʃəs]. Any or all of these representations of words may be used by the mental lexicon in lexical access. Because the weak syllable [fə] is ambiguous in terms of various idealizations, it should activate a sizable word-initial cohort, and because it is a noncanonical version of a number of these lexical candidates, many of them should be only weakly active.

Strong syllables should be less confusing. Although they may well be phonologically ambiguous in my sense of the term, they are more resistant to distancing from canonical forms and are unlikely to be reduced beyond all recognition. The lexical hypotheses activated by such syllables will be relatively fewer and more strongly active, since strong syllables suffer less deformation in connected speech and therefore produce more intelligible accounts of the words they represent.

In this model, while intelligibility determines bottom-up excitation, word activation should also depend on word frequency. It is important, however, that frequency should affect activation levels to a lesser degree than bottom-up excitation does. This proposal follows from consideration of the recognition of function words, where frequency must have a relatively limited effect.

Unlike Cutler and Norris's model, TRACE lacks an a priori indicator of the probable location of function words and so must allow them to compete with all other words which resemble them phonetically. If frequency correlates with activation in such a system, the great frequency of function words, which typically exceeds the frequency of content words by an order of magnitude, would give any function-word hypothesis an overwhelming advantage. A device linearly reflecting this frequency difference would, for example, recognize the word *a* wherever any word contained a schwa. To prevent this, a function of frequency must be used which brings the top and bottom of the range closer together. Moreover, activation levels must depend more on bottom-up excitation than on frequency so that the activation levels of function-word candidates reflect the poor intelligibility generally associated with functors. The suppression of functor candidates will also follow from the fact that short function words will accumulate less activation than longer words containing them, as Frauenfelder and Peeters illustrate.

Now consider association of strong and weak initial syllables with particular word classes. When input from a strong syllable is broadcast to the recognition elements in the mental lexicon, the competitors most strongly activated on grounds of similarity to the input will be words starting with that same strong syllable, among which there will tend to be more content words than function words. While weak syllables may activate a broader, weaker cohort, function words will tend to be in the majority and initially, at least, may rise sharply in activation because of their great frequency of occurrence. Neither of these tendencies predicts which word will be recognized in a given instance, of course. Nor does it predict when the word will be recognized. As I suggested with reference to Frauenfelder and Peeters' work, all that is required is that the correct word candidate is active enough to survive until the many lexical claims on its acoustic material have resolved, either by means of lexical competition or by means of selection on syntactic or semantic grounds.

With these provisos the model should accommodate the results of Cutler and Norris. When *mint* is presented in *mintayve*, there is established a relatively small set of strongly activated competitors competing with *mint* for possession of the [t]. When *mintesh* is presented, the set is larger but much less active. Because of this difference in competitor sets, the experimental result could be simulated with or without lateral inhibition, as we have come to expect. Without lateral inhibition the highly active lexical hypotheses established for strong syllables (*take, tame, taint, tailor, tape, tasty,* etc.) will delay the recognition of *mint* until these strong-onset competitors die a natural death because none of them matches *tayve*. The maximal activation of any weak-onset competitor established by *tesh* is lower, however, for the reasons enumerated earlier, and it probably has a shorter duration because the weak syllables will contain shorter vowels than their strong controls. With the same rate of decay, the shorter, less active weak-onset competitors will always maintain a smaller proportion of the total activation than the longer, more active strong-onset competitors. Thus the weak-onset competitors will more quickly reach the point where *mint* is left with the criterial proportion of all activation, and the activation of *mint* in *mintesh* will achieve the critical advantage over its decaying competitors sooner than it will in *mintayve*. With lateral inhibition, competitors also delay the recognition of *mint* by lowering its activation in proportion to their own strength. Since strong syllables should produce more active competitors, they should suppress the embedded word more and so delay its recovery further when they themselves decay.

It is worth repeating that the model under discussion here is the sort of competition model developed earlier to account for other experimental results. The different competitor sets for strong- and weak-onset words, like the shape of cohort frequency distributions, are taken as characteristics of the language rather than of the model. Treating such a model as a variant of TRACE is merely an expository device which exploits the reader's presumed familiarity with TRACE and its extreme flexibility. What is important about such a competiton model is its parsimonious use of a single mechanism to deal with both word recognition and word segmentation.

It is also worth noting that modifying TRACE to cover these results and observations is almost too easy to be instructive in itself. When the basic device allows us to be imaginative along some ten parameters, eliminating an eleventh is not much of an accomplishment. If we believe the quip attributed to Arnold Sommerfeld, four parameters allow us to draw an elephant; five to tie a knot in its tail. In comparison to sketching elephants, drawing the surface described by three or four experimental results should be simple. It is unfortunate for psycholinguists that further specifying the details of the behavioral surface is currently so much more laborious than modeling those details once they are known. And it is also unfortunate that so little explicit direction can be taken from models which, like TRACE, have many degrees of freedom. Since models can tie knots in anything, establishing more points in the behavioral surface may be the only way forward in our understanding of the processes involved in human speech recognition.

Acknowledgments

This paper was produced with the support of SERC Project Grant GR/E19541 to the author and H. Thompson and of the IED/SERC Large Scale Integrated Speech Technology Demonstrator Project (SERC grants D/29604, D/29611, D/29628, F/10309, F/10316) to the University of Edinburgh in collaboration with Marconi Speech and Information Systems and Loughborough University of Technology. I would like to thank Uli Frauenfelder and William Marslen-Wilson for making data available and for discussing an earlier version of this paper. Thanks are also due to Anne Cutler, Dennis Norris, Steve Isard, Jan McAllister, Richard Shillcock, and Gerry Altmann for helpful discussion and to Jan Charles-Luce and David Pisoni for instructive reviews. None of the above-named is responsible for any persisting errors or misconceptions.

Notes

1. A graded bottom-up contribution seems to be a necessity, however it is expressed. Although Luce (1986b) does not link activation directly to similarity between token and phonological entry, his neighborhood activation model nonetheless contains a continuous variable which corresponds to the joint probability that the phones in a word can be correctly identified.

2. In both cases the input level of the stronger competitor is 1.5 times that of the weaker competitor, the decay rate is .1, maximum activation level is 1, and minimum and resting levels are 0. The exponential transformation of activation levels for use in the Luce rule is e^{4a}.

3. Cutler and Norris (1988) considered a similar account that could not be empirically distinguished from their own model on the basis of the result they presented.

4. These cumulating errors might be avoided if it could be guaranteed that the average listener perceived the strong/weak distinction categorially and that the boundary was at least as useful as the one operating in the corpus analysis. Cutler and her colleagues make no such claim, of course. It is likely that the strong/weak distinction is perceived continuously rather than categorially because other distinctions between vowels characteristically display continuous perception. It is not relevant that listeners can accurately identify vowels in running speech despite the noncategorical nature of vowel perception. Vowel recognition in running speech almost certainly has a top-down component. Strong-syllable recognition might be just such a *post*lexical process, but if it is, it is of no use to Cutler and Norris's theory, where segmentation is *pre*lexical.

References

Balota, D. A., and Chumbley, J. I. 1985. The locus of word frequency effects in the pronunciation task: Lexical access and/or production? *Journal of Memory and Language* 24:89–106.

Bard, E. G., Shillcock. R. C., and Altmann, G. T. M. 1988. The recognition of words after their acoustic offsets in spontaneous speech: Effects of subsequent context. *Perception and Psychophysics* 44:395–408.

Briscoe, T. 1989. Lexical access in connected speech recognition. Twenty-Seventh Congress of the Association for Computational Linguistics, Vancouver. Submitted.

Brown, G. D. A. 1987. Constraining interactivity: Evidence from acquired dyslexia. *Proceedings of the Ninth Annual Conference of the Cognitive Science Society*, pp. 779–793. Hillsdale, N.J.: Erlbaum.

Brown, G. D. A., and Watson, F. 1987. First in, first out: Word learning age and spoken word frequency as predictors of word familiarity and word naming latency. *Memory and Cognition* 15:208–216.

Butterfield, S., and Cutler, A. 1988. Segmentation errors by human listeners: Evidence for a prosodic segmentation strategy. In R. Lawrence, W. A. Ainsworth, and J. N. Holmes (eds.), *Speech '88: Proceedings of the Seventh FASE Symposium*, Book 3, pp. 827–833. Edinburgh: Institute of Acoustics.

Cutler, A., and Carter, D. M. 1987. Predominance of strong initial syllables in the English vocabulary. *Proceedings of the European Conference on Speech Technology*, vol. 1, pp. 207–210.

Cutler, A., and Norris, D. 1988. The role of strong syllables in segmentation for lexical access. *Journal of Experimental Psychology: Human Perception and Performance* 14:113–121.

Francis, W. N., and Kučera, H. 1982. *Frequency Analysis of English Usage: Lexicon and Grammar*. Boston: Houghton Mifflin.

Frauenfelder, U. H., and Henstra, J. 1988. Activation and deactivation of phonological representations. In *Proceedings of the Third International Morphology Meeting* (Krems, Austria), vol. 7, 10–12.

Gernsbacher, M. A. 1984. Resolving twenty years of inconsistent interactions between lexical familiarity and orthography, concreteness, and polysemy. *Journal of Experimental Psychology: General* 113:256–281.

Grainger, J., O'Regan, J. K., Jacobs, A. M., and Segui, J. 1988. On the role of competing word units in visual word recognition: The orthographic neighborhood effect. *Perception and Psychophysics* 45:189–195.

Luce, P. A. 1986a. A computational analysis of uniqueness points in auditory word recognition. *Perception and Psychophysics* 34:155–158.

Luce, P. A. 1986b. Neighborhoods of words in the mental lexicon. Research on Speech Perception, technical report no. 6. Speech Research Laboratory, Department of Psychology, Indiana University, Bloomington.

Luce, R. D. 1959. *Individual Choice Behavior*. New York: Wiley.

McClelland, J. L., and Elman, J. L. 1986. The TRACE model of speech perception. *Cognitive Psychology* 18:1–86.

McClelland, J. L., and Rumelhart, D. E. 1988. *Explorations in Parallel Distributed Processing: A Handbook of Models, Programs, and Exercises*. Cambridge: MIT Press.

Marslen-Wilson, W. 1987. Functional parallelism in spoken word recognition. In U. H. Frauenfelder and L. K. Tyler (eds.), *Spoken Word Recognition*. Cambridge: MIT Press.

Marslen-Wilson, W. 1988. Activation, competition, and frequency in lexical access. Paper delivered to the Experimental Psychology Society, Edinburgh, July.

Zipf, G. K. 1935. *The Psycho-biology of Language*. Boston: Houghton Mifflin.

Zwitserlood, P. 1985. Activation of word candidates during spoken word-recognition. Paper presented to the Psychonomic Society Meetings, Boston.

Chapter 10
Lexical Statistics and Cognitive Models of Speech Processing

Gerry T. M. Altmann

Statistical studies of large lexicons provide psycholinguists with an important tool for exploring new insights into the process of lexical access. On the one hand, these studies provide simple statistics for describing approximations to the target language over which the human device for word recognition must operate. On the other hand, they provide a useful perspective on the kinds of processes that the recognition device may or may not employ. Most contemporary studies of word recognition use lexical statistics to some degree, whether as the basis for evaluating, or even constructing, theories or as a tool for devising experimental materials that exhibit certain well-defined characteristics.

Lexical statistics typically involve the manipulation of information contained within a large computerized dictionary of a specified language. In their simplest form they are concerned with the sheer numbers of items in a dictionary that exhibit certain specified characteristics. These may include purely structural characteristics, such as an item's phonological or orthographic form, its length, its stress pattern, and so on; functional characteristics, such as the item's syntactic form class; or distributional characteristics, such as the frequency of that particular item in the language at large. On the basis of these, the relationship of any one lexical item to the other items in the dictionary can be explored. Of particular interest are the numbers of items that either do or do not satisfy certain criteria. Words that share the same crucial characteristics would not be distinguishable from one another if those characteristics were all that a recognition device had to go by. In such a case the words would fall within the same *equivalence class*. I return to this notion below.

An integral part of calculating lexical statistics are the various manipulations of the information contained within the dictionary. For instance, by underspecifying the phonological form of each item, the confusability of that item with its neighbors can be made to increase, since more words will fall within any one equivalence class. By systematically degrading the phonological information in ways that perhaps conform with the empirical data on phonetic confusability (Miller and Nicely 1955, Luce 1986), one can assess the degree to which the input to the human word recognition device is ambiguous.

The ultimate aim of research that makes use of lexical statistics is to discern properties of the *language* at large and not simply properties of the specific *dictionary* used to derive the statistics. The following example makes the distinction clearer. Pisoni, Luce, and Nusbaum (1986) have shown that knowing only the length of an item in terms of the number of segments can reduce the search space by around 95 percent from an original size of 126,000 to just 6,342. That is, the average size of each equivalence class defined in terms of length alone is just 5 percent of the size of the lexicon taken as a whole. By adding in very limited phonetic information, such as whether each segment is classified as a vowel or a consonant, the search space reduces considerably further to just 0.1 percent of the lexicon. Such studies, although simple, provide important information about the kinds of constraints that can be brought to bear during the recognition process. However, short words occur much more frequently in the language than they do in a dictionary. If one were to weight lexical statistics to reflect this preponderance of short words or to reflect the relative frequencies in the language of *each* word in the dictionary, the statistics calculated on the basis of word length alone would look very different: whereas the search space defined by the (unweighted) dictionary would be much reduced, the search space defined by the language (that is, by the weighted dictionary) would not. Thus, knowing only the length of a word would *not* aid the recognition device by as much as the initial figures suggest. By weighting the lexical statistics to take into account word-frequency information, the lexicon can be used to approximate the target language over which the recognition device is to operate.

A number of studies in the present volume have made use of lexical statistics. Cutler derived lexical statistics to evaluate the efficacy of the Metrical Segmentation Strategy, whereby a lexical boundary is postulated at the onset of every strong syllable (Cutler and Norris 1988). By taking into account the relative frequencies of each word in the language, Cutler and Carter (1987) could assess the proportion of occasions on which the segmentation strategy leads to the correct segmentation (an incorrect segmentation arises through postulating a boundary where there wasn't one or missing a boundary where there should be one). The statistics supported the theory insofar as the majority of frequency-weighted content words in the lexicon started with a strong syllable. This suggested that the correct segmentation should be found in the majority of cases. Moreover, these statistics, although based on a dictionary, agreed quite closely with those found in actual speech.

Shillcock used statistical methods to derive a set of experimental materials with very precise characteristics. By looking at the population of word-initial syllables in the dictionary, he identified syllables that were either very common in word-initial position or very rare. A word like *combat* starts with a relatively common word-initial syllable: there were approximately 55 other words in his 18,000-word dictionary that started with the syllable *com*. The word *wombat*, on the other hand has a rare word-initial syllable: only 2 words started with that syllable. Using materials like these, he could thus test whether or not the activation of the extraneous word *bat* in *combat/wombat* is determined by the number of lexical competitors that might be activated by the end of the word-initial syllable. As it happens, they are not.

Luce (1986 and this volume) used lexical statistics in a rather different way. He was primarily interested in whether the neighborhood structure of a lexical item affected the recognition of that item. Neighborhoods were defined and calculated in two ways. In the first way the neighbors of a word were defined as any words that differed from the target word by only one phoneme. The words *beach* and *peach* would thus be neighbors. The number of words in the neighborhood and their respective frequencies could thus be calculated. Words would then be characterized according to whether they had high or low neighborhood densities—that is, whether there were many or few words in the neighborhood—and whether these neighborhoods had high or low mean frequencies. Luce (1986) found that high- and low-frequency words tended to have similar numbers of neighbors. High-frequency words also tended to have higher-frequency neighbors than low-frequency words, which suggests that high-frequency words are more likely to be confused with other high-frequency words than low-frequency words are likely to be confused with other low-frequency words. However, the difference in frequency between a high-frequency word and its neighbors was greater than that between a low-frequency word and its neighbors—they were more distinctive relative to their neighborhoods than were low-frequency words. In a separate study Luce defined the neighborhood in terms of the phonetic confusability, as determined empirically, of one item with any other item in the dictionary (see Luce's chapter for further details of the actual method employed). By correlating the various measures concerning neighborhood structure with the data from various behavioral studies on word recognition, Luce showed that neighborhood structure *does* influence word recognition.

The remainder of this chapter considers a further application of lexical statistics rather different from those just described. This concerns attempts to determine whether any parts of word and more *informative* than any other parts. For instance, word beginnings may convey more information about the identity of a word than word endings. At issue are whether the human recognition device is likely to capitalize on such facts (if true) and whether automatic speech recognizers could be designed to capitalize on them too. In the following sections I consider this issue in more detail and the implications for research on both human and machine speech-recognition devices. First I deal with some preliminary issues concerned with the gathering of lexical statistics themselves.

Lexical Statistics and Information Theory

As described earlier, an equivalence class is a set of words in a lexicon that are indistinguishable from one another following the application of a particular selection procedure, or *partition*. Lexical statistics help establish the constraining power of a given partitioning of the lexicon. For instance, if words are selected according to just their stress patterns, the two words *fatten* and *glutton* are not distinguishable, because they share the same pattern (stressed-unstressed). Partitioning the lexicon by stress pattern alone does nonetheless lead to equivalence classes with membership sizes that are considerably smaller than the size of the lexicon as a whole, between 15 and 19 percent of the original size (Waibel 1982, Aull and Zue 1984, Carter 1987). Although knowing the stress pattern alone does provide some constraint, it is by no means enough to identify the word in question.

A variety of studies have investigated how the candidate search space reduces as more, or less, phonemic detail is included in the transcription of any one word. The 1986 study described earlier by Pisoni, Luce, and Nusbaum attached one of only two different symbols (consonant versus vowel) to each of the 46 or so phonemes in the English language. Shipman and Zue (1982) reported (unweighted) statistics that distinguished between six different "broad class" categories of segments corresponding to manner of articulation: vowel, nasal, strong fricative, weak fricative, stop, and liquids or glides. Thus the word *piston* would be transcribed as /stop, vowel, strong fricative, stop, vowel, nasal/. They found that these broad-class transcriptions reduced the search space quite considerably: the maximum class size (that is, the worst case) reduced the lexicon from 20,000 to just 200, 1 percent of the original size. The average class size was around 2 (0.01%), and about 32 percent of the items were uniquely identifiable.

Huttenlocher (1984) pointed out that the measures used by Shipman and Zue were inadequate because they were insensitive to variations in size between equivalence classes. Consider a lexicon consisting of just 10 words and a partition that leads to one equivalence class of 6 items and two others each containing just 2 items. The average class size would be 3.3. Huttenlocher suggested that class-size measures should reflect the uneven distribution of words across equivalence classes and that a more appropriate measure than average class size could be derived by multiplying the size of each class by the proportion of the lexicon represented by that class and then summing across these. For the 10-word lexicon this would lead to an *expected class size* (ECS) of $(6 \times 6/10) + (2 \times 2/10) + (2 \times 2/10)$, that is, 4.4. Huttenlocher then repeated the Shipman and Zue study using a frequency-weighted version of expected class size, and he showed that whereas the maximum class size of course remained the same, the percentage of the lexicon that was uniquely identifiable fell to just 6 percent and the expected class size was 34 (0.17%).

Altmann and Carter (1989) explored the use of partial phonetic information even further. We used 13 "mid class' categories (Dalby, Laver, and Hiller 1986), in which distinctions are made between voiced and voiceless stops; voiced and voiceless, weak and strong fricatives; liquids; glides; front, back, and central vowels; diphthongs; and nasals. We used a 12,850-word dictionary and found, not surprisingly, that the search space was reduced considerably more. Our study used a rather different measure, however, than the mean equivalence-class size used in the Huttenlocher 1984 studies. We based our evaluation measure on some notions borrowed from information theory and developed in Carter 1987. Carter argued that it is misleading to use equivalence-class sizes as the basis on which to evaluate any given partitioning of the lexicon. If a 10,000-word lexicon were to be partitioned into 10 equivalence classes each containing 1,000 members, the search space has apparently been reduced by 90 percent. That is, if one knows which equivalence class to look in, the remaining equivalence classes, which amount to 90 percent of the lexicon, can be rejected. This simple state of affairs is schematized in figure 1. But this figure of 90 percent is misleading because the partitioning of the lexicon into 10 equivalence classes of 1,000 words each is only one of the *four* 10-fold reductions in the search space that are required to *uniquely* iden-

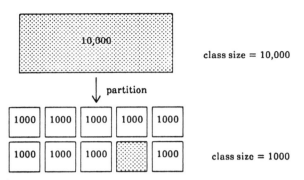

Figure 1
The application of a single lexical partition that decreases the size of the search space by a factor of 10

tify a given item. This process of successive application of partitions is schematized in figure 2. Consequently, Carter argued, the partition that reduced the search space by 90 percent has in fact only extracted *one quarter* of the information required to achieve complete discriminability. Carter moreover showed that his measure of *percentage of information extracted* (PIE) is superior to class size because it can be weighted to reflect the relative frequencies of words within an equivalence class. The class-size measures used by Huttenlocher were at best sensitive only to total class frequency. We shall see later that there is another motivation for using the information-theoretic approach to lexical statistics advocated by Carter: it enables effects to be quantified that could not be investigated using equivalence-class size alone.

Carter's PIE values and Huttenlocher's ECS measure lead to radically different views of how powerful various constraints are in terms of reducing the search space. For instance, the ECS for a 12,850-word dictionary transcribed into broad classes is 31.1 (Carter 1987), approximately 0.25 percent of the original lexicon, 99.75 percent having been eliminated. The PIE value, however, is 79.8 percent, so that approximately *one fifth* of the total information necessary for complete discrimination is *still to be found.*

Using his 12,850-word dictionary, Carter also repeated the study by Pisoni, Luce and Nusbaum (1986), in which only length information was preserved and in which the search space was apparently reduced by 95 percent. Carter's PIE figures demonstrated, however, that 73.5 percent of the information necessary to achieve unique discrimination was still to be extracted. At the other end of the scale, using the mid class transcriptions

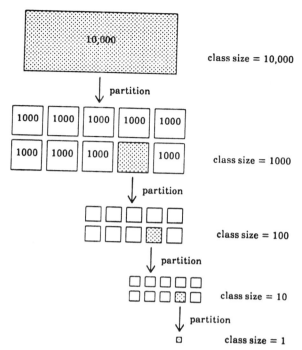

Figure 2
Successive applications of lexical partitions each of which decreases the size of the search space by a factor of 10. Four such partitions are required before the search space contains just a single member.

described earlier, Altmann and Carter (1989) obtained a PIE value of 94.06 percent, which leaves just 5.94 percent of the critical information to be found. The comparisons between the different statistical measures ECS and PIE show that in general statistics based on ECS values paint a far more optimistic picture of how a given partitioning of the lexicon reduces the search space. The former tells us more or less how many words we must discriminate between to reduce the search space completely, while the latter tells us how much *information* is required to achieve this reduction. As such, PIE is the more useful measure.

The studies described in this section transcribed each segment in every word in the same way: they were all transcribed to either mid classes, broad classes, or the same single class. In the following section I consider transcriptions that affect only *some* of the segments in each word as a means to determine which parts, if any, convey the most information about the identity of that word.

Information Content with the Word

The relative informativeness of different parts of the same word can be assessed by manipulating the specificity of information within the word, for instance, by providing full phonemic information for one part of the word but not for another. For example, one could explore whether the phonemic content of the first half of an arbitrary word constrains the candidate search space more or less than the phonemic content of the second half. If the first half is more constraining, equivalence classes (to return briefly to class size as an evaluation metric) should be smaller when phonemic information is preserved in the first half of the word and ignored in the second half than when it is preserved in the second half of the word and ignored in the first. Pisoni, Luce, and Nusbaum (1986) ran the relevant experiments and found that the information in the first half reduced the search space from 126,000 to just 1.7 words, while the information in the second reduced it to 1.9. There was thus only a slight difference in information value (as defined by equivalence class sizes) between the two halves. Huttenlocher (1984) suggested a more principled account of where the main information content might be found. He pointed out that stressed syllables tend to be acoustically more reliable than unstressed syllables and thus more likely to be successfully recognized. It would be maximally efficient if the syllables that are most reliably recognized are also the most informative. To test this hypothesis, he compared two different transcriptions. In the "stressed" condition he transcribed every segment in the lexically stressed syllable into its broad class but used the same covering symbol (*) for each unstressed syllable. Thus the words *piston* and *sultan* are respectively transcribed as /stop, vowel, strong fricative, */ and /strong fricative, vowel, liquid, */. In the "unstressed" condition he transcribed each segment in the unstressed syllable, using the wildcard symbol for each stressed syllable. Thus, the transcriptions for *piston* and *sultan* both became /*, stop, vowel, nasal/. This example illustrates that in the stressed condition the two words can be discriminated but in the unstressed condition they occupy the same equivalence class and are therefore not discriminable. On the basis of the ensuing ECS value—40 in the stressed condition and 2,013 in the unstressed condition—Huttenlocher concluded that even with just broad-class information there was a clear advantage to be found by transcribing only stressed syllables.

Carter (1987) repeated Huttenlocher's experiment with his 12,850-word dictionary and calculated both ECS *and* PIE values. In addition, he used either a broad-class transcription for the syllables to be transcribed or a

Table 1
ECS and PIE values for polysyllabic words
from Carter 1987

	Syllables transcribed	
Transcription used	Stressed	Unstressed
Fine class		
PIE	91.4	83.2
ECS	5.53	29.9
Broad class		
PIE	68.0	69.0
ECS	80.4	111

fine-class transcription (using all 46 phonemes). His results, excluding
monosyllabic words, which do not have both stressed and unstressed
segments, are given in table 1. Carter's results demonstrate that ECS
values suggest an informational advantage associated with transcribing
just stressed syllables for both broad *and* fine class transcriptions but PIE
values show an advantage only in the fine-class condition. So lexically
stressed syllables do seem to be more informative in information-theoretic
terms, but this informational advantage does not manifest itself at a broad
level of segment classification.

Accounting for the Informativeness of Stressed Syllables

The finding that lexically stressed syllables are more informative than
lexically unstressed syllables opens up some interesting issues for research
into both human and machine speech recognition. It might seem fortuitous
that those syllables most likely to be successfully recognized are also those
syllables that constrain the search space within the lexicon more than any
other syllable. But the existence of this relationship between likelihood of
recognition and informativeness does not of itself offer any explanation as
to just why this relationship holds (but see below). Is the mental lexicon
somehow structured to take advantage of the acoustic reliability of stressed
syllables? Is this structuring language-specific? Is the assignment of lexical
stress conditioned by the informational structure of the lexical item? This
last suggestion seems unlikely. But if we reject such an idea, we must seek
some alternative explanation to explain exactly how it is that in English at
least the lexicon does appear to be structured in some informationally
efficient way.

Altmann and Carter (1989) offer one possibility. We proposed that the increased informativeness of stressed syllables might be due to an uneven distribution of *vowel* categories across stressed and unstressed position. The latter are dominated by central vowels, generally the schwa. In the frequency-weighted lexicon there thus might be more vowel categories to choose between in stressed syllables than in unstressed syllables. If one knows whether or not a syllable is stressed and has to guess the category of the vowel, there is a greater probability of success in the unstressed case (with schwa being a safe bet) than in the stressed case. Thus, knowing the identity of the vowel in the stressed syllable, where it could be one of several different categories with roughly equal probability, is more informative than knowing its identity in unstressed position.

There are two ways in which to proceed at this point. Both involve deriving further lexical statistics of one form or another. One of these is to inspect frequency-weighted distributions of the different vowel types in stressed and unstressed position. If there is a relatively even distribution in stressed positions but a relatively uneven distribution in unstressed positions, the hypothesis will have been verified. Presumably, the distributions for *consonants* should look roughly the same if the informativeness of stressed syllables is due simply to properties of the *vowel*. The distributions are shown in figures 3 to 6.

If we look first at the consonants, there is relatively little difference in the overall shape of the histograms in figures 3 and 4. The distribution of consonants in stressed syllables does appear to be slightly more even than the distribution in unstressed syllables, but it is unclear to what extent this would help in trying to guess the identity of a consonant in unstressed position. But from figures 5 and 6 it appears that guessing the identity of the vowel in unstressed position as either /@/ (the schwa) or /i/ is much more likely to succeed than guessing its identity in stressed position.

It appears, then, that the increased informativeness of stressed syllables *is* due to simple differences in vowel distribution. The histograms in figures 3 to 6 are unsatisfactory, however, because they fail to *quantify* the effect. It is impossible to determine just how much *more* informative a vowel is in stressed position than in unstressed position, and it is unclear whether the slight distributional differences between the consonants carry any informational weight. The ECS measure used by Huttenlocher is likewise unsatisfactory: although the informational advantage of stressed syllables shows up, it is unclear whether the ECS values give any way of quantifying how much more information is conveyed by stressed syllables than by unstressed syllables. Altmann and Carter (1989) demonstrate, however,

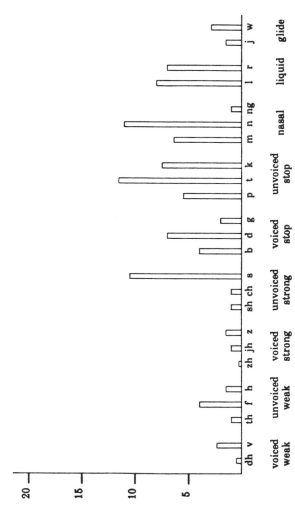

Figure 3
The frequency-weighted distribution of fine-class consonants in stressed syllables, expressed as percentages of the total of such segments

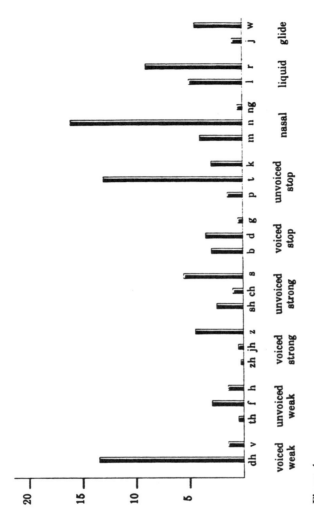

Figure 4

The frequency-weighted distribution of fine-class consonants in unstressed syllables, expressed as percentages of the total of such segments

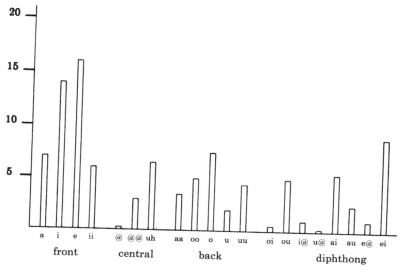

Figure 5

The frequency-weighted distribution of fine-class vowels in stressed syllables, expressed as percentages of the total of such segments

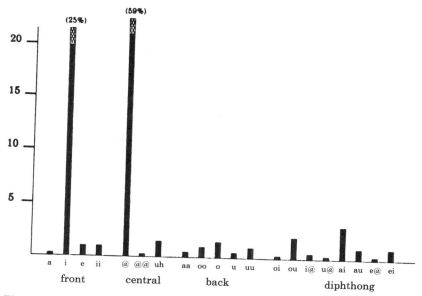

Figure 6

The frequency-weighted distribution of fine-class vowels in unstressed syllables, expressed as percentages of the total of such segments

that by extending the information-theoretic approach in Carter 1987, it *is* possible to quantify the effect.

PIE Values, Entropy Values, and Distributions of Consonants and Vowels

As a first step toward attempting to quantify the increased informativeness of stressed syllables, Altmann and Carter (1989) compared three different kinds of transcriptions. At issue was how much more information is present if a syllable is transcribed into fine-class categories rather than to mid-class categories, as well as whether this depends on whether the syllable in question is stressed or not. To determine this, we compared the following transcriptions:

1. Each segment in the word was transcribed into mid-class categories. This served as the baseline against which to compare the other two transcriptions.

2. Each segment that fell within a stressed syllable was transcribed into fine-class categories, and all the other segments were left in mid-class categories. This gave a measure of how much information is gained by knowing fine-class information in the stressed syllable.

3. Each segment in a specified number of randomly selected *unstressed* syllables was transcribed into fine-class categories, and the others were left in mid-class categories. The precise number of unstressed syllable transcribed in this way was calculated so that the *same* (frequency-weighted) number of segments were transcribed to fine-class categories in this condition as in the previous condition (40%). This condition thus gives a measure of how much information is gained by knowing fine-class information for the same number of segments as in transcription (2) but this time for segments located in unstressed positions.

The results of these three different transcriptions are given in table 2. Because so much information is extracted with mid classes anyway, the results are reported as *percentages of information not extracted* (PINE),

Table 2
PINE values from Altmann and Carter 1989

Transcription	PINE
1. All segments to mid class	5.94
2. Stressed segments to fine class	3.27
3. Unstressed segments to fine class	5.08

which reflects the information that must still be found to achieve total discrimination (i.e., 100 − PIE).[1] The figures in table 2 show that fine-class information in stressed syllables gives approximately 2.7 percent more information compared to the case in which all the segments are transcribed into mid-class categories. Adding in the additional fine class information in unstressed syllables gives only 0.9 percent additional information. Thus, stressed syllables appear to convey about three times more information in terms of the fine-class and mid-class differences than unstressed syllables.

As it stands, however, this study does not distinguish between informational effects due to vowels' being in stressed or unstressed positions and those due to consonants. On the basis of the frequency-weighted distributions shown in figures 3 through 6, one should expect the bulk of this threefold advantage to be located on the vowel and not on the surrounding consonants. To quantify the relative contributions of consonants and vowel segments to the stress effect, Altmann and Carter calculated their *entropy* values.

The entropy in a system reflects the degree of uncertainty about which state the system is in. For instance, if we are given the 46 or so phonemes of the English language and if we assume that any one phoneme is as likely as any other at any given time (although entropy values can be weighted to take into account nonequiprobable distributions), then the entropy of each phoneme (its information content) reflects the fact that at any moment any one of 46 phonemes could be present. The entropy value can be approximately and intuitively thought of as the minimum expected number of bits of information required to encode a random member of the character set, and in the case of English, this is $\log_2 46$. The higher the entropy value, the more choices there might be. Consequently, the higher the entropy value of a phoneme, the more information is conveyed by that phoneme. If a phoneme detector recognized a phoneme that could have been easily guessed, little information has actually been extracted, and this is reflected in a low entropy value for that phoneme. If the phoneme is very unpredictable, recognizing that phoneme means that more information has been extracted.

Table 3 shows the frequency-weighted entropy values for stressed and unstressed syllables with both fine-class and mid-class transcriptions. These values indicate how much information has been extracted by knowing the identity of a syllable, and how this varies depending on whether it is in stressed or unstressed position and whether it has been transcribed to fine class or mid class. The figures in table 3 show that the difference in entropy between fine- and mid-class categories is larger in stressed positions (1.74)

Table 3
Entropy values for stressed and unstressed
syllables from Altmann and Carter 1989

	Position	
Transcription used	Stressed	Unstressed
Fine class	9.87	6.70
Mid class	8.12	6.11
Fine-class — mid-class	1.74	0.59

than in unstressed positions (0.59). Thus more information has been extracted by making fine-class distinctions in stressed positions than by making fine-class distinctions in unstressed positions. And once again it appears that stressed syllables convey about *three* times more information in terms of the difference between fine-class and mid-class categories than unstressed syllables.

The next stage is to calculate entropy values not for syllables but for consonants and vowels, with fine-class or mid-class transcriptions and in stressed or unstressed position. The prediction here is that the entropy values for stressed and unstressed consonants will be about the same whether transcribed to fine-class or mid-class categories, whereas the entropy values for fine-class stressed vowels will be higher than those for fine-class unstressed vowels (and presumably there won't be so much of a difference between mid-class stressed and unstressed vowels). The entropy values are given in table 4. As predicted, there is little difference in the entropy values of different consonants across stress positions: for both fine-class and mid-class transcriptions the entropy values are about the same (as evidenced by the fact that the ratios of the values in the two positions are so close to 1.0). There are, however, substantial differences for fine-class vowels, with a ratio of 0.57, and smaller differences for mid-class vowels, with a ratio of 0.78. We can determine how much more information is provided by a fine-class vowel (as opposed to a mid-class vowel) in stressed position than in unstressed position by subtracting the mid-class stressed entropy value from the fine-class stressed entropy value (3.83 − 1.84) and comparing this to the corresponding figure for the unstressed entropy values (2.19 − 1.44). Once again, it would appear that knowing fine-class information rather than mid-class information in stressed vowels gives approximately three times more information than knowing the corresponding information in unstressed vowels (2.7 times, to be exact).

Table 4
Entropy values for arbitrary consonants and vowels in stressed (S) and unstressed (U) positions from Altmann and Carter 1989

	Fine-class transcription			Mid-class transcription		
	S	U	U/S	S	U	U/S
Consonants	4.07	3.93	0.97	2.87	2.99	1.04
Vowels	3.83	2.19	0.57	1.84	1.44	0.78

To answer the original questions posed by Huttenlocher's and Carter's findings, the increased informativeness of stressed syllables appears not to have arisen because of any fortuitous structuring of the lexicon. It arises because lexical stress preserves distinctions between vowels that are lost is lexically unstressed positions. As long as an acoustic front end can be made sensitive to these distinctions, it will inevitably take advantage of the increased informational value of stressed syllables. Moreover, the results suggest that the effect is language-specific. It is not so much that stressed syllables are more informative as it is that *unstressed* syllables are *less* informative. Consequently, any language that does not have a predominance of reduced, unstressed, or weak syllables will not suffer the informational disadvantages associated with unstressed syllables in English.

In this and the previous section a variety of studies have been described that demonstrate the power of lexical statistics as a tool for exploring certain properties of the lexicon, with consequences for theories of speech processing. In our investigation of stressed syllables, it appears that the consequences are surprisingly limited. The relationship between acoustic reliability and informativeness is in fact quite straightforward: one of the benefits of acoustic reliability is that it allows the speech processor to make distinctions, perhaps even category judgements, that cannot be reliably made elsewhere in the input. This means that it is inevitable, if not actually a tautology, that these segments will be the most informative. Any processor that is sensitive to this increased reliability will therefore be capitalizing on their inherent informativeness. Of course, our investigation of lexical stress does actually ignore any issues of acoustic realization (but see Huttenlocher 1984), but the argument remains the same: the most acoustically reliable segments allow phonemic-category distinctions to be made that cannot be made elsewhere. No special mechanism, aside from the most commonsense one, need be postulated to take advantage of the informational load associated with stressed segments.

The emphasis in these sections has been on calculating the amount of information extracted when only certain parts of each word have been transcribed into some specified phonemic level (e.g., mid-class versus fine-class). This has allowed an investigation of how the informational load, in terms of partitioning the search space, is distributed over the internal structure of words. In the following section I return to the 1986 study by Pisoni, Luce, and Nusbaum, which suggested some further properties of the internal structure of words that might bear on the issue of how the informational load is distributed.

Partial Phonetic Information and Phonotactic Constraints

In Pisoni, Luce, and Nusbaum's original study, in which the lexicon was transcribed by classifying each segment as either a consonant or a vowel, the search space was reduced to just 0.1 percent of the original size of the lexicon. They noted that much of this reduction might be due to phonotactic constraint. Phonotactic constraints, or correlations, arise because not all sequences of segments are equally likely or indeed possible. Consequently, the ordering of segments in an input stream imposes considerable constraint on what can follow next. When Pisoni et al. removed the ordering of the consonant/vowel categories in each word, the size of the search space rose by an order of magnitude to 1 percent.

Consecutive segments are subject to short range dependencies, that is, phonotactic constraints, which are especially strong within syllables. The probability of one phoneme following a given preceding one is *greater* if that preceding phoneme is in the same syllable than if it is in a previous syllable. Whereas there might exist some dependency within one syllable (so that the phoneme /r/ is highly probable if it is preceded in the same syllable by the sequence /st/), there need be no such dependency across syllables (so that the existence in a prior syllable of a /s/ or /t/ phoneme need have no bearing whatsoever on the likelihood of the phoneme /r/ occurring in some subsequent syllable).

Phonotactic constraints reflect the different probabilities of co-occurrence of any two or more phonemes. Equivalence classes, as defined earlier, also reflect these probabilities of co-occurrence: the larger the equivalence class, the more words in it, and hence the more probable that co-occurrence. Conversely, the less probable a co-occurrence, the smaller the equivalence class, and the *more informative* the transcription that captures that co-occurrence. It follows that a reliable transcription of segments subject to strong phonotactic constraints is *less* informative than a reliable transcription of segments not subject to these constraints (and whose identity is therefore less easy to guess).

It follows that a transcription that extracts partial information about only some of the segments in a word will be maximally informative only if these different segments are as free of phonotactic constraint as possible. This has considerable implications for the study of syllable-based effects on information load, as explored in the previous sections. It is an empirical issue as to whether the increased informativeness of stressed syllables found using *syllable-based* transcription schemes manages to outweigh the disadvantages associated with the transcription of adjacent segments occupying the same syllable, and therefore subject to strong phonotactic constraints. A further question is concerned with what the most informative distribution of reliably transcribed segments should be if phonotactic effects are to be minimized: is it more important that the reliably transcribed segments occupy different syllables or that they be nonadjacent? Perhaps the most informative transcription is one that selects segments occupying different syllables irrespective of whether any of the chosen segments are adjacent to one another.

Altmann and Carter explored these questions by comparing two new systems of transcription with the earlier system, in which stressed segments were transcribed into fine-class categories and unstressed segments to mid-class categories:

4. Segments were chosen *at random* to be transcribed into fine-class categories; all others were left in mid-class categories. The number of random segments was chosen so as to match the number of stressed segments in that word (and hence the number of segments transcribed into fine-class categories in the stressed condition reported earlier).

5. The same number of segments was transcribed to fine-class categories, but this time they were all adjacent. The segment at which this contiguous block of fine-class segments started was selected *at random*.

The rationale for choosing these transcriptions was as follows: First, if stressed syllables are not sufficiently informative to outweigh the phonotactic disadvantages associated with reliable transcriptions of adjacent segments, the stressed condition should extract less information than the random condition. This should be reflected in a larger PINE value for the stressed condition. Second, both the stressed condition and condition (5), the contiguous condition, transcribe adjacent segments to fine-class categories, but only in the latter condition do some of these segments fall in different syllables. Once again, if stressed syllables are not sufficiently informative, we expect the stressed condition to have a larger PINE value than the contiguous condition. Finally, the comparison between the random and contiguous conditions allows us to assess whether any phonotactic disadvantage that accrues from transcribing adjacent segments does so simply because they are adjacent or simply because they fall within the same syllable. In both conditions some of the fine-class segments will lie in different syllables, but in the random condition there will be fewer adjacent fine-class segments than in the contiguous condition. If the PINE value for the random condition is smaller than that for the adjacent condition (which indicates that more information has been extracted in the random condition), this will suggest that it is adjacency per se that leads to the loss of information. If the PINE values are similar, we can conclude that phonotactic constraints can be weakened if the crucial segments occupy different syllables, irrespective of whether some of these segments are also adjacent.

The relevant PINE values for all words, monosyllabic words, and poly-syllabic words are given in table 5. The figures of interest here are those for the polysyllabic words, as only in these cases can a single word contain both mid- and fine-class segments (all three transcription schemes result in the same transcriptions for any given monosyllabic word). The figures demonstrate that the most informative transcription, which leaves least information unextracted, is the random transcription. Phonotactic corre-lations do reduce the informativeness of contiguous transcriptions where the reliably transcribed segments all occupy the same syllable, and the informativeness of stressed syllables does not appear to outweigh the phonotactic disadvantages associated with reliably transcribing adjacent segments. The fact that the random and contiguous conditions are so similar suggests in addition that the crucial determinant of whether phonotactic constraints will affect the informativeness of a transcription is whether or not that transcription applies to segments in different syllables. If it does, the effect on informativeness is minimized, even if the segments affected by that transcription are otherwise adjacent.

It is interesting to note at this point that the effects of coarticulation do in fact make it more likely that a front end will more reliably transcribe

Table 5
PINE values from Altmann and Carter 1989

Transcription	All words	Monosyllabic words	Polysyllabic words
2. Stressed to fine class	3.268	5.332	0.321
4. Random to fine class	3.234	5.332	0.213
5. Contiguous to fine class	3.235	5.332	0.215

adjacent segments than nonadjacent segments. Coarticulation results in information relevant to the identification of one segment being superimposed on information relevant to the identification of an *adjacent* segment. Since the likelihood of a particular segment being successfully recognized, and hence reliably transcribed, depends in part on the successful recognition of the context of that segment, it follows that local context effects due to coarticulation increase the likelihood of reliably transcribing adjacent segments. It would appear that this actually counts against the processor in informational terms, but only when the adjacent segments are strongly correlated phonotactically.

Concluding Observations

The intention of this chapter has been to describe some of the issues in spoken-word recognition that have recently been addressed with lexical statistics. Particular attention has been paid to assessing the degree to which such variables as length, stress pattern, phonemic detail, and so on, narrow down the lexical search space. In addition, lexical statistics have been used to locate the most informative segments within the word. Certain considerations, however, must be taken into account when interpreting these statistics. Lexical statistics are, after all, merely descriptions of the particular lexicon over which the statistics have been gathered.

One consideration is that all the studies described so far have assumed that a target language is made up of *isolated* words and that words are recognized on a word-by-word basis and not as part of a continuous string with little or, more often, no information on word boundaries present. Shipman and Zue (1982) found that 32 percent of the words in their 20,000 word dictionary were uniquely identifiable when transcribed into a broad-class level of phonemic detail. But a *string* of such uniquely identifiable broad-class words are not necessarily uniquely identifiable, because there will often be more than one possible segmentation of the string into discrete words. The two word strings *no notions* and *known oceans* can both be hypothesized from the same single fine-class phoneme string, and if that string is transcribed into broad-class categories, many more strings can be hypothesized as well (including *many chins*). Thus the number of lexical items hypothesized on the basis of single, isolated broad-class, or even mid-class, words will be considerably less than when those same isolated words are strung together. Harrington and Johnstone (1988) report a study in which they performed calculations such as these, and they showed that the space of lexical candidates increased by many thousands as soon as mid-class word strings were considered.

A further consideration concerns the precise interpretation of the specific metrics used. We have already seen that the information-theoretic approach to lexical statistics has certain advantages over the class-size approach. The PIE measure gives an indication of how much information has yet to be extracted to achieve total discrimination. The ECS measure merely gives an indication of the size of the remaining search space without indicating how much more constraint needs to be applied to reduce that search space to the point of total discriminability. It might appear, then, that the PIE value is the more useful of the two measures. In one sense this is true, but it must be borne in mind that the proportion of information still to be extracted does *not* indicate how much *work* must be done to extract that information. While it appears that the bulk of the work has been done in transcribing segments only into broad-class categories if PIE = 80, it is not necessarily the case that only 20 percent more work needs to be done. It is quite conceivable that to extract that remaining 20 percent will require almost as much effort as it took to extract that first 80 percent.

The notion of effort here is necessarily vague. From the perspective of automatic speech recognition, it could indicate that certain kinds of information may be more easily extracted in terms of the machine's (and the programmer's) capabilities and resources than certain other kinds. Whether it is a well-founded notion from the psychological perspective is less clear. But there is a further relevant consideration to be taken into account with lexical statistics. The PIE values reported earlier were derived on the basis of phonological information alone. They thus represent the percentage of *phonological* information extracted. But this is not the only available information by which to discriminate between the words in the search space.

There is increasing evidence in the psycholinguistic literature that considerably more than just acoustic-phonetic information can be brought to bear during the recognition process (see, for example, Marslen-Wilson 1987). Within the domain of automatic speech recognition it has been found that syntactic information, for instance, can often be used to help discriminate between alternative lexical competitors (e.g., Thompson and Altmann, this volume, but Frazier, 1987, takes the opposing view and argues that syntactic information is only of minimal use in restricting the search space). There is considerable *redundancy* in the speech recognition system insofar as different kinds of information or constraints can often be applied at any one time. The relevance of this fact is that the speech recogniser may on occasion be in a position to apply one kind of constraint rather than another, perhaps because of some difference in the temporal availability of the two constraints. For instance, if information concerning the expected form class (or range of form classes) is available quite early, it may be simpler to distinguish between two lexical competitors on the basis of their form classes rather than to have to make the fine phonetic distinctions necessary to distinguish between, say, a palatal fricative and an alveolar fricative. Thus the application of one kind of constraint may require less effort than the application, or derivation, of another. PIE values, which take into account only phonological information, by definition cannot give any indication of when and which other kinds of constraints might be more conveniently applied during the search process.

The notion of redundancy is clearly important if the identification of a lexical item is viewed as a process of constraint satisfaction. A study by Altmann and Shillcock (1986) that uses an unweighted 20,000 word lexicon helps make the point. We investigated the joint constraining power of form class and segmental information. We calculated how many words in the lexicon shared the same first segment, the same first two segments, and so on. These equivalence classes were calculated using either fine classes, mid classes, or broad classes. We then repeated the calculations taking into account form-class information so that words in the same equivalence class also had to share the same form class. We found that the size of the search space was drastically reduced after only the first three segments (to 0.02% for fine-class segments, 0.13% for mid-class segments, and 0.77% for broad-class segments). Form-class information further reduced the size of the search space (although as is implicit in the calculations reported in Altmann and Shillcock 1986, rarely is a word constrained to belonging to only a single form class). But what we also found was that the contribution of form-class information to reducing the search space was greatest when there was *less* phonological information, whether in terms of the number of segments considered or in terms of the specificity of the transcription. Conversely, the contribution of phonological information was greatest when form-class information was lacking. Thus the fewer the constraints, the more each one contributed to reducing the search space.

Studies such as these add weight to the suggestion that speech recognition is the robust process that it is simply because of this redundancy: sufficient numbers of different constraints are used to reduce the search space that the absence of any one of them, even an otherwise quite powerful one, will perturb the system only slightly. Our understanding of the processes responsible for human speech recognition and the transfer of these processes to machines are heavily dependent on our understanding of the nature and power of these constraints. Lexical statistics are just one of the tools we have to further that understanding.

Acknowledgments

This work was supported by ALVEY/SERC grant no. D/29628. My thanks to David Carter for comments on an earlier version of this chapter and to Richard Shillcock and Ellen Gurman Bard for their comments on the work reported here.

Note

1. The transcription that involved choosing a specified number of *random* unstressed syllables was run 1,000 times with monosyllabic words and 200 times with polysyllabic words. This gave a standard error of around 0.04 percent in PINE figures to a likelihood of 0.1 percent.

References

Altmann, G., and Carter, D. M. 1989. Lexical stress and lexical discriminability: Stressed syllables are more informative, but why? *Computer Speech and Language*, 3: 265–275.

Altmann, G., and Shillcock, R. C. 1986. Statistical studies of the lexicon. *Association Européenne de psycholinguistique*, newsletter no. 13.

Aull, A. M., and Zue, V. W. 1984. Lexical stress and its application to large vocabulary speech recognition. Paper presented at the 108th meeting of the Acoustical Society of America.

Carter, D. M. 1987. An information-theoretic analysis of phonetic dictionary access. *Computer Speech and Language* 2: 1–11.

Cutler, A., and Carter, D. M. 1987. The predominance of strong initial syllables in the English vocabulary. *Computer Speech and Language* 2: 133–142.

Cutler, A., and Norris, D. 1988. The role of strong syllables in segmentation for lexical access. *Journal of Experimental Psychology: Human Perception and Performance* 25: 385–400.

Dalby, J., Laver, J., and Hiller, S. M. 1986. Mid-class phonetic analysis for a continuous speech recognition system. *Proceedings of the Institute of Acoustics, Speech, and Hearing* 8 (7): 347–354.

Frazier, L. 1987. Structure in auditory word recognition. *Cognition* 21: 157–188.

Harrington, J., and Johnstone, A. M. 1988. The effects of equivalence classes on parsing phonemes into words in continuous speech recognition. *Computer Speech and Language* 2: 273–288.

Huttenlocher, D. P. 1984. Acoustic-phonetic and lexical constraints in word recognition: Lexical access using partial information. M.S. thesis, Massachussetts Institute of Technology.

Luce, D. 1986. Neighborhoods of words in the mental lexicon. Technical report no. 6. Speech Research Laboratory, Department of Psychology, Indiana University.

Marslen-Wilson, W. D. 1987. Functional parallelism in spoken word recognition. *Cognition* 25: 71–102.

Miller, G. A., and Nicely, P. E. 1955. An analysis of perceptual confusions among some English consonants. *Journal of the Acoustical Society of America* 27: 338–352.

Pisoni, D. B., Luce, P. A., and Nusbaum, H. C. 1986. The role of the lexicon in speech perception. Paper presented to the NATO Advanced Research Workshop The Psychophysics of Speech Perception. Utrecht University, the Netherlands, June 30–July 4, 1986.

Shipman, D. W., and Zue, V. W. 1982. Properties of large lexicons: Implications for advanced isolated word recognition systems. *Proceedings of the International Conference on Acoustics, Speech, and Signal Processing*, 546–549. Paris.

Waibel, A. 1982. Towards very large vocabulary word recognition. CMU-CS-82-144, Department of Computer Science, Carnegie-Mellon University.

Chapter 11

Constraining Models of Lexical Access: The Onset of Word Recognition	Jacques Mehler, Emmanuel Dupoux, and Juan Segui

Years of excellent research at many distinguished institutions may license the conclusion that continuous speech has no obvious cues that facilitate the segmentation processes. However, even if cues indicating boundaries or natural segments have not been found, it would be rash to claim that they cannot be found. The lexicon is acquired, and infants are provided with little information about words pronounced in isolation. They are mostly stimulated by continuous speech. Thus, if word boundaries were not available, the acquisition of a lexicon would be incredibly difficult, if not outright impossible. Unfortunately, studies in this domain are by and large not available. So let us take a step back and ask what is known about how adults access lexical information.

It has classically been assumed that the segmentation of continuous speech into words is made possible by using the lexicon. Models of speech processing that maintain that perception is contingent on lexical access favor the view that the signal is matched against the lexicon without any prior segmentation. Segmentation is viewed in these models as a by-product of lexical access. We correctly parse the sentence "The book is on the table" because *bookiso* is not a word. However, these kinds of procedures rapidly run into difficulties. For instance, barring allophonic variations, it may be argued that the phonological realization of the ortho-graphic strings *booki* and *bookis* can be interpreted as words. Moreover, these solutions are not appropriate for coping with frequent instances of phonetic and phonological ambiguity in natural languages, e.g.,

Good candy came anyways.
Good can decay many ways.

Faced with such potential ambiguities, automatic recognition systems adopt two solutions. The first one is to have speakers segment their own speech by inserting pauses between words and/or syllables before the information is fed to the computer (Bahal et al. 1981). The other solution is to rely heavily on constraints derived from higher levels of processing to disambiguate the various segmentations of words embedded in sentences. Unfortunately, such a solution is not sufficient, as attested by the relatively poor score obtained by recognition systems in continuous speech. An even more severe problem for the first solution is that the proposed routines cannot be used by the young infant who is in the process of acquiring spoken language. For one thing, the infant lacks a lexicon, a syntax, and a semantic and pragmatic system. Yet children have to solve the segmentation problem to acquire the lexicon, and they cannot do this in a top-down fashion. This poses a paradox: if infants have to extract words in order to construct their lexicon, how can this process possibly rely on the lexicon? We are apparently back to square one with what seems an unsolvable problem.

In this chapter we will argue that the problems of segmentation might be lifted if we posit a *prelexical unit* available to infants for the construction of lexical entires and the extraction of the phonological structure of speech sounds. We will also provide evidence that infants use a unit that roughly corresponds to the syllable. We suggest that the same type of processing unit is used for speech acquisition in infants and speech recognition in adults. This proposal is compatible with recent data supporting the role of the syllable in adult speech processing (see Segui, Dupoux, and Mehler, this volume).

SARAH, a framework presented in more detail at the end of this chapter, proposes that a syllable-size unit is necessary for the child to correctly parse continuous speech. Each natural language provides cues that may be used by a speech-processing device. Indeed, we argue that continuous speech incorporates acoustic and prosodic cues that facilitate the identification of linguistically relevant boundaries. Such cues ought to be particularly useful during speech acquisition.

Finally, we address the issue that the details of processing and the specification of linguistic units is a function of linguistic experience (Abramson and Lisker 1965, Cutler et al. 1986). Recent results suggest that infants use less-specific processing units than adults (Trehub 1976; Werker and Tees 1984; Best, McRoberts, and Nomathemba 1988). We present some suggestions concerning the mapping of a *universal* system onto a *specialized* one.

We believe that a good model of speech perception must not only incorporate an explanation of lexical access but also present a credible account of how the organism compiles relevant linguistic information to acquire a lexicon. In view of what we do know about the input available to infants, a speech perception routine that in *principle* cannot be acquired remains an inadequate psychological model. Nonetheless, most models of speech perception pay little attention to such learning constraints. In contrast, we posit a rather close *correspondence* between the structures or modules used by young infants and adults and argue that the data collected at both ages can be used to constrain models of speech processing at the initial and stable states.

Processing Units before the Acquisition of the Lexicon

A variety of computational and psychological models have been proposed for spoken-word recognition in adults. Each of these requires the specification of a code in which lexical entries are expressed. Such a code corresponds to the the basic psychological or computational unit in terms of which the acoustic wave is analyzed. After many decades of research, no consensus has been reached concerning its general properties.

An important factor that distinguishes current models in speech perception from each other concerns the *linguistic status* of the processing units. In most computational models, processing units have no clear linguistic status: vectors of linear-predictive-coding (LPC) coefficients, spectral templates, formant trajectories, etc. Klatt (1989) claims that this is desirable, since premature linguistic categorizations may induce virtually irreparable errors. In such models the only relevant linguistic unit is the word itself.

In contrast, in many of the psychologically motivated models, words are represented in terms of such linguistic units as features, phonemes, syllables, morphemes, etc. What differentiates these models is the degree of linguistic reality postulated. Models that acknowledge *strong linguistic reality* postulate processing units that are isomorphic to linguistic constructs. For instance, TRACE postulates phonemic units, and phonemes are recognized via the activation of distinctive features. Likewise, Treiman (1983) postulates the syllables as a psychological real unit and proposes that the *internal structure* of the syllable (onset, coda, rhyme) as described by metrical phonology (Halle and Vergnaud 1987) is used in processing.

Other models adopt units that have *weak linguistic reality*. The units are usually also *similar* to the ones used by linguists, namely, syllables, morphemes, words. However, no a priori commitment is made to the internal *structure* of the units as postulated by linguistic theory. Empirical investigations seek to determine the nature of processes underlying the activation and are using the units to settle this point. Meanwhile, speech-recognition models are being developed with only adults in mind. How well can such models account for speech perception in young infants before they acquire language?

The first problem that a child has to solve is how to identify auditory inputs relevant to maternal language. Clearly, models of speech acquisition must explain why the child does not attempt to construe every possible sound as a potential lexical item. Otherwise, how could we explain why infants do not acquire a lexicon containing chirps, burps, dogs' barks, engine noises, and so forth in addition to words? Theories of speech acquisition must address this issue.

As a matter of fact, if infants represent potential words in terms of purely acoustic information (e.g., spectral templates of say 10 msec each, LPC coefficients, Fast Fourier Transform parameters, etc.), they would not be able to separate a bark from a syllable, say [ba]. Nor would they be able to class together speech sounds, on the one hand, and Schuman's fantasies on the other. However, children do construct a lexicon leaving out noises, music, etc. Although children can recognize a bell, a dog's bark, or a car, they usually cannot say which dog they heard barking or what make of car has gone by. The only lexical compilation that is spontaneously established corresponds to the one used in speech. Thus it is unlikely that infants rely exclusively on acoustic characterizations of speech sounds. In all likelihood humans represent speech sounds by means of structures that are linguistically specific, as is posited by models that postulate a strong or weak linguistic status for processing units in online speech perception. Thus there is some motivation to view speech processing as different from that of other acoustic signals.

One of the most important hypotheses about speech processing was advanced by Liberman and his colleagues (1967), who postulated a special mode to process speech. The speech mode is different from the one used for processing other acoustic stimuli. The existence of a speech mode has motivated a large number of investigations in the last two decades. Some of these investigations directly explored whether speech is special, while others went about it in an indirect fashion. Some investigators argue that the available data show that infants are attracted toward speech sounds and that this makes it possible to demonstrate differential processing of speech and nonspeech stimuli. Colombo and Bundy (1983) reported that four-month-olds show a strong preference for hearing voices over hearing noises. Moreover, this preference is stronger when the voice is presented on the right side. More recently, Bertoncini et al. (1989) showed that four-day-old infants react differently to speech and musical sounds. Infants show right-ear superiority for dichotically presented syllables and a left-ear superiority for dichotically presented musical sounds. The interaction between ear and type of stimulus was significant. These results suggest that very young infants do not have to learn how to process speech and nonspeech sounds differently. Other studies on young infants corroborate these findings. Indeed, Best et al. (1988) and Segalowitz and Chapman (1980) found similar results with a different technique. The human brain is programmed to process speech differently from other acoustic stimuli.

Eimas et al. (1971) attempted to evaluate the ability of one-month-old infants to distinguish and categorize speech sounds. Eimas (1974, 1975) showed that infants categorize stop consonants, liquids, etc., like adults. In short, the infant is born with the ability to discriminate and later to categorize any potential phoneme in any language. Furthermore, human infants are very skillful when it comes to mastering language. Mills and Meluish (1974) reported that fourteen-week-old infants suck more intensely and longer when hearing the voice of their own mothers as opposed to that of a stranger. A similar result was reported by Mehler et al. (1978) with eight-week-olds and by DeCasper and Fifer (1980) with twelve-hour-old neonates.

In brief, infants process speech sounds differently than nonspeech sounds. Indeed, they recognize individual voices soon after birth. These observations are important for any model of speech acquisition. For instance, a proposal compatible with the behavior observed in neonates is that infants are able to *represent* and *memorize* speech sounds in terms of specific abstract linguistic units. It is in virtue of this fact that speech sounds are special. It would appear that classifying a dog's bark and linguistic utterances as different sounds is not a problem for babies. They are already equipped with specialized machinery for processing and representing speech sounds. Thus the data collected with babies favors what we have called the *linguistic status* of the early speech-perception units. However, it is rather difficult at this time to say whether the data favors a weak or a strong linguistic status.

Fine-grained versus coarse-grained models for capturing phonotactics
We assume that humans rely on the speech mode to process incoming speech utterances and to represent these in an abstract format or a linguistic code. What are the properties of such a code? Two types of models can be distinguished on the basis of the size of the proposed processing units. *Fine-grained models* postulate that transduction is smooth and relies on virtually continuous information.[1] During information uptake, central

lexical representations are gradually activated and rapidly deactivated. The process continues until a unique word candidate is isolated. In lexical access from spectra (LAFS), the basic unit of analysis consists of centisecond spectral templates (Klatt 1977, 1989). Recently Marslen-Wilson (1987) has proposed that cohorts feed on such a flow of spectral templates. These models implement an optimal recognition strategy. The lexical system receives new acoustic information on-line, which enables it to select the best word candidate as soon as possible. Fine-grained models, however, need an additional processor to account for the extraction of the phonetic structure of nonword stimuli. In Klatt's initial proposal, LAFS was complemented by the SCRIBER system, another decoding network, whose purpose was to compute the phonetic structure of utterances directly from spectral templates.

In contrast to fine-grained models, *coarse-grained models* postulate that the information flow between peripheral and central levels is discontinuous and relies on rather large information units. In these models a proper intermediate processing level (the prelexical level) accumulates incoming acoustic information before releasing it to high levels. These models do not implement an optimal recognition strategy for speech, because nothing happens before a critical amount of peripheral information has been processed.

A number of mixed models have been formulated to take advantage of the processing efficiency of fine-grained models while still postulating a prelexical level. In these *intermediate-grained models* the information grains are some fraction of syllables. In TRACE the smallest processing unit that contacts the lexicon is the phoneme (McClelland and Elman 1986).[2] Marslen-Wilson (1984) proposed that the reduction of the cohort takes place phoneme by phoneme. Likewise, Cutler and Norris (1979) claimed that words are recognized via phonemes in English. The intermediate-grained models proposed so far have a special feature: they do not need separate processing routes to cope with words and with nonwords. Indeed, the phonetic code of an utterance can be directly extracted from the prelexical levels.

There are many reasons to prefer coarse-grained models. Intermediate-grained models can be classed within the coarse-grained models because they share with them the assumption that processing is discontinuous and based on an intermediary level between the signal and the lexicon, namely, the prelexical level. In fine-grained models of speech perception, phonology and prosody are not explicitly represented, at least at the front end of the system. This deficiency causes fine-grained models to be too powerful, since they can in principle represent very unsystematic or unnatural sequences, e.g., sequences corresponding to a mixture of Serbo-Croatian, Chinese, and English pronunciations. Coarser representations like syllabic trees, morphemes, or word boundaries are needed. Of course, within a fine-grained framework it is conceivable that phonology (syllabic structure, metrical representation, etc.) is derived directly from spectra by a specialized device analogous to the SCRIBER system proposed by Klatt to compute phonological representations directly from the signal.

However, such models should also specify how phonotactic information interacts with the acquisition of a lexicon. One possibility would be that phonotactic information triggers a flag to signal whether the sound sequence is or is not a legal sequence in the language. For instance, such a flag would signal that *pst* is an interjection, *clapitre* a possible French word, and *dlavotnik* a foreign word. Still, this model is not parsimonious, since many of the phonological regularities have to be acquired again in the lexicon. Another possibility would be to postulate that phonological regularities could be compiled at a level halfway between the lexicon and the signal. Of course, such a proposal maps onto a coarse-grained model.

Coarse-grained models propose a level of representation that can potentially filter out sequences of sounds that are illegal in any language, e.g., *pst* and *dztlkfx*. Phonological representations rest on primitives like the syllabic structure and stress pattern of each word. Attempts to model the phonological representations of languages with systems that do not comprehend rules has been tried, but none has paid off (see Pinker and Prince 1988 and Lachter and Bever 1988).

In fact, the smallest segment that can be a word is the syllable. Thus infants, we suspect, compile a bank of syllables, or *syllable analyzers*. Each syllable is represented as the prototype value of coarse-grain sequences that correspond to a compatible phonetic transcript in the language. As soon as the bank of coarse-grained detectors is compiled, lexical acquisition becomes a matter of storage and retrieval. Indeed, metrical and phonotactic regularities can be used to constrain the extraction of word boundaries and provide cues to the morphological components of the system. From the acquisition point of view a coarse-grained model is thus more plausible than a fine-grained model. We are nonetheless aware that this sketch leaves many problems unsolved.

What are the linguistic levels to which the infant pays particular attention? Are infants sensitive to both coarse- and fine-grained speech information, or do they focus preferentially on one of these? Mehler et al. (1978) showed that babies' differential activation to their mothers' voices is not observed when normal intonation is disrupted, which suggests that *prosodic contour* is an important component of infants' speech processing. This finding is compatible with Fernald and Kuhl's (1987) claim that infants prefer to listen to "motherese" rather than to normal speech passages.

It would be rather unfair, however, to suggest that infants are exclusively limited to processing global parameters. In fact, as we showed before, infants are also excellent at discriminating such minimal speech contrasts as [pa] versus [ba], [ra] versus [la], and [pa] versus [ta]. Moreover, infants discriminate very short CV syllabic onsets (spliced from full syllables) where the consonant or the vowel of the full syllable from which they were spliced differs (Bertoncini et al. 1987). This behavior meshes well with adult perceptions. Indeed, adults claim that the very short stimuli give rise to the same phonological representations as the full syllables from which they were derived. Though the behavior of the infants is compatible with adult perceptions, more studies are necessary before it can be argued that infants categorize these short stimuli in the same way as adults. Since infants are so good at processing speech, the next issue that arises concerns the unit or units used to represent and memorize segments of speech. None of the results reviewed so far bears on this issue. Fortunately, a few results can be mentioned in this context.

Bertoncini and Mehler (1981) showed that neonates find it difficult to discriminate between synthetic [pst] and [tsp]. Yet young infants have no difficulty in discriminating [pat] from [tap]. Notice that the segments that indicate the difference between tokens is the same in the two cases, namely, a difference in serial order. Piaget and his collaborators have demonstrated that infants and very young children are not very good at dealing with serial order. How come, then, infants distinguish [pat] from [tap] but not [pst] from [tsp]? In the [pst]-[tsp] case the signals are not well- formed, while in the [pat]-[tap] case they are. However, when we add a vocalic context to the exact same nonspeech segments, such as [upstu] and /utspu/, infants again discriminate the contrast with great ease. These results suggest that infants organize speech sounds in terms of syllables. A contrast embodied in a syllabic context is discriminated even though the same contrast is neglected in other contexts.

Neonates tend to represent syllables as rather global conglomerates. As they grow older, they tend to elaborate an increasingly refined representation. Indeed, in a series of experiments, Jusczyk and Derrah (1987) and Bertoncini et al. (1988) showed that by two months, infants notice the addition of a new syllable into a corpus of four syllables used during habituation, regardless of whether the new syllable's consonant, vowel, or both differ from the most similar habituation syllable. Furthermore, four-day-old infants notice the presence of a new syllable if it has at least one vowel different from that in the preceding syllables. In summary, these results indicate that the infant is fully capable of organizing speech signals in terms of syllables and prosody, i.e., coarse-grained units. Whether the speech signals are always organized in terms of syllables is an open question. However, we know that at least the ability to do so exists at birth.

Temporal normalization
A major problem that must be met by all models of speech recognition like the ones presented above is the fact that speech segments remain perceptually invariant, according to adults, over considerable changes in rate. Lenneberg (1967) claims that English speakers normally talk at a rate of 210 to 220 syllables per minute. He acknowledges, however, that rates of 500 syllables per minute are easy to attain for any normal speaker. Thus, mean syllable length may vary roughly from 300 msec down to 100 msec without affecting the ease or accuracy of comprehension. Chodorow (1979) and King and Behnke (1989) have shown that speech rates can be increased by as much as 60 percent without disrupting the identification of lexical items. At such rates, mean syllable duration is reduced to less than half of the original duration without changing intelligibility. Thus language users show recognition constancy for syllables and words pronounced at very different rates. Such an achievement is comparable to the perceptual constancies illustrated in the visual domain in most textbooks. As for other perceptual constancies, we have to ask whether speech recognition becomes independent of rate by learning or whether it makes language learning possible in the first place. To the best of our knowledge, all experiments that have assessed the intelligibility of compressed speech have used adult subjects.

It is difficult to say whether pre-lexical subjects recognize a syllable as invariant under many different durations. Yet there are informal indications, that infants identify syllables like _dog_, _mummy_, and _ball_ regardless of speaker and durations. Parents never have to repeat a word uttered before so as to match its duration exactly with that of the prior pronunciation. How can they achieve such a performance? The accounts that provide a ready answer assume that the items are already represented in the lexicon and that the signal is recognized by some networklike routine. However, infants do not have a network with lexical items. They have to construct it.

Models of adult speech perception have proposed processing units with two types of temporal characteristics. The *durational* models claim that the minimal unit of analysis spans over a fixed temporal slice (Tyler and Wessels 1983, Marslen-Wilson and Tyler 1980, Salasoo and Pisoni 1985, Tyler 1984). Many computational models propose a purely durational processing routine, e.g., sampling the spectrum of the signal every 10 msec. *Structural* models postulate that the processing unit is constant under varying speech rates. Thus models that specify the primary inputs of their systems in terms of phonemes or distinctive features are synchronized with the rate of speech and qualify as structural models. This is also true of models that propose syllablelike units (Mehler 1981). We will see below that the structural status of the processing unit is crucial for solving the problem of normalizing the speech rate.

Temporal normalization, or freeing the categorization routines from duration, should be very difficult to learn. Durational models posit units of fixed duration, regardless of speech rate. Consequently, a change in speech should become highly disruptive for constancy extraction. To illustrate our point, let us consider the proposition that the first 150 msec of the signal are the processing unit for lexical access (Salasoo and Pisoni 1985). The contents of these 150 msec can, of course, vary dramatically when the speech rate changes. For example, one syllable in the word *capitain* in normal speech becomes over two syllables with a compression rate of 50 percent. If these 150 msec really function as processing units (units that have no internal structure and merely act as a code for accessing the lexicon), this implies that the child should build two access codes for the word *capitain*: *ca-pitain* and *capi-tain*, and for that matter, one for each possible speech rate. This solution, however, lacks design efficiency and raises serious acquisition problems. Indeed, it is mind-boggling to imagine how such a multitude of access codes can be learned and made to correspond to the same word without prior knowledge that they all represent the same segment of speech at different rates. Thus the absence of a normalization procedure seems to be fatal to strict-durational coarse-grained models.[3]

But how about a fine-grained model? Here the information content of a unit (e.g., a centisecond spectral template) seems relatively unaffected by variations in rate. However, speech compression modifies the time course of the activation of these units. If the speech rate is multiplied by two, the number of spectral frames that constitute each word is divided by two. This raises an important problem, since a given word is represented by a great many possible sequences of fine-grained units. If the lexical entries are multiplied by the speech rates an important acquisition problem arises. Indeed, the child must identify all the lexical entries at all possible speech rates to have a lexicon. But to do this the child must identify words spoken at different rates as tokens of identical types. Although we have no idea as to whether this is feasible or not, we are skeptical. Another possibility, proposed by Klatt in LAFS, is to introduce *self loops* into the decoding network. This amounts to introducing a technique of dynamic time warping directly into the network. Such a move turns a durational model into a structural model.[4] Indeed, how many loops will the network have to complete before it halts? Which cues will be used to make it halt? Only structural cues will do a satisfactory job.

Many models of speech recognition define phonemes as a conglomerate of features. In this manner the temporal characteristics of phonemes can be established over a wide range of speech rates. Indeed, mapping articulation parameters might be implemented in a recognition algorithm. However, this is not sufficient, because in such models, duration cues are established as a parameter within phonemes, rather than between phonemes. But the temporal properties of adjacent segments are by no means negligible. Miller and Liberman (1979) have shown that the duration of the first formant transition that distinguishes [ba] from [wa] varies with the duration of the vowel [a]. Hence, an ambiguous sound somewhere between [ba] and [wa] is perceived as a rapid [wa] if the vowel is short and as a slow [ba] if the vowel is long. Moreover, there is some evidence that the average speech rate of the preceding sentence context influences perceptual boundaries, e.g., voice onset time (VOT) (Summerfield 1975) and vowel-duration cues (Port 1976, Port and Dalby 1982). This implies that durational parameters that span over many adjacent phonemes may play a crucial role in speech perception. Models that normalize for rate only in very short segments should induce the child to wrongly categorize sounds, which would make lexical acquisition very difficult, if not impossible. To account for speech normalization, it seems desirable to have a phonetic prelexical level where sequences contain information that spans several linguistic units.

The only possibility left within the two-dimensional continuum of speech-processing models appears to be a model with a rather large structural unit. This type of model accounts for the normalization problem in a rather neat fashion. For purposes of illustration, take a hypothetical syllablelike unit of processing, and let each syllable be represented in a bank of syllabic analyzers. During the processing of speech signals, dynamic time warping tries to adjust each syllabic frame for speech rate. Thus with fast speakers, the spectral entries for each syllable analyzer are time-compressed by a given factor and compared to the signal. However, a compression or expansion factor should be constant within a given syllable. This constraint is absent in finer-grained models where each phonetic segment can be compressed or expanded independently. Thus coarse-grained models allow for normalization procedures that capture for each speech rate trading relations between the durations of consonants and vowels. Of course, contextual speech-rate effects have to be accommodated by postulating an extra mechanism, for instance, that during speech recognition, the bank of syllabic analyzers can come up with the best matching syllable as well as its duration. Thus, when listening to speech, one can arrive at the mean speech rate by averaging the duration of the syllables. This can, in turn, help to disambiguate such cases as [ba] and [wa]. For an ambiguous syllable, the bank of syllabic analyzers outputs two candidates: a rapid [wa] or a slow [ba]. A unique candidate can be selected by choosing which alternative best corresponds to the average speech rate of the context.

In summary and from the perspective of a speech acquisition, a coarse-grained structural model is desirable, since it allows for separate treatment of the problems of lexical acquisition and temporal normalization. Indeed, if the child has a coarse structural unit, his or her perceptual system can be tuned to factor out variations in speech rate. Once stable and invariant prelexical representations are available, the infant can rapidly compile a large lexicon without having to hear every existing word at every possible speech rate.

Everyday language incorporates important alterations in speech rate. Therefore, even very young children must have the capacity to extract constant categories in spite of major changes in speaking rates. What is the evidence that children perform temporal normalization? Miller and Eimas (1983) have shown that infants, like adults, tend to classify CV (consonant-vowel) syllables with a weighted function of formant transitions and the durations of the vowels, which suggests that infants' categorizations are determined by rate. In addition, infants classify sets of multisyllabic pseudowords by the number of syllables (Bijeljac-Babic, Bertoncini, and Mehler, in preparation). In the first experiment it was shown that infants react when changing from a list of bisyllabic items to a list of trisyllabic items or vice versa. Word durations were roughly matched in a control experiment, and the results stayed the same. A replication of these results would be interesting, since this work has important implications for understanding the relation between durational parameters and structural classifications in very young infants.

To sum up the results from research with young infants, it appears that these subjects tend to focus on coarse and global segments of speech rather than on fine ones. However, it must be acknowledged that there is no *direct* evidence that the young child uses syllablelike units for acquiring a lexicon or compiling prelexical representations. Obviously, the child has to rely on prelexical representations to acquire a lexicon. Thus children must engage in prelexical processing. The exact nature of the representations used and the processing on which young infants rely remains to be discovered. Psycholinguistic research provides some information that may be helpful in trying to establish the prelexical processes and units in children.

Cues to understanding infant and adult processing of language
The above arguments, although they remain inconclusive, bias us toward a model that is weakly linguistic, coarse-grained, and structural. Thus in order to steer a middle course, it would appear advisable to evaluate the syllable as a prelexical representation. Syllables are specific linguistic objects, they correspond to minimal speech gestures, and they are not to be confounded with other natural noises. Syllables are coarse-grained and can be used to compile the phonotactic regularity of the native language. Lastly, syllables are structural and are large enough to allow us to conceptualize algorithms for normalizing speech rates. Of course, we acknowlege that different languages may use different sets of coarse-grained, structural, weakly linguistic units (e.g., moras for Japanese). We will evaluate this issue in the next section.

We have argued on logical grounds that in speech acquisition infants probably use a coarse-grained, syllablelike unit, that is, a weakly linguistic, structural unit. Empirical data is scarce, but consistent with the existence of such a unit. How useful would such a unit be with the problem of segmentation and lexical acquisition?

There are several avenues open to explore the information that infants use in the course of lexical acquisition. In fact, there are many regularities at the prelexical level that the infant could use to discover boundaries between natural constituents of speech. Thus allophonic variations of a phoneme may signal the onset of words. For instance, in English the phoneme /t/ is always aspirated in word-initial position but not in intermediate or final positions. This generalization could be very useful to disambiguate sequences like *fast team* versus *fast steam*. Cutler (this volume) argues that main stress occurs mostly in word-initial position and thus potentially signals word boundaries. A similar proposal can be found in Church 1987. However, for the infant to exploit such regularities, the notion of a word with its boundaries must come before.

In French, tonic accent is always in word-*final* position. Moreover, the distribution of syllables depends on their positions in a word. For instance, the syllables *-ique, -isme, -sion, -men* are very frequent in word-final position and quite rare in initial position. Such distributional properties may be useful. For instance, the words *measure* and *solution*, among many others, end with a syllable that is never realized in word-initial position.

Notice, however, that all these cues are language-specific and become available only after the child has established the proper processing routines for its own language. As was pointed out above, some cues even require the acquisition of the lexicon to become functional. How such language-specific cues are acquired is still an open question. But at least, seeing the segmentation problem from the point of view of speech acquisition obliges us to focus on previously ignored aspects of the linguistic signal. Infants, as we have seen above, show a remarkable capacity for processing speech at the prosodic level. Infants also have rudimentary notions of what counts as *phrase units* (see Hirsh-Pasek et al. 1987). We speculate that besides classifying utterances and identifying sentences and clauses, infants may also detect boundaries around words. For instance, when the child first hears a sentence like "Tommy, mange ta soupe" it will be parsed into clauses and then into syllabic templates. Syllabic templates are recognized by the bank of syllabic analyzers. The potential *word boundary detector* may use tonic accent to segment the sentence into potential words (*Tommy, mange, ta, soupe*). Thereafter the child will construct a lexical entry for each word. Consequently, the word *soupe* is represented by one syllable and the word *Tommy* by two. Notice the relationship of this proposal to Gleitman and Wanner's (1982) claim that children pay attention first to the stressed syllables in the sequence and only at a later age to the unstressed ones. This amounts to a segmentation routine related to the one we have in mind. "The child is prepared to believe that each wordline conceptual unit has an 'acoustically salient' and 'isolable' surface expression [that is] an abstract characterization of the sound wave whose surface manifestation in English is a *stressed syllable*" (p. 17).

Alternative mechanisms for surface acoustic cues have been conceived. For instance, the child may scan the continuous signal and simply store words if they are repeated. Words that occur often become represented and play a special role in lexical acquisition. Unfortunately, repetitions have to be found, and that is a major part of the problem that speech-acquisition models have to explain. First the problem of word identification in continuous speech must be solved. Then maybe it will become possible to understand how the lexicon for speech recognition is compiled. Like Gleitman and Wanner, we argue that the child requires surface acoustic cues to segment the speech stream. Furthermore, we speculate that such cues likely continue to be available to the adult. We are aware that hypothetical cues have been postulated to solve the child's bootstrapping problem but have not been uncovered by psychoacoustical research. This is, of course, a problem. However, there are many examples of cues that had not been psychoacoustically discovered but that we now know to be operational. Thus, although psychoacoustics has not yet determined the nature of the encoding, CV- and CVC-initial syllables are marked as such in the signal, as is shown by results obtained by Mehler, Segui, and Frauenfelder (1981). French subjects have shorter latencies to detect CV targets in words whose first syllable is CV and CVC targets in words whose first syllable is CVC. From the responses of the subjects, it appears that responses were elaborated before the lexicon had been accessed. This suggests that in French, initial syllables must be acoustically marked.

But what are the lessons that can be drawn from the infant data for *adult* models of speech perception? It is clear that the type of problem that the infant faces when it encounters its first utterance in English is not the same as that of recognizing one word out of a lexicon of more than 30,000 items. For adults, the problems of separating speech from nonspeech stimuli, extracting phonotactic regularities, and normalizing speech rates have already been solved. We have to acknowledge that in principle adults might use very different processing devices from those used by infants.

Yet current psycholinguistic investigations suggest that this is not the case. Cutler et al. (1983) claimed that the syllable is used as a prelexical representation by speakers of French (but not by speakers of English). Dupoux and Mehler (1990) provide evidence that the prelexical level relies upon large syllablelike units. These units are used either as codes for accessing the lexicon or to compute the corresponding underlying phonetic structure. The lexical code becomes available once a word is recognized. The prelexical code is used to recognize words and/or nonwords. Both codes share a common representation that is also the level at which the phonotactic generalizations of the language are captured. For more details on this issue, see Segui et al. in this volume and Dupoux and Mehler 1990.

The fact that the units used by adults and those used by infants are both syllablelike suggests that they are linked during development. If this is true, much is to be gained in mutually constraining models by the joint study of adults and infants.

Some Open Issues on Language-Specific Tuning

Our proposal so far does not offer the solution to the child's bootstrapping problem. In fact, our proposal has only moved the bootstrapping problem from the lexical to the prelexical level. We posit that infants first parse continuous speech into discrete units and extract word boundaries. But the units and the word-boundary parameters in all likelihood vary from one language to the next. Each language has its own specificity. All languages use phonemes and distinctive features. However, all languages do not honor the same distinctions. For instance, some of them do not make a distinction between [r] and [l]; others use retroflex consonants, clicks, or tones. All languages have syllables, but some of them have syllabic reduction, ambisyllabicity, foots, or moras. All languages have words, but in some of them stress is in word-final position, in others it is in word-initial position, and in others stress can move and have contrastive value. During language acquisition, children learn the phonological and prosodic properties of their language, as revealed by the ability to classify a sequence as a possible word in the language or not. However, they have to do so before the acquisition of the lexicon.

These problems should be all the more difficult to solve if the child confronts several languages at the same time. However, infants raised in multilingual environments do not encounter any major problems in acquiring several parallel linguistic systems. They do not confuse phonology or prosodic properties across different languages. Obviously, adults easily discriminate the language they have mastered from a foreign one, but how can a child who has not yet mastered any language accomplish a similar *coup de maitre*? The child must have a way of segregating utterances from different languages. The set of criteria that might be available to them cannot be based on lexical representations, since the problem is precisely that of constructing separate lexicons for each language. It thus seems obvious that infants construct a representation of what counts as a permissible sequence in their language as opposed to other languages prior to lexical acquisition. There are many surface cues in terms of which languages might be distinguished, for instance, global prosodic contour, metrical structure, phonetic contrasts, syllable structure, etc. More recently Mehler et al. (1988) have shown that four-day-old infants react differentially to *utterances* in the parental language. Infants tend to suck more when listening to French utterances if their parents speak French than with, say, Russian utterances spoken by a single bilingual speaker. Moreover, four-day-old infants respond differently when listening to a sequence of French sentences after a sequence of Russian sentences. Likewise, two-month-old American infants can also discriminate English from Italian. These results suggest that the human infant is able to classify novel utterances drawn from the parental natural language as tokens belonging to a type. They are not able, however, to discriminate tokens of one unfamiliar language from tokens of another unfamiliar language. Although these results need to be explored in further detail, we venture the prediction that it would be fairly difficult for a chimp or a chinchilla to perform like a human neonate even after a huge number of training sessions. A similar result was reported by Bahrick and Pickens (1988). These observations suggest that before they acquire a lexicon, infants can classify utterances into two categories: familiar and unfamiliar language. Mehler et al. (1988) showed that four-day-old infants are still capable of discriminating sequences of French and Russian after the signal is low-pass filtered, which masks most information with the exception of global prosodic contours.

In short, it seems that very early in life infants have a specialized device that classifies utterances of different languages. Furthermore, as we will see in the next section, within their first year of life, infants tune their perceptual system to the language in their environment.

Phonetic to phonemic convergence
The young infant's phonetic repertoire is far broader than that of adults. Monolingual adults are not very good at making discriminations on *phonetic* contrasts when these contrasts are not used in their language. Conversely, their performance is rather good for *phonemic* contrasts. A phoneme is the minimal difference in sound pattern that gives rise to different words. Thus, since /pet/ and /bet/ do not mean the same thing, [p] and [b] cannot be phonemically equivalent. However, /lad/ means the same as /lad/ regardless of whether [l] is produced with the tip of the tongue touching the upper dental ridge or with it displaced laterally (as for the second /l/ of the word *laterally*). With such a definition, a phoneme is an emergent property of a lexicon.

At about one year, infants make most phonetic discriminations, and yet, as far as is known, their lexicon is virtually empty. How do they map their phonetic knowledge onto a phonemic system? Why not store /spit/ and /phit/ as different words with different meanings? The answer is that the child does not wait to compile the lexicon before deciding whether a phonetic contrast is or is not useful in the language.

The evolution of the categorization of speech sounds by infants has been well documented. Indeed, the superb universal aptitudes for categorization displayed by infants at birth tend to decay after some 8 to 10 months of life according to Werker and Tees (1984). Before they turn 12 months of age, infants begin to neglect contrasts that are not used in their linguistic environment. Thus 10-month-old infants raised by English speakers start to neglect the aspirated/nonaspirated contrast used in Hindi. Likewise, other contrasts not relevant to their linguistic environment are lost at roughly the same age. This loss seems to be due to cognitive and attentional processes and not to the loss of sensory-neural sensitivity. If the native and foreign contrasts are similar, unfamiliar speech sounds are assimilated to familiar native categories, which causes the foreign distinction to disappear. In contrast, when unfamiliar speech sounds are too different to be assimilated to familiar native speech categories (Zulu clicks), they are still perceived categorically by inexperienced adults (Best, McRoberts, and Nomathemba 1988). Notice, however, that in all these studies, unfamiliar sounds are phonemically perceived. This suggests that the child has mastered the phonological regularities of his or her language before compiling a lexicon.

If Werker and Tees are right, by the time infants are about to speak, they have already distinguished the relevant from the irrelevant contrasts in their language. Thus the convergence is likely due to a specialized modular system. It seems plausible that computation of the distributions is sufficient to extract statistical modes in speech sounds from the environment.[5] However, no model has as of yet really succeeded in simulating the child's performance. Whatever the exact mechanism of the phonemic shift may be, this reorganization should play a role within future models.

Syllabic and prosodic convergence

Cutler et al. (1986) claimed that English and French adults use different segmentation routines. Indeed, French subjects are sensitive to the syllabic boundary of words like *ba-lance* and *bal-con*, whereas English speakers are not (see Segui, Dupoux, and Mehler, this volume). How does the infant converge on one or the other of these strategies? Empirical investigation of this question with young infants is not yet available. However, Cutler et al. have addressed this issue by testing adult English-French bilinguals. The subjects were raised from birth in a perfectly bilingual environment and were rated as native speakers in both languages. Subjects rated themselves as English or French dominant. French-dominant subjects showed a clear syllabification strategy when listening to French materials but not when listening to English materials. In contrast, English-dominant subjects did not show syllabification in either language. The authors interpret this result by saying that there are syllabic and nonsyllabic strategies for parsing the speech signal.

The question that arises is how the organism tunes in the cues that help segment the speech signal into words. Here again, phonotactic and metrical properties of a language can be seen as a by-product or a *conspiration* (McClelland and Elman 1986) of the lexical items stored in the adult's lexicon. Yet how does the child ever manage to store a few words if he does not know what type of segmentation strategy is useful for his language?

Dresher and Kaye (1990) explore how part of the problem might be solved. These authors have shown that given the syllabic structures of individual words and their stress patterns, a computational model can learn the metrical rules of the language. Thus, given a handful of words sufficiently representative of the language, the algorithm decides whether the language is stress initial, terminal stress, etc. The algorithm selects a system from 200 possible metrical systems by scanning the input words for some robust cues that allows it to set the correct combinations of 10 metrical parameters.

This result is all the more interesting in that it meshes well with what is known about the processing abilities of the child: it seems that children do have access to a syllabic representation and that they do take stress patterns into account (Gleitman and Wanner 1982). Moreover, since the database for inferring the metrical rules is not huge, it is quite reasonable to assume that children rapidly attain a metrical grammar for their language from isolated words or with the help of a rough word-boundary detector. Once compiled, a metrical grammar may provide an important cue signaling language-specific word boundaries to the child.

A Hypothesis about Acquisition and Accessing the Lexicon

What is the link between word recognition and the acquisition of a lexicon? In this section we will propose a framework that we call SARAH (syllable acquisition, representation, and access hypothesis). SARAH provides a common theoretical vocabulary for the study of adult and infant speech perception. This framework postulates a strong correspondence between the processes used by the young infant and those underlying lexical access in the adult.

Our framework postulates a structural, coarse-grained, and weakly linguistic unit of processing. It identifies a syllablelike prelexical segment used to construct potential lexical entries at the initial state and to mediate lexical access and phonemic extraction at the stable state. In our model we propose a set of constraints on how lexical *entries* for spoken words are elaborated during the first years of life. SARAH is a model of how the *forms* of spoken words are acquired. SARAH is *not* a model of how the *content* of the mental lexicon is acquired and represented.

The stable state

SARAH claims that in adults, the front end of speech perception relies on three levels of processing: syllabic, lexical, and phonological.

Syllabic level   SARAH posits that speech is segmented into elementary units that roughly correspond to the syllable. A *syllabic frame* corresponds to an elementary speech utterance, that is, to the minimal functional unit relevant to speech production. This unit captures invariance across speaking rates. Since the number of syllabic frames relevant for a language is rather reduced (about 6,000 for French), it is reasonable to propose that syllabic frames are recognized by a bank of syllabic analyzers.

Lexical level   The bank of syllabic analyzers becomes the code used to access the lexicon. The first syllable of an item constitutes the access code, i.e., the minimal amount of information that can activate a cohort of word candidates.

Phonological level   SARAH claims that phonemes do not play a direct role in speech perception but are derived from the prelexical code, namely, from the syllabic frames.

In this volume Segui et al. argue that such a model accounts for many results in psycholinguistic research. However, more research is needed to specify the exact nature of syllabic frames. Whether the unit corresponds to the syllable as defined in phonological theory or to diphones, triphones, wickelphones, or whatever is a question open to empirical investigation, and the answer may be language-specific.

The initial state

SARAH claims that infants are equipped with at least three basic routines that make acquisition of a lexicon possible.

Syllabic filter   SARAH postulates a syllabic filter that chops continuous speech into isolated elementary syllabic segments. This filter allows only legal sequences such as CV, CVC, V, and CCVC syllables to be analyzed. Sounds like [pst] or a dog's bark are never included as basic sounds. These syllablelike segments are specified in an abstract format, where the type of speaker and speech rate have been factored out. These syllables can be looked on as a kind of gestalt, like, for instance, a square or a triangle.

Phonetic analyzer   SARAH proposes that the infant uses each syllabic representation to compute the underlying universal phonetic representation of the segment. This phonetic analyzer provides a description of the whole syllable in a format compatible with production routines. We thus postulate that these syllables are mapped onto a code that captures the gestures necessary to produce the syllable. To compare this to visual prototypes, the analyzer extracts elementary descriptions of the figure (curved/straight segments, vertical/horizontal main axis, junctures, etc.) relevant to a production routine (a tracer).

Word-boundary detector   SARAH speculates that a word boundary detector uses syllabic representations and other acoustic information to compute elementary cues (duration, stress, etc.) that indicate the onset and offset of words.

This model of the initial state is compatible with findings that suggest that a baby represents speech both at the syllabic and the phonetic levels. Moreover, it acknowledges that infants are able to use prosodic properties of utterances and extract sentence and clause boundaries. SARAH predicts that syllable and word boundaries may also be represented in the signal.

The transition
SARAH claims that the transition from a phonetic to a phonemic system uses two types of specialized mechanisms:

Unlearning, or selective stabilization   At the initial state the young infants possess a universal device to process speech. For instance, their phonetic aptitude is such that they can discriminate any linguistic contrast found in any existing language. Specialization is a process by which such a *universal phonetic capacity* is restricted to a set of language-specific contrasts. SARAH predicts that the same is true for the other devices, namely the syllabic filter and the word-boundary detector. Presumably the syllabic level is much richer in the initial state than in the stable state. By specialization, the syllabic level retains only syllables permissible in the native language(s). Finally, an infant retains only the *word segmentation strategy* that works best for his or her language. Such a process of specialization should depend not on the prior acquisition of a lexicon but rather on such specialized modular routines as statistical extraction and parameter setting.

Compilation   Another acquisition mechanism that SARAH proposes is the storage of syllabic templates and logogens into long-term memory. If the other devices used by the infant (the syllabic filter and the word-boundary detector) are functional and properly tuned, this process is accomplished quite automatically without reference to higher-level constraints. The set of syllable templates helps to bootstrap the acquisition of lexical entries. This set of potential words in turn bootstraps higher levels that facilitate the establishment of a proper morphology for the language in question.

We insist that during the early stages of speech acquisition the entries constructed by the child may be quite remote from what they are in adults. For instance, it seems very likely that children acquire their first potential words as syllables and then as clusters of syllables taken from sentences. These may include, in addition to words, some extra materials such as adjacent closed-class words or clitics ([ðedog], or [delo] (*de l'eau*) in French). How these entries are cleaned up to converge toward those of adults, although not yet understood, at least requires the joint operation of bottom-up and lexical-morphological indices.

Concluding remarks about SARAH

Most models of speech recognition have focused on the performance of adults. Yet researchers have reached no general consensus as to the specific units used to represent and process speech. We claim that much is to be gained by changing perspective so as to acknowledge strong constraints that can be derived by taking acquisition into account.

The basic structures and routines that operate in adult speakers must come from somewhere. It is unlikely that all structures come from thin air or from the linguistic environment of the infant. In fact, as many linguists, psychologists, and others have pointed out (Chomsky 1957, Fodor 1983, etc.), extreme instructivist models of language acquisition are inadequate. Speech acquisition is fast, it honors biological landmarks, and its pace is relatively immune to environmental variations. In a sense, speech acquisition is like specialized acquisitions in other species due mostly to instinctive learning, parameter setting, or hypothesis testing. Thus the main structures used by the adult depend on the biological makeup of the species and should be linked to information-processing structures present in the infants. The rough sketch we have presented has many loose ends and shortcomings. However, it raises many empirical issues and opens new avenues for modeling. We hope that with further research SARAH will acquire speech better than the famous ape of the same name.

Acknowledgments

This research was carried out with the help of CNET (convention no. 00790 9245 DIT), CNRS (ATP Aspects Cognitifs et Neurobiologiques du Langage), and the European Science Foundation (TW 86/17).

Notes

1. We acknowledge that the senses transduce information continuously. The basilar membrane, for one, is set in motion by the acoustic waves in the environment, and information travels up the acoustic fibers in a complex but basically continuous fashion. This mechanism is elegantly illustrated in Delgutte 1980 and Delgutte and Kiang 1984. Likewise, the retina transmits information continuously when the viewer is stimulated by light energy. So there needs to be little, if any, discussion about the continuous versus discontinuous nature of information *transduction*. Our aim, however, is to understand how continuous sensory information is used in speech perception and how the mapping between acoustic energy and higher levels of representation takes place.

2. However, since phonemes are defined over a configuration of distinctive features and since the information flow between different nodes is rather smooth, it could be argued that TRACE *behaves* like a continuous fine-grained model.

3. Of course, a more indulgent reading of this proposition is that the exact duration of the processing window is not fixed but depends on the speech rate. However, such a proposition should specify in a principled way how the speech rate affects the window. In our view this amounts to positing a structural unit.

4. Since the percolation of information into units is related to the rate of variability in the signal, even a structural version of a very fine-grained model is inadequate. First of all, no information is provided as to the value of the individual loops. Thus very odd noises could be learned as proper words (but a burst spectrum of 10,000 msec followed by a voicing onset spectrum of 20,000 msec before a single vowel midpoint spectrum is not likely to be identified as /ta/ by humans). Second, the duration of spectral components is crucial for consonant identification: voice onset time (VOT), the slope of formant transitions, etc. Self loops at every critical band spectrum are thus likely to disrupt performance. As a result, both potential solutions have shortcomings. However, part of the problem might be overcome by using larger units.

5. Data from Lisker and Abramson 1970 indicate that the statistical distribution of VOT in production of the [ba]–[pa] continuum is affected by the native speaker's

language. Clear modes of production are observed in the region of phonemic categories.

References

Abramson, A. S., and Lisker, L. 1965. Voice onset time in stop consonants: Acoustic analysis and synthesis. In *Proceedings of the Fifth International Congress of Acoustics*, Liège.

Bahal, L., Bakis, R., Cohen, P., Cole, A., Jelinek, F., Lewis, L., and Mercer, R. 1981. Speech recognition of a natural text read as isolated words. In *Proceedings of the ICASSP*, Atlanta, Ga., March–April, pp. 1168–1171.

Bahrick, L. E., and Pickens, J. N. 1988. Classification of bimodal English and Spanish language passages by infants. *Infant Behavior and Development* 11:277–296.

Bertoncini, J., Bijeljac-Babic, R., Blumstein, S., and Mehler, J. 1987. Discrimination in neonates of very short CV's. *Journal of the Acoustical Society of America* 82:31–37.

Bertoncini, J., Bijeljac-Babic, R., Jusczyk, P. W., Kennedy, L., and Mehler, J. 1988. An investigation of young infants' perceptual representations of speech sounds. *Journal of Experimental Psychology: General* 117:21–33.

Bertoncini, J., and Mehler, J. 1981. Syllables as units in infant speech perception. *Infant Behavior and Development* 4:247–260.

Bertoncinci, J., Morais, J., Bijejac-Babic, R., McAdams, S., Peretz, I., and Mehler, J. 1989. Dichotic perception and laterality in neonates. *Brain and Language* 37:591–605.

Best, C. T., McRoberts, G. W., and Nomathemba, M. S. 1988. Examination of perceptual reorganization for nonnative speech contrasts: Zulu click discrimination by English-speaking adults and infants. *Journal of Experimental Psychology: Human Perception and Performance* 14, no. 3:345–360.

Bijeljac-Babic, R., Bertoncini, J., and Mehler, J. In preparation. Discrimination de séquences multisyllabiques naturelles chez le nouveau-né de quatre jours.

Chodorow, M. S. 1979. Time compressed speech and the study of lexical and syntactic processing. In W. E. Cooper and E. T. C. Walker (eds.), *Sentence Processing: Psycholinguistic Studies Presented to Merrill Garrett*. Hillsdale: L. Erlbaum.

Chomsky, N. 1957. *Syntactic Structure*. The Hague: Mouton.

Church, K. W. 1987. Phonological parsing and lexical retrieval. *Cognition* 25:53–70.

Colombo, J., and Bundy, R. S. 1983. Infant response to auditory familiarity and novelty. *Infant Behavior and Development* 6:305–311.

Cutler, A., Mehler, J., Norris, D., and Segui, J. 1983. A language-specific comprehension strategy. *Nature* 304:159–160.

Cutler, A., Mehler, J., Norris, D., and Segui, J. 1986. The syllable's differing role in the segmentation of French and English. *Journal of Memory and Language* 25:385–400.

Cutler, A., and Norris, D. 1979. Monitoring sentence comprehension. In W. E. Cooper and E. C. Walker (eds.), *Sentence Processing: Psycholinguistic Studies Presented to Merrill Garrett*. Hillsdale: L. Erlbaum.

DeCasper, A. J., and Fifer, W. P. 1980. Of human bonding: Newborns prefer their mother's voices. *Science* 208: 1174–1176.

Delgutte, B. 1980. Representation of speech-like sounds in the discharge patterns of auditory-nerve fibers. *Journal of the Acoustical Society of America* 68: 843–857.

Delgutte, B., and Kiang, N. Y. S. 1984. Speech coding in the auditory nerve. Parts 1–5. *Journal of the Acoustical Society of America* 75: 866–918.

Dresher E. and Kaye, J. 1990. A computation learning model for metrical phonology. *Cognition* 34, no. 2.

Dupoux, E., and Mehler, J. 1990. Monitoring the lexicon with normal and compressed speech: Frequency effects and the prelexical code. *Journal of Memory and Language* 29, no. 3: 316–335.

Eimas, P. D. 1974. Auditory and linguistic processing of cues for place of articulation by infants. *Perception and Psychophysics* 16, no. 3: 513–521.

Eimas, P. D. 1975. Auditory and phonetic coding of the cues for speech: Discrimination of the (r-l) distinction by young infants. *Perception and Psychophysics* 18, no. 5: 341–347.

Eimas, P. D., Siqueland, E. R., Jusczyk, P. W., and Vigorito, J. 1971. Speech perception in infants. *Science* 171: 303–306.

Fernald A., and Kuhl, P. 1987. Acoustic determinants of infant preference for motherese speech. *Infant Behavior and Development* 10: 279–293.

Fodor, J. A. 1983. *The Modularity of Mind*. Cambridge: MIT Press.

Gleitman, L. R., and Wanner, E. 1982. Language acquisition: The state of the state of the art. In E. Wanner and L. R. Gleitman (eds.), *Language Acquisition: State of the Art*. New York: Cambridge University Press.

Halle, M., and Vergnaud, J. R. 1987. *An Essay on Stress*. Cambridge: MIT Press.

Hirsh-Pasek, K., Kemler Nelson, D. G., Jusczyk, P. W., Cassidy, K. W., Druss, B., and Kennedy, L. 1987. Clauses are perceptual units for young infants. *Cognition* 26: 269–286.

Jusczyk, P. W., and Derrah C. 1987. Representation of speech sounds by young infants. *Developmental Psychology* 23: 648–654.

Jusczyk, P. W., Hirsh-Pasek, K., Kemler Nelson, D. G., Kennedy, L. J., Woodward, A., and Piwoz, J. Submitted. Perception of acoustic correlates to major phrasal units by young infants.

King, P. E., and Behnke, R. R. 1989. The effect of time-compressed speech on comprehensive, interpretive, and short-term listening. *Human Communication Research* 15, no. 3: 428–443.

Klatt, D. 1977. Review of the ARPA Speech Understanding Project. *Journal of the Acoustical Society of America* 62, no. 6.

Klatt, D. 1989. Review of selected models in speech perception. In W. D. Marslen-Wilson (ed.), *Lexical Representation and Process*. Cambridge: MIT Press.

Lachter, J., and Bever, T. G. 1988. The relation between linguistic structure and associative theories of language learning—A constructive critique of some connectionist learning models. *Cognition* 28:195–247.

Lenneberg, E. 1967. *Biological Foundations of Language*. New York: Wiley.

Liberman, A. M., Cooper, F. S., Shankweiler, D. P., and Studdert-Kennedy, M. 1967. Perception of the speech code. *Psychological Review* 74:431–461.

Liberman, A. M., and Mattingly, I. G. 1985. The motor theory of speech revised. *Cognition* 21:1–36.

Lisker, L., and Abramson, A. S. 1970. Some experiments in comparative phonetics. In *Proceedings of the Sixth International Congress of Phonetic Sciences*. Prague: Academia.

McClelland, J. L., and Elman, J. L. 1986. The TRACE model of speech perception. *Cognitive Psychology* 18:1–86.

Marslen-Wilson, W. D. 1984. Function and process in spoken word recognition. In H. Bouma and D. G. Bouwhuis (eds.), *Attention and Performance vol. 10, Control of Language Process*. Hillsdale: L. Erlbaum.

Marslen-Wilson, W. D. 1987. Functional parallelism in spoken word recognition. *Cognition* 71:71–102.

Marslen-Wilson, W. D., and Tyler, L. K. 1980. The temporal structure of spoken language understanding. *Cognition* 8, no. 1: 1–71.

Mehler, J. 1981. The role of syllables in speech processing: Infant and adult data. *Philosophical Transactions of the Royal Society of London* B295:333–352.

Mehler, J., Bertoncini, J., Barrière, M., and Jassik-Gerschenfeld, D. 1978. Infant recognition of mother's voice. *Perception* 7:491–497.

Mehler, J., Dommergues, J. Y., Frauenfelder, U., and Segui, J. 1981. The syllable's role in speech segmentation. *Journal of Verbal Learning and Verbal Behavior* 20:298–305.

Mehler, J., Jusczyk, P., Lambertz, G., Halsted, N., Bertoncini, J., and Amiel-Tison, C. 1988. A precursor of language acquisition in young infants. *Cognition* 29:143–178.

Mehler, J., Segui, J., and Frauenfelder, U. 1981. The role of the syllable in language acquisition and perception. In Terry Myers, John Laver, and John Anderson (eds.), *The Cognitive Representation of Speech*. Amsterdam: North-Holland Publishers.

Miller, J. L., and Eimas, P. D. 1983. Studies on the categorization of speech by infants. *Cognition* 13:135–165.

Miller, J. L., and Liberman, A. M. 1979. Some effects of later occuring information on the perception of stop consonants and semivowels. *Perception and Psychophysics* 25:457–465.

Mills, M., and Meluish, E. 1974. Recognition of the mother's voice in early infancy. *Nature* 252:123–124.

Piaget, J. 1977. *La construction du réel chez l'enfant.* 6th ed. Paris: Delachaux et Niestlé.

Pinker, S., and Prince, A. 1988. On language and connectionism: Analysis of a parallel distributed processing model of language acquisition. *Cognition* 28:73–193.

Port, R. F. 1976. The influence of speaking tempo on the duration of stressed vowel and medial stop in English trochee words. Doctoral dissertation.University of Connecticut.

Port, R. F., and Dalby, J. 1982. Consonant/vowel ratio as a cue for voicing in English. *Perception and Psychophysics* 32:141–152.

Salasoo, A., and Pisoni, P. A. 1985. Interaction of knowledge sources in spoken word recognition. *Journal of Memory and Language* 24:210–231.

Segalowitz, S. J., and Chapman, J. S. 1980. Cerebral asymmetry for speech in neonates: A behavioral measure. *Brain and Language* 9:281–288.

Summerfield, A. Q. 1975. Aerodynamics versus mechanics in the control of voicing onset in consonant-vowel syllables. In *Speech Perception*, no. 4, Department of Psychology, Queen's University of Belfast.

Trehub, S. E. 1976. The discimination of foreign speech contrasts by infants and adults. *Child Development* 47:466–472.

Treiman, R. 1983. The Structure of spoken syllables: Evidence from novel word games. *Cognition* 15:49–74.

Tyler, L. K. 1984. The structure of the initial cohort: Evidence from gating. *Perception and Psychophysics* 36:217–222.

Tyler, L. K., and Wessels, J. 1983. Quantifying contextual contributions to word-recognition processes. *Perception and Psychophysics* 34:409–420.

Werker, J. F., and Tees, R. C. 1984. Cross-language speech perception: Evidence for perceptual reorganization during the first year of life. *Infant Behavior and Development* 7:49–63.

Chapter 12

The Role of the Syllable in Speech Segmentation, Phoneme Identification, and Lexical Access	Juan Segui, Emmanuel Dupoux, and Jacques Mehler

In previous papers we proposed that the syllable is a natural unit in speech processing (Mehler, Segui, and Frauenfelder 1981; Mehler 1981; Segui 1984). According to this position, syllabic units are constructed from the continuous speech signal and constitute the input for lexical access and eventually for more detailed phonemic analysis. This hypothesis is independent of the phonological properties of different natural languages. In the three sections of this chapter we review some recent experimental findings concerning the role of the syllable in speech segmentation, phoneme identification, and lexical access.

The Role of the Syllable in Speech Segmentation

In an initial study Mehler, Dommergues, Frauenfelder, and Segui (1981) investigated the role of the syllable as a unit in speech segmentation. These authors demonstrated that subjects responded faster to a phonemic target sequence when it corresponded to the initial syllable of the target-bearing word than when it did not. For instance, the target *pa* was detected faster in the word *pa-lace* than in the word *pal-mier*, whereas the target *pal* was detected faster in *pal-mier* than in *pa-lace*. In this experiment, target-bearing items began with a stop consonant (/p/, /t/, /k/, /b/, or /g/) followed in all cases by the vowel /a/. The interaction between target type (CV or CVC) and word type (CV or CVC) was highly significant (C = consonant; V = vowel). According to Mehler, Dommergues, et al. (1981), these results indicate that the syllable constitutes a basic intermediary unit in speech perception.

These experimental findings were recently replicated in Spanish by Sanchez-Casas (1988) and Bradley, Sanchez-Casas, and Garcia-Albea (1988), who used a larger number of experimental words beginning with a step consonant, a fricative, a liquid, or a nasal followed by any single vowel permitted in Spanish. As in French, when the target syllabic structure (CV or CVC) and the syllabic structure of the experimental word (CV or CVC) matched, response times (RTs) were shorter than in the nonmatching case. The syllabic effect was larger when the target sequence was specified auditorily rather than visually.

Some caution is necessary concerning the interpretation of these results, since the global RTs obtained by Sanchez-Casas and Bradley et al. were much greater than those observed in French (600 msec versus 360 msec, respectively). Differences in RTs may result from the use of alternative processing strategies, namely prelexical versus lexical strategies. This is important for interpreting the obtained results. In particular, if detection responses are derived from a lexical code, they can reflect the syllabic format of this code and not necessarily the syllabic nature of a prelexical segmentation strategy.

Finally, Morais et al. (1989) observed a syllabic effect in Portuguese with illiterate and ex-illiterate subjects using a modified version of the experimental procedure of Mehler, Dommergues, et al. (1981). In this experiment the dependent variable was the number of correct detections rather than RTs, and the targets were, of course, specified auditorily. A significant interaction was found between target type and word type: detections were more numerous when the target coincided with the first syllable of the experimental word than when it did not. The syllabic effect was similar for the two populations even if ex-illiterate subjects performed better than illiterate ones. This result suggests that Portuguese subjects tend to represent spoken words as a sequence of syllabic units. Furthermore, the comparability of the syllabic effect on the two populations indicates that this form of representation depends essentially on informal experience with the language rather than on formal instruction.

The syllabic effect observed in the three previously examined experiments was obtained with romance languages having clear syllabic boundaries and rather restricted syllabic structures. But what about other families of languages, and in particular, languages having unclear syllabic boundaries? The results obtained on this point are ambiguous.

To test the generality of the syllabic hypothesis, Cutler et al. (1983, 1986) conducted their first English experiment. Contrary to French, many English words do not have a clear syllabic structure. For instance, the syllabic boundary for the word *balance* falls neither clearly before nor after the phoneme /l/. When English subjects are asked to segment this type of word, they do not agree about the location of the syllabic boundary

(Treiman and Danis 1988). To represent the syllabic structure of these words in which an intervocalic consonant precedes an unstressed vowel, linguists have proposed that, in fact, the intervocalic consonant belongs to both the first and the second syllable. In other words, this phonetic segment is ambisyllabic.

In the 1986 experiment by Cutler et al. subjects received words with clear initial syllabic structure like *bal-cony* (CVC words) and words with ambisyllabic second consonants like *ba(l)ance* (CV(C) words). As in the original French experiment, the target sequences used in this English experiment were CV and CVC. No trace of syllabifying segmentation found in this experiment for CVC and CV(C) words. Monitoring latencies for CV and CVC targets were practically identical in both types of words.

The absence of a target effect runs counter to the syllabic hypothesis. In particular, if CVC targets corresponded to the initial syllable of CVC words and at least in some cases to that of CV(C) words, a global CVC target advantage should be found. This was not the case, however. Nevertheless, a word-type effect was observed, CV(C) words being responded to faster than CVC words. The faster RTs for CV(C) words than for CVC words was attributed to the fact that alternating consonant-vowel patterns like CVC (*balance*) lend more readily to segmentation than nonalternating strings like CVCC (*balcony*). Thus the faster response to CVC words over CV words may be interpreted by pointing to the facility with which subsyllabic units were identified.

To interpret the total absence of a syllabic effect in English, Cutler et al. proposed that English subjects used a phonological, rather than a syllabic, segmentation device. The output of this device, which may be used to process languages with irregular syllabic structure, is a phonological representation of speech without any intermediate representation. The hypothesis of a phonological segmentation device may explain the differences observed in detecting target sequences as a function of the initial structural properties of the carrier word. Some sequences of phonemes (alternating consonant-vowel sequences) seem to be easier to deal with than others (nonalternating sequences). In any case, it is clear at this point that a purely phonetic segmentation device does not explain the absence of a difference between CV and CVC targets. Indeed, if words are computed phoneme by phoneme, one should predict shorter RTs for CV than for CVC targets.

More recently Sanchez-Casas (1988) and Bradley et al. (1988) confirmed the absence of an interaction between word type and target type for English. However, contrary to the 1986 results of Cutler et al., these authors observed that CVC targets are generally responded to faster than CV targets. This result was observed independently of the structure of the experimental words, CVC or CV(C). As noted above, these results may be considered to reflect the use of a syllabic strategy if we assume that the initial syllable of CV(C) words may be, at least in some cases, the initial CVC sequence. Nevertheless, Sanchez-Casas and Bradley et al. assumed that the advantage of CVC targets over CV targets is best explained in terms of the ease with which the mental representation of the target can be developed and maintained rather than as reflecting the use of a syllabic-segmentation routine. Independently of the different theoretical interpretations, it is clear that there is an empirical discrepancy between the results of Cutler et al. and those obtained by Sanchez-Casas and Bradley et al.

The hypothesis of Cutler et al., according to which French and English listeners employed two qualitatively different speech-perception routines, can be further evaluated on the basis of some recent results that Zwitserlood et al. (in preparation) observed in Dutch. Like English, Dutch is a language with widespread ambisyllabicity. In particular, in Dutch a syllable with a short vowel is *necessarily closed by a consonant*. Furthermore, if this consonant is followed by another vowel, this consonant is the onset of the second syllable, which results in ambisyllabicity (e.g., *bo(k)en*). However, if the second consonant is followed by another consonant, the second consonant belongs unequivocally to the first syllable (e.g., *bok-ser*). On the other hand, words having a long vowel following the initial consonant have clear syllable boundaries of either the CVV type (e.g., *maa-gen*) or the CVVC type (*maag-den*).

In the experiment by Zwitserlood et al. subjects monitored CV, CVV, CVC, and CVVC words with clear and unclear syllabic boundaries for the presence of target sequences consisting of two or three phonemes. The results obtained for words having a clear syllabic structure and a long vowel reproduce the interaction obtained in French between target type and word type (CVV targets are detected faster in CVV-C words than in CVVC words, whereas CVVC targets are detected faster in CVVC words than in CVV-C words). These results corroborate those previously observed in French.

The main finding in this experiment was the presence of a clear target-type effect for syllabically clear CVC words and for ambisyllabic CV(C) words. Reaction times for these two types of words were significantly shorter for CVC targets than for CV targets. On the other hand, monitoring times for CVC targets were identical in clear syllabic words like *win-de* and in ambisyllabic words like *wi(n)en*. According to the authors, these results indicate that Dutch listeners used a syllabification strategy for clear and ambisyllabic words, since they were just as successful in segmenting both word types.

The experiments examined in this first section confirm the existence of a syllabic effect in syllable monitoring in languages having clear syllabic boundaries like French, Spanish, and Portuguese. However, as noted above, only the results obtained in French and eventually to be obtained in Spanish may be considered to reflect the use of an on-line syllabic segmentation strategy. Results obtained in experiments conducted with languages having less clear syllabic boundaries are open to alternative interpretations. In particular, although data obtained in Dutch are compatible with a reformulation of the syllabic hypothesis according to which phonological "knowledge" about the syllabic regularities of the language may be exploited on-line to segment the speech wave (even if no specific syllabic cues are present in the signal), results observed in English do not appear interpretable in the framework of this hypothesis and suggest on the contrary the use of a nonsyllabic segmentation strategy. Independent of the final issue concerning the nature of the segmentation strategy(ies), the experiments examined above indicate the necessity of taking into consideration the precise phonological structure of the languages employed in order to propose a realistic interpretation of the empirical data.

The Role of the Syllable in Phoneme Identification

The results obtained in previous experiments on phoneme and syllable monitoring suggest that phoneme detection is highly related to the internal structure of the syllable. In particular, Segui, Frauenfelder, and Mehler (1981) observed a strong correlation between phoneme and syllable RTs for words and nonwords. According to these authors, the syllable can be seen as the structural unit from which subsyllabic phonemic analysis originates. In other words, syllables are used to compute their corresponding underlying phonetic structures. In this section we revise some recent results that agree with this aspect of the syllabic hypothesis.

In a series of experiments conducted with French material, Cutler, Mehler, et al. (1987) report a correlation between the RT to detect the initial phonemes of a syllable and the structural complexity of this syllable. This structural complexity can be expressed in terms of the presence or absence of an initial consonant cluster and the presence or absence of a final consonant.

In their first experiment, conducted with French subjects, Cutler et al. observed shorter RTs to detect an initial phoneme in CV syllables than in CVC or CCV syllables. This effect is independent of the lexical status of the target-bearing item (word or nonword). However, RTs to words were shorter than RTs to nonwords.

In a second experiment English subjects were tested with the French experimental material. The effect of syllabic complexity is clearly replicated (CV RTs < CVC RTs < CCV RTs), whereas the lexical status of the target-bearing items does not have any significant effect. These results indicate that the syllabic-complexity effect seems to be independent of the subject's language. In fact, in an experiment conducted in English, Treiman et al. (1982) obtained results comparable to those reported by Cutler, Mehler, et al. (1987) using the same CV, CVC, and CCV types of syllables. RTs to detect the initial phoneme of CCV syllables differed significantly from those obtained with CVC and CV syllables. CV syllables were responded to faster than CVCs for seven out of the eight phoneme-bearing targets, but the difference was not statistically significant. Thus RTs were ranked in the same order as in the experiment by Cutler, Mehler, et al. (1987), CV < CVC < CCV.

Based on formal linguistic descriptions that ascribe an internal structure to the syllable in terms of onset and rhyme, Treiman et al. (1982) concluded that the onset component of the syllable constitutes a perceptual unit. It is the analysis of the syllable in elementary phonemic segments that accounts for the increase in reaction time to initial phonemes in CCV syllables.

In spite of the importance of the above results, which provide strong evidence that identification of the phoneme target depends on the internal structure of the syllable-bearing target, this effect must be reexamined in the light of Cutler, Butterfield, and William's (1987) critique of the experiments of Treiman et al. (1982). Cutler et al. maintain that the differences in RTs obtained by Treiman et al. for syllables bearing an initial consonant cluster (CCV) and those with a simple onset (CV or CVC) can be attributed to the fact that "phoneme monitoring targets are customarily specified for subjects in the form of a word mode. Morever, these models have usually had single-phoneme onset" (p. 407). Such a specification would lead the subject to represent the phoneme target as appearing in a simple CV context. This means that the "best correspondance" between the representation of the target induced by the experimental model and the properties of the stimulus accounts for the differences in RTs observed for CV and CCV stimuli.

To support this interpretation, Cutler, Butterfield, and Williams (1987) conducted an experiment in which subjects listened for word-initial target phonemes in continuous utterances. The target phoneme was a single onset in a CV syllable, or it corresponded to the first consonant of a consonant cluster onset in a CCV syllable. The model that subjects were given for the target matched or did not match the syllabic onset of the target bearing word. Faster RTs were observed when the target had been modeled with the same onset. Thus, when the instructions are to detect phoneme /b/ "as in *blue*," RTs are shorter for the stimulus *blend* (the same /bl/ consonantic cluster) than for the stimulus *besk* or *break*.

In view of these results it seems important to confirm the existence of a syllabic-complexity effect on phoneme detection with an experimental procedure capable of neutralizing the effect of the experimental model. The following two experiments were conducted to establish this point.

Experiment 1

In this experiment we studied the effect of two structural parameters on the detection of an initial phoneme target: the presence or absence of an initial consonant cluster and the open or closed nature of the syllable (the presence or absence of a final consonant). The crossing of these two parameters produced the four following syllabic structures: CV, CCV, CVC, CCVC. The phoneme targets were the voiced and the unvoiced occlusive consonants /b/, /d/, /p/, and /t/. Each phoneme target was contained in a list made up of 40 monosyllabic items. Most of these items were nonwords. Eight items corresponding to two of each of the four types of syllable were added to two distinct vowels. The consonant clusters bore the liquids /r/ or /l/ for /p/ and /b/ and the liquid /r/ for /d/ and /t/. The final consonant was an occlusive. Thus, for example, for the phoneme target /p/ the following eight items were used: CV, /pa/ and /po/; CVC, /pad/ and /pob/; CCV, /pla/ and /pro/; CCVC, /plad/ and /prob/. The thirty-two filler items were made up of eight items out of each of the four types of syllabic structures. Thus each type of syllabic structure was represented by the same number of items. The lists were recorded by a native speaker of French at regular intervals of two seconds between items.

Subjects were instructed that their task consisted in reacting as fast as possible to a particular target phoneme. Each target phoneme was presented before the corresponding experimental list together with a random list of four nonexperimental CV, CVC, CCV, and CCVC items (e.g., for the phoneme target /p/, "the target is /p/, as in the syllables *pli, pe, pru, pred*"). Before presentation of the experimental lists, subjects were given a trial list

Table 1
Mean response time (msec) to detect the target phoneme as a function of onset type (the presence or absence of a consonant cluster) and syllable type (open or closed)

	Initial consonant cluster	
	− (CV-)	+ (CCV-)
Open syllables (-V)	444	495
Closed syllables (-VC)	483	532

constructed along the same lines as the experimental lists with the target phoneme /g/. Two groups of twenty subjects (students at the University of Paris V) were associated to voiced (/b/ and /d/) and voiceless (/p/ and /t/) targets. The observed RTs are similarly distributed for voiced and unvoiced targets.

The results are presented in table 1 and figures 1 to 4. An analysis of variance shows a significant effect of the type of syllable ($F(3, 114) = 14.9$, $p < .001$), whereas the nature of the phoneme target reveals no significant effect ($F < 1$) and does not interact with syllable type ($F < 1$). Specific comparisons indicated that the two structural parameters introduce highly significant effects: syllables without an initial consonant cluster were responded faster than syllables with an initial cluster (CV and CVC RTs < CCV and CCVC RTs; $F(1, 38) = 35.1$, $p < .001$), and open syllables were responded to faster than closed syllables (CV and CCV RTs < CVC and CCVC RTs; $F(1, 38) = 11.6, p < .005$).

Results obtained in this experiment clearly indicate the existence of a close relation between detection of a phoneme in the initial position in a syllable and the structural complexity of the syllable. This complexity was estimated by taking into account the presence or absence of a consonant cluster in initial position and the open or closed nature of the syllable. Our results agree with those obtained by Cutler, Butterfield, and Williams (1987) and Treiman et al. (1982). The observed syllabic effect cannot be coherently interpreted within the hypothesis of a correspondance between the model and the syllabic context.

Experiment 2

In a second experiment we decided to study more directly the roles of target model and syllabic complexity in an experimental situation similar to that employed in our previous experiments and in the experiment of Cutler, Mehler et al. (1987), i.e., one using very short experimental lists.

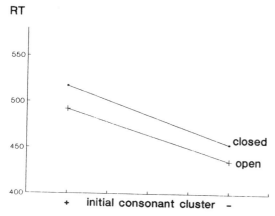

Figure 1

Mean response time (msec) to detect the target phoneme /b/ as a function of onset type (the presence or absence of a consonant cluster) and syllable type (open or closed)

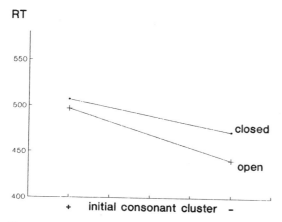

Figure 2

Mean response time (msec) to detect the target phoneme /d/ as a function of onset type (the presence or absence of a consonant cluster) and syllable type (open or closed)

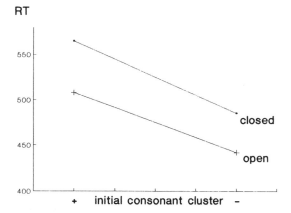

Figure 3
Mean response time (msec) to detect the target phoneme /p/ as a function of
onset type (the presence or absence of a consonant cluster) and syllable type
(open or closed)

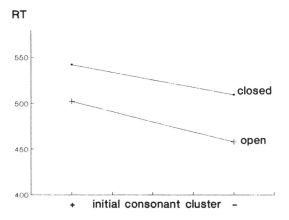

Figure 4
Mean response time (msec) to detect the target phoneme /t/ as a function of
onset type (the presence or absence of a consonant cluster) and syllable type
(open or closed)

Experimental stimuli consisted of six triplets made up of French bisyllabic words. Each triplet had three words beginning with the same initial phoneme. The initial syllable of these words (the structure of the target item) was CV, CVC, or CCV (for the phoneme /p/, for example, the triplet might be *palace, palmier,* and *plateau*). The experimental items were placed at the end of a short sequence (from one to six items). There were three experimental blocks, each including 18 experimental sequences and 12 filler sequences. In each block a particular experimental item was associated with a specific model. The model was a monosyllabic word corresponding to the initial syllable of a member of a triplet. Thus, for example, the experimental sequence bearing the item *palmier* was preceded in one block by the instruction "/p/ as in the word *pal(e),*" in another block by "/p/ as in the word *pa(s),*" and in the third block by the instruction "/p/ as in the word *pla(t).*" Thus, only in one list of a particular block (the first one in this example) did the model correspond to the initial syllable of the experimental item. The three blocks were recorded by a native speaker of French. The pauses between the words in a sequence were 1,500 msec long, and 10 seconds separated the presentation of each sequence. Each subject was given the three experimental blocks in a presentation order counterbalanced across subjects. Thirty subjects, psychology students at the University of Paris V, were tested.

The results obtained in this experiment are presented in table 2. An analysis of variance with subjects as a random variable reveals a very significant effect of type of target-item structure ($F(2, 58) = 16.5$, $p < .0005$), whereas the model structure does not introduce a significant effect ($F(2, 58) = 3.05, p > .10$). The interaction between these two factors is not significant ($F(4, 116) = 2.24, p > .10$).

To confirm the role of target-item structure without interference from the model, we compared the mean values corresponding to the three cases

Table 2

Mean response time (msec) to detect the target phoneme as a function of target-item structure and model structure

Target-item structure	Model structure			Mean RT
	CV	CVC	CCV	
CV	341	378	389	369
CVC	373	390	397	387
CCV	420	414	409	414
Mean RT	378	394	398	

Table 3
Mean response time (msec) to detect the target phoneme as a function of matching and nonmatching target-item and model structures

	CV	CVC	CCV
Matching	341	390	409
Nonmatching	384	385	417
Mean RT	362	387	413

in which there existed a strict matching between the model and the target structure, i.e., the three diagonal cells in table 2. The observed difference is highly significant ($F(2, 58) = 11.3$, $p < .0005$). The order of response times as a function of target structure is the same as in experiment 1: CV < CVC < CCV. Contrary to the suggestion proposed by Cutler, Butterfield, and Williams (1987), this result shows that the differences in RTs introduced by the syllable structure of the target bearing item cannot be attributed exclusively to the degree of correspondence between the model and the target item.

Finally, we compared responses for matching and nonmatching target-item and model structures to estimate the role of model-structure correspondance. The global difference between matching and nonmatching responses was significant ($F(1, 29) = 4.19$, $p < .05$). This effect agrees with Cutler, Butterfield, and Williams's model hypothesis, though this effect interacts with item structure ($F(2, 58) = 4.52$, $p < .02$). As can be seen in table 3, the matching effect is due essentially to CV items.

The results observed in this experiment confirm the role of syllable structure in determining phoneme monitoring latencies. This structural effect is still found when there is a total correspondance between the model used to characterize the target phoneme and the initial syllable of the target-bearing item. In our experimental situation the effect of the correspondance between the model and the target-bearing item is strongly dependent on this latter factor. In fact, only the RTs to CV items are very sensitive to the model used to characterize the target phoneme.

Results obtained in the two previous experiments and in other recent experiments conducted by Dupoux indicate that, *at least for French*, the effect of syllabic complexity on phoneme-monitoring reaction time is robust and well established. This effect cannot be interpreted as being due to the degree of correspondance between the model given to the subject and the structural organization of the stimulus item. The original hypothesis according to which the segmental information necessary for phoneme detection is derived from a syllabic code does account for the data obtained.

The Role of the Syllable in Lexical Access

The syllabic hypothesis assumes that words are accessed by their initial syllable. In other words, initial syllables constitute the access code to the internal lexicon in spoken-word recognition. In this section we present some recent experimental results concerning this particular aspect of the syllabic hypothesis.

If this hypothesis is correct, we can predict that in phoneme monitoring, the role of lexical parameters should be qualitatively different for mono-syllabic and polysyllabic items. Monosyllabic words automatically have access to their corresponding lexical representation without mediation by prelexical syllabic routines. Lexical information becomes immediately available and may be used to detect the initial phoneme of these items. On the other hand, polysyllabic words are accessed through their initial syllable, but the extraction of this syllable is generally not sufficient to isolate a particular word. In this case, phoneme detection may be based exclusively on prelexical information without the intervention of the lexical level.

This hypothesis about the differential nature of processing according to the syllable length of the target-bearing item has been supported in many experiments. In particular, whereas with monosyllabic items, phoneme targets are detected faster in words than in nonwords (Cutler, Mehler, et al. 1987; Rubin, Turvey, and Van Gelder 1976), this effect of lexical superiority is never found with polysyllabic items (Foss and Blank 1981; Segui, Frauenfelder, and Mehler 1981).

Our interpretation of the lexical-superiority effect assumes that the important parameter in these experiments was the *syllabic* length of the target-bearing items rather than the phonetic length or an even more crude, linguistically neutral length parameter, such as the total duration of the target-bearing word (Cutler and Norris 1979). It is clear, however, that these two interpretations, syllabic and durational, are able to explain the observed lexical-superiority effect. Consequently, it is important to obtain new empirical data that will enable us to choose between these two alternative interpretations.

In a recent series of experiments Dupoux and Mehler (in press) attempted to test the validity of the syllabic and durational interpretations. In a preliminary experiment these authors attempted to confirm the existence of a differential lexical effect for mono- and polysyllabic words using as a diagnostic variable the word-frequency effect. Subjects had to monitor initial phonemes of monosyllabic or bisyllabic words. Words were pre-

Table 4
Mean response time (msec) to detect the target phoneme, and percentage of errors, as a function of target syllable length and frequency (normal speech)

	Monosyllabic words	Bisyllabic words
Low frequency	414 (3.7%)	435 (1.7%)
High frequency	377 (2.0%)	422 (2.3%)
Difference	37*	13

*This difference is significant to $p < .001$.

sented in continuous lists, and target phonemes were specified auditorily (e.g., /p/ as in *Paris, Perpignan, Poitier*). Target words were of either high frequency (a mean of 148 for monosyllabic words and 102 for bisyllabic words) or low frequency (a mean of 3 for monosyllabic and bisyllabic words). They were paired according to their initial phoneme and syllabic structure (for example, the high-frequency /poule/ was paired with the low-frequency /pouf/). Identification points (in terms of phonemes) were also matched. Thirty students aged between 18 and 20 served as subjects. RTs were measured from the onset of the burst of the initial phoneme.

The results are presented in table 4. These results agree with those obtained for lexical superiority: in both cases lexical parameters affected the response time only to monosyllabic items ($F(1, 29) = 15.9, p < .001$, for monosyllabic words, and $F < 1$ for bisyllabic words). Monosyllabic words seem to be responded to on the basis of a lexical code, whereas bisyllabic items seem to be responded to on the basis of a prelexical code.

However, as noted before, the syllabic and durational interpretations both predict that with normal speech the lexical effect should be found only or essentially with monosyllabic items. In the syllabic interpretation, it is the number of syllables of the target-bearing item that determines the prelexical or lexical locus of the response, while in nonsyllabic models like Cutler and Norris's (1979) race model, it is the length (or duration) of the target-bearing item that determines the locus of the response. As for the interactive TRACE model (McClelland and Elman 1986), the possibility of obtaining a lexical effect in phoneme monitoring is a function of the level of lexical activation capable of affecting the phoneme unit corresponding to the target-bearing word. For phoneme-initial targets, detection responses cannot be affected by the lexical status of the target-bearing word, since in this case, when the phoneme target occurs, the level of activation of the target-bearing word is very low.

To test these interpretations in a second experiment Dupoux and Mehler (in press) presented subjects the same list of items but at a rate that was

Table 5
Mean response time (msec) to detect the target phoneme, and percentage of errors, as a function of target syllable length and frequency (compressed speech)

	Monosyllabic words	Bisyllabic words
Low frequency	439 (3.3%)	436 (3.8%)
High frequency	410 (1.3%)	434 (2.9%)
Difference	29*	2

*This difference is significant to $p < .002$.

twice as fast. Such a compression was obtained using an algorithm that averages adjacent periods of a 16-kHz digitized signal. This transformation leaves intact the spectral characteristics of speech, such as pitch, timbre, and formant structures. The important point is that in compressed format, bisyllabic words were shorter than uncompressed monosyllabic words but were still very intelligible. Since compression does not modify the number of syllables, the syllabic interpretation predicts the same result as that obtained with normal speech rate. In contrast, a durational interpretation predicts that under compressed presentation, frequency effects should be found with monosyllabic and bisyllabic items. In fact, the identification points of the compressed bisyllabic words occur temporally earlier than those of the normal monosyllabic word.

Thirty subjects participated in this experiment, and the main results are presented in table 5. As can be seen in table 5, only monosyllabic words showed a frequency effect ($F(1, 129) = 11.7$, $p < .002$, for monosyllabic words, and $F < 1$ for bisyllabic words). These results mirror perfectly those obtained in the previous experiment (RTs between these two experiments are significantly correlated; $r = .73$) and agree with the syllabic interpretation.

To reject an alternative interpretation according to which the absence of a frequency effect for bisyllabic items was artifactual and related to a bias in the choice of these items, a lexical-decision experiment was conducted with the same experimental lists. Results showed a robust and comparable frequency effect for monosyllabic and bisyllabic items.

Dupoux and Mehler's results are incompatible with a durational interpretation of the observed frequency effect and agree with the predictions derived from the syllabic hypothesis. The important experimental factor in this research was the syllabic length of the target-bearing words and not their global duration.

In recent papers Cutler proposed an initial-lexical-segmentation strategy well adapted to the structure of English vocabulary (Cutler and Norris

1988; Cutler, this volume). According to Cutler, the speech stream is segmented at strong syllables because these syllables generally occur in the initial position of polysyllabic words. At this level of formulation Cutler's hypothesis can be considered a particular version of the syllabic hypothesis. However, Cutler assumed that the distinction between strong and weak syllables is made not on the basis of the properties of a syllable per se but on the basis of the strong or weak nature of the vowel.

Conclusion

The experimental findings briefly reviewed in the three sections of this chapter generally agree with the predictions derived from a syllabic hypothesis for languages having clear syllabic boundaries, like French. According to this hypothesis, syllables correspond to natural units in speech segmentation and constitute the input to lexical access and phonemic analysis.

In the first section we examined data obtained in syllable-detection experiments indicating that French words and probably Spanish words too are segmented in syllabic units. Results obtained in Portuguese indicate that words are represented in the internal lexicon in a syllabic format. Finally, cross-language research shows that we must take into consideration the phonological structure of the languages studied to interpret the observed results. Segmentation strategies seem to be strongly related to the phonological and prosodic properties of natural languages.

Experimental results considered in the second section show that phoneme-detection RTs vary as a function of the structural complexity of the target-bearing syllables. The time to identify a particular phoneme depends on the manner in which this phoneme is encoded at the syllabic level. In particular, two structural parameters affected RTs: the presence or absence of a consonant cluster at the onset of the syllable and the open or closed nature of the syllable.

In the third section we presented results suggesting that French words are accessed by their initial syllable. The presence of a frequency effect depends on the syllabic length of the words and not on their global duration. According to the syllabic hypothesis, monosyllabic words are responded to from the lexical code, while polysyllabic words are responded to from a prelexical syllabic code.

As noted in Mehler, Dupoux, and Segui, this volume, our syllabic hypothesis may be related in a natural way to the development of language capacities and in particular to the construction of an internal lexicon.

Acknowledgments

The authors would like to thank Marie Eliane Binaghi, Cristophe Bonneuil, and Toby Mintz for assistance in stimulus selection and setting up experiments 1 and 2.

References

Bradley, D. C., Sanchez-Casas, R. M., and Garcia-Albea, J. E. 1988. Language specific segmentation strategies: I, Performance over native language materials. In preparation.

Cutler, A., and Norris, D. 1979. Monitoring sentence comprehension. In W. E. Cooper and E. C. T. Walker (eds.), *Sentence Processing: Psycholinguistic Studies Presented to Merrill Garrett*. Hillsdale, N.J.: L. Erlbaum.

Cutler, A., and Norris, D. 1988. The role of strong syllables in segmentation for lexical access. *Journal of Experimental Psychology: Human Perception and Performance* 14:113–121.

Cutler, A., Mehler, J., Norris, D., and Segui, J. 1983. A language specific comprehension strategy. *Nature* 304:159–160.

Cutler, A., Mehler, J., Norris, D., and Segui, J. 1986. The syllable's differing role in the segmentation of French and English. *Journal of Memory and Language* 25:385–400.

Cutler, A., Mehler, J., Norris, D., and Segui, J. 1987. Phoneme identification and the lexicon. *Cognitive Psychology* 19:141–177.

Cutler, A., Butterfield, S., and Williams, J. N. 1987. The perceptual integrity of syllabic onsets. *Journal of Memory and Language* 26:406–418.

Dupoux, E., and Mehler, J. In press. Monitoring the lexicon with normal and compressed speech: Frequency effect and the prelexical code. *Journal of Memory and Language* 29, no. 3: 316–335.

Foss, D. J., and Blank, M. 1980. Identifying the speech codes. *Cognitive Psychology* 12:1–31.

McClelland, J. L., and Elman, J. L. 1986. The TRACE model of speech perception. *Cognitive Psychology* 18:1–86.

Mehler, J. 1981. The role of syllables in speech processing: Infant and adult data. *Philosophical Transactions of the Royal Society*, series B, 295:333–352.

Mehler, J., Dommergues, J. Y., Frauenfelder, U., and Segui, J. 1981. The syllable's role in speech segmentation. *Journal of Verbal Learning and Verbal Behavior* 20:298–305.

Mehler, J., Segui, J., and Frauenfelder, U. 1981. The role of the syllable in language acquisition and perception. In. T. F. Myers, J. Laver, and J. Anderson (eds.), *The cognitive representation of speech*. Amsterdam: North-Holland.

Morais, J., Content, A., Cary, L., Mehler, J., and Segui, J. 1989. Syllabic segmentation and literacy. *Language and Cognitive Processes* 4:57–67.

Rubin, P., Turvey, M. T., and Van Gelder, P. 1976. Initial phonemes are detected faster in spoken words than in spoken nonwords. *Perception and Psychophysics* 19:394–398.

Sanchez-Casas, R. M. 1988. Access representations in visual word recognition. Ph.D., *Monash University*, Australia.

Segui, J. 1984. The syllable: A basic unit in speech perception? In H. Bouma and D. G. Bouwhuis (eds.), *Attention and Performance*, vol. 10, *Language control mechanisms*. Hillsdale, N.J.: L. Erlbaum.

Segui, J., Frauenfelder, U., and Mehler, J. 1981. Phoneme monitoring, syllable monitoring, and lexical access. *British Journal of Psychology* 72:471–477.

Treiman, R., Salasoo, A., Slowiaczek, L. M., and Pisoni, D. 1982. Effects of syllable structure on adults' phoneme monitoring performance. Progress report no. 8, Speech Research Laboratory, Indiana University.

Treiman, R., and Danis, C. 1988. Syllabification of intervocalic consonants. *Journal of Memory and Language* 27:87–104.

Zwitserlood, P., Schiefers, H., Lahiri, A., and van Donselaar, W. In preparation. The role of the syllable in the perception of Dutch.

Chapter 13

Effects of Sentence Context and Lexical Knowledge in Speech Processing

Cynthia Connine

A complete theory of language processing must describe the way in which various sources of linguistic and nonlinguistic information contribute to language comprehension (Fodor, Bever, and Garrett 1974). The purpose of the present paper is to consider the way in which sentence level (e.g., syntax and semantics) and lexical knowledge contribute to speech processing. There is little disagreement that contextual information influences speech processing. Many studies have focused on the influence of sentence context, and numerous studies have demonstrated that sentence context influences performance in a number of tasks. Some of these experiments have used a gating paradigm, in which subjects must guess the identity of a word from successively larger chunks of speech (Grosjean 1980). In other experiments, subjects were required to shadow sentences as quickly as possible (Marslen-Wilson 1973) or detect mispronunciations (Cole 1973). Marslen-Wilson and Tyler (1980) have used a monitoring paradigm to demonstrate effects of sentence context.

In general, interpretation of the results from studies investigating context effects in speech has been guided by two types of language-processing theories. One class of models, interactive models, can be characterized as having unconstrained use of information during any given computation. The work most closely associated with interactive models is Marslen-Wilson (1973; see also Marslen-Wilson and Welsh 1978) and more recently the TRACE model of speech perception (McClelland and Elman 1986). The TRACE model of speech perception represents a particularly unconstrained version of an interactive theory. In TRACE all sources of information are presumed to directly influence perceptual computations. In particular, sentence-level and lexical knowledge are presumed to be direct sources of evidence for perceptual processing. It should be noted, however, that a potentially important constraint exists in models such as TRACE.

Specifically, TRACE assumes that activation from the context to the perceptual level accumulates over time. One consequence of this aspect of the architecture is that some effects of context may be evident only after sufficient time has elapsed.

An alternative to interactive models is exemplified by the modularity thesis proposed by Fodor (1983). A basic premise of the modularity thesis is that the computations involved in language processing are informed from a restricted domain of knowledge. Specifically, the representations computed at the perceptual level, for example, are not directly influenced by information concerning lexicality, contextual appropriateness, syntactic category, or the like. The final representation computed by perceptual processes is informed only by information within the perceptual domain and not by sentence-level representations. A particularly constrained modular model proposed by Forster (1978, 1979) assumes that processing decisions of any given class do not influence the computations performed in the development of other representations but have access only to the *output* of a lower-level computation. Thus, higher-level information cannot directly intervene in processing decisions in other domains. Information from the sentence context may serve a corrective function in that a decision from a lower level may be overturned once perceptual or lexical output is made available.

Of importance in discussing interactive and modular models is that both sorts of mechanisms can account for the effects of context. The models are distinguished by the class of mechanisms attributed to account for the context effect. In an interactive model, context effects are the result of a mechanism in which perceptual processing is directly influenced by contextual variables. In a modular model, context effects are the consequence of action upon output representation(s). For example, sentence-level representations may function to select among multiple outputs made available by perceptual or lexical processors.

Recently a number of researchers have reviewed studies demonstrating context effects for the particular tasks used (Samuel 1986, Tanenhaus and Lucas 1987; see also Connine 1987). Although an exhaustive review of research relevant to the issues discussed here is beyond the intended scope of this paper, a recent example from the relevant literature may clarify the issues. Seidenberg et al. (1984) have presented evidence consistent with the view that some contextual effects may be attributed to decision-stage processes associated with a particular task. In these experiments, performance on lexical-decision and naming tasks were contrasted in a number of word-priming conditions (e.g., associative, semantic, syntactic, and backward priming). Task-specific patterns of facilitation were found in that responses in the naming task were facilitated only in associative and semantic priming contexts and in the lexical decision task, facilitation was found in all four of the priming conditons. Seidenberg et al. attributed these task-specific patterns of facilitation to an additional postlexical processing component in the lexical-decision task. Facilitation of lexical access is found only in those priming contexts that reflect connections within the lexicon (semantic and associative relationships). Presumably, postlexical access processes facilitate the lexical decision response in the syntactic and backward-priming conditions.

The findings of Seidenberg et al. highlight the importance of considering possible decision effects in tasks that have demonstrated context effects. The specific issue exemplified by the results of Seidenberg et al. is whether a demonstration of an effect of contextual information in a given task can be potentially due to a noninteractive mechanism. Many tasks used to demonstrate context effects in auditory language processing have not been investigated for decision stage factors as possible explanations for context effects. This paper describes a series of experiments designed to investigate the contribution of lexical knowledge and sentence context to speech processing. The specific empirical results detailed here have directly addressed the question of whether contextual effects are attributable to direct influences on perceptual processing (interactive processing) or are the consequence of a decision-stage mechanism. One paradigm that I have recently used to address these issues involves the identification of speech in lexical- or semantic-biasing contexts. A second paradigm, a signal detection analysis of the phoneme restoration effect (Samuel 1981), provides converging evidence for claims based on the speech-identification paradigm.

The conclusions drawn from these experiments are quite straightforward but suggest an interesting alternative to conceptualizations of language processing that are strictly modular or strictly interactive. The results argue for a processing distinction between the sentence-level context and lexical knowledge in their influences on perceptual processing. Specifically, the data suggest a language-processing system that includes both interactive and modular architectures. The data suggest that communication between lexical representations and speech processing may be interactive in nature. In contrast, sentence-context effects on speech processing are argued to be the consequence of a mechanism that influences only the output of perceptual processes, that is, a modular mechanism. My discussion of context effects is divided into two sections, effects of sentence context and the effects of lexical knowledge.

Context Effects

The effects of sentence contexts

One task used in auditory studies of the effects of context on direct influences and decision-stage factors is the phoneme-restoration phenomenon (Warren 1970; see also Warren and Obusek 1971). In these experiments a portion of the acoustic signal was spliced out and replaced with a nonlinguistic sound (e.g., a cough). Listeners report hearing an intact word with (in this example) a cough in the background. Samuel (1981) has conducted a series of studies on phoneme restoration using signal-detection methodology to separate perceptual effects from decision bias (for a more detailed description, see Samuel, this volume). In these experiments, word targets were presented with a sound replaced by white noise or a sound presented intact plus white noise. Samuel found that listeners tended to report the targets as intact rather than replaced when the item occurred in a predictable sentence context. If higher-level syntactic and semantic information were directly influencing phonetic processing, discrimination of intact versus replaced items for predicted words should decrease. Decreased discrimination of the intact items would suggest that sentence context was directly contributing to the acoustic evidence for contextually appropriate words. In fact, the data indicated that discrimination actually increased.

One potential way that completely interactive models could account for the lack of interactive effects from sentence context on perceptual processing is to assume that context effects have not had the opportunity to accrue at the perceptual level. A basic assumption in one highly interactive model, the TRACE model of speech perception, is that the feedback from sentence-level context to perceptual processing is a time-constrained process. Specifically, evidence from one level of representation contributes to another level of representation as a function of time. This predicts that the influence of sentence context will be seen only under conditions in which contextual information has had the opportunity to feed back to the lexical level. One consequence of the time constraint is that evidence from sentence context to the perceptual level is slow to develop and context effects will be evident only under conditions in which sufficient time has elapsed. Such models would predict that context effects would not be evident under conditions in which a response was made prior to sufficient feedback from sentence context to the perceptual level.

A very different paradigm used to investigate the effect of sentence context on lexical/phonetic processing, the identification-function shift paradigm (IFSP), is consistent with Samuel's analysis of the phoneme restoration effect (Connine 1987). In the IFSP, listeners are presented tokens from a speech series (e.g., *dent–tent*) embedded in semantically biased sentence contexts (e.g., *She drives the car with the, She saw the show in the*). Typically, listeners identify ambiguous target sounds so as to form a semantically consistent word (Garnes and Bond 1976). For example, stimuli midway along the *dent–tent* series tend to be identified as /d/ when the stimulus occurred as the final word in the context *She drives the car with the* and as /t/ in the context *She saw the show in the*. Connine found that reaction times for categorizations that formed words consistent with the sentence context were faster than categorizations that were inconsistent. However, this effect was confined to endpoint and midrange stimuli. No consistency effect was evident in the category boundary region. It is important to note that overall reaction times were slower for stimuli in the category boundary region. Thus if, as claimed in TRACE, sentence context effects accrue over time, maximal opportunity would be available for ambiguous stimuli. This predicts that maximal consistency effects would have been evidence for stimuli in the category boundary region.

These data are particularly interesting when contrasted with an experiment using the IFSP in which identification responses were influenced by manipulating monetary payoff associated with a given response (Connine and Clifton 1987). In one condition, voiced identification responses were selectively rewarded; in a second condition, voiceless identification responses were selectively rewarded. The monetary-payoff contingencies in effect influenced subjects' identification responses in that more bias-consistent responses were found in the midrange of the continuum. An analysis of the reaction times at the category boundary and endpoints showed a pattern of reaction times similar to the sentence-context effect: no advantage for payoff-consistent responses was found in the boundary region, while a clear advantage for payoff-consistent responses was found at the continua endpoints with unambiguous stimuli. The pattern of reaction times obtained in the monetary-payoff experiment reflect a clear postperceptual influence, and presumably this pattern of reaction times hold for postperceptual phenomena. It appears, then, that the effects of sentence context operate in a fashion similar to payoff bias and influence processing decisions after the stimulus item has been encoded.

Effects of lexical knowledge

The previous section reviewed some effects of sentence context on perceptual processing that have been interpreted as support for a modular architecture between the sentence context and perceptual processing. Conditions in which there was an opportunity for sentence-context feedback to accrue at the perceptual level did not result in increased availability of a contextually consistent word.

In contrast to sentence-context effects, a number of researchers have argued that lexical knowledge is used directly in perceptual processing (Connine and Clifton 1987, Samuel 1986, Tanenhaus and Lucas 1987). In one set of experiments, Connine and Clifton (1987) investigated the effect of lexical status on speech identification using a paradigm first reported by Ganong (1980). Two types of voicing continua were presented to listeners for identification. In one continuum the voiced endpoint formed a word (*dice–tice*); in a second continuum the voiceless endpoint formed a word (*dype–type*). Subjects tended to label perceptually ambiguous stimuli, typically those stimuli in the midrange of the continuum, so that the phonetic sequence resulted in a real word. Reaction time analyses similar to those in Connine 1987 were performed for stimuli in the region of the category boundary and at the continua endpoints. In this experiment, categorization responses that formed a word were faster than nonword categorization responses in the boundary region; no word advantage was found at the continua endpoints. These data contrast with effects found for sentence context and monetary payoff. For sentence context and monetary payoff, an advantage for responses consistent with context and monetary bias was found only for endpoint stimuli; no consistency advantage was found at the endpoints.

The pattern of reaction times was taken as support for a mechanism in which lexical status operates to directly contribute to the information obtained from the acoustic input. Lexical feedback contributed maximally to the acoustic evidence when categorization was delayed by insufficient input (ambiguous information). In the ambiguous boundary region, lexical information increased the availability of a response consistent with the lexical status of the string, and consequently, word reaction times were faster. At the endpoints a response was quickly made on the basis of the unambiguous input prior to the availability of evidence from the lexical level, and no word advantage was evident. Thus the reaction-time data supported Ganong's original claim that lexical status directly contributes to evidence for sound segments. Additional evidence for this position that used this paradigm is available from Fox 1984. Fox replicated the lexical-effect and recategorized responses in terms of fast, medium, and slow reaction times. Fox found more word responses for slow and medium reaction times in comparison with the range for the fastest reaction times. These data have been attributed to a mechanism in which evidence from the lexicon was available to a greater extent for slower responses (McClelland and Elman 1986, Connine and Clifton 1987; but see Miller and Dexter 1988 for an alternative interpretation).

Recently Elman and McClelland (1988) have investigated the lexical effect and used a slightly different methodology to argue for an interactive mechanism. Here a compensation for coarticulation effect was combined with effects of lexical bias. The compensation for coarticulation effect exploited by Elman and McClelland was the finding by Mann and Repp (1982) that more /k/ responses were found in identification of a /t/ to /k/ continuum when preceded by a context stimulus ending in /s/ than with a context stimulus ending in /š/. For example, consider a stimulus such as *tapes–capes*. If stimuli from a tapes–capes continuum are preceded in the context by an item ending in /s/, such as *christmas*, more /k/ responses are found than when the stimuli are preceded by a unambiguous /š/, as in *foolish*. To determine whether coarticulation compensation could be triggered by the lexical status of the context item, Elman and McClelland prepared context stimuli in which the final sound was ambiguous. Specifically, a stimulus was prepared in which the final phoneme was ambiguous between /s/ and /š/ (e.g., *christma?* and *fooli?*). It was reasoned that if the lexical bias presumed to be present in the ambiguous context items directly influenced perceptual processing, such perceptual processes as coarticulatory compensation would occur in the identification of the *tapes–capes* continuum. In fact, when the ambiguous context words were presented prior to stimuli from a *tapes–capes* continuum, more /k/ responses were found in identification of a *tapes–capes* continuum in the *christma?* context than in the *fooli?* context. Elman and McClelland argued that the results supported interactive use of lexical knowledge and the perceptual process of coarticulatory compensation.

The time course of lexical effects

One issue concerning effects of lexical knowledge on perceptual processing is the way in which such effects are distributed across the length of a lexical item. Specifically, are effects of lexical knowledge on speech processing dependent upon the sequential position of the target phoneme? If lexical evidence accrued at the perceptual level over time, sequentially late phonemes would receive relatively more lexical evidence than sequentially early phonemes.

Constraints available from early portions to later portions of a word have been investigated by a number of researchers using a variety of tasks. Some evidence for an increase in lexical effects as a result of sequential position has been reported by Marslen-Wilson and Welsh (1978). In one experiment, lexical constraint was manipulated by changing the position of a mispronunciation in a lexical item from the first to the third syllable. Mispronounced lexical items were embedded in high-contextual-constraint and low-contextual-constraint passages. Subjects were instructed to shadow the passages as quickly as they could. The shadowing data showed that in high-contextual-constraint passages, subjects fluently restored a higher percentage of mispronunciations in the third syllable than in the first syllable. Using the phoneme-restoration paradigm, Samuel (1981) investigated lexical effects in short versus long words. He also observed effects of target position under conditions in which target items were preceded by primes. Phoneme-restoration effects increased for targets occurring later in the word. Further, these effects proved to be direct effects of constraint: a signal-detection analysis of discriminability of intact versus replaced segments showed significant effects of d' but not beta. Samuel concluded that constraints provided by the initial portions of primed words contributed to a perceptual component of the phoneme-restoration effect.

In discussing the effects of lexical status on identification functions, Connine and Clifton (1987) argued that lexical evidence can accrue positively over some time interval. Recall that a reaction-time advantage for word categorizations was found only at the category boundary. This pattern of data was attributed to a mechanism in which sufficient time elapsed for feedback to accrue from the lexicon. Under conditions of ambiguity, effects of lexical information on reaction time (and on identification) were evident. An alternative way in which evidence from the lexicon can accrue for individual sound segments is under conditions in which the target sound sequentially occurs relatively late in a given lexical item. As evidence from the lexical level is activated and feeds back to the sound level, relatively less acoustic information may be required for a given categorization of a sequentially late sound. On this logic there are a number of predictions for sequentially late target sounds in the identification-function shift paradigm. First, lexical status would be expected to influence identification responses in that more word categorizations are expected than nonword categorizations (a replication of the lexical effect). Second, reaction times for word categorizations would be faster than nonword categorizations for stimuli in the midrange of the continua. This prediction follows from an interactive account of the lexical effect and is also expected on the basis of previous results (Connine and Clifton 1987). The final prediction concerns the pattern of reaction times for unambiguous stimuli, that is, at the continua endpoints. If lexical information has accrued for sequentially late sound segments, we should also find a word advantage for categorizations at the continua endpoints. Specifically, as activation from the lexicon begins to operate as a source of evidence at the perceptual level, processing of the acoustic input will be facilitated by the presence of this additional source of evidence. For unambiguous sounds that occur in a sequentially late position in a word, lexical information will have more opportunity to accrue than for unambiguous sounds that occur toward the beginning of a word. The additional source of evidence from the lexicon for perceptual processing and for the lexically consistent categorization predicts an increased availability for lexically consistent categorizations. The increased availability for the lexically consistent categorizations would be reflected in a reaction-time advantage for word categorizations for unambiguous stimuli (at the endpoints).

To test these predictions, I (Connine, in preparation) conducted an experiment using the IFSP in which two lexical items that differed in place of articulation of the medial stop consonant were chosen (*bagel, cradle*) and two sets of speech continua were synthesized (*bagel–badel* and *cragle–cradle*). In one continuum the alveolar endpoint formed a word (*cradle–cragle*); in the second continuum the velar endpoint formed a real word (*badel–bagel*). Subjects were presented the stimuli and simply instructed to identify the medial consonant.

The percentage of /d/ responses are plotted as a function of stimulus in figure 1. In figure 1, stimuli are labeled 1 through 8, where 1 indicates the /d/ endpoint and 8 indicates the /g/ endpoint. As expected, lexical status significantly influenced identification responses in that more /d/ responses were observed for the *cradle–cragle* continuum than for the *badel–bagel* continuum.[1]

Consider next the effects of reaction time on identification responses. Reaction times were analyzed at the category boundary region and at the continua endpoints. Table 1 displays reaction times for category boundary responses. Overall, categorization responses that formed words were significantly faster than those that formed nonwords (993 msec versus 1,048 msec, respectively). The effect of lexicality replicates the results of Connine and Clifton (1987), in which reaction times for stimulus-initial targets were facilitated for word categorizations. These results are consistent with an interactive mechanism underlying the lexical effect in which perceptual ambiguity permits accrual of lexical evidence.

Consider next reaction times at the continua endpoints as a function of word/nonword and continuum (table 2). Overall, words were significantly

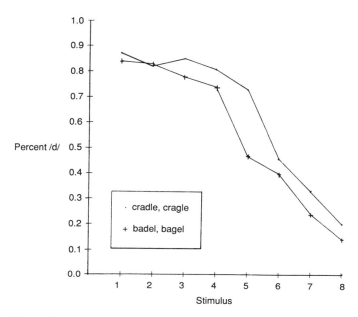

Figure 1

Table 1
Word and nonword categorizations at
the category boundary as a function of
stimulus continuum

	Continuum	
Response	*badel–bagel*	*cradle–cragle*
Word	976	1,010
Nonword	1,018	1,078

Table 2
Word and nonword categorizations at
the endpoints as a function of stimulus
continuum

	Continuum	
Response	*badel–bagel*	*cradle–cragle*
Word	957	994
Nonword	990	1,063

faster (+52 msec) than nonwords (975 msec versus 1,027 msec for words and nonwords, respectively).

Thus, an advantage for word categorizations was found for relatively unambiguous stimuli in medial position targets. This contrasts with the results of Connine and Clifton (1987), in which no word advantage was evident at the continua endpoints. The endpoint word advantage for stimulus medial targets is consistent with an interactive mechanism in which lexical evidence accrued for sequentially late sounds. Presumably, a lexical representation was activated for a sufficient length of time for evidence to accrue for sequentially late sounds. The additional evidence from the lexical level increased availability of lexically consistent sounds.

Concluding Comments

The above discussion focused on a distinction between effects of sentence context and of lexical knowledge on speech processing based on the decision and direct perceptual components of the context effect under consideration. It was argued that lexical knowledge directly informs perceptual processing with evidence for lexically consistent phonemes. In addition, I presented evidence from the IFSP that lexical influences accrue for sequentially late sound segments. These data are consistent with TRACE, a model of speech perception that accounts for lexical effects in speech. One virtue of the feedback mechanism embodied in a model such as TRACE is that it provides a specific mechanism for interaction between knowledge sources. In TRACE a distributed pattern of activation occurs when a lexical item is presented that feeds back to lexically consistent phonemes as an additional source of evidence.

I then argued that the few studies that have directly addressed the issue provided evidence for a decision-stage use of semantic context in speech processing. According to this view, these sentence-context effects are accounted for by selection of a semantically consistent lexical item. Sentence context does not directly influence the interpretation of the acoustic input or the lexical access process. Rather, sentence context functions to resolve ambiguity when a number of hypotheses concerning the input are available or to overturn a contextually inconsistent output of a lower-level processor.

In view of these considerations, it is not obvious how a PDP feedback mechanism can coexist within a general model of language processing that involves symbol processing of the sort familiar to psycholinguists. Specifically, how can we reconcile approaches to language processing as diverse as the modular theory of mind proposed by Fodor (1983) and the TRACE model of speech processing? While a solution is not currently available for language processing, researchers in other domains have recently attempted to provide a synthesis between connectionist models and information-processing models of memory (Estes 1988). In his discussion of the interrelations between distributed network activations and symbolic representations, Estes considers the possibility that "outputs of states of activity in a distributed network in the brain project to other neural structures that have properties more like the local representations conceived in information processing models" (p. 199). Estes's discussion suggests the possibility that connectionist and information-processing models may coexist as explanatory mechanisms in ways that may enlighten the process under study.

Acknowledgments

This research was supported by NRSA (MH-09357) from NIH, and preparation of the manuscript was supported in part by NINCDS Grant NS 26587. I would like to thank David Pisoni for the use of the Speech Research Laboratory at Indiana University and Albrecht Werner Inhoff for comments on the manuscript.

Note

1. It should be noted that a lexical effect is evident at the /g/ endpoint, though this effect was not significant. Inspection of the data indicated that the effect was attributable to contributions from a small subset of the subjects tested.

References

Cole, R. A. 1973. Listening for mispronunciations: A measure of what we hear during speech. *Perception and Psychophysics* 13:153–156.

Connine, C. M. 1987. Constraints on interactive processes in auditory word recognition: The role of sentence context. *Journal of Memory and Language* 16: 527–538.

Connine, C. M. In preparation. Lexical constraints in speech processing.

Connine, C. M., and Clifton, C., Jr. 1987. Interactive use of lexical information in speech perception. *Journal of Experimental Psychology: Human Perception and Performance* 13:291–299.

Elman, J. L., and McClelland, J. L. 1988. Cognitive penetration of the mechanisms of perception: Compensation for Coarticulation of Lexically Restored Phonemes. *Journal of Memory and Language* 27:143–165.

Estes, W. K. 1988. Toward a framework for combining connectionist and symbol processing models. *Journal of Memory and Language* 27:196–212.

Fodor, J. 1983. *The Modularity of Mind.* Cambridge: MIT Press.

Fodor, J., Bever, T., and Garrett, M. 1974. *The Psychology of Language: An Introduction to Psycholinguistics and Generative Grammar.* New York: McGraw-Hill.

Forster, K. 1978. Accessing the mental lexicon. In E. Walker (ed.), *Explorations in the Biology of the Language Processor.* Montgomery, Vt.: Bradford Books.

Forster, K. 1979. Levels of processing and the structure of the language processor. In W. E. Cooper and E. C. T. Walker (eds.), *Sentence Processing: Psycholinguistic Studies Presented to Merrill Garrett.* Hillsdale, N.J.: Erlbaum.

Fox, R. A. 1984. Effects of lexical status on phonetic categorization. *Journal of Experimental Psychology: Human Perception and Performance* 10:526–540.

Ganong, W. F. 1980. Phonetic categorization in auditory word perception. *Journal of Experimental Psychology: Human Perception and Performance* 6:110–125.

Garnes, S., and Bond, Z. A. 1976. The relationship between semantic expectation and acoustic information. *Phonologica* 3:285–293.

Grosjean, F. 1980. Spoken word recognition and the gating paradigm. *Perception and Psychophysics* 28:267–283.

McClelland, J. L., and Elman, J. L. 1986. The TRACE model of speech perception. *Cognitive Psychology* 18:1–86.

Mann, V. A., and Repp, B. H. 1982. Fricative-stop coarticulation: Acoustic and perceptual evidence. *Journal of the Acoustical Society of America* 17:1562–1567.

Marslen-Wilson, W. 1973. Linguistic structure and speech shadowing at very short latencies. *Nature* (London) 244:522–523.

Marslen-Wilson, W., and Tyler, L. K. 1980. The temporal structure of spoken language understanding. *Cognition* 8:1–71.

Marslen-Wilson, W., and Welsh, A. 1978. Processing interactions and lexical access during word recognition in continuous speech. *Cognitive Psychology* 10:29–63.

Miller, J. L., and Dexter, E. R. 1988. Effects of speaking rate and lexical status on phonetic perception. *Journal of Experimental Psychology: Human Perception and Performance* 14, no. 3: 369–378.

Samuel, A. G. 1981. The role of bottom-up confirmation in the phonemic restoration illusion. *Journal of Experimental Psychology: Human Perception and Performance* 7:1124–1131.

Samuel, A. G. 1986. The role of the lexicon in speech perception. In E. C. Schwab and H. C. Nusbaum (eds.), *Pattern Recognition by Humans and Machines,* vol. 1, *Speech Perception.* Orlando, Fla.: Academic Press.

Seidenberg, M. S., Waters, G. S., Sanders, M., and Langer, P. 1984. Pre- and post-lexical loci of contextual effects on word perception. *Memory and Cognition* 12:315–328.

Tanenhaus, M. K., and Lucas, M. 1987. Context effects in lexical processing. *Cognition* 25:213–234.

Warren, R. M. 1970. Perceptual restoration of missing speech sounds. *Science* 167:392–393.

Warren, R. M., and Obusek, C. J. 1971. Speech perception and phonemic restorations. *Perception and Psychophysics* 9:358–362.

Chapter 14

Using Perceptual-Restoration Effects to Explore the Architecture of Perception

Arthur G. Samuel

Perception abhors a vacuum. In vision and audition (and probably the other senses as well), when the perceptual system encounters an incomplete pattern, it often fills the void, creating a complete pattern from the incomplete input. Consider, for example, a line drawing of an almost complete circle. Under normal conditions, people can accurately report that such a figure is incomplete. However, when the perceptual process is deprived of input about the gap in the pattern, the resulting percept is consistently the complete circle. For example, if an occluding figure overlaps the gap, people see the circle as complete (but occluded). A more striking case is one in which the perceiver is an individual with damage to the visual cortex. Such individuals may suffer from a scotoma, a "blind" region, because the cortical cells that would process that part of the visual field do not function. I put *blind* in quotes because a person with a deficit of this sort typically does not report any blindness. The perceptual system produces a filled-in output that appears complete. If a person with such a scotoma were shown the circle with the gap within the scotoma, the person would report an intact circle.

A skeptic might chalk this up to some aberrant compensation process that developed as a result of the brain damage. However, it is easy to demonstrate perceptual completion effects in normal subjects. Each of us has a scotoma caused by the optic nerve's interruption of the retinal mosaic. If the gap in the stimulus circle is aligned to fall on this blind spot (and the other eye is closed), the percept is of a complete circle. Thus, whether the input is degraded by occlusion, neural damage, or neural design, the perceptual process apparently is obligated to produce a completed pattern.

One very general way to talk about this situation is to consider the activation of the sensory receptors as the input, the percept as the output, and the perceptual process as the infamous black box. Given this simplistic breakdown, we must determine how information flows within the black box, and between the box and any other relevant mental processes or structures. In addition to issues of flow of information, there are issues of flow of control: how does the system allocate its processing resources?

One way to approach these difficult issues is suggested by the example considered above. Perhaps the workings of the black box may be illuminated by examining the relationship of the input to the output. By definition, the detailed structure of the black box cannot be inferred in this way. However, a *functional description* of the perceptual process may be attainable. In particular, when we can specify the input and obtain some measure of the output, interesting discrepancies between the two may provide insights into the workings of the black box. The focus of this chapter is the class of discrepancies in which the input is incomplete, while the output appears complete. Under these circumstances we may conclude that the black box adds information to the input to derive the output. If so, it then becomes important to determine the source of the added information (e.g., intrabox or interbox), and the conditions under which such addition occurs (e.g., when the input is degraded or the system is overloaded). These issues should be recognizable as instantiations of the problems of information flow and flow of control.

As noted at the outset, the tendency for perception to complete incomplete stimulus patterns is by no means limited to the visual modality. There are many examples in the literature of incomplete acoustic stimulation yielding complete percepts. Warren and his colleagues have described a number of these effects (Warren 1970, 1984; Warren and Obusek 1971), as has Dannenbring (1974). Warren, Obusek, and Ackroff (1972) have reported that a tone that repeatedly starts and stops is heard as continuous (complete) if it is accompanied by a louder tone. Similarly, Dannenbring found that a repeating pair of tones (one ascending and the other descending) sounds continuous (gliding up and down) if the tones are presented with noise bursts interspersed. In both examples the gaps in the tone presentation are filled in by the perceptual process; the input is incomplete, and the output is complete. As in the visual example, when the stimulus structure is not degraded (by some sort of masking), perception is essentially veridical. When the stimulus *is* degraded, the perceptual system produces a complete, though factually inaccurate, output.

A particularly interesting case of perceptual completion occurs when the interrupted signal is speech. Warren (1970) found that if a bit of a word (a phoneme) was removed and replaced with an extraneous noise, listeners nevertheless perceived the utterance as intact; he called this "phonemic restoration." This case is particularly interesting because the missing piece, unlike the restored percepts in all of the other examples cited here, is not some straightforward physical extrapolation of the remaining parts of the percept. That is, if the /s/ in *legislature* is replaced, there is no mathematical extrapolation of the /ɪ/ or /l/ that could be used to derive the /s/. One can at least imagine such an extrapolation for the incomplete circle or the interrupted tone patterns. The phonemic restoration effect thus appears to be a case in which the black box adds a very complicated sort of information to the input to produce its output.

In considering an input-output discrepancy of this sort, it is important to be aware that we are somewhat constrained by the input specification and greatly limited by the output assessment. In particular, if we are interested in *perception*, we as experimenters cannot directly observe it in subjects (except for our own subjective introspections). As such, we must make inferences based on some sort of *report* of the output. The problem, of course, is that a subject's report of the output of perceptual processing may well be contaminated by processing that occurred after perception and before report.

Most of the data that will be discussed in this chapter have been collected using a paradigm specifically designed to partition perceptual and post-perceptual effects. The goal is to use the pattern of results to clarify the architecture of perception. Two schools of thought regarding this architecture have recently become quite influential. Unfortunately, these two approaches are fundamentally incompatible. One school—the interactive or connectionist approach—assumes that essentially all knowledge structures are interconnected; information flows in all directions. The second view—the modularity approach—assumes that information flow is highly restricted; processing is handled by modules that by definition cannot use information that may be available outside of the module.

In the context of these analyses of perceptual architecture, it should be clear that it is critical to delineate where information does and does not flow. The results to be discussed here are used to begin such a delineation. Two dimensions of possible modularity will be considered: *Vertical* modularity occurs to the extent that high-level knowledge within a particular stimulus domain does not get used in perceptual processing of stimuli within that domain. The issue of vertical modularity thus boils down to an empirical test of how far top-down information flow reaches. In contrast, *horizontal* modularity revolves around the definition of a stimulus domain. In a modular architecture there should be a well-defined stimulus domain over which a module operates. At the sensory level, for example, we can certainly consider audition and vision modular in the sense that the ear is sensitive to one kind of stimulation and the eye is sensitive to another. Such sensory issues aside, the more profound question is whether the perceptual system sorts its inputs by means of modular processing, processing in which a module is essentially blind or deaf to a stimulus because that stimulus is not within the domain of the module.

Some Tests of Flow of Information and Control during Speech Perception

The issue of vertical modularity has a fairly extensive history. Researchers in various areas have debated whether top-down processing plays a role in perception, and if so, the extent of its influence. Samuel's (1981) exploration of the phonemic restoration effect was primarily intended to address this question. This study introduced a methodology designed to reveal any top-down effects in phonemic restoration while factoring out any post-perceptual components. This methodology involves the construction of two types of stimuli and the use of signal detection analyses to isolate perceptual effects. One type of stimulus is very similar to the stimuli used in earlier studies of phonemic restoration (Sherman 1971, Warren 1970, Warren and Obusek 1971, Warren and Sherman 1974). In this stimulus type a phoneme is excised from an utterance and replaced by another sound (such as white noise). The second stimulus type differs from the first by virtue of its having nothing deleted. In these stimuli the extraneous noise is simply superimposed on the phoneme that was deleted in the first stimulus type.

The rationale for the stimuli is based on the phenomenology of perceptual restoration. To the extent that listeners perceptually restore the deleted phoneme in the first stimulus type, the perceptual output should be an intact utterance with an extraneous sound superimposed. This is in fact what subjects typically report. The role of the second stimulus type is in some sense to provide subjects with a model of what an intact utterance with superimposed noise *really* sounds like. On each trial, subjects hear either an intact utterance or one with a phoneme deleted; the task is to report which. In most experiments using this method, each word is presented once in its "added" form and once in its "replaced" form. By testing restoration in a discrimination format, this procedure provides responses that are suitable for analysis with the method of signal detection.

The signal-detection model basically assumes that there are two possible states of the world (in this case, that a phoneme has been deleted or that it hasn't). Each state of the world leads to a distribution of internal states, corresponding to the degree to which the listener perceives the utterance to be intact. Presumably, the distribution of such perceived intactness is on average greater for the truly intact state of the world, than for the phoneme deleted state of the world. However, if this judgment is based on the output given after the black box has added information to the incomplete input, the two distributions may be very similar. The signal detection parameter d' is an estimate of how far apart the two distributions are. To the extent that the black box is successful in restoring the incomplete input, the distributions will not differ: d' will approach zero. If the output for intact stimuli differs from the output for incomplete ones, then d' will be greater than zero. In the signal detection model, factors that do not affect the separation of the distributions, but do affect listeners' bias show up in another parameter, beta.[1]

About a decade has passed since the first subjects were tested in this restoration paradigm. In a sense, this chapter is an attempt to step back and ask what this technique has told us about the architecture of perception. In this respect, no attempt will be made to be exhaustive in considering the literature more generally. Instead, the focus will be on how studies of perceptual restoration constrain models of speech perception.

The first use of this methodology (Samuel 1981, experiment 1) was designed to test whether the phonemic restoration illusion is primarily due to perceptual processing or postperceptual effects. Recall that a perceptual basis would be indicated by very low discriminability of the two stimulus types. However, low d' scores could arise for a less interesting reason: if the superimposed noise in an intact stimulus was very loud, it could mask the coincident phoneme, effectively matching the stimulus in which noise replaced the phoneme. For this reason, control segments were constructed by removing the word context from the critical portions of the stimuli. For an intact stimulus, the control segment was the critical phoneme with its coincident noise; for an incomplete stimulus, the control segment was the noise that replaced the missing phoneme. If the critical portions are easily discriminated out of their word contexts, but these same segments are poorly discriminated in context, the low d' scores may be attributed to perceptual restoration rather than simple masking. In fact, that was the observed pattern of data. Discrimination of the control segments was quite good (with mean d' scores around 2.7), while discrimination of the same acoustic information in word contexts was poor (mean d' less than 1.0). This result indicates that our perceptual black box is capable of transforming an incomplete input into an output that is virtually indistinguishable from the output produced from a complete input.

Given this validation of perceptual completion effects, we may address issues of information flow. In particular, we may investigate what sources of knowledge the black box uses to transform the incomplete input into the complete output. A series of experiments using the restoration paradigm have pursued this question (Samuel 1981, 1987; Samuel and Ressler 1986). An obvious source of information that bears on what phoneme is needed to complete a word is knowledge of the word itself. The role of such *lexical* knowledge in phonemic restoration has been tested in several different ways.

The first test of lexical effects using Samuel's discrimination task involved a comparison of restoration in utterances for which lexical representations should exist, familiar words, and utterances without such representations, pseudowords (Samuel 1981, experiment 2). If the black box relies (at least in part) on information in the lexicon to complete the input, incomplete pseudowords (which by definition are not represented in the lexicon) should yield less complete outputs than those of words. The test basically involved constructing intact and incomplete versions of words (as before) and appropriately matched pseudowords in the same two forms. Each pseudoword was matched to a word in terms of syllabic length, overall phonological structure, stress pattern, and location and identity of the critical phoneme.

The actual experiment involved one methodological complication. It is well established that listeners are extremely poor at temporally localizing sounds that fall into different perceptual streams (Bregman and Campbell 1971). The noise used as the replacement/additon in this study had this property: listeners were generally poor at specifying exactly when the noise occurred relative to the speech stream. Because of this, the pseudoword task in its simplest form is essentially impossible for a subject. For example, if a subject heard *ucrip* with a poorly localized accompanying noise, there is no way to decide whether anything was missing; the pseudoword might have been *ucrip* or *lucrip* or *ucript*, to name just a few possibilities. For this reason, the pseudowords (and words) were presented in a cued format: the test item (with noise either added to or replacing a phoneme) was preceded by an unmanipulated rendition of the word or pseudoword. Subjects were therefore in a position to judge whether the pseudoword was intact or not, even if they could not localize the noise.

Note that because of the structure of the task, if the black box uses lexical information to transform the input into the output, performance should actually be worse on familiar words than on unfamiliar pseudowords. This is so because use of lexical information would produce an output for an incomplete input that is more complete, i.e., more like the output for a veridically complete input: restoration will be stronger for words, and stronger restoration drives discrimination performance down. The obtained results followed exactly this pattern: average discrimination for word stimuli (a d' of about 0.8) was significantly worse than the performance on pseudowords (a d' of about 1.3).[2]

The cued presentation mode used in the word-pseudoword comparison, though methodologically motivated, has an interesting theoretical spin-off. In most tasks, cuing subjects about the identity of an imminent stimulus enhances performance. However, if cuing in the restoration paradigm activates a lexical representation and activated lexical information is used by the black box to restore missing parts of the input, cued words should show greater restoration (i.e., lower discrimination) than uncued words. Interestingly, this is what was found. Moreover, the difference between cued and uncued words depended on the location of the critical phoneme: performance on uncued words was essentially unaffected by whether the critical phoneme occurred at the beginning, middle, or end of the word, while performance on cued stimuli declined through the course of the word. These results are consistent with the view that when the perceptual system expects a particular word, the beginning of the word serves to confirm the expectation sufficiently to produce greater restoration. Apparently, without such prior expectations, the initial part of the incoming word is generally not sufficient to enhance restoration of the remainder.

Several other aspects of the data in Samuel's (1981) study indicate that the perceptual black box utilizes lexical information to construct its output, but the cuing and pseudoword results are the most important. A more recent study (Samuel 1987) provides additional evidence that meshes nicely with these findings. In this study the focus was on how a word's relationship to other words in the mental lexicon might affect perception. More specifically, two experiments explored the effects of "lexical uniqueness," the extent to which an acoustic stimulus uniquely specifies a particular lexical entry. One version of lexical uniqueness can be illustrated with the words *dozen* and *dungeon*. If the initial consonant in *dozen* is excised and replaced with noise, the resulting stimulus is lexically ambiguous—either *dozen* or *cousin* could be perceived. In contrast, when the /d/ in *dungeon* is replaced by noise, the resulting stimulus is lexically unique—only *dungeon* is consistent with the input.

If the perceptual process accesses lexical representations in transforming its input into its output, there are a number of ways that lexical ambiguity (or uniqueness) could affect phonemic restoration. The observed results reflected two significant effects: one perceptual and the other postperceptual. Perceptually, the existence of two (or more) possible lexical candidates led to more restoration, which suggests that the black box was better able to find a means of completing its input when there were multiple possibilities. This perceptual effect was complemented by a reduced overall bias toward reporting lexically ambiguous stimuli as intact; apparently some decision process is sensitive to the fact that such stimuli do not uniquely specify a particular word and scales responses accordingly. For the present purposes, the main lesson to be drawn from this experiment is that the perceptual process is sensitive to the relationship of a word to other words in the lexicon.

The second experiment in this study explored lexical uniqueness in a somewhat different way. Marslen-Wilson and his colleagues (Marslen-Wilson 1987, Marslen-Wilson and Tyler 1980, Marslen-Wilson and Welsh 1978) have argued that a word is recognized when enough of it has been heard to rule out all other lexical candidates; we can tell this "temporal lexical uniqueness." Samuel (1987, experiment 2) tested this notion with the restoration paradigm in a manner analogous to an experiment by Jakimik (1980). In Jakimik's study, subjects were asked to respond when they heard a mispronounced word. Jakimik found that subjects responded more quickly to second-syllable mispronunciations in words whose first syllables were lexically unique. This would be expected if listeners accomplish lexical access sooner in such words and the availability of an accessed lexical representation speeds the detection of a mispronunciation (because of its mismatch).

The restoration test involved four-syllable words whose initial syllables were either very common (*transportation*) or very unusual (*vegetation*). In the first case, lexical uniqueness is delayed because of the many *trans-* words in the lexicon; in the second case, a unique candidate can emerge rapidly. If the perceptual process uses lexical information to complete incomplete inputs, differences in phonemic restoration may be observed as a function of temporal lexical uniqueness. Such differences would be expected to emerge toward the end of the words, since lexical access is hypothesized to occur when enough of the word has been heard to uniquely specify it. In fact, more restoration was found in the third syllable of words like *vegetation* than in words like *transportation*, which supports both the theory of lexical access and the role of lexical information in perception.

A study of attentional control in phonemic restoration (Samuel and Ressler 1986) also demonstrated lexical influences in the illusion. The basic hypothesis tested in this study was that restoration is due in part to a failure to attend to the necessary level of analysis: normally, we attend to words, whereas the stimuli used in restoration experiments require attention to sublexical details. To test this hypothesis, Samuel and Ressler used two manipulations that have proven effective in other studies of attention: training and attentional cues. If inappropriate attentional allocation promotes restoration (nonveridical perception), extensive practice with restoration stimuli might be expected to lead to reduced restoration as subjects learn to allocate attention appropriately for the task. Similarly, if subjects receive information prior to a test item, they may be able to attend to relevant aspects of the stimulus and thereby achieve more veridical perception.

Several kinds of attentional cues were tested. In one condition, subjects were shown a printed version of the impending test word. In another they saw the identity and location of the critical phoneme but not the word (e.g., they might see "p – – – –" when the test word was *piano* and the critical phoneme was the initial /p/). In a third condition, listeners received both lexical and phonemic information. Performance in these conditions was compared to performance in a control condition in which subjects received an uninformative string of dashes as the precue.

The results for these attentional cues were clear-cut. Restoration was unaffected by providing either lexical or phonemic cues; performance in these cases matched the control case. However, when *both* lexical and phonemic cues were provided, restoration was significantly reduced. This pattern suggests that listeners can focus attention on the phonemic level, but that this must be routed via the lexicon; it was not possible to enhance performance by trying to process an initial /p/ in the abstract. Instead, the perceptual black box appears to access lexical structures and to process its input in the context of information from these lexical representations.

The results of the training manipulation are consistent with this interpretation. The only condition to show any improvement with training was the "lexical only" condition, in which subjects saw the word to be tested. Over the course of 600+ trials, there was a small but significant improvement in this condition, suggesting that subjects were learning the location of the critical phonemes in these words (there were 54 words presented 12 times). This item-specific lexical interpretation is bolstered by the results of a transfer test: when new words were presented, performance in the lexical-cue condition returned to the baseline, whereas it remained at its elevated level for subjects receiving both lexical and phonemic information. The overall pattern indicates that if listeners have both lexical and phonemic (positional) information, restoration may be reduced; the black box can reduce its tendency to produce complete outputs from incomplete inputs. The data suggest that the box works directly with lexical representations.

At this point it might be useful to briefly review the findings that implicate the lexicon as an important source of information for the perceptual process. First, known words produce more restoration than unfamiliar pseudowords. Second, priming a word increases restoration of its missing parts. Third, whether or not a stimulus uniquely specifies a lexical item affects the strength of perceptual restoration; this is true for words as a whole and for uniqueness from a temporal perspective. Finally, attentional cues are only effective in reducing the illusion if a lexical route is available for directing attention. Taken together, these results indicate that the perceptual black box must have access to lexical information. Thus, if one wants to interpret the box as an enclosed structure, as a module, one is obligated to include the lexicon in the box (see Fodor 1983 for such a claim).

The results just reviewed indicate that there is a top-down flow of information from the lexical level to the phonemic. These results necessitate either a modular architecture that incorporates the lexicon in the black box, as just noted, or alternatively, a less modular architecture. Interative models, such as Marslen-Wilson's (Marslen-Wilson and Welsh 1978) or McClelland and Elman's (McClelland and Elman 1986, Elman and McClelland 1984) can accommodate these results particularly well, since top-down information flow is a basic property of such models. In fact, these models posit very general use of top-down processing, including both lexical information and higher-level sources (e.g., sentential).

There are a number of studies in the literature that have demonstrated effects of sentential predictability on, for example, shadowing performance (Marslen-Wilson and Welsh 1978) and detections of mispronunciations (Cole and Jakimik 1978). However, as noted above, there is ample opportunity for postperceptual processing to influence responses in many tasks, and there is some reason to believe that this may be the case for these results (see Samuel 1986 for a discussion). The restoration paradigm was explicitly designed to isolate perceptual effects from later processes through its signal detection methodology, which suggests that it could provide a useful test of whether sentential predictability does in fact affect perceptual processing of speech.

Samuel's (1981) initial study using the paradigm included such a test. Twenty-seven sentence sets were constructed using word pairs that differed by a single phoneme and could be differentially predicted by small variations in a sentence frame. For example, consider the following two sentences: "The travelers found horrible bats in the *cavern* when they visited it." "The travelers found horrible food in the *tavern* when they visited it." In each case, syntactic and semantic constraints serve to predict the italicized word. Test stimuli were constructed by presenting noise either in addition to, or instead of, the initial phoneme in these words (critical phoneme position and phone class were balanced across the stimulus set). Along with these predictive contexts, nonpredictive contexts were constructed by using sentences with critical words swapped: "The travelers found horrible bats in the *tavern* when they visited it." "The travelers found horrible food in the *cavern* when they visited it".

Subjects were asked to make the usual intactness judgment for each test sentence. In addition, they were then shown two words (in this case, *tavern* and *cavern*) and asked to indicate which one had been in the sentence; they were obliged to guess if they did not know. The central issue for the present purpose is whether the predictive context produced stronger perceptual restoration, just as knowing a word (versus a pseudoword) and priming increased restoration. Recall that if restoration is stronger, a stimulus with an excised phoneme should sound more like an intact one—d' should be reduced. In fact, this did not occur: Discriminability was actually reliably *better* in predictive contexts (average $d' = 1.60$) than in less predictive ones (average $d' = 1.38$). Apparently, subjects could focus their attention more successfully with consistent information. There was also a reliable post-perceptual effect of predictability: subjects were more biased to report all stimuli as intact when the words fit the context. One interpretation of this result is that the bias measure reflects an overall satisfaction index—when things all make sense, listeners are biased to report that everything was normal. The signal detection analyses allow this effect to be separated out from the measure of perceptual restoration.

The studies of speech recognition reviewed here speak to the issue of vertical modularity raised earlier. The collection of lexical influences on perception indicates that either perception of speech is interactive (non-modular), or that the lexicon is embedded in the perceptual module. In contrast, the results for sentential predictability indicate that syntactic/semantic information does not get used by the perceptual black box. In this sense, the box does appear to be vertically modular. This leaves us with an architecture that is either partially interactive and partially modular (if one rejects the inclusion of the lexicon in a perceptual module) or entirely modular (if one accepts such embedding). My own bias is toward the first choice, on the grounds that the lexicon seems to contain information needed for many cognitive functions (see Gerrig 1986). To the extent that modules are "informationally encapsulated" (Fodor 1983), such widespread utility argues against modularity. The modular alternative can only be maintained under these circumstances by postulating multiple lexicons: the lexicon in the module, plus one or more lexicons to be used by other modular or nonmodular processes (e.g., to compose poetry). Parsimony favors a single lexicon, which implies an interactive architecture up to the lexical level and a modular organization more globally.

Some Tests of Flow of Information and Control during Music Perception

To this point the discussion has focused on vertical modularity, an issue that presupposes a particular stimulus domain (in this case, speech). In a recent series of experiments, Dewitt and Samuel (in press) used the restoration methodology in a nonspeech stimulus domain, music. This research program is intended to determine whether the results found with speech are domain-specific, or whether the same pattern holds true of music. Two general possibilities exist: (1) We might find quite different patterns of interaction/modularity in music than those reviewed here for speech. If so, we may postulate different black boxes for each domain, operating under different principles. This would be a case of horizontal modularity. (2) We might find quite similar patterns of interaction/modularity across speech and music. In this case we could either assume a single black box that operates on inputs of various types or different black boxes that operate on individual domains but with the same principles.

Dewitt and Samuel's first experiment was essentially a demonstration that music restoration occurs and can be measured using the noise addition/replacement paradigm. Familiar portions of common melodies played on a piano were digitized, and one note in each melody was chosen as the critical note. A version with the note replaced by noise was constructed, as was a version with the noise superimposed. Control segments like those used by Samuel (1981) were made by deleting the melodic context, which left either just noise or noise plus a note. Subjects judged melodies as being intact or not and control segments as having notes or not. As with speech, good discriminability of controls coupled with poor discriminability of the same sounds in context is evidence for perceptual restoration. Performance on the controls (average $d' = 3.74$) was in fact much better than on the melodies (average $d' = 1.74$), supporting an inference of perceptual restoration.

Several follow-up experiments explored the degree of vertical modularity in the perception of music. These experiments had the general form of comparing restoration in melodies under conditions in which some kind of higher-level information is available to performance when that information is not available. As a representative case, consider melodies that the listener is familiar with and melodies that are unfamiliar. If people store melodies in some sort of melodic lexicon, this manipulation is analogous to Samuel's (1981) comparison of familiar words and unfamiliar pseudowords. On this analysis, we would expect that because familiar melodies have such a representation, the black box would use such information to fill in an incomplete melodic input, producing more perceptual restoration (and therefore lower d' values). The actual results contradict this expectation: discriminability was reliably better for notes in familiar melodies ($d' = 1.69$) than for notes in matched unfamiliar melodies ($d' = 1.37$). This pattern held across several different manipulations (e.g., familiarity, rhythmic regularity, priming): providing additional information aided performance rather than leading to decreased discriminability because of stronger activation of the representation of a melody.

There are at least two interpretations of the discrepancy between the results of familiarity of words and familiarity of melodies. One possibility is that there are different black boxes for speech and music—horizontal modularity—and that different principles operate in the different modules. Alternatively, it may be that the analogy between words and melodies is not apt. Perhaps melodies are more analogous to sentences; in songs, for example, a melody maps more directly onto a sentence (or sentences) than onto a word. There is no way to decide this issue a priori precisely because speech and music *are* different domains. The theoretical issue is whether the two domains are processed by separate modules.

One way to approach this issue is to assume for the moment that speech and music are processed in a unitary fashion and to see whether the same overall pattern holds across the two domains. We have already seen that if there is to be parsimony, we must assume that melodies are in some way more like sentences than words. In fact, the observed effect of predictability in melodies (via familiarity, for example) is very similar to that found for sentences: In sentences, predictive context yields better discriminability ($d' = 1.60$) than the unpredicted case ($d' = 1.38$), with comparable values for predictable notes in melodies ($d' = 1.69$) versus unpredictable ones ($d' = 1.37$). If this rough analogy is to work, we must find a musical structure somehow more basic than the melody (as words are, compared to sentences) that shows an empirical pattern like that for words.

Dewitt and Samuel hypothesized that a musical scale might have the desired properties: it is reasonably short and invariant under many transformations (e.g., amplitude, key, rhythm). Two tests of restoration of notes in scales were interwoven in one experiment. In one test, subjects heard seven piano notes in an ascending major scale, followed by the critical note, followed by two more ascending notes. For example, in the key of C, subjects heard C, D, E, F, G, A, B, [critical note], D, E. The critical note could be any note (white or black keys) between the initial note (C in this example) and its octave, inclusive. If listeners' expectations influence perception, they should restore the appropriate note (in this example, high C), which would yield lower d' scores in this case than for trials in which the critical note is another one.

The second test involved presentation of varying amounts of a scale: listeners heard from two to six preceding notes in a scale, followed by the critical note, followed by two more ascending notes. In this case, the critical note was always the appropriate one in the scale being played. If activation of the representation of a scale provides information used by the black box, restoration should covary with the amount of the scale presented. Trials from this experiment were randomly interspersed with trials from the other scale experiment, which prevented subjects from adopting any strategy that focused on a particular note (such as the eighth one, the location always probed in one version of the scale experiment).

The results of both experiments indicate that scale information is used by the perceptual process to complete degraded inputs. Restoration was stronger for trials in which the critical (eighth) note fit in the ascending scale than when it did not. Similarly, discriminability of intact and replaced notes was reduced as the amount of scale activation (manipulated by varying the number of preceding scale notes) was increased. These results parallel the findings of lexical manipulations.

The overall pattern found for perceptual restoration in music is quite similar to that for speech. In both cases, high-level information (sentential or melodic) does not appear to be accessible to the perceptual black box; in both cases, information stored in more entrenched representations (word, scales) does seem to be used perceptually. The music domain thus appears to reflect the same perceptual architecture as the speech domain: interactive processing at lower levels of representation and modularity of those levels with respect to higher-level information.

Before drawing any final conclusions regarding the similarity of speech and music, it would be useful to consider flow of control as well as flow of information. Recall that Samuel and Ressler (1986) addressed this issue with regard to phonemic restoration. Their major conclusion was that restoration is due (at least in part) to a failure of attentional control: listeners do not normally attend to the acoustic details. Moreover, it is difficult to induce such a focus. Subjects could only do so if they had both lexical and phonemic/positional precuing or possibly if they had lexical cuing and extensive practice. The results for the first case were much more clear-out than the second, which suggests that much more training (thousands rather than hundreds of trials) might be needed to achieve attentional control in the absence of explicit positional specification.

To date there have not been any studies of attentional control using restoration measures with musical stimuli. However, Watson and his colleagues have conducted a thorough examination of perceptual performance using musical tones that is formally quite similar to Samuel and Ressler's study (Watson et al. 1975; Watson, Kelly, and Wroton 1976; Espinoza-Varas and Watson 1986). In these studies the stimuli were ten-note sequences with a total duration of about a half second, a good approximation to the average duration of spoken words. In most of the experiments, subjects heard a target ten-note sequence, followed by a test sequence that was either identical to the target or slightly different; the difference could be a small frequency shift of one note (Watson et al. 1975, 1976) or a small duration change (Espinoza-Varas and Watson 1986). Subjects were required to determine whether the two sequences were identical or not, and thresholds for making these judgments were measured.

For the present purposes, two factors in these studies are of particular interest: stimulus uncertainty and training. The level of training of subjects in this research program was exceptional: across various conditions, subjects reached asymptotic performance after 20,000 to 30,000 trials; training continued for many thousands of trials beyond this point. The implication for the restoration work is that even though Samuel and Ressler (1986) used a very long training period by speech perception standards (subjects were run through about a thousand trials with feedback), relatively small effects would be expected if the data from the tone stimuli are applicable. As noted earlier, training effects were in fact very small.

The manipulation of stimulus uncertainty may be of greater interest. In the tone-series experiments, stimulus uncertainty was manipulated by varying the number of contexts, the number of different tone sequences the critical note was embedded in. Discrimination performance was strongly influenced by this factor. When subjects could focus their attention on a particular note, their discrimination performance approached levels found for notes presented in isolation; when such focus was not possible, discriminability was an order of magnitude worse.

Espinoza-Varas and Watson (1986) interpret their results in terms of the development of a representation of a note sequence in memory. When such a representation is established (e.g., through training under minimal uncertainty conditions), it may be used to focus attention. As the authors put it, discrimination performance is determined by the subject's knowledge of "what to listen for and where. . . . Performance is limited by the ability to use an internal standard to guide the analysis of the comparison pattern" (p. 1692).

This analysis is precisely the one offered by Samuel and Ressler (1986) to account for performance on the phonemic-restoration discrimination task. In that study, discrimination improved only when listeners knew what to listen for and where: subjects succeeded when they were given lexical and positional information and to a lesser extent when they practiced with lexical cuing (which implicitly provided positional information because the critical phoneme remained constant throughout training). The results for speech and music are thus extremely consistent: attentional focus is achieved by accessing an established representation in memory and then narrowing the focus to the particular position within the required representation. For words, the representations are lexical entries; for note sequences, some comparable representations are evidently established.

Conclusions

The goal of this chapter has been to clarify the architecture of perception. The tactic has been to examine cases in which the output of the perceptual black box is more complete than the input. Such cases give us theoretical leverage because the discrepancy between the input and output may be attributed to the operation of the perceptual process. In particular, perceptual restoration effects provide evidence bearing on the knowledge sources that are available to, and used by, the perceptual black box.

The results of the various studies cited here speak to a number of aspects of the perceptual architecture. As noted earlier, these issues basically revolve around questions of information flow and flow of control. At the risk of oversimplification, the results of a decade's research using Samuel's (1981) restoration paradigm may be sorted into four claims:

1. There is a level of representation that the perceptual process uses in a top-down fashion; information flow is not strictly bottom-up. For speech, the lexical level serves this function. For music, a level of entrenched knowledge behaves in an analogous fashion. The available evidence indicates that extremely well-defined and familiar patterns (such as scales) or exceptionally well-practiced and short patterns (like those studied by Watson and his colleagues) can be used by the perceptual process.

2. Higher-level knowledge sources do *not* appear to be used by the black box to complete incomplete inputs. For speech, sentential constraints fall in this category. For music, the available evidence indicates that melodic structure is in this group. These higher-level sources of information may affect postperceptual processing (and therefore bias reports).

3. Perceptual processing is dependent on attentional allocation, and this allocation is accomplished through two levels: attention is first directed to an existing representation, and then it is focused on a particular location within that representation. The representations that can serve as conduits of attention appear to be the same ones that can be used to provide top-down information flow.

4. The final claim is actually implicit in the other three: Perceptual restoration effects appear to display the same basic properties in the musical domain as they do in the speech domain (see claims 1–3).

These four claims have interesting implications for theories of perceptual architecture. Recall that there are competing schools of thought on this architecture that differ in the hypothesized degree of interaction among various knowledge sources. I have used the term *vertical modularity* to refer to the extent to which the perceptual process is isolated from higher-level knowledge structures. In a vertically modular architecture the perceptual process has no top-down inputs. As discussed previously, the data summarized in claim 2 support at least a partially vertically modular architecture. For the reasons discussed previously, claim 1 seems most consistent with an interactive, rather than a modular, architecture. Thus, the first two claims support an architecture that is interactive at relatively low levels of representation and vertically modular with respect to higher levels.

The results summarized in claim 3 speak primarily to process rather than structure but are nonetheless relevant to theories of perceptual architecture. The data currently available suggest that attentional cuing is only effective when there is a structure of the sort described in claim 1 to serve as a pathway. If this pattern proves to be reliable, it lends additional support to the distinction between low-level and higher-level components of mental representation. Further research in this area could be very useful. The final claim bears directly on the issue of horizontal modularity. Recall that an architecture can be considered horizontally modular to the extent that there are well-specified domains over which different modulus operate. In the present case, horizontal modularity would be indicated if different patterns of performance were observed for speech and music. Indeed, a recurring theme in speech perception research over the last two decades has been that "speech is special" (see, e.g., Liberman et al. 1967). The results cited here do not support this claim; the perceptual mechanisms do not appear to be horizontally modular. This position follows from the parallelism of the speech and music results with respect to interactive, low-level perceptual processing, modular high-level effects, and allocation of attention by means of well-established low-level representations.

In sum, the results of a decade of experimentation with the restoration paradigm have provided interesting constraints on theories of the architecture of perception. Moreover, the type of architecture suggested by the results of this method (Samuel 1981, 1986) is converging with architectural claims based on other considerations (e.g., Connine 1987, Marslen-Wilson 1987, Tanenhaus and Lucas 1987). This convergence of theorizing suggests that we may be closing in on a valid model of perceptual architecture.

Acknowledgments

I would like to thank Donna Kat for all her help in many aspects of the research reviewed in this paper. Lucinda Dewitt and Bill Ressler played important roles. I would also like to thank Dominic Massaro for rekindling my interest in perceptual bias and for drawing my attention to Watson's work. I certainly appreciate Gerry Altmann and the Edinburgh group's invitation to the conference for which this paper was prepared; the workshop was both productive and fun. Finally, the Air Force Office of Scientific Research has provided support for some of the research cited and for preparation of this paper.

Notes

1. This basic formulation of signal detection theory has no provision for what might be termed "perceptual bias." Consider a case in which an experimental manipulation shifts *both* hypothesized distributions. For example, suppose that telling subjects the identity of the impending test word produces a stronger percept both for stimuli in which something is really missing and for truly intact stimuli. This shift of both distributions will yield no change in d' but will shift beta. The

discussion that follows will ignore this possibility (as does almost everyone else). However, this is an interesting possibility that is worth exploring.

2. Samuel (1981) noted that the pseudowords in this study were not perfectly matched to the words. For example, the pseudowords were about 10 percent longer on average than the words. For this reason he suggested that this result be viewed cautiously, pending its replication. Such a replication experiment is currently underway.

References

Bregman, A. S., and Campbell, J. 1971. Primary auditory stream segregration and perception of order in rapid sequences of tones. *Journal of Experimental Psychology* 89:244–249.

Cole, R. A., and Jakimik, J. 1978. Understanding speech: How words are heard. In G. Underwood (ed.), *Strategies of Information Processing*. London: Academic Press.

Connine, C. M. 1987. Constraints on interactive processes in auditory word recognition: The role of sentence context. *Journal of Memory and Language* 26:527–538.

Dannenbring, G. L. 1974. Perceived auditory continuity with gliding frequency changes. Doctoral dissertation, McGill University.

Dewitt, L. A., and Samuel, A. G. In press. The role of knowledge-based expectations in music perception: Evidence from musical restoration. *Journal of Experimental Psychology: General*.

Elman, J. L., and McClelland, J. L. 1984. Speech as a cognitive process: The interactive activation model. In N. Lass (ed.), *Speech and Language*, vol. 10. New York: Academic Press.

Espinoza-Varas, B., and Watson, C. S. 1986. Temporal discrimination for single components of nonspeech auditory patterns. *Journal of the Acoustical Society of America* 80:1685–1694.

Fodor, J. A. 1983. *The Modularity of Mind*. Cambridge: MIT Press.

Gerrig, R. J. 1986. Process and products of lexical access. *Language and Cognitive Processes* 1:187–195.

Jakimik, J. 1980. The interaction of sound and knowledge in word recognition from fluent speech. Doctoral dissertation, Carnegie-Mellon University, Pittsburgh.

Liberman, A. M., Cooper, F. S., Shankweiler, D. P., and Studdert-Kennedy, M. 1967. Perception of the speech code. *Psychological Review* 74:431–461.

McClelland, J. L., and Elman, J. L. 1986. The TRACE model of speech perception. *Cognitive Psychology* 18:1–86.

Marslen-Wilson, W. D. 1987. Functional parallelism in spoken word-recognition. *Cognition* 25:71–102.

Marslen-Wilson, W. D., and Tyler, L. K. 1980. The temporal structure of spoken language understanding. *Cognition* 8:1–71.

Marslen-Wilson, W. D., and Welsh, A. 1978. Processing interactions and lexical access during word recognition in continuous speech. *Cognitive Psychology* 10:29–63.

Samuel, A. G. 1981. Phonemic restoration: Insights from a new methodology. *Journal of Experimental Psychology: General* 110:474–494.

Samuel, A. G. 1986. The role of the lexicon in speech perception. In E. C. Schwab and H. C. Nusbaum (eds.), *Perception of Speech and Visual Form: Theoretical Issues, Models, and Research*. New York: Academic Press.

Samuel, A. G. 1987. The effect of lexical uniqueness on phonemic restoration. *Journal of Memory and Language* 26:36–56.

Samuel, A. G., and Ressler, W. H. 1986. Attention within auditory word perception: Insights from the phonemic restoration illusion. *Journal of Experimental Psychology: Human Perception and Performance* 12:70–79.

Sherman, B. L. 1971. Phonemic restoration: An insight into the mechanisms of speech perception. Master's thesis, University of Wisconsin, Milwaukee.

Tanenhaus, M. K., and Lucas, M. M. 1987. Context effects in lexical processing. *Cognition* 25:213–234.

Warren, R. M. 1970. Perceptual restoration of missing speech sounds. *Science* 167:392–393.

Warren, R. M. 1984. Perceptual restoration of obliterated sounds. *Psychological Bulletin* 96:371–383.

Warren, R. M., and Obusek, C. J. 1971. Speech perception and phonemic restorations. *Perception and Psychophysics* 9:358–363.

Warren, R. M., Obusek, C. J., and Ackroff, J. M. 1972. Auditory induction: Perceptual synthesis of absent sounds. *Science* 176:1149–1151.

Warren, R. M., and Sherman, G. L. 1974. Phonemic restoration based on subsequent context. *Perception and Psychophysics* 16:150–156.

Watson, C. S., Kelly, W. J., and Wroton, H. W. 1976. Factors in the discrimination of tonal patterns: II, Selective attention and learning under various levels of stimulus uncertainty. *Journal of the Acoustical Society of America* 60:1176–1186.

Watson, C. S., Wroton, H. W., Kelly, W. J., and Benbasset, C. A. 1975. Factors in the discrimination of tonal patterns: I, Component frequency, temporal position, and silent intervals. *Journal of the Acoustical Society of America* 57:1175–1185.

Chapter 15

The Relationship between Sentential Context and Sensory Input: Comments on Connine's and Samuel's Chapters

Lorraine K. Tyler

In this discussion I am going to concentrate upon one of the common themes in Connine's and Samuel's contributions to this volume: the relationship between sentential context and sensory input. The specific question they both address in their papers is, At what point in the processing of a word does context exert its effects?

Although no one now disputes that sentential context affects the process of recognizing spoken words, there is still considerable debate about the exact locus of these effects (Tyler and Frauenfelder 1987, Tyler and Marslen-Wilson 1982, Marslen-Wilson and Tyler 1980, Tanenhaus and Lucas 1987). This is an important issue because of its implications for the structure of the language-processing system. Depending on how sentential context affects the word-recognition process, the system can be characterized as being either autonomous or interactive[1] with respect to how information flows between and within levels.[2]

To evaluate the various theoretical options, we have to first consider the major phases involved in recognizing spoken words. I will assume that word recognition involves something like the three phases that Marslen-Wilson (1987) has labeled *access* (the way in which the sensory input is mapped onto representations of lexical form), *selection* (the way in which a single element is chosen out of the total ensemble of activated elements), and *integration* (the way in which the semantic and syntactic properties of the word being recognized are integrated into the higher-level sentential representation).

For the language-processing system to be autonomous, sentential context can only have an effect after a word has emerged as the best fit with the sensory input. In other words, context cannot affect either the access or selection phases of lexical processing. This is the position currently favored by Marslen-Wilson (1987) and, although they do not use the same terminology, by Forster (1976), Seidenberg et al. (1982), and Swinney (1979), among others. These models share the same basic structure, although they differ in the type of selection process they incorporate. In Forster's model, for example, lexical elements are contacted and searched by a serial process until a single candidate is found that best matches the sensory input, whereas in Marslen-Wilson's model, selection is a parallel process.

In contrast, if context affects either access (Morton 1969, Grosjean 1980, McAllister 1988) or selection (Marslen-Wilson and Welsh 1978, Marslen-Wilson and Tyler 1980, Tyler and Wessels 1983, Zwitserlood 1989), then the processing system can be said to be interactive. For context to affect the access phase, it must directly affect the activation level of elements in the mental lexicon. This is what happens in Morton's logogen model. The prior context can raise or lower activation levels of lexical elements according to the extent to which they are contextually appropriate. For context to affect the selection phase, it must directly contribute toward the choice of a unique candidate. In early versions of the cohort theory (Marslen-Wilson and Welsh 1978, Marslen-Wilson and Tyler 1980), context did this by rejecting candidates (accessed on the basis of the sensory input) that were not contextually appropriate and accepting those that were. Although the mechanism of acceptance and rejection was never adequately specified, the implicit assumption was that it involved context being able to affect the activation levels of lexical elements.

To determine exactly how context affects word recognition, we need to find experimental tasks that selectively tap these different phases of the word-recognition process. Considerable effort has been directed toward this end, and for some time it has been thought that so-called "on-line" tasks tap the access and/or selection phases (Marslen-Wilson and Tyler 1980, Tyler and Wessels 1983). Recently some doubts have been raised about the appropriateness of on-line tasks in this context. Tanenhaus and Lucas (1987), for example, have claimed that they do not distinguish between perceptual processes (which we can think of as consisting of the access and selection phases) and postperceptual processes (equivalent to the integration phase). They also claim, however, that there is one task currently in use which does indeed distinguish between perceptual and postperceptual analyses, and that is the task that Samuel uses in his experiments: phoneme discrimination in conjunction with a signal detection analysis. Similarly, Connine claims the same advantages for the task she uses. But do these tasks in fact present us with the solutions we have been waiting for?

Samuel uses the phoneme-restoration effect in the following way to investigate the relationship between sentential context and word recognition. Subjects hear a word that has had one of its segments either replaced by white noise or has had white noise added to it. This word is heard in a sentential context that may or may not bias toward the target word. Subjects are asked to report whether the word was intact (i.e., whether it had noise added to it) or whether the critical phoneme had been replaced by white noise. From subjects' reports, two measures are calculated: d' and β. The measure d' is a measure of the subject's ability to discriminate between an added and replaced stimulus. A low d' value means that the subject thinks that the added and replaced versions sound alike. The d' measure, then, is taken to reflect perceptual processing. This is in contrast with β, which measures the postperceptual effect of response bias and is sensitive to shifts in criterion. That is, a subject can vary his or her criteria for deciding that there is sufficient perceptual evidence that a stimulus has occurred. Samuel's various studies (1981) show that context has no effect on d', but it does have an effect on β. However, there are a number of problems in using signal-detection analysis to separate the effects of perceptual and postperceptual processing.

First, the reason that signal detection analysis is appealing is that it presumes to separate the sensory coding and decision phases of lexical processing. For this to be the case, d' and β need to be independent; d' should not vary as a function of shifts in criteria. Although this is assumed to be the case in Samuel's research, it is in fact never tested. For Samuel to be sure that d' and β are indeed independent in his studies, he needs to obtain the empirical ROC (receiver operating characteristic) curves (where d' is plotted as a function of shifts in criterion) for the stimuli he uses. Until these are obtained, he is making an assumption that is not adequately tested.

The importance of testing the validity of this assumption is highlighted by research in other cognitive domains. For example, in studies of divided attention, people typically used signal-detection analysis to partial out the effects of d' and β, on the assumption that they are independent (e.g., Duncan 1980). However, subsequent research by Shaw (1982) showed that in fact they were not independent, since they could both be affected by the same variables. Before we assume that signal-detection analysis solves our problems and is a task we can use to tease apart the different phases of the word-recognition process, we must make sure that it is indeed appropriate for this purpose.

Another difficulty with Samuel's data concerns the interaction between the acoustic properties of the target phonemes and those of the white noise. It is particularly difficult, for example, to tell whether noise has been added or replaced to either a stop or fricative, whereas this discrimination is much easier for other phonemes, e.g., nasals (Samuel 1981). This might interact in complex ways with context. Assume, for a moment, that if context affects perceptual processing, it does so by making it more difficult to discriminate between an added or replaced segment, i.e., it reduces d'. But if d' is already very small (because the segment is a stop or fricative), it may well be impossible to see any effect of context, because d' is already at the floor and thus performance cannot get worse. Although Samuel used three different phone classes in his 1981 paper, he did not look at the effect of sentential context upon these phone classes separately. Clearly, the best test is to see how context affects d' for segments such as liquids and nasals, which are more discriminable in white noise.

Another problem concerns the way in which a signal-detection analysis of phoneme-restoration data maps onto a model of lexical processing. In a model such as the cohort theory (Marslen-Wilson and Welsh 1978, Marslen-Wilson and Tyler 1980, Marslen-Wilson 1987), which distinguishes between access, selection and integration, how do d' and β relate to these different phases? Does d' tell us about both access and selection or just about one of them? And does β only reflect the integration phase? This is not just a problem for Samuel's methodology. The relationship between task and theory always needs to be made explicit. Otherwise, it is very difficult to evaluate empirical findings with respect to the claims made by different models (see Tyler and Frauenfelder 1987).

In the phoneme restoration task as it is standardly used, listeners are not asked to make their decision as rapidly as possible. It is possible that they have plenty of time to reflect upon their decisions and even to alter them. It is generally thought that in such situations, postperceptual, reflective processes might obscure the effects of perceptual processing. To reduce the possibility of this type of postperceptual process, in a pilot study Marslen-Wilson, Tyler, Warren, and Jefsioutine (1989) modified the task by having subjects produce their responses quickly. In this study we had pairs of stimuli, such as *crate/crane*, that diverged from each other in their final phoneme. We varied the phone class of the final segment, using both voiced and voiceless stops as well as nasals. The final segment of each member of the pair was either masked by white noise (the "noise added" condition) or it was excised and replaced by white noise (the "noise replaced" condition). These tokens were heard either in a neutral context (where both

Table 1
Restoration RTs (in msec)

	Appropriate	Inappropriate	Difference
Neutral context	1,217	1,230	13
Biasing context	1,130	1,271	141

members of the pair were equally acceptable, as determined by pretests) or a context that biased toward one member of the pair. Subjects were asked first to decide whether the word was added or replaced and press an appropriately labeled response key. They were encouraged to do this as rapidly as possible and we recorded their response times (RTs) to make the decision. They then had to indicate what word they thought they had heard by making a forced selection between the two words (e.g., *crate/crane*) on a computer screen. The question was whether, when a word appeared in a biasing context, subjects would be more likely to restore a missing phoneme, that is, to think that a "replaced" item was in fact an "added" item. We thought that if, like Samuel, we did not find an effect of context on d', it might show up in RTs to make the added/replaced decision.

When we examined d' values, we found the same results reported by Samuel: context had no effect. But we did find an effect on RTs, as can be seen in table 1, which shows the restoration latencies. Restoration RTs are the time it takes subjects to press the "added" response key when in fact the target phoneme has been replaced by noise.

The first point to note is the RTs were quite long, which indicates that the decision was a difficult one for subjects to make.[3] Second, as the table shows, RTs to words occurring in a neutral context are not significantly different from each other, which is what one would expect, since in the neutral condition both members of the pair are equally appropriate. However, in the biasing-context condition, restoration RTs are faster when the word is contextually appropriate.[4] It would be reasonable to interpret the RT data as showing that sentential context does indeed play a role in lexical selection. That is, as showing that context affects perceptual processing. But then we are in the position of having to explain why the two measures (d' and RT) give a different pattern of results. The easiest thing to do would be to assume that the RT measure is contaminated by postperceptual analyses in a way that d' is not. But there is no rational basis for drawing this conclusion.

In fact, the only way to make sense of the data is to relate the different aspects of the task to a model of lexical processing that specifies the entire sequence of events involved in recognizing a spoken word. Unfortunately, we're not yet in a position to do this, because we don't fully understand the tasks that we use, which makes it difficult to relate task and theory.

Like Samuel, Connine also claims to use a task that does not confound perceptual and postperceptual components of the word-recognition process (Connine 1987, Connine and Clifton 1987). She examines how identification functions shift when words appear in context. In her 1987 paper, for example, she used target words that differed in the voicing value of the word-initial stop consonant (e.g., *dent/tent, dime/time*). Two sentences were constructed, each biased toward either the voiced member of the pair (e.g., *dent, dime*) or the unvoiced member (*tent, time*). In a third condition, the sentence was neutral. She constructed voice onset time (VOT) continua for her target words and asked subjects to indicate (by pressing a labeled response key) the sound they heard at the beginning of the last word. She recorded subjects' responses and their RTs. Stimuli in the middle range of the continua, where the signal is ambiguous, provided the most important test of the effect of context in that they showed whether a biasing context resulted in more contextually appropriate identifications.

As expected, Connine found that context shifted identification functions. Since she had earlier found that identification functions are also affected by monetary payoffs (Connine and Clifton 1987), she argued that such shifts must be postperceptual. She also found that RTs to contextually appropriate categorizations were faster than those to inappropriate categorizations only when the stimulus was perceptually unambiguous, that is, at the endpoints of the continua. When the stimulus was perceptually ambiguous, subjects' RTs were no faster when the word they thought they were hearing was contextually appropriate compared to when it was contextually inappropriate. She claimed that this showed that context does not intervene in the formation of a percept but rather operates after the percept has been constructed.

Although Connine assumed that the paradigm she used avoids many of the pitfalls associated with tasks that may confound perceptual and postperceptual processes, it is not clear that it in fact does so. One questionable aspect of the task is that it generates very long RTs, around 1,200 msec.[5] Tasks assumed to selectively tap perceptual processes usually produce RTs in the region of 250 to 500 msec. The long RTs in Connine's task may mean that subjects find the task very difficult, or they may be slow because the task includes a "metalinguistic" component. By this I mean that subjects have to make an explicit judgement about what they hear. This forces them to pay attention to particular aspects of the linguistic representation they have constructed.[6] This can be contrasted with tasks where there is an implicit relationship between the variable of interest and the subject's response (e.g., in word-monitoring tasks where the target word occurs after the linguistic element the experimenter is interested in). Subjects invariably take longer to perform tasks that include an explicit decision process than those that do not. Moreover, metalinguistic tasks are sensitive not only to perceptual processes. They are also affected by postperceptual processes. If the task Connine uses does indeed include a metalinguistic component, it is not at all clear that her RT measure is in fact capable of selectively tapping perceptual processing.

Apart from problems of methodology, there are also problems of interpretation. Connine assumes that in the ambiguous region of the VOT continua, both voiced and unvoiced members of a pair are activated and that what her data show is that context doesn't affect any aspect of the activation process. But perhaps both members are not activated. Perhaps, when the sensory input is fully ambiguous, it is not sufficient to initiate a set of activated candidates. If the cohort model is correct in assuming that context can operate only on a set of candidates initiated on the basis of the sensory input, then when the sensory input cannot initiate a cohort, context has nothing to operate on. Furthermore, if a cohort cannot be initiated on the basis of the initial sound sequence, the listener has to engage a nonstandard process (i.e., not a first-pass-analysis process) to try to figure out what the word is. In this case, context might also function in a manner that is different from the way it operates during the first-pass analysis of the signal.

The purpose of this critical analysis of Connine's and Samuel's papers is to illustrate the difficulties inherent in using an experimental technique whose properties are not clearly rooted in a model of the cognitive process one is studying. Although Connine and Samuel claim that the tasks they use tap particular aspects of the recognition process, this claim needs to be related to a specific model of word recognition. In different models perceptual and postperceptual processing can mean different things. This in turn means that their data cannot be taken as conclusive evidence in favor of an autonomous lexical processing system where context intervenes only after a unique candidate has emerged.

My own view is that the situation is currently at a stalemate. There is as much evidence in favor of an interactive system, where context affects the selection phase of lexical processing (Marslen-Wilson and Tyler 1980,

Tyler and Wessels 1983, Zwitserlood 1989), as there is in favor of an autonomous system. Unfortunately, many of the tasks that generate the data can be criticized as being incapable of selectively tapping that aspect of the process that they are intended to tap. What we are left with is a situation where we have a number of models of the word-recognition process (some more fully developed than others) but not enough adequate data to distinguish between them.

Notes

1. For simplicity I am assuming that there is a clear dichotomy between interactive and autonomous models, whereas in fact the distinction is not so clear cut (Tyler and Marslen-Wilson 1982, Tyler and Frauenfelder 1987).

2. It is important to keep clear the distinction between the context that arises from higher-level representations of an utterance and context effects that are due to interlexical associations (e.g., semantic associates). The former case involves different levels within the system, whereas the latter case involves only a single level.

3. Since the RTs are so long, we cannot assume that this task selectively taps perceptual processing. Nevertheless, the fact that the results from the RT task differ from those of the standard signal-detection task is something that needs to be explained.

4. The interaction was significant is an analysis by subjects but not in an analysis by items.

5. RTs were measured from the onset of the burst of each target word.

6. There is some neuropsychological evidence to support the distinction between implicit and explicit processes in many different cognitive domains, e.g., in memory (Weiskrantz 1986) and in spoken-language comprehension (Tyler 1988).

References

Connine, C. 1987. Constraints on interactive processes in auditory word recognition: The role of sentence context. *Journal of Memory and Language* 26: 527–538.

Connine, C., and Clifton, C. 1987. Interactive use of lexical information in speech perception. *Journal of Experimental Psychology: Human Perception and Performance* 13: 291–299.

Duncan, J. 1980. The locus of interference in the perception of simultaneous stimuli. *Psychological Review* 87: 272–300.

Forster, K. 1976. Accessing the mental lexicon. In R. Wales and E. Walker (eds.), *New Approaches to Language Mechanisms*. Amsterdam: North-Holland.

Grosjean, F. 1980. Spoken word recognition processes and the gating paradigm. *Perception and Psychophysics* 28: 267–283.

McAllister, J. 1988. The use of context in auditory word recognition. *Perception and Psychophysics* 44, no. 1: 94–97.

Marslen-Wilson, W. D. 1987. Functional parallelism in spoken word recognition. *Cognition* 25:71–102.

Marslen-Wilson, W. D., and Tyler, L. K. 1980. The temporal structure of spoken language understanding. *Cognition* 8:1–71.

Marslen-Wilson, W. D., Tyler, L. K., Warren, P., and Jefsioutine, M. 1989. The effects of sentential context on coarticulation. In preparation.

Marslen-Wilson, W. D., and Welsh, A. 1978. Processing interactions and lexical access during word recognition in continuous speech. *Cognitive Psychology* 10:29–63.

Morton, J. 1969. Interaction of information in word recognition. *Psychological Review* 76:165–178.

Samuel, A. 1981. Phonemic restoration: Insights from a new methodology. *Journal of Experimental Psychology: General* 110:474–494.

Seidenberg, M., Tanenhaus, M., Leiman, J., and Bienkowski, M. 1982. Automatic access of the meanings of ambiguous words in context: Some limitations of knowledge-based processing. *Cognitive Psychology*, 14:489–537.

Shaw, M. 1982. Attending to multiple sources of information: I, The integration of information in decision making. *Cognitive Psychology* 14:353–409.

Swinney, D. 1979. Lexical access during sentence comprehension: (Re)consideration of context effects. *Journal of Verbal Learning and Verbal Behavior* 14:645–660.

Tanenhaus, M., and Lucas, M. 1987. Context effects in lexical processing. *Cognition* 25:213–234.

Tyler, L. K. 1988. Spoken language comprehension in a fluent aphasic patient. *Cognitive Neuropsychology* 5:375–400.

Tyler, L. K., and Frauenfelder, U. 1987. Spoken word recognition: An introduction. In U. Frauenfelder and L. K. Tyler (eds.), *Spoken Word Recognition*. Cambridge: MIT Press.

Tyler, L. K., and Marslen-Wilson, W. D. 1982. Conjectures and refutations: A reply to Norris. *Cognition* 11:417–427.

Tyler, L. K., and Wessels, J. 1983. Quantifying contextual contributions to word recognition processes. *Perception and Psychophysics* 34:409–420.

Weiskrantz, L. 1986. *Blindsight*. Oxford: Clarendon Press.

Zwitserlood, P. 1989. The locus of the effects of sentential-semantic context in spoken-word processing. *Cognition* 32:25–64.

Chapter 16

Modularity Compromised: Selecting Partial Hypotheses

Henry Thompson and Gerry T. M. Altmann

Like many concepts in cognitive psychology, the concept of modularity appeals to the relatively high-level modeling of the mind. Yet its applicability to actual computational systems is often somewhat unclear because the level of detail present in these systems tends to obscure the higher-level issues. The kind of reality such systems represent, irrespective of whether or not they have any claim to *psychological* reality, may nonetheless provide a useful basis for insight into issues concerning the architecture of the mind.

Below are some of the word pairs that have been used when discussing architectural issues. It often seems that they refer to the same distinction.

impenetrable	penetrable
modular	nonmodular
weak interaction	strong interaction
selective	instructional
encapsulated	unencapsulated

There are two relatively distinct sorts of issues to which these terms might be applied. The original *computational* usage of the term *modular* focused on active issues concerning the *flow of control* and the possible division of the computational system into distinct subsystems. Its use in *architectural* discourse, on the other hand, often focused on passive issues of *information localization*. In this chapter we are primarily concerned with the active issue.

It will be useful to consider the issue of *selection* versus *instruction* (to choose one of the many possible word pairs) in the context of Swinney's (1979) cross-modal priming experiments. The relevant fact that Swinney exhibited is that during lexical access, all readings of polysemous words are retrieved, regardless of their contextual appropriateness. Only some time *after* retrieval are the contextually inappropriate readings discarded, presumably as the contextually appropriate readings are incorporated by the interpretational process.

Several aspects of this simple finding deserve comment. First, the findings suggest that there is some *division of labor* between that part of the system responsible for lexical access and that part of the system responsible for the construction of interpretations. We shall call these aspects *stages* to avoid prejudging the issue. Second, there is an *inherent ordering* between the two stages in that interpretation cannot precede lexical access. Third, there exists some potential for *ambiguity*, at least locally, insofar as the first stage is capable of producing more than one analysis for a given input. And finally, it is assumed that the interaction between the two stages has a particular *granularity*, namely whole word meanings. That is, the mechanism that somehow chooses between the alternatives offered by lexical access has to adjudicate over whole words. This leads to the explicit claim that the interaction is weak, selective, and impenetrable—in other words, that the two stages operate in lock-step, where all the processing at one stage is completed before processing commences at a subsequent stage, and that all hypotheses possible at the first stage are realized, even if they will not be used by the second stage.

The following are necessary characteristics of a system before we can even ask whether the interactions are selective or instructive: (1) there must be inherently ordered stages; (2) there must exist a division of labor between these stages; (3) the analyses performed by the first stage must be potentially ambiguous; (4) the interactions between the two stages must take place with some specified granularity. Once these characteristics have been established one can then ask, Are all hypotheses possible at the first stage realized? If the answer to this question is yes, we would claim that the interactions are selective; if no, instructive. A subsequent processing stage has to somehow instruct that first stage to abandon certain hypotheses before they were fully realized.

In this chapter we shall consider a number of models which are susceptible, by virtue of their differing processing characteristics, to different analyses in terms of the selection/instruction distinction. We start by considering a prototypically selective system (section 1) and a prototypically instructive system (section 2). We then describe a system in secion 3 that, although selective, approximates (in behavior, at least) the instructive system of section 2. In section 4 we describe an extension of this system that goes even further, to the extent that it too becomes an instructive system. Finally, we consider a further system that, although exhibiting the same behavior as this instructive system, is nonetheless selective. We conclude the chapter with a consideration of the implications of this equivalence for the modularity debate.

1   A Prototypical Selective System

The relationship between lexical access and syntactic filtering in an early version of the Edinburgh University Speech Input Project (EUSIP) system exhibits the system characteristics described above. The system architecture is pipelined, using a chart parsing framework to communicate data between processing stages and to manage control flow. Figure 1 outlines the system architecture, with representations in italics and processing stages in bold. For present purposes it is the relationship between syntactic filtering and lexical access which is relevant. The syntactic parser attempts to incorporate each lexical hypothesis as soon as it is realized (i.e., added to the word lattice), and the interaction between the parser and lexical access is purely selective; all words accessible from the phoneme lattice are inserted into the word lattice, regardless of whether or not they are syntactically consistent. Word beginnings are hypothesized only at the beginning of the utterance and at the ends of words already found. Figures 2 through 4 illustrate the process of lexical access and syntactic filtering for a simplified example phoneme lattice.

Figure 1
EUSIP system architecture (version 1)

In figure 2 and subsequent figures, time is horizontal and alternative analyses for the same interval are stacked vertically. Thus some degree of uncertainty about the phonemic identity of three out of four segments is represented in figure 2 as well as the expected lack of bottom-up acoustic information about word boundaries. It is assumed that no prosodic or allophonic information that might contribute to word-boundary location is available.

Figure 3 shows the state of the lattice once lexical access has taken place. There are two alternative segmentations of the phoneme lattice into words (after the first segment /uh/, corresponding to the word *a*, or after the next segment, corresponding to the word *up*). For each of these different segmentations a number of alternative words could arise. The phoneme /g/ has been struck out in figure 3 to indicate that one can infer from a post hoc analysis of the words found that this phoneme was not incorporated into any lexical hypothesis and that the hypothesis that there is a /g/ here can thus be discarded.

Figure 4 shows the state of the lattice after syntactic filtering (with left and right contexts added for the sake of the example). With a fairly robust left and right context, only one path through the word lattice is selected, which allows the system to retrospectively eliminate first the words not

```
   g
   b   a   t
uh p   i   d
```

Figure 2
A phoneme lattice

```
      at
up    it
   g
   b   a   t
uh p   i   d
a  pit
   bit
   pat
   bat
   bid
   bad
   pad
```

Figure 3
Phoneme and word lattices

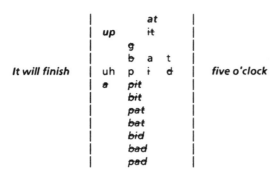

Figure 4
Phoneme and word lattices with syntactic filtering

used in that path and then the phonemes not incorporated into that word path.

Syntactic filtering does not, however, influence what is actually entered onto the word lattice in the first instance. The interaction is purely selective.[1]

2   A Prototypical Instructive System

The relationship between lexical access and syntactic filtering in the Bolt Beranek and Newman HWIM system, constructed as part of the ARPA SUR effort in the early 1970s (see Woods et al. 1976) is rather different, however. It too was pipelined, with stages corresponding more or less to the traditional speech chain. But once it got to lexical access, the system became more complex. Figure 5 outlines the system architecture, again with representations in italics and processing stages in bold.

Again, we are concerned here with the relationship between lexical access and syntax. This system is rather more complex than the purely selective one described earlier. The account given here is slightly simplified but preserves the relevant aspects of the system. The first phase of lexical access is only partial and is an attempt to form a few robust word hypotheses centered around relatively highly valued phonemic hypotheses (these being hypotheses that the system believes have a high probability of being correct). Grammatical information is then used to suggest candidate words on either side of these so-called islands. These candidates are in turn matched directly against the acoustic values in the adjoining intervals (i.e., on either side of the island) by means of analysis by synthesis. That is, the second stage of lexical access involves synthesising sequences of acoustic values appropriate to the candidate words in their hypothesized context and matching the results with the observed values. The successful matches are then entered into the word lattice and, if necessary, the process is repeated until a well-connected word lattice is found. Figures 6 through 9 illustrate one cycle of this process for a similar example to that used in section 1, using the same phoneme lattice but for a *different* utterance.

Figure 6 gives a phoneme lattice. We suppose that only the /a/ is a highly valued phonemic hypothesis. Hence its appearance in bold. In figure 7 we further suppose that only the word *bat* had a sufficiently high match against the lattice to warrant entry onto the lattice, that none of the other alternative words incorporating the /a/ hypothesis (*at, pat, bad, pad*) had high enough scores. In figure 8 we assume that *bat* only occurs as a noun in the system's lexicon, and this information is then used in conjunction with the grammar to predict a preceding determiner. Finally, in figure 9 this syntactic information is used to predict actual determiners (*a* and *the*), which are then matched against the acoustic parameters by means of analysis by synthesis.

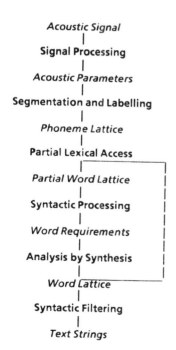

Acoustic Signal
|
Signal Processing
|
Acoustic Parameters
|
Segmentation and Labelling
|
Phoneme Lattice
|
Partial Lexical Access
|
Partial Word Lattice
|
Syntactic Processing
|
Word Requirements
|
Analysis by Synthesis
|
Word Lattice
|
Syntactic Filtering
|
Text Strings

Figure 5
HWIM system architecture

```
      g
      b   a   t
uh    p   i   d
```

Figure 6
A phoneme lattice

```
      g
      b   a   t
uh    p   i   d
      bat
```

Figure 7
Phoneme and partial word lattices

```
      g
      b   a   t
uh    p   i   d

      bat
 |     |
 D     N
  \   /
   NP
```

Figure 8
Phoneme and partial word lattices with syntactic prediction

```
      g
      b   a   t
uh    p   i   d
a
the   bat
 |     |
 D     N
  \   /
   NP
```

Figure 9
Phoneme and partial word lattices with syntactic and lexical prediction

Clearly, the syntactic predictions have significantly influenced what is actually put onto the word lattice, the processing stages that map from acoustic parameters onto words can be influenced by processes that occur at the higher-level syntactic stages, and in some cases syntactic hypotheses play a determining role in what will or will not be hypothesized by lexical access. For instance, in figures 6 through 9 the word *up* will never be hypothesized even though, if searched for, it would be found. The interactions here are clearly instructive.

3 Interleaved Lexical Access and Syntactic Filtering: A Middle Case

In section 1 we pointed out that syntactic filtering could take place before the entire lattice had been constructed. But in fact no advantage was taken of that fact. The whole word lattice could have been constructed before any syntactic processing took place, for all the difference that syntactic filtering would have made. The possibility arises, however, of discarding word hypotheses as soon as it is clear that they will not be incorporated into any supervening syntactic structure. In the EUSIP system, where syntactic filtering is accomplished via a chart parser using a GPSG-like phrase-structure grammar, this would mean discarding word hypotheses not incorporated into at least some partial syntactic hypothesis. For this to happen, one simply has to allow all possible syntactic hypotheses to be developed as each word is hypothesized and note when a word fails to be incorporated by any of the syntactic hypotheses that precede it.[2]

The significance of discarding unincorporable word hypotheses lies not so much in their absence from the lattice per se but in the consequential effect of this absence on where other words will be searched for. This will become clear if we consider again the example from figure 4 (*It will finish ... five o'clock*). The relevant phrase-structure rules from the presumed grammar are given in below. The category symbols used are all straightforwar with the exception of PV, which is used for phrasal verbs (*finish up*).

S → NP VP
VP → Aux VP
VP → PV PP
PV → V P
PP → P NP

For the sake of illustration we suppose that these are the *only* grammar rules that can analyze phrases including *finish*. Below is the traditional tree structure that would be associated with the phrase *it will finish* ....

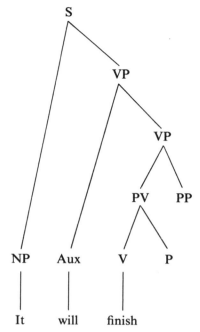

It   will   finish

Figures 10 through 13 show a sequence of snapshots of the chart, in which partial hypotheses ("active edges") are represented as thin edges with light text and complete hypotheses ("inactive edges") are represented as thick edges with bold text. The text associated with each edge looks similar to the rules expressed in the above grammar: the symbol to the left of the arrow represents the identity of the edge (i.e., the kind of hypothesis that the edge represents: S, NP, VP, etc.). The symbols to the right of the arrow represent the constituents that are dominated by that edge. And the dot indicates which constituents have already been found (to the left of the dot) and which constituents remain to be found (to the right of the dot).

Figure 10 shows the syntactic part of the chart that corresponds to the tree diagram as well as that portion of the phoneme lattice about to be encountered following the phrase *it will finish*. The first step of lexical access is to find all words starting from the ends of words most recently incorporated into syntactic edges. In Figure 8a, the most recent such word is "finish," whose incorporation is manifest by the presence of at least one active edge incident at its right end (in this case the "PV → V · P" edge).

In figure 11 the new words *up* and *a* are thus the result of running lexical access from the right-hand end of the *finish* edge.

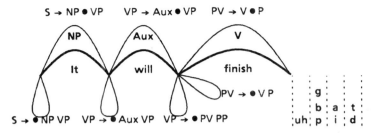

Figure 10
Phoneme lattice with left syntactic context

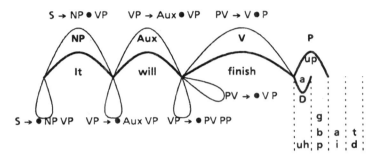

Figure 11
One step of lexical access done

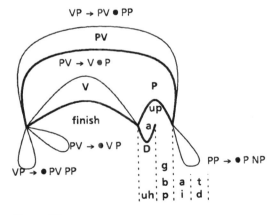

Figure 12
Syntactic processing advanced

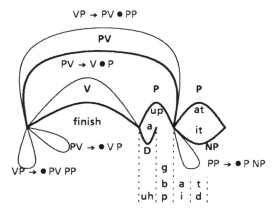

Figure 13
Lexical access advanced

The next step in the process (figure 12) is for the "PV → V·P" edge to combine with the newly found *up* edge to produce a complete PV, which in turn combines with the "VP → ·PV PP" edge to produce a "VP → PV·PP" edge. Top down invocation produces the "PP → ·P NP" edge which is also shown in figure 12. However, no active syntactic edge was available to consume the new *a* edge, so new active edges were built incident at its right-hand end. Therefore, no new words will be searched for from that point.

The existence of the "PP → ·P NP" edge, however, means that in the next stage of the process (figure 13) lexical access will be invoked at the right-hand end of the *up* edge, and this leads to the addition of two new edges, labeled *at* and *it*, to the chart. Only the *at* edge will combine with any preceding syntactic edge (the "PP → ·P NP" edge, in fact) and processing continues in this manner until the entire string, *It will finish up at five o'clock*, has been discovered.

The evident difference between this example and the processing of the prototypically selective system illustrated in figures 2 through 4 is that the seven three-letter words that are all syntactically inappropriate (*bat, bit, bad, bid, pit, pat, pad*) have not been found and consequently have not been entered on the chart. They would have been found if the lexical hypothesis *a* had been incorporated into any higher-level syntactic structure. But since it wasn't, the lexical look-up process was not invoked at its right-hand end. Thus the benefit to the system is not simply that the hypothesis *a* is effectively discarded but rather that none of the spurious words that follow *a* in the lattice have been entertained.

This is still a selective account: when lexical access is invoked, it operates without guidance from above. The only substantial difference between this account and the earlier one described in figures 2 through 4 is the *means* whereby lexical access is invoked. In the earlier case this was determined from within lexical access itself, in that all word endings were candidate word beginnings. In the case just described, candidate word beginnings are only a syntactically determined subset of word ends.

4   Interleaved Lexical Access with Top-Down Filtering: EUSIP (Version 2)

In this section we consider a modification to the interleaved system just outlined that goes one step further and avoids realizing any syntactically inappropriate words at all.

Enough information is available in principle to avoid entering any syntactically inappropriate words on the chart. In the above example this would mean that the explicit hypothesization of the words *a* and *it* would be avoided. The algorithmically simplest way to accomplish this is to divide the lexicon into a set of lexicons, one for each part of speech. Then when lexical access is invoked top down by some active edge needing a preterminal, only the lexicon for that preterminal would be used. In the example above, only the preposition lexicon would be used in the two relevant steps, and neither *a* nor *it* would be found. It is unclear whether such an account would be selective or not. It clearly goes a step further than the previous account in that although the internal workings of lexical access are still monolithic and impenetrable, it is not just *where* to look for words that is determined from above but also *what* words to look for. This takes it almost all the way to the HWIM approach described in section 2 and has a distinctly instructive flavor about it.

But there is another problem with this account, which in some sense preempts the issue. The sheer number of words with multiple parts of speech (54 percent of the 4,500-word lexicon used on EUSIP) argues against having a separate lexicon for each part of speech, if only because of the massive replication of information that would be required across lexicons. Moreover, evidence of the kind provided by Swinney (1979) suggests that a phonemic word has only one "entry" in the mental lexicon. If one is tempted by arguments that make use of psychological validity, this provides a further reason for abandoning a mechanism consisting of multiple lexicons.

There are several other ways, however, to avoid all syntactically inappropriate words. The first one, described in this section, is actually employed in the current version of the EUSIP system. We shall argue that it is *neither* a selective system (as defined at the beginning of this chapter) *nor* an informationally encapsulated one. The model to be discussed in the section that follows will be computationally equivalent to this one, but we shall argue that although still not selective, it *is* informationally encapsulated. By *informationally encapsulated* we mean a module that has reference only to knowledge proper to its task, that is, to syntactic structure for syntactic modules, to lexical structure for lexical modules, etc.

To explain the approach employed in EUSIP, it is first necessary to briefly set out the internal workings of lexical access. (This in itself should be a signal that modularity is about to be compromised.)

A lexicon is divided into a lexicon proper and an index to that lexicon. Consider the example below:

1 *an*   D
2 *at*   P
3 *ant*   N
4 *atom* N
5 *it*   NP
6 *in*   P
7 *inn*   N

The number simply identifies each entry, and the entry contains the orthographic form of the word and the form class of that word. The lexicon is accessed not directly in the course of lexical access but via a tree-structured index. This index is constructed off-line, from all the pronunciations of all the words in a particular lexicon, by folding together initial substrings of pronunciations.

The index shown in figure 14 corresponds to the lexicon above. The filled circles in figure 14 indicate nodes in the index where words may be found. The associated numbers uniquely identify entries in the lexicon. Nondeterminism arises during lexical access when a filled node is encountered that is not a leaf of the tree: having processed /a t/, we don't know whether we have found the word *at* or just the beginning of *atom*. Homophony is also a source of ambiguity, as in the case of *in* and *inn*.

The index is processed against the phoneme lattice by means of a finite-state parser implemented on top of the active chart-parsing mecha-

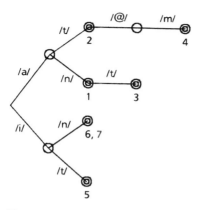

Figure 14
An index

nism, which automatically handles this nondeterminism as well as that arising from the lattice itself. This means that just as there are active syntactic edges representing partial syntactic hypotheses, there are also active lexical edges representing partial lexical hypotheses. These identify phonemic sequences with nodes in the lexical index. The sequence /a t @/ would be identified with the node between those marked 2 and 4 in figure 14.

To allow top-down syntactic filtering to take effect as efficiently as possible in the course of lexical access, it is necessary to modify the index to record at each node the set of all parts of speech of any entries in the lexicon at that node or farther along the tree from that node. This results in the index shown in figure 15, which also uses the above sample lexicon (we have omitted the explicit indices for the sake of readability).

At the end of the preceding section we remarked how lexical access was invoked once the right-hand end of a word had been reached, provided some active syntactic edge subsequently appeared incident at the right-hand end of the word's edge. For instance, in figure 12 it is the active edge "PP → · P NP" incident at the end of the *up* edge that enables lexical access to be invoked so that the lexical hypotheses *at* and *it* are subsequently found. And it is the absence of any syntactic edge incident at the end of the *a* edge that prevents lexical access from wasting effort on all the purious three-letter words that start there.

From the modified lexical index illustrated in figure 15 it is now a simple matter to modify the algorithm for lexical access so that an active *lexical*

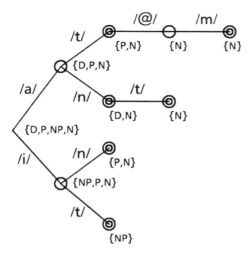

Figure 15
An index with parts of speech

edge (partial lexical hypothesis) will be entered into the chart only if the syntactic hypothesis that invoked the current lexical-access process requires a part of speech consistent with the nodes in the lexical index to which the lexical edge points. In figure 12 the crucial syntactic hypothesis is represented by the "PP → · P NP" edge, and the required part of speech is P. Without going into detail, we can see that whereas the new lexical-access algorithm will succeed in finding, and entering on the chart, the word *at*, it will fail to discover the word *it*. The search will fail after the final /t/ branch in the lexical index because the part-of-speech specification on the subsequent node ({NP}) does not match the specification (P) required by the active edge ("PP → · P NP") that allowed the invocation of the current access process.

It should be clear that this is no longer a purely selective account. The granularity at which syntactic filtering takes place has had to be changed (from whole words to partial lexical hypotheses) to allow spurious lexical hypotheses to be avoided. On the other hand, the reification of partial hypotheses, embodied in the chart's use of active edges, allows us to maintain that this account is not purely instructive either. However, this is clearly not an informationally encapsulated model in that the processor is guided by high-level (syntactic) information distributed *within the lexical index* in its search for candidate words (we return to this point below).

5 Interleaved Lexical Access with Top-Down Filtering: Individuated Partial Hypotheses

In this section we consider a model that appears to be functionally equivalent, within the limited syntactic domain we have adopted here, to the model just described but that is radically different in that it no longer violates information encapsulation.

Thus far our intention has been to shed some light onto the modularity debate from the computational perspective *irrespective* of psychological plausibility. One can ask, however, whether the psychological perspective can nonetheless shed some insight on computational issues and whether a consideration of the two perspectives taken together can somehow further the modularity debate. We might therefore ask whether this last proposal is psychologically plausible, supposing, of course, that we abstract away from the details of the chart implementation.

That there is selection of partial hypotheses appears to be required by the finding that the recognition of a word may often precede the acoustic offset of that word (Marslen-Wilson and Welsh 1978, Marslen-Wilson and Tyler 1980). Of course, we expect that the human top-down filter, which is presumably responsible for the contextual influences on this effect (see Marslen-Wilson 1987 for data pertinent to this), incorporates semantic and pragmatic constraints as will as purely syntactic ones. Also, any cohort-style model (Marlsen-Wilson 1987) would seem to be functionally equivalent to one in which lexical access makes use of shared left subpronunciations (that is, partial lexical hypotheses), as hypothesized here. However, it seems less plausible that syntactic information is distributed through the index, as is also hypothesized here. Such an architecture would imply that on the basis of acoustic information alone one might "know" that one is hearing an adjective, without yet "knowing" which one (and this would suggest that there ought to be some equivalent to the tip-of-the tongue phenomenon in the auditory perception domain).

There does exist an alternative mechanism for producing exactly the same results as those described in the previous section while avoiding this problem, if indeed we view it as such. In the previous system, syntactic information could cause the processor to abandon a particular partial lexical hypothesis only by way of abandoning a whole group of words (that is, all the words of a particular form class). In the new system we present below, these partial hypotheses are individuated.

The alternative approach supposes that the tree-structured index only covers, say, the first syllable of each word in the lexicon, after which

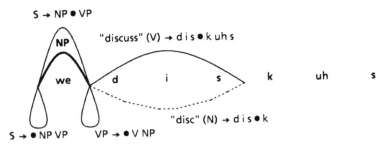

Figure 16
A chart with explicit partial lexical hypotheses

separate partial hypotheses are entered into the chart for each word in the selected cohort. Because the resulting edges each contain part-of-speech information for the words that would result if the rest of the required phonemes were found, these edges can be filtered in a manner similar to that described above but without internal lexical index nodes annotated with part-of-speech information.

Figure 16 illustrates the chart with the lexical item *we* followed by the string /d i s k uh s/, *discuss*, within which the word *disc* would be accessed were it not for its syntactic incompatibility with the noun phrase *we*. Two explicit partial lexical hypotheses are shown, one for the word *discuss* and the other for the word *disc*. In each case the part of speech is also included. The hypothesis for *disc* is dotted because we can prevent it from being entered on the chart simply by specifying that a (partial) lexical hypothesis is entered on the chart only if its part of speech matches the requirements of the syntactic hypothesis that enabled the invocation of the current round of lexical access (the "VP → · V NP" edge in this case). Thus, only the partial hypothesis for *discuss* is entered, the consequences of which are that a lexical boundary is not erroneously postulated after the /k/. In the earlier *it will finish up* ... example, this corresponds to preventing the three-letter words *bat, bit, bad*, etc., from being found (see section 4).

What makes this model rather different from the earlier one is that the matching of acoustic-phonetic input to the internal representations of words is not confined solely to "the lexicon." Once the initial portion of the word has been identified, the entire, syntactically filtered cohort is added to the chart, and it is *there* that any remaining matching is done.

This model is also different from the previous one in that it is clearly informationally encapsulated and partial hypotheses are individuated. Syntactic context still selects from the lexical cohort the appropriate partial hypotheses to entertain on the chart, but now there are separate (sets of) edges for each member of the cohort. Insofar as encapsulation is judged to be a criterion for psychological models, this model fares better than its predecessor when considered from the psychological perspective. A further difference is that there are now two different phases within lexical access: a nonfiltered one that uses the tree-structured index, followed by a filtered one that does not.

To summarize this and the preceding section, we have considered two mechanisms for meeting the same objectives. One of these was an extension of the selective model described in section 3, with lexical information folded back through the lexical index. The other involves a more explicit, individuated representation of partial lexical hypotheses and a division into two phases. In each phase only those partial hypotheses compatible with existing syntactic requirements are entered on the chart. One might ask, however, what the point is of considering these different models, which apparently accomplish the same thing. The simplest answer is that each model is susceptible to a different analysis in terms of the information structures that support context effects (top-down filtering) and in terms of the fine structure of lexical access. We consider these points in further detail in the next section.

6 Computational Equivalence and the Locus of Context Effects

To the extent that the models we considered in the previous section all lead to the realization of the *same* (complete) lexical hypotheses, they are equivalent. The essential difference between them concerns the locus of the context effect. In the model presented in section 4, the effect occurs internally to the lexical-access process. High-level information is used not only to enable the invocation of the lexical access process itself (this much is the same across both models) but also to actively direct the lexical processor to consider only certain branches of the tree-structured lexical index. Some of the branches rejected on syntactic grounds are quite acceptable on the basis of bottom-up acoustic phonetic information alone. It is this fact, enabled by the violation of information encapsulation by incorporating higher-level information in the lexical index, that gives that model its instructive flavor. It no longer realizes all acoustically possible (complete) hypotheses. This is in contrast to the second model, in which the first phase of lexical access is immune to the syntactic requirements of the environment surrounding the cohort of words in question.

This second model, in which individuated partial hypotheses are represented on the chart once the first syllable is past but only those whose part-of-speech specification matches the syntactic requirements of the preceding context, is computationally more complex than the first, involving as it does two phases where before there was one. The first stage is impenetrable and encapsulated, and the second stage occurs after the individuated partial lexical hypotheses identified by the first stage have been entered on the chart. Although processing in the first phase is relatively unchanged, an additional mechanism has been postulated to generate individuated partial lexical hypotheses, and an extra level of (lexical) description has been added to the chart, thereby complicating its operations. In terms of the distinction among *access*, *selection*, and *integration* (Marslen-Wilson 1987 and also Norris 1982), the first phase of lexical access in this model can be construed as corresponding to access, the second phase, in which top-down filtering of individuated partial hypotheses with appropriate parts of speech occurs, can be construed as selection, and finally, the incorporation of a lexical hypothesis into a syntactic hypothesis corresponds to integration.[3] Consequently, the locus of the context effect in this model is at the level of selection. In contrast, the first model does not really admit a distinction between access and selection—it mixes both indiscriminately.

To summarize briefly, we have considered two functionally equivalent models, the second more computationally complex than its predecessor and incorporating context effects within a distinguished phase. As the models become more complex, it becomes possible to identify distinctions held to be psychologically significant. We make no claims about whether such a relationship between complexity and accommodation of theoretical characterization necessarily holds. We are merely concerned with the fact that it is possible to devise systems that exhibit these characteristics.

7 Concluding Remarks

If the modularity or nonmodularity of a system is to be judged according to the simple question, Are all hypotheses possible at the first stage realized? then evidently neither of the models summarized in the preceding section is modular. But the second model is more modular. Its first phase is not subject to top-down filtering, and so all acoustically possible sub-first-syllable partial hypotheses are realized. And it is informationally encapsulated, whereas the first is not.

In view of its relative computational simplicity the first model is clearly to be preferred over the other, even though the alternative model might be preferred on other grounds (such as psychological plausibility perhaps, although any such arguments are beyond the scope of this chapter). One may wonder, then, what the modularity debate has to offer the computational linguist. Indeed, on the assumption that the human speech-processing architecture is itself a computational mechanism that has some-how evolved into a maximally efficient form (a moot point), we may wonder whether a criterion for choosing one model of this system over another should really be based on such considerations as whether or not there is modularity between the different processing stages.

On the other hand, two things stand out among the contributions of system building to the modularity debate. First, the development of real computational system helps clarify the distinction between *representational* modularity (the encapsulation of the long-term information that informs processing at various stages) and *process* modularity (how the process of analysis is shared between stages). This chapter has been concerned pri-marily with the latter issue, but it should be clear that these two aspects of modularity can vary independently. More significant, perhaps, is the fact that much, although not all, of the nonmodularity of the models considered here dissolves if we admit partial hypotheses as full-fledged theoretical entities, as the chart implementation of active edges invites us to do. It is only at the level of whole words that the models fail the test of, Are all hypotheses possible at the first stage realized? Once we reduce the granular-ity of interaction to the level of partial hypotheses, the test is passed. Perhaps this is just the thin end of a wedge that will destroy the distinction altogether, but we think not. Indeed, there are hopeful parallels between the issues discussed here and those confronted by work one level up, as it were, where the issue is the fine structure of the influence of pragmatic context on the processing of syntactic ambiguity (see Altmann and Steed-man 1988, Crain and Steedman 1985).

Acknowledgments

The work reported here was supported by the Science and Engineering Research Council under grants SERC C/78377, D/29611, D/29628, D/29604, and E/93223. Many of the ideas were developed in the course of discussions with Ellen Bard, Richard Shillcock, and Mark Steedman. Our special thanks to Greg Filz, who first implemented the system described in section 4 after realizing its equivalence to the system in section 5.

Notes

1. It should be noted that a general-purpose English syntax is evidently insufficient to provide enough filtering to produce unique word paths through the kind of word lattices that current continuous-speech-recognition systems are capable of producing for large vocabularies. It appears unlikely that we will see sufficient improvement to the word lattices themselves to overcome the resulting poor performance. Either reduced performance will have to be accepted and catered for, as in the original EUSIP proposal for an incremental, interactive speech input system, or domain constraints will have to be applied, and these either by producing so-called semantic grammars that encorporate those constraints directly or by interpretation and inferencing with respect to some representation of domain content.

2. We assume, for the sake of discussion, an essentially left-to-right processor.

3. Although it is implicit in our description of the chart framework that integration can occur only after an inactive lexical edge is created (that is, after all the phonemes required by an active, partial, lexical edge have been found), this is not a necessity. It is possible in principle to modify the chart algorithm so that an active syntactic edge can combine with an active lexical edge. This would allow the integration of partial lexical hypotheses and would correspond in some sense to the recognition of words prior to their acoustic offset.

References

Altmann, G., and Steedman, M. 1988. Interaction with context during human sentence processing. *Cognition* 30: 191–238.

Crain, S., and Steedman, M. J. 1985. On not being led up the garden path: The use of context by the psychological parser. In D. Dowty, L. Kartunnen, and A. Zwicky (eds.), *Natural Language Parsing: Psychological, Computational, and Theoretical Perspectives*. Cambridge: Cambridge University Press.

Marlsen-Wilson, W. D. 1987. Functional parallelism in spoken word recognition. *Cognition* 25: 71–102.

Marslen-Wilson, W. D., and Tyler, L. K. 1980. The temporal structure of spoken language understanding. *Cognition* 8: 1–71.

Marslen-Wilson, W. D., and Welsh, A. 1978. Processing interactions and lexical access during word recognition in continuous speech. *Cognitive Psychology* 10: 29–63.

Norris, D. 1982. Autonomous processes in comprehension: A reply to Marslen-Wilson and Tyler. *Cognition* 11: 97–101.

Swinney, D. A. 1979. Lexical access during sentence comprehension: (Re)considerations of context effects. *Journal of Verbal Learning and Verbal Behaviour* 18: 645–659.

Woods, W., Bates, M., Brown, G., Bruce, B., Cook, C., Klovstad, J., Makhoul, J., Nash-Webber, B., Schwartz, R., Wolf, J., and Zue, V. 1976. Speech understanding systems: Final technical progress report. Bolt Beranek and Newman, report no. 3438, Cambridge, Mass.

Chapter 17

Representation and Structure in Connectionist Models   Jeffrey L. Elman

Introduction

Connectionist models appear to provide a new and different framework for understanding cognition. It is therefore natural to wonder how these models might differ from traditional theories and what their advantages or disadvantages might be. Recent discussion has focused on a number of topics, including the treatment of regular and productive behavior (rules versus analogy), the form of knowledge (explicit versus implicit), the ontogeny of knowledge (innate versus acquired), and the nature of connectionist representations.

This last issue is particularly important because one of the critical ways in which cognitive theories may differ is in the representational apparatus they make available. Our current understanding of connectionist representations is at best partial, and there is considerable diversity of opinion among those who are actively exploring the topic (see Dolan and Dyer 1987; Dolan and Smolensky 1988; Feldman and Ballard 1982; Hanson and Burr 1987; McMillan and Smolensky 1988; Hinton 1988; Hinton, McClelland, and Rumelhart 1986; McClelland, St. John, and Taraban 1989; Pollack 1988; Ramsey 1989; Rumelhart, Hinton, and Williams 1986; Shastri and Ajjanagadde 1989; Smolensky 1987a, 1987b, 1987c, 1988; Touretzky and Hinton 1985; Touretzky 1986, 1989; van Gelder, in press).

In this chapter I will focus on some of the specific questions raised by Fodor and Pylyshyn (1988). Fodor and Pylyshyn express concern that whereas classical theories (e.g., the language of thought, Fodor 1976) are committed to complex mental representations that reflect combinatorial structure, connectionist representations seem to be atomic, and therefore finite in number (because of the limited and fixed resources available to them). And this appears to be at odds with what we believe to be necessary for human cognition in general and human language in particular.

I believe that Fodor and Pylyshyn are right in stressing the need for representations that support complex and systematic patterning, that reflect both the combinatorics and compositionality of thought, and that enable an open-ended productions. What their analysis does not make self-evident is that these desiderata can only be achieved by the so-called classical theories or by connectionist models that implement those theories. Fodor and Pylyshyn present a regrettably simplistic picture of current linguistic theory. What they call the classical theory actually encompasses a heterogeneous set of theories, not all of which are obviously compatible with the language of thought. Furthermore, there have in recent years been well-articulated linguistic theories that do not share the basic premises of the language of thought (Chafe 1970, Fauconnier 1985, Fillmore 1982, Givon 1984, Hopper and Thompson 1980, Kuno 1987, Lakoff 1987, Langacker 1987). Thus the two alternatives presented by Fodor and Pylyshyn (that connectionism must either implement the language of thought or fail as a cognitive model) are unnecessarily bleak and do not exhaust the range of possibilities.

Still, it is possible to phrase the questions posed by Fodor and Pylyshyn more generally in a way that might be profitably pursued: What is the nature of connectionist representations? Are they necessarily atomistic or can they possess internal structure? Can that structure be used to account for behavior that reflects both general and ideosyncratic patterning? Can connectionist representations with finite resources provide an account for apparently open-ended productive behavior? How might connectionist representations differ from those in the language of thought? One strength of connectionist models that is often emphasized is their sensitivity of context and their ability to exhibit graded responses to subtle differences in stimuli (McClelland, St. John, and Taraban 1989). But sometimes language behavior seems to be characterized by abstract patterns less sensitive to context. So another question is whether models that are fundamentally context-sensitive are also able to arrive at generalizations that are highly abstract.

In this chapter I present results from two sets of simulations. These simulations were designed to probe the above issues with the goal of providing some insight into the representational capacity of connectionist models. The paper is organized in two sections. The first section reports empirical results. Two connectionist networks were taught tasks in which an abstract structure underlay the stimuli and task. The intent was to create problems that would encourage the development of internal representations reflecting that abstract structure. Both the performance of the networks as well as the analysis of their solutions illustrates the development of richly structured internal representations. These results are discussed at greater length in the second section and are related to the broader question of the usefulness of the connectionist framework for modeling cognitive phenomena and possible differences from the classical approach.

Simulations

Language is structured in a number of ways. One important kind of structure has to do with the structure of the categories of language elements (e.g., words). The first simulation addressed the question of whether a connectionist model can induce the lexical-category structure underlying a set of stimuli. A second way in which language is structured has to do with the possible ways in which strings can be combined (e.g., the grammatical structure). The second simulation addresses that issue.

Lexical category structure

Words may be categorized with respect to many factors. These include such traditional notions as *noun, verb*, etc.; the argument structure they are associated with; and their semantic features. One of the consequences of lexical category structure is word order. Not all classes of words may appear in any position. Furthermore, certain classes of words, e.g., transitive verbs, tend to co-occur with other words (as we shall see in the next simulation, these facts of co-occurrence can be quite complex).

The goal of the first simulation was to see if a network could learn the lexical-category structure implict in a language corpus. The overt form of the language items was arbitrary in the sense that the form of the lexical items contained no information about their lexical category. However, the behavior of the lexical item, defined in terms of co-occurrence restrictions, reflected their membership in implicit classes and subclasses. The question was whether or not the network could induce these classes.

Network architecture

Time is an important element in language, and so the question of how to represent serially ordered inputs is crucial. Various proposals have been advanced (for reviews, see Elman, in press; Mozer 1988). The approach taken here involves treating the network as a simple dynamic system in which previous states are made available as additional input (Jordan 1986). In Jordan's work the prior state was derived from the output units on the previous time cycle. In the work here, the prior state comes from the hidden unit patterns in the previous cycle. Because the hidden units are not taught to assume specific values, this means that they can develop, in the course of learning a task, representations that encode the temporal structure of the task. In other words, the hidden units learn to become task-specific memory.

The type of network used in the first simulation is shown in figure 1. This network is basically a three-layer network with the customary feed-forward connections from *input units* to *hidden units* and from hidden units to *output units*. There is an additional set of units, *context units*, which provide for limited recurrence (and so this may be called a *simple recurrent network*). These context units are activated on a one-for-one basis by the hidden units, with a fixed weight of 1.0.

The result is that at each time cycle the hidden-unit activations are copied onto the context units; in the next time cycle the context combines with the new input to activate the hidden units. The hidden units thus take on the job of mapping new inputs and prior states onto the output. Because they themselves constitute the prior state, they must develop representations that facilitate this input-output mapping. The simple recurrent network has been studied in a number of tasks (Elman, in press; Hare, Corina, and Cottrell 1988; Servan-Schreiber, Cleeremans, and McClelland 1988). In this first simulation there were 31 input units, 150 hidden and context units, and 31 output units.

Stimuli and task A lexicon of 29 nouns and verbs was chosen. Words were represented as 31-bit binary vectors (two extra bits were reserved for another purpose). Each word was randomly assigned a unique vector in which only one bit was turned on. A sentence-generating program was then used to create a corpus of 10,000 two- and three-word sentences. The sentences reflected certain properties of the words. For example, only animate nouns occurred as the subject of the verb *eat*, and this verb was only followed by edible substances. Finally, the words in successive sentences were concatenated so that a stream of 27,354 vectors was created. This formed the input set.

The task was simply for the network to take successive words from the input stream and to predict the subsequent word (by producing it on the output layer). After each word was input, the output was compared with the actual next word, and the back-propagation-of-error learning algorithm (Rumelhart, Hinton, and Williams 1986) was used to adjust the

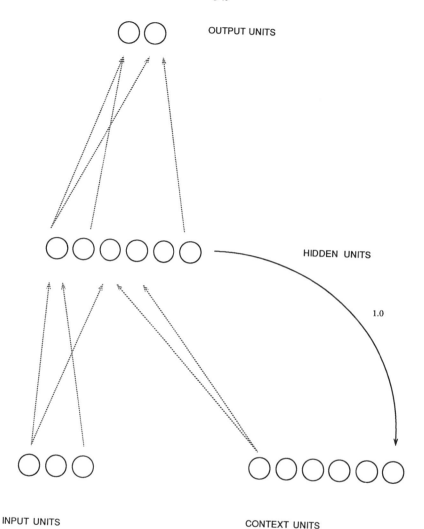

Figure 1
The network used in the first simulation. Hidden-unit activations are copied with fixed weights (of 1.0) onto linear context units on a one-to-one basis. In the next time step the context units feed into hidden units on a distributed basis.

network weights. Words were presented in order with no breaks between sentences. The network was trained on six passes through the corpus.

The prediction task was chosen for several reasons. First, it makes minimal assumptions about special knowledge required for training. The teacher function is simple, and the information required is available in the world at the next moment in time. Thus there are no a priori theoretical commitments that might bias the outcome. Second, although the task is simple and should not be taken as a model of comprehension, it does seem that much of what listeners do involves anticipation of future input (Grosjean 1980, Marslen-Wilson and Tyler 1980, Salasoo and Pisoni 1985).

Results Because the sequence is nondeterministic, short of memorizing the sequence, the network cannot succeed in exact predictions. That is, the underlying grammar and lexical-category structure provides a set of constraints on the form of sentences, but the sentences themselves involve a high degree of optionality. Thus, measuring the performance of the network in this simulation is not straightforward. Root mean squared error at the conclusion of training had dropped to 0.88. However, this result is not impressive. When output vectors are sparse, as those used in this simulation were (only 1 out of 31 output bits was to be turned on), the network quickly learns to reduce error dramatically by turning all the output units off. This drops error from the initial random value of ~ 15.5 to 1.0, which is close to the final root mean squared error of 0.88.

Although the prediction task is nondeterministic, it is also true that word order is not random or unconstrained. For any given sequence of words there are a limited number of possible successors. Under these circumstances it would seem more appropriate to ask at each point in time whether or not the network has learned what the class of valid successors is. We might therefore expect that the network should learn to activate the output nodes to some value proportional to the probability of occurrence of each word in that context.

Therefore, rather than evaluating final network performance using the root mean squared error calculated by comparing the network's output with the actual next word, we can compare the output with the probability of occurrence of possible successors. These values can be empirically derived from the training database (for details, see Elman, in press). Such calculation yields a *likelihood output vector* for each input, which reflects the context-dependent expectations derived from the training base (where context is defined as extending from the beginning of the sentence to the input). Note that it is appropriate to use these likelihood vectors only for the evaluation phase. Training must be done on the actual successor words because the point is to force the network to learn the context-dependent probabilities for itself.

Evaluated in this manner, the error on the training set is 0.053 (s.d. = 0.100). The cosine of the angle between output vectors and likelihood vectors provides a measure of performance that normalizes for length differences in the vectors. The mean cosine is 0.916 (s.d. = 0.123), which indicates that the two vectors on average have very similar shapes. Objectively, the performance appears to be quite good.

The question to be asked now is how this performance has been achieved. One way to answer this is to see what sorts of internal representations the network develops to carry out the prediction task. This is particularly relevant for the focus of this chapter. The internal representations are instantiated as activation patterns across the hidden units evoked in response to each word in its context. These patterns were saved during a testing phase, during which no learning took place. For each of the 29 unique words a mean vector was then computed, which averaged across all occurrences of the word in various contexts. These mean vectors were then subjected to hierarchical clustering analysis. Figure 2 shows the tree constructed from the hidden-unit patterns for the 29 lexical items.

The tree in figure 2 shows the similarity structure of the internal representations of the 29 lexical items. The form of each item is randomly assigned (and orthogonal to all other items), and so the basis for similarity in internal representations is the way in which these words behave with regard to the task.

The network discovered that there are several major categories of words. One large category corresponds to verbs; another category corresponds to nouns. The verb category is broken down into those that require a direct object, those that are intransitive, and those for which a direct object is optional. The noun category is divided into animates and inanimates. Animates are divided into human and nonhuman; nonhumans are subdivided into large animals and small animals. Inanimates divided into breakables, edibles, and miscellaneous.

This category structure reflects facts about the possible sequential ordering of inputs. The network is not able to predict the precise order of specific words, but it recognizes that in this corpus there is a class of inputs (verbs) that typically follow other inputs (nouns). This knowledge of class behavior is quite detailed: from the fact that there is a class of items that

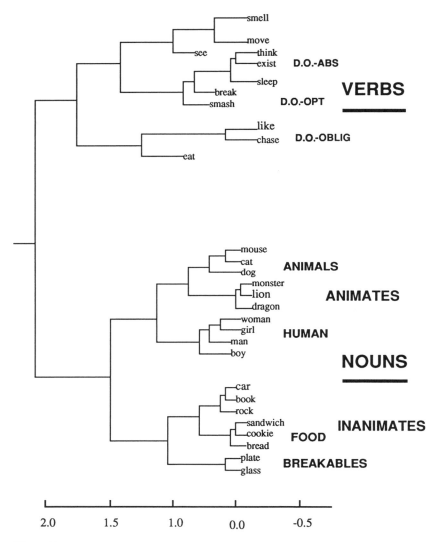

Figure 2
Hierarchical clustering of mean hidden-unit vectors after presentation of each
of the lexical items in context. The similarity structure of the space reflects
distributional properties of the lexical items.

always precedes *chase*, *break*, and *smash*, it infers a category of large animals (or possibly aggressors).

Several points should be emphasized. First, the category structure appears to be hierarchical. *Dragons* are large animals but are also members of the class [−human, +animate] nouns. The hierarchical interpretation is achieved through the way in which the spatial relations of the representations are organized. Representations that are near one another in representational space form classes, and higher-level categories correspond to larger and more general regions of this space.

Second, hierarchicality and category boundaries are soft. This does not prevent categories from being qualitatively distinct by being far from each other in concept space with no overlap. But there may also be entities that share properties of otherwise distinct categories, so that in some cases category membership may be marginal or ambiguous.

Finally, the content of the categories is not known to the network. The network has no information available that would ground the structural information in the real world. This is both a plus and a minus. Obviously, a full account of language processing needs to provide such grounding. On the other hand, it is interesting that the evidence for category structure can be inferred so readily solely on the basis of evidence internal to the language.

The tree shown in figure 2 was constructed from activation patterns averaged across contexts. It is also possible to cluster activation patterns evoked in response to words in the various contexts in which they occur. When context-sensitive hidden-unit patterns are clustered, it is found that the large-scale structure of the tree is identical to that shown in figure 2. However, each terminal leaf is now replaced with further arborization for all occurrences of the word (there are no instances of lexical items appearing on inappropriate branches).

This finding bears on the type/token problem in an important way. In this simulation the context makes up an important part of the internal representation of a word. Indeed, it is somewhat misleading to speak of the hidden-unit representations as word representations in the conventional sense, since these patterns also reflect the prior context. As a result, every occurrence of a lexical item literally has a separate internal representation. We cannot point to a canonical representation for *John*; instead, there are representations for $John_1$, $John_2$, ..., $John_n$. These are the tokens of *John*, and the fact that they are different is how the system marks what may be subtle but important meaning differences associated with the specific token. The fact that these are all tokens of the same type is not lost, however. These tokens have representations that are extremely close in space, closer to each other by far than to any other entity. Even more interesting is that the spatial organization within the token space is not random but reflects contextual differences also found among tokens of other items. The tokens of *boy* that occur in subject position tend to cluster together, as distinct from tokens of *boy* that occur in object position. This distinction is marked in the same way for tokens of other nouns. Thus the network has not only learned about types and tokens, and categories and category members; it also has learned a grammatical-role distinction that cuts across lexical items.

This simulation involved a task in which the category structure of inputs was an important determinant of their behavior. The category structure was apparent in their behavior only; their external form provided no useful information. We have seen that the network makes use of spatial organization in order to capture this category structure.

Representation of grammatical structure
In the previous simulation there was little interesting structure of the sort that related words to one another. Most of the relevant information regarding sequential behavior was encoded in terms of invariant properties of items. Although lexical information plays an important role in language, it actually accounts for only a small range of facts. Words are processed in the contexts of other words; they inherit properties from the specific grammatical structure in which they occur. This structure can be quite complex, and it is not clear that the kind of category structure supported by the spatial distribution of representations is sufficient to capture the structure that belongs not to individual words but to particular configurations of words. I turn next to a problem in which the lexical category structure provides only one part of the solution and in which the network must learn abstract grammatical structure.

As we consider this issue, we also note that till now we have neglected an important dimension along which structure may be manifest, *time*. The clustering technique used in the previous simulation informs us of the similarity relations along spatial dimensions. The technique tells us nothing about the patterns of movement through space. This is unfortunate, since the networks we are using are dynamic systems whose states change over time. Clustering groups states according to the metric of Euclidean distance, but in so doing, it discards the information about whatever temporal relations may hold between states. This information is clearly relevant if we are concerned with grammatical structure.

Consider these sentences:

(1) a. The man saw the *car*.

    b. The man who saw the *car* called the cops.

On the basis of the results of the previous simulation, we expect the representations for the word *car* in these two sentences to be extremely similar. Not only are they the same lexical type, but they both appear in clause-final position as the object of the same verb. But we might also wish to have their representations capture an important structural difference between them. *Car* in sentence (1a) occurs at the end of the sentence; it brings us to a state from which we should move into another class of states associated with the onsets of new sentences. In sentence (1b), *car* is also at the end of a clause, but here it occurs in a matrix sentence that has not yet been completed. There are grammatical obligations that remain unfulfilled. We would like the state associated with *car* in this context to lead us to the class of states that might conclude the main clause. The issue of how to understand the temporal structure of state trajectories will thus figure importantly in our attempts to understand the representation of grammatical structure.

Stimuli and task   The stimuli in this simulation were based on a lexicon of 23 items. These included 8 nouns, 12 verbs, the relative pronoun *who*, and an end-of-sentence indicator (.). Each item was represented by a randomly assigned 26-bit vector in which a single bit was set to 1 (3 bits were reserved for another puropse). A phrase-structure grammar, shown below, was used to generate sentences.

S → NP VP "."

NP → PropN | N | N RC

VP → V (NP)

RC → who NP VP |who VP (NP)

N → boy | girl | cat | dog | boys | girls | cats | dogs

PropN → John | Mary

V → chase | feed | see | hear | walk | live | chases | feeds | sees | hears | walks | lives

Additional restrictions:

- number agreement between N and V within clause and (where appropriate) between head N and subordinate V
- verb arguments:

Hit, feed require a direct object.

See, hear optionally allow a direct object.

Walk, live preclude a direct object (this is also observed for head-verb relations in relative clauses).

The resulting sentences possessed certain important properties. These include agreement, verb argument structure, interactions with relative clauses, recursion, and viable sentences. Let me say a little about each one of these.

Subject nouns agree with their verbs. Thus, for example, (2a) is grammatical, whereas (2b) is not (the training corpus consisted of positive examples only; thus the starred examples below did not occur).

(2) a. John feeds dogs.
    b. *Boys sees Mary.

Words are not marked for number (singular/plural), form class (verb/noun, etc.), or grammatical role (subject/object, etc.). The network must learn first that there are items that function as what we would call nouns, verbs, etc., then it must learn which items are examples of singulars and plurals and then it must learn which nouns are subjects and which are objects (since agreement only holds between subject nouns and their verbs).

Verbs fall into three classes: those that require direct objects, those that permit optional direct objects, and those that preclude direct objects. As a result, sentences (3a–d) are grammatical, whereas sentences (3e, f) are ungrammatical.

(3) a. Girls feed dogs. (*D.o. required*)
    b. Girls see boys. (*D.o. optional*)
    c. Girls see. (*D.o. optional*)
    d. Girls live. (*D.o. precluded*)
    e. *Girls feed.
    f. *Girls live dogs.

Again, the type of verb is not overtly marked in the input, and so the class membership needs to be inferred at the same time as the co-occurrence facts are learned.

The facts of both agreement and verb arguments are complicated in relative clauses. While direct objects normally follow the verb in simple sentences, some relative clauses have the direct object as the head of the clause, in which case the network must learn to recognize that the slot for the direct object has already been filled (even though it occurs before the verb). Thus the normal pattern in simple sentences (3a–d) appears also in (4a) but contrasts with (4b).

(4) a.   Dog who chases cat sees girl.

   b.   Dog who cat chases sees girl.

   c.   *Dog who cat chases dog sees girl.

Sentence (4c), which seems to conform to the pattern established (3), is ungrammatical.

Similar complications arise for facts of agreement. In simple sentences agreement involves a singular noun linked to a singular verb. In complex sentences, such as (5a), that regularity is violated, and any straightforward attempt to generalize it to sentences with multiple clauses would lead to the ungrammatical (5b).

(5) a.   Dog who boys feed sees girl.

   b.   *Dog who boys feeds see girl.

The grammar permits recursion through the presence of relative clauses (which expand to noun phrases, which may introduce yet other relative clauses, etc.). This leads to such sentences as (6), in which the grammatical phenomena noted above may be extended over a considerable distance.

(6) Boys who girls who dogs chase see hear.

One of the literals inserted by the grammar is ".", which occurs at the end of sentences. This end-of-sentence marker can, of course, potentially occur anywhere in a string where a sentence is viable (in the sense that it is grammatically well formed and may at that point be terminated). Thus in sentence (7), the carets indicate positions where the end-of-sentence marker might legally occur.

(7) Boys see ∧ dogs ∧ who see ∧ girls ∧ who hear ∧

The data in (4) through (7) are examples of the sorts of phenomena that linguists argue cannot be accounted for without abstract representations; it is these representations rather than the surface strings on which the correct grammatical generalizations are made.

A network of the form shown in figure 3 was trained on the prediction task (layers are shown as rectangles; numbers indicate the number of nodes in each layer). The training data were generated from the phrase-structure grammar given in table 1. At any given point during training, the training set consisted of 10,000 sentences, which were presented to the network 5 times. (As before, sentences were concatenated so that the input stream proceeded smoothly without breaks between sentences.) However, the composition of these sentences varied over time. The following training regimen was used in order to provide for incremental training. The network was trained on 5 passes through each of the following 4 corpora.

Phase 1. The first training set consisted exclusively of simple sentences. This was accomplished by eliminating all relative clauses. The result was a corpus of 34,605 words forming 10,000 sentences (each sentence includes the terminal ".").

Phase 2. The network was then exposed to a second corpus of 10,000 sentences, which consisted 25 percent of complex sentences and 75 percent of simple sentences (complex sentences were obtained by permitting relative clauses). Mean sentence length was 3.92 (a minimum of 3 words, a maximum of 13 words).

Phase 3. The third corpus increased the percentage of complex sentences to 50 percent, with mean sentence length of 4.38 (a minimum of 3 words, a maximum of 13 words).

Phase 4. The fourth consisted of 10,000 sentences, 75 percent complex, 25 percent simple. Mean sentence length was 6.02 (a minimum of 3 words, a maximum of 16 words).

This staged learning strategy was developed in response to results of earlier pilot work. In this pilot work it was found that the network was unable to learn the task when given the full range of complex data from the beginning of training. However, when the network was permitted to focus on the simpler data first, it was able to learn the task quickly and then move on successfully to more complex patterns. This allowed earlier training to constrain later learning in a useful way; the early training forced the network to focus on canonical versions of the problems, which apparently created a good basis for then solving the more difficult forms of the same problems.

Results   At the conclusion of the fourth phase of training, the weights were frozen at their final values and network performance was tested on a novel set of data generated in the same way as the last training corpus.

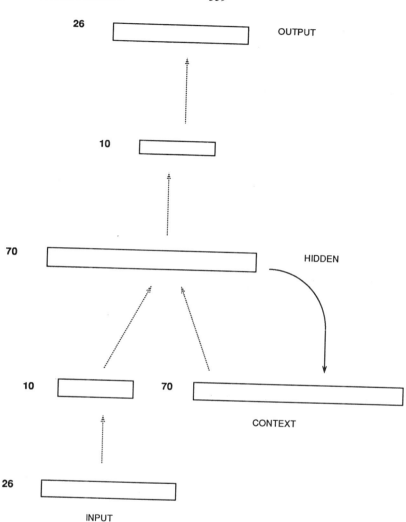

Figure 3

The network used in the second simulation. The architecture is similar to that in figure 1. Additional hidden layers provide for compression of localist input and output vectors.

The technique described in the previous simulation was used; context-dependent likelihood vectors were generated for each word in every sentence. These vectors represented the empirically derived probabilities of occurrence for all possible predictions, given the sentence context up to that point. The root mean square error of network predictions, the likelihood vectors, was 0.177 (s.d. = 0.463); the mean cosine of the angle between the vectors was 0.852 (s.d. = 0.259). Although this performance is not as good as in the previous simulation, it is still quite good. And the task is obviously much more difficult.

These gross measures of performance, however, do not tell us how well the network has done in each of the specific problem areas posed by the task. Let us look at each area in turn.

Agreement in simple sentences is shown in figure 4. The network's prediction following the word *boy* is that either a singular verb will follow (words in all three singular verb categories are activated, since it has no basis for predicting the type of verb) or the next word will be the relative pronoun *who*. Conversely, when the input is the word *boys*, the expectation is that a verb in the plural will follow or else the relative pronoun. Similar expectations hold for the other nouns in the lexicon.

Figure 5 shows network predictions following an initial noun and then a verb from each of the three different verb types. When the verb is *lives*, the network's expectation is that the following item will be "." (which is in fact the only successor permitted by the grammar in this context). The verb *sees*, on the other hand, may be followed by "." or optionally be a direct object (which may be a singular or plural noun or a proper noun). Finally, the verb *chases* requires a direct object, and the network learns to expect a noun following this and other verbs in the same class.

The examples so far have all involved simple sentences. The agreement and verb-argument facts are more complicated in complex sentences. Figure 6 shows the network predictions for each word in the sentence *boys who mary chases feed cats*. If the network were generalizing the pattern for agreement found in the simple sentences, we might expect the network to predict a singular verb following *mary chases* (insofar as it predicts a verb in this position at all; it might also be confused by the pattern N1, N2, V1). But in fact, the prediction of graph 6d, that the next verb should be in the plural in order to agree with the first noun, is correct. In so doing, it has found some mechanism for representing the long-distance dependency between the main-clause noun and main-clause verb, despite the presence of an intervening noun and verb (with their own agreement relations) in the relative clause.

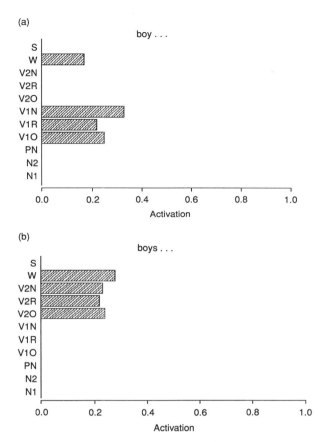

Figure 4
(*a*) Graph of network predictions following presentation of the word *boy*.
Predictions are shown as activations for words grouped by category. S stands for
end-of-sentence (". "), W stands for *who*, N and V represent nouns and verbs, 1
and 2 indicate singular or plural, the type of verb is indicated by N, R, O (direct
object not possible, required, or optional), and PN indicates a proper noun.
(*b*) Graph of network predictions following presentation of the word *boys*.

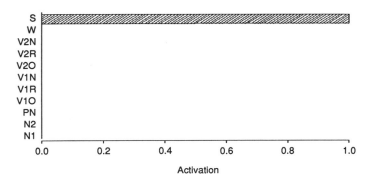

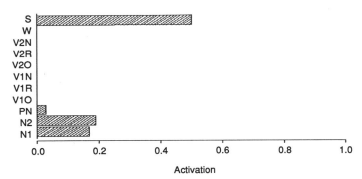

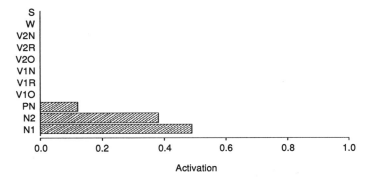

Figure 5
Graph of network predictions following the sequences *boy lives* ..., *boy sees* ...,
and *boy chases* ... (the first precludes a direct object, the second permits a direct
object, and the third requires a direct object).

Note that this sentence also illustrates the sensitivity to an interaction between verb argument structure and relative-clause structure. The verb *chases* takes an obligatory direct object. In simple sentences the direct object follows the verb immediately; this is also true in many complex sentences (e.g., *boys who chase mary feed cats*). In the sentence displayed, however, the direct object (boys) is the head of the relative clause and appears before the verb. This requires that the network learn (1) that some items function as nouns, verbs, etc., (2) which items fall into which classes, (3) that different subclasses of verbs have different restrictions on direct objects, (4) which verbs fall into which classes, and (5) when to expect that the direct object will follow the verb and when to know that it has already appeared. The network appears to have learned this, because in graph 6d we see that it expects that *chases* will be followed by a verb (the main-clause verb in this case) rather than by a noun.

An even subtler point is demonstrated in graph 6c. The appearance of *boys* followed by a relative clause containing a different subject (who mary) primes the network to expect that the verb which follows must be of the class that requires a direct object precisely because a direct-object filler has already appeared. In other words, the network not only correctly responds to the presence of a filler (*boys*) by knowing where to expect a gap (following *chases*); it also learns that when this filler corresponds to the object position in the relative clause, a verb that has the appropriate argument structure is required.

Network analysis   The natural question to ask at this point is how the network has learned to accomplish the task. It was initially assumed that success on this task would constitute prima facie evidence for the existence of internal representations that possessed abstract structure. That is, it seemed reasonable to believe that to handle agreement and argument-structure facts in the presence of relative clauses, the network would be required to develop representations that reflected constituent structure, argument structure, grammatical categories, grammatical relations, and number.

Having gotten the machine to perform successfully, I now want to test this assumption. In the previous simulation, hierarchical clustering was used to reveal the use of spatial organization at the hidden-unit level for categorization purposes. However, the clustering technique makes it difficult to see patterns that exist over time. Some states may have significance not simply in terms of their similarity to other states but also with regard to how they constrain movement into subsequent state space (recall the

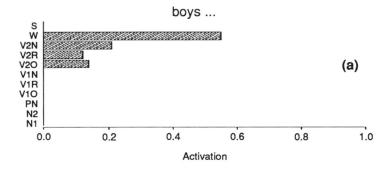

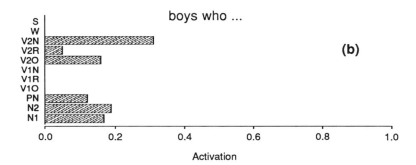

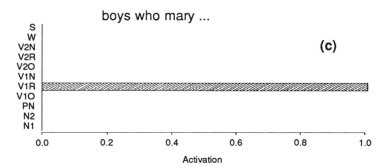

Figure 6
Graph of network predictions after each word in the sentence "boys who mary chases feed cats." is input.

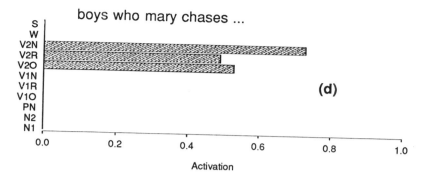

boys who mary chases ...

(d)

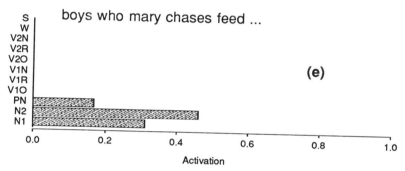

boys who mary chases feed ...

(e)

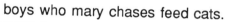

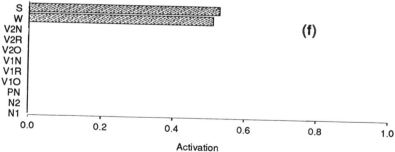

boys who mary chases feed cats.

(f)

examples in (1)). Because clustering ignores the temporal information, it hides this information. It is more useful to follow over time the trajectories through state space that correspond to the internal representations evoked at the hidden-unit layer as a network processes a given sentence.

Phase-state portraits of this sort are commonly limited to displaying not more than a few state variables at once simply because movement in more than three dimensions is difficult to graph. The hidden-unit activation patterns in the current simulation take place over 70 variables. These patterns are distributed in the sense that none of the hidden units alone provides useful information; the information instead lies along hyper-planes that cut across multiple units.

However, it is possible to identify these hyperplanes using principle-component analysis. This involves passing the training set through the trained network (with weights frozen) and saving the hidden-unit pattern produced in response to each new input. The covariance matrix of the set of hidden-unit vectors is calculated, and then the eigenvectors for the covariance matrix are found. The eigenvectors are ordered by the magni-tude of their eigenvalues and are used as the new basis for describing the original hidden-unit vectors. This new set of dimensions has the effect of giving a somewhat more localized description to the hidden-unit patterns because the new dimensions now correspond to the location of meaningful activity (defined in terms of variance) in the hyperspace. Furthermore, since the dimensions are ordered in terms of variance accounted for, we can now look at phase-state portraits of selected dimensions, starting with those with largest eigenvalues.

The sentences in (8) were presented to the network, and the hidden-unit patterns captured after each word was processed in sequence.

(8) a. boys hear boys.
    b. boy hears boys.
    c. boy who boys chase chases boy.
    d. boys who boys chase chase boy.

(These sentences were chosen to minimize differences due to lexical content and to make it possible to focus on differences in grammatical structure. Sentences (8a) and (8b) were contained in the training data; sentences (8c) and (8d) were novel and had never been presented to the network during learning.)

By examining the trajectories through state space along various dimen-sions, it was apparent that the second principle component played an important role in marking the number of the main-clause subject. Figure 7

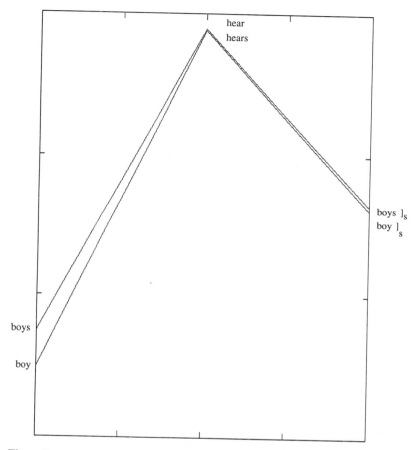

Figure 7
Trajectories through state space for sentences (8a) and (8b). Each point marks the position along the second principle component of hidden-unit space after the indicated word has been input. The magnitude of the second principle component is measured along the ordinate; time (i.e., order of the word in the sentence) is measured along the abscissa. In this and subsequent graphs the sentence-final word is marked]s.

shows the trajectories for (8a) and (8b); the trajectories are overlaid so that the differences are more readily seen. The paths are similar and diverge only during the first word because of the difference in the number of the initial noun. The difference is slight and is eliminated after the verb (*hear(s)*) has been input. This is apparently because for these two sentences (and for the grammar) number information does not have any relevance for this task once the verb has been received.

It is not difficult to imagine sentences in which number information may have to be retained over an intervening constituent; sentences (8c) and (8d) are such examples. In both these sentences there is an identical relative clause that follows the initial noun (which differs with regard to number in the two sentences). This material, *who boys chase*, is irrelevant to agreement requirements for the main-clause verb. The trajectories through state space for these two sentences have been overlaid in figure 8. As can be seen, the differences in the two trajectories are maintained until the main-clause verb is reached, at which point the states converge.

The representation of verb argument structure was examined by probing with sentences containing verbs of the three different classes. Sample sentences are shown in (9).

(9) a. boy walks .
 b. boy sees boy .
 c. boy chases boy .

The first of these contains a verb that may not take a direct object, the second takes an optional direct object, and the third requires a direct object.

The movement through state space as these three sentences are processed is shown in figure 9. This figure illustrates how the network encodes several aspects of grammatical structure. Nouns are distinguished by role: subject nouns for all three sentences appear in the upper right portion of the space, and object nouns appear below them. (Principal component 4, not shown here, encodes the distinction between verbs and nouns and collapses across case.) Verbs are differentiated with regard to their argument structure. *Chases* requires a direct object, *sees* takes an optional direct object, and *walks* precludes an object. The difference is reflected in a systematic displacement in the plane of principal components 1 and 3.

The presence of relative clauses introduces a complication into the grammar in that the representations of number and verb argument structure must be clause-specific. It would be useful for the network to have some way to represent the constituent structure of sentences.

The trained network was given the following sentences.

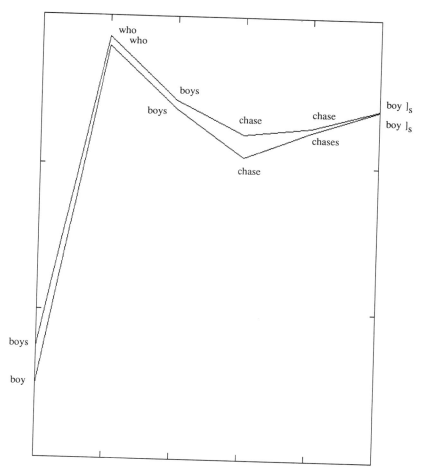

Figure 8
Trajectories through state space during processing of (8c) and (8d).

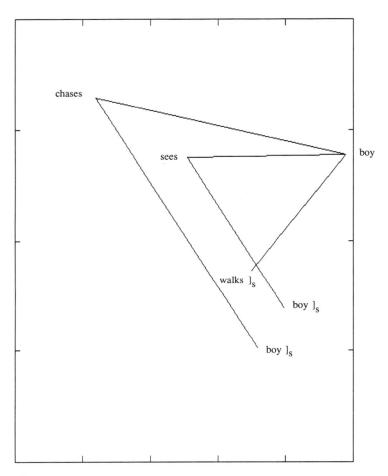

Figure 9
Trajectories through state space for sentences (9a–c). Principle component 1 is plotted along the abscissa; principal component 3 is plotted along the ordinate.

(10) a. boy chases boy .
   b. boy chases boy who chases boy .
   c. boy who chases boy chases boy .
   d. boy chases boy who chases boy who chases boy.

The first sentence is simple; the other three are instances of embedded sentences. Sentence (10a) was contained in the training data; sentences (10b–d) were novel and had not been presented to the network during the learning phase.

The trajectories through state space for these four sentences (principal components 1 and 11) are shown in figure 10. Panel 10a shows the basic pattern associated with what is in fact the matrix sentence for all four sentences. Comparison of this figure with panels 10b and 10c shows that the trajectory for the matrix sentence appears to have the same form: the matrix subject noun is in the lower left region of state space, the matrix verb appears above it and to the left, and the matrix object noun is near the upper middle region. (Recall that we are looking at only 2 of the 70 dimensions; along other dimensions the noun/verb distinction is preserved categorically.) The relative clause appears to involve a replication of this basic pattern but is displaced toward the left and moved slightly downward relative to the matrix constituents. Moreover, the exact position of the relative-clause elements indicates which of the matrix nouns are modified. Thus the relative clause modifying the subject noun is closer to it, and the relative clause modifying the object noun is closer to it. This trajectory pattern was found for all sentences with the same grammatical form; the pattern is thus systematic.

Panel (10d) shows what happens when there are multiple levels of embedding. Successive embeddings are represented in a manner similar to the way that the first embedded clause is distinguished from the main clause: the basic pattern for the clause is replicated in a region of state space displaced from the matrix material. This displacement provides a systematic way for the network to encode the depth of embedding in the current state. However, the reliability of the encoding is limited by the precision with which states are represented, which in turn depends on such factors as the number of hidden units and the precision of the numerical values. In the current simulation, the representation degraded after about three levels of embedding. The consequences of this degradation on performance in the prediction task are different for different types of sentences. Sentences with center embedding (e.g., (8c, d)), in which the level of embedding is crucial for maintaining correct agreement, are more adversely affected than sentences involving so-called tail recursion (e.g., (10d)). In

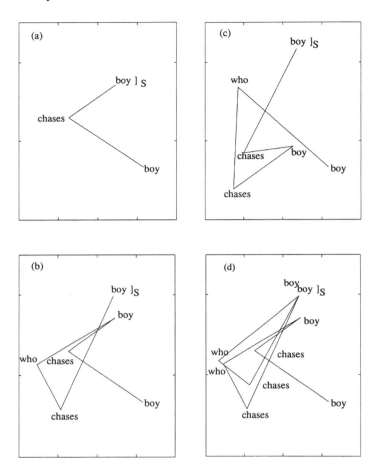

Figure 10
Trajectories through state space for sentences (10a–d). Principle component 1
is plotted along the abscissas; principal component 11 is plotted along the
ordinates.

the latter sentences the syntactic structures involve recursion in principle, but in practice the level of embedding is not relevant for the task (i.e., it does not affect agreement or verb argument structure in anyway).

Panel 10d is interesting in another respect. Because of the nature of the prediction task, it is not actually necessary for the network to carry forward any information from prior clauses. It would be sufficient for the network to represent each successive relative clause as an iteration of the previous pattern. Yet the two relative clauses are differentiated. Similarly, Servan-Schreiber, Cleeremans, and McClelland (1988) found that when a simple recurrent network was taught to predict inputs that had been generated by a finite-state automaton (FSA), the network developed internal representations that corresponded to the FSA states. However, it also redundantly made finer-grained distinctions that encode the path by which the state had been achieved, even though this information was not used in the task. It thus seems to be a property of these networks that while they are able to encode states in a way that minimizes context as far as behavior is concerned, their nonlinear nature allows them to remain sensitive to context at the level of internal representation.

Discussion

The basic question addressed in this chapter is whether or not connectionist models are capable of complex representations that possess internal structure and are productively extendable. This question is of particular interest with regard to a more general issue: How useful is the connectionist paradigm as a framework for cognitive models? In this context the nature of representations interacts with a number of other closely related issues. So to understand the significance of the present results, it may be useful first to consider briefly two of these other issues. The first is the status of *rules* (whether they exist, whether they are explicit or implicit); the second is the notion of *computational power* (whether it is sufficient, whether it is appropriate).

It is sometimes suggested that connectionist models differ from classical models in that the latter rely on rules but connectionist models are typically not rule systems. Although at first glance this appears to be a reasonable distinction, it is not actually clear that the distinction gets us very far. The basic problem is that it is not obvious what is meant by a rule. In the most general sense, a rule is a mapping that takes an input and yields an output. Clearly, since many (although not all) neural networks function as input/output systems in which the bulk of the machinery implements some transformation, it is difficult to see how they could not be thought of as rule systems.

But perhaps what is meant is that the *form* of the rules differs in classical models and connectionist networks. The suggestion has been that rules are stated *explicitly* in the former, whereas they are only *implicit* in networks. This is a slippery issue, and there is an unfortunate ambiguity in what is meant by implicit or explicit. One sense of *explicit* is that a rule is physically present in the system *in its form as a rule* and that physical presence is important to the correct functioning of the system. However, Kirsh (in press) points out that our intuitions as to what counts as physical presence are highly unreliable and sometimes contradictory. What seems to really be at stake is the speed with which information can be made available. If this is true, and Kirsh argues the point persuasively, then explicitness does not belong to data structures alone. One must also take into account the nature of the processing system involved, since information in the same form may be easily accessible in one processing system and inaccessible in another.

Unfortunately, our understanding of the information-processing capacity of neural networks is quite preliminary. There is a strong tendency in analyzing such networks to view them through traditional lenses. We suppose that if information is not contained in the same form as more familiar computational systems, that information is somehow buried, inaccessible, and implicit. For instance, a network may successfully learn some complicated mapping, say, from text to pronunciation (Sejnowski and Rosenberg 1987), but when one inspects the resulting network, it is not immediately obvious how one is to explain how the mapping works or even how to characterize what the mapping is in any precise way. In such cases it is tempting to say that the network has learned an implicit set of rules. But what we really mean is just that the mapping is complicated, difficult to formulate, or unknown. In fact, this may be a description of our own failure to understand the mechanism rather than a description of the mechanism itself. What are needed are new techniques for network analysis, such as the principal-component analysis used here, contribution analysis (Sanger 1989), weight-matrix decomposition (McMillan and Smolensky 1988), or skeletonization (Mozer and Smolensky 1989).

If successful, these analyses of connectionist networks may provide us with a new vocabulary for understanding information processing. We may learn new ways in which information can be explicit or implicit, and we may learn new notations for expressing the rules that underlie cognition. The notation of these new connectionist rules may look very different than that used in, for example, production rules. And we may expect that the notation will not lend itself to describing all types of regularity with equal facility.

Thus the potential important difference between connectionist models and classical models will not be in whether one or the other systems contains rules or whether one system encodes information explicitly and the other encodes it implicitly; the difference will lie in the nature of the rules and in what kinds of information count as explicitly present.

This potential difference brings us to the second issue: computational power. The issue divides into two considerations: Do connectionist models provide *sufficient* computational power to account for cognitive phenomena. Do they provide the *appropriate* sort of computational power?

The first question can be answered affirmatively with an important qualification. It can be shown that multilayer feedforward networks with as few as one hidden layer, with no squashing at the output, and with an arbitrary nonlinear activation funtion at the hidden layer are capable of arbitrarily accurate approximation of arbitrary mappings. They thus belong to a class of universal approximators (Hornik, Stinchcombe, and White, in press; Stinchcombe and White 1989). Put simplistically, they are effectively Turing machines. In principle, then, such networks are capable of implementing any function that the classical system can implement. The important qualification to the above result is that sufficiently many hidden units be provided. What is not currently known is the effect of limited resources on computational power. Since human cognition is carried out in a system with relatively fixed and limited resources, this question is of paramount interest. These limitations provide critical constraints on the nature of the functions that can be mapped; it is an important empirical question whether these constraints explain the specific form of human cognition.

In this context the question of the appropriateness of the computational power becomes interesting. With limited resources it is relevant to ask whether the kinds of operations and repesentations naturally made available are those likely to figure in human cognition. If one has a theory of cognition that requires sorting randomly ordered information, e.g., word frequency lists in Forster's (1979) model of lexical access, then it becomes extremely important that the computational framework provide efficient support for the sort operation. On the other hand, if one believes that information is stored associatively, the ability of the system to do a fast sort is irrelevant. Instead, it is important that the model provide for associative storage and retrieval.[1] Of course, things work in both directions. The availability of certain types of operations may encourage one to build models of a type that are impractical in other frameworks. And the need to work with an inappropriate computational mechanism may blind us from seeing things as they really are.

Let us return now to current work. I want to discuss first some of the ways in which the work is preliminary and limited. Then I will discuss what I see as the positive contributions of the work. Finally, I would like to relate this work to other connectionist research and to the general question raised at the outset of this discussion: How viable are connectionist models for understanding cognition?

The results are preliminary in a number of ways. First, one can imagine a number of additional tests that could be performed to test the representational capacity of a simple recurrent network. The memory capacity remains largely unprobed (but see Servan-Schreiber, Cleeremans, and McClelland 1988). Generalization has been tested in a limited way (many of the tests involved novel sentences), but one would like to know whether the network can inferentially extend what it knows about the types of noun phrases encountered in the second simulation (simple nouns and relative clauses) to noun phrases with different structures.

Second, while the facts of agreement and verb argument structure contained in the present grammar are important and challenging, we have barely scratched the surface in terms of the richness of linguistic phenomena that characterize natural languages.

Third, natural languages not only contain far more complexity in their syntactic structures; they also have a semantic aspect. Indeed, Langacker (1987) and others have persuasively argued that it is not fruitful to consider syntax and semantics as autonomous aspects of language. Rather, the form and meaning of language are closely entwined. Although there may be things that can be learned by studying artificial languages that are purely syntactic, such as the present one, *natural* language processing is crucially an attempt to retrieve meaning from linguistic form. The present work does not address this issue at all, but there are other PDP models that have made progress on this problem (e.g., St. John and McClelland, in press).

What the current work does contribute is some notion of the representational capacity of connectionist models. Such writers as Fodor and Pylyshyn (1988) have expressed concern regarding the ability of connectionist representations to encode compositional structure and to provide for open-ended generative capacity. The networks used in the simulations reported here have two important properties relevant to these concerns.

First, the networks make possible the development of internal representations that are *distributed* (Hinton 1988; Hinton, McClelland, and Rumelhart 1986). While not unbounded, distributed representations are less rigidly coupled with resources than localist representations, in which there is a strict mapping between concept and individual nodes. There is also greater flexibility in determining the dimensions of importance for the model.

Second, the networks studied here build in sensitivity to context. The important result of the current work is to suggest that the sensitivity to context that is characteristic of many connectionist models and that is built into the architecture of the networks used here does not preclude the ability to capture generalizations at a high level of abstraction. Nor is this a paradox. Sensitivity to context is precisely the mechanism underlying the ability to abstract and generalize. The fact that the networks exhibited here behaved highly regularly was not because they learned to be context-insensitive. Rather, they learned to respond to contexts that are more abstractly defined. Recall that even when these networks' behavior seems to ignore context (e.g., panel 10d and Servan-Schreiber, Cleeremans, and McClelland 1988), the internal representations reveal that contextual information is still retained.

This behavior is in striking contrast to that of most classical models. Representations in classical models *are* naturally context-insensitive. This insensitivity makes it possible to express generalizations that are fully regular at the highest possible level of representation (e.g., purely syntactic), but they require additional apparatus to account for regularities that reflect the interaction of meaning with form and that are more contextually defined. Connectionist models, on the other hand, begin the task of abstraction at the other end of the continuum. They emphasize the importance of context and the interaction of form with meaning. As the current work demonstrates, these characteristics lead quite naturally to generalizations at a high level of abstraction where appropriate, but the behavior remains ever rooted in representations that are contextually grounded. The simulations reported here do not capitalize on subtle distinctions in context, but there are ample demonstrations of models that do (e.g., Kawamoto 1988; McClelland and Kawamoto 1986; Miikkulainen and Dyer 1989; St. John and McClelland, in press).

Finally, I wish to point out that the current approach suggests a novel way of thinking about how mental representations are constructed from language input. Conventional wisdom holds that as words are heard, listeners retrieve lexical representations. Although these representations may indicate the contexts in which the words acceptably occur, the representations themselves are context-free. They exist in some canonical form that is constant across all occurrences. These lexical forms are then used to assist in constructing a complex representation into which the forms are inserted. One can imagine that when complete, the result is an elaborate structure in which the words are visible and that depicts the abstract grammatical structure that binds those words. In this account, the process of building mental structures is not unlike the process of building any other physical structure, such as bridges or houses. Words (and whatever other representational elements are involved) play the role of building blocks. As is true of bridges and houses, the building blocks are themselves unaffected by the process of construction.

A different image is suggested in the approach taken here. As words are processed, there is no separate stage of lexical retrieval. There are no representations of words in isolation. The representations of words (the internal states following inputs of words) always reflect the input together with the prior state. In this scenario, words are not building blocks as much as they are cues that guide the network through different grammatical states. Words are distinct from each other by virtue of having different causal properties.

A metaphor that captures some of the characteristics of this approach is the combination lock. In this metaphor, the role of words is analogous to the role played by the numbers of the combination. The numbers have causal properties; they advance the lock into different states. The effect of a number is dependent on its context. Entered in the correct sequence, the numbers move the lock into an open state. The open state may be said to be *functionally compositional* (van Gelder, in press) in the sense that it reflects a particular sequence of events. The numbers are "present" insofar as they are responsible for the final state but not because they are still physically present.

The limitation of the combination lock is, of course, that there is only one correct combination. The networks studied here are more complex. The causal properties of the words are highly dependent on structure, and the networks allow many "open" (grammatical) states.

This view of language comprehension emphasizes the functional importance of representations and is similar in spirit to the approach described in Bates and MacWhinney 1982; McClelland, St. John, and Taraban 1989; and many others who have stressed the functional nature of language. Representations of language are constructed to accomplish some behavior. Obviously, that behavior may range from daydreaming to verbal duels, from asking directions to composing poetry. The representations are not propositional, and their information content changes constantly over time in accord with the demands of the current task. Words serve as guideposts that help establish mental states that support this behavior; representations are snapshots of those mental states.

Acknowledgments

I am grateful for many useful discussions on this topic with Jay McClelland, Dave Rumelhart, Elizabeth Bates, Steve Stich, and members of the UCSD PDP/NLP Research Group. I thank McClelland, Mike Jordan, Mary Hare, Ken Baldwin, Gerry Altmann, Colin Brown, and Dennis Norris for critical comments on earlier versions of this paper. This research was supported by contracts N00014-85-K-0076 from the Office of Naval Research, and contract DAAB-07-87-C-H027 from Army Avionics, Ft. Monmouth.

Note

1. This example was suggested to me by Don Norman.

References

Bates, E., and MacWhinney, B. 1982. Functionalist approaches to grammar. In E. Wanner and L. Gleitman (eds.), *Language Acquisition: The State of the Art*. New York: Cambridge University Press.

Chafe, W. 1970. *Meaning and the Structure of Language*. Chicago: University of Chicago Press.

Dolan, C., and Dyer, M. G. 1987. Symbolic schemata in connectionist memories: Role binding and the evolution of structure. Technical report UCLA-AI-87-11, Artificial Intelligence Laboratory, University of California, Los Angeles.

Dolan, C. P., and Smolensky, P. 1988. Implementing a connectionist production system using tensor products. Technical report UCLA-AI-88-15, Artificial Intelligence Laboratory, University of California, Los Angeles.

Elman, J. L. In press. Finding structure in time. *Cognitive Science*.

Fauconnier, G. 1985. *Mental Spaces*. Cambridge: MIT Press.

Feldman, J. A., and Ballard, D. H., 1982. Connectionist models and their properties. *Cognitive Science* 6:205-254.

Fillmore, C. J. 1982. Frame semantics. In *Linguistics in the Morning Calm*. Seoul: Hansin.

Fodor, J. 1976. *The Language of Thought*. Sussex: Harvester Press.

Fodor, J., and Pylyshyn, Z. 1988. Connectionism and cognitive architecture: A critical analysis. In S. Pinker and J. Mehler (eds.), *Connections and Symbols*. Cambridge: MIT Press.

Forster, K. I. 1979. Levels of processing and the structure of the language processor. In W. E. Cooper and E. Walker (eds.), *Sentence Processing: Psycholinguistic Studies Presented to Merrill Garrett*. Hillsdale, N.J.: Lawrence Erlbaum Associates.

Givon, T. 1984. *Syntax: A Functional-Typological Introduction.* Volume 1. Amsterdam: John Benjamins.

Grosjean, F. 1980. Spoken word recognition processes and the gating paradigm. *Perception and Psychophysics* 28:267–283.

Hanson, S. J., and Burr, D. J. 1987. Knowledge representation in connectionist networks. Bell Communications Research, Morristown, New Jersey.

Hare, M., Corina, D., and Cottrell, G. 1988. Connectionist perspective on prosodic structure. *CRL Newsletter*, vol. 3, no. 2. Center for Research in Language, Univer- of California, San Diego.

Hinton, G. E. 1988. Representing part-whole hierarchies in connectionist networks. Technical report CRG-TR-88-2, Connectionist Research Group, University of Toronto.

Hinton, G. E., McClelland, J. L., and Rumelhart, D. E. 1986. Distributed representations. In D. E. Rumelhart and J. L. McClelland (eds.), *Parallel Distributed Processing: Explorations in the Microstructure of Cognition*, vol. 1. Cambridge, MA: MIT Press.

Hopper, P. J., and Thompson, S. A. 1980. Transitivity in grammar and discourse. *Language* 56:251–299.

Hornik, K., Stinchcombe, M., and White, H. In press. Multi-layer feedforward networks are universal approximators. *Neural Networks.*

Jordan, M. I. 1986. Serial order: A parallel distributed processing approach. Report 8604, Institute for Cognitive Science, University of California, San Diego.

Kawamoto, A. H. 1988. Distributed representations of ambiguous words and their resolution in a connectionist network. In S. L. Small, G. W. Cottrell, and M. K. Tanenhaus (eds.), *Lexical Ambiguity Resolution: Perspectives from Psycholinguistics, Neuropsychology, and Artificial Intelligence.* San Mateo, Calif.: Morgan Kaufmann Publishers.

Kirsh, O. In press. When is information represented explicitly? In J. Hanson (ed.), *Information, Thought, and Content.* Vancouver: University of British Columbia Press.

Kuno, S. 1987. *Functional Syntax: Anaphora, Discourse, and Empathy.* Chicago: University of Chicago Press.

Lakoff, G. 1987. *Women, Fire, and Dangerous Things: What Categories Reveal about the Mind.* Chicago: University of Chicago Press.

Langacker, R. W. 1987. *Foundations of Cognitive Grammar: Theoretical Perspectives.* Vol. 1. Stanford: Stanford University Press.

Langacker, R. W. 1988. A usage-based model. *Current Issues in Linguistic Theory* 50:127–161.

McClelland, J. L. 1987. The case for interactionism in language processing. In M. Coltheart (ed.), *Attention and Performance*, vol. 12, *The psychology of Reading.* London: Erlbaum.

McClelland, J. L., St. John, M., and Taraban, R. 1989. Sentence comprehension: A parallel distributed processing approach. Manuscript, Department of Psychology, Carnegie-Mellon University.

McMillan, C., and Smolensky, P. 1988. Analyzing a connectionist model as a system of soft rules. Technical report CU-CS-303-88, Department of Computer Science, University of Colorado, Boulder.

Marslen-Wilson, W., and Tyler, L. K. 1980. The temporal structure of spoken language understanding. *Cognition* 8:1–71.

Mozer, M. 1988. A focused back-propagation algorithm for temporal pattern recognition. Technical report CRG-TR-88-3, Deparments of Psychology and Computer Science, University of Toronto.

Mozer, M. C., and Smolensky, P. 1989. Skeletonization: A technique for trimming the fat from a network via relevance assessment. Technical report CU-CS-421-89, Department of Computer Science, University of Colorado, Boulder.

Oden, G. 1978. Semantic constraints and judged preference for interpretations of ambiguous sentences. *Memory and Cognition* 6:26–37.

Pollack, J. B. 1988. Recursive auto-associative memory: Devising compositional distributed representations. *Proceedings of the Tenth Annual Conference of the Cognitive Science Society*. Hillsdale, N.J.: Lawrence Erlbaum.

Ramsey, W. 1989. "The philosophical implications of connectionism." Ph.D. thesis, University of California, San Diego.

Rumelhart, D. E., Hinton, G. E., and Williams, R. J. 1986. Learning internal representations by error propagation. In D. E. Rumelhart and J. L. McClelland (eds.), *Parallel Distributed Processing: Explorations in the Microstructure of Cognition*, vol. 1. Cambridge: MIT Press.

St. John, M., and McClelland, J. L. In press. Learning and applying contextual constraints in sentence comprehension. Technical report, Department of Psychology, Carnegie-Mellon University.

Salasoo, A., and Pisoni, D. B. 1985. Interaction of knowledge sources in spoken word identification. *Journal of Memory and Language* 24:210–231.

Sanger, D. 1989. Contribution analysis: A technique for assigning responsibilities to hidden units in connectionist networks. Technical report CU-CS-435-89, Department of Computer Science, University of Colorado, Boulder.

Sejnowski, T. J., and Rosenberg, C. R. 1987. Parallel networks that learn to pronounce English text. *Complex Systems* 1:145–168.

Servan-Schreiber, D., Cleeremans, A., and McClelland, J. L. 1988. Encoding sequential structure in simple recurrent networks. Technical report CMU-CS-88-183, Computer Science Department, Carnegie-Mellon University.

Shastri, L., and Ajjanagadde, V. 1989. A connectionist system for rule based reasoning with multi-place predicates and variables. Technical report MS-CIS-8905, Computer and Information Science Department, University of Pennsylvania.

Smolensky, P. 1987a. On variable binding and the representation of symbolic structures in connectionist systems. Technical report CU-CS-355-87, Department of Computer Science, University of Colorado, Boulder.

Smolensky, P. 1987b. On the proper treatment of connectionism. Technical report CU-CS-377-87, Department of Computer Science, University of Colorado, Boulder.

Smolensky, P. 1987c. Putting together connectionism—again. Technical report CU-CS-378-87, Department of Computer Science, University of Colorado, Boulder.

Smolensky, P. 1988. On the proper treatment of connectionism. *Behavioural and Brain Sciences* 11.

Stinchcombe, M., and White, H. 1989. Universal approximation using feedforward networks with nonsigmoid hidden layer activation functions. *Proceedings of the International Joint Conference on Neural Networks*. Washington, D.C.

Touretzky, D. S. 1986. BoltzCONS: Reconciling connectionism with the recursive nature of stacks and trees. *Proceedings of the Eighth Annual Conference of the Cognitive Science Society*. Hillsdale, N.J.: Lawrence Erlbaum.

Touretzky, D. S. 1989. Rules and maps in connectionist symbol processing. Technical report CMU-CS-89-158, Department of Computer Science, Carnegie-Mellon University.

Touretzky, D. S., and Hinton, G. E. 1985. Symbols among the neurons: Details of a connectionist inference architecture. *Proceedings of the Ninth International Joint Conference on Artificial Intelligence*. Los Angeles.

Van Gelder, T. J. In press. Compositionality: Variations on a classical theme. *Cognitive Science*.

Chapter 18

Combinatory Lexical Information and Language Comprehension

Michael K. Tanenhaus, Susan M. Garnsey, and Julie Boland

This chapter reviews some of our recent work exploring how the combinatory knowledge associated with verbs is used in sentence processing. By *combinatory lexical knowledge* we mean information about how a verb combines semantically and syntactically with other words in a sentence. This information is of two main types: information about verb argument structure and information about control.

Following Tanenhaus and Carlson (in press), we will use the term *argument structure* to refer to information about the types of immediate complements that a verb may take. This includes information about both syntactic subcategorization, which specifies the types of constituents that can serve as the complements of a verb, and thematic structure, which refers to the roles or modes of participation that characterize how the arguments of a verb partake in the event denoted by the verb. Control information refers to the way that a particular verb influences the interpretation of the understood or empty subjects of infinitival complements. For example, the subject of the verb *promise* controls the interpretation of the infinitive (*Tom promised Mary to wash himself/*herself*), whereas the object of the verb *persuade* controls the interpretation of its infinitive (*John persuaded Mary to wash *himself/herself*). Knowledge about verb argument structure and control are clearly used at some point during language comprehension. What is less clear, however, is at *what point during comprehension* these types of knowledge are accessed and used.

Consider first the question of access. There is an extensive literature suggesting that word recognition results in the rapid activation of different types of information (Marslen-Wilson 1987, Seidenberg 1985). If combinatory lexical information acts like other lexical knowledge, one might expect that it too would become available once a word is recognized (Carlson and Tanenhaus 1988; Shapiro, Zurif, and Grimshaw 1987; Tanenhaus,

Burgess, D'Zmura-Hudson, and Carlson 1987). Thus recognition of a verb would make available such information as the semantic representation or sense of the verb, the semantic or thematic roles associated with the verb, the type of constituents that can serve as complements of the verb, and how roles and constituents are to be related to one another.

Take the verb *donate* as an example. If the types of information given above are immediately accessed when *donate* is recognized, the processing system would know that there are three possible roles associated with *donate*: the agent (the one who is doing the donating), the theme (what is being donated), and the recipient (the one receiving the donation). *Donate* is typically followed by an NP and PP, as in *Bill donated money to charity*, in which the subject is the agent, the first postverbal NP the theme, and the PP the recipient. *Donate* can also be used as a simple transitive, in which case no argument is associated with the recipient role. With certain restrictions it can also be used with only a PP, as in *John donates to worthy causes*, in which case the PP is still the recipient and there is no argument associated with the theme.

How and when combinatory lexical information is actually used is, of course, a separate question from when it is accessed. One contrast that has been proposed in the literature is that of *lexical proposal* versus *lexical filtering*. (Frazier 1987, Mitchell 1987). According to the lexical-proposal view, combinatory lexical information can be used to project or propose structure, as suggested in Fodor, Bever, and Garrett 1974. So, for example, after processing a verb that can only be used intransitively, e.g., *cough*, the parser might anticipate that the next phrase would begin a new clause. Or after processing the phrase in (1), the parser might anticipate a verb phrase because the verb *studied*, which is ambiguous between a past tense and a past participle, must be a past participle here because *evidence* can plausibly fill the theme role associated with *studied* but not the agent role.

(1) The evidence studied in the room ...

If the subject is the theme, the ambiguous verb must be a past participle, and therefore the phrase in (1) is a reduced relative clause. In contrast, in (2) a verb would be unexpected because *student* is a good agent for *studied*, and therefore *studied* is treated as the past tense form of a verb in a main clause.

(2) The student studied in the room ...

Whether or not lexical information is used in this way remains controversial (for discussions see Ferreira and Clifton 1986; Frazier 1987;

Mitchell 1987; Stowe 1988; Trueswell, Tanenhaus, and Garnsey, submitted; Tanenhaus, Trueswell, and Carlson 1989).

Alternatively, lexical information might be used to filter or to reject possible analyses proposed by the parser. On this view, lexical information is either not available to initially influence certain processes in parsing, or it is available but is not used as soon as it is available. Thus the parser might initially process a noun phrase following *cough* in the same way as it would a noun phrase that followed an obligatorily transitive verb like *put* (Mitchell 1987). Subcategorization information might then be used to select from among possible parses or perhaps to revise parses that are incompatible with the possible subcategorizations of the verb. Likewise, the parser might not make immediate use of thematic information and thus the phrases in (1) and (2) would initially be processed in the same way, with thematic information coming into play only relatively late in processing.

Unfortunately, the terminology of *lexical proposal* versus *lexical filtering* can be somwhat misleading. For instance, assume that lexical access for *studied* makes available both the past participle and the past tense forms of the verb, much as lexical access makes available multiple senses for words with sense ambiguities. The noun phrase in subject position plays the role of theme for the past-participle form and the role of agent for the past tense. Assume that the thematic fit of the subject noun phrase is used to select between the two forms of the verb. It seems natural to refer to this as lexical filtering or lexical selection, because one of the two possible analyses is being chosen on the basis of lexical knowledge. However, this type of result could also be taken as strong evidence for a lexical proposal, since lexically based information is affecting subsequent syntactic decisions.

Instead of framing the question in terms of *lexical proposal* or *lexical filtering*, we will be asking questions about when certain types of combinatory lexical information are used in processing. The opposition between lexical proposal versus lexical filtering can then be recast in terms of the question of whether or not processing decisions are informed by relevant lexically based knowledge. One consequence of early use of lexical information, we shall see, is that under certain circumstances syntactic structure will be proposed or anticipated in advance of direct syntactic evidence. We will restrict the use of the term *lexical proposal* to cirumstances in which structure is being predicted or anticipated on the basis of lexical information.

Filler-Gap Dependencies

The research that we will be reviewing examines the time course with which verb-argument-structure and verb-control information are accessed and used in comprehending sentences with *wh-* questions. These sentences contain a filler-gap dependency in which the questioned phrase is a filler that must be associated with an empty category or gap that occurs later in the sentence. For example, in (3) the questioned phrase *which customer* must be semantically interpreted as the direct object of *call*.

(3) Which customer did the secretary call _____ about the article?

The research plan we have been following is to determine how verb-based combinatory information influences the assignment of fillers to possible gap positions defined by the verb. Filler-gap sentences are well suited to examining how verb-based lexical information is used in parsing, because the verb plays an important role in defining possible gap positions. Consider, for example, the fragments in (4).

(4) a. Which man did Bill sneeze . . .
     b. Which man did Bill read . . .
     c. Which man did Bill persuade . . .

In (4a) the filler *which man* cannot be the direct object of the verb *sneeze*, because *sneeze* is not subcategorized for a direct object. In (4b) *read* allows both a direct and an indirect object. However, the filler *which man* cannot be the direct object for semantic reasons (if we assume the literal sense of *read*). It could, however, be the indirect object of *read*. In (4c) the filler *which man* could be the direct object of *persuade*, although it need not be, as in *Which girl did the boy persuade the teacher to punish?*

To determine whether lexical structure influences initial filler-gap assignment, we need a method of determining when a filler has been associated with a gap. It is important to note that there is no experimental method that can directly tap gap filling. However, a number of experimental procedures have been shown to be sensitive to the consequences of gap filling. These include *lexical priming* (Clifton and Frazier 1988; Tanenhaus, Carlson, and Seidenberg 1985; Nicol and Swinney 1989), *probe recognition* (Bever and McElree 1988; MacDonald, in press), and a variety of *reading time* measures (Clifton, Frazier, and Connine 1984; Crain and Fodor 1985; Stowe 1986; Frazier, Clifton, and Randall 1983; Tanenhaus, Stowe, and Carlson 1985).

Our experiments made use of the "embedded anomaly" logic developed in collaboration with Laurie Stowe (Tanenhaus, Stowe, and Carlson 1985;

Stowe, Tanenhaus, and Carlson, in preparation), in which fillers that are plausible with respect to a possible gap position are contrasted with fillers that are implausible. Contrast (5a), in which the filler *which book* is a plausible object of *read*, with (5b), in which the filler *which food* is an anomalous object of *read*.

(5) a. Which book did the man read ...

   b. Which food did the secretary read ...

If a gap is posited to follow the verb *read* and the filler is semantically interpreted as its object, sentence (5b) will become anomalous at *read*. The point at which people notice that a sentence becomes implausible provides us with information about when a gap has been posited, filled, and interpreted. As we will see, the embedded-anomaly technique allows us to use the filler as a kind of probe to determine what aspects of verb-based combinatory lexical structure are accessed and used in sentence processing.

Evoked Potentials and Filler-Gap Assignment

The first experiment we will present was designed to distinguish between two gap-filling strategies initially identified by J. D. Fodor (1978): a first-resort strategy, in which a gap is posited following a potentially transitive verb, and a last-resort strategy, in which a gap isn't posited until the grammatical structure of the sentence absolutely requires it to be. A first-resort strategy will cause many gaps to be spuriously proposed, whereas a last-resort strategy will initially miss many gaps. This study uses evoked potentials (EPs) as a response measure. Before describing the conditions in the experiment, we will briefly describe our motivation for exploring the usefulness of evoked potentials as a methodology for studying sentence processing.

   The speed and apparent effortlessness of comprehension typically mask the many moment-by-moment decisions that occur during language processing. As a result, progress in understanding language processing has been closely tied to the development of methodologies that can be used to monitor comprehension processes as they occur in real time. Evoked brain potentials have several characteristics that suggest they might be useful as an "on-line" processing measure. First, EPs can be collected continuously as subjects are listening to or reading sentences. Thus EPs can in principle provide a continuous profile of comprehension processes, as opposed to a mere snapshot of processing at a particular point in time. Second, EPs are unintrusive in that they do not require the sentence to be interrupted or the subject to perform a secondary task. Third, different components of the EP are known to reflect different types of cognitive processes. Thus EPs are an inherently multidimensional response measure. The multidimensional aspect of the response measure is particularly well suited for the study of language comprehension because comprehension involves the rapid integration of different types of linguistic and nonlinguistic information. Thus EPs, if sensitive enough, could provide psycholinguists with an unobtrusive, multidimensional, on-line measure that can be continuously monitored.

The results described below come from an experiment that examined sentences with three types of syntactic ambiguities: *wh-* questions in which the gap location is temporarily ambiguous, sentences with ambiguities of prepositional phrase attachment, and sentences with reduced relatives in which there is an ambiguity between main verb and past participle (for details, see Garnsey, Tanenhaus, and Chapman 1989 and Garnsey, Tanenhaus, and Chapman, in preparation). We will discuss only the results for the filler-gap sentences and associated controls.

Although there is no component of the EP known to be related to gap-filling, using embedded anomalies allowed us to exploit the characteristics of the N400 component. N400 is a negative peak that occurs about 400 msec after the onset of a word that is odd in context (Kutas and Hillyard 1980a, 1980b). There is some controversy about just what kind of processing is reflected by N400 (Kutas and Hillyard 1983, 1984; Nagaishi and Shimokochi 1985; Polich 1985a, 1985b; Besson and Macar 1987; Fischler et al. 1983), but for purposes of our experiment it was sufficient to know that N400 reliably occurs in response to semantically incongruous words.

Our filler-gap sentences contained embedded *wh-* questions in which the filler was either plausible or implausible as the direct object of the embedded verb, which was the first possible position for the gap. For example, in

(7) The businessman knew which customer the secretary called _____ at home.

the filler *which customer* is a plausible direct object of *called*, whereas in

(8) The businessman knew which article the secretary called _____ at home.

the filler *which article* is not a plausible object of *called* on the most frequent sense of *called*, the sense synonymous with phoned. In the experimental sentences we used, the first possible gap position was also the true gap location, as in sentences (7) and (8). However, the position of the gap is ambiguous at the embedded verb because the sentences have possible continuations in which the true gap occurs after the first possible gap, as in sentence (9):

(9) The businessman knew which article the secretary called the customer about _____ .

In (9) not only are the first and true gap locations different, but the filler that is implausible when assigned to the first possible gap is plausible when assigned to the true gap. All of the verbs we used are typically used transitively, as determined by norms collected by Connine et al. (1984), so our study did not address the question of how transitivity preference might interact with gap filling (Clifton, Frazier, and Connine 1984; Fodor 1978; Tanenhaus, Boland, Garnsey, Carlson 1989; Tanenhaus, Stowe, and Carlson 1985). By using transitive preference verbs, we were introducing a lexical bias in favor of the first-resort strategy.

If the parser immediately posits a gap at the embedded verb, and associates and semantically interprets the filler with the gap, then there should be an N400 in response to the verb. If, however, the parser waits until later in the sentence when it becomes clear that there is no other possible gap, the N400 should occur sometime later in the sentence. Thus N400 can be used as a diagnostic for filler-gap assignment.

In addition to the filler-gap sentences illustrated in (7) and (8), a control condition was included in which the plausible and implausible fillers occurred in normal direct-object position. The control sentences were included to demonstrate that N400 was sensitive to the plausibility differences between our fillers in unambiguous sentences. Thus there were four conditions, illustrated in (10):

(10) a. The businessman knew which customer the secretary called at home.
  b. The businessman knew which article the secretary called at home.
  c. The businessman knew whether the secretary called the customer at home.
  d. The businessman knew whether the secretary called the article at home.

Thirty-two subjects read twenty-four sets of sentences similar to the set illustrated in (10). Each subject saw only one of the four sentences in each set, and thus six sentences of each type. Sentences were presented visually one word at a time at a rate of two words per second. This relatively slow presentation rate was used to allow enough time to see N400 develop on each word. (For details of the methodology and data-analysis procedures, see Garnsey et al. 1989).

Figure 1 shows the grand mean waveforms from four midline electrode sites for the control sentences. Responses to the control sentences are shown at the embedded verb, the direct object (*customer* or *article*), and the following preposition (*at*). N400 was quantified as the mean voltage between 300 and 500 msec after word onset with reference to a 100 msec presentence baseline. As expected, N400 is larger in response to the implausible object (*article*) than to the plausible object (*customer*), which confirms that N400 is sensitive to the implausibility of the direct objects used.

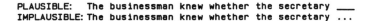

PLAUSIBLE: The businessman knew whether the secretary ___
IMPLAUSIBLE: The businessman knew whether the secretary ...

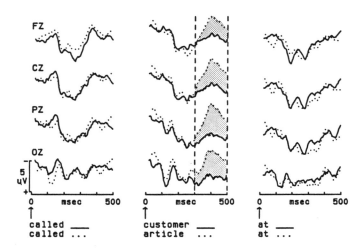

Figure 1
Mean EP waveforms (from 32 subjects) for the plausible (10c) and implausible (10d) control sentences at four midline electrode cites (FZ, CZ, PZ, and OZ; Jasper 1958). Solid lines represent the plausible condition and dotted lines the implausible condition. At the top of the figure appear the portions of the sentences preceding the words whose responses are shown, which appear under each panel. The word *the* was presented between *called* and *article* or *customer*, but its response is not shown here. Vertical dashed lines at 300 and 500 msec in the middle panels indicate the 200 msec range across with N400 was quantified. The shading indicates the plausible-implausible differences found.

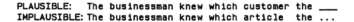

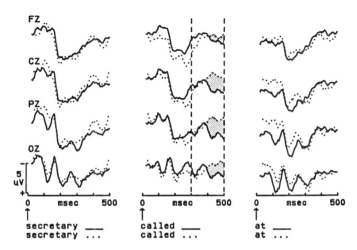

Figure 2
Mean EP waveforms (from 32 subjects) for the plausible (10a) and implausible
(10b) filler-gap sentences. Solid lines represent the plausible condition and dotted
lines the implausible condition. At the top of the figure appear the portions of
the sentences preceding the words whose responses are shown, which appear
under each panel. Vertical dashed lines at 300 and 500 msec in the middle panels
indicate the 200 msec range across which N400 was quantified. The shading
indicates the plausible-implausible differences found.

Figure 2 shows the waveforms for the filler-gap sentences at the embedded subject (*secretary*), the embedded verb (*called*), and the following
preposition (*at*). The question of primary interest was whether N400 would
occur in response to the embedded verb in the implausible filler-gap sentences. Figure 2 shows that there is indeed a larger N400 at the verb for
the filler-gap sentences with implausible fillers. This result demonstrates
that gaps are posited and immediately filled at the verb, as the first-resort
strategy predicts. The results also suggest that it may be possible to use
faster presentation rates and still observe the N400 component. The N400
for the filler-gap sentences continues into the next word. With faster presentation rates, then, the N400 might still be observed, but it would show
up at the beginning of the word that followed the anomaly.

The results clearly demonstrate that the evoked potential can be sensitive
enough to be used with standard psycholinguistic designs. They also pro-

vide clear support for a version of the first-resort strategy in which gaps are posited and filled immediately when a verb is encountered.

This early-filling strategy—Janet Fodor has referred to it as "first resort with a vengeance"—seems counterintuitive because it leads to gaps being spuriously posited when the next constituent would provide definitive evidence against the gap analysis. For instance, in (11), the NP *the boss* is the object of the verb *call*, and thus there can't be a gap following the verb.

(11) Which customer did the secretary call the boss about ____ ?

Fodor (1978) proposed that the the first-resort strategy was coupled with a "try-the-next-constituent strategy" so that the parser would not posit a gap until it first checked the next constituent. This strategy would prevent the parser from incorrectly positing gaps in argument positions that have overt noun phrases. There is now evidence from a variety of experimental paradigms that gaps are posited immediately at the verb. However, the initial studies supporting early gap filling (Crain and Fodor 1985, Stowe 1986) used self-paced reading with word-by-word presentation. It is possible that under these circumstances early filling is induced by slow presentation rates or perhaps whenever sentences are presented one word at a time.

Because of concerns that early filling might be an artifact of word-by-word presentation, Tanenhaus, Stowe, and Carlson (1985) conducted an experiment in which subjects were timed as they judged whether sentences like those illustrated in table 1 make sense (see also Stowe, Tanenhaus, and Carlson 1989 and Tanenhaus et al. 1989 for a description of the results). The *whole* sentence was displayed *at once* on one line of a computer terminal. There were three variables manipulated in this experiment:

• The transitivity preference of the verb (transitive or intransitive preference)
• The position of the gap, which was either after the main verb in the embedded question (early gap) or after a later preposition (late gap)

Table 1
Sample materials for the whole-sentence-presentation study. (The implausible filler is in italics.)

The district attorney found out which witness/*church* the reporter asked ____ about the meeting. (Early gap)

The district attorney found out which witness/*church* the reporter asked anxiously about ____. (Late gap)

• The plausibility of the filler in the early gap position. All fillers were equally plausible for the late-gap position.

We will be concerned here only with the results for the transitive-preference verb.

Table 2 presents the percentage of sentences judged to make sense for the four conditions created by the combination of gap position and filler plausibility. Note that there is an effect of plausibility for both early- and late-gap sentences. The plausibility effect for the early-gap sentences is expected, of course, because plausibility of the filler with respect to the early gap was directly manipulated in the materials. However, there is also a plausibility effect for the *late-gap* sentences. Recall that the fillers were *equally plausible* for the late gap position. Thus the effect of plausibility must have been due to subjects initially associating the filler with the early gap.

Verb Argument Structure

To this point we have established that the embedded-anomaly technique can be used to detect when a gap associated with a verb is posited and filled. We are now in a position to examine how the argument structure and control information associated with a verb influence gap filling. The studies we have reviewed thus far demonstrate that readers posit and fill gaps following transitive-preference verbs. The nature of the evidence is that sentences become implausible at the verb, and the implausibility is due to having interpreted the filler as if it were the direct object of the verb. One explanation for our results would be that gaps are posited following all potentially (or perhaps typically) transitive verbs and the filler is asso-

Table 2
Results for the whole-sentence-presentation study

	Early gap		Late gap	
	% made sense	RTs in msec	% made sense	RTs in msec
Plausible filler	83	4,623	79	4,539
Implausible filler	64	4,864	64	4,832

Note: The percentage of sentences judged to make sense and response-time (RT) latencies in msec for those sentences judged to make sense for each condition in the whole-sentence-presentation study. Note that fillers differ in plausibility *only* with respect to the early gap position.

ciated with the gap. If this story turned out to be correct, studying filler-gap sentences would provide little, if any, information about the use of combinatory lexical information in sentence processing. Fortunately for our present purposes, there is an alternative explanation for our results.

In all of the filler-gap studies in which we found evidence for immediate filling, we predominately used verbs that typically do not take infinitival or sentential complements. In cases where a verb could have more than two possible arguments associated with it, the implausible filler was always implausible in both argument positions. Thus our data are also compatible with a view of gap filling in which lexical access for the verb makes available the full argument structure of the verb and all of the argument positions are available as potential gap positions.

In other work we have been exploring the hypothesis that word recognition makes available all of the thematic roles associated with the subcategorized arguments of a verb (Carlson and Tanenhaus 1988; Tanenhaus and Carlson, in press). If the set of roles or argument positions associated with a verb defines the potential gap sites available to the parser, the parser might be able to see its way ahead to an upcoming gap. Consider, for example, the verb *remind*, which typically takes a direct object and a complement clause. In a sentence beginning *Which movie did Bill remind* . . . , the parser might assume that someone is being reminded about a movie or reminded to do something concerning a movie rather than assume that the movie is the direct object of *remind*. This alternative is not available for verbs that are not subcategorized for complement clauses. According to the argument-structure hypothesis, then, the reason we observed implausibility effects at the verb in previous studies was that the filler was implausible in all of the argument positions made available by the verb. The argument-structure hypothesis predicts that we should not see plausibility effects when the filler is implausible as the direct object of the verb as long as there are other argument positions in which it could be plausible.

We conducted an initial test of this hypothesis by comparing verbs that are typically used with both an object and an infinitival complement (e.g., *remind*) with verbs that do not take infinitival complements (e.g., *call*). We used the embedded anomaly technique in a self-paced word-by-word reading task in which subjects pressed a *no* button as soon as the sentence stopped making sense. A trial terminated after a *no* response. Example sentences are presented in (12). The full set of materials are presented in the appendix.

(12) a. Which customer did the secretary call on the office phone?
   b. Which article did the secretary call on the office phone?
   c. Which child did your brother remind to watch the show?
   d. Which movie did your brother remined to watch the show?

The results are presented in figure 3, which presents the cumulative percentage of sentences with plausible and implausible fillers that were judged to not make sense for words in the critical regions of the sentence. There is a clear interaction between verb-type and plausibility. For the *call*-type verbs, there are more *no* judgments from the verb to sentences with implausible fillers than there are to sentences with plausible fillers. Thus we find the same evidence for early filling that we did in the EP study described above. However, plausibility effects for the *remind*-type verbs do not begin until the complementizer *to*, which provides syntactic information that the filler has to be the object of the verb. Thus the results show a clear difference for *call* and *remind* verbs. For *call*-type verbs, fillers are interpreted as filling gaps in verb-object position even when they are implausible in this position, whereas implausible fillers are not interpreted as filling object gaps for *remind*-type verbs.

Although our results provide strong support for some version of the argument-structure hypothesis, they do not provide a clear picture of when gaps are posited and filled for *remind*-type verbs. With the embedded-anomaly technique, evidence for gap filling is obtained only when a gap is filled with an implausible filler. As we did not find implausibility effects at the verb for the *remind*-type verbs, we can only conclude that the implausible filler was not interpreted as the direct object of the verb. It is possible that the processor adopts a last-resort strategy and does not initially posit a gap following the verb, perhaps because there are several likely places for gaps upcoming. If this were the case, neither the plausible nor implausible filler would be interpreted as the direct object of the verb. An alternative is that object gaps are filled only when the filler is plausible. If it is implausible, the processor assumes that the filler will be associated with one of the other argument positions of the verb. To discriminate between these alternatives, we conducted an experiment relying upon the filled-gap effect (Crain and Fodor 1985, Stowe 1986). Using sentences like

(13) Which guest did the hostess introduce us to at the party?

Crain and Fodor and also Stowe observed an increase in reading times at the noun phrase following the main verb (i.e., at *us* in the example), which indicates that subjects have already filled the gap and are having to revise their interpretation of the sentence.

A: 'Call'-type verbs

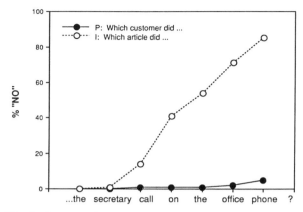

B: 'Remind'-type verbs

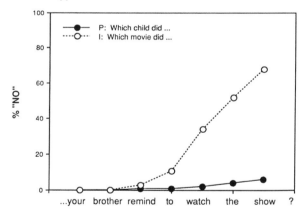

Figure 3
Panel A shows the percentage of sentences judged not to make sense at each word for the *call*-type verbs with plausible and implausible fillers. The words at the top of the panels are words for which we did not collect data. Panel B presents the same information for the *remind*-type verbs.

We used the filled-gap effect to determine whether or not plausible fillers were being assigned to object gaps with *remind*-type verbs. We used three conditions, illustrated in (14).

(14) a. Which movie did Mark remind them to watch this evening?
      b. Which child did Mark remind them to watch this evening?
      c. Sam wondered whether Mark reminded us to watch the movie.

Again, we used the self-paced stop-making-sense task. If filler-gap assignment is delayed for *remind*-type verbs, we should not see a filled-gap effect for either the plausible (14a) or implausible (14b) filler sentences. If, however, plausible fillers are assigned to object gaps, we should see a filled-gap effect for only the plausible fillers. In this experiment, all of the experimental sentences are plausible, so we expected filled-gap effects to result in only a small increase in the percentage of sentences judged to make sense. Thus we also report reading times for the sentences judged to make sense.

Figure 4 presents reading times and makes-sense judgments for the critical regions of the sentences. As in the preceding experiment, there were no plausiblity effects at the verb. For the plausible fillers there was a clear filled-gap effect localized at the complementizer following the object pronoun in both the judgment and reading-time data for the plausible fillers, which indicates that a gap had been posited and filled at the matrix verb. The increase in reading times at the complementizer reflects the reprocessing that takes place when the pronoun forces the processor to revise the gap analysis. However, the implausible fillers did not show a filled-gap effect. Thus for *remind*-type verbs, object gaps are filled only when the filler is a plausible object of the verb. The conclusion we reach from these experiments is that the verb makes available all of the information present in the argument structure of the verb. For a verb such as *remind*, a filler will be associated with the first argument position if it meets the thematic conditions for that position. If not, it will be associated with a subsequent argument position.

It may seem somewhat counterintuitive that the processing system has access to semantic information about a complement of a verb before processing the complement. Thus one would like to see other examples where processing appears to be mediated by a projected verb complement. Null-complement anaphora may such an example. In the absence of context, sentence (15a) seems more natural than (15b).

(15) a. Fortunately, Bill reminded Tom to go to the bank.
      b. Fortunately, Bill reminded Tom.

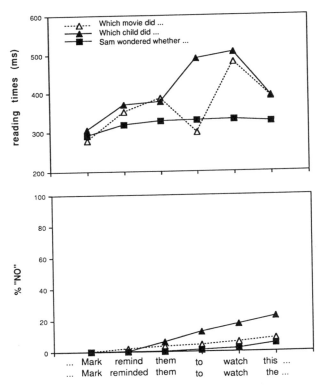

Figure 4

Results for the filled-gap experiment with *remind*-type verbs. The bottom panel of the figure presents the percentage of sentences judged not to make sense up through each word for *wh-* sentences with plausible and implausible fillers and *whether* controls. The top panel presents reading-time data for trials on which a word was judged to make sense.

Sentence (15b) feels incomplete because one doesn't know what Tom is being reminded to do. However, when the context establishes an "antecedent" for the complement, the sentence without the complement appears more natural. Compare sentences (15a) and (15b) when they are preceded by the context sentence *Tom nearly forgot to go to the bank.* Sentence (15a) now seems somewhat infelicitous because the information in the complement is redundant. Although this conjecture requires experimental verification, it seems that the reader has already inferred that Tom was reminded to go to the bank. Since the inference is being driven by the complement, it seems reasonable to conclude that the verb is making information about its complement available before syntactic information about the complement is encountered. We suggest that examples like this are similar to other cases where one of us has argued that syntactic expectations are mediated by thematic knowledge (Carlson and Tanenhaus 1988; Tanenhaus and Carlson, in press). For instance, in the absence of context, sentence (16a) appears to be less natural than sentence (16b).

(16) a. John generously donated some money.

b. John generously donated some money to the charity.

Our explanation is that *donate* generates an expectation for its *recipient* role to be filled, which translates into a syntactic expectation for a PP. Note that this would be a true example of lexical projection of structure as we defined it earlier in the chapter. When the sentences in (16) are preceded by a context sentence that establishes a plausible recipient, such as *Bill told John that the charity had its budget slashed,* (16a) appears more natural, and in fact the PP in (16b) feels redundant. Our account is that the recipient role, which has been activated at the verb, is associated with *charity,* and thus the expectation that it will be filled by a PP in the sentence is reduced. What is common, then, between the *donate* and the *remind* examples is that processing is being mediated by information in the argument structure that is made available when the verb is recognized.

We have been assuming that gap filling involves associating a filler with a thematic role. This runs counter to the more standard assumptions that gap-filling is primarily a syntactic process. Although we do not have direct evidence that gap filling is thematic rather than syntactic, there are several reasons why we favor such an account. First, to account for our data with verbs that take infinitive complements, it seems necessary to assume that the processing system can compare a filler against the thematic or semantic conditions associated with a possible syntactic gap position. Thus we already need to assume that thematic information is available. It also seems more sensible for the processing system to make initial thematic commitments rather than syntactic commitments because mistakes in syntactic analysis are often costly, whereas thematic reassignments seem to be relatively cost-free (Carlson and Tanenhaus 1988). Of course, one would like more direct evidence that gap filling is thematically mediated. Verbs like *donate* may provide an interesting domain for testing the hypothesis that thematic roles mediate gap filling. Recall that *donate* has both a theme role and a recipient role. The theme role is filled by the NP following the verb, and the recipient role by a PP. On our account, recognition of the verb *donate* should make both of these roles available as possible gap sites. In a fragment such as *Which charity did Bill donate . . .* , the filler *which charity* should be associated with the recipient role, even though the processor has not yet encountered the syntactic gap site for the filler. One way to test this is to see when people notice the implausibility of a sentence such as (17).

(17) Which charity did Bill donate his guns to?

The implausibility of the sentence depends upon the reader having interpreted *charity* as the indirect object, because *guns* can be a plausible direct object of donate, as is illustrated by (18).

(18) Which hunting lodge did Bill donate his guns to?

If the implausibility is detected at *guns*, this would indicate that *charity* was being semantically interpreted as if it were the indirect object before the syntactic position of the gap. Research using sentences like these is in progress.

Finally, our experiments with argument structure do not distinguish between two alternative views of gap filling. According to the view proposed by Clifton and Frazier (1988), the filler actively seeks a gap. An alternative is that a filler is associated with a gap only when the lexical representation of the verb makes available a possible argument position that the filler can be associated with. The embedded-anomaly technique can, however, be used to distinguish between a filler-driven and gap-driven system. Consider what might happen with a sentence beginning with the fragment in (19):

(19) Which doctor did the patient cough . . .

Cough is an obligatorily intransitive verb. If gap-filling is filler-driven, there should be a plausibility effect at the verb, because the verb does not make available an argument position for the filler to be associated with that would make the sentence plausible. If, however, gap filling is gap-driven, there should not be a implausibility effect, because the verb does not make available any possible gap sites. Thus the filler would never be associated with the verb. Note that either a gap-driven or filler-driven account of gap filling is compatible with our hypothesis about argument structure. Crucially, however, we do not expect to see anomaly effects at the verb with intransitive verbs, such as *agree*, that have an argument position associated with a subcategorized preposition, as is illustrated in (20).

(20) Which friend did Harry agree with?

The results that we have reviewed thus far suggest that the processor attempts to associate a filler with the first verb encountered. The set of possible gaps considered appear to be those defined by the argument structure of the verb. On the one hand, the processor does not appear to be able to anticipate gap sites that are not directly associated with the verb, such as gaps that are associated with adjuncts. On the other hand, possible gap positions in infinitive complements do seem to be immediately recognized by the processing system as soon as the verb is encountered. Thus the data we have presented demonstrate that word recognition makes available verb argument structure and that this information is immediately used in parsing. We have also suggested that initial filler-gap assignment may be thematic rather than syntactic, with thematic assignment having syntactic-evaluation conditions associated with it. We now turn to a brief consideration of verb control information.

Verb Control

Recall that control refers to the way that particular verbs influence the interpretation of the empty, or understood, subjects of infinitive complements. In object-control verbs, the interpretation of the empty subject is controlled by the object of the controlling verb, whereas in subject-control verbs, it is controlled by the subject of the controlling verb. Thus in sentence (21a), which contains *force* (an object-control verb), *Bill* (the object of *force*) is the understood subject of the infinitival complement *to go to the store*, whereas in (21b), which contains *promise* (a subject control verb), *John* (the subject of *promise*) is the understood subject of the infinitive.

(21) a. John forced Bill to go to the store.
     b. John promised Bill to go to the store.

Frazier, Clifton, and Randall (1983) used a task that involved end-of-sentence comprehension (a got-it task) with sentences like those in (22) using verbs, such as *beg*, that can be used as either subject- or object-control verbs.

(22) a. Which woman did the child beg _____ to sing those silly French songs last Christmas. (Object control, distant filler)

   b. Which woman did the child beg _____ to sing those silly French songs for _____ last Christmas. (Subject control, recent filler)

They found that the object-control sentences were more difficult to understand than the subject control sentences. They suggested that this was because subjects followed a recent-filler strategy and assumed that *the girl* was the subject of the complement *to sing*, which resulted in a garden path for a sentence like (22a) in which the more distant filler, *the woman*, functions as the subject of the infinitive. Surprisingly, they also found the same pattern of results when they used verbs with unambiguous control properties, such as *start* and *force*. Frazier et al. argued that subjects use the recent-filler strategy on a first pass through the sentence even when it violates verb-control information, because access to control information is delayed long enough so that it is not immediately available to guide initial filler-gap assignment. Applying the recent-filler strategy across the board to sentences with *wh-* questions, such as those in (22), results in the subject of the verb being interpreted as the object of the infinitive. This strategy will work for subject-control verbs but not for object-control verbs.

Frazier, Clifton, and Randall's interpretation of their data has been extremely controversial (Crain and Fodor 1985, Fodor 1988, Ford and Dalrymple 1988). Their evidence that verb-control information is initially ignored by the parser is quite indirect, Fodor (1988) has argued. Their results could also be due to differences in complexity between the recent and distant filler sentences that are correlated with verb control.

Boland, Tanenhaus, and Garnsey (forthcoming) used the experimental logic of embedded anomaly to examine when verb-control information is used. They used materials such as those in (23).

(23) a. Which frog/snake did the boy force to hop over the rock?

   b. The boy forced the frog/snake to hop over the rock.

Fillers were either plausible (*frog*) or implausible (*snake*) as the subject of the verb in the infinitive clause, as illustrated in the examples. In the *wh-* sentences, detection of the incongruity introduced by the implausible filler depends upon correctly using verb-control information to interpret the filler as the empty subject of the infinitive. The materials were designed so that the most recent filler was always a plausible subject of the verb in the infinitive clause (e.g., boys can hop). Thus the recent filler strategy would predict that subjects should take longer to detect the incongruity in the *wh-* sentences than in the declarative sentences.

Figure 5 presents judgment and reaction-time data from an experiment using the stop-making-sense variant of the self-paced word-by-word reading task that we used in the preceding two experiments. In the judgment data, the implausible and plausible sentences diverge at the verb in the infinitive clause for both the *wh-* sentences and the declarative sentences. In the reaction-time data, plausibility effects show up one word later. Crucially, plausibility effects are observed at the same point for both types of sentences. Thus verb-control information seems to be accessed and used rapidly, and it seems unlikely that failure to access and use verb-control information could underlie the differences reported by Frazier et al. (1983) and Clifton and Frazier (1987).

Conclusion

We began this chapter with a brief discussion of the types of combinatory information associated with the lexical representation of verbs and how this information might be used in sentence processing. We then raised two questions: When is combinatory lexical information accessed? How is it used in language processing? The line of research we presented suggests that combinatory information is immediately accessed and used when a verb is encountered. This suggests that lexical representations could be used to rapidly coordinate a range of different types of information during language processing. Whether or not the processing system fully exploits the information made available by lexical representations remains a question for further empirical and theoretical exploration.

Appendix

This appendix presents the test sentences comparing transitive (*call*-type) verbs with verbs that typically take an infinitive complement (*remind* type). Fragments are presented up to the main verb, with a slash separating plausible and implausible fillers.

"Call"-type verbs

Which star/meal did the assistant watch . . .
Which leader/market did the rioters follow . . .
Which client/prize did the salesman visit . . .

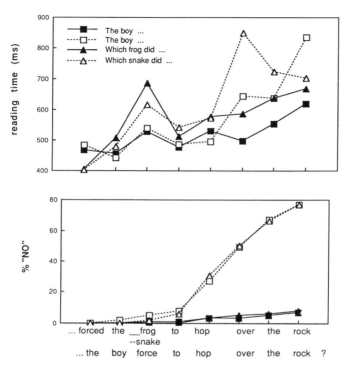

Figure 5
Results for the verb-control experiment. The bottom panel presents the
percentage of subjects who judged sentences not to make sense at each word for
wh- sentences and declarative sentences with plausible and implausible fillers.
The top panel presents reading-time data for trials on which the word was
judged to make sense.

Which room/rate did the maid clean ...
Which truck/crowd did the workers unload ...
Which painting/promise did the firemen save ...
Which customer/contract did the secretary call ...
Which car/eye did the maniac pass ...
Which book/food did the child read ...
Which key/bar did the watchman lose ...
Which structure/afternoon did the biologist see ...
Which package/sentence did the passenger leave ...

"Remind"-type verbs

Which diver/event did the coach persuade ...
Which pen-pal/article did your friend convince ...
Which actor/script did the producer force ...
Which girl/place did the wizard warn ...
Which daughter/disease did the mother urge ...
Which students/classes did the university hire ...
Which administrator/topic did the teacher advise ...
Which aunt/hospital did Martha Simpson coax ...
Which parent/car did the salesman pressure ...
Which actor/style did the drama coach encourage ...
Which child/movie did your brother remind ...
Which suspect/procedure did the detective command ...

Acknowledgments

This research was partially supported by NIH grant HD-22271 and NSF grants BNS-8217738 and BNS-8617738. Many of the ideas discussed in this chapter were developed in collaboration with Greg Carlson. We would like to thank Janet Fodor for helpful discussions about many of the issues addressed in this research, including making the suggestion that datives might provide an informative domain for distinguishing between thematic and syntactic accounts of gap filling.
    Our thinking about these topics has also benefitted from the comments by Janet Fodor (this volume) on our previous work.

References

Besson, M., and Macar, F. 1987. An event-related potential analysis of incongruity in music and other non-liguistic contexts. *Psychophysiology* 24:14–156.

Bever, T. G., and McElree, B. 1988. Empty categories access their antecedents during comprehension. *Linguistic Inquiry* 19:35–43.

Boland, J., Tanenhaus, M. K., and Garnsey, S. M. Forthcoming. Lexical structure and parsing: Evidence for the immediate use of verbal argument and control information in parsing.

Carlson, G. N., and Tanenhaus, M. K. 1988. Thematic roles and language comprehension. In W. Wilkins (ed.), *Thematic Relations*. New York: Academic Press.

Clifton, C., and Frazier, L. 1986. The use of syntactic information in filling gaps. *Journal of Psycholinguistic Research* 15:209–224.

Clifton, C., and Frazier, L. 1988. Comprehending sentences with long-distance dependencies. In G. Carlson and M. K. Tanenhaus (eds.), *Linguistic Structure in Language Processing*. Dordrecht: Reidel Press.

Clifton, C., Frazier, L., and Connine, C. 1984. Lexical expectations in sentence comprehension. *Journal of Verbal Learning and Verbal Behavior* 23:696–708.

Connine, C., Ferreira, F., Jones, C., Clifton, C., and Frazier, L. 1984. Verb frame preferences: Descriptive norms. *Journal of Psycholinguistic Research* 13:307–319.

Crain, S., and Fodor, J. D. 1985. How can grammars help parsers? In D. Dowty, L. Kartunnen, and A. Zwicky (eds.), *Natural Language Parsing*. Cambridge: Cambridge University Press.

Ferreira, F., and Clifton, C. 1986. The independence of syntactic processing. *Journal of Memory and Language* 25:348–368.

Fischler, I., Bloom, P. A., Childers, D. G., Roucos, S. E., and Perry, N. W. 1983. Brain potentials related to stages of sentence verification. *Psychophysiology* 20:400–409.

Fodor, J. D. 1978. Parsing strategies and constraints on transformation. *Linguistic Inquiry* 9:427–474.

Fodor, J. D. 1988. On modularity and sentence processing. *Journal of Psycholinguistic Research* 17:125–168.

Fodor, J., Bever, T. G., and Garrett, M. 1974. *The Psychology of Language*. New York: McGraw Hill.

Ford, M., and Dalrymple, M. 1988. A note on some psychological evidence and alternative grammars. *Cognition* 29:63–71.

Frazier, L. 1987. Theories of sentence processing. In J. Garfield (ed.), *Modularity in Knowledge Representation and Natural Language Processing*. Cambridge: MIT Press.

Frazier, L. 1988. Sentence processing: A tutorial review. In M. Coltheart (ed.), *Attention and Performance*, pp. 559–586. Hillsdale, N.J.: Lawrence Erlbaum Associates.

Frazier, L., Clifton, C. J., and Randall, J. 1983. Filling gaps: Decision principles and structure in sentence comprehension. *Cognition* 13:187–222.

Garnsey, S. M., Tanenhaus, M. K., and Chapman, R. M. 1987. Evoked potential measures of sentence comprehension. Paper presented at the Ninth Annual Meeting of the Cognitive Science Society, Seattle.

Garnsey, S. M., Tanenhaus, M. K., and Chapman, R. M. 1989. Evoked potentials and the study of sentence comprehenson. *Journal of Psycholinguistic Research* 18:51–60.

Garnsey, S. M., Tanenhaus, M. K., and Chapman, R. M. In preparation. The immediate use of verb-based knowledge in the comprehension of WH-questions.

Jasper, H. H. 1958. The ten-twenty system of the International Federation. *Electroencephalography and Clinical Neurophysiology* 10:371–375.

Kutas, M., and Hillyard, S. A. 1980a. Reading senseless sentences: Brain potentials reflect semantic incongruity. *Science* 207:204–206.

Kutas, M., and Hillyard, S. A. 1980b. Reading between the lines: Event-related brain potentials during natural sentence processing. *Brain and Language* 11:354–373.

Kutas, M., and Hillyard, S. A. 1983. Event-related brain potentials to grammatical errors and semantic anomalies. *Memory and Cognition* 11:539–550.

Kutas, M., and Hillyard, S. A. 1984. Brain potentials during reading reflect word expectancy and semantic association. *Nature* 307:161–163.

MacDonald, M. C. 1989. Priming effects from gaps to antecedents. *Language and Cognitive Processes* 18:21–35.

McElree, B., and Bever, T. G. 1989. The psychological reality of linguistically defined gaps. *Journal of Psycholinguistic Research* 18:21–35.

Marslen-Wilson, W. D. 1987. Functional parallelism in spoken word recognition. *Cognition* 25:71–102.

Mitchell, D. C. 1987. Lexical guidance in human parsing: Locus and processing characteristics. In M. Coltheart (ed.), *Attention and Performance*, vol. 12, *The Psychology of Reading*. Hillsdale, N.J.: Lawrence Erlbaum Associates.

Nagaishi, Y., and Shimokochi, M. 1985. The effects of semantic or grammatical incongruity on event-related potentials in Japanese. *Electroencephalography and Clinical Neurophysiology* 61:S32–S33.

Nicol, J., and Swinney, D. 1989. The role of structure in coreference assignment during sentence comprehension. *Journal of Psycholinguistic Research* 18:5–20.

Polich, J. 1985a. Semantic categorization and event-related potentials. *Brain and Language* 16:304–321.

Polich, J. 1985b. N400s from sentences, semantic categories, and number and letter strings? *Bulletin of the Psychonomic Society* 23:361–364.

Seidenberg, M. 1985. Constraining models in word recognition. *Cognition* 14:169–190.

Shapiro, L., Zurif, E., and Grimshaw, J. 1987. Sentence processing and the mental representation of verbs. *Cognition* 27:219–246.

Stowe, L. 1986. Parsing wh-constructions: Evidence for on-line gap location. *Language and Cognitive Processes* 2:227–246.

Stowe, L. A. 1988. Thematic structures and sentence comprehension. In G. Carlson and M. Tanenhaus (eds.), *Linguistic structure and Language Processing*. Dordrecht: Reidel.

Stowe, L., Tanenhaus, M. K., and Carlson, G. In preparation. Filling gaps in-line: Use of lexical and semantic information in sentence comprehension.

Tanenhaus, M. K., Boland, J., Garnsey, S. M., and Carlson, G. N. 1989. Lexical structure in parsing long-distance dependencies. *Journal of Psycholinguistic Research* 18:37–50.

Tanehaus, M. K., Burgess, C., Hudson-D'Zmura, S., and Carlson, G. 1987. Thematic roles in language processing. In *Proceedings of the Ninth Annual Cognitive Science Society Meetings*, pp. 587–596. Hillsdale, N.J.: Lawrence Erlbaum Associates.

Tanenhaus, M., and Carlson, G. 1989. Lexical structure and language comprehension. In W. D. Marslen-Wilson (ed.), *Lexical Representation and Process*. Cambridge: MIT Press.

Tanenhaus, M. K., Carlson, G. N., and Seidenberg, M. S. 1985. Do listeners compute linguistic representations? In D. Dowty, L. Kartunnen, and A. Zwicky (eds.), *Natural Language Parsing: Psychological, Computational, and Theoretical Perspectives*, pp. 359–408. Cambridge: Cambridge University Press.

Tanenhaus, M., Stowe, L., and Carlson, G. 1985. The interaction of lexical expectation and pragmatics in parsing filler-gap constructions. In *Proceedings of the Seventh Annual Cognitive Science Society Meetings*, pp. 361–365. Hillsdale, N.J.: Lawrence Erlbaum Associates.

Tanenhaus, M. K., Trueswell, J. C., and Carlson, G. N. 1989. Thematic roles in language processing. *Journal of Language and Cognitive Processes* 4:211–234.

Trueswell, J. C., Tanenhaus, M. K., and Garnsey, S. M. Submitted. Semantic influences on parsing: Use of thematic role information in syntactic disambiguation.

Chapter 19
Exploring the Architecture   Lyn Frazier
of the Language-Processing
System

Secure knowledge of the structure of the human language-processing mechanism continues to elude us, despite progress in the study of the representations and principles underlying lexical access and syntactic analysis. The distinctness of the principles employed for lexical access versus syntactic analysis suggests that distinct mechanisms, indeed distinct processing subsystems, are involved. In particular, considerable evidence suggests that a strategy of pursuing just the first available analysis (late closure, minimal attachment) is followed in the syntax (Frazier 1987), but not in the lexicon, where multiple lexical entries are accessed in parallel (Swinney 1979, Seidenberg et al. 1982).[1] However, even here the boundaries of the subsystems have not been securely established.

When we turn to the external relation between the grammatical processing system and other cognitive systems, we find that there exists at least one general theory of these relations, namely, Fodor's (1983) proposal that human mental architecture is modular and consists of input systems sensitive only to limited domain-specific information but not to top-down knowledge of a domain-independent variety. Fodor's proposal might be represented as in figure 1, where the relevant constraint is illustrated by the absence of an arrow permitting general domain-independent knowledge of the central system to influence the performance of an input module. Relations within an input system or between distinct input systems fall largely beyond the scope of Fodor's proposal, as does any linguistic processing extending beyond syntactic representation, e.g., computing logical form (LF) to the extent that this is considered a semantic, as opposed to syntactic, level of linguistic representation.

Several arguments may be leveled against the above view and in favor of a language-processing system that extends beyond the purely form-driven components in Fodor's proposal. First, as noted above, substantial

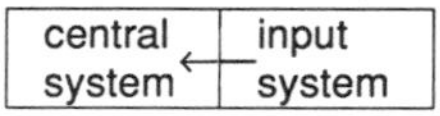

```
┌─────────┬─────────┐
│ central │ input   │
│ system ←│ system  │
└─────────┴─────────┘
```

Figure 1

evidence suggests that constituent-structure processing is serial. The evidence is not explained on the view that the parser computes and interprets multiple syntactic analyses and subsequently discards all but the most plausible or appropriate semantic analysis. Hence, it is problematic how world knowledge (among other factors) influences the reanalysis of unpreferred structures that lead the parser up the garden path. This is a problem for Fodor's view if reanalysis must take place in the language module rather than in some central processor. Rayner, Carlson, and Frazier (1983) found that the pragmatic plausibility of the correct relations in (1b) made for garden-path effects completely comparable to those in (1a), where the pragmatic relations are misleading, but that the ease and probability of accurate recovery was greater in (1b) than in (1a).

(1) a. The florist sent the flowers was very pleased with herself.

   b. The performer sent the flowers was very pleased with herself.

Thus the evidence shows that world knowledge (which determines the likelihood of a performer being the agent rather than the recipient of *send the flowers*) influences reanalysis of this structure. However, reanalysis might be argued to occur outside the language processor for the structures in (1), since reanalysis in this particular case is not always successful, as shown by the complete breakdown of analysis when one first encounters the structurally similar *The horse raced past the barn fell.*

World knowledge in the form of the pragmatic plausibility of various readings of a sentence influences reanalysis in general, however, not just in cases of conscious breakdown of the first analysis. For example, Frazier and Flores d'Arcais (in press) show an effect of the semantic/pragmatic plausibility of a *third* reading of a preposed constituent in Dutch just in case the structurally preferred (subject-preposed) analysis of the sentence (2a) must be eventually abandoned in favor of the object-preposed analysis (2b).

(2) a. De patienten$_i$ bezoek-en [e$_i$ de dokter V].
      The patients visited-en (= plural) the doctor (= The patients visit the doctor).

   b. De patienten$_i$ bezoek-t [de dokter e$_i$ V].
      The patients visit-t (= sing.) the doctor (= The doctor visits the patients).

c. De patienten bezoeken ...
    The patients visit + en (= infinitival marker) (= To visit the
    patients ...)

Hence, increasing the semantic plausibility of the third (ultimately unten-
able) reading increased sentence-comprehension times but only for sentences where the parser was forced to give up the structurally preferred
reading. This again shows an effect of world knowledge on *reanalysis* times
but in a case where recovery from the unpreferred analysis is apparently
automatic. In the experiment a high error rate was observed on certain
object-preposed sentences. However, unlike the examples in (1), under
ordinary nonexperimental circumstances neither the subject- nor object-
preposed sentence forms are consciously experienced as garden paths or
as cases where sentence analysis breaks down altogether. Hence, it is more
difficult in this case to argue that reanalysis depended on a central processing system rather than on the language processor. Indeed, making that
assumption would require the knowledge and mechanisms of the language
processor to be duplicated in the central processing system.

    There are additional problems for the proposal that the grammatical
processing system consists of an encapsulated form-based phonological,
lexical, and syntactic system whose output is interpreted by mechanisms
of an unencapsulated, language-independent, general processing system.
The proposal predicts, or at least leads one to expect, that only general
nonlinguistic information and mechanisms will influence "semantic" processing beyond the shallow interpretation of sentences or discourse. But
this can't be right. The plausibility of an interpretation of a linguistic
input is relative to the linguistic mechanisms available to express the
hypothesized meaning, i.e., the plausibility of form-meaning pairings,
not simply the plausibility of the propositional content describing the
perceived/assumed facts of the world. Hence, focus structure, type of
anaphor, and (cross-sentence) scope of modal operators all influence the
ultimately chosen analysis for ambiguous structures. If world knowledge
comes to bear on the semantic interpretation of a sentence that is outside
of the language system proper but yet must be evaluated in light of the
alternative grammatically permissible form-meaning pairings available in
the language, it seems that grammatical knowledge must be available
outside the language system as well as inside it (see Grice 1968).

    For example, in (3) the perceiver may take *the jerk* to refer to Emmon
even though he may believe Emmon is not a jerk at all and may in fact
believe some individual corresponding to another discourse entity (Dale
or the bully) is a jerk.

(3) I saw Dale fighting with the neighborhood bully. Then Emmon left.
    The jerk ...

Plausibility in the sense of real-world likelihood or consistency with beliefs about the world does seem to influence even early reference and predication assignments (Nicol 1988; Clifton and Frazier, in preparation). But, in contrast to nonlinguistic domains, plausibility is evaluated with respect to the linguistic presentation of information. Thus the relevant notion of plausibility is not who is more likely to be a jerk in view of the real-world properties of Dale, Emmon, and the bully but rather who is more likely to be the referent of *jerk* in view of this real-world information together with the particular reference mechanism used.

This is unexpected if the grammatically permissible analyses of a sentence are determined and then purely nonlinguistic plausibility considerations are used to select the interpretations assigned to a sentence. In short, the interpretation chosen for a given sentence does not seem open to an account based exclusively on domain-independent cognitive principles but rather is tied to plausibility assessed in light of the grammatical options open to the speaker and to the particular referential devices the speaker opted for. Marslen-Wilson and Tyler (1987) make a related point. They argue that certain aspects of discourse processing (pronoun interpretation) are—I would say *can be*—automatic and are not the outcome of sluggish cognitive mechanisms.

In what follows, I will argue that Fodor is essentially correct: the form-driven subsystems ("modules") of the language processor are information-encapsulated and respond only to information represented in their own specialized vocabulary. Further, I will argue that within this form-driven system the identification criteria for subsystems is cast in terms of pre-specified knowledge that must be consulted before any decision is made (the no-bookkeeping constraint). In contrast to Fodor, I will explore the view that the language system proper extends beyond form-driven systems to include linguistic subsystems that are not strictly encapsulated but nevertheless behave like modules in essential respects. There are linguistic constraints on the well-formedness of their output. In advance of an actual input stimulus, there is a specification of their behavior. However, unlike true input modules, where this specification is entirely in term of knowledge used in the analysis, the advance specification of the behavior is in terms of the *task* performed and includes constraints on a well-formed output. In short, I will suggest that Fodor's view of an undifferentiated central system is incorrect. The form-driven subsystems of the language module

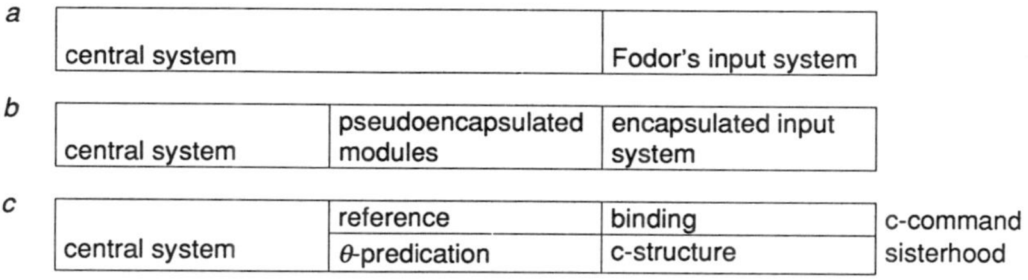

a			
central system			Fodor's input system

b			
central system		pseudoencapsulated modules	encapsulated input system

c				
central system		reference	binding	c-command
		θ-predication	c-structure	sisterhood

Figure 2

are supplemented by the effects of world knowledge once translated *into* the vocabulary of a grammatical module by pseudoencapsulated linguistic systems (Frazier 1985). These pseudoencapsulated subsystems are characterized by linguistic constraints and task specification given prior to actual input or discourse, as indicated in figure 2b. More specifically, I will propose the system in figure 2c. Section 1 sketches in some of the basic properties of the subsystems in figure 2c while ignoring lexical and phonological/orthograpic analysis. Section 2 takes up the relation between modules. Section 3 returns to the issue of whether it is solely information encapsulation that underlies the claimed processing advantages of input modules.

1 Postlexical Modules

Perhaps the best understood module in figure 2c is the constituent-structure (c-structure) module. Numerous studies indicate that it follows a one-analysis strategy, initially pursuing certain structurally identifiable choices at decision points where the grammar allows more than one option (see the references in Frazier 1987). It structures input items essentially as they are encountered (Frazier and Rayner 1982, Ferreira and Henderson 1989). The initial choice of analysis is made using grammatical conditions constrained by strictly local (sisterhood) relations, i.e., case theory, X′ theory, and the formal (theta criterion) aspect of thematic constraints (see Chomsky 1981).

In this chapter the existence of a c-structure input module will simply be assumed on the basis of arguments and evidence presented elsewhere. It is impossible to review here all the material relevant to those arguments. Let me briefly mention the *kinds* of arguments supporting the (present) encapsulation or modular solution to capturing the similarities between syntactic and nonsyntactic grammatical processes. First, in the absence of semantic/pragmatic biases, there exist general, systematic, and structural preferences in the analysis assigned to an ambiguous input (e.g., the complement-clause analysis is preferred in *John told the girl that Bill liked the story*). Second, in tasks permitting subjects lots of time, the structural preferences sometimes appear to be overridden by nonsyntactic information. Nevertheless, in the same structures a processing-time advantage is observed for the preferred syntactic structure if the measurement point is earlier and/or nonsyntactic biases are removed. Third, in some structures (e.g., *John hired Bill a drunk* and *a gift to a boy in a box*) a preferred syntactic analysis will be consciously detected even though it is pragmatically less plausible than the alternative. None of these generalizations is explained by the view that c-structure assignment is part of a content-driven analysis system rather than part of an encapsulated input module. Further, no benefits accrue to the content-driven analysis system, since a syntactic analysis must in any case be constructed at some point during sentence analysis simply to discriminate between meanings that are grammatically licensed and those that aren't. Finally, as argued in Frazier 1990 the modular view offers an explanation for why certain structures are more quickly and readily influenced by semantic information than are others.

A distinct syntactic module is concerned with relations between (potentially) nonadjacent phrases in the constituent structure. The idea that grammatical conditions stated primarily in terms of structural dominance (constituent-commanding or c-commanding) can apply separately from those based on sisterhood derives from several sources (e.g., Frazier, Clifton, and Randall 1983; Crain and Fodor 1985; Fodor 1988; Ford and Dalrymple 1988). Freedman and Forster (1985) show differences between c-structure and binding constraints in a same/different matching task (see also Crain and Fodor 1987, Forster and Stevenson 1987).

What experimental evidence is available suggests that *distinct* processing principles may apply to (1) movement dependencies, (2) coindexing d-linked *wh*- phrases (phrases, like *which girl*, that seem to bear the referential index of a discourse entity), (3) reflexive binding, and (4) control. For example, DeVincenzi (1989) uses reading time data to argue that a minimal chain principle (MCP) applies to (1) but not (2) in Italian. Plunkett (in preparation) provides questionnaire data suggesting the MCP does not apply to (3). Only in early analyses of extraction dependencies (Frazier, Clifton, and Randall 1983) did (4) get classified together with (1) in terms of the processing decisions to which a single processing strategy applied. What, then, unifies these operations into a module if not the processing strategy (e.g., MCP) that the parser uses in recovering the dependency?

At present two characteristics suggest themselves. First, all are stated in terms of c-commanding (structural dominance), not sisterhood. In this sense, there is a natural division in the grammar between c-structure and binding (or structure-evaluation) modules. Second, perceivers don't construct analyses that violate phrase-structure rules. Thus, it seems the c-structure principles participate in a stage of processing that proceeds *regardless* of whether binding information is available *but* not until all sisterhood constraints have been checked. In short, the separation of the two syntactic modules seems warranted by the fact that no bookkeeping principle applies to each.

No-bookkeeping constraint: At each point in the ongoing analysis of a sentence, a decision will not be made within any module without checking that the decision is consistent with all within module information.

The no-bookkeeping constraint (NBC) implies that a c-structure decision will violate a sisterhood principle only when no alternative is available, e.g., when the input is ungrammatical or unparsable. This follows because all intra-module (c-structure) information will be checked, and this will uncover any incompatibilities between the assigned analysis and any c-structure constraints before the parser moves on to the next c-structure decision. However, the above constraint says nothing about delaying the next c-structure decision until the current c-structure decision is proved to be compatible with all the principles of binding theory (BT), bounding theory, and control (i.e., the binding module). Hence, there is no guarantee that binding constraints will have been checked before the parser moves on to new c-structure decisions. Hence, nothing will guarantee that the assigned c-structure is necessarily well formed according to the constraints of the binding module or other constraints lying outside the c-structure module.

The no-bookkeeping constraint is intuitively appealing because it eliminates the need for each module to keep track of which decisions have satisfied the requirements embodied in which grammatical principles/rules/ conditions. To guarantee well-formedness, each parsing decision must be checked to insure that it complies with all grammatical requirements. The no-bookkeeping constraint ensures intramodule well-formedness without any record keeping beyond the analysis assigned to the input. In this respect, the constraint insures an architecture that minimizes computational and memory burdens. To the extent that the boundaries between modules represent natural divisions into classes of grammatical principles that are maximally interdependent within a module but not (reciprocally) interdependent across modules, the memory/computational savings will be gained at low cost in terms of parsing errors that could have been averted by having larger modules, i.e., by delaying analysis until additional grammatical principles had been consulted.

The empirical predictions of the no-bookkeeping constraint are at least consistent with the available data. On the same assumption as before, that case theory is part of the c-structure module, this constraint predicts that the case information in (4a) prevents *he* (nominative) from being misanalyzed as the direct object of the verb *saw*.

(4) a. Mary saw he...
    b. Mary saw a picture of themselves...

Intuitively, one does expect (4a) to continue with a predicate for the subject pronoun. By contrast, the violation of the binding theory in (4b), where *themselves* requires an antecedent, does not prevent a direct-object analysis of this phrase, even though no binder will be accessible on this constituent-structure analysis.[2]

To my knowledge, phrase-structure misanalyses inconsistent with case (or X′ theory or general theta requirements) do not occur. Ongoing eye-movement studies by Chuck Clifton, Greg Lamontagne, and myself are encouraging for this view. The work explicitly tries, but so far has failed, to uncover phrase-structure decisions that violate case theory, at least when the case-bearing element is fixed. This is predicted by the no-bookkeeping constraint. On the other hand, the NBC leads one to expect that phrase-structure analysis can, and at least under some circumstances does, proceed without guaranteeing well-formedness in terms of the constraints in the binding module. Frazier, Clifton, and Randall (1983) and Nicol (1988) report possible examples of phrase-structure analysis continuing without the parser having guaranteed well-formedness according to control theory. Freedman and Forster (1985) suggest that phrase-structure analysis progresses even in the face of a binding-module violation. Quite standard judgments in the syntactic literature also presuppose bounding-theory well-formedness will be sacrificed rather than c-structure well-formedness when both cannot be satisfied.

Take an example like (5), where perceivers seem to interpret *what* as the object of *contruct*, which satisfies case, X′ and theta requirements but leads to a consequent violation of bounding theory (subjacency, see Chomsky 1981).

(5) *What did the man who constructed die of poverty?

Why not satisfy bounding theory at the expense of c-structure by, e.g., interpreting (5) to mean, What did the man who died of poverty construct? This analysis would entail crossed branches in the phrase marker, a clear violation of X' theory. But (5), as interpreted, also involves a violation. Why do people systematically prefer the bounding-theory violation? In view of the no-bookkeeping constraint, this might follow simply from the c-structure parser proceeding with its attempt to find a well-formed c-structure without concerning itself with the fact that no well-formed binding is afforded by this structure.

The arguments above concern the separation of syntactic processing into two distinct modules each satisfying the no-bookkeeping constraint. (See Nicol 1988 and Cowart and Cairns 1987 for arguments that the binding module initially operates using only syntactic information, but see also Tanenhaus et al., this volume.) The arguments above suggest that binding theory, bounding theory, and control are not part of the c-structure module, but they leave open the possibility that these systems form not a single module but several. The empirical issue here is whether, say, the binding-theory constraints on a filler-contained anaphor are checked before a filler-gap decision is made in sentences like *Which picture of himself did Mary see ...?* Experimental evidence on this issue is currently unavailable.

Let us turn to thematic/predication assignment. Few generalizations have been tested widely enough to draw any final conclusions. However, some recent studies of thematic assignment in nominalizations and in adjunct-predication structures lend added support to the idea that one subsystem of the language processor is concerned with thematic and predication assignments (Rayner et al. 1983). In sharp contrast to the c-structure module, this substructure considers alternative analyses in parallel and does not rely on a one-analysis strategy. It evaluates alternatives as arguments are parsed but delays a selection decision until all potential arguments have been received (rather than choosing a thematic role immediately as each argument is parsed).

Rayner et al. (1983) suggested the existence of a thematic-processing subsystem responsible for choosing the most plausible thematic frame listed in the lexical entry for each head of a phrase (but see Taraban and McClelland 1988, Frazier 1990, and the discussion below). Then the chosen frame disconfirms the current c-structure analysis of the input unless the number of internal arguments (and their syntactic category) matches that of the phrases appearing as sisters to the head of the phrase in the current c-structure analysis. In effect, the selected frame can guide the c-structure processor to look for an alternative with the indicated number and type of internal arguments. Thus thematic frame selection serves as feedback from the thematic processor to the c-structure processor. By translating semantic/pragmatic information into a syntactic vocabulary, world knowledge can be brought to bear on issues of syntactic attachment to c-structure.

On this view, thematic-role assignment (and predication) is accomplished by a processing module distinct from the syntactic module. The thematic processor operates temporally in parallel with the c-structure processor, evaluating the input for a best-fit thematic frame once the frame-bearing item is identified as the head of a phrase. However, a selection between frames can usually be made only once all potential arguments of the head are available for assessment, since choosing the most plausible frame (i.e., the best pairing of phrases with thematic roles) implies knowledge of the plausibility of all alternatives. The thematic processor must utilize the structure assigned to the input by the c-structure processor in order to identify heads of phrases, which bear thematic frames, and to identify phrases corresponding to potential arguments. By hypothesis, it also consults real-world and discourse information about potential arguments, typically all of them, to choose the most plausible thematic frame for each phrase head; e.g., it chooses a frame that includes an instrument for *see x with binoculars* but not for *see x with a revolver*.

Below additional evidence for this proposed module is presented. Discussion of whether it is truly an input module in Fodor's (1983) sense will be delayed until later.

Clifton, Seely, and Frazier (in preparation) explore the properties of thematic assignment, arguing that assignment is indeed a matter of frame selection and not of assignment of a thematic role to each individual NP as it is encountered. To begin, consider the examples in (6) through (8).

(6) a. the city's destruction
     b. the army's destruction
     c. the destruction of the city
     d. the destruction of the army
     e. the army's destruction of the city

(7) a. the dam's construction
     b. the company's construction
     c. the construction of the dam
     d. the construction of the company
     e. the company's construction of the dam

(8) a. the produce's preservation
  b. the refrigerator's preservation
  c. the preservation of the produce
  d. the preservation of the refrigerator
  e. the refrigerator's preservation of the produce

Intuitively, there's a tendency for the single argument of a nominalization from a transitive verb to be interpreted as a theme (the internal argument of the corresponding active verb) rather than as an agent (the external argument of the corresponding active verb), as indicated by the (a–d) forms above. In examples where two arguments are present (the (e) forms above), no such preference emerges. Perceivers in this case are happy to take *army*, *company*, and *refrigerator* as the agent of *destroy*, *construct*, and *preserve*, respectively. Thus, if the processor immediately assigns a thematic role to the preverbal NP in specifier position as soon as the deverbal noun is encountered, an on-line preference to assign it as the theme should emerge in cases of temporary ambiguity. However, if the processor delays assignment until it determines how many arguments are present no theme preference is expected. In a self-paced reading study, Clifton, Seely, and Frazier (in preparation) tested this prediction in sentences like (9). The various forms (9a–h) were all followed by the same predicate. Forms (9a, b, e, f) are ambiguous in terms of the plausibility of the semantic relations involved; the others are strongly biased.

(9) ____ was praised by the local newspaper.
  a. The city's excavation of its historic buildings (ambiguous agent)
  b. The city's excavation by the archaeologists (ambiguous theme)
  c. The archaeologist's excavation of the old foundation (unambiguous agent)
  e. The fact that the city excavated the historic buildings (ambiguous agent)
  f. The fact that the city was excavated by the archaeologists (ambiguous theme)
  g. The fact that the archaeologist excavated the old foundation (unambiguous agent)
  h. The fact that the dinosaur was excavated by the paleontologist (unambiguous theme)

Sentences (9a–d) provide the critical examples. If thematic assignment proceeds before the number of arguments of the head (*excavation*) has been established, the temporarily ambiguous forms (9a–b) should be processed most easily when the theme interpretation of the first NP is confirmed.

Hence, (9b) should be read more quickly than (9a). The clausal counter-parts in (9e–h) were tested as a control for lexical differences and to determine whether common thematic assignment mechanisms operate in NPs and in clauses.[3]

Contrary to the prediction of the immediate-thematic-assignment hypothesis, no difference between the ambiguous-theme example (9b) and the ambiguous agent example (9a) was observed. Ambiguous forms (9a, b, e, f) took longer to read than unambiguous ones, but this effect of ambiguity did not interact with whether the true role of the first NP was the theme or the agent. This conflicts with the prediction of an immediate-theme-assignment strategy, which predicts agent sentence forms to be more slowly processed than the theme forms when a temporary ambiguity of relation permitted an immediate theme-assignment to the NP in the specifier position.[4]

Clifton and Frazier explore the processing of adjunct predicates to see if the choice between two potential external arguments (subjects) proceeds like other postulated thematic/predication assignments, e.g., thematic-frame selection. If so, all potential external arguments within the current thematic domain should be considered in parallel.

Clifton and Frazier (in preparation) present preliminary evidence that adjuncts are identified by default and not by an explicit decision to treat a phrase as an adjunct. Phrases following the verb will typically be syntactically analyzed as sisters to the verb, given constituent-attachment principles (e.g., minimal attachment, see Frazier 1987). The parser will initially analyze phrases in this position as arguments (see Clifton and Frazier, in preparation, and the "Sister Constraint" in Chomsky 1965).

Once an adjunct predicate has been identified, it is interpreted according to the following strategy:

Adjunct-interpretation strategy: Predicate an adjunct of the theme or external argument (Williams's (1980) "subject") of the current argument complex.

In a probe recognition study, the adjunct-interpretation strategy was tested by looking at recognition times for a visual probe (presented at the location of one of the asterisks in the examples in (10)).

(10) a. Jonathan ate the broccoli competely na*ked and unwa*shed.
        Probe = *Jonathan*
     b. Jonathan ate the broccoli completely na*ked and unwa*shed.
        Probe = *broccoli*

c. Jonathan ate the broccoli completely ra*w and unwa*shed.
   Probe = *Jonathan*

d. Jonathan ate the broccoli completely ra*w and unwa*shed.
   Probe = *broccoli*

The question of interest was whether the adjunct-interpretation strategy would be applied in a parallel fashion, with both *Jonathan* and *broccoli* being considered simultaneously for possible assignments as external arguments of the sentence-final adjectival phrase, e.g., *completely naked and unwashed*. If so, probe-recognition speed and accuracy should be high whenever the probe corresponds to the actual external argument (the subject) of the sentence-final predicate (e.g., *completely naked and unwashed*). The facilitation effect should be entirely symmetric on the parallel- or multiple-analysis view. By contrast, a serial-analysis application of the adjunct-interpretation strategy might lead us to expect the more recent NP to be checked first, with the distant NP checked only when the recent NP leads to an implausible analysis. In this case, the facilitation effect should not be symmetric but rather should favor object-probe sentences, since the object NP will be checked in all cases as a possible external argument (subject) for the final predicate, but the sentence subject will be checked only in the subject-predication sentences (9a, b).

In fact, probe recognition was both accurate and fast (the latter only marginally significant) when the probe matched the antecedent of the predicate in comparison with when it mismatched. This facilitation effect was equal in size for probes of both subjects and objects, which suggests that both argument assignments were tried in parallel. It must be emphasized that this evidence is preliminary; the study has not yet been replicated. But if it is confirmed by the outcome of subsequent studies, it strongly supports the idea that multiple thematic/predication analyses are considered in parallel.

The above studies are preliminary exploration of processing nominalizations and adjunct-predication structures. Like earlier studies of thematic-frame selection (Rayner et al. 1983) they indicate that thematic/prediction assignments proceed by considering the full set of grammatically possible pairings of arguments and thematic roles and choosing the most plausible one once all potential arguments have been identified. This requires the use of world knowledge, such as that archaeologists are likely agents but unlikely themes of *excavate*. Thus, in all respects—parallelism, nonimmediate selection, and use of world knowledge—these assignments seem to differ from c-structure assignments. These distinct properties of thematic/

predication assignment versus c-structure assignment argue for separate processing subsystems associated with these clusters of decision types and processing principles.

I turn now to the referential semantics. It is fairly standard to (implicitly) assume that some processing operations are concerned with the referents assigned to pronouns and other referential NPs. Given the no-bookkeeping constraint, this implies that either initial referential assignments and thematic/predication assignments are always yoked (one type of decision cannot proceed without checking the constraints imposed by the other) *or* they occur in two distinct modules. Several studies (e.g., Erhlich and Rayner 1983, Nicol 1988) suggest that the search for an antecedent occurs immediately upon encountering a pronoun, even one in subject position, which thus occurs before its theta assigner, the verb, has been received. If the grammatically permissible thematic role assignments are not yet known, this evidence would fit naturally with the existence of distinct modules for referential assignment (NP semantics) and for thematic/predication assignments.

Formulating and trying to defend a principle like the no-bookkeeping constraint may seem wildly premature to some, in view of the paucity of the empirical evidence requiring incorporation of the principle into a theory of the architecture of the human sentence-processing mechanism. The justification for formulating hypotheses even in the face of little evidence is that examining the validity of *some* hypothesis helps to reveal the implications of what evidence is available. In the current case, formulating a stronger principle, say one requiring each decision to be checked against the principles of *all* the modules in figure 2c, would be *too* strong. It conflicts with available evidence about thematic-role assignment (above) and control (Nicol 1988), and it fails to elucidate the role of bounding theory (Freedman and Forster 1985 and my discussion of (5) above). The no-bookkeeping principle is weakened to avoid the known counterexamples to the stronger principle. If it is consistent with available evidence, it seems preferable to the hypotheses that relations between individual processing decisions are arbitrary and that each decision may or may not require prior checking of any other logically independent decisions. The latter position makes no explicit predictions and thus should presumably not be adopted as a first hypothesis.

With this preliminary sketch of the division of the language processor into subsystem, discussion will turn now to the relations between these subsystems or modules.

2   Relations between Modules

From the modularization of the language-comprehension system illustrated in figure 2c, numerous incompatible models could be developed by
stipulating various relations between the modules. But what if we say
nothing at all about these relations? Instead, we might explore the idea that
no principles of mental architecture or language stipulate the relations
between modules. What would be the consequences of the view that
intermodular relations are unregulated?

On this view, whether there is communication between modules, will
depend entirely on intramodular factors. Whether one module is related
to another will depend on whether the computational results of one are
phrased in a vocabulary relevant to the operation of the other. For example, knowing the discourse referent assigned to some NP by the referential
module might in principle have consequences for the binding module, since
referentially independent elements take scope outside referentially dependent ones (scope being defined in terms of c-command, a relation
interpreted by the binding module). Similarly, thematic-frame selection has
potential consequences for c-structure processing, since arguments of a
head are subject to a locality constraint defined in terms of sisterhood
(Williams 1980, 1988). In short, which modules bear what relations to each
other follows from intramodular properties; it needn't be stipulated.

Specifically, we might consider the very strong hypotheses that *only*
the scope principle (a phrase may be referentially dependent only on a
c-commanding phrase) governs the relation between the binding module
and the referential module and that *only* the argument principle (internal
arguments are sisters to the head of phrase) governs the relation between
the c-structure module and the thematic/predication module. Whether in
the long run it will prove possible to maintain such a restrictive hypothesis
is unclear. But the important point for present purposes is that the scope
principle and the argument principle are not principles directly governing
the relations between processing systems. Instead, they are part of the
grammatical specification of the modules themselves, much like X' theory
or the theta criterion (see Chomsky 1981 for definitions; see Frazier 1985,
1990, for a proposal concerning how these (and other) principles define
processing modules).

Whether some module in fact takes notice of intermodular information
from some other potentially related module presumably depends only on
available computational/memory resources. In the normal case, it should
probably be assumed that all relevant intermodular information is regis-

tered and acted on, since processing proceeds smoothly to an interpretation at least consistent with all grammatical requirements. But perhaps computational restrictions imposed by brain damage can limit access to intermodular information that is in principle relevant to processing an input, in effect reducing the number of modules implicated in some task. What is interesting about this possibility is that the particular operative modules may depend on the task. For example, one might interpret the account of agrammatic aphasics provided by Linebarger et al. (1983) in this manner. Restricted computational resources may reduce the effective language system to one pair of modules: when the task requires purely grammatical judgments, the c-structure and binding modules; when the task requires meaning judgments, the reference and thematic/predication modules. The hypothesis that relations between modules are free would explain why this is possible. (For further evidence of the existence of module-independent capacity restrictions, see Waters, Caplan, and Hildebrandt 1987, where it is argued that syntactic and propositional processing both draw on central resources, though they don't interact with each other.)

The effect of intermodular relations may depend heavily on the relative timing of processing decisions. For example, imagine that the referential module finds (or fails to find) an existing discourse entity for a definite noun phrase corresponding to an NP identified by the c-structure processor. This might serve as an error signal to the thematic and c-structure modules. If we assume the late-revisions principle, its effect might depend on how quickly this information is made available.

Late-revisions principle: Confirmed processing decisions take longer to revise than unconfirmed ones.

The late-revisions principle predicts that errors consistent with subsequent items analyzed in the same module and errors confirmed by analysis of other modules will take longer to revise than errors immediately disconfirmed by intramodular or intermodular information. (See, for example, Frazier 1978, Stowe 1989, Pritchett 1987, and Frazier and Rayner 1982 for experimental results that can be interpreted as evidence for the late-revision principle; see Frazier 1987 for a discussion of the relative ease of various types of reanalysis.)

The confirmed-decisions principle accounts for the finding that arguments are processed more quickly than adjuncts (Frazier and Clifton 1987, Smith 1988), since analysis of a phrase as sister to its head is confirmed by thematic-frame selection for arguments but not for adjuncts (on the assumption, as before, that only arguments are sisters to a head and that adjuncts are not listed in thematic frames).

Confirmed-decisions principle: Processing a sentence where initial decisions are confirmed takes less time than processing a sentence where initial decisions are not confirmed.

This needn't be stipulated as a principle (see Abney 1988, for example). What underlies these two principles is presumably the most fundamental of all assumptions (simplicity metrics) in resource-limited domains, namely, performing some operation takes less time performing that operation plus another one drawing on the same resources. The late-revisions principle follows because revising a confirmed decision requires reconsidering decisions other than the error itself, quite apart from any additional effect of the confirming material in obscuring the source of the error. The confirmed-decisions principle follows because decisions that are not confirmed will entail making revisions or at least searching for alternatives. If there are completely free relations between modules, a principle like the late-revisions principle is precisely what we expect to characterize the interplay between modules.

Perhaps the assumption of free relations between modules can also help solve a puzzle in current processing accounts that permit nonsyntactic information to influence reanalysis of an input but not the first syntactic analysis of it. If we assume that not all reanalysis involves conscious puzzle-solving abilities (see my discussion of (1) above), the question is why reanalysis but not first analysis is affected by semantics? On the present proposal, this question may be restated as, Why does the no-bookkeeping constraint apply to each module or subsystem during the first analysis but apply to the entire language system as a whole during reanalysis, including the referential and thematic/predication modules, which translate world knowledge into a syntactic vocabulary? Put this way, the question suggests an answer. On the assumption that a linguistic input must be processed by all potentially relevant language modules (see Forster 1979), the decisions implicated in the first analysis of an input may be checked against just the intramodular principles, and still and global well-formedness of the analysis will be assured. Step-by-step compatibility between a decision about the current representation of the input and intramodular information will guarantee that decisions across modules are grammatically compatible with each other. By contrast, a decision to *revise* one aspect of the representation, say a c-structure attachment, will not guarantee that all previously licensed relations remain well formed once the structure has been revised. For example, reattaching a phrase containing an anaphor (e.g., *himself*) to a position higher in the phrase-structure tree may entail that the anaphor is no longer bound by a c-commanding NP. Thus, in the reanalysis, unlike the first analysis, the only way to guarantee global grammaticality is to ensure that the no-bookkeeping constraint applies to the language system as a whole.

So far the consequence of leaving the relations between modules unregulated has not been disastrous at all. Indeed, the predictions fit rather well with some general considerations about processing capacity and the nature and cost of revising the first analysis assigned to a string. They also receive some support from a consideration of variation in language processing.

In principle, variation in the language-processing system could occur in any of numerous ways: in the principles adopted by the processor, in the structure of the processing mechanism, in the response to ambiguous or complex constructions, etc. Yet variation between individuals, entire populations, or different tasks seems to be attributable to differences in the relative timing of the subsystems implicated.

Apparent variation, say in the role of syntax in language comprehension, often comes about simply because the output of the entire language and cognitive systems is very slow. This apparently masks differences in the complexity of processing various syntactic structures. For example, Cupples and Holmes (1987) find individual differences between readers: slow readers do not exhibit robust garden-path effects. This finding is not too surprising on the view that distinct modules operate simultaneously: intramodule differences in the complexity of processing a sentence influence (overall) response times when they represent the slowest or one of the later modules to contribute to the output. This of course contrasts with a model in which the input-output relation between subsystems is serially ordered and thus each module contributes to overall output times in an additive fashion.

In principle, the facts could have been quite different. For example, it might have turned out that slow subjects exhibited garden-path effects, but not fast subjects. This sort of finding would suggest true variation in the processing systems, with different individuals adopting different strategies.

Another type of variation in the language system might be expected if semantic modules could operate particularly fast under some circumstances. In this case, an early error signal provided by a semantic subsystem might result in there being only a minimal cost associated with revising a syntactic analysis because of early revision (see my discussion of the late-revision principle above). We might speculate that something like this is responsible for the evidence suggesting that individuals with left-handed relatives are less tied to the syntax in various language-processing tasks than individuals without left-handed relatives (Bever et al. 1986, Cowart 1988). Quite simply, the output of (some) lexical/semantic processes may be available particularly early in the sinistrals (left-handers), which gives the appearance that the syntax is less important in the judgments of these individuals. A perhaps comparable contrast is the processing of high versus low semantic-constraint prose. If we increase the semantic or pragmatic constraints, the results of semantic processes are presumably available earlier (absolutely and relative to the syntactic modules), which thus leads to the impression that syntactic factors are less important than when fewer semantic constraints exist.

For example, Flores d'Arcais (1987) finds conscious detection of syntactic violations is greater for low semantic-constraint prose than for high-constraint prose. If a plausible semantic analysis of an input is available very early, this analysis is presumably already available to govern output responses, in contrast to low-constraint prose, where it is expected that the semantic analysis would take longer to develop. As expected, on the assumption of a modular system containing one or more syntactic modules, reading-time evidence indicated that syntactic violations slowed comprehension, whether they were consciously detected or not. In short, speeding nonsyntactic analysis or slowing syntactic analysis should have comparable effects, since it is the relative availability in outputs that will be important in a system in which no principle regulates the relations between subsystems.

3   Are All Modules Input Modules?

I now return to the question of whether the modules in figure 2c are input modules. The c-structure and binding modules seem straightforwardly to satisfy all criteria. To my knowledge, there is no problem at all with simply labeling them as input modules in the ordinary strongest sense laid out by Fodor (1983). They may be influenced by nonlinguistic information but only once it has been translated into the vocabulary of c-command or sister-hood by influencing a referential or thematic/predication assignment. But the reference and thematic/predication modules are problematic in that they require information that goes beyond purely linguistic information. At least, information about discourse context (e.g., imagine a llama just entered the room) must be available to the reference module. Real-world and discourse-representation information must be available to the thematic module. Since information encapsulation is usually viewed as *the* central feature of an input module, this suggests that two of the modules in figure 2c are not input modules at all.

One response to this situation might be simply to draw the line between the language input module and the general cognitive system to the left of the binding and c-structure modules in figure 2c, with only the modules to the right being identified as input modules. This is essentially what Fodor does: he maintains the strongest version of modularity, but only by restricting the domain of language comprehension essentially to form recognition of the sentence structures allowed in the language. What seems to be wrong with that picture is that it ignores the modular behavior of the reference and thematic/predication modules. Specifically, these subsystems fail the criterion for input modules in one vary particular way while maintaining other important properties of input modules, even some concerning information encapsulation.

The reference and thematic modules do not really behave like the general cognitive system on current conceptions of it, namely, that it is modality- and domain-independent, entirely open, with any inconsistencies in the implications of information not necessarily noticed and no privileged access to other systems. Indeed, as argued by Marslen-Wilson and Tyler (1987), the operation of the referential module does not suggest the operation of a sluggish general-purpose processor but instead mimics the behavior of input modules in many respects. For example, the construction of a representation including a discourse entity for referential phrases (at least for arguments in referential positions) seems to occur quickly and automatically.

We can account for the partial similarity between the reference mechanism and c-structure analysis in several ways. Marslen-Wilson and Tyler suggest capturing it by abandoning the view that syntactic analysis is performed by a specialized encapsulated system. This, of course, challenges the view that a central system always behaves as an unconstrained general-purpose system.

Instead, the view pursued here suggests that the notion of a module might be enriched by distinguishing truly encapsulated input modules from pseudoencapsulated modules that import general cognitive knowledge into the language system in a task-dependent manner. The pseudoencapsulation would result from the fact that the task is defined in advance, along with the systematic (grammatical) knowledge used to accomplish it. In essence, a shallow output is defined by the constraints of predication theory together with the linguistic constraints on various referential devices. This prespecification of the task and (nonincidental) knowledge permit many of the advantages of an input module to be shared by an interface module.

The behavior of a Fodorian encapsulated language system is specified in advance in terms of (1) the component tasks involved, (2) the linguistic constraints on possible outputs or solutions, and (3) the knowledge used to accomplish the task. Discussion of modularity or input systems has almost invariably focused on (3) as underlying at least the speed of the language processor if not also its robustness and automaticity. In the experimental literature too, autonomy versus interaction of information sources has captured attention and thus focused discussion almost entirely on (3). But it's unclear *why* advance knowledge of the tasks implicit in solving some problem and advance knowledge of constraints on the possible solutions should not also facilitate rapid automatic processing. What has been argued here is that the pseudoencapsulated reference and thematic modules benefit from these advantages. This indirectly also serves to limit the information imported into the language system on any given occasion. It will be limited to the information required to complete these predetermined tasks, along with whatever additional relevant information has been identified before those tasks have been completed.[5]

4   Summary

It may be inappropriate to call the reference and thematic modules input modules, but it has been suggested here that they are nevertheless module-like. The prespecification of their (closed) information system suffices to permit consistency to be maintained and the no-bookkeeping constraint to be satisfied. Most important of all, a shallow ontput can be defined. By hypothesis, the prior identification of the obligatorily consulted information together with the prior specification of a task results in the modular behavior of the grammatical-semantic systems and permits them to be closed off from the general cognitive system. The grammatical constraints on reference and predication define a shallow output of sorts, in effect a grammatical level of representation optionally supplemented by whatever relevant world knowledge has been imported into the system for the particular input at hand.

Just as the c-structure module maps lexical strings onto well-formed phrase markers meeting all the sister-conditions, the reference module maps syntactic representations onto (new or preexisting) discourse entities in accord with constraints on reference. The thematic/predication module also defines a shallow output, by mapping c-structure representations onto predication structures satisfying the theta criterion, the projection principle, and the requirement that all predicates have an external argument. These shallow-output representations in turn permit a system with access to an open system of information to masquerade as, indeed to share many advantages of, an information-encapsulated one.

Acknowledgments

I am very grateful to Chuck Clifton, Mike Tanenhaus, Gerry Altmann, Janet Fodor, Rene Schmauder, and an anonymous reviewer for comments on an earlier draft of this chapter. This work was supported by NIH Grant HD 18708 to Chuck Clifton and Lyn Frazier.

Notes

1. Gorrell (1987) makes an interesting proposal intended to account both for the evidence for pursuing a structurally favored analysis first and for semantic biases outside the syntactic module. His staggered parallel system has several drawbacks, however. The evidence supporting it suggests alternative (nonpreferred) analyses are available during the processing of a sentence like *The horse raced past the barn fell*. Why, then, is the alternative unavailable when it is needed, e.g., at the end of the sentence? Further, Blosfelds (1988) has been unable to replicate the experimental findings. Crain and Steedman (1985) also propose a system compatible with placing the semantics outside the syntactic system, but they do not show how it is consistent with the evidence for serial analysis.

2. One might think that (4a) differs from (4b) in that rejecting a direct-object analysis leads to a grammatical analysis in (4a) but not in (4b). This is not strictly true. Sentence (4b) could continue *Mary saw a picture of themselves bothered the old men*.

3. This direct comparison of theme-first and agent-first sentences is lexically confounded. Thus the more relevant measure is the interaction of ambiguity with the structurally preferred thematic assignment (theme-first sentences for nominalizations, agent-first sentences for clauses). If assignment proceeded immediately, e.g., upon encountering the specifier and noun, we would expect the difference between ambiguous and unambiguous forms to be greatest when an unpreferred structure was read. This predicts an interaction of ambiguity × (theme/agent) × (NP/S). No such interaction was observed.

4. Stowe (1989) argues that thematic analysis does proceed immediately as each argument is parsed. However, the evidence she presents could be explained simply by assuming that semantically confirmed decisions take longer to revise than semantically implausible or anomalous ones.

5. This predicts that the longer the interval needed to make an obligatory referential or predication assignment, say because the unique possible antecedent occurred far

back in the text, the greater the amount of world knowledge that can penetrate the language system.

References

Abney, S. 1988. A computational model of human parsing. Paper presented at the First Annual CUNY Conference on Human Sentence Processing.

Bever, T. G., Townsend, D., and Carruthers, C. 1986. The quasi-modularity of language. Paper presented at the Annual Meeting of Psychonomics Society, New Orleans.

Blosfeld, M. 1988. Parallel versus serial processing in the parsing of ambiguous sentences. Paper presented at the Sixth Australian Language and Speech Conference, Sydney, Australia.

Chomsky, N. 1965. *Aspects of the Theory of Syntax*. Cambridge: MIT Press.

Chomsky, N. 1981. *Lectures on Government and Binding: The Pisa Lectures*. Dordrecht: Foris.

Clifton, C., and Frazier, L. In preparation. Thematic constraints on adjunct interpretation.

Clifton, C., Seely, D., and Frazier, L. In preparation. Thematic role assignment in nominalizations.

Cowart, W. 1988. Notes on the biology of syntactic processing. Paper presented at the First Annual CUNY Conference on Human Sentence Processing.

Cowart, W., and Cairns, H. 1987. Evidence for an anaphoric mechanism within syntactic processing: Some reference relations defy semantic and pragmatic constraints. *Memory and Cognition* 15:318–331.

Crain, S., and Fodor, J. D. 1985. How can grammars help parsers? In D. R. Dowty, L. Karttunen, and A. Zwicky (eds.), *Natural Language Parsing: Psychological, Computational, and Theoretical Perspectives*. Cambridge: Cambridge University Press.

Crain, S., and Fodor, J. D. 1987. Sentence matching and overgeneration. *Cognition* 26:123–169.

Crain, S., and Steedman, M. 1985. On not being led up the garden-path: The use of context by the psychological parser. In D. R. Dowty, L. Karttunen, and A. Zwicky (eds.), *Natural Language Parsing: Psychological, Computational, and Theoretical Perspectives*. Cambridge: Cambridge University Press.

Cupples, L., and Holmes, V. M. 1987. Reading skill and interpretation of temporary structural ambiguity. *Language and Cognitive Processes* 2:179–204.

DeVincenzi, M. 1989. "Syntactic parsing strategies in a null subject language." Doctoral dissertation, University of Massachusetts.

Erhlich, K., and Rayner, K. 1983. Pronoun assignment and semantic integration during reading: Eye movements and immediacy of processing. *Journal of Verbal Learning and Verbal Behavior* 22:75–87.

Ferreira, F., Henderson, J. M. 1989. The use of verb information in syntactic parsing: A comparison of evidence from eye movements and segment-by-segment self-paced reading. Manuscript, University of Alberta.

Flores d'Arcais, G. B. 1987. Syntactic processing during reading comprehension. In M. Coltheart (ed.), *Attention and Performance*, vol. 12. Hillsdale, N.J.: Lawrence Erlbaum Associates.

Fodor, J. A. 1983. *Modularity of Mind*. Cambridge: MIT Press.

Fodor, J. D. 1988. On modularity in grammar. *Journal of Psycholinguistic Research* 17:125–168.

Ford, M., and Dalrymple, M. 1988. A note on some psychological evidence and alternative grammars. *Cognition* 29:63–72.

Forster, K. 1979. Levels of processing and the structure of the language processor. In W. E. Cooper and E. C. T. Walker (eds.), *Sentence Processing: Psycholinguistic Studies Presented to Merrill Garrett*. Hillsdale, N.J.: Erlbaum.

Forster, K. and Stevenson, B. J. 1987. Sentence matching and well-formedness. *Cognition* 26:171–186.

Frazier, L. 1978. *On Comprehending Sentences: Syntactic Parsing Strategies*. Doctoral dissertation, University of Connecticut.

Frazier, L. 1985. Modularity and the representational hypothesis. *Proceedings of NELS*, vol. 12. Amherst, Mass.: Graduate Linguistics Student Association.

Frazier, L. 1987. Sentence processing: A tutorial review. In M. Coltheart (ed.), *Attention and Performance*, vol. 12. Hillsdale, N.J.: Lawrence Erlbaum Associates.

Frazier, L. 1990. Parsing modifiers: Special purpose routines in the HSPM? In D. A. Balota, G. B. Flores d'Arcais, and K. Rayner (eds.), *Comprehension Processes in Reading*. Hillsdale, N.J.: Lawrence Erlbaum Associates.

Frazier, L., and Clifton, C. 1987. Thematic relations in parsing. In T. Daniel Seely (ed.), *University of Massachusetts Occasional Papers in Linguistics*. Vol. 9, *Special Issue on Psycholinguistics*. Amherst: Graduate Linguistics Student Association.

Frazier, L., Clifton, C., and Randall, J. 1983. Filling gaps: Decision principles and structure in sentence comprehension. *Cognition* 13:187–222.

Frazier, L., and Flores d'Arcais, G. B. In press. Filler-driven parsing: A study of gap filling in Dutch. *Journal of Memory and Language* 28:331–344.

Frazier, L., and Rayner, K. 1982. Making and correcting errors during sentence comprehension: Eye movements in the analysis of structurally ambiguous sentences. *Cognitive Psychology* 14:178–210.

Freedman, S., and Forster, K. 1985. The psychological status of overgenerated sentences. *Cognition* 19:101–132.

Gorrell, P. 1987. "Studies of Human Syntactic Processing: Ranked Parallel versus Serial Models." Doctoral dissertation, University of Connecticut.

Grice, P. 1968. Utterer's meaning vs. sentence-meaning. *Foundations of Language* 4:225–242.

Linebarger, M., Schwarz, M., and Saffran, E. 1983. Sensitivity to grammatical structure in so-called agrammatic aphasics. *Cognition* 13:361–392.

Marslen-Wilson, W., and Tyler, L. 1987. Against modularity. In J. L. Garfield (ed.), *Modularity in Knowledge Representation and Natural Language Understanding*. Cambridge: MIT Press.

Nicol, J. 1988. "Coreference processing during sentence comprehension." Doctoral dissertation, MIT.

Plunkett, B. In preparation. The parsing of anaphors and the Binding Theory. Manuscript, University of Massachusetts.

Pritchett, B. 1987. "Garden path phenomenon and the grammatical basis of language processing." Doctoral dissertation, Harvard University.

Rayner, K., Carlson, M., and Frazier, L. 1983. The interaction of syntax and semantics during sentence processing: Eye movements in the analysis of semantically biased sentences. *Journal of Verbal Learning and Verbal Behavior* 22:358–374.

Seidenberg, M. S., Tanenhaus, M. K., Leiman, J. M., Bienkowski, M. 1982. Automatic access of meanings of ambiguous words in context: Some limitations of knowledge-based processing. *Cognitive Psychology* 14:489–537.

Smith, C. 1988. Structural and other factors in parsing. Manuscript, University of Texas.

Stowe, L. 1989. Thematic structures and sentence comprehension. In M. Tanenhaus and G. Carlson (eds.), *Linguistic Structure in Language Processing*. Kluwer Academic Publishers.

Swinney, D. A. 1979. Lexical access during sentence comprehension: (Re)consideration of context effects. *Journal of Verbal Learning and Verbal Behavior* 18:645–660.

Taraban, R., and McClelland, J. L. 1988. Constituent attachment and thematic role assignment in sentence processing: Evidence for content-guided processing. *Journal of Memory and Language* 27:597–632.

Waters, G., Caplan, D., and Hildebrandt, N. 1987. Working memory and written sentence comprehension. In M. Coltheart (ed.), *Attention and Performance*, vol. 12. Hillsdale, N.J.: Lawrence Erlbaum Associates.

Williams, E. 1980. Predication. *Linguistic Inquiry* 11:203–238.

Williams, E. 1988. The anaphoric nature of theta roles. To appear in *Linguistic Inquiry*.

Chapter 20

Thematic Roles and Modularity: Comments on the Chapters by Frazier and Tanenhaus et al.	Janet Dean Fodor

1 Thematic Processing Solves a Problem

The chapters by Frazier and by Tanenhaus et al. have in common a very high score on the ideas-per-paragraph scale.[1] Both chapters bristle with new proposals for experiments, new data, and new suggestions for their interpretation. With respect to content, the chapters have in common an interest in thematic roles (agent, goal, instrument, etc.) in sentence processing. Frazier's chapter also addresses questions about modularity of the processor, a concern that is shared by almost everyone at the conference even though the modules we care most about may differ.

Since a full-dress review of both chapters is out of the question, I will concentrate on the topics of thematic roles and modularity and will show that there is a rather surprisingly close connection between them which constrains the sorts of models of sentence comprehension that we can develop. I will set out four widely accepted premises about sentence processing, and show that together they create a problem. One way (though there are others) to solve this problem is to posit a thematic processing module. Thus it is appropriate for experimental psycholinguistic research to be on the lookout for signs of this thematic processor at work.

The first premise of the argument is the credo of linguistically trained psycholinguists working on sentence processing: that the processor's source of information about the structures of the language is the mental (competence) grammer. This is a working assumption; it might, of course, turn out to be false, but since that would be unfortunate in all sorts of ways, we put that possibility aside as long as the data continue to permit us to.[2] Along with this basic assumption come several others, though they are not quite logical corollaries of it. For example, it is natural to assume that the modular structure of the grammar is largely reflected in the organization of the processing routines. In particular, we may assume that there is a syntactic processing module, which feeds into, but is not fed by, the semantic and pragmatic processing routines. This is just Chomsky's "autonomy of syntax" principle (1965, 1975) applied to performance and dressed in new terminology.

The second premise is empirical and has been widely (though not universally) accepted since Frazier's dissertation (1978). It is that syntactic analysis is serial, with back-up and revision if the processor's first hypothesis about the structure turns out later to have been wrong.[3] The standard evidence for this assumption is the existence of consistent preferences for one analysis rather than another of an ambiguous word string, and difficulty in the processing of a temporarily ambiguous string which requires the nonpreferred analysis. As just one example among many, the ambiguous string (1) is usually interpreted with *to Mary* as the goal associated with *is reading* rather than as a modifier of *the letter*.

(1) John is reading the letter to Mary.

And the second *to*-phrase in the unambiguous (2) is likely to cause trouble, since it forces the nonpreferred analysis of *to Mary*.

(2) John is reading the letter to Mary to Bill.

The third premise is also an empirical one: that semantic/pragmatic information can influence the processor's choice of a structural analysis. Defenders of the autonomy of syntax have long hoped to show that this is not so. But the arguments marshalled against it over the years have had to become more and more subtle, for at any gross level of observation, semantic/pragmatic influences on sentence comprehension are ubiquitous. One example from Crain 1980 concerns the interpretation of the pronoun *it* in a sentence such as (3).

(3) It frightened the child that John wanted to visit the lab.

With no preceding context, the *it* is usually interpreted as expletive, a mere placeholder for the extraposed *that*-complement clause at the end of the sentence. But there is an alternative interpretation with the *it* as referential and the *that*-clause as a relative clause modifying *the child*. This latter interpretation is strongly encouraged if the prior context contains a possible referent for the *it*, as in (4).

(4) There was an explosion.
    It frightened the child that John wanted to visit the lab.

I will return shortly to questions about the proper interpretation of effects of context such as this.

The fourth and last premise is also empirical but has the status of a widely held hunch, since it has never (to the best of my knowledge) been empirically tested.[4] It is that semantic/pragmatic preferences in processing are comparative, not absolute. That is, the semantic/pragmatic processor does not accept all analyses of a word string that are above some threshold of plausibility and reject all analyses below that threshold; rather, it selects the most plausible of the bunch, which might or might not itself be very plausible.

This kind of comparison is what is generally assumed to be going on, for example, in the sentences in (5), from Rayner, Carlson, and Frazier 1983, adaped from Crain and Coker 1978.

(5) a. The florist sent the flowers was very pleased.
    b. The performer sent the flowers was very pleased.

Subjects in the Rayner et al. experiment correctly paraphrased sentences like (5a) less often than sentences like (5b). What is the relevant difference between (5a) and (5b)? For both sentences the correct analysis of the first five words is as a noun phrase containing a reduced relative clause, but both strings also lend themselves to a misanalysis in which the first two words are the subject noun phrase and the next three words are the verb phrase of the main clause. The sentences were constructed with the intention that for (5b) the correct relative clause analysis is more plausible than the incorrect main clause analysis (assuming that performers are more likely to receive flowers than to send them), while for (5a) this difference is less strong or reversed (since florists are at least at likely to send flowers as to receive them).

The fact that subjects found (5a) more difficult than (5b) might seem to establish the truth of the fourth premise, that comparative plausibility is what matters. But this result does not quite suffice. It would do so only if certain alternative explanations could be excluded, for example that the main clause analysis of (5b) is rejected because it falls below some absolute plausibility threshold, or that the relative-clause analysis of (5a) is rejected because it falls below threshold. These possibilities probably *can* be excluded for the materials used by Rayner et al. But the strongest test of the comparison hypothesis would be to show that the less plausible (relative clause) analysis of (5a), which subjects reject, is just as plausible as the more plausible (relative clause) analysis of (5b), which subjects accept. Then it would be clear that there is no absolute standard that the semantic/pragmatic processor applies. It is more doubtful that this latter condition is satisfied by the materials used by Rayner et al. (i.e. for (5): that florists and performers are equally likely to be sent flowers, though they are not equally likely to send them). In any case, this has not been established. Let me summarize the four premises:

Premise 1. There is an encapsulated syntactic processing module.

Premise 2. Syntactic processing is serial (with back-up where necessary).

Premise 3. There are semantic/pragmatic influences on the choice of analysis.

Premise 4. Semantic/pragmatic choices are comparative, not absolute.

These four premises are mutually inconsistent. The problem is that if the syntactic processor makes its decisions before the semantic/pragmatic processor, then once the syntactic processor has made its selection among possible analyses, there is no room left for the semantic/pragmatic processor to make its choice. All it can do is pass on, or reject, the syntactic choice; it cannot compare the alternatives and decide which of them it considers better. This situation is sketched informally in figure 1.

At least one of the four premises has to go. There are two different opinions (perhaps more) to be found in the literature as to which one should be sacrificed. The first approach I will consider gives up premise 2. If we assert, after all, that alternative syntactic analyses are pursued in parallel, then the semantic/pragmatic processor will be able to consider them all (figure 2). Parallelism of syntactic processing has recently been argued for by Crain and Steedman (1985), Kurtzman (1985), Gorrell (1987), Chodorow and Slutsky (1986), and Altmann and Steedman (1988). Parallel processing has the disadvantage that, since ambiguities can multiply exponentially, computation of all possible analyses can be very costly of resources, but several means have been suggested for limiting this proliferation. Also, a parallel model must, of course, offer some account

Figure 1
Serial syntactic processing

Figure 2
Parallel syntactic processing

of the original data which suggested serial processing. Asymmetric preferences between analyses, as in (1), could be attributed to a ranking of "expectedness" for the alternatives, rather than to the selection of one and garden-pathing on the others. Kurtzman has suggested a conceptual basis for such a ranking. More in keeping with autonomy of syntactic processing, Gorrell has proposed syntactic criteria for ranking analyses, in fact the very same criteria as are assumed by many serial models (e.g., Minimal Attachment). Though I incline toward this parallel syntax solution of the problem, I will not discuss it further here.

A different solution is to give up premise 1, or at least the corollary that makes syntactic analysis precede semantic/pragmatic analysis. If the semantic/pragmatic processor operated in parallel with the syntactic processor, the problem of syntax preempting the semantic/pragmatic processor's right to choose would be solved: each processor could freely choose whichever analysis it thought the best, and then they could compare notes afterward on an equal footing (figure 3). This is what Rayner et al. (1983) proposed to account for their findings on pragmatic preferences. These perferences were observed only in end-of-sentence judgements. On-line tasks showed syntax-based preferences and no effect of semantic/pragmatics. For instance, for sentences like (5a, b), eye movements indicated garden paths of equal severity in the reading of both sentences, though the paraphrase task favored the sentences like (5b) in which plausibility considerations concur with syntactic considerations. Rayner et al. suggest that there is a semantic/pragmatic processor which does not wait for the syntactic processor but operates in parallel with it, selecting the most plausible integration of the predicates and arguments in the sentence. If its selection turns out to be the same as that of the syntactic processor, all is well; if they disagree, some process of resolution must be initiated, such as a search for some other syntactic analysis that does agree with semantics/

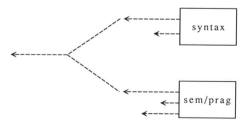

Figure 3
Syntax and semantics in parallel

pragmatics. (The exact nature of this resolution process turns out to be crucial with respect to encapsulation; I discuss it in section 3 below.)

Thus there is parallelism in the model, just as in the previous solution, but now the parallelism is between syntax and semantics/pragmatics, and within semantics/pragmatics, rather than within syntax. The problem with this second solution is that it appears to entail that semantic/pragmatic analysis must proceed without benefit of any input from syntax, which would be a reversion to the kind of unconstrained, grammar-free semantic/pragmatic processing that we took exception to at the outset. Admittedly this crudeness could now be isolated in the processor that runs in parallel with syntax and whose job is to make plausibility judgments. There would *also* be a semantic/pragmatic processor that would be properly in touch with the grammar and whose job would be to interpret the output of the syntactic parse; this would account for the precision of human sentence comprehension. But even so, how could the first of these two gadgets do its job without any syntax to guide it? The answer is that it is not necessary that *all* of the semantic/pragmatic analysis of a sentence be done in parallel with the syntactic analysis. Rather, the currently available data can be accounted for on the assumption that just the thematic roles of noun phrases are established in parallel with syntactic analysis.

Thus we arrive at the hypothesis that there is a thematic processing module whose functioning is independent of the syntactic module, except perhaps for a rough syntactic parse of the sentence into noun phrases and predicates, and whose job is to communicate to the syntactic processor which way of combining the predicates and arguments in the sentence would make most sense even if that is not in fact how they are combined. Just how rough the syntactic parse could be and still provide the thematic processor with what it needs to know is not clear. It is arguable that a complete and accurate identification of the predicate and its arguments in each clause of a sentence would call for something close to a total parse. And if this were necessary, the model would approach one in which both syntax and semantics/pragmatics compute all analyses and rank them, which would be quite similar to Gorrell's model (figure 4). To decide such

Figure 4
Ranked parallel syntactic processing

questions would require subtle experiments to provide estimates of the thematic processor's sensitivity to minor details of syntactic structure. But if we are prepared to accept for now that the thematic processor can cut syntactic corners, then the postulation of this thematic module will resolve the conflict between our other premises. It allows the overall processing system to steer safely between Scylla and Charybdis, between the twin monsters of syntactic parallelism and syntax-free semantic processing.[5] Thus any theory that regards syntactic parallelism as a monster should be strongly inclined to accept the existence of a thematic processor even prior to its being established experimentally. The motivation to go out and look for it in experiments is strong.

There are differences of detail between Frazier and Tanenhaus concerning just how thematic roles fit into the larger processing model, but the general convergence is nevertheless quite striking. This new interest in thematic role structure in processing may have been stimulated by developments in linguistic theory over the last few years. Beginning with Stowell's (1981) dissertation, there have been attempts to dispense with phrase structure rules for characterizing deep syntactic structures and to substitute general principles of grammar that would jointly and indirectly entail the structural facts. Case theory will do some of this work, but Stowell also called on theta theory to guarantee the presence of arguments to predicates, to trigger movement, and so forth. Previously, thematic roles (or their close equivalents) had been invoked in the syntactic component only by theories that were rejected by mainstream transformational linguistics (e.g., Gruber 1965, Fillmore 1968).[6] As we begin to find out just how much contribution thematic roles can make in the formal grammar, it is natural to want to investigate how much contribution they might be making in the application of grammatical knowledge in sentence processing.

My discussion will now bifurcate. In the next section I will comment on Tanenhaus, Garnsey, and Boland's proposal (more clearly articulated in Tanenhaus and Carlson 1989) to reformulate certain earlier hypotheses about processing so that they refer to thematic roles rather than to syntactic constituents. In the final section I will discuss Frazier's proposal about the relationships between language modules. As we have seen, the postulation of a thematic processor can help to defend the syntax module against being swallowed up into a more inclusive nonmodular semantic/pragmatic system. But as long as the syntactic and semantic/pragmatic processors need to talk to each other, worries about modularity still remain.

2   Tanenhaus et al. on Gap-Filling

The characterization of the thematic processor that I gave above, since it is quite sketchy, will cover both Frazier's model and that of Tanenhaus et al. But Tanenhaus et al. appear to be more inclined to give the thematic processor its head and let it make predictions that the syntax then follows up on. The thematic processor is neither the servant of the syntactic processor nor its equal partner but in some cases at least can be the leader.

The sort of evidence that Tanenhaus et al. offer for this has to do with contrasts such as between (6a) and (6b).

(6) a. Bill donated some money.
     b. Bill donated some money to the library.

In isolation, (6b) is more natural than (6a), which suggests that *donate* sets up an expectation of a goal phrase as well as a theme phrase. Tanenhaus et al. argue that this expectation is framed in terms of thematic roles, rather than in terms of syntactic constituents, because the preference is reversed if the sentence is preceded by a sentence that supplies a suitable goal for *donate*, as in (7).

(7) The library had its budget slashed.
     Bill donated some money (to the library).

The phenomenon is intuitively quite robust and is interesting. However, a look at further examples indicates that this is not a case of pure thematic prediction. The processor presumably does *not* expect deletion of a phrase, however redundant in context, if it is syntactically obligatory, as in (8).

(8) The table looked very bare.
     *Bill put the vase of flowers.

If so, thematic roles are not the *only* thing governing expectations; syntactic subcategorization is at least as important. The fact that the goal of *donate* can be omitted if identified by the context is a lexical/syntactic fact about *donate*; the fact that the goal (or location) for *put* cannot be omitted even if identified by the context is a lexical/syntactic fact about *put*.[7] More experimental evidence is needed here, but it does look as if the thematic processor probably restricts itself to analyses approved by the syntactic processor. And that indicates that it is acting *not* as leader but as equal partner at most and possibly only as camp follower.

Much of the chapter by Tanenhaus et al. is concerned with the possible role of the thematic processor in the computations by which "gaps" and "fillers" are associated in sentences where constituents have been deleted or moved away from their underlying positions. Previous work on this topic over the last several years has generally portrayed the processes of gap finding and filling as syntactic. It would be said, for instance, that in (9) there is a filler in the subordinate clause because there are two noun phrases before the verb instead of the usual one, and that there is a gap between *about* and *in* because the preposition *about* must have an NP object and there is no NP after it in the word string.

(9) I wonder who Betty wrote about in her diary.

Even lexical influences on gap finding have generally been construed as structural. For example, whether or not the processor will assume that a position following a verb is a gap depends on what the verb is. It is much more likely to hypothesize a gap after a transitive verb such as *make* than after an intransitive verb like *fall*. And for verbs that can be either—such as *race*, *read*, or *fail*—the processor's hypothesis will be sensitive to whether the verb occurs more commonly as a transitive or as an intransitive. (See Clifton, Frazier, and Connine 1984, Tanenhaus, Stowe, and Carlson 1985.) The transitive/intransitive distinction here is taken to be a matter of syntactic subcategorization, i.e., a lexically specified fact about the syntactic categories of the constituents that can appear as sisters to the verb in a syntactic phrase marker.

But Tanenhaus et al. are taking a fresh look at filler-gap processing, in light of their general claim that thematic roles are computed on-line, generate expectations, can facilitate or inhibit processing, and so forth. Their suggestion is that the hunt for a gap is defined not primarily in terms of syntactic categories but in terms of a suitable thematic role for the filler phrase. Once this has been identified, the thematic processor encourages the syntactic processor to adopt an analysis consistent with it. Once again, the thematic processor is portrayed as the leader. And once again, the empirical motivation for substituting this model for the syntactically driven model is not compelling. In fact it is difficult in this case to get them to generate distinct predictions.

For example, Tanenhaus and Carlson (1989) offer two different accounts, one syntactic (pp. 535–536) and one thematic (p. 551), of the central finding of Tanenhaus, Stowe, and Carlson (1985). What the latter group found is that subjects detect an anomaly in (incomplete) word strings such as (10) but not in those like (11).

(10) The teacher didn't know which song the student read . . .

(11) The sheriff wasn't sure which rock the cowboy raced . . .

The anomaly in (10) presumably results from association of the filler with a gap immediately following the verb.[8] So a postverbal gap is apparently being identified in (10) but not in (11). What is the relevant difference between (10) and (11)? The syntactic account says that perceivers tend to take *read* as a transitive verb, while they tend to assume that *raced* is intransitive. The consequence is that for most perceivers there is "room" for a noun phrase gap after *read* but not after *raced*. The thematic account says that perceivers tend to construe *raced* as a verb that has only a theme role to assign. Since it will necessarily assign that one role to its subject, there is no way in which *raced* could assign a thematic role to the filler. But *read* is likely to be construed as assigning both an agent role and a theme role, and though the subject absorbs the agent role, the theme role is still available to be assigned to the filler.

I have spelled out these competing accounts in some detail just in case there is lurking within them some hint of a difference in their explanatory potential, but if there is, I have not been able to see it. The same is true of the more recent findings of Tanenhaus, Boland, Garnsey, and Carlson (1989), which demonstrate an even more interesting sensitivity of the gap identification routines. This study compared responses to word strings such as (12) and (13).

(12) Which fabric did the lawyer visit ...

(13) Which movie did your brother remind ...

Subjects detected an anomaly in (12) but not in (13). Both *visit* and *remind* are normally taken to be transitive, so this is not the relevant difference between (12) and (13). Rather, what matters seems to be that *remind* takes a complement clause in addition to an object NP, while *visit* takes only the object NP and no clause.[9] A syntactic account of (13) would note that a clause can be a rich source of possible noun phrase positions, any one of which might harbor a gap, so there is no urgency for the processor to associate the filler with the gap after *remind*, given that it knows that a clause is likely to follow. A thematic account of (13), which is what Tanenhaus et al. offer, would say that a clause is a rich source of thematic roles, so there is no urgency for the processor to assign the filler the experiencer role for *remind*. There seems remarkably little to choose between these accounts.[10]

What would it take to prove the thematic account right and the syntactic account wrong, or vice versa? The only attempt I know of in the literature to adjudicate between these two approaches is in Fodor 1979, where dative questions are used as evidence in favor of "position assignment" (syntactic) strategies for gap finding, as opposed to "role assignment" (thematic) strategies. An informal experiment will elicit the relevant property of dative questions. Suppose you are requested to answer a series of questions, as quickly as possible, with complete sentence answers; the content of the answers may be anything you wish. Asked, *What did you order for breakfast?* you might respond, *I ordered calamari for breakfast.* Asked, *Who did Betty speak to on the beach?* you might answer, *Betty spoke to Bernard on the beach.* Asked, *Who did they bring Mary?* you might answer, *They brought Mary Samantha.* Few people answer, *They brought Samantha Mary,* though in principle this should be an equally acceptable answer.[11] Let us now consider how this fact supports the syntactic processing routine.

A dative question has two noun phrases in a row, one of which has been fronted, leaving a trace. The point of interest is which of the two noun phrases is perceived as having been fronted. The question *Who did they bring Mary?* could be assigned structure (14) or structure (15).

(14) Who$_i$ did they bring trace$_i$ Mary?

(15) Who$_i$ did they bring Mary trace$_i$?

The way the question is usually answered indicates that analysis (15) is preferred. This might just be a completely isolated fact about the grammar of English, but there are indications in other constructions and in other languages of a general preference for taking the constituent *in situ* to be the first of the pair. And this is plausibly attributed to a parsing strategy called Try the Next Constituent, or TTNC, by Fodor (1978). This strategy tells the parser not to create a trace until it has checked the input word string for the phrase it is looking for; if suitable words are there, postulating a trace is unnecessary.[12] In a construction with two like constituents in a row, such as a dative question, the result of this strategy will be the preference we have observed, with the trace following the overt constituent. But this decision strategy only makes sense for a parsing routine that is looking for the *position* of the gap. A thematically-based gap-finding routine, by contrast, would have considered the thematic roles associated with *bring* and would have picked the most plausible role for the filler *who*. Since *who* is animate, the more plausible role for it would be the goal (indirect object) rather than the theme (direct object); animate entities probably have things brought to them more often than they are brought to other people. So a thematically-based routine would favor analysis (14), in which the trace associated with *who* is the indirect object.[13] A syntactic routine, which seeks likely positions for gaps, is thus more explanatory than a thematic routine, which seeks likely roles for fillers.

Which model is right is almost less important than the possibility of deciding between them on empirical grounds. Unfortunately, only the special property of dative questions (the sequence of two adjacent NPs, both in principle extractable) permits the two models to be distinguished; we cannot apply excatly the same form of argument to the materials of Tanenhaus et al. The best I can suggest is to find out whether the critical difference between the *remind* constructions and the *visit* constructions is the difference between a verb's taking arguments and its taking only adjuncts. If it is, that is something the thematic approach could explain particularly well, since only arguments, not adjuncts, have thematic roles and would be predictable by the thematic processor. The relevant experiment would contrast potential gap positions following verbs that take additional arguments (e.g., the verb *fill*, which can take a *with*-NP argument after the object NP), with potential gaps following verbs that take no additional arguments (e.g., *destroy*, where everything after the object NP is an adjunct by the criteria of Carlson and Tanenhaus 1988).[14] For both of these verb types, a syntactic gap-finding routine should be able to reason that a later gap could occur, so that it need not grab a gap in direct object position. But the thematic processor could reason along these lines only about later gaps in argument positions.

Even if such a contrast were found, it would not be a definitive result for a number of reasons. First, although arguments are sometimes optional, adjuncts are (almost) always optional, so there is a difference in their predictability that would be sufficient to explain the parser's reacting differently in the two cases. Second, though extraction from adjuncts occurs, it is generally less acceptable than extraction from arguments. So even if their existence were equally predictable, they would not offer equal gap opportunities, and this would be sufficient to account for a parsing difference. Of course, this very difference in extractability might be construed as stemming from a processing asymmetry between adjuncts and arguments, and hence as evidence for the thematic processor, but this is one of those chicken-and-egg situations that are difficult to resolve.

In short, we don't really know at present how to decide between the two explanations of the *visit/remind* results. So far, then, we have little positive reason to make the switch from syntactic to thematic explanation that Tanenhaus et al. recommend.

One final, methodological comment on the chapter by Tanenhaus et al. The semantic/pragmatic anomaly detection task that he and his colleagues are currently using is excellent in several respects: it is rapid and natural for subjects, and yet it also provides word by word information. (Response times are reported to average around 350 msec, which is much less than is characteristic of other continuous tasks, such as lexical decision or syntactic decision or even self-paced word-by-word reading with a different secondary task (see Ford 1983; Crain and Fodor 1985; Stowe 1983; Holmes, Stowe, and Cupples, in press; Chodorow and Slutsky 1986). But the anomaly detection task does, of course, force subjects to engage in semantic/pragmatic processing before responding. It is inherently biased, therefore, toward picking up any semantic/pragmatic influences there may be on processing. And it might conceivably encourage the use of semantic/ pragmatic information even though this information is not used, or is not used so rapidly, or is not used in the same way, in normal sentence processing. The one thing this task cannot be expected to be good at is titrating out any purely syntactic processing phenomena that may precede semantic processing. Thus this method is excellent for revealing semantic/pragmatic influences that might otherwise have gone undetected, but it is quite unsuited to revealing whether semantic/pragmatic influences take precedence over syntactic analysis and guide it, or whether they are secondary to syntactic analysis and merely approve or disapprove what the syntax proposes. To clarify this crucially important aspect of human sentence processing, we will need to devise some more selective experimental paradigm which will tap "pure" syntactic processing—assuming it is there to be tapped.[15]

3 Frazier on Module Geography

Frazier has used the conclusion that there must be a thematic-role processor distinct from the syntax processor as the basis for a novel proposal about module definition and organization. Some standard configurations for complexes of modules are sketched in figure 5.[16] In line with J. A. Fodor's (1983) characterization of modules, there is a minimum of cross-communication between these modules. They are informationally encapsulated; in particular, none of them receives input from the central processor, which houses nonlinguistic, encyclopedic world knowledge. In Frazier's model, by contrast, there are two-way communication channels between some of the modules, and as we track them through, we find that they make information from central processes available to all modules (figure 6).[17] Thus Frazier gives up encapsulation as a criterion for modules (though she does make a terminological distinction between modules which are encapsulated and those which are not; only the former are termed *input* modules). Since this represents a considerable weakening of the concept

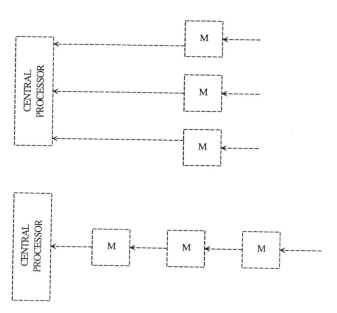

Figure 5
Two modular configurations

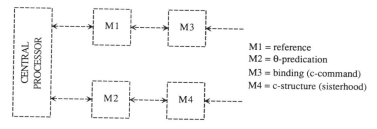

M1 = reference
M2 = θ-predication
M3 = binding (c-command)
M4 = c-structure (sisterhood)

Figure 6
Frazier's model

of modular structure in the mind/brain, we should seek strong evidence in favor of it before adopting it.

In principle, two kinds of evidence are necessary. First, it must be shown that the proposed processing units are indeed distinct, and then it must be shown that they intercommunicate. (Note that the latter is of no interest in the absence of the former; it would not be a fair test of the modularity thesis to first subdivide the putative modules too finely and then point to interactions between them.) Frazier has attempted to provide evidence of both kinds, but as yet it is far from abundant.

The evidence offered for distinctness is that the various subprocessors exhibit different profiles with respect to their operating characteristics. For instance, the syntactic and thematic processors are claimed to be distinguishable on the grounds that the syntactic processor makes its decisions immediately, makes them serially, and uses only grammatical information in doing so, while the thematic processor delays its decisions, makes them in parallel, and consults extragrammatical real world information in doing so. These contrasts may eventually be confirmed, but at present they must be considered extremely tentative.

I have noted already in section 1 the existence of recent empirical arguments for parallelism of syntactic processing, which, if correct, would obliterate the first contrast. The second contrast (immediate/delayed decisions) appears to be based largely on experiment 1 of Frazier's chapter (conducted by Clifton and Frazier), which is supposed to demonstrate that thematic role assignment in a phrase such as (16) is delayed until all the noun phrases associated with the head have been encountered (i.e., to show that the whole thematic grid associated with the head is assigned at once).

(16) the city's excavation of its historic buildings

But I believe that the results of experiment 1 are open to a contrary interpretation.

Frazier observes that the phrase (17) favors a reading with *the city* as theme rather than as agent.

(17) the city's excavation

This contrasts with (16), where the city is agent. She argues that if the assignment appropriate to (17) were made on-line during the processing of (16), a garden path should occur in (16), and hence (16) should be difficult to process. In particular, (16) should be more difficult to process than (18), for which no garden path is predicted since its analysis agrees with (17).

(18) the city's excavation by the archeologists

In fact the data show that (16) is easier to process than (18). And Frazier takes this to show that the thematic processor does *not* make an early decision with a consequent garden path.

However, we may wonder that happens at an even earlier stage of processing these phrases. There is a general tendency for external arguments (subjects) to be interpreted as agents (see Bever 1970 and many discussions since, though these discussions typically refer to clauses rather than to derived nominals). So a processor which made *early* thematic role assignments would be expected to guess first that *the city* is agent, just as it in fact is in many examples (e.g., *the city's announcement, proclamation, demands, activities, attempt,* etc.).[18] When the processor then encountered the head noun *excavation,* there would be nothing to contradict this initial interpretation of *the city* as agent, and by the Revision-as-Last-Resort principle (Fodor and Frazier 1980) this initial assignment should therefore be retained. Hence (16) should be easy. It is true that if the noun phrase were to terminate after *excavation,* as in (17), that *would* constitute counterevidence (though nondecisive) against the agent hypothesis, which would then need to be revised. But since (16) *doesn't* end there, there is no reason why the hypothesis should change.[19] By contrast, in (18) the processor's initial hypothesis would eventually *have* to change, so (18) should be more difficult to process. Thus the greater difficulty of (18) over (16) that Clifton and Frazier observed is predicted without assuming that thematic role assignment is delayed. Hence the second difference that Frazier proposes between the syntactic processor and the thematic processor is also uncertain.[20]

The third proposed difference concerns knowledge sources, and this is where I think Frazier's model is likely to distress those who believe in a module for language encapsulated from general cognition. (A terminological note: The issue concerns little modules within a larger module covering all of language. To keep these distinguished in what follows, I will refer to the little modules as submodules.) The claim that there is a distinct submodule (M2 in figure 6) for processing thematic roles is by itself no threat to the modularity thesis for language as a whole. Nor is it problematic in principle that this submodule is claimed to process thematic roles without regard to relevant linguistic properties of the word string, and on the basis of real-world plausibility. Note, however, that this last claim clearly puts M2 outside the language module, as characterized by J. A. Fodor (1983) and others.

There is still no danger in this as long as M2 outside the language module does not influence the activities of submodules within the language module. In the parallel syntax model (figure 2), it doesn't, and so all is well. But in Frazier's model it does. In the parallel syntax model, thematic processing merely screens the output of the syntactic processor. But in Frazier's model, as far as I can tell, the thematic processor actually makes suggestions to the syntactic processor (to M4, and perhaps also to M3 though figure 6 doesn't show it). It says things like "Could you please try to find a syntactic analysis that would make the performer the recipient rather than the sender of the flowers?"

Deciding just how much interaction between putative modules is or is not consistent with the modularity thesis is a difficult business, and often bears a strong resemblance to hair splitting. But I suspect that this is one hair that cannot be split. This kind of semantic/pragmatic stage whispering to the syntax goes too far for modularity. It is a case of what Crain and Steedman (1985) call "strong interaction" as opposed to the "weak interaction" of systems in which semantics/pragmatics merely evaluates what syntax sends to it.

Thus Frazier takes a clear stand here (clearer, for example, than in Rayner, Carlson, and Frazier 1983) against modularity as it is standardly conceived. While modularists devote effort to reconciling encapsulation with empirical results that often give the appearance of strong interaction, Frazier's goal now is to reconcile nonencapsulation with the empirical results that suggest only weak interaction. Her way of imposing order on the morass of data is to assume (I think) that the syntactic processor always makes one pass through the input uninfluenced by thematic processing and world knowledge. Only after it has formed its opinion does it have to listen to the thematic processor's instructions telling it to try to fix its analysis so that (for instance) the subject NP is the recipient not the agent. That is, she assumes no interaction during the initial parse, but strong interaction during reanalysis.

I would point out that once strong interaction has been limited to second-pass processing in this way, only a very slight modification of the model is required to eliminate it altogether. All that is needed is that the thematic processor decides what pattern of thematic role assignments would be most plausible, but does not communicate its decision to the syntactic processor; it would communicate nothing if it agreed with the outcome of the syntactic analysis, and if it disagreed, it would communicate only the generic instruction that the syntactic processor should look for a different analysis. This reticence makes the thematic processor appear rather coy, but it would work as long as the number of alternative analyses was small; it would lead to the same outcome as if the syntax were told specifically what to look for, and it would not require much extra labor. Yet this model preserves the idea that the feedback channel from semantics/pragmatics to syntax is limited to carrying messages of approval or disapproval only.

Frazier does not attempt to placate modularists by this sort of technical adjustment to the model. The reason seems to be that limiting the interactions between the thematic and the syntactic processors contributes to modularity for the language faculty as a whole *only* if the thematic processor is relegated to the great disorderly mass of nonmodular central processing. And this Frazier does not accept. She believes the thematic processor knows too much grammar for that to be plausible. In short, the thematic processor can no more be excluded from the big language module than it can be fully included within it; it functions as an interface between linguistic and nonlinguistic knowledge.

This frontier status of the thematic processor, also advocated by Tanenhaus (see Tanenhaus and Carlson 1989), will obviously be a focus of future thinking in this area, and deservedly so. I don't know what the outcome of the debate will be; I am merely drawing attention to what is at stake. The thematic processor as characterized in these chapters dissolves the boundary between language and world knowledge. Frazier at one point seems to imply that this doesn't make a *very* big dent in the modularity thesis, because in practice the thematic module won't have time to consult a great deal of real-world information before it has to deliver its decisions. But what is relevant to issues of mental architecture is the existence of accessibility channels, not how often information actually flows through them.[21]

Notes

1. These comments do not align as well as they might with the chapters they comment on. They were written several months before receipt of the chapter by Tanenhaus, Garnsey, and Boland. The discussion of Tanenhaus's work was prepared on the basis of an earlier and different paper (Tanenhaus and Carlson 1989). The discussion of Frazier's proposals was based on an early draft of her chapter.

2. For purportedly grammar-free sentence processing, see Riesbeck and Schank 1978. For a model in which grammatical information is merely implicit in the perception and production algorithms, see Marslen-Wilson and Tyler 1987.

3. For reference to parallel processing models, see below. For a serial model without back-up, see Marcus 1980.

4. Devising appropriate materials to test this premise is difficult (see text, p. 436). Kurtzman (1985) touches on closely related points, but his experiments do not address the issue directly.

5. Ulysses encountered his two "monsters" (actually a rock and a whirlpool respectively) off the coast not all that far from Sperlonga.

6. The term *theta* role is used in Government Binding theory without commitment as to whether these roles, which do work in the syntax, are to be identified with traditional, semantically characterized thematic roles. They are often assigned the same names (*agent, goal,* etc.), but in most syntactic analyses the qualitative differences between roles are of no import; what matters is merely whether a noun phrase has or does not have a theta role. For example, it is argued that in a passive sentence a noun phrase has to move from deep object position to surface subject position because in deep object position it is assigned a theta role but no case, and in surface subject position it is assigned case but no theta role; but it is a matter of indifference to this explanation whether the theta role assigned is, for example, theme (*John was kicked*), goal (*John was sent flowers*), or experiencer (*John was angered by it*). However, role identity does matter to some phenomena that Government Binding theory would treat as syntactic. For example, in constructions like *John lent Mary a book to read* and *John borrowed from Mary a book to read*, what controls the empty subject position in the subordinate clause is not consistently either the subject or the object of the main clause, but the goal. For discussion of theta roles and further references, see Jackendoff 1987 and Rappaport and Levin 1988.

7. Lexically governed sensitivity to context is not uncommon. For example, the verb *read* can appear freely without an overt direct object (*Jane was reading*), the verb *make* never appears without an overt object (**Jane was making*), but the verb *notice* can occur without an overt object just in case its understood object has been identified by the context (*The lights changed. Jane didn't notice*).

8. The experiment also included control sentences that had a plausible filler for a gap in this position.

9. One of the examples classified as of the *visit* type and used, somewhat unfortunately, to exemplify the whole class is *Which food did the child read* .... Note that *read* can be followed by a complement clause, as in *Which food did the child read that doctors disapprove of?* It is true that *read* doesn't take both an object NP and a complement clause at the same time, but at the relevant position in the word string (after *read*) a subject could not know whether an object NP or a clause follows. Fortunately, most of the other examples tested were like *visit* rather than *read*, and so do not raise this complication.

10. Tanenhaus, Boland, Garnsey, and Carlson 1989 note that there is no increase in response time in the anomaly judgement task at the *remind* position in (13), which suggests that the filler is not even temporarily associated with a post-*remind* gap, as it would be if that gap were selected on a purely syntactic basis and then checked for plausibility. But the fact is that we don't know what causes perceivers to exhibit a "boggle" reaction of the kind that would elevate response times. It seems quite possible that merely deciding *whether* "which movie" would be a good

object for "remind" would not cause boggle; plausibly, boggle occurs only when the processor thinks it *has* to accept the anomalous analysis because there is no other. If so, the response time data are completely compatible with a syntactic gap-finding routine.

11. Few people other than New Yorkers (see Langendoen, Kalish-Landon, and Dore 1974).

12. TTNC was proposed to account for intuitive data. It is not confirmed, however, by recent experimental results (e.g., Crain and Fodor 1985; Stowe 1983; Garnsey, Tanenhaus, and Chapman 1989). Perhaps TTNC is wrong, or perhaps, as I suspect, the experimental paradigms that are being used are encouraging subjects to perceive every initial sentence fragment as a whole sentence if possible. (In these paradigms, presentation is slow or at least discontinuous, and a judgement is required before the next word is made available.) This would cause a fragment like *Which fabric did he visit . . .* to be analysed with a gap after *visit*. Stowe (1984) shows how this could account for the subject/object asymmetries in her data. Tanenhaus, Boland, Garnsey, and Carlson's (1989) finding for *remind*-type verbs is the only exception to this pattern, as far as I know, so it is important to find out what the right explanation is.

13. Tanenhaus et al. assume that the thematic processor contemplates suitable thematic roles for a filler only when the verb has been received. At that point in (14)/(15), the only NP so far encountered is the filler *who*, as noted in the argument above. But it might be objected that immediately after the verb is *Mary*, and that the thematic processor might take both noun phrases into account. Instead of trying to decide whether *who* is better as goal or as theme, it would try to decide which is the best way of pairing up *who* and *Mary* with goal and theme. However, since both noun phrases are animate, the processor presumably couldn't choose between them, so this still won't explain the finding that *who* is preferred as theme.

14. It might be possible to sort the *visit*-type verbs of the present experiment into these two kinds to get a preliminary indication of whether this is a relevant factor.

15. A number of studies have isolated syntactic expectations in processing by using syntactically well-formed but semantically/pragmatically anomalous materials (see, for example, Wright and Garrett 1984). The measurement of eye movements in reading gives results which suggest that it separates syntactic from semantic/ pragmatic processes (Rayner et al. 1983, Ferreira and Clifton 1986). This may be because syntactic processing occurs earlier, or, if the two are occurring in parallel, it might be because eye movements are sensitive only to syntactic operations.

16. The first model in figure 5 would be natural for different input modalities such as hearing, touch and vision. The second one is typical of how levels of linguistic processing such as phonetics, phonology, and syntax are often viewed. But these are just for-instances; I don't promise that either is actually correct.

17. This picture of the arrangement of modules is drawn from Frazier's chapter. The arrows I have inserted reflect comments in the early draft of her chapter. The published version suggests that there should be more arrows, that every module has direct access to all the others. One point that is relevant to the discussion in section 1 above but is not brought out in the diagram is that thematic roles would

be assigned at two places in the system. They are assigned on the basis of plausibility and a minimal syntactic analysis by module M2, which is what I have been calling (following Rayner, Carlson, and Frazier 1983) the thematic processor. But roles would also have to be assigned, by some other unit not represented here, on the basis of a full syntactic analysis and without regard for plausibility, as part of the final semantic interpretation of the sentence.

18. It may also be relevant that the possessive form *the city's* in this experiment is temporarily misconstruable as a reduction of *the city is*, which probably also favors *the city* as agent.

19. The whole noun phrase was presented simultaneously, so the parser would not even temporarily think that the phrase in (16) had ended at *excavation*.

20. The search for different operating characteristics of different subprocessors is also reported on in Frazier 1986. A lot of interesting data are presented, but they tend to derive from very various experiments, which differ in method as well as materials, so that it is difficult to be sure whether the different outcomes do reflect real differences between processors.

21. The situation would be very different if it could be shown that there is a qualitative rather than a quantitative limit on what information about the world can be tapped. In particular, the modularity thesis would be safe if linguistic processing were sensitive to only a specific subset of world knowledge that could be regarded as having been grammaticized or lexicalized. I don't think this is completely out of the question in the case of the thematic processor. Conceivably, the plausibility effects that interact with lexical processing are all based on listings in the lexicon of stereotypical agents, themes, instruments, etc., associated with each verb. The stereotypical agent is probably universally an adult human; for *read* the stereotypical theme would be *book*, even though one can also read labels on sauce bottles; for *cut* the stereotypical instrument would be *knife*, even though one can cut one's bonds with a nailfile. However, it is unlikely that this could handle contrasts like *florist* versus *performer*.

References

Altmann, G. T. M., and Steedman, M. 1988. Interaction with context during human sentence processing. *Cognition* 30:191–238.

Bever, T. G. 1970. The cognitive basis for linguistic structures. In J. R. Hayes (ed.), *Cognition and the Development of Language.* New York: John Wiley and Sons.

Carlson, G. N., and Tanenhaus, M. K. 1988. Thematic roles and language comprehension. In W. Wilkins (ed.), *Thematic Relations*, vol. 21 of *Syntax and Semantics.* New York: Academic Press.

Chodorow, M., and Slutsky, H. 1986. Parsing non-deterministic verb phrases: Some psycholinguistic evidence. Paper presented at New York University.

Chomsky, N. 1965. *Aspects of the Theory of Syntax.* Cambridge: MIT Press.

Chomsky, N. 1975. Questions of form and interpretation. *Linguistic Analysis* 2:75–109.

Clifton, C., Frazier, L., and Connine, C. 1984. Lexical expectations in sentence comprehension. *Journal of Verbal Learning and Verbal Behavior* 23:696–708.

Crain, S. 1980. *Contextual Constraints on Sentence Comprehension.* Ph.D. dissertation, University of California, Irvine.

Crain, S., and Coker, P. L. 1978. A semantic constraint on syntactic parsing. Paper presented at the annual meeting of the Linguistic Society of America.

Crain, S., and Fodor, J. D. 1985. How can grammars help parsers? In D. Dowty, L. Kartunnen, and A. Zwicky (eds.), *Natural Language Parsing: Psychological, Computational, and Theoretical Perspectives.* Cambridge: Cambridge University Press.

Crain, S., and Steedman, M. 1985. On not being led up the garden-path: The use of context by the psychological parser. In D. Dowty, L. Kartunnen, and A. Zwicky (eds.), *Natural Language Parsing: Psychological, Computational, and Theoretical Perspectives.* Cambridge: Cambridge University Press.

Ferreira, F., and Clifton, C. 1986. The independence of syntactic processing. *Journal of Memory and Language* 25:348–368.

Fillmore, C. 1968. The case for case. In E. Bach and R. T. Harms (eds.), *Universals in Linguistic Theory.* New York: Holt, Rinehart and Winston.

Fodor, J. A. 1983. *The Modularity of Mind: An Essay on Faculty Psychology.* Cambridge: MIT Press.

Fodor, J. D. 1978. Parsing strategies and constraints on transformation. *Linguistic Inquiry* 9:427–474.

Fodor, J. D. 1979. Superstrategy. In W. Cooper and E. C. T. Walker (eds.), *Sentence Processing.* Hillsdale, N.J.: Lawrence Erlbaum Associates.

Fodor, J. D., and Frazier, L. 1980. Is the human sentence parsing mechanism an ATN? *Cognition* 8:417–459.

Ford, M. 1983. A method for obtaining measures of local parsing complexity throughout sentences. *Journal of Verbal Learning and Verbal Behavior* 22:203–218.

Frazier, L. 1978. *On Comprehending Sentences: Syntactic Parsing Strategies.* Ph.D. dissertation, University of Connecticut. Distributed by Indiana University Linguistics Club.

Frazier, L. 1986. Natural classes in language processing. Manuscript, MIT.

Garnsey, S. M., Tanenhaus, M. K., and Chapman, R. M. 1989. Evoked potentials and the study of sentence comprehension. *Journal of Psycholinguistic Research* 18:51–60.

Gorrell, P. G. 1987. *Studies of Human Syntactic Processing: Ranked-Parallel versus Serial Models.* Ph.D. dissertation, University of Connecticut.

Gruber, J. S. 1965. *Studies in Lexical Relations.* Ph.D. dissertation, MIT. Distributed by Indiana University Linguistics Club.

Holmes, V. M., Stowe, L. A., and Cupples, L. 1989. Lexical expectations in parsing complement-verb sentences. *Journal of Memory and Language* 28:668–689.

Jackendoff, R. 1987. The status of thematic relations in linguistic theory. *Linguistic Inquiry* 18:369–411.

Kurtzman, H. S. 1985. *Studies in Syntactic Ambiguity Resolution.* Ph.D. dissertation, MIT.

Langendoen, D. T., Kalish-Landon, N., and Dore, J. 1974. Dative questions: A study in the relation of acceptability to grammaticality of an English sentence type. *Cognition* 2:451–478.

Marcus, M. 1980. *A theory of Syntactic Recognition for Natural Language.* Cambridge: MIT Press.

Marslen-Wilson, W. D., and Tyler, L. K. 1987. Against modularity. In J. L. Garfield (ed.), *Modularity in Knowledge Representation and Natural Language Understanding.* Cambridge: MIT Press.

Rappaport, M., and Levin, B. 1988. What to do with θ-roles. In W. Wilkins (ed.), *Thematic Relations*, vol. 21 of *Syntax and Semantics.* New York: Academic Press.

Rayner, K., Carlson, M., and Frazier, L. 1983. The interaction of syntax and semantics during sentence processing: Eye movements in the analysis of semantically biassed sentences. *Journal of Verbal Learning and Verbal Behavior* 22:358–374.

Riesbeck, C., and Schank, R. 1978. Comprehension by computer: Expectation-based analysis of sentences in context. In W. I. M. Levelt and G. B. Flores d'Arcais (eds.), *Studies in the Perception of Language.* Chichester: Wiley.

Stowe, L. A. 1983. *Models of Gap-Location in the Human Language Processor.* Ph.D. dissertation, University of Wisconsin, Madison.

Stowe, L. A. 1984. A subject/object asymmetry in parsing. *Proceedings of the North Eastern Linguistics Society.*

Stowell, T. 1981. *Origins of Phrase Structure.* Ph.D. dissertation, MIT.

Tanenhaus, M. K., Boland, J., Garnsey, S. M., and Carlson, G. N. 1989. Lexical structure in parsing long-distance dependencies. *Journal of Psycholinguistic Research* 18:37–50.

Tanenhaus, M. K., and Carlson, G. N. 1989. Lexical structure and language comprehension. In W. D. Marslen-Wilson (ed.), *Lexical Representation and Process.* Cambridge: MIT Press.

Tanenhaus, M. K., Stowe, L., and Carlson, G. 1985. The interaction of lexical expectation and pragmatic information. *Proceedings of the Seventh Annual Cognitive Science Society Meetings.*

Wright, B., and Garrett, M. 1984. Lexical decision in sentences: Effects of syntactic structure. *Memory and Cognition* 12:31–45.

Chapter 21

Syntax and Intonational Structure in a Combinatory Grammar

Mark J. Steedman

What function would we expect prosody and intonation to perform in natural-language understanding if we didn't know what we were up against? I think that most people would expect them to be indicators of surface structure. They might reason as follows: Natural-language understanding consists in the construction of a semantic interpretation and its evaluation in a context. The only semantics we really understand is a Tarskian compositional semantics. Syntax (and morphology) are the rules that map strings onto a compositional semantics. So what *else* is there for prosody to do, expect to reveal that structure?

However, everyone knows that the prosodic phrase boundaries established by intonation and timing are often orthogonal to the syntactic phrase boundaries that linguists usually recognize. For instance, the bracketed strings in the following examples are usually not regarded as syntactic constituents. Nevertheless, they can form single intonational phrases (the examples are adapted from Selkirk 1984):

(1) a. The very eminent professor (was avidly reading about) the latest developments in geomorphology.

    b. (Mary prefers) corduroy.

There are many intonational ways of marking the boundaries of prosodic phrases, and I will not attempt a formal definition of intonational phrase here. One way that is particulary easy to intuitively grasp is to use *contrastive stress* and to end a phrase with a *continuation rise*. This intonation is virtually forced when (1b) is uttered as a response to the question "I know that Harry prefers silk. But what does *Mary* prefer?"[1]

The close relation of intonation to meaning reinforces the expectation that intonation should somehow be related to surface structure. Early generative theories of the relation of syntax to prosodic phonology—for example, those of Chomsky (1971) and Jackendoff (1972)—attempted to salvage the insight by using "annotated" surface structures to syntactically represent such aspects of prosodic meaning as focus. However, such proposals seem to have resisted formalization and to have remained little more than sketches. (They have also been criticized on grounds of descriptive inadequacy by Hajičová and Sgall (1987, 1988).) Later work in the "metrical" theory of prosody seems to have moved further and further from any simple relation to surface syntax.

Selkirk (1984, p. 286) has recently argued for a level of "intonational structure" that is entirely independent of surface structure in the usual sense of the term. This level of structure is subject to an interesting constraint that Selkirk (following Halliday) has called the "sense unit condition." The condition captures the fact that although all manner of strings that are not traditional constituents can constitute an intonational phrase, the one bracketed below cannot:

(2) *Three mathematicians (in ten derive a lemma).

The phrase *in ten* is neither an argument nor a modifier of the predicate *derive a lemma*. It follows that it cannot constitute a sense unit that can be presupposed or focused, and hence it also cannot be a unitary intonational phrase.

The sense-unit condition does seem to capture what is wrong with (2). However, it underlines the fact that the intonational structure of an utterance is directly related to the interpretation or "logical form" (Selkirk 1984, sec. 5.4, esp. fig. 5.2, and sec. 8), since logical form rather than surface structure is the level at which the information structure is represented.[2] This proposal is surprising for two reasons. First, she defines the sense-unit condition in terms of exactly those aspects of meaning that are most directly represented in syntax, namely government and modification (pp. 291, 294). Second, while I have not yet said what information structure actually *is*, it must map on to argument structure in some very direct way, since the sum of presupposition and focus is clearly a complete proposition. It seems strange that there should be two independent paths between sound and meaning dealing with such closely related properties of the sentence, as in the architecture represented in figure 1. Such an architecture amounts to a claim that natural languages have *two* systems of syntax embodying the different but interdependent notions of constituency and interpretation.

I shall assume throughout this paper that some version of metrical phonology will provide a correct account of phonological form, including the association of intonational tunes and timing with intonational

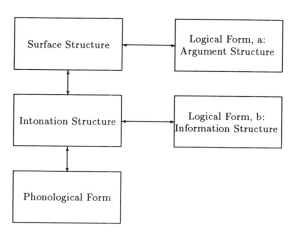

Figure 1
The architecture of current metrical phonologies

phrases (for the various versions see Liberman and Prince 1977, Prince 1983, Selkirk 1984, Pierrehumbert 1980, Nespor and Vogel 1986, Beckman 1986, Beckman and Pierrehumbert 1986, Ladd 1988). My sole concerns are with the concept of intonation structure itself and with the nature of the input to such rules. I shall propose an alternative view of surface structure according to which a much simpler relation holds between it and intonational structure. It permits the assumption that Selkirk's sense-unit condition applies to surface structure and therefore suggests that the rules defining the intonation contour and other prosodic features of intonational phrases can be driven directly from surface syntax. The present theory thus represents a return to the position sketched by Chomsky 1971. However, the concept of surface syntax is radically changed. In effect, surface structure *is* intonation structure. This property makes for a simpler and more modular theory.

Prosody

Prosody is traditionally regarded as conveying distinctions of *focus*, such as the distinction between presupposed, or given, and focused, or new, information proposed by Halliday (1967, 1970) and the Prague School (see Hajičová and Sgall 1987 for a recent review). The given information in an utterance is that part (or those parts) of its meaning that the utterer presupposes or regards as already established in the discourse. New information is the part (or parts) that the utterer regards as having to be established by the utterance itself. I shall assume here that new information is signalled by the presence of a pitch accent, that is, by Halliday's tonic or Pierrehumbert's H*, L*, etc. Further distinctions of emphasis, contrast, and propositional attitude are conveyed by *which particular* Hallidean tone or Pierrehumbert pitch accent is involved.[3]

The kinds of thing which utterers may regard as established or given include various sorts of referential entities about whose formal character there is a fair degree of confusion, and which are not the concern here. But they also include various sorts of propositional entities. As Ellen Prince (1986) has pointed out, these include "open" propositions, that is, incomplete propositions with unfilled arguments or thematic roles. Open propositions are most obviously and reliably introduced into the context of a discourse by a *wh-* question. For example, question (3a) introduces the open proposition that might be visualized as (3b):[4]

(3) a. What are legumes a good source of?
    b. Legumes are a good source of ＿＿＿ .

The question invites the recipient to fill in the blank in the open proposition, by identifying an entity that combines with it to yield a true proposition. In a felicitous reply such as the following (in which the italics indicate a pitch accent), it seems reasonable to argue that the intonation contour indicates the distinction between the given open proposition and the new information, marked by a pitch accent such as Pierrehumbert's H* (see Selkirk 1984, fig. 5.6, p. 257; Hirschberg and Pierrehumbert 1986; Pierrehumbert and Hirschberg 1987):

(4) (Legumes are a good source of) (*vi*tamins).

As Chomsky has pointed out (1971, p. 91), such intonation contours do not *always unambiguously* determine the open proposition. Although intonation breaks must coincide with intonational structure boundaries, the reverse does not hold: intonation structure boundaries may not be marked in this way, and the pitch accent need not occur at the beginning of the new information. So, for example, the following exchange imposes a different information structure on (4). Nonetheless, (4) need not be acoustically distinct from (5b):

(5) a. What are legumes?
    b. (Legumes are) (a good source of *vi*tamins).

Thus I am not claiming that (5a) is *necessary* to make (5b) felicitous, nor am I claiming that this is the *only* felicitous response. But the claim that intonation conveys the entities and open propositions that are in focus is borne out by the fact that other intonation contours which on this hypothesis would convey other information structures inconsistent with the context (3) *are* infelicitous (which I indicate with a hash sign):

(6) a.   What are legumes a good source of?
    b. #(*Le*gumes) (are a good source of vitamins).

Unlike many aspects of discourse semantics and information structure, the semantics of open propositions is a relatively straightforward matter. The open propositions that are introduced by *wh-* questions (and by other constructions dealt with in the next section) are clearly *abstractions*, in the sense of the term embodied in the λ calculus, as Jackendoff (1972) and Rooth (1985) have pointed out. So we might be tempted to write down the information structure of (3), using the λ calculus, as

(7) given $= \lambda x[\text{good}'(\text{source}'\ x)\text{legumes}']$
    new $= \text{vitamins}'$

Such a representation can be interpreted via "β-reduction," or functional application, to yield the following argument structure:

(8) $(\text{good}'(\text{source}'\ \text{vitamins}'))\text{legumes}'$

However, the notation of (7) merely underlines the problem: the division of the sentence into an open proposition "$\lambda x[(\text{good}'(\text{source}'\ x))\ \text{legumes}']$" and an argument *vitamins'* appears to cut right across the traditional subject-predicate surface structure.

Wh- questions are not the only structures that are syntactically and semantically reminiscent of abstractions. So too are the residual fragments in all constructions that generative grammarians would regard as arising from *wh-* movement and deletion under coordination. It is these constructions that motivate the theory of grammar that I shall use to resolve this paradox via a surprising reformulation of the notion of surface syntax and surface constituency. The next two sections of the paper constitute an excursus to establish the lineaments of this theory of grammar.

Categories and Constituents

Almost every current theory of grammar accounts for examples like the topicalized sentence (9a) as arising from a structure like (9b):

(9) a. Lobster, I like!
    b. $\lambda x[(\text{like}'\ x)i']$

Government-Binding (GB) theory does so very directly, using traces, which are explicitly related to bound variables, as in (10), and so in essence does generalized phrase-structure grammar (GPSG).

(10) a. (A man) whom I think that Harry likes *t*.
　　 b. (A man) whom I loathe *t* and you detest *t*.
　　 c. (A book) which I bought *t* without reading *t*.

Relative clauses like those in (10) make the analogy even more tempting. Like the lambda operator, the relative clause may "abstract" upon an indefinitely embedded "variable," here represented by *t*, as in (10a), or upon more than one occurrence of the same "variable," as in (10b, c).

However, a number of puzzles suggest that the analogy may not be quite the right one. The most obvious puzzle is that there is no phonological realization of the putative bound variables. Since the sole purpose of the syntax of a language is to indicate which rules apply to which entities, it seems most odd to think that natural syntax obscures this equation by omitting such a crucial element of meaning. If that were the only paradox, it might be tolerated, since it is after all no odder than the fact that natural languages do not include explicit brackets to indicate structure. But there is a second problem for the analogy with the λ calculus. It arises from the curious gaps among the possibilities for such "abstraction" that are revealed by certain constraints on rules that have been noted by generative linguists. For example, it is impossible in English to relativize on a subject embedded under a complementizer, as in (11a), in contrast to an object.[5] It is also impossible to relativize on a position in only one branch of a coordinate structure, as in (11b).

(11) a. *(A woman) who I think that *t* likes lobster.
　　 b. *(A man) who I loath *t* and you detest him.

There is nothing in the notion of abstraction via bound variables to suggest why this should be so.

It is interesting in this connection that there is a whole family of applicative systems, all of which capture the notion of abstraction or definition of fucntions, and of which the λ calculus is merely the most familiar. It is particularly interesting that one branch of the family, those based on the combinators of Curry and Feys (1985), explicitly eschew the use of bound variables. Instead, they capture the notion of abstraction algorithmically, in terms of a few primitive operations on functions, such as functional composition. These operations correspond to elementary abstractions, in terms of which the familar lambda operator can be defined algorithmically.

A few of the operations used by Curry, together with the equivalent lambda expressions, are given below:

(12) a. $\mathbf{B}FG \equiv \lambda x F(Gx)$ b. $\mathbf{C}F \equiv \lambda x \lambda y Fyx$
     c. $\mathbf{W}F \equiv \lambda x Fxx$ d. $\mathbf{S}FG \equiv \lambda x Fx(Gx)$
     e. $\mathbf{I} \equiv \lambda x x$ f. $\mathbf{K}x \equiv \lambda yx$
     g. $\mathbf{T}x \equiv \lambda FFx$

Only a few of these combinators will be used in the theory, and those will be discussed more fully later. However, it may be helpful to point out now that the clearest intuitive introduction to combinators remains chapters 5 and 6 of Curry and Feys 1958, and that the most entertaining introduction is to be found in Smullyan 1986, a mathematical diversion in which combinators take the form of birds. It should also be noticed that a convention of left association is used here and elsewhere in this chapter, so that an expression like $\mathbf{B}FG$ is equivalent to $(\mathbf{B}F)G$.

Using these functional operations as primitives, elementary functions can be combined to yield complex functions equivalent to lambda abstractions. For example, the abstraction in the lobster sentence (9) can be written without any bound variables as follows:

(13) $\mathbf{B}(\mathbf{T}i')$like$'$

In 1987 and 1988 I argued for an alternative theory of grammar embodying the following simple claims:

• The syntax of coordination and unbounded dependency is as straightforward a reflection of an applicative system as is the syntax of the λ calculus.
• The applicative system in question is based not on variable binding, but on a specific and restricted set of combinators, essentially limited to $\mathbf{B}$, $\mathbf{T}$, and $\mathbf{S}$.[6]
• The syntactic operations corresponding to the combinators allow for a parsimonious explanation of problematic constraints on these constructions in natural languages.

In all other respects, the proposal is a theory of competence of a quite standard kind, and it conforms to all the principles that are standardly accepted within the generative approach. The evidence upon which it stands or falls is entirely linguistic, and is briefly summarized in the next section.

Combinatory grammar

The most fundamental assumption of the theory, from which everything else follows, is the following:

(14) *The principle of adjacency:* Combinatory rules may only apply to entities that are phonologically realized and adjacent.

This principle might as well be called the combinator assumption, because it merely enshrines in linguistic terms a determination to avoid postulating "invisible" variables (or indeed any other syntactic "empty category") and a determination to do the work of abstraction with combinators, which by definition operate on adjacent entities.[7]

Since combinators are operations on functions, we need a grammatical notation that makes function-argument relations explicit. Categorial grammar (CG) provides such a notation. CG associates every lexical item and every constituent with a category, or type, which defines its possible combinations. For example, the information embodied in a phrase-structure rule like (15a), defining the transitive verb phrase, is captured in CG by associating the category of a function from NPs into VPs with transitive verbs, as in (15b):

(15) a. VP → V NP
     b. eat := VP/NP : eat'

Note that the category includes an interpretation (to the right of the colon) whose type is reflected in the syntactic category. In the unification-based realizations of CG discussed in Uszkoreit 1986, Karttunen 1989, Wittenburg 1986, Pareschi 1987, and Zeevat 1987, type and interpretation are represented in a single structure.

Backward-combining functions, such as predicates, are written as follows:

(16) walk := S\NP : walk'

In the present notation the range of a function always appears on the left, and the domain on the right, together with a slash indicating directionality. Functions can have more than one argument, and the arguments can combine in more than one direction. But such functions are always "curried," that is, *n*-place functions are always understood as multiple applications of unary functions, as in (17):

(17) eats := (S\NP)/NP : eat'

Any word or constituent may have more than one lexical category. For example, *eats* is also a predicate:

(18) eats := S\NP : eat' something'

Together with a categorial lexicon of such entries, a categorial grammar includes combinatory rules that combine them to yield complex constituents. In a classical categorial grammar there are just two of these rules, corresponding to backward and forward functional application. They are written here as follows:

(19) a. $X/Y:F \quad Y:y \quad \Rightarrow X:Fy \quad (>)$
     b. $Y:y \qquad X\backslash Y:F \Rightarrow X:Fy \quad (<)$

(The symbols in parentheses are used as abbreviations in the derivations below.) Just as the categories are both syntactic and semantic in nature, so these rules are rules of semantic as well as syntactic combination. The interpretation of the result is obtained by functional application on the input interpretations.

These two rules operate on categories to yield derivations written as follows:

(20) Harry   eats   bagels

     NP   (S\NP)/NP   NP
          ───────────────── >
               S\NP
     ───────────────────── <
               S

The underlines represent the operation of rules on categories and are annotated with mnemonic symbols indicating the rule that has applied. The symbols > and < indicate rules (19a, b) apply. The diagrams are equivalent to trees, and a categorial grammar including only rules of application is context-free.

To accommodate coordination in such a grammar while continuing to adhere to the principle of adjacency, we might add the following rule:[8]

(21) X conj $X \Rightarrow X$ (coord)

Such a rule says that any two like categories can coordinate, including functions.[9] The following derivation is otherwise just like the last one:

(22) I   cooked   and   ate   the beans

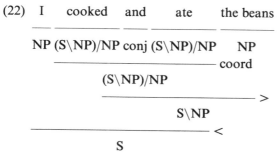

However, the following raised-right-node example is not accepted by the grammar as it stands:

(23) I   will   cook   and   might   eat   the beans which ...

$$\underline{\text{NP}} \quad \underline{\text{(S\backslash NP)/VP}} \quad \underline{\text{VP/NP}} \quad \underline{\text{conj}} \quad \underline{\text{(S\backslash NP)/VP}} \quad \underline{\text{VP/NP}} \quad \underline{\text{NP}}$$

Functional application alone will not allow these two categories to combine to yield S. However, if we add a combinatory rule corresponding to an almost equally basic operation on functions, namely functional *composition*, then the sentence and others like it are accepted immediately. The rule is called forward composition and is written as follows:

(24) Forward composition

$$X/Y : F \quad Y/Z : G \Rightarrow X/Z : \mathbf{B}FG \quad (>\mathbf{B})$$

Composition (**B**) is the most basic of Curry's combinators. (It is the one that Smullyan calls the Bluebird.) Hence the present extension of categorial grammar is called combinatory categorial grammar (CCG). The interpretation of the result in the above rule can therefore simply be written as **B**FG, the composition of the input interpretations. With this rule the tensed verb and the main verb can be composed to yield a composite verb with exactly the same category as a lexical tensed transitive verb. This nonstandard constituent can coordinate, and the rest of the derivation can therefore proceed exactly like the last one, by a forward and a backward application of the conjoined function to the object and the subject, respectively:

(25)

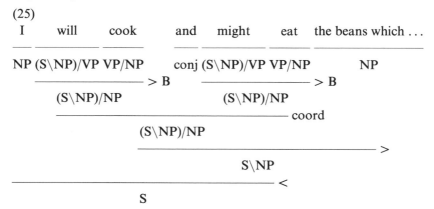

If we assume a suitable semantics for the coordination rule, the fact that the semantics of the composition rule *is* functional composition guarantees that the result will associate the verbs and their arguments correctly.

The following related sentence requires the introduction of one further kind of combinatory rule.

(26)

I	will	cook	and	Betty	might	eat	the mushrooms
NP	(S\NP)/VP	VP/NP	conj	NP	(S\NP)/VP	VP/NP	NP

While *will* and *cook* can again be composed, the result cannot be combined with the subject to yield a single conjoinable category. However, if the subject were a function, it too could compose. It can be made into just the right type of function by introducing an operation of functional "type raising" of a kind familiar from Montague grammars. Type raising turns an argument category X into a function over functions that take X as argument. It corresponds to another of Curry's combinations, which he called C_*. Smullyan follows Rosser in calling it T, the Thrush. Because it occupies a central role in the present system, as it does in those of Church, of Rosser, and of Smullyan, and because T stands for type raising, the present notation follows them. The definition of T is given in (12) above and is repeated here.

(27) $Tx \equiv \lambda FFx$

The above sentence needs the following instance of such a rule, called subject type raising:

(28) Subject type raising

   $NP : x \Rightarrow S/(S\backslash X) : Tx \ (>T)$

The intuition behind type raising is precisely the same as the linguists' notion of *case*. Nominative-case morphology in a language like Latin determines a noun-phrase argument like *Balbus* to be something that must combine with a predicate, like *ambulat*, or *murum aedificat*. In categorial terms, it makes it a function over functions over subjects, whose interpretation is precisely *Tbalbus'*.

The point of the subject-type-raising rule is the following. Since the rule makes subjects into functions *over* predicates, it allows them to compose with functions *into* predicates, that is, with tensed verbs. The problematic sentence can therefore be accepted as follows:

(29)

I	will	cook	and	Betty	might	eat	the mushrooms

NP   (S\NP)/VP VP/NP conj   NP   (S\NP)/VP VP/NP   NP

—————— > T   —————— > T

S/(S\NP)   S/(S\NP)

————————————————— > B   ————————————————— > B

S/VP   S/VP

————————————————— > B   ————————————————— > B

S/NP   S/NP

—————————————————————————————————————— coord

S/NP

——— >

S

The subject-type-raising rule is a special case of the following schema, which allows any category to raise over any function over that category:

(30) $X : x \Rightarrow \Sigma/(\Sigma \backslash X) : \mathbf{T}x$ ($< \mathbf{T}$)

(The symbol Σ is a polymorphically typed variable ranging over categories.) Such a rule is an infinite schema and must be universally restricted if grammars of this type are to be decidable. In English (as opposed to Dutch), this rule (as opposed to another type-raising rule discussed below) appears to be further restricted to subject NPs, so we can finally write the rule in full as follows:

(31) $X : x \Rightarrow \Sigma/(\Sigma \backslash X) : \mathbf{T}x$, where $X = \text{NP}, \Sigma = \text{S}$ ($> \mathbf{T}$)

As I noted in Steedman 1985, p. 554, it is possible to regard type-raising rules either as rules of syntax, as they have been presented so far, or as lexical rules. According to the latter proposal, specifiers of argument categories, such as determiners, would not bear the category NP/N. Rather, they would bear such categories as $(\Sigma/(\Sigma \backslash X))/N$, that is, functions from N to a type-raised NP category, as in effect they do in the system of Karttunen 1986, which is closely related to the present one. My earlier paper (1985, p. 564) notes that at least for languages with case, like German and Finnish, it seems most natural to assume that type raising is associated with the lexicon via the morphology of case. In English it is easier, at least for present purposes, to present type raising as a syntactic process. This should not be taken as a committment against the view that it is a process of the lexicon and of morphology.

Extending categorial grammar with these simple rules of functional composition and type raising captures a wide range of linguistic phenomena. Since subjects, verbs, and the like are all functions or raisable into functions, indefinitely long sequences can be composed, so that the grammar immediately allows right-node raising to be unbounded, as in the following sentence:

(32)

[I believe that Harry eats,]$_{S/NP}$ but [you say that he merely admires,]$_{S/NP}$ the bagels which he buys at the market every Sunday.

Moreover, the grammar provides almost all that is needed to account for *leftward* unbounded movement as well. Since the string *I believe that Harry eats* is a single function of type S/NP and is adjacent to the moved relative pronoun, all that is needed is a way of allowing the application of the one to the other:

(33) (bagels) which [I believe that Harry eats]$_{S/NP}$

The way in which this last detail is dealt with is described in Steedman 1987 and will be passed over here. I merely note that whatever that way is, it will not compromise the adjacency principle.

Limits on possible rules

A grammar must not only allow the sentences that *do* occur in the relevant language; it must also exclude the ones that do not. And the degrees of freedom that are exercised in defining rules and exlcuding others constitute a prediction that those degrees of freedom define the logical space of possible natural grammars and constructions, that is, universal grammar. Some imaginable grammatical phenomena are already ruled out by the central principle of the present theory, the principle of adjacency. For example, the following coordinate structure might be allowed under a theory including deletion or movement to reduce to something meaning that I will cook the mushrooms and Betty will eat the mushrooms:

(34) *[I will cook]$_{S/NP}$ [the mushrooms]$_{NP}$ and [Betty will eat]$_{S/NP}$

However, the adjacency principle means that no coordination rule that will allow such constructions is permitted in the present theory.

Nevertheless, if we allowed *all* of the rules corresponding to Curry's combinators that *could* be written in the notation above, we would have a very unconstrained kind of grammar indeed. It is therefore an important property of the theory that all the rules that we actually want to write appear to be constrained by two very natural limiting principles:

(35) *The principle of directional consistency:* All syntactic combination rules must be consistent with the directionality of the principle function.

(36) *The principle of directional inheritance:* If the category that results from the application of a combinatory rule is a function category, then the slash defining directionality for a given argument in that category will be the same as the one defining directionality for the corresponding argument(s) in the input function(s).

The first of these principles means that a combinatory rule may not override the directionality specified in the lexicon. It rules out the following anomalous instance of functional application:

(37) $*X \backslash Y : F, Y : y \Rightarrow X : Fy$

The second of the two principles implies that directionality of a function is a property of its *argument* and must be inherited under rules like composition, just as the syntactic category of the argument must. This principle rules out the following anomalous instance of functional composition, because the Z slash in the result is not the same as the Z slash in the input:

(38) $*X/Y : F \quad Y/Z : G \Rightarrow X \backslash Z : \mathbf{B}FG$

These principles allow only a very small proportion of the imaginable combinatory rules to occur in natural grammars. The full set of rules are discussed in my earlier papers, where it is hypothesized that all natural grammars can be formulated in terms of a lexicon constructed according to universal principles and combinatory rules drawn from this set and possibly subject to category-specific restrictions on individual rules.

Such grammars provide elegant accounts of many natural constructions. For example, the proposal concerning "nonconstituent coordination" of Dowty 1988 adds the following permitted versions of composition and type raising to the grammar of English:[10]

(39) $Y \backslash Z : G \quad X \backslash Y : F \Rightarrow X \backslash Z : \mathbf{B}FG \quad (<\mathbf{B})$

(40) $X : x \Rightarrow \Sigma \backslash (\Sigma / X) : \mathbf{T}x$, where $X \in$ complements and $\Sigma \in$ sentential categories $\quad (<\mathbf{T})$

(The second rule is a less restricted version of type raising than the earlier subject-type-raising rule. The restrictions on it mean that X must be a category drawn from the set of those subcategorized for by verbs, while Σ is restricted to sentential categories, that is, the set recursively defined as containing S and all functions into members of the set itself.) The construction is then accepted as follows:

(41)

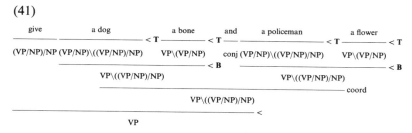

Because of the SVO category of the English tensed verb and the principles of adjacency, consistency, and inheritance, no combinatory rules are permitted that would permit strings like the following to yield the same interpretation:[11]

(42) a. # Give a bone a dog, and a flower a policeman.
   b. * A policeman a flower, and give a dog a bone.

Dowty (1988) and I (1985) point out that well-known universal generalizations concerning gapping and the basic order of constituents follow from these principles. The theory also allows elegant explanations of a number of "parametrically" determined language-specific constraints, such as the fixed-subject constraint or the "*that-t filter," which has been invoked in other frameworks to explain the following subject-object assymmetry:

(43) a. (bagels) which [I believe that]$_{S/S}$ [Harry eats]$_{S/NP}$
   b. *(a woman) who [I believe that]$_{S/S}$ [eats bagels]$_{S\backslash NP}$

The constraint is forced on the grammar of English by the fact that the second, disallowed extraction would require a *different* rule of functional composition because of the backward-looking category of the English predicate. The rule is the following:

(44) $X/Y : F \quad Y\backslash Z : G \Rightarrow X\backslash Z : \mathbf{B}FG \quad (>\mathbf{B}x)$

This rule is allowed by the twin principles of consistency and inheritance, and it is crucially implicated in the grammar of Dutch (Steedman 1985). However, its unrestricted inclusion in a grammar of English would affect the grammar throughout and lead to a partial collapse of word order.[12]

   "Island" constraints are a rather different case. Consider the following contrast between extraction from a nonisland (45a) and an adjunct island (45b):[13]

(45) a.   (articles) which I will [file]$_{VP/NP}$
[before reading your instructions]$_{VP\backslash VP}$
   b.   ?(articles) which I will [read you instructions]$_{VP}$
[before filing]$_{(VP\backslash VP)/NP}$

This restriction is easily captured, since as the categories stand, the incomplete adverbial cannot combine with the VP until it gets its NP, and it cannot get its (extracted) NP until it has combined with the VP because of the adjacency principle. However, if the VP were allowed to undergo type raising, it could become VP/(VP\VP). It could then compose with *before filing*, to permit the extraction. We therefore have to stipulate that such raisings are prohibited. We could do this purely syntactically, restricting lexical type raising to categories like NP and PP. However, the "fuzziness" of these restrictions and their sensitivity to the content of the construction suggests that they are ultimately semantic in origin. The point is illustrated by the following well-known exception (46a) to the complex NP constraint illustrated in (46b):

(46) a.   (a physicist) whom I saw a painting of
   b.   ?(a physicist) whom I own a watch that belonged to

Such vagaries suggest that the origin of these constraints is ultimately semantic, if they should be regarded as constraints on grammar at all. The important fact about them for present purposes is that such limitations on the possibilities for combinatory rules to build constituents corresponding to arbitrary contiguous substrings of sentences find a parallel in the domain of intonation.

The notion of surface structure

The theory just presented has surprising consequences for the conception of surface structure. The claim that fragments like *I believe that Harry eats* are constituents for the purposes of coordination and extraction immediately implies that they must be permissible constituents for ordinary canonical sentences like *I believe that Harry eats bagels*. For example, the following is only one among many alternatives to the usual right-branching analysis:

(47)   I   believe   that   Harry   eats   bagels

$\underline{S/(S\backslash NP)}$ $\underline{(S\backslash NP)/S'}$ $\underline{S'/S}$ $\underline{S/(S\backslash NP)}$ $\underline{(S\backslash NP)/NP}$ $\underline{NP}$

$$\frac{\qquad\qquad\qquad\qquad}{S/S'} > \mathbf{B}$$

$$\frac{\qquad\qquad\qquad\qquad\qquad}{S/S} > \mathbf{B}$$

$$\frac{\qquad\qquad\qquad\qquad\qquad\qquad}{S/(S/NP)} > \mathbf{B}$$

$$\frac{\qquad\qquad\qquad\qquad\qquad\qquad\qquad}{S/NP} > \mathbf{B}$$

$$\frac{\qquad\qquad\qquad\qquad\qquad\qquad\qquad\qquad}{S} >$$

The fact that the present theory not only engenders unorthodox surface structures but engenders *many alternative* unorthodox surface structures might seem to be a disadvantage. However, the semantics of the combinatory rules, and in particular the fact that composition is an associative operation, guarantees that all of the alternative analyses deliver the same function-argument relations. While the existence of this proliferation of alternative analyses is clearly a problem for parsing the written language, Pareschi and Steedman (1987) have argued that it may be possible to exploit the associativity of composition and the property of preserving argument structure of the combinatory rules themselves to render such parsing manageable. For present purposes it is more important to note that this much freer notion of surface structure, together with the property that such structures are fully interpretable and reduce to a canonical set of function-argument relations, is exactly what is needed to account for intonation, a matter to which I can now return.

Prosodic Constituency

The class of nonstandard surface constituents postulated by the account above show a considerable overlap with Selkirk's class of intonational phrases. For example, *Mary prefers* is a constituent under one analysis of the following sentence according to the present theory, and it can also be an intonational phrase (Selkirk 1984, p. 291, ex. 5.128):[14]

(48) (Mary prefers) (corduroy)

Such surface structures are reminiscent of those that arise from Giegerich's "transformational" rule of "W-pairing" in his surface-structure-driven version of the metrical approach (1985, sec. 4.4).

Similarly, as Moortgat (1987) points out, whatever stops composition across (most) modifier boundaries and thereby imposes island contraints appears also to contrain intonational structure. Examples like the following have given rise to various proposals of parsing strategies and "readjustment rules" (Chomsky and Hallé 1968, chap. 2; Kimball 1973; Langendoen 1975; Selkirk 1984):

(49) (This is the cat)(that chased the rat)(that lived in the house) (that Jack built)

As already noted, the inclusion of composition and type raising in the grammar allows a great many surface structures. For example, all of the following bracketings of the string *I want to begin to try to write a play* are grammatical ways of dividing it into two nonstandard constituents independently motivated by the possibility of coordinating the sequences in question:

(50) a. (I)(want to begin to try to write a play)
     b. (I want)(to begin to try to write a play)
     c. (I want to begin)(to try to write a play)
     d. (I want to begin to try)(to write a play)
     e. (I want to begin to try to write)(a play)

All of these nonstandard constituents correspond to possible, distinct intonational phrasings (Selkirk 1984, p. 294, ex. 5.136). Conversely, *in ten derive a lemma* cannot be a constituent of sentence (2), repeated here, and nor can it constitute an intonational phrase (Selkirk 1984, ex. 5.132):

(51) *(Three mathematicians) (in ten derive a lemma)

We know that the crucial string cannot be a constituent of an English sentence, because we can neither extract out of it nor coordinate it:[15]

(52) a. *How many mathematicians do you think *t* in ten derive a lemma?
     b. *Three mathematicians, in ten derive a lemma, and in a hundred can cook a reasonable soufflée.

The theory thus explains the sense-unit condition on the simplest possible ground: sense units are surface syntactic constituents.

The converse relation between syntax and prosody also holds. On the present theory, sentences involving unbounded extraction and/or coordination not only *may* include the nonstandard constituents but *must* do so. These are also sentences where the string corresponding to the nonstandard constituent typically corresponds to an intonational phrase. For example, the many possible prosodies and intonational contours of the first bracketed string in the following right-node-raised examples seem to be identical to the ones that induce the relevant perceptual bracketing on the corresponding strings in the *non*coordinated examples (48) and (50):

(53) (Mary prefers)(corduroy and bombazine)

(54) a. (I)(want to begin to try to write a play and hope to finish it by teatime)

    b. (I want)(to begin to try to write a play and to succeed in finishing it)

    c. (I want to begin)(to try to write a play and to be nicer to my brother)

    d. (I want to begin to try)(to write a play and to make a movie)

    e. (I want to begin to try to write)(a play and a movie)

The same appears to be true of the residue left behind by movement:

(55) a. (Whom)(did you paint a picture of?)

    b. (Of whom)(did you paint a picture?)

    c. (Whom)(do you think you will invite?)

The theory thus explains the fact that intonation contour is constrained by coordination and extraction, because both phenomena depend on surface constituency.

The claim that all intonational phrases are constituents does not, of course, imply the converse: some CCG constituents are smaller than an intonational phrase, while some are larger. It is instructive to look at Selkirk's discussion (1984, p. 292) of the following intonational bracketings of the sentence *Jane gave the book to Mary* into intonational phrases under Pierrehumbert's definition:

(56) a. (Jane gave the book to Mary)

    b. (Jane)(gave the book to Mary)

    c. (Jane gave the book)(to Mary)

    d. (Jane gave)(the book)(to Mary)

    e. (Jane)(gave)(the book to Mary)

    f. (Jane gave)(the book to Mary)

    g. (Jane)(gave the book)(to Mary)

    h. (Jane)(gave)(the book)(to Mary)

Of these, the only two that she regards as ill formed are (56e, f), the two that attempt to assign a single intonational phrase to the string *the book to Mary*. In section 2 we saw that such sequences are possible constituents in a combinatory categorial grammar, assembled via type raising and the backward composition rule ($<$**B**) to capture coordinate sentences like the following:

(57) Jane gave the book to Mary and the record to Sue.

However, such constituents must be made up of *two* intonational phrases.

These examples suggest that the notion of intonational structure can be identified with the notion of surface structure that emerges from the combinatory theory. I conjecture that the combinatory rules can be annnotated using Pierrehumbert's notation to specify simple conditions on the intonation tune fragments that may combine under them. For example, the forward composition rule must be annotated to express the injunction not to apply the rule when the tune indicates a prosodic phrase boundary between the two functions. On the other hand, *backward* composition must be annotated to express the requirement that both functions bear tunes indicating a complete prosodic phrase, while the basic rules of application are presumably not constrained by intonation and may combine all tunes and tune fragments.

The annotated forward-composition rule will then correctly allow the derivation of the nonstandard constituent *Mary prefers* in example (48) because this sequence does not include an intonational marker of an internal prosodic phrase boundary. (I am assuming that the sequence *Mary prefers* is uttered with a pitch accent on the first syllable of *Mary* and a "continuation rise" on the last syllable of *prefers*.)

(58) *Q*: I know that Fred perfers silk. But what does *Mary* prefer?
     A: (*Ma*-ry prefe-rs)(*cor*duroy).

The same rule will also accept sequences in which the same L + H* LH% contour is spread over more lengthy open propositions, such as *Mary says she prefers* . . . , as in the following version:

(59) *Q*: I know that Fred prefers silk. But what does *Mary* prefer?
     A: (*Ma*-ry says she perfe-rs)(*cor*duroy).

Such constituents are guaranteed to come with interpretations corresponding to the relevant open propositions. The annotated rule will similarly *forbid* the derivation of such a constituent when the intonation indicates that *Mary* ends with a prosodic phrase boundary and thus cannot compose with the material to its right. I conjecture that many of the examples considered by Jackendoff (1972, esp. p. 261) can be accepted by such rules to yield only the appropriate structures and the contextually appropriate interpretations.

A Cautious Conclusion

The above proposal is clearly in need of further research and refinement, and it may be wrong in details. However, I hope to have demonstrated that it is possible to salvage the intuition that intonational phrasing, syntax, and interpretation are very closely related levels of structure. According to the present theory, surface structure is identical to intonational structure, and prosodic phrase boundaries invariably coincide with syntactic ones. Information structure consists in the interpretations that the combinatory rules associate with nodes in this unified structure, and it denotes the contextually relevant open propositions and foci of the discourse in the form of functional abstractions over the propositions and their arguments. All of the diverse analyses and associated interpretations for a given proposition reduce via functional application to the same canonical function-argument relations. A number of important conditions on permissible intonational phrases, including Selkirk's sense-unit condition, follow as inevitable consequences of the theory, rather than from stipulation.[16] Moreover, the complex theoretical architecture of figure 1 can be replaced by the simpler one shown in figure 2, in which there is a single path between logical form and phonological form via surface syntax.

As noted earlier, this proposal represents a return to the architecture proposed by Chomsky and Jackendoff. The difference is that the concept of surface structure has been radically changed. It is now *just* surface

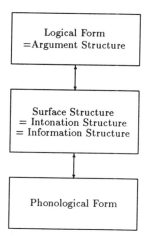

Figure 2
The architecture of a CCG-based prosody

structure, supplemented only by annotations. indicating the information-structural status of certain *constituents*. The kind of surface structure already embodies intonational structure and is assumed to serve as the direct input to the phonology.

While many problems remain both in parsing written text with grammars that include associative operations and at the signal-processing end, the benefits for automatic spoken-language understanding are likely to be significant. Most obviously, where in the past parsing and phonological processing have delivered conflicting structural analyses and have had to be pursued independently, they now are seen to work in concert. So we can devise processors that use both sources of information at once, thus simplifying both problems. For example, intonation may to a great extent determine syntactic structure in the present sense, although, of course, many genuine local and global syntactic ambiguities must be resolved by other means (see the discussions in Altmann and Steedman 1988; Marcus, Hindle, and Fleck 1983; and Pareschi and Steedman 1987 for alternative proposals). And a syntactic analysis that is so closely related to the structure of the signal should be easier to use to filter the ambiguities arising from lexical recognition. What is likely to be more important in the long run, however, is that the constituents that arise under this analysis are also semantically interpreted. I have argued that these interpretations are directly related to the concepts, referents, and themes that have been established in the context of discourse, say as the result of a question. The shortening and simplification of the path from speech to these higher levels of analysis offers the possibility of using these probably more effective resources to filter the proliferation of low-level analyses as well.

Acknowledgments

I am grateful to Elisabet Engdahl, Julia Hirschberg, Stephen Isard, Aravind Joshi, Ewan Klein, Bob Ladd, Mitch Marcus, Janet Pierrehumbert, Henry Thompson, and Bonnie Lynn Webber for comments and advice. This research was supported in part by an ESPRIT grant, project 393, to the University of Edinburgh and by DARPA grant no. N0014-85-K0018, ARO grant no. DAAG29-84-K-0061, and NSF grant no. CER MCS 82-19196 to the University of Pennsylvania.

Notes

1. While I am appealing to intuition in making such assertions about intonational structure in these examples, they and most other examples in this chapter are taken from elsewhere in the intonation literature and are not intended to be controversial.

2. Selkirk uses the term *focus structure* rather than the more general term *information structure* used here.

3. These remarks are informal and are intended to do no more than to provide intuitive background for the theory of prosody offered below. Nothing there hinges on the question of how such distinctions are actually grounded in a theory of discourse.

4. The example originates with Pierrehumbert.

5. See Steedman 1987 for a discussion of relative clauses like "(A woman) who(m) I think t likes lobster."

6. In Smullyan's terms, it is a forest containing the Bluebird, Thrush, and Starling. Certain generalizations of these basic combinators, such as Curry's $\mathbf{B}''$ are allowed. $\mathbf{T}$ is sometimes written $\mathbf{C}_*$.

7. Actually, the prinicple is a little stronger. Since combinators themselves are not phonologically realized, combinatory rules cannot apply to combinators. We therefore have a system in which combinators can apply only to *terms*.

8. We could achieve the same end with a category of the form $(X \backslash X)/X$. However, it is simpler for present purposes to use a syncategorematic rule.

9. The semantics of the rule depends upon the number of arguments, or "arity," of the function, a point which we will pass over here.

10. Again, the presentation of type raising as a rule of syntax, as opposed to a rule of the lexicon, is a matter of expository convenience rather than a commitment on the question.

11. The first is, of course, accepted to yield a *different* (and semantically anomalous) interpretation, indicated by a hash sign. The second has no analysis, as indicated by the asterisk.

12. In Steedman 1989 I proposed that a very restricted instance of this rule is implicated in the English gapping construction. However, this proposal does not affect the rest of the grammar.

13. See Steedman 1987 for an account of "parasitic" exceptions to this island constraint.

14. The proposal to account for prosodic constituency in terms of related grammars, including associative operations, has a precedent in Moortgat 1987, 1988a; Oehrle 1988; and Steedman 1985, p. 540). Related points concerning "bracketing paradoxes" in morphology are made by Moortgat (1988a, 1988b), Hoeksema (1985), and Hoeksema and Janda (1988). See also Wheeler 1981, 1988, and Schmerling 1980.

15. It is likely that this restriction is universal. But its origin is probably semantic or conceptual, not syntactic. A suitable choice of categories and combinatory rules (which it might amuse the reader to identify) would permit such constructions, just as it would in the case of the island violations discussed in the last section.

16. Among Selkirk's other conditions, the basic focus rule (1984, p. 207) and the condition of focus domination of pitch accent (1984, pp. 280–282) follow trivially from the fact that surface structure reflects focus information. I passed over these rules above because (as Selkirk points out) they would also follow trivially from the original Chomsky-Jackendoff proposal.

References

Altmann, Gerry, and Mark Steedman. 1988. Interaction with context during human sentence processing. *Cognition* 30:191–238.

Beckman, Mary. 1986. *Stress and Non-Stress Accent*. Dordrecht: Foris.

Beckman, Mary, and Janet Pierrehumbert. 1986. Intonational structure in Japanese and English. *Phonology Yearbook* 3:255–309.

Chomsky, Noam. 1971. Deep structure, surface structure, and semantic interpretation. In D. Steinberg and L. Jakobovits, *Semantics*. Cambridge: Cambridge University Press.

Chomsky, Noam, and Morris Hallé. 1968. *The Sound Pattern of English*. New York: Harper and Row.

Curry, Haskell, and Robert Feys. 1958. *Combinatory Logic*. Amsterdam: North-Holland.

Dowty, David. 1988. Type raising, functional composition, and nonconstituent coordination. In Richard T. Oehrle, E. Bach, and D. Wheeler (eds.), *Categorial Grammars and Natural Language Structures*. Dordrecht: Reidel.

Giegerich, Heinz. 1985. *Metrical Phonology and Phonological Structure*. Cambridge: Cambridge University Press.

Halliday, Michael. 1967. Notes on transitivity and theme in English, Part II. *Journal of Linguistics* 3:199–244.

Halliday, Michael. 1970. Language structure and language function. In John Lyons (ed.), *New Horizons in Linguistics*. London: Penguin.

Hajičová, Eva, and Petr Sgall. 1987. The ordering principle. *Journal of Pragmatics* 11:435–454.

Hajičová, Eva, and Petr Sgall. 1988. Topic and focus of a sentence and the patterning of a text. In János Petöfi (ed.), *Text and Discourse Constitution*. Berlin: De Gruyter.

Hirschberg, Julia, and Janet Pierrehumbert. 1986. Intonational structuring of discourse. *Proceedings of the Twenty-Fourth Meeting of the Association for Computational Linguistics*, New York.

Hoeksema, Jack. 1985. *Categorial Morphology*. New York: Garland Press.

Hoeksema, Jack, and Richard Janda. 1988. Implications of process-morphology. In Richard T. Oehrle, E. Bach, and D. Wheeler (eds.), *Categorial Grammars and Natural Language Structures*. Dordrecht: Reidel.

Jackendoff, Ray. 1972. *Semantic Interpretation in Generative Grammar*. Cambridge: MIT Press.

Karttunen, Lauri. 1989. Radical lexicalism. In Mark Baltin and Tony Kroch (eds.), Chicago: University of Chicago Press, to appear.

Kimball, John. 1973. Seven principles of surface structure parsing in natural language. *Cognition* 2:15–47.

Ladd, D. Robert. 1986. Intonational phrasing: The case for recursive prosodic structure. *Phonology Yearbook* 3:311–340.

Ladd, D. Robert. 1988. Metrical representation of pitch register. In John Kingston and Mary Beckman (eds.), *Papers in Laboratory Phonology*, vol. 1. Cambridge: Cambridge University Press, to appear.

Langendoen, D. Terence. 1975. Finite state processing of phrase structure languages and the status of readjustment rules in grammar. *Linguistic Inquiry* 6:533–554.

Liberman, Mark, and Alan Prince. 1977. On stress and linguistic rhythm. *Linguistic Inquiry* 8:249–336.

Marcus, Mitch, Don Hindle, and Margaret Fleck. 1983. D-theory: Talking about talking about trees. In *Proceedings of the Twenty-First Annual Meeting of the Association for Computational Linguistics*, Cambridge, Mass., June 1983.

Moortgat, Michael. 1987. Lambek categorial grammar and the autonomy thesis. Instituut voor Nederlandse Lexicologie, working paper 87-03, Leiden.

Moortgat, Michael. 1988a. *Categorial Investigations*. Dordrecht: Foris.

Moortgat, Michael. 1988b. Mixed composition and discontinuous dependencies. In Richard T. Oehrle, E. Bach, and D. Wheeler (eds.), *Categorial Grammars and Natural Language Structure*. Dordrecht: Reidel.

Nespor, Maria, and Irene Vogel. 1986. *Prosodic Phonology*. Dordrecht: Foris.

Oehrle, Richard. 1988. Multi-dimensional compositional functions as a basis for grammatical analysis. In Richard T. Oehrle, E. Bach, and D. Wheeler (eds.), *Categorial Grammars and Natural Language Structures*. Dordrecht: Reidel.

Pareschi, Remo, and Mark Steedman. 1987. A lazy way to chart parse with categorial grammars. *Proceedings of the Twenty-Fifth Annual Conference of the Association for Computational Linguistics*, Stanford, July 1987.

Pierrehumbert, Janet. 1980. *The Phonology and Phonetics of English Intonation*. Bloomington, Ind.: Indiana Linguistics Club.

Pierrehumbert, Janet, and Julia Hirschberg. 1987. The meaning of intonational contours in the interpretation of discourse. Manuscript, Bell Labs.

Prince, Alan. 1983. Relating to the grid. *Linguistic Inquiry* 14:19–100.

Prince, Ellen F. 1986. On the syntactic marking of presupposed open propositions. In *Papers from the Parasession on Pragmatics and Grammatical Theory at the Twenty-Second Regional Meeting of the Chicago Linguistic Society*.

Rooth, Mats. 1985. Association with focus. Ph.D. dissertation, University of Massachusetts, Amherst.

Schmerling, Susan. 1980. The proper treatment of the relationship between syntax and phonology. Paper presented at the fifty-fifth annual meeting of the Linguistic Society of America, December 1980, San Antonio, Texas.

Selkirk, Elisabeth. 1984. *Phonology and Syntax*. Cambridge: MIT Press.

Smullyan, Raymond. 1986. *To Mock a Mockingbird*. New York: Knopf.

Steedman, Mark. 1985. Dependency and coordination in the grammar of Dutch and English. *Language* 61:523–568.

Steedman, Mark. 1987. Combinatory grammars and parasitic gaps. *Natural Language and Linguistic Theory* 5:403–439.

Steedman, Mark. 1988. Combinators and grammars. In *Categorial Grammars and Natural Language Structures*, ed. by Richard T. Oehrle, E. Bach, and D. Wheeler. Dordrecht: Reidel.

Steedman, Mark. 1989. Coordination and constituency in a combinatory grammar. In Mark Baltin and Tony Kroch (eds.), *Alternative Conceptions of Phrase Structure*. Chicago: University of Chicago Press.

Szabolcsi, Anna. 1987. On combinatory categorial grammar. *Proceedings of the Symposium on Logic and Language*, Debrecen. Budapest: Akadémiai Kiadó.

Uszkoreit, Hans. 1986. Categorial unification grammars. In *Proceedings of the Eleventh International Conference on Computational Linguistics*, Bonn.

Wheeler, Deirdre. 1981. Aspects of a categorial theory of phonology. Ph.D. dissertation, University of Massachusetts, Amherst.

Wheeler, Deirdre. 1988. Consequences of some categorially motivated phonological assumptions. In Richard T. Oehrle, E. Bach, and D. Wheeler (eds.), *Categorial Grammars and Natural Language Structures*. Dordrecht: Reidel.

Wittenburg, Kent. 1986. Natural Language parsing with combinatory categorial grammar in a graph-unification based formalism. D.Phil. dissertation, University of Texas at Austin.

Wittenburg, Kent. 1987. Predictive combinators: A method for efficient processing of combinatory grammars. *Proceedings of the Twenty-Fifth Annual Conference of the Association for Computational Linguistics*, Stanford.

Zeevat, Henk, E. Klein, and J. Calder. 1987. An introduction to unification categorial grammar. In N. Haddock et al. (eds.), *Edinburgh Working Papers in Cognitive Science*, vol. 1, *Categorial Grammar, Unification Grammar, and Parsing*.

Chapter 22

Description Theory and Intonation Boundaries

Mitchell Marcus and Donald Hindle

1 Introduction

This paper is a first step towards an account of obligatory and optional intonation boundaries within an analysis of natural-language phrase structure that we call description theory (Marcus, Hindle, and Fleck 1983; Marcus 1987; and Hindle and Marcus, in preparation). In what follows, we will develop a computational analysis of intonation boundaries in which these boundaries directly affect the behavior of a postulated phrase-structure (PS) analyzer. We will argue that in view of the nature of description theory, intonation boundaries are optional just in those cases where the syntactic analysis is unaffected by either the presence or absence of these boundaries. We will argue that environments in which boundaries are obligatory have the property that the presence of these boundaries causes the syntactic analyzer to output structures that are fundamentally different than when they are absent.

This analysis will depend upon the view, incorporated description theory, that phrase-structure analysis results in an underspecified description of syntactic structure in which multiple chunks of syntactic description can be freely combined in post-phrase-structure processing by the simple use of equality over variables. In contrast to the free combination of multiple chunks, a single chunk that is the output of phrase-structure analysis may not be broken up later. Description theory is a deterministic framework in which whatever structure is assigned at each stage of analysis cannot be undone. If we assume these notions, the fundamental claim of what follows is just this: an intonation boundary is obligatory exactly in those environments where it prevents phrase-structure analysis from incorrectly attributing structural details to the utterance at hand, while a boundary is optional in cases where either it changes the output of PS analysis only by its own presence or the boundary splits the resulting description of syntactic structure into two chunks that can be transformed into the description created when the boundary is absent just by equating some of the variables in terms of which the structures are described. This paper will not provide an account of where optional boundaries are and are not possible; the reader should note that Steedman (in which volume) provides just such an account in a rather different framework.

Part and parcel to this claim is the further claim that the PS analyzer itself is sensitive only to the presence of boundary tones and to the distinction between major and minor boundaries, but not to any other details of either the intonation contour as a whole or to further details of the boundaries themselves (see Pierrehumbert 1980 for a thorough analysis of intonation structure as a whole). Certainly a full syntactic analysis cannot be established until other details of the intonation contour (e.g., the exact nature of the boundary tones) have been examined and taken into account, but this is done by processes following the level of analysis considered here.

Our approach to the interaction of intonation and syntax is intended in the long term as a serious test of our description-theory approach. As will be seen below, once we assume that intonation boundaries are part of the lexical stream, an adequate account of their effect on syntactic analysis falls out from the structure of description theory with no other assumptions unique to intonation boundaries.[1]

The organization of the chapter is as follows. Section 2 characterizes the intonational phenomena we are concerned with. Section 3 lays out the concepts of description theory needed to develop our account of the interaction of intonation and syntax, and it describes the phrase-structure component in some detail, providing an example to illustrate the key properties of phrase-structure descriptions. Outlined is one post-phrase-structure component essential to the account of obligatory boundaries, the theta-role component. Section 4 presents the central argument of this paper, illustrated with examples from English. Section 5 discusses a case of obligatory intonation boundaries in Japanese, providing an extended description of the processing involved in the syntactic recognition of the ambiguous particle *no* and offering an explanation of why the presence or absence of an intonation boundary forces a particular interpretation of this particle.

2 Optional and Obligatory Intonation Boundaries

In spoken language the speech stream does not constitute an undifferentiated string of words. Even within a single clause, the word stream is often broken up into a series of phonological subunits called intonation phrases. The phonological events that divide speech into these intonation phrases, which often cut across traditional syntactic constituents, are called intonation boundaries.

To characterize the interation of these intonation boundaries with syntactic structure, it is useful to classify such boundaries, following Downing (1970), into two functional categories: optional boundaries and obligatory boundaries. *Optional* boundaries can be inserted optionally (not surprisingly) at many but not all points in the speech stream, as determined by roughly the same as yet ill-specified pragmatic systems that determine assignment of abstract intonation contours in general. (Some pioneering studies into the pragmatics of these contours include Liberman and Sag 1974, Ladd 1980, Ward and Hirschberg 1985, and Pierrehumbert and Hirschberg, in press.) These optional boundaries freely cut across syntactic constituents; it is often said that they leave intact not syntactic units but the semantic units that Selkirk (1984) refers to as "sense units." The presence or absence of optional boundaries has no impact on the underlying syntactic structure; it is exactly from this particular perspective that the boundaries are optional. *Obligatory* boundaries, on the other hand, directly affect the well-formedness of the utterance in which they occur. If an obligatory boundary is deleted, the resulting speech either becomes unacceptable (and, we will argue, ungrammatical) or else is assigned a different grammatical analysis than the same string of words uttered with the boundaries present.

An illustration of the difference between obligatory and optional intonation boundaries is the pronunciation of (1) below.[2]

(1) John % he's the guy I told you about yesterday % stopped by this morning.

Here, as in parentheticals in general, the parenthetical is set off from the surrounding sentence by obligatory preceding and following intonation boundaries; if these boundaries are dropped, the sentence becomes unacceptable. It also appears that the parenthetical here must be uttered with a compressed pitch range relative to the surrounding context.

In some cases it superficially appears that the deletion of obligatory boundaries does not render the sentence unacceptable but merely changes the syntactic analysis of the word string. A little thought reveals that this occurs when two syntactic structures share terminal strings that differ only in intonation boundaries. In these cases the boundaries themselves distinguish between the two structures. Often it occurs that one or more boundaries are obligatory for one particular structure, while these boundaries are optional for a second structure. (Why these boundaries are optional, and not forbidden, will be discussed below.)

So, for instance, consider (2a).

(2) a. We only suspected % they all knew % that a burglary had been committed.

   b. *We* only sus*pect*ed % *they* all kn*ew* % that a burglary had been committed.

   c. We only suspected (%) they all knew that a burglary had been committed.

When pronounced with the fundamental frequency (F_0) contour shown in figure 1 (i.e., the intonation indicated schematically in (2a)), the utterance is interpreted as a matrix sentence with an inserted parenthetical. That is, *We only suspected that burglary had been committed* is taken as the matrix, with the parenthetical comment *they all knew* (presumably that we only suspected) inserted into that matrix.[3] To receive this interpretation, the major intonation boundaries before and after the parenthetical are obligatory and cannot be eliminated. It also appears that this parenthetical, like parentheticals in general, must be uttered with reduced pitch range.

These same intonation boundaries are obligatory if the utterance is to be given a "right-node-raised" interpretation, with a typical F_0 contour

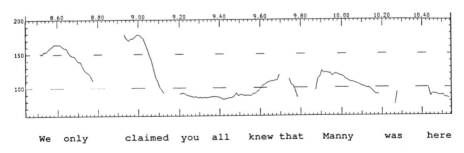

Figure 1
The fundamental frequency contour for an inserted parenthetical. The *x*-axis measures time in seconds, and the *y*-axis measures pitch in hertz.

shown in figure 2 and schematized in (2b). In this utterance, *we* and *suspected* are both contrasted with *they* and *knew*; each of these four words receives a pitch prominence. With this intonational detail, the utterance means something like that we only suspected that a burglary had been committed, but they (in contrast) knew that one had been committed.

If this same string of words is uttered as in (2c), without a boundary after *knew*, with something like the fundamental frequency contour shown in figure 3, the sentence can only be read as stating that we suspected that they knew that a burglary had been committed. The intonation boundary after *suspected* is optional; it can be added or deleted without changing the meaning of the sentence. Most interesting, an optional boundary can be inserted after *knew* that gives the same reading as (2c). This case differs intonationally from (2a) and (2b) by the lack of compression of pitch range relative to (2a) and the clear lack of pitch prominences in the final clause, as in (2b).

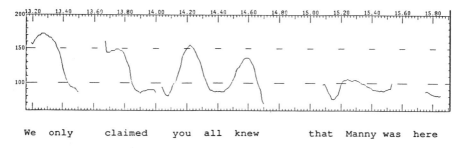

Figure 2
The fundamental frequency contour for a raised-right-node interpretation. The *x*-axis measures time in seconds, and the *y*-axis measures pitch in hertz.

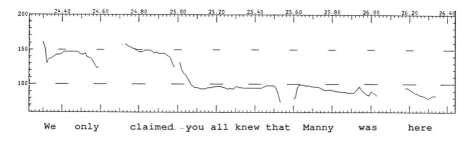

Figure 3
The fundamental frequency contour with no boundary after *knew*. The *x*-axis measures time in seconds, and the *y*-axis measures pitch in hertz.

These three different readings of the same lexical string demonstrate that optional boundaries have no effect on syntactic structure, while the presence or absence of obligatory boundaries affects the acceptability of a sentence as dramatically as the presence or absence of grammatical formatives.

3 An Outline of Description Theory

Description theory (D-theory) is intended to provide an account of both the operation and the output of aspects of human syntactic processing. In this paper we will sketch only those aspects of D-theory necessary for our present discussion of intonation boundaries. We will not attempt to discuss at length many other consequences of the theory. For more detail on an earlier formulation of this theory (as well as an earlier formulation of our analysis of intonation), see Hindle and Marcus, in preparation. In this section we will first lay out the key assumptions about phrase-structure (PS) analysis in D-theory. The principles presented here (rather compactly) are illustrated in the rest of the paper. This general discussion of the basics of phrase-structure analysis is followed by an example intended to illustrate key aspects of the D-theory account. The final part of this section briefly describes the theta-role component, an essential part of our account of obligatory intonation boundaries. The key assumptions about phrase structure analysis are as follows.

Strict X-bar grammar The first stage of syntactic analysis proper is phrase-structure analysis, which is done according to the specifications of an X-bar phrase-structure grammar. We take this grammar to consist of two components, the first of which is a context-free grammar roughly equivalent to the base component of a traditional generative grammar. The phrase-structure grammar itself instantiates a strong form of so-called X-bar theory (Jackendoff 1977). In particular all phrasal categories in this grammar must project nonvacuously to maximal projections, i.e., all lexical items of phrasal categories have maximal projections that include more than the head.

Leading-edge templates Associated with each phrase-structure rule is a set of templates, each of which is a short ordered list of maximal projections and particular lexical items. The phrase-structure analyzer will use these templates to initiate syntactic structures. The set of lexical items mentioned in the set of templates over an entire grammar forms the set of *specified* *lexical items* with respect to that grammar. These specified lexical items need be of no phrasal category, in the sense discussed immediately above. We assume that each template has associated with it a set of features, unary predicates predicated of any constituent whose leading edge is triggered by that template.

As a simple example of the interaction of phrase-structure rules and templates, consider (3), a highly simplified rule for NPs in English.

(3) PS rule: $N' \to Q' \, A' \, N$
    Templates: a. [N]
              b. [the]: $\{+\text{definite}\}$
              c. [*a*]: $\{-\text{definite}, +\text{singular}\}$

From only what has been said so far, the phrase structure rule (3) is to be interpreted to mean that an NP consist of a QP, followed by an AP, followed by a single head. Template (3a) states that a noun always initiates an NP; this is just an instance of the principle that *every* constituent is triggered by its head. We assume that such triggers need not be specified explicitly at all; we do so here only to clarify the use of templates in this grammar. Templates (3b, c) state that the lexical items *the* and *a* each trigger NPs, as discussed above. Template (3b) says if an NP is initiated by *the*, that NP is given the feature $+\,definite$; template (3c) says if initiated by *a*, it is given the features $-\,definite$, $+\,singular$.[4]

Constituents may form piles   Each rule of the CF grammar component (but not each template) is interpreted to permit an arbitrary number of constituents of each maximal projection occurring on its right-hand side. Thus a rule of the form

(4) $X \to A^{\text{max}} \, B^{\text{max}} \, X^{n-1}$

is interpreted to mean

(5) $X \to (A^{\text{max}})* \, (B^{\text{max}})* \, X^{n-1}$,

where the Kleene star (*) indicates zero or more constituents of the specified type. Thus phrase-structure rule (3) is actually interpreted to mean that an NP consists of *any number* of QPs, followed by *any number* of APs, followed by a single head. One motivation for this interpretation of phrase-structure rules is to replace the common rule schema

(6) $X \to X$ and X,

which captures conjunction in many grammars. In addition, the Kleene-star interpretation licenses appositives, multiple adjuncts, and multiple NP complements in VPs. We will refer to the set of constituents that instantiate a single maximal projection in the right-hand side of a phrase-structure rule as a *pile* of constituents. This interpretation gives us a three-dimensional analysis of conjunctions similar to that proposed by Goodall (1987) and discussed in a computational context by Fong and Berwick (1985). Another, more interesting motivation, discussed below, is central to the point of this chapter. While we will not dwell on the operation of the parser in much detail here, it is crucial that the parser follows a "late closure" strategy (Frazier 1978) while building piles: once initiated, the parser will add constituents onto a pile unless something intervenes.

The proposal embodied in these points may seem radical, but it is motivated by the desire to provide a clean and simple account of a wide range of largely unnoticed facts:

• The leading edges of constituents, but only the leading edges, can be idiosyncratic. The remainder of each maximal projection must be regular and simple.

• There can be many such idiosyncratic leading edges per maximal projection.

• The only syntactically obligatory elements of maximal projections are in the leading edge of each projection.

• Specified lexical items that initiate maximal projections appear to have very simple semantics that can be captured through sets of binary features assigned to the constituents they initiate.

Thus, it is consistent with this proposal that determiners like *the* and *a* are specified lexical items in that one and only one determiner can appear per NP, that determiner is phrase-initial, determiners are obligatory for singular NPs, and the semantics of these words appears to be adequately captured through a set of simple features including definite/indefinite, singular/plural/, and a few others.[5]

Descriptions, not trees   The output of phrase-structure analysis is not a tree but rather, to a first approximation, a *description* of a tree in that the output of PS analysis consists of a set of predications about a set of variables. Each variable will ultimately be taken as a name referring roughly to some temporally contiguous chunk of the spoken utterance. Crucially, the PS analyzer makes no claims about such an alignment. In particular, the components that further specify the output of phrase-structure analysis make no assumption that the values of these variables are disjoint.

Categories are feature bundles   Consistent with much current linguistic practice, we assume that categories like NP are really just a shorthand for a complex of features. For the purposes of this chapter we will assume a feature for the part of speech of the head of the construction, in this case N, and the bar level of the maximal projection. To keep figures simple yet complete, we will use a single bar to represent the maximal projection. Consistent with (4), these features are in fact simply predicates on names, so that "NP(*a*)" is really just a shorthand for "N(*a*) and Barlevel (*a*, 1)."

An illustration of phrase structure analysis
To make the operation of the phrase-structure analyzer clear, consider an example discussed in Marcus, Hindle, and Fleck 1983, which illustrates that this notion of description interacts with the notion of piles to yield a simple factoring of conjunction ambiguities, as illustrated in (7).

(7)   a.

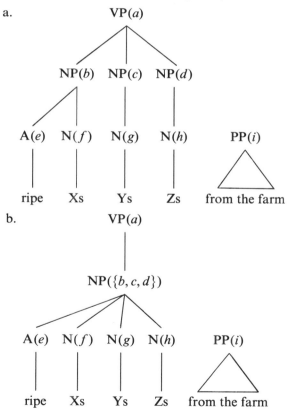

(For expository reasons, the conjunction *and* is ignored here. We'll deal with this briefly below.) Note that this example will most naturally receive a reading as a conjunction of nouns if X, Y, and Z are replaced with the lexical items *apples, peaches,* and *cherries* respectively, but as a conjunction of NPs if replaced with *cheese, bread,* and *cider.* Note also—and this is the crucial point—that b, c, and d are variables that may or may not ultimately refer to the same NP. If the variables b, c, and d are each ultimately taken to refer to different NPs, the interpretation of this structure will be the NP conjunction, roughly equivalent to the standard interpretation of the graphical representation shown in (7a). But while (7a) is a graphical representation of the output of PS analysis, its intended interpretation is *not* standard, because it graphically represents *the set of predications* made of the tree by the PS analyzer, but not the tree itself. Thus, "VP(a)" represents the predication that a is a VP, and the line from "VP(a)" to "NP(b)" represents the predication that a dominates b. With this much less direct representation, there is another consistent interpretation of the set of predications represented by (7a), namely that the variables b, c, and d all refer to the same NP. A system for analyzing natural language in our view would choose such an analysis when post-phrase-structure pragmatic processes decide that $b = c$ and $c = d$ and thereby reduce the three descriptions to one single description, as shown in (7b).

This example illustrates one key aspect of the relationship between the phrase-structure component in D-theory and later components: components that further specify the output of phrase-structure analysis, such as the mechanism that assigns theta roles, and pragmatically sensitive processes that determine the scope of conjunction in cases like that discussed above *cannot create names or add domination assertions*, with the exception to be discussed below that the theta-role mechanism can copy from the lexicon structures that serve to project the theta-structure of the verb. The phrase-structure component is also constrained: *the phrase structure mechanism cannot make use of equality.*

But now, consistent with the partiality of descriptions, this representation enables us to say of a node b that its head is an N without specifying its bar level simply by asserting N(b) but not Barlevel(b, 1) or Barlevel(b, 0). Conversely, we can say of a node c only that it is a maximal projection, Barlevel(c, 1), without saying what lexical category it projects. In this case c, could be equated by post-phrase-structure processes with any maximal projection. Similarly, one can have names about which nothing at all is predicated. In particular, the preterminal nodes above specified lexical elements are unspecified both as to bar level and as to lexical category.

This representation allows us to specify elements like *and* as being a template for a maximal projection that is unspecified as to lexical category:

(8) PS rule: XP

  Template: [*and*]

(Here and elsewhere, we will use "XP(*a*)" as a shorthand for "Barlevel(*a*, 1)." Note that the "X" here is not a variable. Rather, it stands for the lack of any predication at all.) We will stipulate that although such descriptions can be created, they cannot further expand into anything at all. The net result of the above rule, then, is that whenever the parser encounters the word *and*, it will create a new description for a maximal projection that will dominate only the otherwise unspecified preterminal node above the token of *and*.

What is the parser to do when it encounters such an XP during the parsing process? If the parser is building a pile of some particular maximal projections, it is reasonable for the parser simply to add this XP onto the pile. After all, if the parser has begun a pile of NPs, say, and it encounters a description of a node *b* that says merely that *b* is a maximal projection, such a description is perfectly consistent with *b* being an NP. But such an XP cannot initiate a pile. What kind of pile would it initiate? So we will assume that XPs can never be pile-initial.

One result of this is that an XP that immediately follows the head of a constituent will terminate the construction of that constituent, because the head of a constituent is never a maximal projection, by strict X-bar theory.

A brief sketch of theta-role assignment

In what follows, we postulate the operation of a very simple, very greedy theta-role component. We assume that whenever a lexical item is determined to project complement structure, for example, a verb, its theta structure is immediately projected from the lexicon. This is done by creating a copy of a skeletal tree from the lexicon with unique names for the various levels of projection of the verb and for each of its arguments, with domination assertions enforcing which arguments are internal and which external. Appropriate predications of case and number agreement are made of the arguments that promote the correct alignment of surface NPs with theta roles.

So, for example, merging the descriptions shown in (9a) and (9b) results in the description shown in (9c).

(9)   a.   S(*b*)   b.   *B*

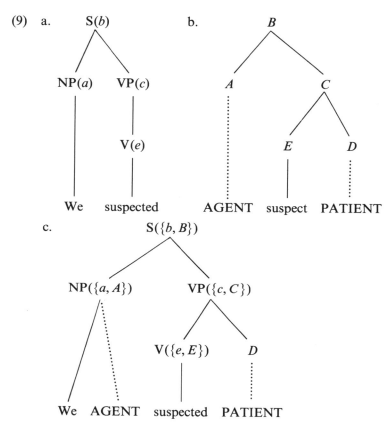

c.   S({*b, B*})

        NP({*a, A*})   VP({*c, C*})

                        V({*e, E*})   *D*

        We   AGENT   suspected   PATIENT

In (9a) we show a graphical depiction of the mental description of the phrase structure of the fragment *we suspected*; the description states that the structure *a* is an NP dominated by *b*, which is an S, which itself dominates the VP, *c*, etc. Upon encountering the verb *suspected*, the lexical component projects the lexical skeleton graphically depicted in (9b). This skeleton says merely that the verb *suspect* takes both a complement that (roughly) is either an entity or a proposition and also an external argument that must be animate. The details of the subcategorization here are much less important than the observation that the distinction between internal and external arguments can be made by such a lexical skeleton without further describing the nonterminal nodes in this description.

With this skeletal tree, theta-role assignment is done by equating its argument nodes with argument nodes describing appropriate constituents in the phrase-structure description and equating the internal nodes in the lexical skeleton to the appropriate internal nodes in the phrase-structure description. In the case of the descriptions of (9a) and (9b), c is equated with C, then b with B, and a with A, which results in the description depicted graphically in (9c), with the variable D in the lexical skeleton left unequated with any lexical material. For the moment, following a wide range of newly emerging experimental results in psycholinguistics, we assume that once the lexical head of a constituent has been encountered, surface-structure parsing of complements is not done per se. We assume that the theta mechanism equates potential argument NPs to theta roles as quickly as the NPs are created by the parser, running in parallel with the operation of the parse itself.[6]

4   Intonation Breaks and Theta-Role Assignment

With these preliminaries on the table, a simple account of intonation boundaries follows almost immediately. We need stipulate only that major intonation boundaries are introduced into the lexical stream fed to the parser and that the parser knows nothing about them. All else is but consequence! Upon encountering an utterly unknown "lexical" item, a deterministic parser simply terminates the constituent at hand, declaring that constituent complete. It continues to terminate successive constituents in its stack until the stack is empty, at which point the parser discards the offending item (at this point there really isn't anything else to do with it). The parser then begins to analyze the structure that continues after the intonation break.

The net result of treating intonation boundaries as unknown lexical items is that the parser generates a separate syntactic *description* for each intonation phrase. That the output consists of a string of descriptions of trees and not a string of trees themselves is crucial, because, as is well known, intonational phrases often do not divide sentences into some simple factorization of the grammatical structure. Often intonational phrases consist of fragments of constituents, as in

(10) This is the cat % that chased the rat % that ate the cheese.

and not, as Langendoen (1975) points out, something like

(11) *This is % the cat that chased % the rat that ate the cheese.

The key idea is that because these are descriptions, the judicious use of equality can in effect "glue" tree fragments back into reasonable trees once more, *just as long as no wrong attachments have been made.* So, for example, the parser can build a description for each relative clause in sentence (10) indicating that there is some NP that dominates that relative clause, as shown in (12).

(12)

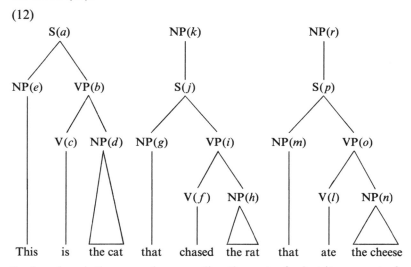

This is the cat that chased the rat that ate the cheese

Such a description encodes very directly part of what it means to know that an S serves as a relative clause, i.e., that it is dominated by an NP. Note the crucial point that because these are descriptions, there is no presupposition that each name for a node refers to a unique node. Thus some process after phrase structure, presumably some aspect of pragmatic processing that determines something like Altmann and Steedman's (1988) principle of referential support, will eventually simply assert that $d = k$ and $h = r$, which results in the structure that one expects in this case. This account is consistent with the experimental results of Crain and Steedman (1985) and Altmann and Steedman (1988) if we assume (rather more narrowly than these researchers themselves interpret their results) that the exact attachment of adjuncts like relative clauses and prepositional phrases is determined only after pragmatic information comes into play.

Another simple consequence of this account is that intonation boundaries are obligatory in sentences like (13), taken from Frazier and Rayner 1982, where an intonation break is required in speech between *drank* and *the strange looking water*.

(13) After you drank the strange looking water was discovered to be polluted.

If this sentence is pronounced as a single intonation phrase with no intonation break, the sentence reliably causes a garden path. The key point here is that *drank* potentially subcategorizes for NP complements like *the water*, but the NP here is to be analyzed not as filling such a theta role of the verb but rather as serving as the subject of the following major clause.

By our account, if the NP is contiguous with the verb, the theta-role mechanism will immediately appropriate the NP to fill a role in its theta grid, which will lead the phrase-structure analyzer down a garden path. If an intonation boundary intervenes, however, the theta-role mechanism cannot immediately equate a following NP with a role in its theta grid. In general, then, the theta-role mechanism will immediately appropriate all noun phrases encountered as complement structures unless an intonation boundary intervenes (in both sense of *intervenes*). We should note that we believe that the comma functions similarly in text, which accounts for the very clear and obvious conscious garden-path effect caused by such a sentence when presented visually in text form without the comma.

Now let us turn our attention to the obligatory and optional intonation boundaries of the various readings of sentence (2), repeated here.

(2) a. We only suspected % they all knew % that a burglary had been committed.

b. *We* only sus*pec*ted % *they* all kn*ew* % that a burglary had been committed.

c. We only suspected (%) they all knew that a burglary had been committed.

As it turns out, the obligatory and optional character of each of the intonation boundaries for (2a–c) follows from the general principles stated above, given the single output of the phrase structure analyzer and the form of the final structures that must result for each of the readings of (2).

Consider first the form of the output of the phrase-structure analyzer. The intonation boundary immediately after the verb *suspected* causes the phrase-structure analyzer simply to output the description it has constructed for the first intonation phrase. This occurs before the theta-role processor can assign any syntactic structure to the theta role of its complement, associated with the variable D in (15).

(15)

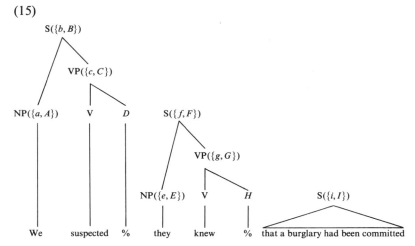

Similarly, the boundary after "knew" terminates the surface structure analysis of the second intonation phrase; this prevents the theta-role processor from immediately filling the complement associated with the variable H in the theta-projection. Thus, the presence of the two boundaries causes the parser to produce a string of three descriptions, as shown in (15).

The various visible root nodes and unfilled theta roles in this forest now allow a range of additional equations to be made during post-phrase-structure analysis. Crucially, both the variable D in the description of the theta grid of *suspected* and the variable H in the description of the theta grid of *knew* remain unequated with any lexical NPs, which licenses the assertion of equalities in later processing. Also, both the S node f and the S node i (and of course the root node b) remain undominated by other nodes. Thus they are candidates for additional equality assertions in later processing.

Consider first the parenthetical reading of (2a). This reading results if later processes, interpreting in part the compressed pitch range in the second phrase, equate variable D with i, so that the clause *that a burglary had been committed* is now taken as complement of *we suspected*. The clause fragment *they knew* is taken as a parenthetical fragment interposed between the two discontinuous segments of the main clause. But with what is H to be equated to saturate the theta grid of the parenthetical? The only visible node not equated to any other node is the root node b! Thus, this node is equated with H, yielding the reading that (a) we suspected that a burglary had been committed and, parenthetically, that they knew (a).

In the case of the right-node-raised reading (2b), the equations are slightly more complex. By means of some kind of mapping operator, we assume, D is equated with i, which fills the complement of *we suspected* with the clause *that a burglary had been committed*, and H is equated with i, which fills the complement of *they knew* with *that a burglary had been committed* as well.

The simple reading (2c) is also straightforward to derive. This reading results from equating D with f and, if there is a boundary between *know* and *that*, equating H with i. This last analysis, (2c), shows why the intonation boundaries are optional in this structure. According to our account, what would have been immediately achieved by the greedy theta grabbers can be achieved by processes that consider and then reject more complex options. The key point is that the intonation boundaries inserted into this particular analysis are optional, as it turns out, exactly because they do not change the analyses of the individual fragments from what they would have been had the boundaries not been present. Thus, optionality of boundaries need not be explicitly represented anywhere within the processing system itself.

But now we need to consider why the two intonation boundaries are obligatory in readings (2a–b). The key point here is that if either of these boundaries were missing, whichever NP would then be contiguous with the proceeding verb would be immediately incorporated into its theta grid during the first-pass processing. If the intonation boundary after *suspected* were absent, for example, then the theta-role mechanism would immediately equate D with f during the first pass. This would make it superfluous for second-pass processes to attempt to equate anything with these nodes. But that would mean that D would no longer be available to be equated with i to yield either the parenthetical or the raised-right-node interpretations of (2). Similarly, if the intonation boundary after *knew* were absent, the theta-role mechanism would immediately equate H with i. This would make i no longer available to be equated with D to derive the parenthetical interpretation or to be equated with both D and H to derive the right-node-raised interpretation. Thus it is that both of these boundaries are obligatory if either the parenthetical or the right-node-raised interpretations are to be obtained.

5   Intonation Boundaries and the Japanese Particle "No"

In the section above, we have given an account, for the particular case of English, of why intonation boundaries are obligatory in some contexts while optional in others. In essence, we have argued that intonation boundaries cause the phrase-structure analyzer to output a string of tree fragments, with root nodes and unexpanded nonterminal nodes, which can then be equated to other nodes by post-phrase-structure processes. This analysis immediately leads to the question of whether this account provides an idiosyncratic analysis of English for some reason or other, or whether it will generalize to apply across languages. While answering this question in full will require a careful examination of a very broad range of languages, we will show in the remainder of this paper that this same analysis appears a hold for at least one language unrelated to English, namely Japanese.

A sketch of Japanese syntax

A few brief comments about Japanese syntax may be useful to those unfamiliar with the structure of this language. First of all, word order in Japanese and English are distinctly different. While English sentences typically have the pattern SVO (subject, verb, object), in Japanese the surface order is SOV, with the verb final. More generally, Japanese is strongly *head-final*. Thus in the NP (16), the noun *tegami* ('letter'), which is the head of NP, is final and is preceded by the relative clause *John no Mary ni yondeyatta* 'which John read to Mary'.

(16) a. [$_{NP}$ [$_S$ John no   Mary ni   yondeyatta $_S$] tegami $_{NP}$]
     b.   John NOM Mary DAT read-to   letter
     c. 'the letter (which) John read to Mary

Similarly, in this relative clause, as in all sentences, the verb *yondeyatta* 'read-to' comes at the end of the VP *Mary ni yondeyatta* 'read to Mary', and the PP *Mary ni* 'to Mary' is a *post*positional phrase, with the head of the PP, the postposition itself, the final element.

A second key difference between Japanese and English is that Japanese sentences regularly follow a topic-comment structure, with a topicalized constituent followed by the particle *wa* in sentence initial position. If either the subject or object of the verb serves as topic, the nominative or accusative case marking is missing. Hence,

(17) a. John wa   tegami o   yonda.
     b. John TOPIC letter   ACCUSATIVE read
     c. 'John read the letter.' *or*
        'Speaking of John, (he) read the letter'.

(18) a. Tegami wa   John ga   yonda.
     b. Letter   TOPIC John NOMINATIVE read.
     c. 'Speaking of the letter, John read (it).'

Two final facts. To a first approximation, the order of NPs in a sentence can be freely permuted, but the verb must remain final. Japanese also freely allows zero anaphora; all elements of the sentence that are (roughly) recoverable from context can be deleted, except for the verb.

For Japanese, we assume a phrase structure component that extends rules like those given below:

(19) PS rule: S → P V'
    Templates: a. [V']
            b. [P'$_{+case}$]
(20) PS rule: P' → N' P
    Templates: a. [P]
            b. [N']

Rule (19) says that an S consists of any number of PPs, followed by any number of VPs. Template (19a) states that an S is initiated by a VP, and template (19b) states that an S is initiated by a PP bearing case. Rule (20) states that postpositional phrases consist of any number of NPs followed by a postposition. According to this rule, PPs are triggered by one of two constituents: its head (template (20a)) or an NP (template (20b)). A consequence of template (20b) is that all NPs will immediately initiate dominating PPs. Thus this analysis states that there are no bare NPs in Japanese, that all apparently bare NPs are in fact PPs with zero postpositions.

The uses of the particle "no"

The analysis we will sketch here is a part of a larger grammatical analysis that attempts to unify the various uses of the Japanese particle *no*, a particle which can play a dizzying variety of grammatical roles in different contexts. (The full analysis is discussed in Hindle and Marcus, in preparation. The analysis we give here differs in subtle but crucial ways from the earlier analysis given in Marcus 1987.) As a postposition, *no* can mark either the genitive case or (in relative clauses only) the nominative case. It can also serve as an appositive marker, making the NP it follows an appositive of the following NP. Thus, for example, (21a) is ambiguous between a reading where *no* is a genitive marker with the reading given in (21c) and a reading where *no* marks an appositive with roughly the reading of (21d).

(21) a. isha   no sensei
    b. doctor *no* teacher
    c. 'the doctor's teacher'
    d. 'the teacher, who is a doctor'

In the NP given in (16) above, *no* serves as a nominative marker; this is grammatical only because the sentence whose subject it marks is a relative clause. The particle *no* also can follow a PP or an S to signal a headless relative clause, as in (22) and (23), respectively. (Note that if it follows an NP in a matrix S, the interpretation is of a possessive, as in (24). Hindle and Marcus, in preparation, deals with such cases in detail.)

(22) a. Sore wa [NP [PP New York kara] no] hikooki desu
     b. that TOPIC   New York from *no* plane   be
     c. 'That plane's the one from New York.'

(23) a. [NP [S Asoko   ni   suwatte iru] no] ga   John desu
     b.   over-there DATIVE sitting be *no* NOM John be
     c. 'The one who is sitting over there is John.'

(24) a. Sono hon   wa   John no   desu.
     b. that book TOPIC John GENITIVE be
     c. 'That book is John's.'

While we will not give examples here, the particle *no* can also appear sentence-finally as a particle that signals a question or to weaken the force of declaratives, typically in so-called women's speech.

The particle "no" in the spoken language
While the analysis of *no* that we will sketch below resulted from our search for a unified analysis of this particle, what is most crucial to our present concerns is that this analysis interacts with exactly the same assumptions made about the processing of intonation boundaries for English to provide an account of the following fact:

While the particle *no* is completely ambiguous in some contexts in the written language, these contexts are completely disambiguated in speech by the presence or absence of an intonation boundary immediately following *no*.

Thus in the written form of the NP (25a) *no* is ambiguous between marking nominative and genitive case, as indicated by (25c, d). The reading glossed in (25c) has roughly the meaning of (25e), while the reading glossed in (25d) has the meaning of (25f), with a zero pronoun serving as subject. While these facts are not well known, we are told by many native speakers of Japanese that these judgments are quite clear.

(25) a. John no   kodomo ni   yondeyatta tegami
     b. John *no*   child   DATIVE read-to   letter
     c. John NOMINATIVE child   DATIVE read-to   letter
     d. John GENITIVE   child   DATIVE read-to   letter
     e. 'the letter that John read to the child'
     f. 'the letter that x read to John's child'
     g. John no % kodomo ni yondeyatta tegami

In speech, however, (25a) has the interpretation (25c), with reading (25e), only if an intonation boundary intervenes between *no* and *kodomo*, as in (25g), while it has only the interpretation (25d), with reading (24f), if there is no intervening boundary.

We will not lay out a sketch of our analysis of *no*, focusing on how this analysis gives accounts of the genitive and nominative usages of *no*. We will then show how this analysis interacts with the assumptions about intonation boundaries given above to account for the data in (25).

The phrase structure of the particle "no"

Our analysis of *no* consists of two parts: the handling of *no* by the phrase-structure component and a set of rules that specify the subsequent processing of the resulting structures by post-phrase-structure components. The particle *no* is handled within the phrase-structure component by the single phrase-structure rule given below.

(26) PS rule: $X' \rightarrow$?

     Template: [*no*]

The defective phrase-structure rule shown as (26) says only that a phrase that is a maximal projection of unknown category has some unspecified expansion. The template given in (26) says that the particle *no* initiates a maximal projection of unknown type.

The net effect of (26) is that whenever the parser encounters an instance of the particle *no* in its input stream, it will initiate the description of a new node, say x, of which the parser will assert Barlevel(x, 1) without asserting what category x is. As discussed above, if the parser is currently attempting to attach constituents of some maximal projection or other, say NP, it will attach this new XP (i.e., this new maximal projection of unknown category) to the constituent under construction because its description is consistent with x's being an NP. Note that unification is not done at this point in the analysis process, so that x remains partially described.

The phrase-structure analysis in detail

Let us turn to a concrete example. Assume that (21a) above is part of a *ga*-marked postpositional phrase (i.e., *isha no sensei ga*), which is input to a description-theory parser for Japanese that incorporates this grammar fragment. This input will result in the structure shown in (27).

(27)

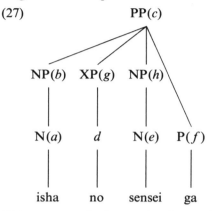

This structure is the result of something like the following process: The noun *isha* is parsed into an NP represented by node variable b, by a phrase-structure rule unspecified here. This NP description matches template (20b), which causes the parser to initiate the description of the PP c and to assert that c dominates b. Next, the particle *no* matches template (26), which causes the parser to initiate the description of the XP g. Since there is no right hand side to this phrase-structure rule, the XP g is immediately completed, and the parser attempts to find a parent for this node. Given phrase-structure rule (20), the parser will assert that node c dominates all the nodes immediately following b that are indistinguisable from NPs, and hence the parser asserts that the XP g is dominated by c.

The rest of the analysis is straightforward. The noun *sensei* causes the parser to construct a description for the NP h, and the parser, still looking for nodes indistinguishable from NPs, asserts that c dominates h. The parser next encounters f, the postposition *ga*, and asserts that c dominates f. But now nothing can continue the PP c, since a constituent can have only one head, and so the constituent c is complete.

But what are post-phrase-structure processes to do with this output? It is not hard to see that some further specification of the structure shown in (27) must be provided. The grammatical analysis of an input is finished only when every node in that input has been assigned a complete analysis according to the grammar. It is not enough that the analysis is consistent with the (albeit highly unspecified) phrase-structure grammar. For semantic analysis to take place, post-phrase-structure processes must complete what the phrase-structure analyzer has started. This means that two aspects of the output of the analyzer shown in (27) must be further specified: First, the pile of maximal projections dominated by node c in (27) must be assigned some further structure. Second, the incomplete descriptions of nodes g and d must be somehow completed. But how can this be done *with only equality between existing nodes and without creating any further structure*? The key question is simply this: what completely specified nodes can g and d be equated with such that the result is a fully specified legal structure?

All this must be accomplished within one key constraint imposed by Japanese: whatever structures result must be head-final except for any morphology, and all morphology must follow the head. We have no account of why this should be so for Japanese, and so must stipulate this behavior here, but the rigidity of the head-final nature of Japanese is uncontestable.

One simple possibility is to equate node variable g with node variable h, and node variable d with node variable b. These assertions of equality are legal because the descriptions of g and h are compatible, which allows these nodes to be equated, and because d is completely unspecified and therefore can be equated with any node at all. Also, both g and h are directly dominated by the same node, b and d are both dominated by c, the first node directly, the second through g. In the resulting structure, shown in (28), the node with variable b is still dominated by the node with c, although node g now mediates this domination relation.[7]

(28)   PP(c)

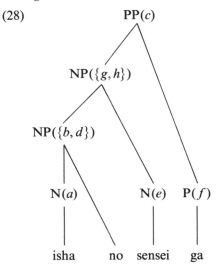

NP($\{g, h\}$)

NP($\{b, d\}$)

N(a)   N(e) P(f)

isha   no   sensei   ga

Note that all node variables are now fully specified, because g has inherited the description of h by equality and b has inherited the structure of d.

But now examine (28) carefully. The structure that results from these two equations is a standard analysis for genitives, like the genitive reading of sentence (21a) above, i.e., the reading given as (21c). The result of the two equality assertions is that two sibling structures have now been incorporated into one structure, with the left sibling subordinated to the right sibling. The particle *no* in this analysis serves not as a postposition but merely as a morphological flag of the subordination relation. Also, note that the head-final constraint for Japanese is observed and that the particle *no*, here serving as a morphological particle, follows the head of its constituent.

Were it not for the head-final nature of Japanese, a mirror-image analysis to the above, equating g with b and d with h, would also be possible. But this would result in subordinating the left sibling to the right sibling, which violates the head-final nature of Japanese. Similarly, equating g, h, *and* d yields a structure with a morphological particle phrase internal. This analysis is also blocked by the stipulation on Japanese phrase structure.

But what if node variable g is equated to variable c? The two variables can be equated because the descriptions of g and c are compatible and the domination relation is reflexive. However, if g is equated with c, then d must be equated with some other fully specified variable to result in a legal structure. One possibility is to equate d with b, which results in two sister NPs, the first of which is morphologically marked by *no*. Again, the particular constraints for Japanese are met: the head of the structure is final, and the morphological marking of the first NP follows its head. This structure (29) is a plausible analysis for appositives like the reading of (21a) given as (21d).

(29)   PP($\{g, c\}$)

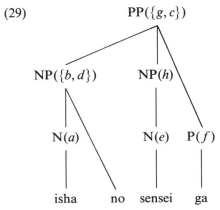

This exhausts all possible equations involving node g. (We will discuss a few more impossible equations below.)

Now consider a slightly different case where no other NP immediately follows the particle *no*, as in (30a) below.

(30) a. John no yonda tegami
  b. John *no* read letter
  c. 'the letter John read'

In this case, post-phrase-structure processes can yield a very different structure from those discussed above. If no NP follows *no*, the phrase-structure analysis will be exactly equivalent to the initial segment of (31a), except that the XP, here node e, will be the last child of the PP, here c.

(31) a. PP(c)

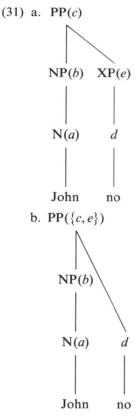

  b. PP($\{c, e\}$)

As in the appositive case above, the node variable e can be equated with c, which yields the structure represented in (31b). In this case, however, there is no necessity that the node variable d be equated with any other node. Why? After node variables c and e are equated, there is a natural interpretation of node-variable d that follows from the phrase-structure rule itself for completing the grammatical description of the tree fragment under c. Since (1) node d dominates a lexical item, (2) it is immediately dominated by a node at the first bar level, (3) that node dominates no head, and (4) node d is phrase final, it follows by a simple theorem that node d must be the head of the structure. Thus we can simply assume that any node in this configuration will be interpreted by post-phrase-structure processes as being the head of the larger structure. In this particular case it follows that *no* is a postposition that is the head of the PP *John no*. It is structure (31b) that can yield the interpretation of *no* as a subject marker, i.e., the head of the PP.

Why is this structure available only if no NP follows the particle *no*? The answer to this question explains why an intonation boundary disambiguates the two readings of (25a), why *no* cannot be taken as a subject marker if it is followed by an NP without an intervening intonation boundary. Without an intonation boundary following *no*, the initial segment of (25a) results in exactly the same phrase-structure analysis given in (27) on the assumption that the parser greedily analyses all constituents that can be placed into a pile of constituents. This structure is shown in (32a).

(32) a. PP(c)

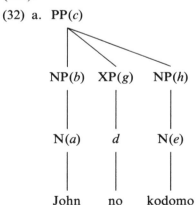

b. PP(*c*)

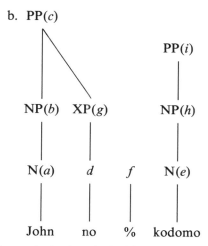

John   no   %   kodomo

The analysis given in (31) is not simply not available, given the head-final constraint of Japanese syntax. Most simply put, the node *d* is followed by the N *e*, so that it cannot be the head of either *c* nor *h*, given head-final constraint. As a secondary consideration, if *d* were described as a post-position, the NP *h* would no longer have any place in the phrase structure, given the particular rule for PPs considered here.

If, however, a boundary is present following the *no*, the parser will turn out two separate PP descriptions for the initial segment of this utterance, as shown in (32b). In this case the intonation boundary causes the parser to terminate the description of the PP *c*. Subsequently, the NP *h* after the intonation break triggers a new PP. In this analysis the description of the first PP is exactly parallel to that of (31), and the particle *no* here can be assigned a structure where it can serve as a postposition without grammatical violation. The second PP will then dominate whatever postposition follows it and will serve a grammatical function distinct from PP *c*. Thus the availability of the interpretation of *no* as a subject marker when followed by a noun depends crucially on the presence of an intonation boundary after the *no*.

6 Conclusion

In this paper we have argued that when intonation boundaries are obligatory, it is because their absence would lead the syntactic analyzer to a syntactic misanalysis. In particular, the absence of an obligatory boundary leads the phrase-structure analyzer and the theta-role component wrongly to join together phrases that later have to be broken apart. In contrast, optional boundaries cause the phrase-structure analyzer merely to have as output a greater number of unconnected pieces, which subsequent analysis components can appropriately join together as permitted by the properties of syntactic descriptions in description theory.

This account falls out naturally from several assumptions basic to description theory (assumptions that we have outlined in this paper without giving their full motivation). The key assumptions are as follows: Syntactic analysis is deterministic—syntactic pieces once built cannot easily be taken apart. Phrase-structure analysis is a process of incremental description by a series of components; pieces output by the phrase-structure analyzer can be glued together by subsequent components through the use of equality. Intonational boundaries are entered into the lexical stream just like standard lexical items. With these assumptions our account follows from the fact that intonation boundaries have no lexical properties that the phrase-structure analyzer can interpret. This paper is, of course, just a beginning at accounting for the relationship of intonation and syntax. We have restricted our attention to one level of boundary (major-phrase boundaries), ignoring those aspects of (post-pharse-structure) sentential analysis that are sensitive to intermediate phrase boundaries and tune type. Within these restrictions we have illustrated how the description-theory framework provides an account of obligatory intonation boundaries for in two unrelated languages: English and Japanese.

Acknowledgments

We would like to thank O. Fujimura, M. Beckman, J. Pierrehumbert, J. Hirschberg, A. Joshi, M. Liberman, M. Tanenhaus, J. Henderson, G. Altmann, and R. Ladd for many valuable comments. Preparation of this chapter was supported in part by DARPA grant N00014-85-K0018 and ARO grant DAA29-84-9-0027.

Notes

1. We will assume in this paper that the acoustic-phonetic and phonological components of the language-understanding system will isolate and transcribe intonation boundaries into the lexical stream. For a discussion on the relation between acoustics-phonetics and phonology, see, for example, Pierrehumbert 1980. For a discussion of automatic extraction of boundaries, see Pierrehumbert 1983 and Ljolje 1986.

2. We will transcribe intonation breaks with the % symbol.

3. In figures 1–3, instead of the exact string of words of sentence 2, we show F_0 contours for the syntactically equivalent word string *We only claimed you all knew that Manny was here* to minimize local segmental perturbations of F_0 that might

obscure the relevant F_0 pattern. Obviously, the discussion of the interpretation of F_0 contours in these sentences is independent of the particular word string.

4. It might seem that these templates would initiate two separate NPs for a phrase like *the boy*, the first by template (3b) and a second by template (3a). In this case, after the first NP is initiated, general rule-ordering principles, which we will not discuss here, will cause a potential subconstituent also specified in templates to be attached rather than trigger a new constituent of the same kind.

5. While we will not further pursue this issue in this chapter, it is important to note that the PS grammar itself describes only underlying structure. Variations between this underlying structure and the surface string result first from a small collection of local transformations, which are "undone" by the PS analyzer as it runs in much the same way as local transformations are undone in Parsifal (Marcus 1980) or Fidditch (Hindle 1983).

6. While we don't have time to explore this here, this mechanism has much in common with the notion of lexicalized TAGs introduced in Schabes and Joshi 1988.

7. The domination relation between b and c is not shown in (28). After additional equality assertions are made by post-phrase-structure processes, such redundant (but still true) domination relations are simply ignored.

References

Altmann, G., and M. Steedman. 1988. Interaction with context during human sentence processing. *Cognition* 30:191–238.

Crain, S., and M. Steedman. 1985. On not being led up the garden path: The use of context by the psychological syntax processor. In D. Dowty, L. Kartunnen, and A. Zwicky (eds.), *Natural Language Parsing: Psychological, Computational, and Theoretical Perspectives*. Cambridge: University of Cambridge Press.

Downing, B. 1970. Syntactic structure and phonological phrasing in English. Ph.D. dissertation, University of Texas at Austin.

Fong, S., and R. Berwick. 1985. New approaches to parsing conjunctions using Prolog. In *Proceedings of the Twenty-Third Annual Meeting of the Association for Computational Linguistics*. Chicago.

Frazier, L. 1978. On comprehending sentences: Syntactic parsing strategies. Ph.D. dissertation, University of Connecticut.

Frazier, L., and K. Rayner. 1982. Making and correcting errors during sentence comprehension: Eye movements in the analysis of structurally ambiguous sentences. *Cognitive Psychology* 14:178–210.

Goodall, G. 1987. *Parallel Structures in Syntax*. Cambridge: Cambridge University Press.

Hindle, D. 1983. Deterministic parsing of syntatic non-fluencies. In *Proceedings of the Twenty-First Annual Meeting of the Association for Computational Linguistics*. MIT.

Hindle, D., and M. Marcus. In preparation. A description theory account of intonation boundaries in Japanese.

Jackendoff, R. 1977. *X' Syntax: A Study of Phrase Structure.* Cambridge: MIT Press.

Ladd, D. R. 1980. *The Structure of Intonational Meaning.* Bloomington, Ind.: Indiana University Press.

Langendoen, T. 1975. Finite state parsing of phrase-structure languages and the status of readjustment rules in grammar. *Linguistic Inquiry* 4, no. 4.

Liberman, M., and I. Sag. 1974. Prosodic form and discourse function. In *Papers from the Tenth Regional Meeting of the Chicago Linguistics Society.*

Ljolje, A. 1986. Intonation and phonetic segmentation using hidden markov models. Ph.D. dissertation, Cambridge University.

Marcus, M. 1980. *A Theory of Syntactic Recognition for Natural Language.* Cambridge: MIT Press.

Marcus, M 1987. Deterministic parsing and description theory. In P. Whitelock et al., (eds.), *Linguistic Theory and Computer Applications.* London: Academic Press.

Marcus, M., D. Hindle, and M. Fleck. 1983. D-theory: Talking about talking about trees. In *Proceedings of the Twenty-First Annual Conference of the Association for Computational Linguistics.* MIT.

Pierrehumbert, J. 1980. The phonology and phonetics of English intonation. Ph.D. dissertation, Massachusetts Institute of Technology.

Pierrehumbert, J. 1983. Automatic Recognition of Intonational Patterns. In *Proceedings of the Twenty-First Annual Meeting of the Association for Computational Linguistics.* MIT.

Pierrehumbert, J., and M. Beckman. 1988. *Japanese Tone Structure.* Cambridge: MIT Press.

Pierrehumbert, J., and J. Hirschberg. In press. The meaning of intonation contours in the interpretation of discourse. In M. Pollack and P. Cohen (eds.), *Plans and Intentions in Communications and Discourse.* Cambridge: MIT Press.

Schabes, Y., and A. Joshi 1988. An Earley-type parsing algorithm for tree adjoining grammars. In *Proceedings of the Twenty-Sixth Annual Meeting of the Association for Computational Linguistics.* Buffalo, N.Y.

Selkirk, E. 1984. *Phonology and Syntax: The Relation between Sound and Structure.* Cambridge: MIT Press.

Ward, G., and J. Hirschberg. 1985. Implicating uncertainty: The pragmatics of fall-rise intonation. *Language* 61:747–776.

Chapter 23

| Phrase Structure and Intonational Phrases: Comments on the Chapters by Marcus and Steedman | Aravind K. Joshi |

This chapter is based on my notes prepared for oral comments on "Description Theory and Intonation Boundaries" by Mitch Marcus and Donald Hindle and "Syntax and Intonational Structure in a Combinatory Grammar" by Mark Steedman. Since the reader will have read their chapters before reading these comments, I will not reproduce their detailed discussions but only refer to some of their key points as I need them.

What Are They Trying to Do?

Both Marcus and Steedman are concerned with intonational phrasing and its relationship to syntactic structure. Marcus subscribes to the more conventional X-bar syntax. His parser, however, produces not phrase-structure trees but descriptions of trees, which, on occasion, may underspecify the structure. Steedman has developed a combinatory categorial (CG) framework, which leads to nonstandard constituents (and hence gives rise to flexible phrase structures).

Intonational phrases (IP) and intonational boundaries (IB) do not necessarily line up with the conventional phrase structure and phrase boundaries. This is especially true for the so-called optional IBs. The term *optional* makes sense only in the case where there is a fixed phrase structure specified for a sentence, as is the case for Marcus. Marcus completely ignores these optional boundaries because for him these boundaries do not affect the syntactic structure. He assumes that these boundaries are specified by some mechanism that relates pragmatics to the intonational contours.

Marcus is concerned with obligatory boundaries, i.e., those boundaries that if deleted would result in an unacceptable sentence or would be incorrectly analyzed by his parser. Steedman is more concerned (at least in this paper) with the so-called optional boundaries. Strictly, the optional/

obligatory distinction is not relevant for Steedman's grammatical framework, as there is often no unique analysis for a sentence but rather a class of grammatically equivalent derivations. I will continue to use these terms for convenience. Marcus and Steedman are not talking about exactly the same aspects of intonational phrasing. They have focused on certain aspects of intonational phrasing that relate in interesting ways to certain key features to their theories of grammatical/processing systems. I will discuss these in the next section.

How Do They Do It?

Marcus's description-theory (D-theory) parser produces descriptions of trees and not the phrase-structure trees directly. In general, it underspecifies the structure. Marcus's parser is deterministic and on occasion gives the wrong reading. Marcus assumes that the obligatory IBs will be marked by some input available to his parser. He then uses this extra input to make sure that his parser does not give a wrong reading, which it would give without this extra input. Thus the obligatory IBs help Marcus's parser; in other words, the obligatory IBs and D-theory fit together well.

Steedman's categorial grammar (CG) in general provides for a sentence a multiplicity of analyses (which are all semantically equivalent). This aspect of a CG enables it to provide nice analyses of several coordination phenomena. Steedman suggests that the multiplicity of analyses CG provides for a sentence are also relevant to intonational phrasing. Out of all the possible equivalent analyses for a sentence, Steedman will pick the analysis that gives the syntactic phrasing that lines up with the intonational phrasing. Thus Steedman uses the IPs to help select one of the many equivalent analyses. The nonstandard analyses that a CG provides are thus relevant because the IPs in general cut across the standard syntactic boundaries in various ways. Steedman claims that the flexibility of structure possible in a CG is adequate for capturing the IPs. Thus a separate mechanism is not needed for specifying the IPs, as is the case if standard constituency is assumed. The result is a simpler architecture for metrical phonology.

Although both Marcus and Steedman adopt some notion of flexible constituent structure (D-theory for Marcus and a CG for Steedman), their architectures for relating the systems of constituent structure and the generation of intonational phrases are quite different. The major difference between these architectures is shown in figures 1 and 2.

Figure 1
The architecture implicit in Marcus's work

Figure 2
The architecture proposed by Steedman

In Marcus's implicit architecture (figure 1) the two components, phrase-structure component and the generator of IPs, are separate components. The relationship between these two components is not direct. Rather it is loose and not strictly defined. Hence the jagged line in figure 1. An appeal to some additional condition such as the "sense-unit" condition (referred to in Steedman's paper and attributed to Selkirk) is made to explicate this relationship. These assumptions are not made explicit by Marcus, but he does assume a conventional architecture for metrical phonology.

In the architecture proposed by Steedman (figure 2), the two components are not really distinct. The system of flexible constituent structure given by the CG also provides the IPs. Thus the two components are really identical and therefore the relationship between them is clearly well defined. This is shown by a solid straight line in figure 2.

Later I will describe an architecture that has a phrase-structure-like component for the constituent structure and a generator for IPs that is well defined and directly linked to the first component but not identical to it, as in Steedman's work. But first I will return to the work of Marcus and Steedman.

Some Problems with What They Have Done

Marcus used the obligatory IBs to help his D-theory parser prevent some unwanted readings. Since Marcus's D-theory is a processing account, it is difficult to formalize it in that it is not possible to state precisely which analyses are supported by his system and which are not supported. It is clear from his paper how some of the obligatory IBs prevent the parser from getting wrong readings. However, it is difficult to see exactly what is the set of all wrong readings prevented by the obligatory IBs. In other words, although the relationship between the obligatory IBs and the D-theory parser is clear for the specific examples discussed, the general character of this relationship is not obvious. This is so largely because the distinction between obligatory IBs and optional IBs seems to be tied to the D-theory parser itself.

Steedman's CG formalism is a grammar formalism. So in principle, it is possible to figure out the set of possible (equivalent) analyses for a sentence. Each one of these analyses corresponds to a different syntactic phrasing. Each phrase is semantically coherent as a "sense unit." This follows from CG theory itself. Steedman identifies the required IP with one of these phrasings. This part of Steedman's argument is very clear. It is not clear, however, whether each one of the possible analyses corresponds to some IP in some appropriate context, or only some of these analyses correspond to IPs in appropriate contexts. If the latter situation holds, it is necessary to give an independent characterization to this subset, and it is not clear to me how this can be done. Steedman's CG provides a collection of analyses in which it is possible to find one that corresponds to the required IP. The claim for the flexibility provided by the CG would be stronger and more interesting if it could be shown either that all the analyses are relevant to IPs in suitable contexts or that only some are, and that this subset of analyses has some natural characterization. In the case of coordinate constructions Steedman takes the position that all these analyses are relevant for coordination. Thus it is important to raise a similar question in the case of IPs. If such a claim could be supported, it would make a much stronger case for Steedman's revised version of the architecture for metrical phonology.

Since the multiplicity of analyses is exploited by Steedman for both coordination and the specification of IPs, there is a potential problem when coordination and IP require different phrasing. Consider the following situation:

(1) a. Q: What does Mary prefer?

　　b. A: Mary prefers oysters.

Question (1a) suggests the open proposition

(2) λx. Mary prefers x,

and this corresponds to the IP in (3):

(3) (Mary prefers) (oysters),

which is one of the analyses provided by the CG. However, let us suppose that the response to (1a) is (4):

(4) R: Mary prefers oysters but hates clams.

Now the coordination in (4) requires (in CG) that the syntactic phrasing be

(5) (Mary) (prefers oysters)

for the left conjunct in (4). This is different from (3), so there is a potential conflict between the phrasing required in (3) and that required in (5). Of course, we could say in this case (as Steedman suggested in his response to my comments at the workshop) that R has a different open proposition in mind when responding to (1a) as in (4). In the discourse in (1) the syntactic phrasing of (1a) (in accordance with the CG) suggests the open proposition (2), which then serves to pick the appropriate phrasing for (1b). This is an attractive part of Steedman's proposal. If (4) can be a response to (1a), the open proposition suggested by the phrasing of (1a) is irrelevant to the phrasing of (4). The syntactic phrasing required for (4) can be related to some appropriate open proposition that is different, of course, from that suggested by (1a), but then this makes the open proposition suggested by (1a) irrelevant in predicting the phrasing in (4). If (4) can be uttered with the first conjunct in (4) receiving the IP as in (Mary prefers) (oysters), there is a problem here.[1] If one adopts the proposal that there can be multiple analyses *simultaneously* holding for the sentence, there is no problem. (I don't think Steedman would subscribe to this position). Note that this proposal of simultaneously holding multiple analyses is not the same proposal as what is implied in the conventional architecture for metrical phonology. The conventional architecture requires that a phrase-structure component gives the syntactic structure and some other machinery provides the IP. The phrase-structure component does not provide the IP. The proposal suggested above is different. The different analyses that hold simultaneously are all given by the same grammatical system. I will pursue this point later in a little more detail.

Nonstandard Syntactic Analyses

Both Marcus and Steedman have used nonstandard syntactic analyses, Marcus only marginally and Steedman substantially. As I pointed out earlier, Marcus uses the standard X-bar syntax, and his parser constructs (partial) descriptions of trees rather than the trees themselves. He assumes, as in the conventional architecture for metrical phonology, that the syntax specifies a fixed phrase structure and the IPs are specified by some other mechanism, the IPs are not specified by the phrase-structure component. In contrast, Steedman's CG formalism gives a flexible phrasing. In fact, a sentence has multiple analyses (all semantically equivalent), all of which are given by the grammar itself. An appropriate phrasing can then be selected as determined by the required IP.

The space of possibilities of nonstandard syntactic analyses provided by different formalisms is not limited to those considered by Marcus and Steedman. I will briefly discuss some of the implications of the formalism for the tree-adjoining grammar (TAG) for some of the issues raised in these two chapters, especially the issue of flexible phrasing raised by Steedman. TAGs are interesting to look at in this context because it has been shown that a number of different grammatical formalisms are equivalent to TAG, for example, the head grammars (HG) of Pollard, linear indexed grammars discussed by Gazdar, and more important for the present discussion, combinatory grammars (CG) of Steedman (Gazdar 1985; Joshi 1987; Joshi, Weir, and Vijay-Shanker, to appear; Pollard 1984).

The elementary TAG trees provide an extended domain of locality (in comparison with context-free grammars), and these allow factoring recursion from the domain of dependencies. Dependencies such as agreement and subcategorization and even the so-called long-distance dependencies such as topicalization and *wh-* movement are all defined on the elementary trees and are thus local. The long-distance nature of the dependencies is then a consequence of adjoining auxiliary trees to elementary trees or derived trees. The extended domain of locality and the consequent encapsulation of the predicate argument structure in each one of the elementary trees is relevant to the issue of flexible structure.

I will consider a lexicalized TAG that consists of a finite set of structures (trees being a special case) associated with each lexical item intended to be the *anchor* of these structures and two operations for composing these structures.[2] These operations are substitution and adjoining. Instead of giving formal definitions for these two operations, I will illustrated them by means of examples later. The finite set of trees consists of two disjoint sets of trees: initial trees and auxiliary trees. Each elementary tree encapsulates the predicate argument structure. The following example illustrates a lexicalized TAG. Some elementary trees (initial trees and auxiliary trees) are shown below.

(6) man:

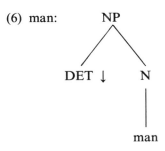

(7) Harry:

(8) the: DET

(9) that: COMP

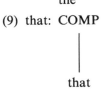

(10) who: COMP

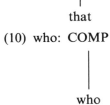

(11) likes:

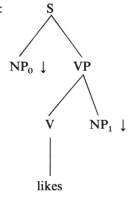

(12) sings:

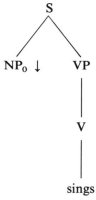

(13) thinks:

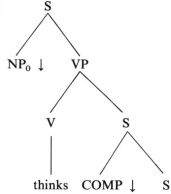

(14) quickly:

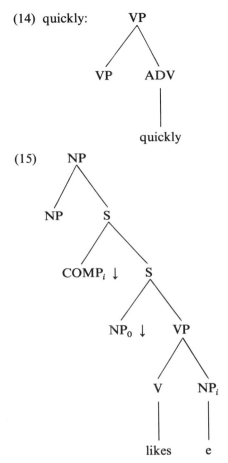

(15)

Trees (6) through (13) are initial trees. Trees (14) and (15) are auxiliary trees. For $X \neq S$, X-type initial trees correspond to the trees that can be substituted for one of the argument positions of elementary trees. Trees (11) to (13) are examples of S-type initial trees. They are structures that encapsulate all arguments of the verb, including the subject. The downward arrow ($\downarrow$) near a node indicates that an appropriate substitution has to be made at that node. Unless it is a terminal, a node without a downward arrow is a possible site for adjoining. In particular, note that the foot node of an auxiliary tree (e.g., tree (15)) does not have a downward arrow because this tree is an auxiliary tree, which can be adjoined at some appropriate node in some tree.

As I said, trees (14) and (15) are auxiliary trees (these are modifiers or predicates taking sentential complements). Tree (14) corresponds to an adverbial modifier, and tree (15) corresponds to a relative clause. Tree (14) has VP as the root node and VP as the foot node. Tree (15) has NP as the root node and NP as the foot node.

Complex structures are built by substitution and adjoining. Substituting tree (8) in tree (6) for DET, tree (6) at the NP_0 node in tree (11), and tree (7) at the NP_1 node of tree (11), we get (16).

(16) The man likes Harry

With appropriate substitutions in tree (15) and then by adjoining tree (15) to the tree corresponding to (16) at the subject NP node, we get (17).

(17) The man who Mary likes likes Harry

Adjoining can be thought of as excising the subtree at a node, inserting an auxiliary tree of the right type, and then attaching the excised subtree at the foot node of the auxiliary tree. It has been shown that by using adjoining together with substitution, we can obtain a lexicalized TAG as shown above, with each elementary tree encapsulating the predicate and its arguments. In this representation it is easy to see the relationship between a lexicalized TAG and a CG. Although a TAG provides a phrase structure at the level of elementary trees and a new tree is derived at each step of the derivation, these trees are *object-language* trees and not derivation trees, as in a context-free grammar. The derivation structures of TAG are in terms of these elementary trees; i.e., they record the history of the derivation of the *object-language* tree in terms of the elementary trees and the nodes where substitution or adjunctions are made. Therefore, the resulting system is not a standard phrase-structure grammar. Thus although CGs are weakly equivalent to TAGs in terms of the strings they generate, TAGs represent a system intermediate between the standard phrase-structure grammars and a CG.

The question now is, How can we assign structures to strings that correspond to nonstandard constituents (in terms of a CG)? Suppose we have the following elementary trees:

(18) John: NP

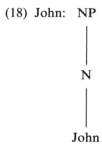

(19) likes:

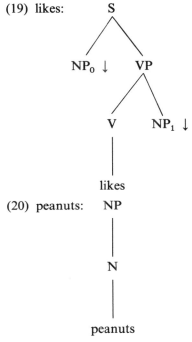

(20) peanuts:

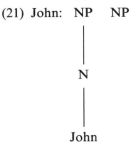

We can use these trees to associate structures to the following strings. On the right hand side of each structure I have shown its associated syntactic (functional) type to bring out the relationship to the CG.

(21) John: NP   NP

     N

     John

(22) likes:

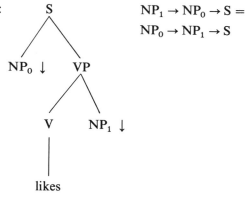

$$NP_1 \to NP_0 \to S =$$
$$NP_0 \to NP_1 \to S$$

(23) John likes:

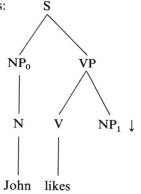

$$NP_1 \to S$$

(24) likes peanuts:

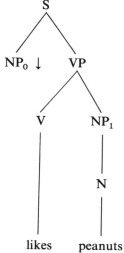

$$NP_0 \to S$$

(25) John likes peanuts:

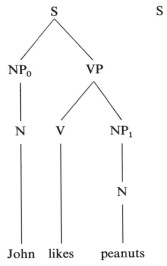

Thus *John likes* is of the type $NP_1 \to S$ (the indices are for convenience only; the tree addresses distinguish the NPs), *likes peanuts* is of the type $NP_0 \to S$, and *John likes peanuts* is of the type S. Note that *likes* is of the type $NP_1 \to NP_0 \to S$ or $NP_0 \to NP_1 \to S$, and in fact we must assert an equality between these two types.

The Curry CG notation captures the argument structure (e.g., for *likes* one has $(S\backslash NP)/NP$ corresponding to the elementary tree for *likes*, as shown above). However, with this Curry notation comes the requirement that the arguments must be bound in a specific order. What I have shown in the above example is that if we work with structures (as shown above), we can bind the arguments in any other, which thus allows the assignment of types to strings such as *John likes* without doing away with phrase structure at the level of elementary trees. Thus in this representation there appears to be a way of assigning types to such strings as *John likes* as well as to *likes peanuts*, i.e., to the possible intonational phrasings.[3]

We can regard the elementary trees of the lexicalized TAG, for example, trees (6) through (15), as a representation of categories as *structured objects*. Thus for the representation of the category for *likes* we have the structured object (11).

Thus with operations of substitution and adjoining as defined above, a lexicalized TAG is like a *categorial* grammar, in that the categories are structured objects, the basic categories are structured objects, and the operations of substitution and adjoining derive structured objects from structured objects. A basic structured object can be associated with a (curried) functional type or types as described earlier. Derived structured objects can also be associated with a (curried) functional type or types in the obvious manner. Thus the operations of substitution and adjoining play a role analogous to function composition.[4]

I have associated (curried) functional types with the structured objects to bring out the relationship to a CG. However, since one of my major objectives is to avoid the Curry notation, it is better to associate an (uncurried) functional type to a structured object. Thus for the tree (11) we can associate the (uncurried) functional type $NP_0 \, X \, NP_1 \rightarrow S$. The derived objects can also be associated with (uncurried) functional types. Substitution and adjoining give rise to derived structured objects, and the derived (uncurried) functional types are obtained by composition of functions. This approach with (uncurried) functional types is the appropriate one to pursue in the context of lexicalized TAGs, where the elementary trees are viewed as categories represented as structured objects. However, since the immediate concern is the relationship between a TAG and a CG, I will continue to talk in terms the associated (curried) functional types.

Since we have avoided the Curry notation, the order in which the arguments of a function are filled in is arbitrary, and this freedom gives us the ability to assign (functional) syntactic types to lexical strings that are not constituents in the conventional sense. Of course, this freedom will give rise to some functions that we would like to rule out. Thus, for example, consider the elementary tree (26) corresponding to a topicalized sentence. Tree (26) can be regarded as another category (structured object) associated with *likes*.

(26)

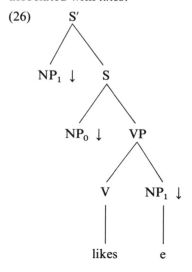

Substituting (18) for NP_0 in (26), we get (27).

(27)   S′ $NP_1 \rightarrow S'$

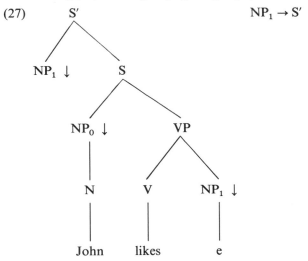

The lexical string corresponding to (27) is *John likes*. Let us call *John likes* the string *spelled out* by (27) or by the function corresponding to (27).[5] Note that *John likes* can be coordinated with, say, *Bill hates*, as in (28).

(28) Apples John likes and Bill hates.

Thus *John likes and Bill hates* is of the functional type $NP_1 \rightarrow S'$. The idea is that the lexical strings spelled out by the structured objects are fragments that can be coordinated (and therefore can also serve as appropriate intonational phrases, as in Steedman's idea). Of course, sometimes the lexical string spelled out by a structured object will not be a fragment that can be coordinated (or serve as an intonational phrase). Thus in tree (27) if we first substitute (20) for NP_1, we have the derived object tree (29).

(29)

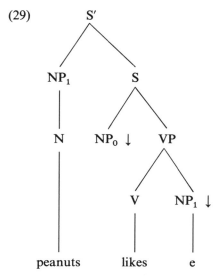

The lexical string spelled out by (29) is *peanuts likes*. However, this string is not an appropriate fragment for coordination (or for serving as an intonational phrase). If it were, we would get

(30) *Peanuts John likes and almonds hates

(meaning that John likes peanuts and John hates almonds). So we want to rule out the functional type corresponding to (29) as a possible candidate for coordination. We can rule out (29) by specifying a requirement on the lexical string spelled out by the structured object. The lexical string spelled out by (29) is not a contiguous string in that it is interrupted by NP_0; i.e., in the frontier of the tree (29) *peanuts* and *likes* are not contiguous.

It appears that we can develop an account of coordination (and therefore for the possible intonational phrases suggested by Steedman) in a lexicalized TAG by requiring that only functional types that spell out a contiguous lexical string are appropriate for coordination (or can serve as functional types associated with intonational phrases).[6] This requirement of contiguity of the lexical string appears to be well motivated if we want to treat these fragments as possible candidates for IPs. This contiguity condition can be thought of as a phonological condition and not as a syntactic condition.

I have thus shown (albeit rather briefly and informally) that if we start with categories as structured objects (trees of lexicalized TAGs, for example), we can assign (syntactic) functional types in the conventional sense to strings that are nonconstituents (as well as as those that are constituents,

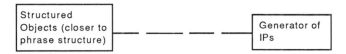

Figure 3
The architecture that I propose

of course) without giving up the phrase structure at the level of elementary trees. Thus in contrast to the two architectures described in figures 1 and 2 earlier, we have now a new architecture as described in figure 3. The two components are systematically related, but they are not identical, as in a CG. So I have shown the relationship between these two components with a dashed line.

In conclusion, in this section I have suggested that the space of non-standard phrase-structure analyses is large. I have shown that it is possible to have a nonstandard syntactic analysis that combines standard phrase structure and intonational phrasing in a systematic manner, in contrast to the conventional architecture for metrical phonology (as in figure 1), which has a separate IP generator very loosely coupled to the phrase-structure component. The architecture in figure 3 combines a key aspect of the architecture proposed by Steedman (figure 2) but still retains phrase structure in a certain sense.

Conclusion

Both Marcus and Steedman have made very interesting contributions to the interface between syntax and metrical phonology by showing how their respective theories of grammar/processing interact with IPs. I have commented briefly on their respective approaches, pointing out the different aspects of IPs they are concerned with and bringing out some of the problems with their respective theories. I have also briefly discussed a phrase-structure-like approach that is able to support some flexible phrasing and thus permits a set of analyses holding *simultaneously*. Clearly there are a number of different ways to set up the interface between syntax and metrical phonology, and there will be theory-internal criteria for selecting one theory over another. There are, of course, two external criteria highly relevant to this workshop. These are psycholinguistic relevance and computational efficiency. Both Marcus and Steedman have said very little in their chapters with respect to these issues. Marcus's commitment to determinism and Steedman's commitment to incremental processing in their other papers clearly reflect their concern for these issues. I expect them to develop these issues further in their future work on the interface between syntax and metrical phonology.

Acknowledgments

This work was partially supported by NSF grants MCS-8219196-CER, IRI84-10413-A02, DARPA grant N0014-85-K-0018, and ARO grant DAA29-84-K0061.

Notes

1. This example is perhaps not as convincing as I would like. Steedman certainly claims that such conflicts cannot arise. My point here is that the potential conflict between IPs and coordination phrases should be looked into further. The lack of conflict between these two types of phrases should not be accepted a priori, as Steedman has done.

2. The notion of an anchor here really corresponds to that of a functor in a CG. The elementary tree associated with a lexical item can be regarded as a *structured* object that is its syntactic type. For example, in tree (3) the lexical anchor is *man*. In this case it is also the head of the structure, but this will not always be the case. Thus in tree (9) the lexical anchor is *quickly*, which is clearly not the head of the structure in tree (9). It is a functor in the CG sense. In tree (3) *man* is also a functor in the CG sense. In some of my earlier papers, the term head was used instead of anchor, with quotation marks around head and an explanation that the notion of head really corresponds to the notion of a functor in CG. In retrospect that was a bad choice of terminology. I should have adopted a neutral term such as *anchor* from the beginning to avoid unnecessary confusion.

3. The representation provided by a lexicalized TAG is crucial here. It can be shown that substitution alone cannot lexicalize a context-free grammar, but substitution and adjoining together can lexicalize a context-free grammar. The resulting system is then a lexicalized TAG! For details, see Schabes, Abeille, and Joshi 1988.

4. Substitution corresponds directly to function composition. Adjoining can be shown to be a kind of function composition also. An auxiliary tree is a function of the type $X \to X$. Adjoining is then a composition of a function obtained by abstracting on the node in a tree where adjunction is to be made and on the function corresponding to the auxiliary tree to be adjoined at that node. Function application is a special case of substitution.

5. Strictly, the lexical string spelled out by (27) is *John likes e*, but I will disregard the trace. It is not crucial to our present discussion. Also, a lexicalized TAG by itself does not demand traces. Analyses without traces can also be given in a lexicalized TAG.

6. A detailed development of this approach is being worked out at present and will be described elsewhere later. The discussion presented here represents my initial attempt at this problem. It is only after reading Steedman's paper that I began to pursue the approach briefly described above.

References

Gazdar, G. 1985. Applicability of indexed grammars to natural languages. Technical report CSLI-85-34, Center for Study of Language and Information, Stanford University.

Joshi, A. K. 1987. An introduction to tree adjoining grammars. In A. Manaster-Ramer (ed.), *Mathematics of Language*. Amsterdam: John Benjamin.

Joshi, A. K., Vijay-Shanker, K., and Weir, D. To appear. The convergence of mildly context-sensitive grammar formalisms. In S. Shieber and T. Wasow (eds.), *The Processing of Linguistic Structure*. Cambridge: MIT Press.

Pollard, C. 1984. Generalized Phrase Structure Grammars, Head Grammars, and Natural Language. Ph.D. dissertation, Stanford University.

Schabes, Y., Abeille, A., and Joshi, A. K. 1988. Parsing strategies with "lexicalized" grammars: Application to tree adjoining grammars. In *Proceedings of the Twelfth International Conference on Computational Linguistics* (*COLING 88*), Budapest.

Contributors

Gerry T. M. Altmann
Laboratory of Experimental
Psychology
University of Sussex

Ellen Gurman Bard
Centre for Speech Technology
Research
University of Edinburgh

Julie Boland
Department of Psychology
University of Rochester

Jan Charles-Luce
Department of Communicative
Disorders and Sciences
SUNY, Buffalo

Michael S. Cluff
Department of Psychology
SUNY, Buffalo

Cynthia Connine
Department of Psychology
SUNY Binghampton

Anne Cutler
MRC Applied Psychology Unit
Cambrige

Emmanuel Dupoux
Laboratoire de Sciences Cognitives
et Psycholinguistique
Centre National de la Recherche
Scientifique
Paris

Jeffrey L. Elman
Department of Linguistics
University of California, San Diego

Janet Fodor
Graduate Centre
CUNY

Uli Frauenfelder
Max-Planck Institut für
Psycholinguistik
Holland

Lyn Frazier
Department of Linguistics
University of Massachusetts,
Amherst

Susan M. Garnsey
Department of Psychology
University of Rochester

Steven D. Goldinger
Speech Research Laboratory
Department of Psychology
Indiana University

Donald Hindle
AT&T Bell Laboratories
New Jersey

Aravind K. Joshi
Moore School of Engineering
University of Pennsylvania

Paul A. Luce
Department of Psychology
SUNY, Buffalo

Mitchell Marcus
Moore School of Engineering
University of Pennsylvania

William Marslen-Wilson
MRC Applied Psychology Unit
Cambridge

Jacques Mehler
Laboratoire de Sciences Cognitives
et Psycholinguistique
Centre National de la Recherche
Scientifique
Paris

Dennis Norris
MRC Applied Psychology Unit
Cambridge

Guus Peeters
Max-Planck Institut für
Psycholinguistik
Holland

David B. Pisoni
Speech Research Laboratory
Department of Psychology
Indiana University

Arthur G. Samuel
Department of Psychology
Yale University

Juan Segui
Laboratoire de Psychologie
Experiméntale
Centre Nationale de la Recherche
Scientifique
Paris

Richard Shillcock
Centre for Speech Technology
Research
University of Edinburgh

Mark Steedman
Moore School of Engineering
University of Pennsylvania

Michael K. Tanenhaus
Department of Psychology
University of Rochester

Lorraine K. Tyler
Department of Experimental
Psychology
University of Cambridge

Henry Thompson
Centre for Speech Technology
Research
University of Edinburgh

Index